AF827367

t published 2003 by Ashgate Publishing

ssued 2018 by Routledge
rk Square, Milton Park, Abingdon, Oxon OX14 4RN
Third Avenue, New York, NY 10017, USA

ledge is an imprint of the Taylor and Francis Group, an informa business

right © Paula M. Pevato 2003.
opyright of individual articles please refer to the Acknowledgements.

hts reserved. No part of this book may be reprinted or reproduced or utilised in any form or by lectronic, mechanical, or other means, now known or hereafter invented, including opying and recording, or in any information storage or retrieval system, without permission in from the publishers.

or corporate names may be trademarks or registered trademarks, and are used only for cation and explanation without intent to infringe.

r's Note
lisher has gone to great lengths to ensure the quality of this reprint but points out that some tions in the original copies may be apparent.

er
isher has made every effort to trace copyright holders and welcomes correspondence from have been unable to contact.

of Congress record exists under LC control number: 2002074717

978-1-138-71286-7 (hbk)
78-1-315-19921-4 (ebk)

International Environmental Law
Volume I

The Library of Essays in International Law
General Editor: Robert McCorquodale

Titles in the Series

International Human Rights Law, Volumes I and II
Michael K. Addo

International Law and Indigenous Peoples
S. James Anaya

Law of the Sea
Hugo Caminos

The Law of Treaties
J. Scott Davidson

Humanitarian Law
Judith Gardam

International Peacekeeping
Boris Kondoch

International Economic Regulation
Jane Kelsey

Sources of International Law
Martti Koskenniemi

International Dispute Settlement
Mary Ellen O'Connell

International Crimes
Nikos Passas

International Environmental Law, Volumes I and II
Paula M. Pevato

State Responsibility in International Law
René Provost

Jurisdiction in International Law
Michael Reisman

Title to Territory
Malcolm Shaw

The Nature of International Law
Gerry Simpson

International Environmental Law
Volume I

Edited by

Paula M. Pevato

Public International Lawyer, Barrister and Solicitor, Canada

Routledge
Taylor & Francis Group
LONDON AND NEW YORK

Contents

Acknowledgements

The editor and publishers wish to thank the following for permission to use copyright material.

American Association for the Advancement of Science for the essay: Garrett Hardin (1968), 'The Tragedy of the Commons', *Science*, **162**, pp. 1243–8. Copyright © 1968 American Association for the Advancement of Science.

American Society of International Law for the essays: Edith Brown Weiss (1990), 'Our Rights and Obligations to Future Generations for the Environment', *American Journal of International Law*, **84**, pp. 198–207. Copyright © 1990 American Society of International Law; Robin R. Churchill and Geir Ulfstein (2000), 'Autonomous Institutional Arrangements in Multilateral Environmental Agreements: A Little-Noticed Phenomenon in International Law', *American Journal of International Law*, **94**, pp. 623–59. Copyright © 2000 American Society of International Law.

Blackwell Publishers Limited for the essay: Paula M. Pevato (1999), 'A Right to Environment in International Law: Current Status and Future Outlook', *Review of European Community and International Environmental Law*, **8**, pp. 309–21. Copyright © 1999 Blackwell Publishers Ltd.

Chicago-Kent College of Law for the essay: A. Dan Tarlock (1992), 'The Role of Non-Governmental Organizations in the Development of International Environmental Law', *Chicago-Kent Law Review*, **68**, pp. 61–76.

Indiana University for the essay: Daniel Bodansky (1995), 'Customary (And Not So Customary) International Environmental Law', *Global Legal Studies Journal*, **3**, pp. 105–119.

International Music Publications Ltd for the Lyrics: 'Goodbye To A River', Words and Music by Donald Henley, Stanley Lynch, Jay Winding and Frank Simes. Copyright © 2000 Wisteria Music, Matanzas Music, Dobbs Music Inc and Frank Simes Music, USA. (75%) Warner/Chappell North America Ltd, London W6 8BS. Reproduced by permission of International Music Publications Ltd. All Rights Reserved.

Kluwer Law International for the essay: Günther Handl (1990), 'Environmental Security and Global Change: The Challenge to International Law', *Yearbook of International Environmental Law*, **1**, pp. 3–33. Copyright © 1991 Graham & Trotman. With kind permission of Kluwer Law Review.

Melbourne University Law Review for the essay: Patricia Birnie (1995), 'Environmental Protection and Development', *Melbourne University Law Review*, **20**, pp. 66–100.

O'Brien Center for Scholarly Publications for the essay: David D. Caron (1991), 'Protection of the Stratospheric Ozone Layer and the Structure of International Environmental Lawmaking', *Hastings International and Comparative Law Review*, **14**, pp. 755–80. Copyright © 1991 Hastings College of the Law.

Oxford University Press for the essays: Allen L. Springer (1977), 'Towards a Meaningful Concept of Pollution in International Law', *International and Comparative Law Quarterly*, **26**, pp. 531–57; Owen McIntyre and Thomas Mosedale (1997), 'The Precautionary Principle as a Norm of Customary International Law', *Journal of Environmental Law*, **9**, pp. 221–41. Copyright © 1997 Oxford University Press.

Southern California Law Review for the essay: Christopher D. Stone (1972), 'Should Trees Have Standing? – Toward Legal Rights for Natural Objects', *Southern California Law Review*, **45**, pp. 450–501.

Tulane Journal of International and Comparative Law for the essay: Günther Handl (1997), 'Compliance Control Mechanisms and International Environmental Obligations', *Tulane Journal of International and Comparative Law*, **5**, pp. 29–49. Copyright © 1997 Tulane Journal of International and Comparative Law.

University of Michigan for the essay: Pierre-Marie Dupuy (1991), 'Soft Law and the International Law of the Environment', *Michigan Journal of International Law*, **12**, pp. 420–35.

Every effort has been made to trace all the copyright holders, but if any have been inadvertently overlooked the publishers will be pleased to make the necessary arrangement at the first opportunity.

Series Preface

Open a newspaper, listen to the radio or watch television any day of the week and you will read or hear of some matter concerning international law. The range of matters include the extent to which issues of trade and human rights should be linked, concerns about refugees and labour conditions, negotiations of treaties and the settlement of disputes, and decisions by the United Nations Security Council concerning actions to ensure compliance with international law. International legal issues have impact on governments, corporations, organisations and people around the world and the process of globalisation has increased this impact. In the global legal environment, knowledge of international law is an indispensable tool for all scholars, legal practitioners, decision-makers and citizens of the 21st century.

The Library of Essays in International Law is designed to provide the essential elements for the development of this knowledge. Each volume contains essays of central importance in the development of international law in a subject area. The proliferation of legal and other specialist journals, the increase in international materials and the use of the internet, has meant that it is increasingly difficult for legal scholars to have access to all the relevant articles on international law and many valuable older articles are now unable to be obtained readily. These problems are addressed by this series, which makes available an extensive range of materials in a manner that is of immeasurable value for both teaching and research at all levels.

Each volume is written by a leading authority in the subject area who selects the articles and provides an informative introduction, which analyses the context of the articles and comments on their significance within the developments in that area. The volumes complement each other to give a clear view of the burgeoning area of international law. It is not an easy task to select, order and place in context essays from the enormous quantity of academic legal writing prublished in journals – in many languages – throughout the world. This task requires professional scholarly judgment and difficult choices. The editors in this series have done an excellent job, for which I thank and congratulate them. It has been a pleasure working with them.

ROBERT McCORQUODALE
General Series Editor
School of Law
University of Nottingham

Preface

> I went to the woods because I wished to live deliberately, to front only the essential facts of life, and see if I could not learn what it had to teach, and not, when I came to die, discover that I had not lived.
>
> Excerpt from chapter entitled 'Where I Lived, and What I Lived For', in Henry David Thoreau, *Walden; or, Life in the Woods* (1854)

During a speech to the General Assembly gathered in New Delhi for the 1968 meeting of the Swiss-based International Union for the Conservation of Nature and Natural Resources, Senegalese forestry engineer and ecologist Baba Dioum could not have said it any better when he declared:

> *In the end we will conserve only what we love. We will love only what we understand. We will understand only what we are taught.*

How true it is that without instruction, we might never comprehend the fragile state of our global environment. Once the global community was made aware of that state, and the potential irreversible losses of habitat, species and entire ecosystems, an international conservation agenda ensued. But was it out of love or necessity? Whatever basis for that reaction, it is indeed a fact that the global community needs to be reminded constantly of the following: why we must preserve the earth's fragile ecosystems; how nature is inextricably linked with and affected by humankind's activities; where damage has already occurred to the global environment, what we can do to halt or even reverse that damage; that ongoing destruction of habitats and entire ecosystems endangers some of the world's most unique species inhabiting them, such as the elusive cloud leopard of Russia or the lion-tailed macaque in India's Western Ghats living in closed-canopy forests; and, what we do to the environment today determines the state of the environment we will pass on to future generations. It is only after we contemplate these questions seriously that we might begin to understand how utterly delicate our natural world is and the complicated environmental structure it supports. Thus the study of international protection of the environment is so critical today given that it contributes to understanding the international community's legal and policy responses to resolving global environment concerns and achieving some measure of ecological security. Those measures taken at the international level then have a trickle-down effect, with the ultimate obligation to implement international norms and standards into domestic law and policy.

It is my most sincere desire that this collection of essays assembled within these two volumes contributes to the study of international environmental law. Whether the reader is a newcomer to a field that operates within the normative system comprising public international law, or seasoned academic, or practitioner facing daily challenges on behalf of clients, or undergraduate and graduate student alike, whether reading law or environmental science and other related topics, this collection of essays offers something for everyone. This collection reflects upon past ecological crises – both underlying and immediate – triggering the progressive development of international environmental norms and standards, assesses critically international legal and policy norms and standards, and their effectiveness in achieving global environmental security, in addition to pondering whether or how environmentally responsible are those decisions that our political leaders take to achieve such security, and ultimately to hold those in decision-making authority accountable for the state of the world we intend to pass on to future generations.

But the ongoing struggle to realise ecological security does not stop at the international level. For 'when one tugs at a single thing in nature', wrote John Muir, 'he finds it attached to the rest of the world'. It is hard to imagine that our present actions, their effect upon our surroundings, and what we do each day to preserve our own little corner of the universe, our personal space, our tiny environment, every single action contributes to broader international environmental goals. So it is not only our political leaders who are accountable for decision-making that may contribute positively (or, regrettably, negatively) to international environmental security, but also ourselves as individuals, each and every day, from multinational corporate decision-makers in the private sector to the small and medium sized businesses operating at the grass roots level, to public sector entities, and to individual households participating in community recycling and energy saving programmes. Published just in time for the 1992 Rio Earth Summit, Al Gore reminded us in *Earth in the Balance: Ecology and the Human Spirit* that,

> *[t]he world's ecological balance depends on more than just our ability to restore a balance between civilisation's ravenous appetite for resources and the fragile equilibrium of the earth's environment . . . . Each of us must take a greater personal responsibility for this deteriorating global environment.*

Help save the environment, not only through participation in democratic processes, namely, in choosing to vote for political leaders with platforms that have an ecologically sound vision, but in your actions each and every day: reduce waste, recycle, if possible bike to work, car pool or take public transit, go for a long walk through a public park, choose environmentally friendly products, volunteer to plant trees in your local community, teach your children about preserving the environment. Education matters. Every action counts. 'The creation of a thousand forests', according to Ralph Waldo Emerson, 'is in one acorn'. Likewise, the creation of a global environmental consciousness begins in one person. Volumes I and II contain twenty-five distinct visions represented by twenty-four authors who critically analyse and interpret international environmental problems and the proposed solutions to those global issues. Every written contribution matters to the teaching and study of international environmental law. These essays in turn expand our understanding of the subject from an international legal perspective. Our passion for protecting and preserving the global environment may be escalated, thereby helping us to appreciate our natural world. Hopefully, in the end, the reader is encouraged now more than ever to conserve what is appreciated, even loved: the earth's fragile, unique and glorious environment.

Now for a few housekeeping notes. The ratification status of treaties referred to in the Introduction was reviewed on an ongoing basis, particularly near final drafting and editing stages from August to October 2001. However, it may seem odd that many of the ratification status dates cited do not reflect those periods. This is simply because the actual dates cited reflected that particular treaty Secretariat's own latest updates according to the most up-to-date information presented on each respective website. In other words, a treaty's status checked in September 2001 may record the status updated last by the Secretariat in January 2000. Hence, the apparent discrepancy. I hope this clears up any potential confusion. Additionally, with exceptions, research reflects most developments as at October 2001.

In the 1980s, developers planned to build residential and commercial units at the infamous sight considered the birthplace of the American environmental movement: Walden Woods. Fortunately, the pristine sight of Henry David Thoreau's infamous retreat, where the author and philosopher wrote his literary masterpiece *Walden*, was saved by developers thanks to Don Henley, who in 1990 founded The Walden Woods Project, a not-for-profit land conservation organisation. Through its mission – to protect land of ecological and historic significance at Walden Pond's environs, and to support educational initiatives pertaining to the study of the environment and the humanities via the Thoreau Institute at Walden Woods – collectively the Project, Institute and Thoreau Society (the latter founded in 1941) are exemplary of locally organised, donor-funded and grass roots driven initiatives that contribute to the preservation of a particular local environment's ecological heritage and historical integrity for present and future generations. Additionally, the Project contributes to broader international environmental goals: conservation, education, preservation, protection, and ultimately, ecological security. It is thus with profound respect that I express my affable appreciation to Don Henley, his publishing administrator Lisa Thomas, music companies and collaborating colleagues on the song for having given their kind and generous permission to excerpt lyrics from a most humbling and prescient 'Goodbye To A River'.

Similarly, I support and reiterate recognition towards all authors and/or publishing houses referred to in the Acknowledgements pages of Volumes I and II. Their collective permission to reprint articles contained herein means much more to me than giving *carte blanche* authority to reproduce a previously published essay. It is much more than that: their permission is symbolic of what might perhaps be characterised as an unwritten solidarity when it comes to presenting issues pertaining to international protection of the environment. Taken at face value, some of the essays may seem dated (as elaborated upon later within the Introduction to these volumes). Yet, open-minded authors (whether scientist, international legal scholar or international law practitioner) and their publishers undoubtedly recognise that each essay has had something important to say – notwithstanding the date when it was conceived, written, and published – and certainly every individual author was influenced by current challenges, debates and developments surrounding the international community during those times when she or he were immersed in writing their respective essay. For instance, less recent articles are still relevant today because they contribute to a better understanding of various historical dimensions and subsequent evolution of more contemporary issues, theories and achievements. Some authors were, and still are to a great extent, considered mavericks during their times, having recorded provocative, even *avant garde* doctrines. Since their publication, great strides have been gained within international environmental law, thanks in part to those challenging, dare we say even radical, contributions made for their time. The past should never be dismissed. Rather, it should be embraced, celebrated and recognised so that one understands current legal and policy issues pertaining to international environmental protection. Therefore, all essays contained herein have stood the test of time, are in no way outdated, each having contributed intelligent opinions and commentaries on the progressive development of international environmental law and policy. Authors' and publishers' kind reprinting permission is illustrative of a mature confidence in granting said rights. Thus, it is a privilege and honour to commend all authors and/or their publishing representatives who have had the grace and enthusiasm to participate in these exciting volumes. My thanks are courteously extended to all of you.

On a more personal note, I am grateful to Professor Robert McCorquodale for having invited me to participate in this most ambitious project. His guidance and helpful suggestions throughout the drafting processes were invaluable. My sister, Linda Pevato, BEd, BA, reviewed many drafts (without a single complaint I might add!) and provided expert guidance on presentation, content and technique. I am lucky to have both Robert and Linda as friends and mentors. Any omissions and oversights are my responsibility alone.

My gratitude would be incomplete without thanking the wonderful team of editors and other staff at Ashgate. In particular, I must extend my warmest appreciation to John Irwin (General Editor), Jacqueline Cox (Reference Manager, Rights & Permissions) and Maureen Campbell (Desk Editor). What a wonderful experience to have worked with such professional, enthusiastic and supportive people!

Finally, according to Song Hun, 'a clear breeze has no price, the bright moon no owner'. I am indebted to my family for their enduring encouragement and for having given me the priceless gift of respecting and loving our natural world. I embrace wholeheartedly their love and friendship. *Con mille auguri, abbracci e baci.*

Dr. Paula M. Pevato
Toronto, Canada
October 2001 and May 2003

Introduction

> Great indeed are the things which in this brief treatise I propose for observation and consideration by all students of nature. I say great, because of the excellence of the subject itself, the entirely unexpected and novel character of these things, and finally because of the instrument by means of which they have been revealed to our senses.
>
> *The Starry Messenger* (Galileo Galilei, 1610)

> The evolving framework of international environmental law and the development of national law provide a sound basis for addressing the major environmental threats of the day. It must be underpinned by a more coherent and coordinated approach among international environmental instruments.
>
> *Malmö Ministerial Declaration* (UNEP, 2000)

International Law and Environmental Protection: Casual Musings

The natural environment when viewed as a resource is a finite one. That might be a paradoxical reality difficult to reconcile with popular attitudes represented within many economically developed societies where a 'disposable mentality' prevails. In other words, if something is broken, replace it! This is a maxim that is not so easily applied to the protection and preservation of the environment: thus there are no spare unpenetrated ozone layers, no back-up uncontaminated oceans, no surplus of 'closed canopy' ecosystems to be purchased at local shopping malls. If exploitation of the earth's fragile ecosystems and the resources they accommodate continues along unsustainable depletion patterns fully taking into account what has happened to the natural environment during the past two centuries without the intervention, development and implementation of new environmental protection norms and standards in international law and policy (along with regional and municipal environmental management plans or other legal and policy initiatives expressing those standards), grave consequences are predicted. The global environment is irreplaceable. Following decades of prolonged, substantial, and often irreversible, environmental harm, it became a matter of grave urgency that the restoration, preservation and protection of the environment was necessary – especially for damaged fragile ecosystems, over-exploited non-renewable resources, and over-harvested renewable natural resources – once the global community accepted that pervasive harm to the natural world had to be redressed by legal and other means. Numerous technological achievements marked significant turning points in history. Those achievements were attained via developments within specific scientific and engineering disciplines which, at the same time, also contributed to ecological degradation in many cases (for example, the automobile). Consequently, new paradigms and innovative fields needed to be developed within traditional disciplines, particularly law and environmental sciences, to respond to the adverse effects of persistent environmental abuse. In reaction to many pressing issues facing the international community in relation to global environmental degradation, international law evolved to provide an assortment of legal and policy frameworks offering solutions to those environmental challenges. Thus, when ecological changes were classified as physical limits to the global environment's non-renewable natural resources within singular and interdependent ecosystems, some international lawyers concluded that global environmental degradation had reached a 'precrisis stage' by the 1990s (Timoshenko, 1990, 127ff, quoted in Chapter 1, p. 3, Volume I). Others such as Handl determined that the global environment was experiencing an 'unavoidable global environmental change that threatens possibly catastrophic economic, social and political consequences': in short, the protection and preservation of the environment became a matter of 'global security' (see further Chapter 1, p. 3, Volume I).

Contemporary ecological concerns may be succinctly characterised as environmental issues. According to Caldwell, an 'environmental issue' is an issue formulated as 'a result of an emergent change in the environment, caused or influenced by human activity, with consequences arousing social concern or creating problems leading to political action'. Furthermore, he suggests that environmental issues 'interact with and interrelate with other seemingly mutually exclusive developments . . . air quality issues interlink with health, energy, and economic problems; and endangered species issues entail questions of habitat, land use, recreation, commerce, and ethics' (Caldwell, 1990, p. 11). This view is reminiscent of renowned British astrophysicist Sir Arthur Eddington's rather dire predictions in relation to the natural world, given that he observed an earlier period farther back in time when the earth was less disorganised or, as Sir Arthur put it, 'less shuffled'. Certainly, an incontrovertible amount of unnatural 'disorder' now exists within a more advanced, or 'shuffled', world today. Eddington further observed that entropy,[1] as time's arrow, points forward only: thus the world was in a constant state of evolution, so had to be less disorderly, less shuffled in the past. He also surmised that the amount of energy for use in the universe was finite (Eddington, 1928). As such, just as there is a finite component to energy, so too is there a calculable component to the natural environment.

It is within the context of the environment that this particular disorder is relevant, a category of disorder that cannot be attributed solely to an inevitable, evolutionary process. Rather, it is disorder marked, and marred, by human intervention and activities aptly categorised by Caldwell into twelve broad groupings, many of which are examined throughout the various chapters in these two volumes. The first six were deemed critical and required immediate action: genetic loss; ecosystem disruption and destruction; devegetation; desertification; contamination of the environment (air, water, soil and biota); and degradation and depletion of fresh water. The remaining six were at various stages of proceeding to critical levels (for example, 'precrisis stage'): overpopulation by humans; deterioration and erosion of topsoil; climate change and deterioration of atmospheric quality and resultant adverse effects including sea-level rise (Chapter 18, Volume II); ozone depletion and acid rain (Chapter 7, Volume I); progressive reduction in existing sources of energy and the adverse environmental effects of such use; disruption of biogeochemical cycles; and maintenance of mankind's built environment and loss of cultural heritage in arts and architecture, including large-scale public works such as dams, canals and highways (Caldwell, 1990, pp. 17–18). Furthermore, it is disorder identified by patterns of unsustainable development, irresponsible use of finite resources, neglect, abuse, greed and ignorance or lack of respect for and understanding of the earth's variegated patchwork of fragile ecosystems, inextricably linked, interdependent and indivisible. It is disorder capable of taking on assorted identities: endangered or extinct species, depleted forests, land or ship based sources of marine pollution, threats to and loss of biological diversity (Chapter 19,

Volume II), nuclear testing carried out amidst highly sensitive environments (Sands, 1996), careless transfers of hazardous wastes (Chapters 21 and 22, Volume II), oil fields set afire during armed conflicts thereby creating environmental disasters (Schmitt, 1997),[2] industrial factories spewing toxic effluents into air and water and dispersing them beyond state borders, threats to local river ecosystems, to rain forest watersheds, to species inhabiting those environments, and adverse health and social consequences from unsustainable development, all resulting from development projects such as the construction of hydro dams that damage water quality and ecosystems,[3] these are just some scenarios that would have tragic consequences for the planet, its environment and inhabitants.

Applied metaphorically to an international legal inquiry, the views of Sir Arthur Eddington – a celebrated mathematician, astronomer and physicist – would have one imagine that many centuries or even decades ago, when the entropy arrow had not yet pierced forward to the extent one sees today, global pollution was of little concern to humankind. Before the 1970s, very few international legal textbooks referred to the environment. It was perhaps discussed more in fiction than fact, for instance in Tolkien's *Lord of the Rings* trilogy and its prequel *The Hobbit*, wherein the fire-breathing dragon 'Smaug' was created as a metaphor for the author's own personal dismay over environmental pollution, starkly evident in a post-industrial revolution society.[4] Similarly, very few global treaties expressing environmental protection regimes had been ratified, or declarations adopted, prior to 1972. Most of the early treaties concentrated on regional or bilateral concerns, such as the conservation of wildlife (birds, fisheries, seals) as expressed in the 1902 Convention for the Protection of Birds Useful to Agriculture,[5] or the protection from pollution of jointly managed boundary waters, exemplified by the 1909 Boundary Waters Treaty[6] between the United States (US) and the United Kingdom, on behalf of Canada (Sands, 1995, pp. 26–9). In contrast, hundreds of treaties and declarations were ratified or adopted at global, regional, sub-regional and bilateral levels by the end of the twentieth century.[7] Scenarios described in the previous paragraph illustrate just a few of many urgent conditions triggering development of international norms and standards. In direct contravention of entropy laws, if one could peer backwards in time using Galileo's 'instrument', known today simply as a telescope, the metaphysical eye would reveal a less 'shuffled' natural environment, unlike today's natural world with its critical pollution levels.

Assembled against an elaborate backdrop scattered with images of what Aldo Leopold characterised as a 'world of wounds', (Leopold, 1978, p. 197) the collection of essays presented within Volumes I and II expands upon those images and the international legal solutions that have been formulated to resolve global environmental problems. The essays chosen convey pivotal breakthroughs in 'international environmental law', delineated by the following broad categories:

- historical developments and milestones achieved in standard-setting;
- traditional and modern sources of international law;
- a myriad of governance issues pertaining to international institutions, inter-governmental organisations (IGOs) and non-governmental organisations (NGOs);
- the progressive development of international environmental law, featuring a selection of global treaties;
- two essays comparing and contrasting approaches to controlling the hazardous wastes trade to and from developed and developing states; and

- challenges to be addressed concurrent with the progressive development of international environmental law, including tensions, cross-cutting issues, international financing dilemmas, and general deficiencies within the international normative system for environmental protection.

Despite the broad array of topics covered by these essays, this anthology does not seek to replace comprehensive texts on the subject.[8] Nor does it attempt to cover issues of international environmental politics and policy,[9] and national, sub-regional or regional developments,[10] such as those within economic or politically integrated zones, for example, the European Union (EU),[11] UN Economic Commission for Europe (UNECE), Organisation of American States (OAS), African Union (AU) replacing the Organisation of African Unity (OAU) in 2002, Organisation for Economic Cooperation and Development (OECD), and Asia Pacific Economic Cooperation (APEC),[12] to name but a few.

Hence, this particular compilation must be viewed as a prelude to a broader spectrum of perspectives and approaches captured within many studies on international protection of the environment, and an invitation to further exploration. Given that international environmental law is anything but static, it is logical to observe that more recent essays will represent up-to-date developments. Others in the collection should be read within an historical context, especially where certain treaties or protocols either were not in force or did not exist when that specific essay was written. However, the essence of less recent essays is not diminished by the passage of time, for many of them are just as insightful and original now as they were when published decades ago. For example, Hardin's metaphoric thesis on the tragedy of the commons (Chapter 2, Volume I) has only gained momentum over time, having become entrenched within the symbolic pathos of international environmental law and policy. Others, such as Springer's 1977 essay on the meaning of pollution (Chapter 3, Volume I), Stone's chapter pleading the case for assigning rights to natural objects (Chapter 4, Volume I), or Brown Weiss's theory on a planetary trust for the environment (Chapter 5, Volume I), may be viewed comparatively when measuring current developments and progress achieved. Certain essays might also serve as significant benchmarks to determine how far the international community has come since those individual theories were introduced, observations proposed, and what obstacles remain on the path to achieve Handl's state of international environmental security.

In short, these oft-cited essays presenting original ideas and novel perspectives are all worthy of inclusion within these two volumes for many reasons: they challenge conventional ways of thinking about international law through the addition of environmental protection issues and resultant layers of new and emerging norms and standards; they provide richly descriptive commentaries on historical developments, institutional frameworks, and achievements in treaty-making; they navigate through complex dispute resolution and compliance issues; they emphasise South–North tensions conveyed by environmental protection proponents versus economic development supporters; or, they leap outside of the traditional international law box by confronting more controversial topics related to diverse competing interests, emerging concepts, tensions and cross-cutting issues. This carefully chosen assemblage of essays is based upon the premise that to understand the present and future of international environmental law and security, one must first understand and acknowledge the past. The chapters included within both volumes are loyal to that maxim because they do not ignore historical positions in favour of current ones. Contemporary theories often evolved from earlier ones, even if those theories were less sophisticated than current approaches. Henceforth, the reader is invited to join an academic journey in defiance of entropy and temporal laws through a representative selection of past, present and future international legal responses to global environmental challenges. This introduction seeks to assist the reader upon that journey, commencing with a few philosophical reflections.

Conceptual Issues

The formidable task of situating the environment within an international legal context, thereby transporting the reader into an international environmental law frame of mind, is accomplished with skill in the opening essay by Günther Handl, 'Environmental Security and Global Change: The Challenge to International Law' (Chapter 1, Volume I). Handl's essay, when appreciated for its discerning philosophical viewpoint, is the perfect starting point for introducing other essays in this first section – particularly but not exclusively Brown Weiss' essay on intergenerational equity (Chapter 5, Volume I) – as well as embodying a treasure chest of issues for both volumes in this particular series, given that he familiarises the reader with many themes to follow. In fact, besides introducing thematic issues, Handl sets the tone for the entire series by posing a central question that might be considered the unofficial leitmotif for Volumes I and II: can the international legal system meet the challenges posed by global environmental concerns, thus providing present and future generations with a 'modicum of environmental security in the face of rapid global change'?

Published during the interregnum period between Stockholm and Rio, this essay evaluates the state of international law for environmental protection 'on the eve of the 1992 United Nations Conference on Environment and Development' (UNCED), a significant turning point for international law and environmental protection and an important fact to bear in mind when reading Handl's assessment of various techniques available at that time to achieve international environmental security. In particular, one might consider whether or not Handl's evaluation of international environmental security, conventional techniques, and corresponding problems they might pose when applied to international environmental issues, remains relevant today despite post-UNCED accomplishments. Additionally, it is prudent to ask whether significant progress has been made in the international legal system's ability to respond to global environmental concerns. Techniques assessed consist of the use of framework conventions and implementing protocols (see Chapters 6 and 7, Volume I, and Chapter 18, Volume II), 'soft law' (see Chapter 9, Volume I, as well as Chapter 11, Volume I, and Chapters 16 and 17, Volume II), and the possibility of establishing uniform environmental standards and the harmonisation of local, regional and global standard-setting. Handl familiarises the reader with key areas of implementation, enforcement and compliance with international environmental standards (see Chapters 13 and 14, Volume I), observing that whilst certain disadvantages might be perceived by the 'reluctance of states to submit to third-party decision-making' in this area – particularly the effectiveness of international environmental regimes to monitor compliance – other advantages offset those drawbacks, such as the increasing use of reporting techniques, peer review and other internal controls on states parties' obligations; the difficulty of using solely legal criteria 'to adjudge the merits of a legal dispute' where the precautionary principle is utilised (see Chapter 10, Volume I); and the increasing role of NGOs in assisting with the 'application and enforcement of international environmental standards' (see Chapter 15, Volume I).

Furthermore, Handl acquaints the reader with the concept of sustainable development (see Chapter 17, Volume II), viewed as a 'cardinal principle of international environmental decision-making', and its 'conceptual or philosophical' counterpart, that of intergenerational equity (see Chapter 5, Volume I). Although his pre-UNCED predictions classify sustainable development as a concept with 'international normative weakness', can the same be true today? Has sustainable development remained a concept that guides policy or has it taken on normative character? That question will be explored further by Sands in Chapter 17 in Part V of Volume II. Finally, in the course of his review of other traditional means of encouraging international environmental cooperation (IEC – the term is clarified in Chapter 11, Volume I) via legal means, Handl emphasises the importance of adopting less conventional methods, such as redefining sovereignty or inviting non-state actors to be participants, most notably transnational corporations (TNCs) and multilateral lending institutions responsible for financing sustainable development, thereby achieving a measure of equity for less developed countries (LDCs), and in turn, assisting in meeting economic and logistical obstacles LDCs inevitably encounter in complying with minimum environmental standards (see Chapters 24 and 25 in Volume II). The 'North–South Issue' is a recurring theme in subsequent essays wherein competing interests between environmental goals and developmental needs are considered (see Chapter 12, Volume I); methods for the transboundary movement of hazardous waste evaluated (see Chapters 21 and 22 in Volume II); and the Global Environmental Facility (GEF), a 'proposal' at the time of Handl's writing, updated and assessed in light of subsequent developments (see generally Chapter 6, Volume I and Chapters 17 and 25, Volume II).

The inherent dangers in embracing unfettered development without consideration of environmental consequences are predicaments for which solutions are not limited exclusively to legal parameters. Thus, it is less idiosyncratic that entropy would factor into a collection of essays on international environmental law than one might assume, since the subject matter itself is multidisciplinary, reaching far beyond the study of international law into the social and natural sciences, philosophy, micro- and macro-economics, politics and diplomacy, and making parallels drawn between 'time's arrow' and the evolution of the global environment harder to repudiate. Just as entropy cannot move in reverse, the natural world cannot evolve backwards into a pristine state tantamount to Elysian Fields. As a corollary to matters within the science of astrophysics, there exist separate but overlapping concerns identified as environmental issues, many of which have been gleaned from the natural and social sciences. It is fitting that this section includes what is considered a classic treatise written by an ecologist.

In Garrett Hardin's essay 'Tragedy of the Commons' (Chapter 2, Volume I), his venerable parable of the herdsman's flock grazing on the commons portrays how seemingly harmless individual pursuits could lead to unavoidable detrimental consequences. His thesis illustrates that in a world where resources such as land are finite, the open, unfettered and unregulated access to commonly owned resources results ultimately in their over-exploitation, with ruinous repercussions. Hardin analyses the pollution problem as a function of population density. Whilst the case of one herdsman seeking to maximise his flock and personal wealth is not so 'tragic', many herdsmen adding to their flocks will generate collective degradation by over-maximising the benefits of commonly owned spaces. If his thesis concerns solely herdsmen's flocks grazing on land in the historical sense, utilising Hardin's tragedy of the commons as a metaphor for modern environmental problems would be obsolete. Yet, when applied to a contemporary framework, his thesis transforms into a practical metaphor facilitating explanations for many global environmental problems that exist in today's common spaces: problems such as acid rain, climate change, ozone depletion, over fishing, polluted oceans, mismanaged forests and desertification.[13] In short, left unregulated, shared resources became a 'cesspool'. 'Freedom in a commons', wrote Hardin, 'brings ruin to all'. Consequently, external controls were deemed desirable, without which the pursuit of individual interests would lead to tragedy.

Whether viewed as having provided a foundation for 'free-market environmentalism' or as having influenced limited command-and-control models of environmental regulation, Hardin's thesis led to the strong belief for many decades that tight regulatory controls were the only solutions to limit individual freedom of usage within the commons. These limited controls have been criticised for failing to address underlying causes of environmental problems.[14] Contemporary approaches seek to reconcile individual and collective competing interests through various means, such as carrying out environmental impact assessments,[15] taking into account social, economic, environmental and political factors, incorporating better environmental management practices that recognise various values (ancestral, cultural, societal) at each stage of proposed development projects, and providing greater transparency through access to environmental information.

But what does Professor Hardin mean by 'pollution' and is it a term delimited in an international legal context? As Allen Springer illustrates with precision in his essay, 'Towards a Meaningful Concept of Pollution in International Law' (Chapter 3, Volume I), no single legal definition of pollution evolved during the post-Stockholm era, that is, the period following the 1972 UN Conference on the Human Environment (UNCHE), convened in Stockholm, Sweden. Springer adopted the view that pollution is an indication of 'a threshold level of damage or interference *which is legally significant*' (emphasis added). Bourne expanded Springer's observations in his recommendations to proceed with caution when using the word 'pollution', for it 'is a slippery word', he wrote, 'especially when used in relation to water resources':

> It denotes nothing precise about the state of any given waters; it is thus capable of meaning different things to different people. Moreover, it is an emotional word, full of unpleasant connotations; and, of course, it is a key word in the rhetoric of all those who now labour in the cause of saving mankind from self-destruction by environmental pollution. It is a term that should be avoided by lawyers. Its use obscures the real issues raised by the utilisation of water resources and thus hinders fruitful legal analysis; it tends to lead one to think that any act that renders water impure is wrong and ought to be illegal. (Bourne, 1971, p. 194)

Certainly, from an international legal perspective the term 'pollution' has evolved in accordance with Springer's opinion: activities that create pollution that in turn cause damage to the environment will trigger responsibility for environmental damage at different levels, measured according to prescribed rules and norms of domestic and international law (Francioni and Scovazzi, 1991, pp. ix–x). Decades before Springer's essay was published, when emissions from a Canadian smelter in Trail, British Columbia, caused damage to farmland via air pollution in the US State of Washington, the arbitration panel concluded in the *Trail Smelter* case that 'no state has the right to use or permit the use of its territory in such a manner as to cause injury by fumes in or to the territory of another'.[16] This decision is said to have evolved into the customary international law principle of harm prevention, expressed as a state's duty to control and regulate activities within their jurisdiction, not to cause transboundary environmental harm, and a corresponding right of an injured state to be compensated for any damage. The 'no harm principle' is considered as having universal acceptance, being expressed within Principle 21 of the Declaration of the UNCHE (Stockholm Declaration) and Article 2 of the Rio Declaration on Environment and Development (Rio Declaration),[17] thereby affirming a global consensus for this principle, albeit codified in non-legally binding documents (Birnie and Boyle, 1992, pp. 89–92; Hunter, Salzman and Zaelke, 1998, pp. 345–49; Sands, 1995, pp. 190–94).

'Pollution' is a 'slippery word'. No single definition of 'environment' exists in international law either (Birnie and Boyle, 1992, pp. 2–3; Sands, 1995, pp. 17–19). Undoubtedly, it is difficult to define narrowly that which is not narrow. Thus, treaties adopt definitions of various aspects of the environment, such as 'dumping' in the London Dumping Convention;[18] 'ozone layer' in Article 1, Vienna Convention for the Protection of the Ozone Layer (Vienna Ozone Convention);[19] 'climate change' in Article 1(2), Climate Change Convention (UNFCCC);[20] 'wastes' in Article 2(1), Basel Convention;[21] and 'air pollution' in the Convention on Long Range Transboundary Air Pollution.[22] Rather than delimit terms within the treaty itself, other conventions adopt 'listing' techniques whereby lists such as controlled substances,[23] or endangered species are included within annexes, thereby facilitating flexibility in content and accuracy in their status. The Convention on International Trade in Endangered Species of Wild Fauna and Flora (CITES) includes three annexes of flora and fauna ranging from the most endangered, to those currently at risk of becoming endangered in absence of regulation, and species under national jurisdiction and control.[24] Despite obvious difficulties in settling upon one uniform legal definition of the environment, the International Court of Justice (ICJ) has stressed the 'great significance it attaches to respect for the environment, not only for States but also for the whole of mankind'.[25] The ICJ concluded in its Advisory Opinion on nuclear weapons that,

> the environment is not an abstraction but represents the living space, the quality of life and the very health of human beings, including generations unborn. The existence of the general obligations of States to ensure that activities within their jurisdiction and control respect the environment of other States or of areas beyond national control is now part of the corpus of international law relating to the environment.[26]

Two further essays continue the elaboration in this section on conceptual rather than visceral approaches to international environmental law. Hardin generated spirited debate in the academic world, a debate that continues today. Christopher Stone, too, provoked ongoing deliberations by posing 'the famous environmental question' (Krämer, 1996, p. 15): should trees have standing? Similarly, Brown Weiss's seminal theory on intergenerational equity proposed that the present generation held the planet in trust for future generations. Whether by coincidence or not, Stone's essay was published in the same year that the UN held the first global conference to address the environment, the UNCHE (Stockholm Conference), a title referring to the 'human environment' and suggestive of a more anthropocentric approach than that author might have desired. In his thought-provoking essay, 'Should Trees Have Standing? – Toward Legal Rights for Natural Objects' (Chapter 4, Volume I), Stone argued that although 'corporations, states, infants, incompetents, municipalities or universities' cannot speak, they nevertheless have legal standing to sue. If a corporation can possess a legal identity, so too should forests and streams, which cannot speak for themselves either. Stone concluded natural objects should be represented by a legal guardian who would be able to protect their rights and collect legal judgments on those objects' behalf. But what rights and corresponding duties would a tree hold? Stone's thesis broke new ground by presenting a fresh perspective towards conservation and by applying rights-based theories to inanimate objects. The problem with his theory arises in delineating those specific rights and duties, a predicament carried over into the twenty-first century, given that non-state actors continue to be excluded from most significant international fora, including from the ICJ and World Trade Organisation (WTO) (Hunter, Salzman and Zaelke, 1998, p. 204; on NGOs as well as more recent developments within the WTO, see further below for commentary on Chapter 15, Part IV, Volume I).

Just as a trust fund benefits members of future generations, Edith Brown Weiss introduces a similar concept to protect and preserve the natural environment for future generations in Chapter 5's essay, 'Our Rights and Obligations to Future Generations for the Environment'.[27] According to her thesis, the essence of a trust is a fiduciary relationship, one that imposes on trustees a duty to act for the benefit of beneficiaries with respect to trust matters. It follows, then, that a 'planetary trust' works as follows: humans have a duty to hold the natural environment in common with all other humans, past, present and future generations alike. The basis for this duty is the concept of fairness between generations, or 'intergenerational equity'. The holders of the planetary trust, the present generation, are also beneficiaries of that trust because they are entitled to use and benefit from it, without compromising the trust in a manner that diminishes the inheritance that is to be passed on to the next generation. In other words, the planetary trust must not be passed on in a condition worse than that in which it was received. Brown Weiss explains that the corpus of the planetary trust includes both the natural heritage of the planet and the cultural heritage of the human species. Supporters of her thesis take the position that 'the idea of protecting the interests of future generations has already been introduced into international politics and international law'; accordingly, norms and standards should be elaborated further via treaty law rather than reliance on the development of customary norms and *opinio juris*, so that 'the duty of future generations should have a prominent place in the framework' of a convention (Gündling, 1990, p. 212).

This position is not without critics. D'Amato suggests rather than limit actions 'to those we are able to determine now as directly or indirectly benefitting ourselves or our descendants . . . we should cultivate our natural sense of obligation not to act wastefully or wantonly even when we cannot calculate how such acts would make any present or future generation worse off' (D'Amato, 1990, p. 1980). When regarded as a concept of IEC, intergenerational equity has less legal than policy significance in contemporary public international law. As a fundamental concept integral to the definition of sustainable development – development that meets the needs of present generations without sacrificing the needs of future generations – intergenerational equity is more likely a cross-cutting issue than emerging norm of customary international law or principle of international environmental law.

Both scenarios, rights for natural objects and planetary trusts – as 'seductive as the idea might be to bring actions in the name of whales, seals, trees or future generations' (Krämer, 1996, p. 15) – encompass actions that are generally not admissible in international law. Krämer noted that even by 1996, almost a quarter of a century after Stone's essay was published and more than a decade after Brown Weiss first introduced her thesis, legal actions in Europe in the name of trees or future generations were not admissible by any domestic court of an EU Member State:

> [t]he main objection against the admissibility of such actions is, in my opinion, the uncertainty of what rights such environmental items have or should have. Is one square metre of soil enough for a tree or are fifty square metres necessary? And who can decide whether an action is in the interest of a future generation or whether it is more appropriate not to take action, and which generation is one talking of? (Krämer, 1996, p. 15)[28]

Accordingly, cautious public international law practitioners dismiss theories of legal rights for natural objects and planetary trusts, despite their 'intellectual attractiveness' (Krämer, 1996, p. 15), and given that, in practice, trees do not have standing and planetary trusts do not exist in *lex lata*. As a matter of *lex ferenda*, on the other hand, it remains to be argued that either or both theories may represent emerging norms of customary international law or principles of international environmental law, deliberations that no doubt will continue among present generations, and someday carried on by those 'generations yet unborn'.

Traditional Sources of International Environmental Law: Treaties and Custom

Although it was impossible to turn back the clock and defy entropy, the global community still heeded nature's own stifled pleas, by recognising, at least by the 1970s, that unsustainable patterns of growth, consumption and development would contribute to Sir Arthur Eddington's own theory, an inevitable 'running-down of the universe'. Thereafter, international law evolved in reaction to the reality that, in absence of international norms and standards for environmental protection, current consumption habits, population growth, food insecurity, development policies – among many other social, economic and political variables integral to the ecological equation – would devastate further an already damaged, and often irreparable, global environment, left unchecked and unregulated. In many ways, 1972 signifies a magical date for international environmental law, with the Stockholm Conference representing a catalyst for the elaboration of global environmental protection treaties, while three relevant treaties were being drafted at that time: CITES, the United Nations Convention on the Law of the Sea (UNCLOS) and the UN International Watercourses Convention.

Firstly, CITES was adopted and opened for signature in 1973 and represented the first comprehensive attempt by the global community to regulate international trade in endangered species, plant and animal life alike. Considered as the most successful of all international treaties pertaining to wildlife conservation, subsequent developments included the 1997 decision to move the African elephant from its listing from Appendix I to II and the adoption of an EU Council Regulation protecting wild flora and fauna through regulating their trade, measures thought to yield superior controls, to be more effective and likely to achieve sustainable development (Ong, 1998, pp. 291–2). Renowned wildlife expert Simon Lyster attributes CITES's success to 'its basic principles, which most States have proved willing to accept, and by the way in which it operates, which ensures that on the whole it is better enforced than many other treaties' (Lyster, 1985, p. 240).

Coinciding with the elaboration of CITES was the ongoing work, often arduous, on combining various standards for the protection of the marine environment within one treaty. For decades, various UN conferences on the law of the sea sought to regulate marine pollution, albeit in piecemeal fashion. According to Oxman, nowhere is the link between the rule of law in international affairs and strengthening the global environment more apparent than in UNCLOS. He eloquently demonstrates that UNCLOS's promotion of the environment need not be antithetical to promotion of economic development or other human activities. Rather, drawing a nexus between the objectives of strengthening the rule of law in oceans governance and the objectives of promoting the marine environment, in fact advances both sets of objectives. Oxman argues that this link stimulates 'stronger public support throughout the world for both legal and environmental goals' (Oxman, 1996, p. 364). Furthermore, Boyle's own chronicle of the negotiating history of marine pollution norms recalls that during the Stockholm Conference, 'recommendations called on states to accept and implement existing instruments on the control of marine pollution to ensure the effectiveness of controls on vessel-source pollution and dumping at sea and to participate in new efforts to bring all sources of marine pollution, including land-based sources, under appropriate controls' (Boyle, 1985, p. 349).[29] By 1982, in the second of three examples of global treaties under brief review here, UNCLOS was adopted inclusive of a basic duty of states to protect and preserve the marine environment as expressly recognised in Articles 192 and 194.[30]

Thirdly, an equally laborious initiative of the UN General Assembly in 1970 concerned work on regulating the non-navigational uses of international watercourses, with a view towards its progressive development and codification. By 1974, the International Law Commission (ILC) had begun preliminary work on the subject and appointed the first of four special rapporteurs (McCaffrey, 1995, pp. 396–7). Two decades later, an international convention was adopted in 1997 that included articles on protection, preservation and management of international watercourses, signalling yet another milestone in international law and environmental protection (McCaffrey and Mpazi, 1998).[31]

Norms and standards expressed within CITES, UNCLOS and the International Watercourses Convention represent the final products of ambitious visions. Conventions cradling those goals were tantamount to the international community's acknowledgement of a rapidly depleting environment. That collective visceral response often found support in the form of cautionary scientific data, as in the case of endangered species, or reflective of a collective desire to protect, preserve and, where possible, improve environmental quality, whilst fully cognisant that pollution respects no political boundaries, as in the separate but inter-related cases of marine pollution and international watercourses noted above. Additional solutions based upon international law and cooperation were also deemed necessary to prevent further environmental erosion, such as ozone depletion, climate change and loss of biodiversity.

The selection of essays featured in this portion of the volumes are descriptive of major achievements in regulating activities that pollute the environment at the global level. Analyses are put forth for two of the three primary sources of international law as defined by Article 38(1)(a)–(c) of the ICJ Statute, treaties and custom; whilst the third and less lucid general principles of law is discussed further in the next section in the context of 'soft law', principles and emerging norms. Subsidiary sources – judicial decisions and writings of publicists – though not considered directly here should be mentioned as well, given that they may clarify important emerging rules for international environmental law, in the case of judgments, or provide intricate interpretations of the law, in the case of academic publications, or within reports published by international organisations such as the UN.[32] For instance, in *Gabcíkovo–Nagymaros*, the ICJ observed 'new norms and standards have been developed, set forth in a great number of instruments during the last two decades'[33] for environmental protection, these norms and standards considered as components forming part of the general corpus of international law (Hunter, Salzman and Zaelke, 1998, p. 238).

In the context of environmental protection, treaties are considered 'the most frequent method of creating binding international rules relating to the environment' (Birnie and Boyle, 1992, p. 11). Generally speaking, treaties are a source of rights and obligations agreed by the parties to them, rather than a formal source of law.[34] In the *Reservations to the Genocide Convention Case*, dissenting Judges Guerrero, McNair, Read and Hsu Mo jointly cautioned that the legislative or quasi-legislative nature of conventions 'must not obscure the fact that the legal basis of these conventions, and the essential thing that brings them into force, is the common consent of the parties'.[35] Treaty obligations apply only to the parties and may be contrasted with customary international law and municipal statutory law in this sense. Given that no central law-making authority exists in the international community, treaties are only binding upon parties.[36]

In Chapter 6, Andronico Adede chronicles the status of pre-UNCED environmental treaty-making and provides a useful synopsis of the main areas regulated by existing treaties in his essay, 'Towards New Approaches to Treaty-Making in the Field of the Environment'. One such area is described in David Caron's award-winning essay, 'Protection of the Stratospheric Ozone Layer and the Structure of International Environmental Lawmaking' (Chapter 7, Volume I). Both authors trace histories of treaty-making processes for multilateral environmental agreements (MEAs), generally in the first essay, and specifically in the second pertaining to the case of protecting the stratospheric ozone layer, 'an area in which there already has been a relatively large amount of lawmaking activity'. Each author recognises several key points, most notably that the process of elaborating environment and development issues requires 'an interdisciplinary approach' involving 'scientists, lawyers, economists, development strategists', among others. Furthermore, both write that even though international legal principles are applied during the process of drafting MEAs, within the normative system governing environmental concerns, 'new grounds [were] broken by international law through the development of new concepts', thereby distinguishing international environmental law-making as 'different from international lawmaking in general'. Adede's piece is instructive for contributing a useful summary of standard clauses in MEAs, thereby drawing out common elements among them, as well as indicating when and what non-legally binding environmental agreements have been adopted, so-called 'soft law' instruments (see Part III, Volume I).[37] The arduous road to Rio is introduced, as well as contributions by the World Commission on Environment and Development (WCED) and the Legal Working Group of UNCED's Preparatory Committee during that journey. Adede emphasises throughout his essay that the needs of developing states must be taken into consideration in any and all instruments, including those negotiated to finance sustainable development or tackling pressing environmental problems via the GEF, without diversion of such funds earmarked for such projects from developed states.

Using an example of an international legal regime pre-dating UNCED, Caron renders an expertly crafted account of how and why the international community adopted new standards to protect the ozone via the 1985 Vienna Ozone Convention, 1987 Montreal, and the London Amendment. Further amendments subsequent to the publication of his essay, and thus not chronicled therein, include those at Copenhagen in 1992 pertaining to non-compliance procedures.[38] Ostensibly, a 1985 publication by British scientists outlining their discovery of a hole in the ozone layer over Antarctica had triggered more rapid negotiations for a comprehensive protocol to the Vienna Ozone Convention, a view that is a matter of debate (Benedick, 1991, pp. 9–19). Once again the importance of scientific knowledge is underscored in Caron's essay, reaffirming the view that '[p]erhaps more than any other international environmental issue, the legal response to ozone depletion has been inextricably linked to our evolving understanding of the underlying science' (Hunter, Salzman and Zaelke, 1998, p. 545).

A second primary source of international law is custom, a source that according to some writers is considered preferable over the cumbersome, time-consuming processes of drafting and ratifying treaties (Birnie and Boyle, 1992, p. 15). In the *North Sea Continental Shelf Cases*, the ICJ determined that uniform, consistent state practice and *opinio juris* – the belief by a state that they are conforming to a legal obligation – were necessary conditions to recognise an international customary norm.[39] In Chapter 8, in his essay 'Customary (And Not So Customary) International Environmental Law', Bodansky reexamines custom in the context of international environmental law, concluding that so-called customary international environmental norms, such as the 'no harm principle' established in *Trail Smelter*, and later codified within Principle 21 of the Stockholm Declaration, among other environmental concepts, do not represent customary international law per se. Rather, these norms represent a new kind of law that he calls 'declarative international law'.[40] Given that legal institutions do not exist to apply international environmental norms nor do such norms comprise adequately precise substance to guide state behaviour, the question of their legal status is not significant. Instead, he argues that this particular source of international environmental law represents community standards that may guide state behaviour, set parameters for debate and provide a framework for negotiation of more specific norms, but generally possesses inconsequential normative force. Bodansky's position refutes the classical approach to customary international law-making based upon state practice and *opinio juris*, maintaining that those traditional approaches may have been appropriate when the scope of international law and the number of states were limited. Nonetheless, the increasing number and diversity of states coupled with expanded subject matters, such as international environmental law, are considered as rendering the traditional approach inappropriate (Charney, 1993, pp. 543–8). The question remains, however, whether these authors are talking about a new form of custom or whether such norms are more related to 'soft law' discussed in the next section.

Contemporary Sources of International Environmental Law: 'Soft Law', 'Principles' and Emerging Norms

The subject of non-traditional sources of international environmental law is said to be 'a highly controversial' one (Birnie and Boyle, 1992, p. 26); these represent another feature that might distinguish international environmental law-making from general international law-making, such as the persistent use of non-legally binding instruments known generically as 'soft law'. In fact, it is difficult to ignore this particular 'source' of international environmental law, given that the frequent resort to non-binding instruments is a reoccurring motif discussed throughout many chapters in this collection. Why do states prefer the practice of adopting non-legally binding instruments?

According to Alberto Székely, who is quoted in Chapter 11's essay in Volume I, the deliberate choice of states to express many obligations via 'soft law' in international environmental law represents their conscious intention 'not to create or develop international law, and if possible not to allow necessarily for the eventual formation of an international legal rule' (Székely,

1997, p. 190). An alternative view is advanced in the course of his examination of the creation, form and content, and legal effect of 'soft law' in Pierre-Marie Dupuy's essay 'Soft Law and the International Law of the Environment' (Chapter 9, Volume I). Essentially, he considers 'soft law' to have an indirect legal effect on the international law-making process but distinguishes it from customary law, categorising it as 'a sign and product of the permanent state of multilateral cooperation and competition among heterogeneous members of the contemporary world community'. Hillgenberg views non-binding agreements as not subject to treaty law and the principle of *pacta sunt servanda*. He concludes in part that such agreements are not indifferent in legal terms: if these agreements contain certain rules governing relations between parties, then 'they are a source of a self-contained legal regime subject to legal thinking and thus deserve the international lawyer's attention' (Hillgenberg, 1999, p. 516).

In contrast, other public international lawyers are not so keen to embrace 'soft law', 'a highly controversial subject', for which certain 'lawyers harbour such strong dislike of the appellation that they refuse even to mention it, especially in connection with sources [of law]' (Birnie and Boyle, 1992, p. 26). Malgosia Fitzmaurice does not accord source of law status to 'soft law' instruments such as non-binding annexes to treaties or resolutions and declarations, despite the fact that certain legal disputes may be settled by reference to these instruments. Most legal norms, in her view, are contained within treaties that occasionally have special structures, for instance, framework conventions that later elaborate more precise duties in protocols, or opting-out provisions enabling flexible adaptation to technological or environmental developments and facilitating consensus. One paramount customary norm, according to Fitzmaurice, is the obligation of states not to harm another state, or 'no harm principle', reaffirming the legal effect in international law on states, other than 'persistent objectors', of *Trail Smelter* and Principle 21 (Fitzmaurice, Chapter 16, Volume II).

The international legal status of other so-called customary principles or emerging norms are not so easily ascertained. Brown Weiss considers intergenerational equity as an obligation *erga omnes* and an emerging customary norm (Brown Weiss, 1984, pp. 540–44). This thread is followed in Chapter 10's essay 'The Precautionary Principle as a Norm of Customary International Law', wherein Owen McIntyre and Thomas Mosedale trace the development of sources enunciating the precautionary principle to ascertain its status in international law, concluding that it 'has indeed crystallised into a norm of customary international law'. Although this concept has been sewn into international documents, most often those documents are non-legally binding, expressed for instance within Article 15 of the Rio Declaration. Statements referring to the precautionary principle or 'precautionary approach' generally proclaim the notion introduced by the WCED that a lack of scientific certainty is an insufficient reason to postpone environmental protection measures where there are threats of serious or irreversible damage. Some international lawyers, however, are more sceptical of its legal status, expressing impracticality of implementation and that 'it is too vague to serve as a regulatory standard because it does not specify how much caution should be taken' (Bodansky, 1991, p. 4). More recently, the precautionary approach was included within the preambular paragraphs and Article 1 of the Cartagena Protocol[41] to the Biodiversity Convention[42] (see further Chapter 19, Volume II). It was hailed as the first protocol to initiate a binding global biosafety regime establishing significant international obligations for the transboundary movement of living modified organisms (LMOs). Yet, references to a precautionary approach are not considered as establishing 'any obligations beyond those explicitly articulated' within that protocol (Hagen and Weiner, 2000, pp. 710–11). Whether or not this particular protocol is evidence of consensus that the precautionary principle is a customary norm remains equivocal, and a highly debatable position.[43]

In contrast to those authors who embrace IEC concepts as evidence of emerging customary norms, others are not so quick to draw premature conclusions. For instance, my article in Chapter 11 entitled 'A Right to Environment in International Law: Current Status and Future Outlook' surveys the status of a so-called human right to environment in international law. I take the position that, in absence of a global treaty expressly recognising this concept as an internationally legally binding norm, and/or without consistent and uniform state practice expressing *opinio juris*, it is difficult to bestow a right to environment with anything other than cross-cutting issue status or that of an IEC concept. As with arguments about intergenerational equity and the precautionary principle as customary norms, most writers are 'sceptical of the view that a right to a decent environment presently forms part of international law' (Birnie and Boyle, 1992, p. 191). Not only do *travaux préparatoires* suggest otherwise, an international human right to environment is not considered to be a peremptory norm (*jus cogens*), and no uniform approach has evolved in municipal law.[44] It is difficult to find any consensus suggestive that *opinio juris* has developed, especially when no single global treaty recognises this concept as a human right. What is more, the only two regional treaties expressing variations of a human right to environment experienced slow ratification, poor implementation and questionable compliance by parties.[45]

Quite frankly, it is unclear what is meant precisely by an international human right to environment in the first place. Is it a right to a decent, healthy, safe or sound environment; is it a right to environmental protection; or is it a right to conservation? Is it a substantive or procedural right? Is it an individual or collective right? Is it a civil, political, economic, social or cultural right? Is it an emerging norm, third or fourth generation, or solidarity right? Even its proponents cannot agree on a single, uniform characteristic. In some cases, states express environmental protection in constitutions as procedural rights to information and access to justice for environmental matters. But these procedural rights can hardly be said to be novel, given that their foundation is based upon the rule of law and due process. What is more, there is a distinct tendency for proponents of new human rights to fall into the 'rights trap', as in the case of environmental protection wherein classification of legal rights and obligations in terms of narrowly defined human rights cannot effectively address the plethora of ecological concerns that face contemporary decision-makers. Furthermore, just because expressly recognised international human rights, such as the rights to life, health, privacy and property, can be linked to environmental issues does not automatically lead to the conclusion that an international human right to environment exists as an inherent human right or emerging norm. Rather, it suggests that environmental degradation is but one of many issues that can be added to an ever-expanding roster of issues and relevant scenarios applicable during the assessment of whether or not expressly recognised international human rights have been violated in contravention of global human rights treaty obligations.

In terms of general principles of law, conservative approaches consider that Article 38(1)(c) is limited to legal procedures commonly applied in all municipal legal systems (Birnie and Boyle, 1992, pp. 21–4). The more controversial interpretation has evolved from the interchangeable usage of expressions 'general principles of law' and 'principles of international environmental law'. Some authors refer to 'principles and rules of general application' (Sands,

1995, pp. 183–237) or 'international environmental law principles and concepts' (Hunter, Salzman and Zaelke, 1998, pp. 325–84). Conversely, the current trend emanating from members of the ICJ, from legal officers within the UN and its specialised agencies, and from international legal scholars like Adede, is to identify emerging principles or rules as new 'concepts' comprising intergenerational equity, common but differentiated responsibility, common concern of mankind, the precautionary principle, and sustainable development among others (see further Chapter 6, Volume I, pp. 85–6). The confusion lies in whether or not such principles are those of the Article 38(1)(c) variety or simply IEC concepts shaping and defining global environmental policy, more closely associated with non-legally binding tenets of 'soft law'.

International Institutions and Non-Governmental Organisations: Their Evolving Roles and Influence in Elaborating International Environmental Law through Standard-Setting, Implementation, Monitoring, Enforcement, Compliance and Dispute Resolution Procedures

Previous chapters reviewed above are useful as building blocks in this part, essentially to underscore additional achievements in international law for the protection of the environment. In this subsection, the general themes presented within these essays endeavour to assist the reader in taking a closer look at diverse institutional arrangements, whether within the UN system, IGOs, or multilateral environmental institutions (MEIs), also referred to in this section as 'autonomous institutions'[46] – the latter specifically created to administer MEAs – or whether operating on the periphery of the UN, IGOs and MEIs, such as NGOs independently monitoring the implementation of and compliance with MEAs by member states.

One of the earliest MEAs is said to date back to 1868. Today, over 500 international treaties and other agreements related to the environment have been concluded, of which the United Nations Environment Programme (UNEP) estimates over 320 are regional in scope. Approximately 60 per cent of the total number of agreements in existence post-date the Stockholm Conference, illustrating the accelerated rate at which agreements were negotiated since 1972, with well over 300 new agreements coming into existence during that period (UNEP/IGM, 6 April 2001, 'Executive Summary', para. 4; Part I, 'Status of MEAs', para. 9; UNEP/IGM, 4 April 2001, para. 45). At last, following the Stockholm Conference, pre-existing, new and emerging environmental problems were brought to the attention of the international community, thereby raising an international environmental consciousness. But a huge challenge remained: how would these treaties be administered? Certainly, pre-existing multilateral institutions, especially, but not exclusively UN entities as a convenient starting point, had to be modified, whilst completely new treaty organs had to be created to address global environmental concerns, to meet environmental obligations, and to fulfil clauses expressly stating that these new treaty bodies must be established, all obligations encapsulated within individual MEAs themselves. This section looks at two specific areas of international institutions: first, MEIs within the UN system; and second, MEIs established pursuant to MEAs, where core environmental conventions and related agreements of global significance are either associated with UNEP or negotiated independently of UNEP and UN organs in general.

Consequent to rapid proliferation of MEAs and the ever-growing number of states' parties participating in their conception, ratification and implementation, a resultant debate was triggered that focuses upon several issues under the broad theme of 'international environmental governance' (IEG). The President of UNEP's Governing Council identified the 'current debate on the requirements for a more coherent and more effective' IEG were predicated upon 'a continuation of international efforts over the past decade to develop institutional responses [underpinning] international action to confront the increase of environmental threats faced by all countries'. Not only is a coherent framework for coordinated international action necessary to address specific environmental problems, limited resources available needed to be deployed 'in the best possible manner for optimal effect' (UNEP/IGM, 16 January 2002, para. 1).

With specific reference to UN organs, Patricia Birnie confirms in her essay 'Environmental Protection and Development' (Chapter 12, Volume I), that the founding member states of the UN did not envisage environmental protection as one of its mandates when it was established over half a century ago. Nor does the UN Charter make any reference to the environment. In fact, the principal organs of the UN – General Assembly, Secretariat, Security Council, Economic and Social Council (ECOSOC), and ICJ – as well as its specialised agencies, subsidiary organs and related agencies initially were not created with environmental problems in mind.[47] Subsequent to the landmark global conferences held at Stockholm and Rio de Janeiro, the mandates of those principal and subsidiary organs have become increasingly cognisant of environmental issues, recognising global environmental concerns within various political agendas. (Iwama, 2002, (uwp); Caldwell, 1996, pp. 127–39; Morrison and Wolfrum (eds), 2000, pp. 71–110; Szasz, 1992, pp. 340–51). In fact, Birnie demonstrates this point by describing how the UN, its specialised agencies and numerous conferences organised under its auspices, most notably at Stockholm and Rio, have taken added environmental issues to their agendas in response to addressing environmental challenges. She credits the establishment of UNEP, by the General Assembly (a principal agenda-setting and policy-making body within the UN system) as having contributed to the progressive development of international environmental law, as well as having reconciled competing interests of environment and development. Birnie acknowledges the Stockholm Conference's leading role in placing the environment front and centre upon a UN conference's agenda for the very first time, and she sees the Stockholm Declaration as influencing subsequent standard-setting for environmental protection. Birnie's view finds strong support in Louis Sohn's superbly crafted essay featuring intricate details of negotiations alongside a clause-by-clause analysis of the Stockholm Declaration, comparing it with the 1948 Universal Declaration of Human Rights as triggering the eventual drafting of several international treaties for the protection of human rights. Given the plethora of MEAs drafted after Stockholm, Sohn's prescient observations have proven reliable:

> In the new ambience of international relations thus established, this first step toward the establishment of international environmental law on a firm foundation might prove to be more decisive than originally anticipated. Having accepted the responsibility for the preservation and improvement of the human environment, the international community will find in the Stockholm Declaration a source of strength for later, more specific action. (Sohn, 1973, p. 515)[48]

Despite these seemingly lofty international environmental achievements by and through UN organs, an impartial profile of existing UN organs illustrates that presently, only UNEP, the Commission on Sustainable Development (CSD),[49] and the GEF are directly concerned with issues pertaining to IEG within their specific mandates. What is more, only 8 out of 16 UN specialised agencies are directly involved in environmental protection (Iwama, 2002, uwp).[50] This reality has led many commentators to call for a complete overhaul of the UN organs presently dealing with environmental matters. Recommendations to reform the current system are numerous and most often conclude with the creation of a completely new international environmental agency. Sir Geoffrey Palmer's frequently cited essay proposed the creation of 'a proper international environmental agency within the [UN] system that has real power and authority', not simply the creation of a UN General Assembly resolution (as in the case of UNEP); rather, Sir Geoffrey proposed the creation of a UN specialised agency he named the International Environment Organisation (IEO). This new entity could build upon existing entities, like UNEP, but be constructed with a similar tripartite structure to that of the ILO – wherein delegations comprise members of government, as well as workers' and employers' organisations – with the IEO model to include representatives from government, industry and environmental organisations that would make up delegations sent to participate in transparent decision-making processes at the IEO Secretariat (Palmer, 1991, pp. 262, 280–82; Iwama, 2002, uwp). Desai proposed the creation of a specialised agency called the United Nations Environment Protection Organisation (UNEPO) (Desai, 2000, pp. 495–98); Farr, that of a Global Environmental Organisation (GEO) modelled on the WHO (Farr, 2000, pp. 510–25); Iwama, for a vertical approach (that is, creating a new UN agency and/or a specialised agency)[51] in concert with a horizontal approach (that is, revitalising existing UN organs including the General Assembly, Security Council, Secretariat, ECOSOC, specialised agencies, strengthening UNEP, reforming UNDP, among others), but cautioning that unless the political climate is 'ripe enough', in reality it 'seems unlikely for a new UN principal organ to be created, because of the limited UN budget, an unwillingness of member states to bear the expense of creating new institutions, their resistance to the expansion of the UN organs and a foreseeable difficulty of amending the UN Charter' (Iwama, 2002, uwp).

The preceding cautious viewpoint may find some comfort in the fact that IEG reform projects have already been undertaken within the UN itself. When the UN Secretary-General established a Task Force on Environment and Human Settlements, the reports that followed led to the creation of the Global Ministerial Environment Forum (GMEF). Then, against the backdrop of the 2002 World Summit on Social Development's (WSSD) preparations, the UNEP Governing Council's adoption of Decision 21/21 entitled 'International Environmental Governance' established the Open-Ended Intergovernmental Group of Ministers or Their Representatives (IGM). The IGM's mandate was to undertake a comprehensive policy-oriented assessment of existing institutional weaknesses as well as future needs and options for strengthened IEG, including but not limited to financing UNEP (UNEP/IGM, 16 January 2002, paras. 3, 4, and 6). The IGM has already produced a number of working papers, background reports, summaries of selected relevant publications on IEG by governments, NGOs and individual authors, in addition to identifying key weaknesses and strengths in the current IEG system, upon which several proposals and recommendations were made.[52] Twenty MEA Secretariats – dealing specifically with core environmental conventions and related agreements of global significance, whose negotiation, development and/or activities are associated with UNEP's work – were asked to complete a questionnaire ('MEA questionnaire') according to one UNEP/IGM report. In response to the MEA questionnaire, those secretariats identified a number of issues for discussion, among the following key points:

- **Strengths:** clustering core MEAs with common ground; exploring opportunities for synergies and scientific cooperation; and, increasing arrangements for cooperation among MEAs (UNEP/IGM, 30 March 2001, paras. 39–41; ibid., 6 April 2001, para. 16);
- **Weaknesses:** reluctance of some agreements to cooperate with others; inadequate attention to the harmonisation of national reporting; inadequate implementation and coordination efforts at the national level; inadequate enforcement and compliance; lack of environmental performance indicators measuring effectiveness of an MEA; insufficient funding for certain agreements (UNEP/IGM, 30 March 2001, paras. 42–46, 48; ibid., 6 April 2001, para. 16);
- **Issues not being addressed effectively by MEAs:** a long wish list identified many areas, such as forests, tropical timber, river ecosystems, control of new ozone-depleting substances, among many others (UNEP/IGM, 30 March 2001, para. 47; ibid., 6 April 2001, para. 17).[53]

Another UNEP report prepared for the WSSD willingly admitted that IEG in its present form faces many challenges, namely,

> [that the] present proliferation of structures, agreements and conferences, [results] in a heavy burden placed upon developing countries in particular, many of which simply do not have the necessary resources either to participate in an adequate and meaningful manner, or to comply with the complex and myriad reporting requirements associated with [MEAs] (UNEP/IGM, 4 April 2001, para. 7).

The challenges do not stop there: weak policy coordination is considered a major cause in missed opportunities to enhance coherence and synergy among various instruments. The number of MEAs is also on the rise, whilst the average time taken to negotiate each and every treaty is decreasing. At the same time, both the scale and magnitude of problems to be addressed have widened, corresponding with a similarly gradual burgeoning number of sovereign states participating in complex negotiations of legal arrangements addressing environmental problems; and, although MEAs represent outstanding achievements on the part of the international community, the urgent need for policy coherence at all levels is prevalent (UNEP/IGM, 4 April 2001, para. 7). Although the path of reform is uncertain, whatever path reform eventually takes, Bodansky sensibly advocates the importance of strong, authoritative, and internationally legitimate institutions, considered a major requirement to achieving effective international reactions and solutions to global environmental problems (Bodansky, 1999).

Besides the UN system and reform proposals therein, several MEIs exist primarily to monitor the implementation of and compliance with a single MEA embedding standards of international environmental law. Certain kinds of MEIs have been established as a result of negotiation, their detailed structure outlined within an MEA itself specifying an institutional arrangement must be set up, dedicated solely to the administration of that particular MEA once the treaty has been concluded. Thereafter, a conference of the parties (COP) with decision-making powers, a secretariat, advisory bodies, clearing-house and financial mechanisms, and if necessary, additional specialised subsidiary organs may be created as part of the MEA's administrative structure (UNEP/IGM, 30 March 2001, para. 21). These particular treaty bodies collectively may be categorised as MEIs (Iwama, 2002, uwp), or alternatively, what Robin Churchill and Geir Ulfstein refer to as 'autonomous institutions', a thesis presented in their impressively researched essay, 'Autonomous Institutional Arrangements in Multilateral

Environmental Agreements: A Little-Noticed Phenomenon in International Law' (Chapter 13, Volume I). Fundamentally, the authors distinguish IGOs initiated under MEAs from more traditional IGOs, the former having established 'autonomous institutional arrangements' (AIAs). On the one hand, AIAs are distinct from both states parties to a particular MEA and from existing IGOs, and on the other hand, AIAs have their own law-making powers, compliance and enforcement mechanisms. Churchill and Ulfstein suggest AIAs signify 'a distinct and different approach to institutionalised collaboration between states, being both more informal and more flexible, and often innovative in relation to norm creation and compliance', a phenomena they consider has gone without much notice by international lawyers. The authors link the emergence of AIAs with increasing interdependence among states – as distinguished from more traditional approaches to international law and security where the preservation of a peaceful coexistence among nations was paramount – a phenomenon derivative of a more contemporary approach to international law requiring an international law of cooperation. This also supports the concept introduced earlier regarding the emergence of IEC concepts, part and parcel of a cooperative approach in dealing with international environmental issues. Churchill and Ulfstein conclude such AIAs, ultimately, 'demonstrate that international cooperation may take innovative forms designed for specific needs, presenting challenges to the international lawyer'.

Whatever form an MEI takes, whether established within the UN system or not, the overall effectiveness of international environmental standards are fundamentally considered to be directly dependent on 'the establishment of international institutions which are empowered to take measures with the view to ensure compliance with the established standards' (Wolfrum, 1998, p. 48). Succeeding in that task requires establishing effective and sound reporting, monitoring, compliance and dispute resolution procedures, collectively considered less than perfect procedures with current MEAs as summarised within the aforementioned UNEP/IGM reports. Sachariew defines the general characteristics of a reporting system as 'premised on an institutional framework (permanent organisation, meetings of the parties, secretariat or special organ) within which reports on measures taken by the parties are received, studied and assessed'. He describes 'monitoring' as 'a method of studying the effects of human activities on natural ecosystems in order to understand the cause-effect relationships involved'. 'Reporting' is characterised by Sachariew as the more 'elaborate procedure' of the two, due to the 'soft' role in the cases of monitoring, research and fact finding as supervisory techniques in international environmental law (Sachariew, 1991, pp. 35, 40–41).

A contemporary reporting system provides one example of a 'more sophisticated' regime, and consequently further evidence in support of Sachariew's observations. Articles 7 and 8 of the Kyoto Protocol to the UNFCCC[54] – the latter examined closely in Chapter 18 of Volume II – expand the two basic reporting requirements established under the treaty: namely, national inventories and accounts of greenhouse gas emission budgets; and periodic national communications providing detailed information on states parties' implementation. All states parties must provide information necessary to ensure compliance with their obligations under the Protocol, as part of its annual inventory. That inventory must comply with prescribed methods, failure to do so resulting in adjustments to account for uncertainties. The Protocol also strengthens the review of information procedures by requiring annual reviews of national inventory and emission target information as part of a centralised accounting of assigned amounts. The Secretariat is responsible for collecting, compiling and publishing inventories, as well as coordinating expert teams that review states parties' reports and forwarding any perceived problems identified by expert teams' report for consideration at a Meeting of Parties. This reporting procedure is said to have 'transformed from an information-collecting device into a true monitoring system' (Wolfrum, 1998, p. 43).

Paying closer attention to categories of compliance, enforcement, and dispute resolution, with regard to the first category, compliance with MEAs may be achieved through a variety of confrontational and non-confrontational methods: in the first instance, through countermeasures on the basis of Article 60 of the 1969 Vienna Convention on the Law of Treaties,[55] withdrawing membership privileges or via MEAs imposing trade restrictions; or, in the second instance, through economic incentives as in the case where MEAs balance environmental commitments by potential economic benefits, including financial incentives from multilateral financial institutions (Wolfrum, 1998, pp. 56–150).[56] In the case of non-compliance, Günther Handl expands on issues of implementation and compliance (introduced in Chapter 1, Volume I) in his second essay included in this volume, 'Compliance Control Mechanisms and International Environmental Obligations' (Chapter 14, Volume I). Handl pays close attention to typical attributes of non-compliance procedures within MEAs, rather than and in addition to the techniques reviewed earlier.[57] From a conceptual perspective, Mitchell suggests that 'compliance is neither a necessary nor sufficient condition for effectiveness'. His theory is premised on the notion that an MEA can be effective without necessarily being complied with, as long as the treaty produces 'the environmental improvements that motivate their negotiation in the first place'. On the other hand, greater compliance may increase environmental improvements, thus delineating compliance as a valuable proxy for effectiveness (Mitchell, 1996, pp. 24–6).

UNEP's IGM made several observations and recommendations with respect to the current state of monitoring implementation, compliance and enforcement of MEAs. Responses to the MEA questionnaire noted weaknesses in current capacities to monitor the state of compliance with MEAs. Even though the current processes in place call for the regular submission of reports to each and every MEA as a means of monitoring levels of implementation and compliance with conventions, some countries do not submit reports, and others 'do so belatedly'. At the same time, MEA Secretariats have small budgets. Solutions to these problems include establishing an authoritative body with the capacity to verify the information supplied by governments; resolving the issue of reviewing implementation status on a country-by-country basis as opposed to an agreement-by-agreement basis; and, reinforcing surveillance mechanisms to monitor the implementation of MEAs. To improve compliance, many MEA Secretariats complained that there were not enough financial measures and incentives to encourage implementation. In addition, they cited that proliferation of MEAs placed huge financial burdens on many countries that simply could not keep up with the demands of the international community. In order to improve compliance, incentives and measures such as additional financing, adoption of a centralised reporting process, encouraging ratification and making some agreements enforceable even against non-signatories were a few recommendations. Finally, several tools were suggested to improve all categories noted above:

- revising environmental exceptions to the WTO (discussed further below, Part IV, Volume I);
- establishing a complaints system with defined roles for MEA Secretariats in processing complaints, for COP powers to rule on them and a range of measures that could be taken (that is, assistance measures, economic sanctions, and so on);

- establishing a dispute settlement mechanism (conciliation, negotiation, and so on), whether centralised or specific to each agreement, within a new court, the ICJ or otherwise;
- creating an office for an environmental ombudsman (already in existence at the national level of many states including Canada), or alternatively a centre for amicable settlement of environmental disputes, possibly under UNEP (or a new international environmental agency);
- implementation of common regulations on the subject of environmental liability as an instrument promoting States parties to respect their obligations; and,
- imposition of sanctions and penalties for non-jurisdictional aspects (UNEP/IGM, 4 April 2001, paras. 150–52).

Another means of ensuring compliance with MEAs is via transparent procedures in which NGOs can monitor implementation of obligations through active and effective participation. The history of NGO participation is traced succinctly in Dan Tarlock's essay, 'The Role of Non-Governmental Organizations in the Development of International Environmental Law' (Chapter 15, Volume I).[58] Not considered a traditional 'subject' of international law, non-state actors like NGOs have increasingly had tremendous influence in ensuring compliance with MEAs. In accordance with the policy science or New Haven School of thought, Judge Rosalyn Higgins of the ICJ has argued that international law is a particular decision-making process wherein the notion of 'subjects' and 'objects' has no credible reality and, within that process there are many participants other than states, including IGOs, TNCs and NGOs.[59] In fact, NGOs and other non-state actors played crucial roles generally in environmental diplomacy, applied to international environmental treaty-making efforts,[60] for instance during arduous negotiations of the Montreal Protocol (Benedick, 1991, pp. 68–76). During the preparatory process of UNCED, the UN decided to provide roster status to non-ECOSOC/NGOs in order to expand the number involved at Rio. More than 1400 UNCED NGOs were thus accredited via liberal and flexible accreditation rules that were subsequently adopted by the CSD. Accredited NGOs are allowed to participate in CSD meetings as observers, where they are permitted to submit written statements at their own expense and to address meetings at the chair's discretion (Mori, 2002, uwp).

NGOs may also take part in COP meetings to MEAs with observer status. The main functions of NGOs at such meetings are considered to ensure that obligations are enforced under MEAs, to inform the public and to voice concerns, among others. Exceptionally, NGOs may monitor the implementation of agreements on behalf of IGOs, as in the case of the World Conservation Monitoring Unit assigned to track state reports of imports and exports of listed species under CITES, or may have observer status, as in the case of the Vienna Ozone Convention and Montreal Protocol. Very few agreements provide rights of access to environmental information, thereby preventing transparency and limiting NGOs' abilities to monitor compliance. A third method in which NGOs may become instrumental in ensuring compliance is when its members become part of national delegations at intergovernmental conferences. NGOs have become important facilitators in raising funds in 'debt-for-nature swaps' wherein an environmental organisation will purchase a state's debt and, in turn, finance environmental projects in the debtor state using bonds or other types of security issued in exchange for the debt (Wolfrum, 1998, pp. 52–4; Sachariew, 1991, pp. 48–9). NGOs may have greater access to the world's trade institutions. In an 'unexpected move', the WTO's Appellate Body issued an 'Additional Procedure' to deal with submissions from 'non-parties'. This procedure will allow NGOs, academics and industry groups the opportunity to present *amicus curiae* briefs, providing an increased level of transparency and recognising civil society's interest in participating in certain cases. Furthermore, this development has significant 'implications for NGOs promoting health and environmental protection and sustainable development in the context of international trade' (Palmer and Werksman, 2001, pp. 125, 130).[61] The next step for NGOs would involve more formalisation of NGO involvement in MEIs, a role that would include voting rights, although highly unlikely to be accepted anytime soon (Charnovitz, 1997, p. 283; Mori, 2002, uwp). Nevertheless, one cannot dismiss an increasingly important role that NGOs have played, particularly in representing views of civil society through broader participation in previously restricted access global sessions exploring and debating critical global environmental issues.

The Progressive Development of International Law in the Contexts of Environment and Sustainable Development: Assessing Achievements at the Stockholm and Rio Conferences

The collection of essays chosen for this part outlines advancements made in international environmental law after Stockholm and particularly during the post-UNCED period. In Chapter 12, where Birnie left off in her summary of developments at Stockholm, this section picks up on that theme in Chapter 16, Volume II, wherein Malgosia Fitzmaurice's essay 'International Environmental Law as a Special Field', opens with a conceptual approach reminiscent of the collection of essays presented in Part I of Volume I. Fitzmaurice ponders the question of the environment as a special 'field' of international law and reviews treaties and 'soft law' as sources of law, subjects reviewed in previous chapters. However, she quickly changes pace, confronting pressing issues not raised in the essays included within Volumes I and II. The distinguishing features of her essay are twofold: first, an informative synopsis of the ILC's complex work on state responsibility; and second, an enumeration of states' various duties and entitlements in relation to environmental protection and preservation, whilst contemporaneously analysing those duties in light of the ILC liability draft.

In the case of state responsibility and liability for environmental damage,[62] it was the escalating international recognition of the irreversible disposition of environmental harm that led research within various forums which produced drafts of specific rules addressing distinct environmental damage, beginning in the 1960s with the International Law Association's 'Helsinki Rules' (ILA, 1966), the ILC, and the *Institut de Droit International*. Since Fitzmaurice's essay was published, the ILC draft liability articles were presented to the Commission's session in 1996 by Special Rapporteur Barboza. A Working Group established at that session subsequently reported to the Commission, the latter considering substantial advances on the draft had been attained. In 1997, Mr Pemmaraju Sreenivasa Rao was appointed Special Rapporteur to focus on prevention of transboundary damage from hazardous activities. Rao's first report discussed procedural obligations that the general duty of prevention entailed: prior authorisation; international environmental impact assessment; cooperation; exchange of information; notification; consultation and negotiation in good faith; dispute prevention or avoidance and settlement of disputes; and non-discrimination. Concerning substantive obligations, Special Rapporteur Rao considered the precautionary principle, the polluter-pays principle, and the principle of equity, capacity-building and good governance. In 1998, the ILC adopted, on first reading, a set of 17 draft articles pertaining to prevention of transboundary damage from hazardous activities.[63] This latest draft was submitted to the UN Secretary-General for dissemination to governments for their comments, a process that was ongoing at the time of writing.

Complementing the ILC's work in this area is that of the *Institut de Droit International*, whose members have considered state responsibility and liability in the context of the environment. In September 1997, the *Institut* adopted a resolution, 'Responsibility and Liability Under International Law for Environmental Damage',[64] that sets up a two-tiered framework: primary liability is assigned to private operators; secondary liability is assigned to states. At the heart of this resolution one finds procedures that promote the prevention of environmental damage ('Preventive Mechanisms'), thereby incorporating a precautionary approach, and providing compensation and reparation for damage – for instance, where the source of environmental damage is unidentified or compensation is unavailable, then collective reparation is envisaged in Article 12. The preamble stresses prominent themes in international environmental law that are 'developing new links with the concepts of intergenerational equity, the precautionary approach, sustainable development, [and] environmental security', as well as principles of common but differentiated responsibility, in addition to other areas of international law, such as human rights. It also takes into account 'evolving principles and criteria governing State responsibility . . . under international and national law', inferring perhaps the ILC's work in that regard as well as national schemes. In mirroring many of the ILC's observations, the *Institut*'s Special Rapporteur's study emphasises: the need to prevent harm rather than focus on reparation of injuries; encouraging the use of environmental impact assessments; the obligations to notify and consult states that might be affected by harmful activities; implementation of pre-paid collective reparation funds; provision of comprehensive private or national insurance schemes; and shifting the burden of proof via strict liability whilst drawing a demarcation between responsibility and liability. To put it plainly, responsibility conjures up the notion of fulfilling obligations, thus preventing harm in the first place, or triggering consequences when a state fails to meet its obligations; whereas liability recognises traditional methods relating to restoration and compensation (Orrego Vicuña, 1996). The international legal effect of this draft on environmental protection is, at best, to provide a workable set of guidelines that, as one author views it, might 'spur international lawyers to create flexible and effective regimes to meet current and future environmental challenges' (Berwick, 1998, p. 267).

In closing her essay, Fitzmaurice surveys the latest 'trends and developments in international environmental law', among which she includes her perception of the concept of 'sustainable development', which she does not view as a norm of international law, thus providing a convenient bridge into the next essay. In fact, the concluding sections of both Birnie's and Fitzmaurice's essays in Chapters 12, Volume I and 16, Volume II respectively end with brief speculation on the evolving concept of sustainable development in international environmental law, a subject that is expertly examined by Philippe Sands. In Chapter 17, Volume II, Sands' essay, 'International Law in the Field of Sustainable Development' shifts the focus of international law from the field of 'environment' (for example, Fitzmaurice's perspective) to that of 'sustainable development', raising pertinent questions as to its nature and scope whilst challenging international lawyers to contemplate this new lingua franca within international environmental law, a focus described by another author as 'a major paradigm shift' (Sand, 1993, p. 377). According to Sands, Principle 27 of the Rio Declaration suggests that 'international law in the field of sustainable development' already exists, a field he describes as 'a broad umbrella accommodating the specialised fields of international law which aim to promote economic development, environmental protection and respect for civil and political rights', cautioning that it is not 'an independent and free-standing body of principles and rules, and it is still emerging'. In the course of his in-depth analysis of sustainable development, from historical roots to UNCED, Agenda 21 and the Rio Declaration, Sands undertakes adeptly the challenging task of ascertaining what is meant by sustainable development in international law. After classifying six broad issues as critical to international law and sustainable development, he describes with clarity and precision areas that may be cross-referenced to other chapters in both Volumes I and II, for instance: emerging principles (some of which are considered in Chapter 16, Volume II); new and restructured institutional arrangements, including the CSD and the GEF (see Chapters 12 and 13, Volume I, and Chapter 25, Volume II); governance, with emphasis upon NGOs and access to environmental information (see Chapter 15, Volume I); international regulation (see generally Part II in Volume I); implementation, compliance and enforcement (see Chapters 13 and 14, Volume I); and financing sustainable development for and transfer of technologies to developing states (see Chapter 25, Volume II). Sands encourages integration of separate fields of international law, rather than compartmentalising 'worlds of environmental and economic law'.

Overall, Sands' essay is far more optimistic than other essays critically assessing the Rio Declaration.[65] Kovar considers the Rio Declaration a disappointment for not having met the expectations raised by UNCED Secretary-General Maurice Strong, who had called for, but failed to achieve, consensus on an 'Earth Charter',[66] though ending on a more upbeat note by characterising the Rio Declaration as 'an important step forward' (Kovar, 1993, pp. 119, 140). A more extreme assessment by Pallemaerts claims that it represents a profound step backwards, regressing from sustainable development to 'sustained growth' for subordinating 'environmental policies to economic imperatives'. Pallemaerts maintains the position that the 'new ideology of sustainable development undermines the autonomy of environmental law as a body of rules and standards designed to restrain and prevent the environmentally destructive effects of certain kinds of economic activity' (Pallemaerts, 1993, pp. 13–14, 16–17, 18–19). Regional approaches suggest that sustainable development has become an underlying policy within regional organisations such as the EU,[67] APEC (Lin, 1995, p. 32),[68] and the OAS (Ascencio Herrera and Pevato, 1996, p. 13).[69]

In reference to the Rio conference in general, even Strong was convinced afterwards 'that the future of our planet and its people cannot be left in the hands of our political leaders' (Strong, 1993, p. 34). Regardless of diverging viewpoints pertaining to the Rio Declaration itself, or to the outcome at UNCED, it is certain that two treaties opened for signature at UNCED represent qualified successes. The first, being the UNFCCC, is recounted meticulously by Donald Goldberg in 'As the World Burns: Negotiating the Framework Convention on Climate Change' (Chapter 18, Volume II). Indeed, as the title of his essay implies, the scientific and diplomatic gatherings debating climate change produced as much drama and intrigue as any soap-opera plot. In comparison to Goldberg's essay, Bodansky's detailed evaluation of the UNFCCC provides a more sombre reminder that many governments and commentators had very high and unrealistic expectations – assuming for instance 'that it would be able to build on the progress achieved in international environmental agreements such as the Montreal Protocol' – particularly given the gravity of global warming predictions. The Montreal Protocol established stringent control measures requiring phase-out of most ozone depleting substances.

In contrast, the UNFCCC failed to include binding stabilisation commitments, leading Bodansky to characterise this treaty as 'a modest achievement'. According to Bodansky, this deficiency was the treaty's 'greatest disappointment', because it fell short of existing agreements. To address deficiencies, Bodansky recommends reducing uncertainties about the basic science of climate change, developing an information base about national conditions and options, and establishing a strong institutional structure (Bodansky, 1993, pp. 554–8). Ostensibly, commitments and other details were to be specified later. Certainly, this was the case during recent negotiations in Bonn on changes to the Kyoto Protocol, the legal stimulus wherein those commitments were clarified, albeit after eleventh-hour negotiations and diplomatic compromises. That Protocol commits 178 states to cutting greenhouse gas emissions to 94.8 per cent of 1990 levels by 2012, and applies to six gases, three of which are released by human activity: carbon dioxide (CO_2), nitrous oxide and methane, hydrofluorocarbons, perfluorocarbons and sulphur hexafluoride. Developed states commit to assisting less developed states to create projects that reduce emissions, then receive tradeable credits to offset their own emissions limits. It also introduces innovations such as the 'Clean Development Mechanism'.[70] Other states may offset their obligations by counting proper management of forests and farmlands that absorb CO_2, known as 'carbon sinks'. Yet some environmentalists claim last-minute compromises will reduce cuts to less than 2 per cent. The Protocol becomes legally binding when 55 states ratify it, including industrialised states accounting for at least 55 per cent of the total 1990 CO_2 emissions.

The biggest failure of the Kyoto Protocol, however, is considered to be the inability to convince the US, where 25 per cent of the world's greenhouse gas emissions are produced, to ratify the Protocol due to its seemingly intransigent stance that signing the treaty would hurt its domestic economy (Fife, 2001, A1). One editorial noted the ineffable irony that in 'an era of anti-globalisation fervour, the Bonn meeting passed the world's greatest globalisation compact without a peep of protest' (Corcoran, 2001). In that regard, MEAs have yet to address effectively many environmental issues that were identified within the MEA questionnaire, including the control of new ozone-depleting substances and the impact of climate change on migratory waterbirds (UNEP/IGM, 6 April 2001, para. 17).

A second treaty opened for signature at UNCED is featured in Abdulqawi Yusuf's essay, 'International Law and Sustainable Development: The Convention on Biological Diversity' (Chapter 19, Volume II). He emphasises access to and transfer of technology, and financial commitments of developed countries to less developed states as integral to the success of this treaty. Biodiversity is a crucial issue in regions such as Latin America, given that six of thirteen states containing 70 per cent of existing biological diversity on the planet are states located within that region: Brazil, Colombia, Ecuador, México, Perú and Venezuela. It is not surprising, then, to find that the OAS and regional offices for UNEP have placed great importance on the Biodiversity Convention, the implementation of sustainable development via Agenda 21 and the Rio Declaration, and continue to develop regional approaches via treaties and declarations for environmental protection (Ascencio Herrera and Pevato, 1996, pp. 1–2, 9–10, 13). More recent developments such as the well-documented opposition of the US delegation to the Kyoto Protocol recall its negotiations in Rio de Janeiro – where the US objected to the Biodiversity

Convention's final text and did not sign it at UNCED. This was depicted by Chandler, an American legal advisor to the US delegation, as a decision 'grounded on several legal and policy objections, including the treatment of intellectual property rights, proprietary business information, biotechnology, and financial issues' (Chandler, 1993, pp. 141, 174). It was noted earlier by Hagen and Weiner that the Cartagena Protocol establishes a regime for the safe transfer of LMOs. This Protocol presents an additional challenge in the quest to preserve the world's biological diversity, which is considered by Johnston as supporting 40 per cent of the world's economy and 80 per cent of the needs of the world's poor. Consequently, further loss of biodiversity threatens ecosystem services, food security, climatic stability, freshwater security and health needs of living beings around the world dependent upon its maintenance (Johnston, 1997, pp. 219, 221, 228). Hence, whether acclaimed as a milestone in international environmental law for its thorough ecosystem approach to address conservation, sustainable use and equitable sharing of benefits, or chided as a flawed agreement, the Biodiversity Convention certainly represents an important step towards achieving a workable foundation for continued action and diplomatic dialogue.

It is appropriate that the next essay follows the Biodiversity Convention because it ties in with the recognition in that Convention (in Article 8(j)) of preserving indigenous knowledge and practices. In 'Indigenous Peoples, International Law and Sustainability' (Chapter 20, Volume II), Benjamin Richardson surveys international environmental law to ascertain the extent to which indigenous peoples and their special relationship with the environment has been recognised and preserved. Given that Principle 22 of the Rio Declaration and Chapter 26 of Agenda 21 identified indigenous peoples as one of several 'special groups' with crucial interests in achieving sustainable development, UNCED at least recognised (albeit via 'soft law') their special relationship with their land and the traditional knowledge they possess. Richardson hopes that international environmental law increasingly aims to achieve effective participation of indigenous peoples within decision-making processes. One might expand on Richardson's views by adding that those processes should take into consideration traditional indigenous models for decision-making and dispute-resolution, rather than impose Western-style methods that are often too confrontational, intimidating, and utterly foreign from many indigenous cultural perspectives, with experiments in circle-sentencing procedures in Canada and Australia as precedents for 'new' approaches based upon traditional practices.

Whereas climate change and biodiversity were considered qualified successes, other issues have not been dealt with successfully. For example, UNCED failed to achieve ratification of a legally binding treaty to protect the world's forests, linked to both climate change and biodiversity for their ability to act as carbon sinks and for holding incalculable amounts of biological diversity. Thus, for each and every loss of forest acreage there are adverse effects on climate change and biodiversity. Following a 'big showdown' between developing states with thriving forestry industries and developed states, the best UNCED could achieve was a non-legally binding statement of forest principles (as described in Chapter 12, Volume I and Chapter 17, Volume II), confirming a lack of international consensus on this issue (see Schally, 1993). To date, the international community has failed to achieve consensus, a serious deficiency given the dire predictions expressed within a recent UNEP report, warning that the world's remaining healthy forests are in jeopardy of extinction within decades. 'Short of a miraculous transformation in the attitude of people and governments', the report reads, 'the Earth's remaining closed-canopy forests and associated biodiversity are destined to disappear in the coming decades' (UNEP,

2001). Providing, as it were, the first comprehensive global snapshot of how much forest cover is left on Earth, scientists studied satellite photographs of all the world's forests, determined how many had enough density to support wildlife, then examined pressures that could destroy those ecosystems. Approximately 21 per cent of the planet's land area (2.9 billion hectares) is covered with what the report calls closed-canopy forests, defined as forests with a canopy closure of more than 40 per cent. In effect, forest's trees are interlocked, creating a forest ecosystem healthy enough to support some of the world's rarest and most unique wildlife, protect watersheds and able to perform all its known environmental functions effectively. Most of those forests are in 15 states whilst three states (Russia, Canada and Brazil) contain nearly half of the world's canopied forests. Given that only a small percentage of those closed-canopy forests are protected, UNEP has called upon governments to pinpoint conservation funds to protect forests most worth saving and counted on the outcome at Bonn on the Kyoto Protocol negotiations, where governments agreed to spend money on transferring new technologies to developing states in an effort to reduce burning fossil fuels. Those funds in turn could assist states in saving forests (Mitchell, 2001, A10). Other specific global environmental issues not being dealt with at all, or effectively within MEAs, besides forests and the tropical timber trade, were identified in the MEA questionnaire as follows:

- freshwater resources;
- river ecosystems;
- commercial fishing from an environmental perspective;
- coastal zone management and information;
- impact of population, poverty and urbanisation on coastal resources; and,
- the role of poverty and corruption in relation to bad environmental management practices (UNEP/IGM, 6 April 2001, para. 17).

Regrettably, deforestation and climate change both contribute to another environmentally disastrous phenomena: desertification, another issue addressed at UNCED, where delegations committed themselves to negotiating a future treaty. In 1994, the UN Desertification Convention was opened for signature and ratification.[71] The ultimate success or failure of this Convention is considered to 'speak volumes as to the future viability of international environmental agreements'. That success or failure is said to depend upon the following factors: 'sufficiency of financial resources, effectiveness of research programmes, responsiveness to socio-economic factors; attention to the role of women in land use and stewardship; and commitments to local decision-making' (Burns, 1995, pp. 863, 882).

Reconciling South–North Tensions: The Case of Transboundary Traffic in Hazardous Waste

This section provides a case study in an area where the differences between developed and developing states are delineated drastically: the international hazardous waste trade. Modern industrial societies generate increasing amounts of hazardous waste. Apart from domestic incineration and other disposal methods, many developed states began shipping hazardous waste for disposal abroad, usually because it was more economical to do so rather than undertaking expensive disposal processes at home. The careless attitude towards shipping hazardous waste abroad is attributed to the 'not in my back yard', or NIMBY, syndrome. Tragically, numerous disposal sites were located within LDCs, where the dire need for revenues from accepting and disposing of such waste outweighed any perceived environmental dangers in receiving them. As a result of several environmental disasters associated with illegal or improper shipment of hazardous waste from developed to less developed nations (events that were documented by many governments and environmental NGOs), the international community responded by developing comprehensive legal regimes (pre-dating UNCED) to govern the transboundary traffic of hazardous waste (Hunter, Salzman and Zaelke, 1998, pp. 856–7).

The challenges in achieving the first international regime to address this growing global problem are skilfully demonstrated by Katharina Kummer in her essay 'The International Regulation of Transboundary Traffic in Hazardous Wastes: The 1989 Basel Convention' (Chapter 21, Volume II). Kummer's expertise acquired during negotiations of the Basel Convention undoubtedly gave her a practical, unique and hands-on perspective on this issue and the competing interests it generated, and contributes layers of perception to her essay. The Basel Convention establishes a global notification and consent system for transboundary shipments of hazardous and other wastes among parties, and prohibits the parties from trading in wastes with non-parties. Since the publication of Kummer's essay, further developments include: 1995 amendments to ban immediately the shipment of wastes destined for disposal from developed to less developed states; and to obligate parties to ban shipment of hazardous waste covered by the Convention that are destined for recovery from developed to less developed parties by 31 December 1997 (Hunter, Salzman and Zaelke, 1998, p. 862). In her assessment of the Convention, Kummer concedes that critics view the legal regime is bound to fail because it does not ban all transboundary movement of hazardous waste. However, in response, she points out that a complete ban would not have been appropriate since it would prevent transboundary waste disposal 'even in cases where it presents the best solution from an environmental viewpoint', precluding for instance establishing joint disposal facilities by neighbouring industrialised countries. Nevertheless, it is generally characterised as 'a step in the right direction'.

Principles 6 and 7 of the Rio Declaration give express recognition to the special needs of LDCs, those nations having common but differentiated responsibilities based upon different contributions to global environmental degradation. When regional organisations enact their own treaties to address those special needs, it is commendable but at the same time raises questions regarding the reasons why diplomatic processes such as those during the Basel Convention negotiations would marginalise LDCs to the point of driving them out of negotiations altogether, such as the African delegation. LDCs face both external and internal challenges, including what one author refers to as 'internal colonisation'.[72] Accelerated development and growth of urban settlements in less developed states, for example, has serious implications for the environment. All states should be reminded, then, that the goals expressed within the Rio Declaration and Agenda 21 are not exclusive to developed states at the expense of less developed ones. Although inclusion of all states as participants was stressed at UNCED, developing countries may still feel left out in the cold.

The highly significant perspectives of less developed nations regarding international environmental law-making are concisely summarised by Wordsworth Filo-Jones in his comparative essay 'The Evolution of the Bamako Convention: An African Perspective'

(Chapter 22, Volume II). Filo-Jones considers the regional legal regime provided for in the Bamako Convention on the Ban of Import into Africa and the Control of Transboundary Movement and Management of Hazardous Waste within Africa[73] (a pre-UNCED treaty regime) vis-à-vis the Basel Convention. Without an outright ban on hazardous waste trade, AU/OAU member states found the Basel regime simply too weak and entirely unacceptable. Despite efforts made to ban hazardous waste from the African continent, LDCs in Africa still in theory could have received waste from the Basel Convention parties through the Article 11 exception. However, the AU/OAU addressed this loophole by initiating Article 4 in the Basel Convention forbidding a party from shipping waste to a state or economic integration organisation which has banned all hazardous waste imports. By January 1991, all AU/OAU states (except for South Africa, not an AU/OAU member at that time) had banned hazardous waste imports by signing the Bamako Convention. In spite of these efforts, the capacity of AU/OAU member governments to implement the Bamako Convention, which is now in force, is said to be limited. Significantly, both the Basel and Bamako Conventions initiate pollution prevention strategies, to prevent, reduce and control the generation of hazardous waste in the first place thereby adopting a life-cycle approach rather than end-of-the-pipe pollution control methods (Hunter, Salzman and Zaelke, pp. 878–9).

As an aside, one might also consider Basel and Bamako in another light by posing a significant question: to what extent are these specific international and regional environmental regimes – designed and/or initiated by richer industrialised nations to address various sources of pollution originating in those developed nations – in fact imposing highly advanced conservation agendas upon LDCs wherein the source of pollution, and the problem, did not originate?

A Selection of Prevailing Challenges for International Environmental Cooperation: International Trade, Transnational Corporations, and Financing Sustainable Development Through Multilateral Development Banks

This final section features three among a multitude of challenges that remain to be resolved within international environmental law. The first provides an examination of international trade and environmental issues. Often described as complex and multifaceted, the trade and environment debate has fuelled enormous anti-globalisation demonstrations aimed against international institutions such as the WTO, whose meetings have been disrupted by protestors as witnessed during the November 1999 Seattle debacle (Hornblower, 1999). From a political perspective, the trade–environment debate is characterised by a polarisation of participants that either support or reject liberalisation of free trade. On the one hand, supporters argue that free trade levels the playing field by maximising wealth and alleviating poverty; on the other hand, unrestricted free trade may encourage the unfettered sacrifice of environmental values and sustainable development goals in favour of development needs in the face of economic pressures, triggering a so-called 'race to the bottom' because states permit lax environmental standards in order to gain a larger market share (Hunter, Salzman and Zaelke, 1998, pp. 1167–79). The international trade–environment saga is superbly recounted in Thomas Schoenbaum's essay, 'International Trade and Protection of the Environment: The Continuing Search for Reconciliation' (Chapter 23, Volume II). As in the case of other UN organs reviewed earlier, the General Agreement on Tariffs and Trade (GATT) used to be a development-oriented international organisation without much to say about the environment, except for Article 25 of the GATT. When in 1994 the final act of the Uruguay Round of trade negotiations established the WTO, included in the Marrakesh Agreement's preamble was the recognition of sustainable development as the WTO's overarching objective. In response to overwhelming criticism of being 'insufficiently responsive to environmental consequences' of world trade, the WTO shortly thereafter set up the Committee on Trade and Environment (CTE) in 1995 (Iwama, 2002, uwp).

In considering the 1995 report issued by the WTO's CTE merely as a timid first step towards reconciling competing interests and tensions represented within the trade and environment debate, Schoenbaum offers specific suggestions to resolve trade–environment issues within existing WTO agreements and jurisprudence, whilst advocating the establishment of an ongoing process to address those conflicting issues. But will sustainable development as a policy objective or cross-cutting issue flourish or perish in a globalised world of 'free international trade'? Or is it the case that environment-friendly rules are developing more quickly within regional trade regimes than in the WTO, such as the EU or pursuant to the North American Free Trade Agreement (NAFTA), and if so why? (Steinberg, 1997). Seattle closed the twentieth century on a sour note in the context of international trade law, appearing to exacerbate the trade–environment divide even further. Will the global environment continue to lose out in the trade wars of the twenty-first century? Given that MEAs containing trade measures continue in principle to be in conflict with WTO rules and agreements, despite Article XX exceptions, the success rate of invoking those exceptions will be likely to remain scant. After Seattle two camps emerged – either favouring the status quo or recommending clarification of Article XX (Schwartz, 2000, p. 69) – giving little hope that the relationship between MEAs and WTO rules will be reconciled any time soon. This sombre conclusion is supported by the reality that the WTO is a trade organisation first and foremost. The dispute resolution procedures, comprising *inter alia* a panel and appellate body, must consider whether measures in question taken by a state party have breached WTO trade rules, such as erecting non-tariff trade barriers (NTBs). NGOs from the environmental and health sectors monitoring WTO disputes often do so with guarded optimism, but too often encounter disappointment with end results, as outlined by Schoenbaum's analysis of cases before the WTO.

The recent case of asbestos is illustrative of how seemingly 'bizarre' conclusions can be reached in the name of upholding free trade, especially 'bizarre' from environmental and health perspectives. The WTO panel report indicated that French measures taken to ban asbestos amounted to unfavourable treatment between 'like' products, that is, products similar to a harmful carcinogenic substance 'like' asbestos (WTO, 2000). Although the panel eventually found the toxicity of asbestos to warrant measures 'necessary to protect human . . . life or health' under Article XX(b), it did so only after finding that France's trade restrictions on asbestos violated the GATT's basic rules requiring all 'like' imported products to be treated in a non-discriminatory manner. Palmer and Werksman characterised the panel's decision as 'a bizarre interpretation of GATT law and practice', a decision that if left to stand, in their view would 'allow trade rules to challenge even the most basic regulatory judgments'. Additionally, they predicted that the judgment would 'place any regulator wishing to distinguish between hazardous and non-hazardous (but otherwise 'like') products, the burden of meeting the GATT's narrowly drawn exceptions under Article XX' (Palmer and Werksman, 2001, pp. 125, 127). The Appellate Body reversed the panel's initial findings namely, that France's actions amounted to unfavourable treatment. Both decisions, in fact, ultimately upheld France's ban of the asbestos products. But it was the panel's initial findings that were troublesome from an environmental perspective. If products 'like' asbestos are viewed by the WTO's dispute resolution panel purely from a trade perspective without any regard for their toxicity, it may create difficulties for national health regulators as the panel's decision brought into question municipal health regulator's authority 'to develop measures to protect their populations in a manner that does not violate GATT' (Palmer and Werksman, 2001, p. 130). As a matter related to the broader topic of IEG reform, UNEP's IGM proposed undertaking a revision of the environmental exceptions to WTO rules so as to clarify that trade measures taken in pursuance of MEAs are protected from challenges at that trade body (UNEP/IGM, 4 April 2001, para. 152(a)). This might prevent further 'bizarre' decisions, whereas some states might argue using the environment as an excuse to erect NTBs for some hidden agenda would be subject to abuse. Would using the environment as an excuse to erect NTBs, and perhaps avoiding future 'bizarre' conclusions, be a small political and economic price to pay for protecting the environment itself?

With reference to the final two essays included within Volume II, in promoting and implementing sustainable development policies in LDCs, Hecht considers access to financial resources to be a necessary precondition for investment in environmentally sound technologies, conversion from existing technologies, or simply achieving the ambitious goals enunciated within the Rio Declaration and Agenda 21. Three factors are considered as preconditions to assist in making sustainable development a more realistic goal in developing states, factors that will be considered directly and indirectly within Volume II's last two essays:

- domestic policy actions such as taking steps towards creating accessible, free market economies, sound and enforceable environmental policies and public participation in decision-making;
- private sector investment and clean technology development; and,
- environmentally sound financing policies of bilateral and multilateral lending institutions (Hecht, 1999, p. 111).

The first two points are related to the penultimate chapter of Volume II. Handl suggests the importance of adopting less conventional methods, for example, the inclusion of non-state actors as participants, most notably TNCs and multilateral lending institutions. As previously noted Higgins views TNCs as participants within processes of authoritative decision-making, not non-state actors according to traditional demarcations that apply subject/object paradigms. Traditionally, the controls that international environmental law exert over TNCs are framed as soft-law propositions (Sornarajah, 1995, p. 284). TNCs are active participants in the global trading regime, as well as increasingly active regarding international environmental governance,[74] corresponding and overlapping regimes part of an economic system generating levels of growth and prosperity unsurpassed for many industrialised states. At the same time, the economic regime has produced relentless imbalances within LDCs. Strong viewed these disparities within the context of a new global partnership – a redefined economic–security–legal triad – one that would be incomplete without the essential component of a new economic regime (Strong, 1993, pp. 26–9). A prototype for this new regime was examined by the World Business Council for Sustainable Development (WBCSD) comprising of 48 CEOs from the world's leading

TNCs. Essentially, the WBCSD advocated an ambitious 'eco-industrial revolution', driven by full integration of the environment into economic life, including efficient use of materials and energy, sustainable recycling and waste disposal, revamping national fiscal systems to reward environmentally sound and sustainable corporate behaviour, internalising environmental costs in all economic transactions, and striking a balance that will not reward imports from developing states that destroy the environment while, at the same time, addressing developing states' needs to export and to encourage environmentally sound techniques in that process (Schmidheiny, 1992). These issues were addressed at UNCED: first, Principle 9 of the Rio Declaration encourages transfer of technologies that contribute to sustainable development, whilst Principle 12 promotes 'a supportive and open international economic system' conducive to economic growth and sustainable development simultaneously. Second, Chapter 30 of Agenda 21 expands on that concept, encouraging business and industry leaders to participate in sustainable development through many means, including adopting cleaner production via environmentally sound manufacturing processes and management practices and responsible entrepreneurship.

According to Fowler, TNCs wield absolute economic power globally: 1 per cent of TNCs control over half of global direct foreign investment, and the ten largest companies control over 25 per cent of TNCs' total assets. By the early 1990s, he notes there were almost 37,000 TNCs in the world. Certainly, their 'influence on the global economy is enormous' (Fowler, 1995, p. 1). He points out that TNCs have grown beyond the control of national governments and operate in a 'legal and moral vacuum', free to choose their own corporate agendas. Related concerns are examined with skill in David Ong's comparative essay, 'The Impact of Environmental Law on Corporate Governance: International and Comparative Perspectives' (Chapter 24, Volume II). Traditionally, international law played a limited role in governing TNCs, because, as Ong points out, states were considered the primary subjects of international law, not multinational corporations. As a result, he remarks, 'the classical exposition of public international law as the law governing states presents an initial jurisdictional problem for legal control of companies in the environmental field'. Exceptionally, voluntary codes of conduct, such as the draft UN Code of Conduct for Transnational Corporations, or the OECD's guidelines introduced in the 1970s,[75] have represented marginal achievements in this area. But international law's demarcation of TNCs as non-state actors has created a double-edged sword effect for international environmental law, since it excludes participants that are simultaneously part of the problem and potential solution to global ecological issues (Hunter, Salzman and Zaelke, pp. 434–5, 1385, 1388). Thus, Ong considers 'whether environmental principles and norms developed by international law and applied in domestic jurisdictions justify the progressive reform of corporate governance law'. In the course of examining this dilemma, he provides useful examples from both international law and national developments in several jurisdictions.

Following UNCED, a number of corporate environmental standards have evolved: for instance, the Coalition for Environmentally Responsible Economies Principles (CERES Principles); the International Chamber of Commerce's Business Charter for Sustainable Development; the EU's Environmental Management and Audit Scheme (EMAS), and the International Organisation for Standardisation's (ISO) 14000 series (Hunter, Salzman and Zaelke, Chapter 19, pp. 1385–415). Additionally, the OECD created a new section on 'Environmental Protection' in June 1991 to encourage TNCs to undertake a number of measures to protect the environment by considering environmental consequences of their activities in decision-making processes (Sands, 1995, p. 98), besides revising its 1976 guidelines. Apart from 'soft law' voluntary codes of conduct and non-legally binding documents such as Agenda 21 and the Rio Declaration, the Mälmo Ministerial Declaration also makes reference to the roles that TNCs can play in sustainable development. It identifies the private sector as a global actor with significant impact on environmental trends through investment and technology decisions. In expanding on the two factors necessary to achieve sustainable development noted earlier, it encourages the private sector to engender a new culture of environmental accountability by applying the polluter-pays principle, environmental performance indicators and reporting, and the precautionary approach in investment and technology decisions, with a view of contributing to sustainable development. Also, it requires that a precautionary approach be linked to cleaner and more efficient technologies developed by the private sector and to the promotion of the safe transfer of environmentally sound technologies with a view of encouraging a life-cycle economy. To achieve these commitments, interaction between the government and private sector is necessary, with the former establishing an institutional and regulatory environment to create incentives for the latter's participation in these initiatives. Consideration of the relationship between foreign direct investment and the environment should continue within the auspices of UNEP. Moreover, this Declaration encourages participation in the UN Global Compact[76] by the private sector (UNEP, 2000, paras. 11–13).

In addition to broadly worded 'soft-law' declarations, consumers have more direct and immediate economic power to choose eco-friendly products, such as recycled papers, and other manufactured using environmentally friendly technologies. Ominously, Fowler echoes Székely's sentiments expressed earlier, by recognising that the international business community's preference for soft techniques 'highlights the fragility of any support alleged to exist among TNCs for the development of international environmental standards' (Fowler, 1995). That in turn mirrors states' own practices in choosing to adopt non-legally binding documents expressing environmental protection aspirations. In order to ensure that foreign investment does not deviate from the goals of sustainable development in host states where TNCs operate, Sornarajah recommends creating duties on home states to impose liability on TNCs that cause environmental harm abroad and to develop further the concept of an international crime for environmentally injurious activities in accordance with the general principles of international law (Sornarajah, 1995, pp. 289–93). Nevertheless, Ong distinguishes between corporate environmental responsibility and governance: he concludes that whilst achievements have been made at the national level to import liability upon corporate directors for environmental damage, thereby lifting the corporate veil and assigning responsibility, reforms are needed in corporate governance to implement environmentally sound management techniques and processes.

A less confrontational method than Sornarajah's is to encourage TNCs' participation in sustainable development at the national level, as exemplified by Canada's introduction in 2001 of an 'environmental indicators' (EIs) programme. The federal government's objective is that EIs will provide quantitative data to ensure a sound basis for both environmental and economic policy development, and would represent ongoing protection against environmental complacency. EIs will be used to assess the national environment's health, including air quality, forests and fisheries, and will be compared with traditional measures of GDP, unemployment and inflation to assist the Canadian Government to shape national policy. Participation by business leaders is considered integral to the initiative's success (NRTEE, 2001, p. 1). Another method would be to quantify and publicise the economic benefits from good environmental practices, an environmental issue identified by MEA Secretariats as not being addressed effectively within MEAs (UNEP/IGM, 6 April 2001, para. 17).

According to Hecht, the third factor noted above considered necessary to assist developing states in meeting sustainable development goals is environmentally sound financing policies of bilateral and multilateral lending institutions such as the World Bank (the Bank) and the International Monetary Fund (IMF) (Hecht, 1999, p. 111). The South–North debate is ever present when development financing issues are considered, given that the UNCED Secretariat estimated the cost of financing Agenda 21 between 1993 and 2000 would have been around US$125 billion, funds that needed to be transferred from developed to less developed states in order to meet sustainable development targets. In reality, official development assistance after UNCED flowing from OECD states declined to US$59 billion, with very few states meeting a voluntary target of donating 0.7 per cent of their GDPs to fund UNCED. The final chapter of this volume contemplates multilateral financing issues by examining the world's largest development assistance lender, in 'The World Bank and the Environment: A Legal Perspective', an essay written by the late Ibrahim Shihata (Chapter 25, Volume II). With over US$20 billion in loans and credits annually, the Bank is unquestionably the most influential of all multilateral lending institutions. Having served as the Bank's general counsel for a number of years, Shihata lends an experienced hand in delivering his treatise which describes the Bank's evolving policies and procedures in relation to funding development projects that may have adverse effects upon the environment. Admittedly, the Bank is not the most popular institution amongst environmentalists because it financed some of the world's most environmentally disastrous development projects in the past, the most notorious of which were the Kedung Ombo and Sardar Sarovar dams. Nor has the fact that the Bank operates the GEF escaped criticism. An independent evaluation undertaken following the GEF's completion of its three-year pilot phase exposed serious shortcomings, particularly given LDCs' mixed experiences and concerns for more transparency and policy formulation that better reflects their own environmental and development priorities (Hunter, Salzman and Zaelke, 1998, pp. 1460–84). Inadequate financing for the global environment and significant lack of debt relief for LDCs continue to be identified by MEA Secretariats themselves as serious weaknesses hindering effective implementation of MEAs, besides overall weaknesses of UNEP's tenuous financial situation (UNEP/IGM, 6 April 2001, para. 17; UNEP/IGM, 16 January 2002, paras. 11–14; UNEP/IGM, 4 April 2001, paras. 98, 102–19; UNEP/IGM, 30 March 2001, para. 48).

Sources of funding for multilateral environmental agreements are not limited to the GEF, and financing opportunities are not solely the responsibility of the World Bank. Besides the GEF, traditional trust funds supported by states parties to MEAs help to finance secretariat operations and the implementation of work programmes activities. The Multilateral Fund for the Montreal Protocol assists LDCs to meet their normative obligations pursuant to that agreement. Kyoto Protocol mechanisms for instance comprise the Clean Development Mechanism to assist states parties not listed in Annex I (that is, developing countries) in achieving sustainable development and in contributing to the ultimate objective of the UNFCCC, namely, to stabilise interference with the climate system. Joint Implementation (JI) and Emission Trading (ET) are project-based mechanisms under the Kyoto Protocol whereby under JI a country can receive emission reduction credits when it funds projects in other countries where the emissions are actually reduced. In the case of ET projects, a party listed in Annex I to the UNFCCC 'may transfer to, or acquire from, any other such Party emission reduction units resulting from projects aimed at reducing anthropogenic emissions by sources or enhancing anthropogenic removals by sinks of greenhouse gases' for the purpose of meeting its targets under the Protocol. Still, other sources of funding comprise external donor funding for implementation of various decisions and resolutions of the meetings and COPs, and for special projects for which funding is not available from trust fund budgets (UNEP/IGM, 30 March 2001, paras. 51–7). Besides the World Bank, other financing opportunities may be found within regional development banks, bilateral arrangements with donor countries, foundations such as the UN Foundation, private-sector donors and NGOs (ibid., para. 51).

With respect to the World Bank, Shihata readily concedes that 'the Bank, like others, is still a beginner in this field and inevitably makes mistakes in the learning process'. Nevertheless, he traces the Bank's greening renaissance, including the requirement of environmental impact assessments prior to funding approval and newly elaborated 'green' operational directives. At the same time, Shihata admits that the 'inherent and circular relationship between poverty and environmental degradation' requires that a 'judicious and workable balance be struck' between environment protection and development goals. This current century will prove whether or not an equitable balance can be achieved.

International Environmental Law for the Twenty-First Century: Concluding Thoughts

> The Universe requires an eternity . . .
> thus they say that the conservation of
> this world is a perpetual creation and that
> the verbs 'conserve' and 'create', so much at odds here,
> are synonymous in heaven.
> *Historia de la Eternidad* (Jorge Luis Borges, 1936)

> Lakes and levees, dams and locks,
> They put that river in a box
> It was running wild
> And men must have control
> We live our lives in starts and fits
> We lose our wonder bit by bit
> We condescend and in the end
> We lose our very souls
> Goodbye to a river
> Goodbye to a river
> So long
>
> 'Goodbye To A River'[77]

This Introduction finds a certain amount of symmetry with Handl's captivating essay presented in Chapter 1, the latter having been published on the eve of UNCED, whilst this essay was written before the dawn of the WSSD, a ten-year review of UNCED scheduled for Johannesburg, 2–11 September 2002.[78] Also known as Rio +10, participants will include governments, UN agencies (most notably UNEP, as well as the CSD, the Summit's acting preparatory committee), multilateral financial institutions, concerned citizens, IGOs, NGOs and other major groups, gathering together to assess sustainable development and global change since UNCED.

According to the WSSD's latest PrepCom documents, its draft agenda is packed and focused, having tabled no less than twenty thematic reports covering an array of topics, the essence of which have already been raised and discussed in Volumes I and II, topics that may be divided into four broad areas:

- specific global environmental concerns (biodiversity; climate change; desertification; forests; oceans and seas; hazardous and radioactive waste; and fresh water);
- cross-cutting issues (changing consumption patterns; poverty; demographic dynamics; education and public awareness; information and institutions for decision-making; and health issues);
- cross-sectoral issues (energy and transport; major groups; human settlements and environmentally sound management of solid waste; and tourism); and,
- issues relating to economics and science (finance and trade; transfer of environmentally sound technologies; and biotechnology).

UN Secretary General and Nobel Laureate Kofi Annan's most recent update at the time of writing reports significant progress made in preparation of the WSSD. From Jakarta to Santiago, Addis Ababa to Barbados, Bucharest to New York, national and IGO meetings, regional roundtables and stakeholder consultations were planned to elaborate on issues to be discussed in Johannesburg. Regional PrepComs were scheduled for Africa (Kenya), Asia and Pacific (Phnom Pehn), West Asia (Cairo), Latin America and the Caribbean (Rio de Janeiro) and Europe (Geneva) between September–November 2001. Forums have already produced initiatives such as the Arctic Message adopted by the Arctic Council, an IGO composed of all Arctic states, with those regions' indigenous peoples taking part in its work on a permanent basis. Their message reiterates the challenge of securing sustainability in the use of natural resources in Arctic regions and encourages all Arctic states to assess the environmental, social and economic impacts on their territory whilst taking into consideration the latest research on special circumstances in those regions (UNGA, 2001, para. 16). The Arctic Council's statement accords with legal regimes that have been negotiated to protect the Arctic environments, such as the 1991 Madrid Protocol to the 1959 Antarctic Treaty, the first of its kind to create an integrated environmental protection regime in Antarctica (Rothwell, 2000). The report encourages contributions from and active participation by major groups and civil society, viewed as 'essential to a transparent, dynamic and interactive preparatory process' (UNGA, 2001, para. 28). Although international environmental law was not specifically mentioned in that particular update, it is certain that decisions taken at PrepComs and at the Summit will have impact both directly and indirectly upon international environmental law and policy.

Socrates employed the method of creating knowledge by questioning, a procedure that has become well-known to lawyers as the Socratic method. Certainly, many questions have been raised for consideration at the Johannesburg Summit, evoking a similarly maieutic process to that of Socrates, given that it seeks to bring about the birth of ideas and thoughts from the Summit's participants by means of a series of questions. In the case of international environmental law, the Summit will consider to what extent states have ratified pertinent MEAs such as those introduced at UNCED to prevent biodiversity loss or further climate change, in accordance with promises made during UNCED. These assorted queries provide a convenient *segue* into summoning Handl's question posed at the outset: whether the international legal system is capable of meeting challenges posed by global environmental concerns. The essays presented within Volumes I and II collectively supply a cautiously measured degree of validation in support of the international legal community's response to those challenges. By enacting a series of global treaties and declarations for environment protection and preservation over the past few decades, a great deal has certainly been accomplished from a standard-setting perspective. But much work remains. Some view that progress made to date as inadequate, falling short of goals and expectations that require far-reaching and effective solutions to protect and preserve the environment for present and future generations.[79] In particular, critics argue that international legal solutions, especially those embodied within MEAs are pointless without meaningful serious commitments to realising sustainable development in national law and policy, political will, stronger international institutions administering efficient international environmental governance, additional financing and debt relief, and uncompromising mechanisms to administer non-compliance procedures, among many other recommendations (UNEP/IGM, 4 April 2001, paras. 70–87).

Imagine using Galileo's telescope in an entropy-induced trance. Picture in your mind polluted oceans, disappearing ice caps, diminishing habitats threatening exotic species, and other scenarios. Consider that the past environmental damage cannot be reversed. Then ask yourself: what will the future bring for international environmental law during the next century? The answer depends largely upon whether or not the international community will manage to curb its edacious appetite, reverse unsustainable consumption and production patterns (Principle 8, Rio Declaration), and work towards increasing sustainable management, conservation and protection of the natural world in accordance with the conditions laid out in Agenda 21 and the Rio Declaration. In fact, Chapter 39[80] ('International Legal Instruments and Mechanisms') of Agenda 21, along with Principle 11 (states 'shall enact effective environmental legislation') and Principle 27 (states and people shall cooperate 'in the further development of international law in the field of sustainable development') of the Rio Declaration feature the importance of national and international environmental law-making as a significant contribution to the multidisciplinary process of achieving sustainable development. Therefore, Johannesburg should provide the appropriate forum to review and discuss the status of international environmental law-making since UNCED, and the national implementation of those norms, so that an accurate inventory of some remaining challenges can be compiled and assessed. Is international environmental law-making of any practical significance or is the political process the true catalyst that will make or break global environmental security?

Another position considers that the legal weight attached to 'soft' law instruments in the field of environmental protection may be of little significance given that their political function provides parties to international arrangements with the power 'to justify and persuade' (Hillgenberg, 1999, p. 516). Koskenniemi shatters an allegedly 'inherited ideal' which views a world order based upon the rule of law. He contends that this perspective 'thinly hides from sight the fact that social conflict must still be solved by political means'. Furthermore, he suggests that any common legal rhetoric among international lawyers must rely upon contested political principles to justify outcomes to international disputes (Koskenniemi, 1990, pp. 5–6).

When considering the success or failure of international environmental law-making, a trend in the legal literature is starkly apparent: the tendency of authors to make a number of recommendations, for instance to strengthen existing institutions, to implement international environmental obligations, to sign MEAs in the first place, and so on. Of approximately 41 MEAs reviewed by UNEP's Open-Ended Intergovernmental Group of Ministers, only six were not legally binding. Given that MEAs have been negotiated, ratified and implemented to some extent, the problem does not seem to be the legal framework of core MEAs in itself. So why is the pursuit of global environmental security so arduous? For argument's sake, assume for a moment that part of the problem lies not with making those particular recommendations per se or in reminding parties of their international commitments. Rather, that after so many decades these seemingly primitive reminders are still necessary. Such wish lists are beginning to sound like one collective broken record. That assumption leads to questions that remind us of Handl's essay in Volume I's opening chapter: has the international community taken threats to ecological security seriously? Are many environmental norms not respected and if so, why not? In the spirit of optimism, it is appropriate at this point to quote from the Mälmo Declaration's framers, who summed up that mood within their concluding remarks. Their 'common vision' included slashing abject poverty in half by 2015, without degrading the environment; acknowledging the 'emergence of a new consciousness'; and conceding that by the twenty-first century's genesis, human and material resources were already available to achieve sustainable development, no longer an abstract concept, but 'a concrete reality'. They envisaged ensuring environmental security through early warning procedures (conjuring up Handl's discussion, Chapter 1, Volume I), implying that this specific goal is an ongoing concern yet to be resolved. A final component of their common vision is to address major environmental threats through better coordination of international environmental instruments, both with other international legal instruments and with national laws, so as to achieve a more cohesive framework for international environmental law. Yet, one senses the ominous feeling of déja vu from the foregoing commitments.

So, to paraphrase Handl's query posed in Chapter 1 of Volume I, the international legal system appears to have taken bold steps towards meeting threats posed by global environmental problems. Certainly, the international environmental law-making process has been extremely active, having been called upon time and time again, repeatedly utilised in that regard. Admittedly, the international legal framework for MEAs is but one of many important roads to travel upon the path leading towards sustainable development. That process alone is not the panacea for the earth's ecological woes. Ideally, coordination of legal instruments involves reforms such as those identified by UNEP's IGM, and further entails strengthening existing international environmental norms rather than seeking to develop new ones, ensuring current standards are complied with through efficient secretariats, cooperation between and among various MEA Secretariats, comprehensive monitoring techniques, and preventative, results-oriented non-compliance mechanisms. These procedures must be integrated within a rejuvenated universal environmental consciousness that no longer accepts anything less than sustainable development as an IEC concept or cross-cutting issue prevalent within international environmental law and policy, and a responsibility passed on to the appropriate political entities at the national, regional and sub-regional levels.

Successful implementation remains dependent upon international environmental cooperation and actions by individual states to adopt international environmental norms into domestic law and policy, given that states remain predominant participants in ensuring international environmental conventions fulfil their intended purposes when they send delegations to global conferences (Lin, 1995, p. 31). That cooperation includes equitable participation, not just richer states dictating an environmental agenda that LDCs cannot hope to achieve, if they were able to partake in the decision-making process at all given often prohibitive costs of sending delegations from LDCs in the first place. As UNEP's Intergovernmental Group of Ministers admitted, the 'ability of developing countries to participate meaningfully in the development of international environmental policy and to undertake the requisite implementation of international agreements at the national level must be strengthened if environmental policy is to be translated into sustainable development' (UNEP/IGM, 16 January 2002, para. 18). Whilst the price tag of achieving international environmental security may seem high, what is the price of depleting the earth's precious resources, its fragile ecosystem, the ozone layer, the oceans and forests? The cost of saving the planet may seem like a bargain compared with the high price that the earth and its inhabitants will end up paying if global environmental security as a whole continues to be ignored or inadequately addressed. Despite international environmental law's 'novel character' and moral appeal, until an environmental consciousness is universal in both spirit and practice – with political decision-making setting aside national interests and addressing economic imbalances in favour of global community interests – and only when economic, political, legal and social policies are harmonised with international environmental norms, then global environmental security, even a 'modicum', will at best remain an elusive objective.

Notes

1 Defined as a measure of the amount of energy unavailable for useful work in a system undergoing change.
2 See also International Committee of the Red Cross Guidelines for Military Manuals and Instructions on the Protection of the Environment in times of Armed Conflict, attached to UNGA, 1994, pp. 49–53.
3 Besides the well-publicised Three Gorges Dam Project in China, critics of other development projects considered threats to fragile habitats, such as a rainforest habitat along Belize's Macal River Valley, argue that electricity costs will only increase rather than provide residents of San Ignacio and environs affordable, clean energy: see further 'www.riverkeeper.org'.
4 Tolkien, 1991, and ibid., 2000.
5 (Paris, 19 March 1902), *British and Foreign State Papers*, **192**, p. 969. In force 20 April 1908.
6 Treaty Between the United States and Great Britain Respecting Boundary Waters Between the United States and Canada (Washington, 11 January 1909), *American Journal of International Law* (Suppl.), **4**, p. 239. In force 5 May 1910.
7 For compilations of international treaties in the field of the environment, see Adede, 1993; Birnie and Boyle, 1995; Burhenne (ed.), 1975– (looseleaf); Rüster and Simma (eds), 1975–83 and 1990– (looseleaf); and Sands, 1994.
8 Among the leading texts, see in particular Birnie and Boyle, 1992 (2nd ed. forthcoming, 2002, not available at time of writing); Hunter, Salzman and Zaelke, 1998; and Sands, 1995.
9 See in particular Caldwell, 1990 (2nd ed.) and 1996 (3rd ed.), and Conca and Dabelko, 1998 (2nd ed.).
10 See Morrison and Wolfrum (eds), 1999.
11 For expert treatment on EU environmental law, see Krämer, 1993; ibid., 1997; ibid., 1999.
12 See further Lin, 1995, pp. 31–3.
13 See further De Young and Kaplan, 1988, pp. 273ff; and Feeny *et al.*, 1990, pp. 1ff.
14 Smith *et al.*, 1996, observed that Hardin's call for 'mutual coercion, mutually agreed upon' became the 'intellectual justification for nearly three decades of environmental legislation in the United States'.

15 See, for example, the Convention on Environmental Impact Assessment in a Transboundary Context (Espoo, 25 February 1991), in force 10 September 1997, 29 (+EU) signatories and 37 (+EU) ratifications. This convention was drafted under the auspices of the UNECE.

16 (1941), *American Journal of International Law*, **35**, p. 716.

17 Both texts available at 'www.unep.org'.

18 Article III(1), Convention on the Prevention of Marine Pollution by Dumping of Wastes and Other Matter (London, 29 December 1972), 11 ILM 1294 (1972). In force 30 August 1975, 78 parties. As amended in 1978, 1980, 1989, and by the 1996 Protocol (15 parties, not in force). The 1996 Protocol contains definitions of 'dumping' (Articles 4.1–4.2) and 'pollution' (Article 10).

19 Convention for the Protection of the Ozone Layer (Vienna, 22 March 1985), 26 ILM 1529 (1987). In force 22 September 1988, 28 signatories, 181 parties. See further Protocol on Substances that Deplete the Ozone Layer (Montreal, 16 September 1987), 26 ILM 1550 (1987). In force 1 January 1989, 46 signatories, 180 parties (Montreal Protocol). London Amendment (1990), in force 10 August 1992, 153 ratifications. Copenhagen Amendment (1992), in force 14 June 1994, 128 ratifications. Montreal Amendment to the Montreal Protocol (1997), in force 10 November 1999, 63 ratifications. Beijing Amendment to the Montreal Protocol (1999), in force 25 February 2002, 22 ratifications.

20 United Nations Framework Convention on Climate Change (New York, 9 May 1992), 31 ILM 849 (1992). In force 21 March 1994, 186 ratifications.

21 Convention on the Control of Transboundary Movements of Hazardous Wastes and their Disposal (Basel, 22 March 1989), 28 ILM 657 (1989). In force 5 May 1992, 148 ratifications. See further amendments, including Amendment 1 to Annex 1, and adoption of Annexes VIII and IX, in force 6 November 1998; the Basel Ban Amendment (adopted 22 September 1995), incorporated into the Convention's text at COP5 (Decision III/1), 26 ratifications, not in force; and Basel Protocol on Liability and Compensation (adopted 10 December 1999), 13 signatories.

22 Convention on Long-Range Transboundary Air Pollution (Geneva, 13 November 1979), 18 ILM 1442 (1979), Article 1(a). In force 16 March 1983, 33 signatories, 48 parties (LRTAP). Includes 8 protocols. See further 'www.unece.org/env/lrtap'.

23 See, for example, Vienna Ozone Convention and Montreal Protocol (listing controlled substances); London Dumping Convention (listing prohibited substances in Annex I; substances requiring 'special care' and a special permit for their disposal, in Annex II; and provisions establishing criteria for dumping at sea); LRTAP (annexes and protocols that set, *inter alia*, sulphur emission levels and reductions); and Basel Convention (annexes include categories of wastes to be controlled, those requiring special consideration, and a list of hazardous characteristics).

24 Convention on International Trade in Endangered Species of Wild Fauna and Flora (Washington, 3 March 1973), in force 1 July 1975, 155 parties. As amended, 1979 Bonn Protocol (in force 13 April 1997, 42 parties); 1983 Gaborone Protocol, adopted 30 April 1983, 39 parties). See further Ong, 1998.

25 *Case Concerning the Gabcíkovo–Nagymaros Project (Hungary/Slovakia)*, Judgment of 25 September 1997, para. 53 [hereinafter, *Gabcíkovo–Nagymaros*]. The text of this judgment and subsequent references are to ICJ judgments as available at 'www.icj-cij.org', unless otherwise indicated.

26 *Legality of the Threat or Use of Nuclear Weapons, Advisory Opinion*, 8 July 1996, para. 29.

27 For more comprehensive versions of her thesis, see Brown Weiss, 1996, and ibid., 1984. Due to page restrictions, Brown Weiss' 1984 article could not be included in Volume I of this series.

28 Cf. *Minors Oposa* v *Secretary of the Department of Environment and Natural Resources*, 33 ILM 173 (1994). The Supreme Court of the Philippines granted standing to a group of minors representing their generation, as well as 'generations yet unborn', to sue for environmental damage caused by granting timber licenses. The Court noted that the State's 1987 Constitution provided for 'the right of the people to a balanced and healthful ecology in accord with the rhythm and harmony of nature'.

29 Boyle's essay is contained in H. Caminos (ed.) *Law of the Sea* Chapter 17 and hence the issue of marine pollution is not considered further here.

30 21 ILM 1261 (1982).

31 Convention on the Law of the Non-Navigational Uses of International Watercourses, UN Doc A/51/869, adopted by the UN General Assembly on 21 May 1997.

32 Article 38(1)(d), ICJ Statute. See further Birnie and Boyle, 1992, pp. 24–6; and Sands, 1995, pp. 125–6.

33 *Gabcíkovo–Nagymaros*, para. 140.
34 *Oppenheim*, 1992, p. 31, §11; and Brownlie, 1990, p. 11.
35 ICJ Rep (1951), p. 32.
36 *Oppenheim*, 1992, p. 32, §11.
37 UNEP divides MEAs into five clusters: biodiversity-related conventions, atmospheric conventions, land conventions, chemicals and hazardous wastes conventions and regional seas conventions and related agreements: UNEP/IGM, 6 April 2001, 'Scope of the Core Environmental Conventions and Related International Agreements', paras. 15, 18–23. For a useful summary of major MEAs, see tables annexed to UNEP/IGM, 30 March 2001.
38 See note 19 above.
39 ICJ Rep (1969), p. 3, para. 77.
40 For a comprehensive examination of new means of creating customary international law, see Mendelson, 1998, Chapter V, pp. 347–95.
41 Cartagena Protocol on Biosafety (Cartagena, 23 February 2000), 103 signatories, 7 parties.
42 Convention on Biological Diversity (Rio de Janeiro, 5 June 1992), in force 29 December 1993, 168 signatories, 182 parties.
43 The International Tribunal for the Law of the Sea (ITLOS) ordered Japan to refrain from conducting an experimental fishing programme, in the *Southern Bluefin Tuna cases*. For a discussion on whether or not ITLOS' Order represents a 'missing link', such that the precautionary approach to fisheries has evolved into a norm of customary international law, see Marr, 2000.
44 Advocates of a right to a safe environment as representing the most basic human right at the municipal (national) level often link this right with passionate and eloquent accounts of environmental activism aimed at protecting fragile ecosystems at the local level. Such activism is commendable. Yet, the main distinctions from grassroots advocacy groups, such as the Hudson Riverkeeper network, and international approaches to environmental protection is how such initiatives affect the normative character of emerging concepts of international environmental cooperation and whether there is uniform state practice to accord such concepts with international normative characteristics. For an excellent account of effective grassroots environmental activism and advocacy, see Cronin and Kennedy, 1997. In the US, for instance, where environmental lawyer and activist Robert F. Kennedy Jr. has accused the Bush administration of waging 'a secret war against the environment' by 'eviscerating America's environmental laws [via] 100 proposed rollbacks of environmental regulations' (Leahy, 2003, p. 40), it is difficult to evaluate, purely from an international legal perspective, how the recognition of an international human right to a decent environment would reverse reckless federal political decision-making, until and unless such a right is first expressly recognised at the international level, then either incorporated into domestic law and policy and/or entrenched within a national constitution, to be justiciable. Even so, there is no guarantee that an international human right to environment, in whatever manner defined, would ensure, in turn, that federal environmental laws will be upheld and enforced or access to environmental justice expanded. That is perhaps more a matter of viewing the environment as a priority in all decision-making and less about international human rights, apart from improving procedural mechanisms or other access to environmental justice issues that are not necessarily dependent upon viewing the environment as a basic human right.
45 Article 11, Additional Protocol to the American Convention on Human Rights in the Area of Economic, Social and Cultural Rights (San Salvador, 17 November 1988), in force 16 November 1999, 12 parties; Article 24, African Charter on Human and Peoples' Rights (Banjul, 27 June 1981), in force 21 October 1986, 33 signatories, 53 ratifications.
46 See further Röben, 2000; and Chapter 13, Volume I in these two volumes.
47 For a more detailed description of the UN organs and their relationship with environmental issues, see further Iwama, 2002, section entitled 'Existing Multilateral Institutions', unpaginated working paper (uwp).
48 Due to its length, Sohn's essay could not be included within these volumes.
49 For a critical analysis, see Carpenter, 2002, who explores the possibility of reforming existing UN organs – particularly the CSD, ECOSOC, and the General Assembly – with a view to establishing 'greater coordination and coherency among environment-related UN activities'.
50 The eight specialised agencies are: Food and Agriculture Organisation (FAO), International Bank

for Reconstruction and Development (IBRD), International Labour Organisation (ILO), International Maritime Organisation (IMO), United Nations Educational, Scientific, and Cultural Organisation (UNESCO), United Nations Industrial Development Organisation (UNIDO), World Health Organisation (WHO), and World Meteorological Organisation (WMO). On the World Trade Organisation (WTO), see Introduction 'A Selection of Prevailing Challenges . . .', and the accompanying essays reproduced in Part VII, Volume II of these volumes.

51 Suggestions include a World Environmental Organisation (WEO), a World Environment and Development Organisation (WEDO), or a new UN principal organ, the Economic Security Council (ESC) dealing with economic, social and environmental issues: Iwama, 2002, 'Conclusion', uwp. On IEG reform, including proposals to reform existing UN bodies and creating a new international environmental organisation, see further Carpenter, 2002; Charnovitz, 2002; Elliot, 2002; and Mori, 2002, among several working papers developed for a study on IEG undertaken by the United Nations University, Institute of Advanced Studies, Tokyo, available to download at 'www.ias.unu.edu'.

52 On existing strengths and weaknesses within the current IEG regime, see for instance UNEP/IGM, 30 March 2001, p. 9, paras. 39–49; ibid., 4 April 2001, paras. 62–87; ibid., 5 April 2001, excerpts from Canada and Norway; ibid., 6 April 2001, pp. 27–30; among other IGM reports. See also 'Needs and Options', including at the MEA level, ibid., paras. 148–50. As for recommendations, overall a 'prudent approach to institutional change' was favoured 'with preference given to making better use of existing structures: ibid., 12 January 2002, para. 8(a). Consult the foregoing reports for a complete list of more specific recommendations. It remains to be seen how or whether an internally conducted review by UNEP addressing weaknesses in UN treaty organs could maintain an independent and impartial position to achieve meaningful reforms.

53 Consult UNEP/IGM, 6 April 2001, paras. 16–17 for the complete list.

54 UN Doc FCCC/CP/1997/7/Add.1, 84 signatories, 40 parties, not in force. For a critical analysis of compliance techniques as prescribed within the Kyoto Protocol, see Lanchbery, 1998.

55 (Vienna, 22 May 1969), 8 ILM 679 (1980). In force 27 January 1980. Article 60 provides the opportunity for states to terminate or suspend the operation of a treaty as a consequence of its breach.

56 For an outstanding review of compliance in international environmental law, see Rüdiger Wolfrum's Hague Academy of International Law lecture, published in Wolfrum, 1998.

57 On dispute resolution generally, and the establishment of a separate World Environment Court specifically, see further Pauwelyn, 2002.

58 For a comprehensive historical overview of NGO involvement from 1775 to the late 1990s, see also Charnovitz, 1997, pp. 183–286. Given the length of Charnovitz's essay, it was not included in these volumes due to page restrictions. Charnovitz covers the emerging influence of NGO participation in the League of Nations, UN and related organisations (particularly ECOSOC). He considers that there is a cyclicality of NGO involvement and impact, having gone through periods of underachievement followed by intensification and empowerment. After an elaborate review of benefits and problems of NGO roles, aims of participation, techniques of involvement, and future prospects, Charnovitz concludes that the two greatest virtues of NGOs are the improvement of IGOs and promotion of peace.

59 Higgins, 1994, pp. 48–55.

60 See further Susskind, 1994.

61 In the dispute between France and Canada over asbestos products, five applications for leave to appeal were submitted to the Appellate Body. All were rejected. A series of admissibility criteria must be met before leave to appeal is granted: Palmer and Werksman, p. 125.

62 The ILC's text of draft articles on 'Responsibility for Internationally Wrongful Acts' (the 'Responsibility Draft'), under the current direction of Special Rapporteur James Crawford, is distinct from the ILC's draft articles on 'International Liability for Injurious Consequences Arising Out of Acts Not Prohibited by International Law' (the 'Liability Draft'). For the latest Responsibility Draft, see ILC, 2001.

63 The text of the 1998 draft and commentary therein is available at 'www.un.org/law/ilc/reports/1998/chp4.htm'.

64 Resolution of the Eighth Commission, adopted at Strasbourg, 4 September 1997, 37 ILM 1474 (1998).

65 See, for example, Stone, 1995, pp. 5–17.

66 On 29 June 2000, an Earth Charter was launched in The Hague. This non-legally binding document was a private or 'civil society initiative', the product of a consortium of NGOs, including the Earth Council, IUCN, Green Cross International, and the Amazonian Parliament. It consists of four parts and is not written in the legal language of international instruments. Instead, it 'is written in an ambitious and informal, sometimes even poetic, style and is meant to serve as a common standard for a sustainable way of life by which the conduct of individuals, organisations, businesses, governments, and transnationals is to be guided and assessed'. It remains unclear how states and international institutions will view the Earth Charter, other than or beyond a source of inspiration for the progressive development of international environmental law and policy (ILA, 2000, pp. 12–13). For the Earth Charter's text, see 'www.earthcharter.org'.

67 The EU adopted its 6th Environmental Action Programme (EAP) for 2000–2010 on 24 January 2001. Priority issues include climate change; nature and biodiversity; health and environment; and sustainable use of natural resources and waste management. Sustainable development remains an underlying policy objective.

68 APEC's first Ministerial Meeting on Sustainable Development, held in Manila from 11–12 July 1996; the Action Programme expresses desire 'to advance cooperation on sustainable development' in all APEC member states. See further 'www.apecsec.org'.

69 The OAS' Unit for Sustainable Development and Environment oversees implementation of the objectives expressed at UNCED and reiterated in the Bolivia Summit Plan of Action. During the Summit on Sustainable Development, held from 7–8 December 1996, a declaration and plan of action were produced. The Declaration of Santa Cruz de la Sierra reaffirms 'determination to move forward toward sustainable development and to implement the decisions and commitments set forth in the Rio Declaration and Agenda 21': see further 'www.oas.org'.

70 See further, Rowlands, 2001.

71 UN Convention to Combat Desertification In Those Countries Experiencing Drought And/Or Desertification, Particularly in Africa (Paris, 17 June 1994) 33 ILM 1328 (1994). In force 26 December 1996, 115 signatories, 176 ratifications.

72 'Internal colonisation' is used to designate the process by which, on the pretext of 'development', large parts of many Southern states are still in effect being colonised by their own ruling elite: Calvert, 2001. One might add that a certain amount of external colonisation is at hand, given the explosion of third world debt and the financial dependency that has ensued.

73 (Adopted at Bamako, 30 January 1991), in force 22 April 1998, 18 parties (10 ratifications and 8 accessions), and 12 signatories without ratification. The Convention's text is reprinted in 30 ILM 775.

74 See further Usui, 2002.

75 Revised in 2000.

76 An inter-organisational initiative by UNEP, ILO, and the UN High Commission for Human Rights. See further 'www.unglobalcompact.org'.

77 Henley *et al.* (2000).

78 This Introduction was drafted before the conclusion of the WSSD and thus cannot for practical reasons present conclusions from that global conference. Thus, for conclusions and further reports, see the official website listed at 'Further References' below.

79 For instance, critics since UNCED have been many in number. For a critical analysis in general, see Pallemaerts, 1993. Following UNCED, the case of global forest regulation is one area that has received a lot of criticism, as noted earlier in the introduction to this volume. In the context of elaborating a global forest regime, in an article by Steiner, she recalls the decade following UNCED. During that time, 'a lengthy and contentious battle on how to shape international forest policy' emerged. She views the recently elaborated UN Forum on Forests (UNFF) as a new regime that raises many questions, for instance, how will existing institutions fit into this new institution? Steiner concludes that the UNFF's success will depend upon, *inter alia*, better coordination of an ineffective, inefficient and confusing 'fractioned approach' to global forestry governance, and engaging all relevant stakeholders 'through the multitude of different treaties, organisations, institutions and processes that already exist' (Steiner, pp. 98–9, 104–5).

80 On Chapter 39, see further Sands's article, reproduced in Chapter 17, Volume II.

References

Adede, A.O. (1993), *International Environmental Law Digest: Instruments for International Responses to Problems of Environment and Development 1972–1992*, Amsterdam and New York: Elsevier Science.

Ascencio Herrera, A. and Pevato, P.M. (1996), 'Legal Framework for Environmental Co-operation in Latin America: An Overview', *Review of European Community and International Environmental Law*, **5**, pp. 1–17.

Benedick, R. (1991), *Ozone Diplomacy: New Directions in Safeguarding the Planet*, Cambridge, MA: Harvard University Press (and see 1998 'Enlarged Edition').

Berwick, T.A. (1998), 'Responsibility and Liability for Environmental Damage: A Roadmap for International Environmental Regimes', *The Georgetown International Environmental Law Review*, **10**, pp. 257–77.

Birnie, P.W. and Boyle, A.E. (1992), *International Law and the Environment*, Oxford: Clarendon Press.

Birnie, P.W. and Boyle, A.E. (1995), *Basic Documents on International Law and the Environment*, Oxford: Clarendon Press.

Bodansky, D. (Sept. 1991), 'Scientific Uncertainty and the Precautionary Principle', *Environment*, **33**, pp. 4–5, 43–4.

Bodansky, D. (1993), 'The United Nations Framework Climate Change Convention: A Commentary', *Yale Journal of International Law*, **18**, pp. 451–558.

Bodansky, D. (1999), 'The Legitimacy of International Governance: A Coming Challenge for International Environmental Law?', *American Journal of International Law*, **93**, pp. 596–624.

Bourne, C.B. (1971), 'International Law and Pollution of International Rivers and Lakes', *University of Toronto Law Journal*, **21**, pp. 193–202.

Boyle, A. (1985), 'Marine Pollution under the Law of the Sea Convention', *American Journal of International Law*, **79**, pp. 347–72.

Brown Weiss, E. (1984), 'The Planetary Trust: Conservation and Intergenerational Equity', *Ecology Law Quarterly*, **11**, pp. 495–581.

Brown Weiss, E. (1996), *In Fairness to Future Generations: International Law, Common Patrimony, and Intergenerational Equity*, New York: Transnational Publishers.

Burhenne, W.E. (ed.) (1974–), *International Environmental Law: Multilateral Treaties*, (looseleaf), Berlin: Erich Schmidt Verlag.

Burns, W.C. (1995), 'The International Convention to Combat Desertification: Drawing a Line in the Sand?', *Michigan Journal of International Law*, **16**, pp. 831–82.

Caldwell, L.K. (1990), *International Environmental Policy*, 2nd edn, Durham, North Carolina: Duke University Press.

Caldwell, L.K. (1996), *International Environmental Policy*, 3rd edn, Durham, North Carolina: Duke University Press.

Calvert, P. (2001), 'Internal colonisation, development and environment', *Third World Quarterly*, **22**, pp. 51–63.

Carpenter, C. (2002), 'Strengthening IEG by Reforming Existing UN Bodies', *International Environmental Governance (Gaps and Weaknesses/Proposals for Reform), Working Paper*, Tokyo, Japan: United Nations University, Institute of Advanced Studies (UNU/IAS).

Chandler, M. (1993), 'The Biodiversity Convention: Selected Issues of Interest to the International Lawyer', *Colorado Journal of International Environmental Law and Policy*, **4**, pp. 141–75.

Charney, J. (1993), 'Universal International Law', *American Journal of International Law*, **87**, pp. 529–51.

Charnovitz, S. (2002), 'A World Environment Organization', *International Environmental Governance (Gaps and Weaknesses/Proposals for Reform), Working Paper*, Tokyo, Japan: UNU/IAS.

Charnovitz, S. (1997), 'Two Centuries of Participation: NGOs and International Governance', *Michigan Journal of International Law*, **18**, pp. 183–286.

Conca, K. and Dabelko, G.D. (1998), *Green Planet Blues. Environmental Politics from Stockholm to Kyoto*, 2nd edn, Boulder, Colorado: Westview Press.

Corcoran, T. (2001), 'Editorial: Canada's Kyoto policy chaos', *Financial Post*, Tuesday, 24 July 2001.

Cronin, J. and Kennedy Jr., R.F. (1997), *The Riverkeepers. Two Activists Fight to Reclaim Our Environment as a Basic Human Right*, New York: Scribner.
D'Amato, A. (1990), 'Do We Owe a Duty to Future Generations to Preserve the Global Environment?', *American Journal of International Law*, **84**, pp. 190–98.
Desai, B.H. (2000), 'Revitalizing International Environmental Institutions: The UN Task Force Report and Beyond', *Indian Journal of International Law*, **40**, pp. 455–504.
De Young, R. and Kaplan, S. (1988), 'On averting the tragedy of the commons', *Environmental Management*, **12**, pp. 273–83.
Eddington, Sir A. (1928), *The Nature of the Physical World* (Gifford Lectures 1927), Cambridge: Cambridge University Press.
Elliott, L. (2002), 'Expanding the Mandate of the UN Security Council to Account for Environmental Issues', *International Environmental Governance (Gaps and Weaknesses/Proposals for Reform), Working Paper*, Tokyo, Japan: UNU/IAS.
Farr, K.T. (2000), 'A New Global Environmental Organization', *Georgia Journal of International and Comparative Law*, **28**, pp. 493–525.
Feeny, D., Bekres, F., McCay, B.J. and Acheson, J.M. (1990), 'The Tragedy of the Commons – 22 Years Later', *Human Ecology*, **18**, pp. 1–19.
Fife, R. (2001), 'Greens laud PM for Kyoto revival', *National Post*, Tuesday 24 July, pp. A1, A13.
Fowler, R.J. (1995), 'International Environmental Standards for Transnational Corporations', *Environmental Law*, **25**, pp. 1–30.
Francioni, F. and Scovazzi, T. (eds) (1991), *International Responsibility for Environmental Harm*, London/Dordrecht/Boston: Graham and Trotman.
Gore, A. (1992), *Earth in the Balance: Ecology and the Human Spirit*, Boston: Houghton Mifflin Company.
Gündling, L. (1990), 'Our Responsibility to Future Generations', *American Journal of International Law*, **84**, pp. 207–12.
Hagen, P.E. and Weiner, J.B. (2000), 'The Cartagena Protocol on Biosafety: New Rules for International Trade in Living Modified Organisms', *The Georgetown International Environmental Law Review*, **12**, pp. 697–717.
Hecht, A.D. (1999), 'The Triad of Sustainable Development: Promoting Sustainable Development in Developing Countries', *Journal of Environment and Development*, **8**, pp. 111–32.
Henley, D., Lynch, S., Winding, J. and Simes, F. (2000), 'Goodbye To A River', Wisteria Music BMI/WB Music Corp./Matanzas Music/Dobbs Music/Frank Simes Music ASCAP.
Higgins, R. (1994), *Problems and Process: International Law and How We Use It*, New York: Oxford University Press.
Hillgenberg, H. (1999), 'A Fresh Look at Soft Law', *European Journal of International Law*, **10**, pp. 499–516.
Hornblower, M. (1999), 'The Battle in Seattle: Antiglobalisation forces are threatening to turn the WTO's meeting on free trade into a free-for-all', *Time Europe*, **154**, 6 December, as available on 'www.time.com/time/europe/magazine/1999/126/seattle.html'.
Hunter, D., Salzman, J. and Zaelke, D. (1998), *International Environmental Law and Policy*, New York: Foundation Press.
ILA (1966), *Helsinki Rules on the Uses of International Rivers*, adopted 20 August 1966, reprinted in 52 ILM 484 (1967).
ILA (2000), *Committee on Legal Aspects of Sustainable Development, Fourth Report*, London Conference, 2000.
ILC (2001), *Responsibility of States for Internationally Wrongful Acts*, UN Doc A/CN.4/L.602/Rev.1, 26 July 2001.
Iwama, T. (2002), 'Multilateral Environmental Institutions and Coordinating Mechanisms', *International Environmental Governance (Gaps and Weaknesses/Proposals for Reform), Working Paper*, Tokyo, Japan: UNU/IAS.
Jennings, R. and Watts, A. (eds) (1992), *Oppenheim's International Law*, 9th edn, New York: Longman.
Johnston, S. (1997), 'The Convention on Biological Diversity: The Next Phase', *Review of European Community and International Environmental Law*, **6**, pp. 219–30.
Koskenniemi, M. (1990), 'The Politics of International Law', *European Journal of International Law*, **1**, pp. 4–32.

Kovar, J.D. (1993), 'A Short Guide to the Rio Declaration', *Colorado Journal of International Environmental Law and Policy*, **4**, pp. 119–40.

Krämer, L. (1993), *European Environmental Law Casebook*, London: Sweet and Maxwell.

Krämer, L. (1996), 'Public Interest Litigation in Environmental Matters Before European Courts', *Journal of Environmental Law*, **8**, pp. 1–18.

Krämer, L. (1997), *Focus on European Environmental Law*, 2nd edn, London: Sweet and Maxwell.

Krämer, L. (1999), *EC Environmental Law*, London: Sweet and Maxwell.

Lanchbery, J. (1998), 'Verifying Compliance with the Kyoto Protocol', *Review of European Community and International Environmental Law*, **7**, pp. 170–75.

Leahy, S. (2003), 'An Imbalance of Power. Q & A with Robert F. Kennedy Jr.', *Macleans*, 31 March 2003, pp. 40–41.

Leopold, A. (1978), *A Sand County Almanac: With Essays on Conservation from Round River*, New York: Ballantine Books.

Lin, S. (1995), 'Implementation of Environmental Conventions: A Regional Perspective', in Kurukulasuriya, L. (ed.), *UNEP's New Way Forward: Environmental Law and Sustainable Development*, Nairobi, Kenya: UNEP.

Lyster, S. (1985), *International Wildlife Law*, Cambridge: Grotius Publications.

Marr, S. (2000), 'The Southern Bluefin Tuna Cases: The Precautionary Approach and Conservation and Management of Fish Resources', *European Journal of International Law*, **11**, pp. 815–32.

McCaffrey, S.C. (1995), 'The International Law Commission Adopts Draft Articles on International Watercourses', *American Journal of International Law*, **89**, pp. 395–404.

McCaffrey, S.C. and Mpazi, S. (1998), 'The 1997 United Nations Convention on International Watercourses', *American Journal of International Law*, **92**, pp. 97–102.

Mendelson, M.H. (1998), 'The Formation of Customary International Law', *Recueil des Cours*, **272**, pp. 165–395.

Mitchell, A. (2001), 'Forests Face Global Extinction, Study Says', *The Globe and Mail*, A10, Tuesday, 21 August 2001.

Mitchell, R. (1996), 'Compliance Theory: An Overview', in J. Cameron, J. Werksman and P. Roderick (eds), *Improving Compliance with International Environmental Law*, London: Earthscan Publications.

Mori, S. (2002), 'What is the Missing Link? Multilateral Environmental Governance, Regimes, Structural Integration and the Possibility of a World Environment Organization', *International Environmental Governance (Gaps and Weaknesses/Proposals for Reform), Working Paper*, Tokyo, Japan: UNU/IAS.

Morrison, F.L. and Wolfrum, R. (eds) (2000), *International, Regional and National Environmental Law*, The Hague: Kluwer International Law.

National Round Table on the Environment and the Economy (NRTEE) (Summer 2001), *Review*, Ottawa: NRTEE.

Ong, D.M. (1998), 'The Convention on International Trade in Endangered Species (CITES, 1973): Implications of Recent Developments in International and EC Environmental Law', *Journal of Environmental Law*, **10**, pp. 291–314.

Orrego Vicuña, F. (1996), *Final Report prepared for the Eighth Commission of the Institut de Droit International by Francisco Orrego Vicuña, Rapporteur on the subject of Environmental Responsibility and Liability*, 12 December 1996, reprinted in 1998, 'Responsibility and Liability for Environmental Damage under International Law: Issues and Trends', *The Georgetown International Environmental Law Review*, **10**, pp. 279–308.

Oxman, B. (1996), 'The Rule of Law and the United Nations Convention on the Law of the Sea', *European Journal of International Law*, **7**, pp. 353–71.

Pallemaerts, M. (1993), 'International Environmental Law From Stockholm to Rio: Back to the Future?', in P. Sands (ed.), *Greening International Law*, London: Earthscan Publications Ltd., pp. 1–19.

Palmer, A. and Werksman, J. (2001), 'World Trade Organisation, European Communities – Measures Affecting Asbestos and Asbestos-Containing Products, Panel Report', *Review of European Community and International Environmental Law*, **10**, pp. 125–30.

Palmer, G. (1992), 'New Ways to Make International Environmental Law', *American Journal of International Law*, **86**, pp. 259–83.

Pauwelyn, J. (2002), 'A World Environment Court', *International Environmental Governance (Gaps and Weaknesses/Proposals for Reform), Working Paper*, Tokyo, Japan: UNU/IAS.

Röben, V. (2000), 'Institutional Developments under Modern International Environmental Agreements', *Max Plank Yearbook of United Nations Law*, **4**, pp. 363–442.

Rothwell, D.R. (2000), 'Polar Environmental Protection and International Law: The 1991 Antarctic Protocol', *European Journal of International Law*, **11**, pp. 591–614.

Rowlands, I.H. (2001), 'The Kyoto Protocol's "Clean Development Mechanism": A Sustainability Assessment', *Third World Quarterly*, **22**, pp. 795–811.

Rüster, B. and Simma, B. (eds) (1975–83), *International Protection of the Environment: Treaties and Related Documents*, **I–XXXI**, Dobbs Ferry, NY: Oceana Publications.

Rüster, B. and Simma, B. (eds) (1990), *International Protection of the Environment: Treaties and Related Documents*, looseleaf, Dobbs Ferry, NY: Oceana Publications.

Sachariew, K. (1991), 'Promoting Compliance with International Environmental Legal Standards: Reflections on Monitoring and Reporting Mechanisms', *Yearbook of International Environmental Law*, **2**, pp. 31–52.

Sand, P. (1993), 'International Environmental Law After Rio', *European Journal of International Law*, **4**, pp. 377–89.

Sands, P. (1995), *Principles of International Environmental Law*, Manchester and New York: Manchester University Press.

Sands, P. (1996), 'Observations on International Nuclear Law Ten Years after Chernobyl', *Review of European Community and International Environmental Law*, **5**, pp. 199–204.

Sands, P., Tarasofsky, R. and Weiss, M. (1994), *Documents in International Environmental Law*, 2 vols, Manchester and New York: Manchester University Press.

Schally, H.M. (1993), 'Forests: Toward an International Legal Regime?', *Yearbook of International Environmental Law*, **4**, pp. 30–50.

Schmitt, M.N. (1997), 'Green War: An Assessment of the Environmental Law of International Armed Conflict', *Yale Journal of International Law*, **22**, pp. 1–109.

Schwartz, R. (2000), 'Trade Measures Pursuant to Multilateral Environmental Agreements – Developments from Singapore to Seattle', *Review of European Community and International Environmental Law*, **9**, pp. 63–70.

Smith Jr., F.L., Simmons, R.T. and Georgia, P.J. (1996), 'The Tragedy of the Commons Revisited: Politics vs. Private Property', monograph available at 'www.privateconservation.org'.

Sohn, L. (1973), 'The Stockholm Declaration on the Human Environment', *Harvard International Law Journal*, **14**, pp. 423–515.

Sornarajah, M. (1995), 'Foreign Investment and International Environmental Law', in L. Kurukulasuriya (ed.), *UNEP's New Way Forward: Environmental Law and Sustainable Development*, Nairobi, Kenya: UNEP.

Steinberg, R.H. (1997), 'Trade–Environment Negotiations in the EU, NAFTA, and WTO: Regional Trajectories of Rule Development', *American Journal of International Law*, **91**, pp. 231–67.

Steiner, M. (2001), 'After a Decade of Global Forest Negotiations, Where Are We Now?', *Review of European Community and International Environmental Law*, **10**, pp. 98–105.

Stone, C. (1995), *The Gnat is Older than Man. Global Environment and Human Agenda*, Princeton, NJ: Princeton University Press.

Strong, M. (1993), 'Beyond Rio: Prospects and Portents', *Colorado Journal of International Environmental Law and Policy*, **4**, pp. 21–35.

Susskind, L.E. (1994), *Environmental Diplomacy: Negotiating More Effective Global Agreements*, Oxford: Oxford University Press.

Szasz, P.C. (1992), 'Restructuring the International Organizational Framework', in E. Brown Weiss (ed.), *Environmental Change and International Law*, Tokyo: United Nations University Press.

Székely, A. (1997), 'Non-Binding Commitments: A Commentary on the Softening of International Law as Evidenced in the Environmental Field', in UN, *International Law on the Eve of the Twenty-First Century. Views of the International Law Commission*, New York: United Nations.

Thoreau, H.D. (2000), *Walden; or, Life in the Woods*, Toronto: HarperCollins Canada/Harper Trade.

Timoshenko, A. (1990), 'Ecological Security: Global Change Paradigm', *Colorado Journal of International Environmental Law and Policy*, **1**, pp. 127–45.

Tolkien, J.R.R. (1991 edition), *The Lord of the Rings*, New York: HarperCollins.
Tolkien, J.R.R. (2000 edition), *The Hobbit*, Toronto: HarperCollins Canada.
UNEP (2000), *Mälmo Ministerial Declaration*, Adopted by the Global Ministerial Environment Forum, Sixth Special Session of the Governing Council of the United Nations Environment Programme, Fifth Plenary Meeting, 31 May 2000.
UNEP (2001), *An Assessment of the Status of the World's Remaining Closed Forests*, UNEP/DEWA/TR 01-2, Nairobi: DEWA/UNEP.
UNEP/IGM (16 January 2002), *Draft Report of the President of the United Nations Environment Programme Governing Council for Consideration by the Open-Ended Intergovernmental Group of Ministers or Their Representatives on International Environmental Governance*, UNEP/IGM/5/2.
UNEP/IGM (6 April 2001), *International Environmental Governance. Multilateral Environmental Agreements (MEAs)*, UNEP/IGM/1/INF/3.
UNEP/IGM (4 April 2001), *International Environmental Governance. Report of the Executive Director*, UNEP/IGM/1/2.
UNEP/IGM (30 March 2001), *Multilateral Environmental Agreements: A Summary. Background paper presented by the secretariat*, UNEP/IGM/1/INF/1.
UNEP/IGM (5 April 2001), *Summary of Selected Papers. Note by the secretariat*, UNEP/IGM/1/INF/2.
UNGA (1994), *Report on the UN Decade of International Law*, UN Doc A/49/323, Annex, 19 August 1994.
UNGA (2001), *Report in Preparatory Activities for The World Summit on Sustainable Development*, UN Doc A/56/50, 14 September 2001.
Usui, M. (2002), 'The Role of Private Business in International Environmental Governance', *International Environmental Governance (Gaps and Weaknesses/Proposals for Reform), Working Paper*, Tokyo, Japan: UNU/IAS.
Wolfrum, R. (1998), 'Compliance with International Environmental Law', *Recueil des Cours*, **272**, pp. 25–154.
WTO (2000), *European Communities – Measures Affecting Asbestos and Asbestos-Containing Products, Report of the Panel*, 18 September 2000, WT/DS135/R.
WTO (2001), *European Communities – Measures Affecting Asbestos and Asbestos-Containing Products, Report of the Appellate Body*, 12 March 2001, WT/DS135/AB/R.

Further References

A selection of relevant websites for updates on international environmental law and related issues:

African Union (AU) [successor to the OAU, see below]	www.african-union.org
Convention on Biological Diversity	www.biodiv.org
Convention on International Trade in Endangered Species of Wild Fauna and Flora	www.cites.org
European Union official website	www.europa.eu.int
Food and Agriculture Organisation (FAO)	www.fao.org
Friends of the Earth	www.foe.org
Greenpeace	www.greenpeace.org
Intergovernmental Panel on Climate Change (IPCC)	www.ipcc.ch
International Atomic Energy Agency (IAEA)	www.iaea.org
International Court of Justice (ICJ)	www.icj-cij.org
International Labour Organisation (ILO)	www.ilo.org
International Organisation for Standardisation (ISO)	www.iso.ch
International Union for the Conservation of Nature (IUCN)	www.iucn.org
Organisation for Economic Cooperation and Development (OECD)	www.oecd.org
Organisation of African Unity (OAU) [predecessor to the AU]	www.oau-oua.org
Organisation of American States (OAS)	www.oas.org

Ozone Secretariat	www.unep.org/ozone
Secretariat of the Basel Convention on the Control of Transboundary Movement of Hazardous Wastes and Their Disposal	www.basel.int
United Nations (containing useful information on the Commission on Sustainable Development (CSD), International Law Commission (ILC), Law of the Sea and other topics)	www.un.org
United Nations Development Programme (UNDP)	www.undp.org
United Nations Environment Programme (UNEP)	www.unep.org
United Nations Framework Convention on Climate Change (UNFCCC)	www.unfccc.de
United Nations Global Compact	www.unglobalcompact.org
United Nations Secretariat of the Convention to Combat Desertification (CCD)	www.unccd.int
Walden Woods Project, Thoreau Institute and Thoreau Society	www.walden.org
World Bank	www.worldbank.org
World Business Council for Sustainable Development (BCSD)	www.wbcsd.ch
World Health Organisation (WHO)	www.who.org
World Summit on Sustainable Development (WSSD)	ww.johannesburgsummit.org
World Trade Organisation (WTO)	www.wto.org
Worldwide Fund for Nature (WWF)	www.wwf.org

Part I
Conceptual Issues

[1]

ENVIRONMENTAL SECURITY AND GLOBAL CHANGE: THE CHALLENGE TO INTERNATIONAL LAW*

Günther Handl

I. Introduction

In 1972, Maurice Strong, noted:

> "The essential theme of modern age is interdependence, the interdependence of all the elements which sustain . . . life on the planet, of man with those elements, of the natural system with man's needs and aspirations and most of all man with man".[1]

Today, almost twenty years later, on the eve of the 1992 United Nations Conference on Environment and Development, global environmental interdependence has become painfully obvious, its manifestations distinctly threatening, its ramifications all-engrossing. Some commentators conclude that global environmental degradation has reached a "precrisis stage".[2] Others, quite persuasively, maintain that we are in the middle of a process of unavoidable global environmental change that threatens possibly catastrophic economic, social and political consequences.[3] Whatever the perspective on the present state of affairs, there is broad agreement that environmental resource management has become a matter of paramount importance, an issue involving national security[4] and thus, by definition, international, indeed global security.[5]

If, therefore, the present state of the global environment poses a serious challenge to both national and international decision-makers and to the international public order system itself, it offers also an opportunity for, indeed holds out the promise of unprecedented international cooperation. The end of the cold war signals the possibility of broad and intensifying East–West accomodation and, in its wake, of global cooperation. In general, we see, as Prof. Falk has pointed out, a "dramatic shift from the perception of international relations as a zero-sum

* This is a revised version of a paper given at a Conference on Environmental Protection and International Law, in Vienna, October 11, 1990. I would like to thank conference participants for their comments, especially, however, Luzius Wildhaber, Peter Sand, Yves van der Mensbrugghe and Konrad Ginther. Thanks are also due to Joseph Weiler. Any shortcomings of the paper obviously are my own responsibility.

[1] U.N. Doc.A/C.2/SR.1466 (1972).

[2] *See, e.g.*, Timoshenko, "Ecological Security: Global Change Paradigm", 1 *CoJIELP* 127 (1990).

[3] *See, e.g.* Döös, "Challenges to the Environment Requiring International Action," in W.Lang & H.Neuhold, eds., *Environmental Protection and International Law* (forthcoming); and *cf.* Brown, "The New World Order", in *State of the World 1991* 3, at 20 (1991).

[4] *See, in particular*, Mathews, "Redifining Security", 68 *Foreign Affairs* 163 (1989); and M.Renner, *National Security: The Economic and Environmental Dimensions*, Worldwatch Paper 89 (May 1989).

[5] *See, e.g.*, Vinogradov, "International Environmental Security: The Concept and its Implementation", in A.Carter and G. Danilenko, eds., *Perestroika and International Law* 196 (1990).

game to a positive sum game".[6] The notion of "spaceship earth", long accepted as a metaphor for the existence of a global community in an ecological sense, may finally inspire international political and legal action. Successful responsive action, however, will depend on whether and how decision-makers act upon the special characteristics of todays' environmental crisis and its specific implications for the international legal system.

The scientific, economic and social context in which the global environmental crisis unfolds is subject to change at increasing speed.[7] Indeed, certain features of the factual setting change at exponentially increasing speed. The result has been an enormous strain on the capability of the international legal system, and particularly, of the international legislative process,[8] to keep up with the rate of change, to reorder regulatory priorities and, most importantly, to adjust procedurally and institutionally to increasing demand for quick legislative action.

A second characteristic ingredient of the crisis is the fact that environmental issues that rise to the level of international concern have progressively advanced from purely local transboundary, to regional/continental and, lately, global dimensions. This has meant that the international regulatory focus had to expand accordingly, ultimately necessitating the building of environmental global regimes. The geographically expanding scope, in turn, has rendered international standard-setting a much more delicate task, an exercise in balancing the objectives of minimum state participation, discouragement of free-riders and avoidance of unreasonably low levels of environmental protection.

Finally, the present global environmental situation acquires crisis proportions because of the intensity or severity of its present or potential manifestations.[9] There is a risk of serious irreversible or cumulative effects, of an environmental system overload producing cascading effects throughout ecological sub-systems.[10] Thus, international environmental law must come to reflect a much greater emphasis on precautionary policies and a systematic rather than segmented approach to environmental resource management.

The question thus arises whether the international legal system can meet these challenges, whether it will be able to ensure to this and future generations a

[6] Falk, "The Capacity of International Law to Respond to the Environmental Challenge", [1989] *Proceedings, Canadian Council on International Law* 35, at 47.

[7] As Talbot points out, the current acceleration is unique to the extent that change is now being experienced within a lifetime. *See* Talbot, "Man's Role in Managing the Global Environment", in D.Botkin, M.Caswell, J.Estes & A.Orio, eds., *Changing the Global Environment – Perspectives on Human Involvement* 17, at 23 (1989).

[8] Indeed, growing concern about the characteristically slow response to change by the traditional multilateral law-making process is well documented in Szasz, "Reforming the Multilateral Treaty-Making Process: An Opportunity Missed?", in Y. Dinstein, ed., *International Law at a Time of Perplexity. Essays in Honour of Shabtai Rosenne* 908, at 926 (1989).

[9] The threat of global climatic change is an obvious illustration of this point. For an indication of the dimension of the problem see, *e.g.*, *Intergovernmental Panel on Climate Change, First Assessment Report: Overview, 31 August 1990*, 4.

[10] *But see* A.Hawley, *Human Ecology: A Theoretical Essay* 123 (1986), who urges caution with regard to predicting limits of cumulative change.

modicum of environmental security in the face of rapid global change. The following review thus will attempt to sketch an answer by identifying critical policy themes[11] and by evaluating evolving international community responses to specific issues that are likely to bear on success or failure of the international legal system.

II. INTERNATIONAL PROTECTION OF THE ENVIRONMENT: THE EVOLVING PROCESS

A. Legal Instruments and Law-Making Techniques

(i) Framework Conventions and Implementing Protocols

If international protection of environmental resources requires an increasingly high degree of adaptability or responsiveness of the legal system to rapid and frequent change,[12] a traditional, ad hoc treaty-based approach to international environmental standard-setting, is evidently ill suited to meet the task. The disadvantages of the classic treaty approach are obvious: The drafting, adoption and putting into effect of treaties as well as revisions or amendments involve elaborate and time-consuming exercises in diplomacy. In the aggregate, transaction costs of this approach become unacceptably high because, as legislative international intervention will be repeatedly required to respond to an evolving international environmental problem, this approach offers simply too many opportunities to states for "opportunistic" behavior.

The need to facilitate international environmental decision-making of a less cumbersome and time-consuming nature without sacrificing at the same time on the objective of broad state adherence to adequate environmental standards, has prompted a restructuring of multilateral legislative processes: Diplomatic "*ad hocracy*"[13] is being abandoned for institutionalized, periodic and informal review of international regulatory regimes with simplified amendment procedures.

While there are other indications of this development in international environmental standard setting – note, for example, the simplified amendment procedures of Article 313 of the United Nations Convention on the Law of the Sea[14] – it is only in the context of more recent environmental framework conventions and implementing protocols, that the trend has become conspicuous.

[11] Although the institutional aspects of global environmental management are of major importance, anything more than a perfunctory discussion of issues involved would far exceed the limits of this paper. For coverage of some of the institutional issues, see instead Thacher, "Alternative Legal and Institutional Approaches to Global Change", World Resources Institute, *Greenhouse Warming: Negotiating a Global Regime* 37 (1991).

Other important issues, such as international liability for and compensation of harm to the environment, or of how to operationalize a system of international responsibility for the protection of the global commons, are not being reviewed here for similar reasons.

[12] For an exemplary exposition of these factors and their impact on international environmental standard-setting, see P.Sand, *Lessons Learned in Global Governance* (1990).

[13] A.Toffler, *Future Shock* 124 (1970), *cited in* P.Sand, *ibid.* 5.

[14] United Nations Convention on the Law of the Sea, UN Doc. A/CONF.62/122, 7 October 1982 [hereafter: UNCLOS], *reprinted in* 21 *ILM* 1261 (1982).

For example, the Montreal Protocol on Substances that Deplete the Ozone Layer expressly provides for the periodic review and assessment of control measures taken and their adjustment or supplementation whenever deemed necessary.[15] Similarly, the 1989 Basel Convention on the Transboundary Movement of Hazardous Wastes (although, strictly speaking, not a framework convention[16]) authorizes the regularly scheduled meetings of the Conference of the Parties to take legislative initiatives to ensure the effectiveness and continuous improvement of the regime.[17] Significantly, as regards adoption of technical annexes under either regime, parties must "opt out" so as to avoid being bound by the new standards.[18] Simplification of the formal standard-setting procedure is, moreover, accompanied by an acceleration of meetings of the parties, thus increased opportunities for legislative initiatives. In the case of some of the regimes concerned, this may well offer the prospect of a virtually continuous legislative enterprise.[19]

The resulting intrinsic flexibility or adaptability of the legislative process comes, as some might be apt to object, with a substantial price-tag. The framework-*cum*-implementing protocols approach necessarily entails a significant degree of indeterminacy of the normative landscape thus being created: States tend to settle first broad policy outlines through the device of framework conventions and leave nettlesome details to be worked out in future protocols. This institutionalizes international law-making within the individual environmental context as defined by the framework convention. By necessity, this approach thus also signals a certain open-endedness of the legislative enterprise.

More significantly still, states may leave the definition of key legal parameters regarding the scope and very nature of conventional obligations to which they contract to be settled at a later date. Consider, for example, the Basel Convention: The finalization of at least two such concepts, namely that of "environmentally sound management of wastes" and of "liability", have been left for decision by the parties until after the Convention formally enters into force.[20]

International legislation under this guise is no longer a single well-defined product carried by expectations of stability for a forseeable future. It is rather a fragile, temporary legal sign-post in an institutionalized process in which legal

[15] *See* Articles 6 and 11 of the Montreal Protocol on Substances that Deplete the Ozone Layer, Final Act, *text in* 26 *ILM* 1544 (1987).

[16] *But see infra* text at note 20.

[17] *See* Article 15, paragraph 5 (b) – (e) of the Basel Convention, in *United Nations Environment Programme, Basel Convention on the Control of Transboundary Movements of Hazardous Wastes and Their Disposal, Final Act.*

[18] *See* Article 10, paragraph 2 (b) and (c) of the Vienna Convention for the Protection of the Ozone Layer, *reproduced in* 26 *ILM* 1516 (1987); and Article 18, paragraph 2 (b) and (c) of the Basel Convention.

[19] Note, *e.g.*, that the third meeting of the parties to the Montreal Protocol has been scheduled within a year of the last: Decision II/20, Report of the Second Meeting of the Parties to the Montreal Protocol on Substances that Deplete the Ozone Layer, U.N. Doc. UNEP/OzL.Pro.2/3, 11, at 18 (1990).

[20] *See* especially Article 12 of the Basel Convention which provides for consultations on liability after entry into force of the Convention. *See also* Resolution 3 of the Final Act (regarding the interim development of a protocol on liability and compensation to be submitted to the parties at their first meeting), and Resolution 8 of the Final Act calling for the elaboration of technical guidelines for the environmentally sound management of wastes, again, for consideration by the parties at their first meeting.

positions are subject to constant review and susceptible to frequent and speedy alteration. Those who might be troubled by this fact might do well to heed Prof. Sax's admonition on the function of domestic environmental law which applies with equal, indeed greater force to international legal mechanisms for protecting environmental resources globally:

> "[W]e must put aside the dominating idea that the legal system is to be designed to institutionalize stability and security. Probably nothing is more urgently required than institutions for controlled instability".[21]

Some aspects of this development may be undesirable. For example, the institutional dynamics of multilateral regimes (with regard to both the setting and implementation of standards[22]), may be such as to de-couple decision-making within the regime from traditional national processes of control and supervision. In this sense, the new type of environmental regime may signal an emerging "democratic deficit".[23] Other implications of such regimes might be merely inconvenient. However, on balance, there can be little doubt that the evolving international legislative process represents progress towards better international legal management of increasingly demanding global enviromental problems.[24]

(ii) "Soft Law"

It is against the background of the special regulatory exigencies of international environmental problems that so-called "soft law"[25] plays an important role in the evolution of international environmental law. "Soft law" denotes international prescriptions that are deemed to lack the requisite characteristics of international legal norms proper, but which, notwithstanding this fact, are capable of producing certain effects. "Soft law", of course, travels in tandem with "hard law", its counterpart on the other side of the threshold of international normativity.[26]

There are international lawyers who habor serious reservations about usage of the term, defining it as a "pathological phenomenon"[27] of international law; as introducing a graduated scale of normativity; as a practice that lends itself to

[21] Sax, "A General Survey of the Problem", in *Science for Better Environment, Proceedings of the International Congress on the Human Environment* 753, at 755-56 (1976).

[22] *See infra*, § II.B.

[23] One facet of this development, namely the relative loss of control over the legislative process by individual states to the collectivity of parties, is that domestic review and control may become commensurately more attenuated.

[24] For an in-depth exposition of the merits of these developments, see Gehring, "International Environmental Regimes: Dynamic Sectoral Legal Systems", 1 *Ybk. Int'l Env. L.* (1990).

[25] In French, "soft law" is sometimes quite appropriately referred to as "droit vert". Remarks of Prof. Pierre Dupuy, during panel discussion on "A Hard Look at Soft Law", ASIL Annual Meeting, Washington D.C., April 22, 1988.

[26] *See, generally,* "A Hard Look at Soft Law" (remarks by Handl, Reisman, Simma, Dupuy and Chinkin), [1988] *ASIL Proceedings* 371-93.

[27] Weil, "Towards Relative Normativity in International Law", 77 *AJIL* 413, at 417 (1983).

legal pretension. The concept, so the argument goes, tends to blur the line between law and non-law, be that because merely aspirational norms are accorded "legal" status, albeit of a secondary nature; be that because the effect of the usage of the term may be to undermine the status of an established legal norm.

On the other hand, "soft law" can be a valuable instrument for enhancing or supplementing international law proper. In fact, frequently "soft law" will capture emerging notions of international public order and thus help extend the realm of legitimate international concern to matters of previously exclusive national jurisdiction. This is especially true of the use of soft law with regard to the protection of the environment. In this sense, soft law is the thin end of the normative wedge of international environmental law, perhaps the "Trojan Horse of environmentalists".[28]

There is, of course, abundant and well-known evidence of the effectiveness of soft law declarations as catalysts in the evolution of international environmental law proper. The so-called Helsinki Rules on the Uses of Waters of International Rivers,[29] the 1972 Stockholm Declaration on the Human Environment,[30] or the 1982 General Assembly Resolution entitled "World Charter for Nature"[31], to name only a few,[32] all have proved to be agents in the "legalization of international environmental protection."[33]

In the final analysis, though, soft law concepts, pose both a challenge for and an obligation on international lawyers. First, the declining reliability of formal criteria as guideposts to what actually constitutes international law,[34] – a phenomenon that, as intimated, may be prevalent in the context of international environmental decision-making – requires an adequate theory about international law, namely as a process of communication,[35] and thus sensitivity to those signals indicating international normativity and those that do not. Second, international environmental lawyers, must heed the normative dividing line and avoid misrepresenting aspirational norms for "hard law" and thereby rendering a disservice to the very cause they purport to serve, namely the strengthening of the legal protection of the environment globally.

(iii) Uniform Environmental Standards and Asymmetrical Rights & Obligation

In his recent study on international environmental standard-setting, Peter Sand[36] endorses asymmetrical standards or differential obligations as a way to

[28] Lang, "Die Verrechtlichung des internationalen Umweltschutzes", 22 *AVR* 283, at 303 (1984).

[29] *See, International Law Association, Report of the Fifty-Second Conference, Helsinki 1966*, 484.

[30] Declaration on the Human Environment, in Report of the United Nations Conference on the Human Environment, Stockholm June 5-16, 1972, UN Doc. A/CONF.48/14, *reproduced in* 11 *ILM* 1416 (1972).

[31] World Charter for Nature, G.A. res. 37/7, *GAOR, Thirty-Seventh Sess. Supp. No.51* (A/37/51).

[32] For additional references, see Dupuy, *supra* note 26, at 381.

[33] *See* Lang, *supra* note 28, at 303-05.

[34] *See, especially*, McDougal & Reisman, "The Prescribing Function in World Constitutive Process: How International Law is Made", 6 *Yale Studies in World Public Order* 249 (1980).

[35] For a masterly exposition of the process, see Reisman, "International Law-Making: A Process of Communication", [1981] *ASIL, Proceedings* 101.

[36] *See* P. Sand, *supra* note 12, at 6–8.

induce broad state acceptance of a regulatory regime, yet beat the "lowest common denominator problem". The usefulness, indeed indispensability of selective incentives, is, of course, a reflection of the fact that expected benefits and costs of any regime will vary from state to state. Thus, incentives such as delayed compliance schedules or economic/financial assistance, may be necessary to offset the absence of reciprocal state interest in the proposed regime. As an axiom of international co-operation,[37] such measures have long been part and parcel of international standard-setting efforts.[38] By the same token, the intrinsic merit of differentiating standards that account for variations in state parties' contributions to the problem to be regulated, is equally self-evident.[39]

Nevertheless, from a legal policy perspective, any asymmetry in rights and obligations is a sensitive matter. Sometimes, the nature, possibly also the scope, of asymmetrical standards may raise a fundamental question about the appropriateness of such multilateral regime-building devices. Indeed, in the absence of special justifications, such as causation-related allowances in the case of environmental regimes addressing a transnational pollution problem, any international regulatory system that discriminates among states with regard to its core obligations, is bound to be problematical in the long run.[40]

Consider, for example, the Nuclear Non-Proliferation Treaty[41] to which Sand refers as an example of a successful incentive-based regulatory approach.[42] To many observers the NPT may illustrate also the dangers inherent in any asymmetrical standard-setting: the persistence of the temporarily sanctioned legal discrimination along the lines of nuclear "haves" and "have-nots" has exacerbated diplomatic controversies over implementation of the treaty and repeatedly threatened to unravel the whole regime.[43]

As regards international environmental legislation, asymmetrical normative standards that bear on the essence of the regulatory regime, unlike incentives, are generally undesirable. First, they invariably entail higher administrative costs given the greater complexity of the system; second, inevitable distortions in international trade are likely to be more difficult to reverse than would be the case if brought about by, for example, financial incentives to induce disadvantaged states to comply fully with internationally uniform, but stringent standards;

[37] As to the importance of reciprocity, see R. Axelrod, *The Evolution of Co-operation* (1984); and Pinto, "Reflections on International Liability for Injurious Consequences Arising out of Acts Not Prohibited by International Law", 16 *Netherlands Yearbook Int'l L.* 17, at 41–42 (1985).

[38] *See, e.g.*, F. Morgenstern, *Legal Problems of International Organizations* 132–33 (1986).

[39] *See* also Magraw, "Legal Treatment of Developing Countries: Differential, Contextual and Absolute Norms", 1 *CoJIELP* 69 (1990).

[40] A case in point are "flexible" international labour standards. Thus, as Morgenstern points out, during the 1984 session of the International Labour Conference, many delegates insisted that "international standards must be intransigent when they are a matter of fundamental rights". F. Morgenstern, *ibid.* 133, fn.125.

[41] Treaty on the Non-Proliferation of Nuclear Weapons, 161 UNTS 72.

[42] *See supra* note 12, at 7.

[43] Thus, at the most recent Review Conference of States Party to the NPT, delegates failed to adopt a final conference declaration as a result of irreconcilable differences over the United States' refusal to commit itself to abandon nuclear testing by 1995: *See* "Deadlock Threatens Future of Nuclear Treaty", *N.Y. Times*, September 16, 1990, 5, col.1.

third, such standards might be counterproductive in terms of long-term environmental benefits, especially where less developed countries are involved: A dilution of the normative demands on developing countries is likely to impede progress by those countries towards an adequate level of local environmental protection, the acquisition of technological know-how and managerial ability on which "sustainable development" locally will depend. Thus, developing country status cannot justify in and by itself an automatic lowering of international standards.

To oppose such differentiation in environmental standards does not imply rejection of a state's ability to control the risk of untoward enviromental impacts – quite apart from its contribution to the problem – as the ultimate basis of international responsibility for safeguarding internationally sensitive environmental resources. As a matter-of-fact, retaining uniformity with regard to core obligations while taking into account states' socio-economic conditions, are entirely compatible objectives for multilateral regulatory regimes.

Take, for example, the Basel Convention on the Transboundary Movement of Hazardous Waste. It establishes very broad international obligations for the protection of would-be-importing countries. Yet, there is little evidence that the regime reflects the abandonment of the rules of classic state responsibility or the ascendancy of social welfare concepts in international relations, as some might be tempted to argue. Rather, rights and obligations within the essentially bilateral context of exporting and importing states are fairly well balanced.[44] They are in line with the traditional international principle to allocate responsibility to the state party best able to act towards minimization of the costs of untoward waste transfers.[45] In particular, the Convention does not proceed from the unwarranted assumption that the responsibility of the state of import is automatically diminished whenever the latter falls into the developing country category.[46]

In the end, rejection of a purely wealth-sensitive or development status-oriented international standard-setting philosophy, quite obviously brings into sharper focus the issue of equity in North–South relations and the need for alternative mechanisms to redress the problem of underdevelopment as it bears on international environmental regime building.[47]

(iv) The Formal Legal Structure of Regulatory Regimes

To be effective, international environmental regimes must not only attract the support of all relevant states, but also reach effectively the activities of major transnational non-state actors, especially transnational corporations (TNCs) and multilateral lending institutions. Given the immense influence of activities of

[44] For details, see, *e.g.*, Handl, "The 1989 Basel Convention on the Transboundary Movement of Hazardous Waste: A Preliminary Assessment", [1989] *Canadian Council on International Law, Proceedings* 367.

[45] *See* Handl, "State Liability for Accidental Transnational Environmental Damage by Private Persons", 74 *AJIL* 525, at 530-35 (1980).

[46] For the policy arguments against a status-dependent diminuition of importing state responsibility, see Handl and Lutz, "An International Policy Perspective on the Trade of Hazardous Materials and Technologies", 30 *Harvard ILJ* 351, at 363 (1989).

[47] *See infra* § III.C.

some of these non-state actors on national policies and operational decisions affecting internationally sensitive environmental resources,[48] as well as these actors' often quasi-autonomous conduct in the transnational arena,[49] the question arises of how best to formally structure environmental regulations.

One possibility might be to legally treat these entities as formally independent of states in recognition of their frequent *de facto* independence in the transnational arena. Another would be to couch international regulations in terms of private legal obligations directly incumbent on the principal actors, instead of in language that focuses on states' international responsibility as the underlying cardinal principle. Indeed, the definition of the relationship between private legal obligations and explicit norms of state responsibility has become a significant issue in recent efforts at international standard-setting related to environmental protection.[50]

Some transboundary regulatory regimes of a highly technical nature, most notably those relating to liability for transboundary damage,[51] already evince a so-called "private law" approach. While the legal instruments by which these regimes are established represent formal international agreements among states proper, their objective is the regulation of rights and obligations not among states themselves, but among private individuals. Similarly, the OECD Guidelines for Multinational Enterprises[52] as well as the proposed U.N. Code of Conduct on Transnational Corporations[53] directly address responsibilities of TNCs. Finally, there is the phenomenon of limited direct international regulation of environmentally sensitive private conduct as in the Convention on the Regulation of Antarctic Mineral Resource Activities (CRAMRA),[54] or the draft regulations drawn up by the UN Preparatory Commission for the International Sea-Bed Authority and for the International Tribunal for the Law of the Sea.[55]

48 "Internationally sensitive environmental resources" as used in this paper denotes environmental resources the use of which by any one country is a matter of intrinsic international concern, be that because of spatial, i.e. injurious transboundary, or temporal, i.e. burdensome intergenerational effects associated with usage. *See also infra* § III.D.

49 *See, e.g.*, The Impact of Multinational Corporations on the Development Process and on International Relations, UN Doc.E/5500/Add.1 (1974).
For an argument strongly in support of an enhanced legal status of TNCs in the international legal system, see Charney, "Transnational Corporations and Developing Public International Law", [1983] *DukeLJ* 748.

50 Note the debates within the IAEA Standing Committee on Nuclear Damage as to how to relate satisfactorily private and state liability in a comprehensive liability regime. For details, see, *e.g.*, Report of the Standing Committee on Liability for Nuclear Damage, Second Session, Vienna 15–19 October 1990, IAEA Doc. SCNL/2/INF2.

51 Examples of this phenomenon include the Paris and Vienna nuclear liability conventions, *texts in* 55 *AJIL* 1082 (1961), and 2 *ILM* 727 (1963), respectively; the 1969 Brussels Convention on Civil Liability for Oil Pollution Damage, *text in* 9 *ILM* 45 (1970); and the 1989 Convention on Civil Liability for Damage Caused During Carriage of Dangerous Goods by Road, Rail and Inland Navigation Vessels (CRTD), UN Doc. ECE/TRANS/79.

52 *Text in* 15 *ILM* 969 (1976).

53 *Reproduced in* 23 *ILM* 626 (1984).

54 *See* Article 8 of CRAMRA, *text in* 27 ILM 859 (1988).

55 *See* Preparatory Commission for the International Sea-Bed Authority and for the International Tribunal of the Law of the Sea, Draft Regulations on Prospecting, Exploration and Exploitation of Polymetallic

cont.,

However, neither existing "private law" liability regimes, nor other, presently proposed, international regulations that might directly address private conduct more broadly, should obscure the fact that the ability to invoke state responsibility principles remains a necessary alternative to asserting non-state actors' responsibility. Thus, to single out TNCs, it is unlikely that any time soon, their international legal status would be upgraded to the point where they could be both direct claimant and respondent under international law without any mediation by states.[56] Nor is it likely that international control, for example under United Nations auspices, would replace present "home" state control, and that thereby United Nations responsibility would replace "home" state responsibility.[57]

In short, the principle of state responsibility proper is likely to remain an essential legal underpinning of any transboundary regulatory regime. States are the repository of ultimate power to enforce transnational community standards. Accordingly, in the interest of strengthening international environmental regulations, the principle of state responsibility should be made explicit especially where it already extends implicitly to controlling activities of nationals, including multinational corporations. At the same time, it will be necessary to continue to strengthen the direct transnational accountability of key actors, such as TNCs. This will not, however, diminish state responsibility for the conduct of corporate nationals abroad. Rather, greater specificity of TNC obligations will strengthen the hand of host states in dealing with TNCs while introducing a more demanding standard against which to assess "home" state compliance with its international obligation to control corporate nationals.

(v) The Interplay of Local, Regional and Global Environmental Standard-Setting

Heightened awareness of international environmental interdependence and rising threats to globally shared resources, such as the atmosphere, have had a dramatic impact on the *locus* of standard-setting bearing on internationally sensitive environmental resources. Two basic trends are discernible. First, international law-making on environmental matters is rapidly becoming more centralized, thus reducing the room for standard-setting at individual state level. Evidence of this shift can be found in many regulatory contexts, including, for example, marine pollution. Unlike the early 1970s, when Canada could unilater-

55 cont. Nodules in the Area, Addendum, Part VIII, Protection and Preservation on the Marine Environment from Activities in the Area, Working Paper by the Secretariat, U.N. Doc. LOS/PVN/SCN.3/WP.6/Add.5 (1990).

56 This is not to deny that TNCs at times do act or are treated as partial or functional "subjects" of international law. However, codes of conduct for TNCs were not intended to raise TNCs to the level of both autonomously entitled and responsible formal "subjects" of international law. For further details, see Lutz & Aron, "Codes of Conduct and Other International Instruments", in G.Handl & R.Lutz, *Transferring Hazardous Technologies and Substances: The International Legal Challenge* [hereafter: *Transferring Hazardous Technologies and Substances*] 129 (1989); and Hailbronner, "Völkerrechtliche und staatrechtliche Überlegungen zu Verhaltenkodizes für transnationale Unternehmen", in I. von Münch, ed., *Festschrift für Hans-Jürgen Schlochauer* 338–41 (1981).

57 For a summary of an illustrative debate on this point in the Institute of International Law, see I.Seidl-Hohenveldern, *Corporations under International Law* 22–26 (1987).

ally set offshore pollution prevention standards which, though primarily intended to protect national environmental interests, cut broadly across international interests,[58] today, in an analoguous situation, national discretion would be severely limited: UNCLOS and special international marine pollution legislation establish clear international procedures for authoritative standard-setting that preempt unilateralism.[59] At the same time, global regimes are susceptible to the *de facto* veto power of strategic individual countries. Consider, for example, the recent United States Oil Pollution Liability and Compensation Act[60] which allows federal states to set higher than internationally agreed upon limits on liability. Most observers agree that this legislation will seriously undermine, if not kill,[61] the 1984 Protocols amending the 1969 Oil Pollution Liability Convention[62] and the 1971 Fund Convention.[63]

Second, international standard-setting tends to occur – not surprisingly – at a level consistent with what in a different context is often referred to as the principle of "subsidiarity" of legislation.[64] Frequently, the appropriate level for international environmental legislative action will be the regional one. Regionalization, as Sand points out, offers an opportunity for custom-built regimes and more stringent environmental standards as limited membership is likely to imply a higher common denominator.[65] Recognition of the merits of this approach, can

[58] *See* the Arctic Waters Pollution Prevention Act (Bill C-202), *text in* 10 *ILM* 543 (1970). For the ensuing diplomatic conflict between the United States and Canada, see Department of State Press Release No.121 of April 15, 1970, and the Canadian Note of April 16, 1970, *reproduced ibid.* 605–15. The Canadian position was eventually fully vindicated in Article 234 of UNCLOS.

[59] Thus, in 1989, when, after a series of tanker mishaps, the United States proposed creation of a 10-mile tanker free zone off Florida to prevent further environmental damage from oil spills, the U.S. sought from the outset international authorization for its plan: *See* "Coast Guard Leader Backs Plan for Tanker-Free Zone off Florida", *N.Y. Times*, August 23, 1989, 10, col.5; and 55 *Federal Register*, May 9, 1990, 19418. Only upon IMO approval in September 1990, was designation of the Florida Keys as "an area to be avoided" enacted. *See* § 6 of the Florida Keys National Marine Sanctuary and Protection Act, P.L. 101–605, 104 Stat. 3089.

[60] Oil Pollution Act of 1990, P.L. 101–380, 104 Stat. 484.

[61] *See* "U.S. Failure to Ratify Protocols Could Undermine Pollution Control, IMO Says", *BNA, Int'l Env. Reporter, Curr. Rpt.* 240 (1990).

[62] *Supra* note 51; 1984 amendments in International Maritime Organization, *International Conference on Liability and Compensation in Connexion with the Carriage of Certain Substances by Sea, 1984* 57 (1985).

[63] 1971 International Convention on the Establishment of an International Fund for Compensation of Oil Pollution Damage, 11 *ILM* 284 (1972); as amended in 1984: *text in* International Maritime Organization, *supra* note 62, at 26.

[64] Thus, in the current debate over the institutional development of the European Community, "subsidiarity" refers to the principle according to which Community legislation in an area of concurrent competence (EC/member states) would be permissible only if the tasks concerned "may be undertaken more effectively in common than by Member States acting seperately . . .": "Editorial Comments", 27 *CMLRev.* 181 (1990), quoting Altiero Spinelli. As to the applicability of the principle to EC environmental action, see Article 130r(4)(i) of the EEC Treaty.
"Subsidiarity", of course, is, as Jacqué and Weiler remind us, a fundamental concept that underlies any federal-type allocation of powers and competences. *See* Jacqué & Weiler, "On the Road to European Union – A New Judicial Architecture: An Agenda for the Intergovernmental Conference", *ibid.* 185, at 202–03.

[65] Provided limited membership reflects some affinity among the states concerned: P. Sand, *supra* note 12, at 9.

be seen in the fact that many global regimes leave room for supplementary regulation at regional or bilateral levels. For example, the Basel Convention specifically accomodates bilateral, multilateral or regional agreements or arrangements regarding the transboundary movement of hazardous wastes, provided "environmentally sound management" at least equivalent to that required under the Convention will be assured.[66] By contrast, the 1986 Conventions on Early Notification of Nuclear Accidents[67] and on Assistance[68] represent bare-bones framework conventions which in effect render bilateral or regional implementating regimes a necessity.

Regional standard-setting, of course, is not only a process of intrinsically regional importance. The dynamics of the "small group-high common denominator" function may result in stringent or innovative environmental standards at regional level. Such standards are often precedent-setting for the larger community of states. Indeed, it would be difficult to overlook the major contribution of regional organizations to the evolution of general international environmental law. Mention need only be made of various OECD initiatives, such as Council recommendations or decisions related to the "polluter-pays-principle", equal right of access, or "risk communication".[69] Yet, there are intrinsic limits to the ability of regional organizations to offer precedent-setting environmental legal solutions for global problems. Often, global issues render globally arrived at solutions simply inevitable.[70]

There is yet another problematical and critically important aspect to the phenomenon of environmental standard-setting at various levels of territorial organization. The problem is that of legal precedence among conflicting standards, and specifically, of the interrelationship between local standards that vary from those of the larger communities involved. By and large, treatment of the issue on an international/global level mirrors that at regional, e.g., within the European Community[71] or, at national levels, within federal systems of government.[72] Uniformity, even at the cost of the lowest common denominator, tends to be given preference to acceptance of stricter local or national standards whenever the latter are deemed to restrain national or international trade and to

[66] *See* Article 11.

[67] Convention on Early Notification of a Nuclear Accident, *text in* 25 *ILM* 1370 (1986).

[68] Convention on Assistance in the Case of A Nuclear Accident or Radiological Emergency, *ibid.* 1377.

[69] *See infra* text at note 108.

[70] A case in point, prominently mentioned by Sand, is the OECD project for an international agreement on control of transfrontier movements of hazardous waste. When experts came to realize that the effect of a stringent regional convention might be to redirect the hazardous waste stream to non-member states with less demanding regulatory standards, the OECD abandoned its convention project. *See* P. Sand, *supra* note 12, at 9–10; and see Note by the Secretariat, "Implications and Modalities of Further Restricting Hazardous Waste Exports from OECD Member Countries to Developing Countries", OECD Doc. ENV(89)7, 8 March 1989.

[71] *See infra* note 73.

[72] Note, however, that § 1018 of the recently enacted United States Oil Pollution Liability and Compensation Act, *supra* note 60, expressly preserves states' rights to impose additional liability or clean-up requirements.

amount to a level of environmental protection that is "disproportionate" to the effect on trade.[73]

It is true that neither GATT's general rules[74] nor the Tokyo Round's Subsidy Code[75] or Agreement on Technical Barriers to Trade[76] prohibit states from adopting standards that affect the international trade in goods for the *bona fide* purpose of protecting the local environment.[77] On the other hand, a state's unilateral environmental standard-setting that nullifies or impairs another state's pre-existing trade concession, might open the former to claims for compensation even if the standards themselves are found not to violate GATT.[78] For the moment, this provision of GATT remains a dead letter.[79] That might change. In any event, the present Uruguay Round of negotiations on further liberalization of world trade, especially the push for a reduction or elimination of agricultural subsidies, has rekindled justified concerns that multilateral progress in facilitating international trade, may come at the price of eliminating individual states' freedom to set stricter than international minimum standards and thereby endanger local natural resource conservation.[80] Conversely, GATT negotiations could result in a strengthening of the hand of those governments that might seek to impose countervailing duties on imports from countries with liberal or non-existent environmental protection standards, on the grounds that the export of such goods is indirectly subsidized.[81]

Conceivably, Peter Sand's conclusion that "it is the trade regime that determines, if not the 'bottomline', at least the margin of tolerable asymmetries in the EEC's environmental regime"[82] might well come to characterize also global environmental standards. Yet, if ultimately, economic aspirations must be compatible with the principle of "sustainable development",[83] very careful attention

[73] *See, e.g.*, the decision of the European Court of Justice in *Re Disposable Beer Cans: E.C. Commission v. Denmark* (Case 302/86), [1989] *1 CMLR* 619, at 632.

A very similar balancing standard applies to local or state regulations affecting interstate commerce in the United States. *See Pike v. Bruce Church, Inc.*, 397 U.S. 137, at 142.

[74] *See* Article XX (b) and (g) of GATT, 55 *UNTS* 187.

[75] *See* Article 11, paragraph 1 (f) of the Agreement on Interpretation and Application of Articles VI, XVI and XXIII of the General Agreement on Tariffs and Trade, in *General Agreement on Tariffs and Trade, Basic Instruments and Selected Documents*, 26th Supplement, 56 (1980).

[76] *See, especially*, Article 2, paragraph 2 of the Agreement on Technical Barriers to Trade, *ibid.* 8.

[77] *Cf.* also Article 609 of the Canada-United States Free Trade Agreement, 27 *ILM* 281, at 316 (1988).

[78] For a discussion, see Koh, "The Responsibility of the Importer State", in *Transferring Hazardous Technologies and Substances* 170, at 186 (1989).

[79] *See* Rehbinder, "Environmental Protection and the Law of International Trade", in R. Dupuy, ed., *The Future of the International Law of the Environment* 357, at 359 (1985).

[80] *See, e.g.*, Ritchie, "GATT, Agriculture and the Environment: The US Double Zero Plan", 20 *The Ecologist* 214 (1990); and Shrybman, "The Environmental Costs of Free Trade", *Multinational Monitor* 20 (March 1990).

[81] *See* Raman, "Corporate Responsibility to Protect the Global Environment: Emerging Issues of Law and Equity", in *Preserving the Global Environment*, [1989] *Proceedings of the Canadian Council on International Law* 93, at 109. *But see* Rehbinder, *supra* note 79, at 359.

[82] P.Sand, *supra* note 12, at 13–14.

[83] Note, *e.g.*, Paragraph 14 (i) of the Conclusions of the Siena Forum on International Law of the Environment, calling for adapting international trade rules to "generally accepted goals for the protection of the environment"; *Text in 1 Ybk. Int'l Env. L.* (1990). *See further infra* § III.B.

will have to be paid to the finalization and subsequent application of emerging new GATT, regional or bilateral trading rules so as to avoid setting up an international regulatory system in which the trade tail wags the environmental dog.[84]

B. Implementation and Enforcement of International Environmental Law

A first observation concerns the dearth of arrangements for compulsory third-party decision-making in environmental disputes. The well-known general reluctance of states to submit to third-party decision-making,[85] may pose a particularly severe threat to the effectiveness of international environmental regimes. International disputes involving environmental problems are as likely to arise over underlying issues of science and technology as over conflicting views on applicable legal principles and detailed norms. Thus, the absence of in advance agreed to impartial fact-finding, or, generally speaking, of authoritative third-party decision-making, can be a significant impediment to full realization of the respective regime's environmental protection objectives.

There are, however, some offsetting factors that must be mentioned here. First, in the decision-making environment characteristic of some of the regimes described above – a prime example of which is the ozone protection layer regime – in which formal legal criteria might be disregarded for the sake of pragmatic advancement of the regulatory agenda,[86] the absence of compulsory formal dispute settlement procedures may actually be an advantage: any third-party institution, especially, however, any international tribunal or court might be overtaxed when asked to adjudge the merits of a legal dispute. Measured against formal international legal criteria, some of the decisions that have evolved within these environmental regimes might be found not to meet the test of "legality".

Second, some of these regulatory regimes[87] feature special internal implementation mechanisms based on reporting requirements and review procedures somewhat akin to supervisory procedures in the field of human rights.[88] For example, within the framework of the ECE Convention on Long-Range Transboundary Air Pollution, the Protocols on sulphur and nitrogen oxides emissions, establish national reporting requirements vis-a-vis the Executive Body for the Convention and provide for the independent calculation of pollutant budgets, transboundary fluxes and deposition by EMEP, the Co-operative Programme for

[84] Indeed, it is already being suggested that a new round of trade talks address the myriad of international trade-enviromental issues. *See* "Environment versus Freer Trade", *N.Y. Times*, February 11, 1991, C4, col.1.

[85] Diplomatic negotiation is by far the states' choice of preference for settling international disputes. For a detailed analysis of the reasons why, see Bilder, "An Overview of International Dispute Settlement", 1 *Emory J.Int'l Dispute Resolution* 23, fn.36 (1986).

[86] For a detailed description of this phenomenon, see Gehring, *supra* note 24.

[87] CRAMRA, is, of course, a special case because it establishes an international regime under special circumstances, i.e. for an area with a special international status.

[88] *See, e.g.*, Meron, "Norm Making and Supervision in International Human Rights: Reflections on Institutional Order", 76 *AJIL* 754 (1982).

the Monitoring and Evaluation of the Long-Range Transmission of Air Pollutants in Europe.[89] It is against this data base that national reports are being reviewed at annual meetings of the Executive Board and individual states' compliance with obligations under the Protocols is being evaluated. Leaving asied the formal dispute settlement mechanisms of the respective Protocols, this process of verifying compliance is an essential element in the regimes' enforcement mechanisms.

Institutionalized periodic peer review of states' performance is a basic feature also of the Montreal Protocol. Article 8 specifically calls upon the parties to consider procedures and institutional mechanisms for determining non-compliance with the Protocol.[90] The 1990 London amendments to the Montreal Protocol now establish an "Implementation Committee" which reviews allegations of non-compliance and acts as an initial arbiter in disputes over the implementation of obligations under the Protocol.[91] This approach thus internalizes, at least to some extent, dispute settlement that might otherwise be entrusted to third parties.[92]

A second observation concerns the increasingly important role of non-governmental organizations (NGOs), in the application and enforcement of international environmental standards. Of course, environmental NGOs, like those working in the field of human rights, have a long history of active participation in international legal decision-making.[93] Most notable among these involvements is the gathering and dissemination of environmental information,[94] policy advocacy,[95] and the appraisal of failure or success of policies in the light of avowed public policy objectives.[96]

89 *See* Articles 4 and 5 of the Protocol to the 1979 Convention on Long-Range Transboundary Air Pollution on the Reduction of Sulphur Emissions or Their Transboundary Fluxes by at least 30 Per Cent, 27 *ILM* 707 (1988); and Articles 8 and 9 of the Protocol to the 1979 Convention on Long-Range Transboundary Air Pollution Concerning the Control of Emissions of Nitrogen Oxides or Their Transboundary Fluxes, 28 *ILM* 212 (1989).

90 *See* Report of the Parties, *supra* note 19, at 15-16; and Note on Procedures and Institutional Mechanisms for Determining Non-Compliance with the Montreal Protocol on Substances that Deplete the Ozone Layer (prepared by the Secretariat), U.N. Doc UNEP/OzL.Pro.LG.1/2 (1989).

91 *See* Annex III, U.N. Doc. UNEP/OzL.Pro.2/3, 40.

92 *See also* Gehring, *supra* note 24.

93 International law is best analyzed from the perspective of a decision-making process with distinct decision functions, many of which are open to participation by non-state actors. *See* McDougal, Lasswell & Reisman, "The World Constitutive Process of Authoritative Decision", in M.McDougal & M.Reisman, *International Law Essays: A Supplement to International Law in Contemporary Perspective* 191, at 269–86 (1980).

94 A most spectacular example of this kind is the unauthorized landing, in 1983, of a Greenpeace fact-finding party at the Lorino whaling station in Siberia to verify Soviet compliance with International Whaling Commission regulations. *See* "Whaling Protesters Say Chase Followed Incursion into Siberia", *N.Y. Times*, July 20, 1983, A6, col.3.

95 An example of such policy advocacy is the recent proposal by the Natural Resources Defense Fund for an environmental commission of inquiry to review World Bank activities. *See* E.Christensen, *Green Appeal. A Proposal for an Environmental Commission of Enquiry at the World Bank*, September 1990.

96 For an example of such appraisal activity by an NGO, see the report prepared for Greenpeace International by P.Sands, *The International Law of Liability for Transboundary Nuclear Pollution: The Existing Regime, Its Deficiencies and A Framework for a New Regime*, August 1989. The report has provided the policy platform for Greenpeace International's participation in the work of the IAEA Standing Committee on Nuclear Liability on which Greenpeace has observer status.

Against the background of an explosive growth of interest and grass-root political activism regarding international environmental issues,[97] NGO involvement in international decision-making related to enforcement of and compliance with international environmental standards, is likely to continue to intensify and expand. Consider, for example, the emerging international regime on the transboundary movement of hazardous waste. Experience shows that, at the national level, controlling movements of hazardous wastes is notoriously difficult, notwithstanding relatively strict reporting requirements and elaborate monitoring and policing efforts.[98] On the international level, these difficulties are bound to be significantly greater.[99] Thus, although the Basel Convention establishes a formal procedure for the verification of compliance and leaves room for the establishment of subsidiary bodies to assist in this task,[100] the Convention's effectiveness may ultimately turn on various informal monitoring and verification processes involving non-state actors. In the past, NGOs have been key players in the tracking of hazardous waste exports, and in alerting both would-be importing countries and the international public of illegal or unsound waste disposal plans and operations.[101] Clearly, NGO input in the international system of supervision thus can be expected to be an indispensable factor in rendering the Basel Convention an effective regime.

Private enforcement of environmental legal standards through "citizen suits" is an essential component in the effectiveness of domestic law.[102] An analoguous enhancement of NGOs' status on the transnational environmental plane therefore might be highly desirable.[103] NGOs, it has recently been suggested, could

[97] For an indication of the scope of activities by some of the key environmental NGOs during 1990, see "Reports from Organizations: 2. Non-Governmental Organizations (NGOs)", 1 *Ybk. Int'l Env. L.* (1990).

[98] *See, e.g.*, "A Black Market Arises in the Disposal of Debris", *N.Y. Times*, October 15, 1989, L112, 1, col.1; and "Mob Looks at Recycling and Sees Green", *N.Y. Times*, November 28, 1990, B1, col.2.

[99] As an indication of the problem involving only transboundary movements within North America, see, *e.g.*, Uva & Bloom, "Exporting Pollution: The International Waste Trade", 31 *Environment* 4 (1989); "Hitting the Road: Hazardous Waste Hauling on the Rise", 6 *The Great Lakes Reporter* No.2, 1 (1989); and the Report of the Secretary-General, Illegal Traffic in Toxic and Dangerous Products and Wastes, U.N. Doc. A/44/362, 18 July 1989, 30–32.

[100] *See* Article 19. Moreover, pursuant to Article 15, paragraph 5, the Conference of the Parties "shall keep under continuous review and evaluation the effective implementation" of the Convention, and for that purpose establish such subsidiary bodies as are deemed necessary.

[101] For an indication of the role of NGOs in monitoring hazardous waste movements, see, *e.g.*, *Ad Hoc* Working Group of Legal and Technical Experts with a Mandate to Prepare a Global Convention on the Control of Transboundary Movements of Hazardous Waste, Report of the Ad Hoc Working Group on the Work of its Third Session, Doc. UNEP/WG.189/3, 16 November 1988, 5–6.

[102] *See, generally*, Greve "The Private Enforcement of Environmental Law", 65 *Tulane L.Rev.* 339 (1990).
In the United States, experience with private environmental law enforcement in the context of the Federal Clean Water Act has been so encouraging that § 707 of the 1990 amendments to the Clean Air Act now substantially strengthen that Act's private enforcement provisions.

[103] Indeed, outside international environmental regimes that effectively develop and update their own compliance data, such as, for example, the ECE long-range transboundary air pollution regime, the case for strong private party involvement in decision-making processes related to ensuring implementation of and abidance by environmental law, is even more persuasive on the international plane than might be in a domestic legal setting.

"actually be appointed to perform inspections or serve even as expert mediators or arbitrators of disputes".[104]

While a few environmental NGOs have formal consultative status with international organizations, some more may have observer status on specific international bodies entrusted with environmental matters, NGOs continue to suffer from limited access to environmental decision-making bodies in the transnational arena. As a minimum, existing relationships between international organizations and NGOs, therefore, ought to be expanded and formalized so as to allow for a more effective NGO input in the international environmental decision-making process which would most likely benefit the quality of the decision outcome.[105]

Directly related is a third observation that regards empowerment at local level. By now it is almost a truism that, as the Conclusions of the Siena Forum note, "environmental protection begins at the local level".[106] Protection of internationally sensitive natural resources, including the global commons, depends on support at local level. This "think globally, act locally" maxim, however, can only be realized if citizens have access to pertinent environmental information as well as to relevant enviromental decision-making fora.

Traditionally, international legal efforts had focused on ensuring access by individuals, potentially or actually affected by injurious transboundary activities, to foreign decision-making fora on a basis of equality with nationals of the foreign state concerned.[107] More recently, the international regulatory focus has begun to expand beyond the limited transboundary context to environmental empowerment of citizens in general.[108] For example, a 1989 OECD Council Decision commits member countries to ensure local hazard communication: The public must be provided with and have access to pertinent information about local industrial hazards. The Decision also obliges member states to ensure the affected public of an opportunity to participate in decisions concerning hazardous installations and the development of community emergency preparedness plans.[109] The European Council Directive on freedom of access to information on the environment,[110] goes a significant step beyond the OECD Decision by establishing a general obligation for member states to make environmental information held by public authorities available to any person. Finally, the World

[104] Kimball, "International Law and Institutions: The Oceans and Beyond", 20 *ODIL* 147, at 155 (1989).

[105] Note in this context the European Convention on the Recognition of the Legal Personality of International Non-Governmental Organisations, *discussed in* Drzemczewski, "The Role of NGOs in Human Rights Matters in the Council of Europe", 8 *Human Rights L.J.* 273, at 274–75 (1987). The Convention's purpose is to facilitate cross-border work of NGOs.

[106] See *supra* note 83.

[107] For a summary, see Handl, "Internationalization of Hazard Management in Recipient Countries: Accident Preparedness and Response", in *Transferring Hazardous Technologies and Substances* 106, at 116–17.

[108] For details of this process as it evolves hazardous industrial installations, see Handl, *ibid.* 111–15.

[109] *See* Decision-Recommendation of the Council concerning Provision of Information in Decision-Making Processes Related to the Prevention of, and Response to, Accidents Involving Hazardous Substances, OECD Doc. C(88)85(Final), 2, paragraph 1.

[110] EC Council Directive of 7 June 1990 on the freedom of access to information on the environment (90/313/ECE), *Official Journal* No L 158/56, 23.6.90.

Charter of Nature endorses a general or broadly conceived right of individuals to be involved in decisions bearing on the environment. Article 23 stipulates that "[a]ll persons . . . shall have the opportunity to participate, individually or with others, in the formulation of decisions of direct concern to their environment. . .".[111] Although the Article does not amount to an unqualified endorsement of local environmental empowerment,[112] it signals recognition in principle of the fundamental importance of extending participatory democracy to local and national environmental decision-making processes to ensure success at protecting the global ecological system as a whole.

III. THE CHANGING NATURE AND SCOPE OF STATES' ENTITLEMENT TO THE USE OF ENVIRONMENTAL RESOURCES

A. *The Precautionary Principle*

(i) State Autonomy and Significant Transboundary Risk

The self-evident truth that an ounce of prevention is better than a pound of cure, has for some time now been reflected in the international law related to the environment, even though unto this day the notion has persisted that customary international law does not yet include such an obligation. The evolution of a duty of prevention can be traced from its conceptual origin in the venerable *Trail Smelter* decision,[113] all the way to the International Law Commission's focus on prevention in its work on the liability topic.[114] Evidence of state practice supportive of the existence, in principle, of a customary international legal duty to prevent transboundary harm, includes such relatively early multilateral environmental treaties as the Baltic Sea Convention,[115] the 1974 Paris Convention for the Protection of Marine Pollution from Land-Based Resources,[116] and the 1982 United Nations Law of the Sea Convention,[117] quite apart from more recent multilateral environmental regimes.[118]

[111] World Charter for Nature, *supra* note 31.

[112] These rights of individuals are subject to the qualifying language of "in accordance with [individuals'] . . . national legislation": *Ibid.*

[113] *See* Kirgis, "Technological Challenge to the Shared Envrionment: United States Practice", 66 *AJIL* 290, at 294 (1972); and Handl, "An Internationally Legal Perspective on the Conduct of Abnormally Dangerous Activities in Frontier Areas: The Case of Nuclear Power Plant Siting", 7 *ELQ* 1, 32-33 (1978).

[114] Note draft Article 8 as proposed by the Commission's special rapporteur. *See* Barboza, Fifth Report on International Liability for Injurious Consequences Arising out of Acts not Prohibited by International Law, UN Doc. A/CN.4/423, 22-23, paragraphs 64–68 (1989); and the Report of the International Law Commission on the Work of its Fortieth Session, 9 May–29 July 1988, GAOR, Forty-Third Session, Supplement No.10 (A/43/10) 40-42, paragraphs 92–95 (1988).

[115] Convention on the Protection of the Marine Environment of the Baltic Sea Area, Article 3, paragraph 1, *text in* 13 *ILM* 546 (1974).

[116] Article 1, paragraph 1 of the Convention, *reproduced ibid.* 352.

[117] *See especially* Article 194 of UNCLOS.

[118] For example, all Regional Seas Conventions contain provisions on prevention of harm, as do CRAMRA (Articles 2–4), and the draft Regulations on Prospecting, Exploration and Exploitation of Polymetallic Nodules in the Area proposed by the Preparatory Commission for the International Sea-Bed Authority and for the International Tribunal of the Law of the Sea (especially Articles 104–112), *supra* note 55.

The obligation concerned is one of due diligence and requires a state to abstain from conduct that carries a significant risk of harm.[119] It is an obligation that has several procedural companion- elements, namely the duty of prior information and of consultation. By now, both these obligations have become part of customary international law.[120] A third procedural obligation, namely to analyze the risk of transboundary environmental impact, is, logically speaking, a necessary appendix of the obligations of prior information and consultation. However, the life of the law has seldom been logic, but experience.[121] International acknowledgment of the intimate relationship among these procedural obligations – all of them geared towards prevention of significant transboundary environmental harm – and concomitant acceptance that transboundary environmental assessment, as much as prior information and consultation, would be required under international law, has not been clearly reflected in the practice of states.[122] However, in light of recent state practice,[123] including finalization of an ECE draft Convention on Environmental Impact Assessment in Transboundary Context[124] which is to be adopted in early 1991, as well as recent national legislative

[119] For details see Handl, "National Uses of Transboundary Air Resources: The International Entitlement Reconsidered", 26 *NRJ* 405, at 429–30 (1986). *See also* R. Pisillo Mazzeschi, *"Due Diligence" e responsabilità internazionale degli stati* 382 (1989).

Note that while accepting due diligence as the customary standard for international environmental obligations, Pisillo Mazzeschi rejects the idea that, as a general principle, states might be required to abstain from conduct that could cause significant transboundary environmental injury. As long as the conduct concerned is not per se impermissible, due diligence, he maintains, limits the state's obligation to act towards avoidance of significant transboundary environmental harm, not to guarantee avoidance by abstaining from conduct altogether: *Ibid.* 383. Although he acknowledges that in cases involving especially hazardous activities due diligence might come to reflect a standard characteristic of an obligation of result, in his view, states would still be free to carry on such activities: *Ibid.* 385–86. Although this might be a reasonable interpretation of state practice, recent developments, in particular expressions of support for "precautionary action" are difficult to reconcile with Pisillo Mazzeschi's position. Moreover, even earlier international practice can well justify the conclusion that states are obliged to abstain from conduct whenever the transboundary risk of harm associated is particularly significant. *See*, Handl, *supra* note 113, at 35–39.

[120] *See, e.g.*, § 601, Comment (e), ALI, *Restatement, Third, Foreign Relations Law of the United States* (vol.2) 107 (1987). For a detailed analysis, see G.Handl & B.Simma, *Grenzüberschreitendes nukleares Risiko und völkerrechtlicher Schutzanspruch* §§ 3.2.1–3.2.2. (forthcoming).

[121] O. Holmes, *The Common Law* 5 (M. DeWolfe Howe, ed. 1963).

[122] Note, *e.g.*, the recommendatory language ("should") used in Article 5, paragraph 2 (addressing environmental assessment) of the International Law Association's Montreal Rules of International Law Applicable to Transfrontier Pollution. *See International Law Association, Report of the Sixtieth Conference, Montreal* 1, at 2 ((1982); and Rauschning, "Legal Aspects of the Conservation of the Environment", *ibid.* 157, at 74, paragraph 15. *See* further Handl, "The Environment: International Rights and Obligations", [1980] *ASIL Proceedings* 223, at 226; and Wirth, "International Technology Transfer and Environmental Impact Assessment", in *Transferring Hazardous Technologies and Substances* 83, at 103–04.

[123] *See, e.g.*, CRAMRA, Articles 2–4; the programmatic commitment to environmental impact assessment in Article 37 of the Fourth ACP-EEC Convention signed in Lomé on 15 December 1989, [*hereafter*: Lomé IV Convention] *text in 29 ILM* 809, at 819 (1990); and Article 13 of the 1990 Protocol Concerning Specially Protected Areas and Wildlife to the Convention for the Protection and Development of the Marine Environment of the Wider Caribbean Region, *text in* 1 *Ybk. Int'l Env. L.* (1990). *Cf.* also Paragraph X of the ECE Code of Conduct on Accidental Pollution of Transboundary Inland Water, Doc. E/ECE/1225, ECE/ENVWA/16 (1990), *ibid.*

[124] U.N. Doc. ENWA/R.36, 5 November 1990.

developments,[125] it will be increasingly difficult to maintain that states are not (yet) obliged under customary international law to assess potential transboundary effects.

An essential aspect of precautionary environmental policy, then, is the taking of remedial action even in the absence of provable environmental harm, simply upon evidence of a significant risk thereof. This is, of course, the approach that inspires the international ozone layer regime. On the other hand, in the context of, for example, the North American acid rain problem, when Canada proposed that the United States take specific remedial action as required under international law, the U.S. government invoked "scientific uncertainty" regarding "traceability" and thus "redressability" of pollutant emissions as a reason for non- compliance.[126]

Today, it should be axiomatic that the greater the risk of harm threatened, the lower the evidentiary burden concerning source-specific causal linkage and injurious transboundary environmental impact. Obviously, only such a conceptual starting point is appropriate in addressing the global warming issue[127] or in attempting to ensure biological security. It is not surprising, therefore, that the Ministerial Declaration adopted at the Bergen Conference on Sustainable Development,[128] focuses attention on this crucial aspect of precautionary action: "Environmental measures must anticipate, prevent and attack the causes of environmental degradation". It goes on to emphasize that "[w]here there are threats of serious or irreversible damage, lack of full scientific certainty should not be used as a reason for postponing measures to prevent environmental degradation". By the same token, the parties to the third International Conference of the North Sea, in committing themselves to apply the "precautionary principle", pledged "to take [preventive] action . . . even when there is no scientific evidence to prove a causal link between emissions and effects".[129]

(ii) "Precautionary Action" As a General International Canon of Environmental Conduct?

These and other recent references to precautionary action[130] have encouraged advocacy of a "precautionary principle" as a basic restraint on environmentally

125 Note, *e.g.*, the recently federal Canadian environmental assessment process (Bill C-78) that would extend to environmental effects outside of Canada. *See* Hunt, "Canada", 1 *Ybk. Int'l Env. L.* (1990).

126 *See* Handl, "Acid Rain in United States–Canada Relations: The Politics of Procrastination and International Law", [1987] *Proceedings, Canadian Council on International Law* 131.

127 However, at the February 1991 session of the United Nations Intergovernmental Negotiating Committee on Climate Change, the U.S. government declined yet again to commit itself to a reduction of greenhouse gases on the grounds that scientific evidence warranting such action was not conclusive enough. *See* "U.S. to Negotiate Steps on Warming", *N.Y. Times*, February 15, 1991, All, col. 1.

128 Bergen Ministerial Declaration on Sustainable Development in the ECE Region, *text in 1 Ybk. Int'l Env. L.* (1990).

129 Final Declaration of the Third International Conference on the Protection of the North Sea, the Hague, 7–8 March, 1990, 4.

130 However, at the recent special Antarctic Treaty Consultative Meeting in Viñar del Mar, Chile, some states unsuccessfully sought to persuade the Commission of the Convention on the Conservation of Antarctic Marine Living Resources, to adopt a "precautionary approach" to the development of krill fisheries: *See* Kimball, "Antarctica", 1 *Ybk. Int'l Env. L.* (1990).

sensitive action generally.[131] Indeed, state practice,[132] resolutions of international organizations,[133] and other pertinent indicia[134] point to the emergence of community expectations that, at least as a matter of basic international policy, activities potentially affecting the environment be subject to restraint. Three general notions underlie these emerging expectations. First, although precautionary action is advocated as an international standard of conduct, its application is not limited to transboundary risks of harm, but instead reaches environmentally sensitive activities generally, i.e., irrespective of a direct transnational impact potential. Second, restraint is advocated not just in face of present and clear danger to environmental resources, but as a corollary of our inherently limited knowledge of the ecological implications of human activities through time and space.[135] Third, "precautionary action" implies a broad, systemic approach to global environment management. The "react and correct model" of international environmental legislation must, as the Conclusions of the Siena Forum emphasize, be complemented by a "forecast and prevent approach".[136]

Notwithstanding the relative clarity of these notions, at present, the precautionary principle is not a term of art. The principle's exact political and, *a fortiori*, legal implications remain "elusive".[137] One reason for this is the fact that postulations of precautionary action evince also a strong undercurrent of preservationist concerns.[138] It must remain open to doubt, therefore, whether, ambiguous as it may be as a broadly defined concept, "precautionary principle" can evolve into an effective international canon of environmental conduct. On

[131] *See, generally*, Gündling, "The Status in International Law of the Principle of Precautionary Action", 5 *IJECL* 23 (1990).

[132] *See, e.g.*, paragraph 7 of the Ministerial Declaration of the Second World Climate Conference, 7 November 1990, *text in* 1 *Ybk. Int'l Env. L.* (1990); and paragraph 12 of the Baltic Sea Declaration, adopted September 2–3, 1990, *text ibid.*

[133] *See, especially*, paragraphs 10 and 11 of the World Charter for Nature, *supra* note 31, at 17; Principles 1–6 of the Stockholm Declaration on the Human Environment, *supra* note 30; and the Nairobi Declaration on the State of the Worldwide Environment, U.N. Doc.UNEP/GC/10/INF/5, 1982, 21 *ILM* 676 (1987).

Note also the recommendation by UNEP's Governing Council that "governments adopt the 'principle of precautionary action' as a basis for their policy with regard to the prevention and elimination of marine pollution": Decision 15/27 "Precautionary Approach to Marine Pollution, including Waste-Dumping at Sea", 25 May 1989.

[134] *See, e.g.*, Art.3 of the Legal Principles for Environmental Protection and Sustainable Development, in *Experts Group on Environmental Law of the World Commission on Environment and Development, Environmental Protection and Sustainable Development*, [hereafter: *WCED Legal Principles*] 7, at 8 (1986).

[135] *See* the discussion in Nollkaemper "Deep Sea-Bed Mining and the Protection of the Marine Environment", 15 *MP* 55, at 61 (1991).

[136] Paragraph 4 of the Conclusions of the Siena Forum, *supra* note 83.

[137] Gündling, *supra* note 131, at 25.

[138] Economic utilitarianism, the idea that restraint is warranted simply to render long-term exploitability of natural resources possible, may be the dominant facet of the "precautionary principle". However, the principle appears also to be inspired by non-instrumentalist concerns about the environment. Note, for example, preambular paragraph (a) of the World Charter for Nature, *supra* note 31: "Every form of life is unique, warranting respect *regardless of its worth to man* . . ." (emphasis added).

For a tracing of the complex mix of considerations that might influence any environmental protection policy, see Hargrove, "The Historical Foundations of American Environmental Attitudes", 1 *Environmental Ethics* 209 (1979).

the other hand, there is no denying that international environmental law already addresses some of the concerns epitomized in the principle of preautionary action, such as the call for restraint on state autonomy in creating significant risks of transboundary environmental harm, or for conserving biological diversity of the planet.[139] By the same token, a limited number of general maxims of environmental action, such as adoption of "best available pollution control technology", "controlling pollution at the source", or the setting of reasonable margins of safety in environmental policy-making[140] which are basic ingredients of precautionary environmental action, appear to be well on their way to becoming part of the customary international law of the environment.[141]

B. Sustainable Development/Intergenerational Equity

Sustainable development might be defined as "development that meets the needs of the present without compromising the ability of future generations to meet their own needs".[142] This concept of living off nature's "income", rather than squandering its "capital", is a key tenet of the report of the World Commission on Environment and Development,[143] and has since been supported by a number of decisions of the United Nations or other international orgnizations,[144] agencies within the U.N. system, and various conferences of states.[145] It is thus fast becoming the basic criterion against which international or transnational environmental initiatives and, increasingly so, ostensibly merely "local" environmental activities are being evaluated politically.

Its potential normative reach is narrower than that of "precautionary action".[146] "Sustainable development" evinces a strictly utilitarian view of environmental protection: It imposes restraints on developmental activities only

[139] *See, e.g.*, Report of the *Ad Hoc* Working Group on the Work of its Second Session in Preparation for a Legal Instrument on Biological Diversity of the Planet, Doc. UNEP/Bio.Div.2/3, 23 February 1990.
For a general overview of recent international action regarding conservation of wildlife and biological diversity, see de Klemm, "Nature Conservancy: Natural Lands and Biological Diversity", 1 *Ybk. Int'l Env. L.* (1990); and Robertson, "United Nations Educational, Scientific and Cultural Organization (UNESCO)", *ibid.*

[140] As to the analogous domestic debates, see, *e.g.*, *NRDC v. U.S. EPA*, 824 F.2d 1146 (D.C. Cir. 1987).

[141] For a discussion of the international legal status of these notions see Handl, *supra* note 119, at 463–65.

[142] Resolution Concerning Environment, Development Employment and the Role of the ILO, International Labour Conference, Provisional Record, Seventy-Seventh Session, 29/32 (1990).

[143] *See World Commission on Environment and Development, Our Common Future* (1987).

[144] *See, e.g.*, Recommendation 1130 (1990) (1) of the Parliamentary Assembly of the Council of Europe on the formulation of a European charter and a European convention on environmental protection and sustainable development.

[145] *See, e.g.*, the Bergen Ministerial Declaration, *supra* note 128; the preambular reference to "common objectives of sustainable development . . ." in the Final Document adopted at the 1990 meeting in Bonn of the Conference on Security and Co-operation in Europe: Document of the Bonn Conference on Economic Co-operation in Europe Convened in Accordance with the Relevant Provisions of the Concluding Document of the Vienna Meeting of the Conference on Security and Co-Operation in Europe, Doc. CSCE/KWZEB.15/Rev.1, 11 April 1990, *reprinted in 29 ILM* 1055 (1990).

[146] Note, however, that at times "sustainable development" is viewed as the overarching objective, while "precautionary action" merely as a necessary implementing strategy. *See, e.g.*, paragraph 7 of the Bergen Ministerial Declaration, *supra* note 128.

insofar as these would undermine the environmental basis for further development in the long run. Indeed, "sustainable development" is non-preservationist; it reflects a commitment to promote development, albeit of a special qualitative nature.[147] This perspective, in contrast to the no-growth strands that are part of the complex policy fabric of the precautionary principle, makes "sustainable development" internationally a broadly attractive concept. Not surprisingly, it has thus turned out to be a notion around which legally significant expectations regarding environmental conduct have begun to crystallize.[148] Indeed, before long the concept might turn into a mandatory standard of international legal evaluation, a peremptory norm of international law.

The reasons for such a possible ascendancy are intuitively persuasive. "Sustainable development" is a *conditio sine qua non* for human life on this planet in the long run. It stands to reason, therefore, that other legal arrangements would have to measure up to the principle. "Sustainability" thus would safeguard not simply individual state interests but act as a restraint in "the higher interest of the whole international community"[149] in preserving the ecological basis for human civilization.

To ascribe *ius cogens* character to the objective of "sustainable development", however, tends to highlight the special problems any peremptory norm raises in the co-hierarchical and decentralized decision-making process of the international legal system.[150] Without authoritative third-party decision-making, conflicting claims about the concept's specific normative implications will abound and disputes over application will be exceedingly difficult to resolve.[151] This will be all the more so because "needs" will vary from country to country, and the consistency of state conduct with "sustainable development" will thus depend on context.[152]

For the moment, in any event, the concept *per se* poses a more preliminary, i.e., fundamentally definitional problem. Thus, while the prospect of "sustainable development" eventually gaining *ius cogens* status cannot be ruled out, it is difficult to see how the concept could be readily operationalized. To begin with, the concept suffers from internal tension: "Sustainable develop-

[147] *See Our Common Future, supra* note 143, 49–54; and Statement by the UNEP Governing Council on Sustainable Development, Doc. UNEP/GC 15/L.37, Annex II (1989).

[148] *See, e.g.*, Articles 33–35 of the Lomé IV Convention.

[149] Verdross, "*Ius Dispositivum* and *Ius Cogens* in International Law", 60 *AJIL* 55, at 58 (1966). *See also* Christenson, "*Ius Cogens*: Guarding Interests Fundamental to International Society", 28 *Virginia J. Int'l L.* 585 (1988).

[150] For a recent restatement of the issue, especially the implicit threat to the stability of the international normative system, see Weil, *supra* note 27, at 423–30.

[151] Thus, it has all along been recognized that the effectiveness of peremptory norms would depend on compulsory third-party dispute settlement. *See, e.g.*, Lauterpacht, "Règles générales du droit de la paix", 62 *Recueil des Cours* 95, at 308 (1937). *See also*, C. Rozakis, *The Concept of Ius Cogens in the Law of Treaties* 6–7 (1976).

[152] Thus, while for developing countries "sustainable development" will mean some economic growth, for developed countries it may well imply steady-state economic activities only. *See* Handl, "Environmental Protection and Development in Third World Countries: Common Destiny – Common Responsibility", 20 *N.Y.U. J. Int'L. & Politics* 603, at 606–07 (1988).

ment" as an international policy or legal concept, clearly implies some measure of international accountability; yet, as generally endorsed, it is also accompanied by an express disclaimer of any intended encroachment upon state sovereignty.[153] The initial challenge, therefore, will be to reach a clear international understanding on pathways to sustainable development[154] and agreement on the specific markers that lead to that goal.[155]

Notwithstanding increasingly frequent affirmations of "sustainable development" as a cardinal principle of international environmental decision-making, we are still at a very early stage of this task. Recent calls for "sustainable development practices" as, for example, in the Bergen Ministerial Declaration,[156] by the Council of Europe's Parliamentary Assembly,[157] or the Interparliamentary Conference on the Global Environment,[158] are couched in fairly abstract and general terms. On the other hand, the list of criteria developed within the U.N. Centre on Transnational Corporations,[159] as well as, for example, the 1989 OECD Council Recommendation concerning an Environmental Checklist for Development Assistance,[160] or the World Bank's Environmental Assessment Operational Directive,[161] provide more specific guidance to decision-makers at corporate management, national governmental or international organizational levels.

[153] "Sustainable development is development that meets the needs of the present without compromising the ability of the future generations to meet their own needs and does not imply in any way encroachment upon national sovereignty": Statement by the UNEP Governing Council, *supra* note 147.

[154] For an overview, *see, e.g.* B. Long, *Sustainable Development and the International Environmental Research Agenda for the 1990's* (Manuscript of a paper delivered at the Tenth Session of the International Co-ordinating Committee for the Man and the Biosphere Programme (MAB), UNESCO, Paris, 15 November 1988).

[155] However, for "sustainability" to be a meaningful operational concept, current systems of national income measurements will have to be adjusted to include environmental and resource accounting. *See also* Mathews, *supra* note . . ., at 173. Only a thus revised system of national accounts can provide a true picture of the sustainability of existing patterns of production and consumption. *See, generally*, Y. Ahmad, S. El Serafy & E. Lutz, eds., *Environmental Accounting for Sustainable Development* (1989). As environmental degradation and depletion of natural resources translates into negative GNP factors in such a system of analysis, effective political pressure will be generated to curtail non-sustainable policies and practices. Some countries, like the Netherlands and Germany, have already launched ambitious efforts at incorporating national resource accounting into their calculations of national economic activity. Encouragingly, the OECD Council recently adopted a recommendation that calls upon member states to "develop environmental indicators and related environmental accounting to measure environmental performance and better integrate environmental and economic decision-making": Recommendation of the Council on Environmental Indicators and Information, OECD Doc. C(90) 165/Final, 3 (1991).

[156] *See, especially*, parts II–IV of the Declaration, *supra* note 128.

[157] *See supra* note 144.

[158] *See* The Interparliamentary Conference on the Global Environment, April 29–May 2, 1990, Washington D.C., Decision on Sustainable Development, *reproduced in 20 EPL* 112, at 114 (1990).

[159] *See* Criteria for Sustainable Development Management, in Annex I to the Report of the Secretary-General, Transnational Corporations and Issues Relating to the Environment, UN Doc. E/C.10/1990/10, 28 March 1990, 25.

[160] *See* Recommendation of the Council concerning an Environmental Checklist for Possible Use by High-Level Decision-Makers in Bilateral and Multilateral Development Assistance Institutions, OECD Doc. C(89)2(Final), March 3, 1989, *reprinted in 28 ILM* 1314 (1989).

[161] For details, see Ofosu-Amaah & Lausche, "World Bank", 1 *Ybk. Int'l Env. L.* (1990); and *The World Bank and the Environment. First Annual Report: Fiscal 1990*, 62–63 (1990).

Irrespective of the concept's international normative weakness at the moment, it is evident that "sustainable development" is shaping environmental policy debates in a fundamental way. More significantly, it has begun to act as a de facto constraint on environmental decision-makers,[162] both internationally as well as domestically.[163]

The conceptual or philosophical underpinning of this emerging obligation to reorient natural resource use towards sustainability, is the notion of intergenerational equity. The idea that present generations accept restraints on their use of natural resources for the benefit of future generations, has attracted overwhelming international support ever since the Maltese proposal of a "common heritage of mankind" to the United Nations General Assembly in 1967.[164] States have expressly re-endorsed the principle of intergenerational responsibility ever since it was first formally adopted by a conference of states in the 1972 Stockholm Declaration.[165]

Today, few could thus deny that the concept of intergenerational responsibility is a fundamental tenet of international public policy. Rather, if there is a debate about the concept *per se*, it will be, first, over whether the obligations of restraint emanating from the concept are of an international legal, rather than of a merely moral nature; and, second, whether they arise vis-a-vis future generations for which the present generation holds the planet in trust[166] or, whether they are obligations of conduct on behalf of future generations that members of the present generation owe each other directly.[167]

As indicated above, the twin notion of "sustainable development" appears close to becoming an international legal standard for the evaluation of state conduct bearing on the environment. It appears also to be the one that would be more readily acceptable from an ideological viewpoint.[168] As regards the second issue, the normative basis of obligation for intergenerational responsibilities, it is

[162] For an assessment by business leaders of the impact of the concept of "sustainable development" on business practices, see J.-O. Willums, ed., *The Greening of Enterprise* (1990).

[163] For example, in the United States, the so-called Valdez Principles, a new environmental code of conduct, seek to bring about the greening of corporate boardrooms by committing corporations to follow sustainable development policies in their business activities. *See* "Group Sets Corporate Code on Environmental Conduct", *N.Y. Times*, September 8, 1989, 25, col.1.

[164] "Common heritage of mankind" clearly includes the notion that natural resources, such as the deep seabed, are not the fruit of the labour of the present generation and that, therefore, any use thereof must be exercised with due regard to the "rights" of future generations: Fleischer, "The International Concern for the Environment: The Concept of Common Heritage", in M.Bothe, ed., *Trends in Environmental Policy and Law* 321, at 338 (1980).

[165] *See, especially*, Principles 1–5 of the Stockholm Declaration, *supra* note 30.

[166] *See, e.g.*, E. Brown Weiss, *In Fairness to Future Generations: International Law, Common Patrimony, and Intergenerational Equity* 45 (1989); and Brown Weiss, "Our Rights and Obligations to Future Generations", 84 *AJIL* 198 (1990).

[167] On this issue, *cf.* d'Amato, "Do We Owe a Duty to Future Generations to Preserve the Global Environment?", *ibid.* 190; Brown Weiss, *supra* note 166; and Gündling, "Our Responsibility to Future Generations", *ibid.* 207.

[168] *See supra* text at note 147. As to the formidable size of the "motivational problem" that accompanies any attempt at establishing intergenerational responsibilities, see *e.g.*, N.Care, *On Sharing Fate* 108–11 (1987).

evident that the protection or insulation of norms guaranteeing sustainable development or fairness to future generations against unwarranted changes or tampering by members of the present generation ought to be a matter of concern. But as to the quality of protection provided, it is not self-evident which conceptual basis would be more effective.[169] In any event, and whatever the underlying philosophical justification for sustainability obligations, Lothar Gündling reminds us that "without equity within the present generation, we will not be able to achieve equity among generations".[170]

C. The North-South Issue

Against the backdrop of the existing North-South divide, one of the most contentious issues in international standard-setting for globally sensitive environmental resources is the question of incentives to poor countries. Protection of such resources typically will require wide-spread, if not universal international co-operation, thus rendering Third World participation essential to securing the environmental objectives of the regimes concerned.[171] Traditionally, Third World aid demands and, conversely grants and concessions by developed countries, had been viewed in terms of a moral obligation of donor countries to redress past wrongs of colonialism or to respond to calls for international solidarity. Now, with international concern over the conservation of internationally sensitive natural resources on a sharp rise, developing countries have begun to insist publicly that conservation measures they are being asked to undertake locally, be paid for by developed nations. Thus, development assistance in general, and selective treaty incentives to developing countries in particular, have become the focus of an entitlement re-interpretation. A peak in this development thus far has been the debate accompanying the diplomatic drive to increase state participation in the ozone layer protection regime.[172] Another high point will probably be

[169] Obviously, the issues raised here cannot be adequately addressed within the scope of this paper. Suffice it to say that, for any intergenerational responsibility to be effective as a legal obligation, a norm to this effect would depend on the consensus among members of the present generation. Relying on the concept of "rights" of future generations even though they lack in particularity, hence in the absence a readily accepted motivational basis for present restraint, is probably a less promising strategy for protecting sustainability or intergenerational fairness norms. Rather, the legal basis of an obligation on behalf of future generations should be seen in the fact that non-sustainable development practices that endanger future generations, impose value deprivations directly upon members of the present generation(s). An essential defining aspect of the human experience is one's understanding of oneself as part of a larger, intergenerational body of humanity. Any disturbance of this sense will amount to a basic value deprivation. Thus members of the present generation faced with the implications of non-sustainable present-day policies, would incur losses that can and should be actionable. Of course, in this conceptualization, norms bearing on fairness to future generations would be dependent on the support from the living generations; but so would norms rooted in different concepts.

[170] Gündling, *supra* note 131, at 211.

[171] For a discussion of these problems in the context of protecting atmospheric resources, see Handl, "International Efforts to Protect the Global Atmosphere: A Case of Too Little Too Late?", 1 *EuJIL* 250 (1990).

[172] For a discussion, see, *e.g.*, Handl, "Law and Protection of the Atmosphere", 71 *Economic Impact* 36 (1990).

reached when negotiations begin in earnest on an international convention on climate change.

There is no denying that, more often than not, incentives to encourage developing country participation in global environmental regimes are justified as a matter of fundamental international equity. International regulations, for example, for the protection of the ozone layer or of climate stability, tend to become necessary because past uses and abuses of the environment have created an environmental crisis situation. While the benefits of such regulations, in terms of mitigation or avoidance of harm, might be spread among developing and developed nations alike, the costs of compliance would weigh more heavily on developing countries. More importantly, while developed nations would be asked to pay up belatedly for globally experienced or threatened environmental costs associated with their economic and social development, developing nations whose contribution to the problem might be minor,[173] are asked to share the burden of controls without having derived comparable compensating socio-economic benefits. Finally, international regulations deemed necessary to protect crictical global resources, may preempt developing nations from exercising what might have been their "natural" development options.

It can be hardly surprising, therefore, that in such a situation, developing countries should insist on compensatory and/or technical incentives in exchange for support of international regulatory restrictions. Indeed, if a Third World country incurs opportunity costs by forgoing a natural development option to preserve environmental resources that are of global interest or special interest to other states, it should be recognized as entitled to compensation. The fact that restraint would also be in the long-term interest of the developing country itself should not detract from compensation as a matter of right. For such claims for compensation merely amount to a vindication of the principle of equitable utilization, a principle long recognized as a basic legal tenet that underlies the use of internationally shared natural resources.[174]

The moral, political and, ultimately, legal persuasiveness of claims by developing countries to financial or technical assistance in protecting resources of global significance, are foreshadowed in the declarations adopted at the U.N. Environmental Conferences in Stockholm in 1972 and in Nairobi in 1982.[175]

[173] As regards the ozone depletion problem, note that in 1989 North America, Europe and Japan alone accounted for more than 80% of the total consumption of substances subject to control under the Montreal Protocol. *See* Open-Ended Working Group of the Parties to the Montreal Protocol, Final Report, Second Session of the First Meeting, Nairobi, 28 August – 5 September 1989, UN Doc. UNEP/OzL.Pro.WG.1(2)4, 26 (1989). As regards emissions of greenhouse gases, it was estimated that in 1990 3/4 of all emissions were the responsibility of developed countries: *See* Ministerial Declaration of the Second World Climate Conference, *supra* note 132, at 5, paragraph 12.

[174] *Cf., e.g.*, Articles IV and V of the Helsinki Rules, *supra* note 29, at 486–88.

[175] These declarations strongly endorse the principle that developing countries should be assisted in redressing conditions of underdevelopment causing local environmental disruption. *See*, in particular, Principle 9 of the Stockholm Declaration on the Human Environment, *supra* note 30, at 1418; and Paragraph 7 of the Nairobi Declaration, *ibid.* 676. Claims by developing countries to financial or technical assistance in protecting resources of global significance are, of course, much stronger.

Since then, the basic international consensus on support measures for developing countries' environmental efforts has matured into a strong conviction about international burden-sharing with regard to the preservation of internationally sensitive environmental resources. Thus, innovative financial assistance arrangements, such as debt-for-conservation swaps,[176] international debt forgiveness strategies,[177] and the proposal for a Global Environmental Facility[178] as well as numerous formal and informal declarations by conferences of states, etc.[179] all testify to growing recognition of the legitimacy of developing countries' claims.

At an international regulatory level, the change in the entitlement perspective can be seen in specific concessions granted to developing countries. Thus Article 5 of the Montreal Protocol invites parties to undertake to facilitate access by developing countries, to alternative technology as well as to provide them with financial assistance for the use of alternative technology and for substitute products. At the Second Meeting of the Parties to the Protocol, finally, agreement was reached on an international financial mechanism in fulfillment of the mandate of Article 5.[180]

Environmental interdependence as reflected in the need to enlist the co-operation of key developing countries in order to ensure the success of international regimes for the protection of globally sensitive natural resources thus may be a turning point in North–South relations. Unlike the postulation of a "new economic order" in the 1970s, presently proposed strategies to counter the threat to global environmental security may lead to the empowerment of developing countries. By forcing developed countries to squarely face the effects of underdevelopment on global environmental protection objectives, developing

[176] A first such swap was arranged between Bolivia and Conservation International: see "Bolivia to Protect Lands in Swap for Lower Debt", *N.Y. Times*, July 14, 1987, C2, col.3. Since then countries such as Costa Rica, Ecuador, Madagascar, the Philippines, Zambia, and, most recently, Mexico have joined the rank of nations that have participated in debt-for-nature swaps.

In September 1990, the United States proposed a general debt-for-nature program for Latin American and Caribbean countries in connection with its "Enterprise for the Americas Initiative": *See* "Bush Proposal on Latin America, Caribbean Would Trade Debt for Environmental Programs", *BNA, Environment Reporter, Current Report* 1101 (1990).

[177] Such as, for example, the so-called "Brady Plan". Most recently, the European Community proposed cancellation of $2.1 billion of Third World debt and conversion of a further $2.1 billion of promised loans into grants. *See* "Plan to Cancel 3d World Debt", *N.Y. Times*, February 14, 1991, C6, col.1.

[178] The purpose of this pilot project which is co-sponsored by the World Bank, several potential donor countries and UNEP as well as UNDP, would be to provide grants or concessional loans to developing countries to allow them to participate in and implement international regimes for the protection of globally sensitive resources. Negotiations on the facility, including establishment of a Global Environmental Trust Fund, are at an advanced stage. *See* Ofosu-Amaah & Lausche, *supra* note 161.

[179] *See, e.g.*, the Declaration of the Hague of March 11, 1989, *reprinted in 28 ILM* 1308 (1989); the Economic Declaration adopted at the 1989 Paris Economic Summit, paragraph 38, *ibid.* 1293, at 1297; the Conclusions of the Siena Forum, paragraph 24, *supra* note 83; and the Ministerial Declaration of the Second World Climate Conference, paragraphs 15–17, *supra* note 132.

Cf. also the Report of the Secretary-General, Progress Achieved in the Implementation of Resolution 44/207 on Protection of Global Climate for Present and Future Generations of Mankind, UN Doc. A/45/696/Add.1, 8 November 1990, 13, paragraph 2.

[180] *See* Decision II/8 on Financial Mechanisms, and Annex IV of the Report of the Second Meeting of the Parties, *supra* note 19, at 12 and 42, respectively.

countries might succeed in shedding their traditionally marginal roles as international actors. In any event, the new dialogue and evolving patterns of North-South co-operation can only work to the benefit the community of states as a whole.

D. Redefining Sovereignty

Any student of transnational environmental issues will readily acknowledge that the nature and scope of state sovereignty or autonomy is undergoing dramatic change. Across-the-board, decision-making powers on matters that hitherto had been exclusively in the national domain, are increasingly shared with other states or have completely devolved upon the international community at large.

This process is at work also with regard to "local" natural resource management. Its focal point is an increasingly restrictive interpretation of the classic international entitlement rule which – absent special circumstances – limits states' autonomy only in the sense of enjoining domestic environmental pratices from causing transboundary harm or posing a significant risk thereof.[181]

Restrictions on state autonomy are hinted at in concepts such as "intergenerational equity", "sustainable development", or "common concern of mankind".[182] Notwithstanding frequent disclaimers, all of these notions have been invoked authoritatively to intimate limits on nation-states' freedom of action for the sake of protecting the larger community interest at stake. Together they provide a conceptual platform from which the international community advances its claim to review or participate in certain national decision-making processes related to internationally sensitive environmental resources, irrespective of their location or the presence of direct or immediate transnational environmentally harmful effects.

Whether a certain matter is or is not solely within the domestic jurisdiction of a state is, as the Permanent Court of Justice noted, "an essentially relative question; it depends upon the development of international relations".[183] By this standard, protection of globally sensitive natural resources is a matter of legitimate international concern. However, it is equally clear that general acquiescence in expressions of international concern over local environmental management is one thing; states' acceptance of specific international normative standards and rules that might impose severe limits on natural resource policies locally, is quite

[181] While states have the sovereign right to exploit their own resources pursuant to their own environmental policies, they are required "to ensure that activities within their jurisdiction or control do not cause damage to the environment of other States or of areas beyond the limits of national jurisdiction": Principle 21 of the Stockholm Declaration, *supra* note 30, at 1420. Today, this principle is a universally accepted expression of customary international law.

[182] *See* General Assembly Resolution on Protection of Global Climate for Present and Future Generations of Mankind, UN Doc. A/RES/43/53, 27 January 1989, which recognizes "that climate change is a common concern of mankind"; thus, it did not follow stronger language suggested by Malta which had referred to the conservation of climate "as part of the common heritage of mankind".

[183] Advisory Opinion, *Tunis – Morocco Nationality Decrees*, [1923] PCIJ Ser.B, No. 4, 24.

another.[184] Frequent allegations of foreign interference with national environmental decision-making[185] or the reiteration of a "sovereign right to administer freely [national] natural resources"[186] are reminders of the extreme sensitivity of the "internationalization process". Still, as vehement as some of these objections may be, in the final analysis, they represent rearguard action by defenders of an anchronistic view of national sovereignty.[187]

It is well to remember that state sovereignty is a functional concept. Territorial sovereignty, Max Huber noted in the *Island of Palmas* case, "serves to divide between nations the space upon which human activities are employed, in order to assure them at all points the minimum of protection of which international law is the guardian".[188] Today the rights that emanate from the concept of sovereignty, are not, as Philipp Allott reminds us, unfettered freedoms but powers shared between the holder of the power and the community of states.[189] In other words, sovereignty signals no longer a simple *status negativus*, a legal basis for exclusion, but has become the legal basis for inclusion, or of a commitment to co-operate for the good of the international community at large: *Souveraineté oblige*.

IV. CONCLUSIONS

Not that long ago, any generalization of the notion that a "community of interest" among states in an internationally shared natural resouce would entail common legal rights,[190] was derided as an exercise of a most primitive *Begriffsjurisprudenz*.[191] Today, few would deny that, from an environmental view-

[184] Recall, for example, the express disclaimer incorporated into the definition by the UNEP Governing Council of "sustainable development". *See supra* note 147.

Similarly, at its second session, the Working Group of Experts on Biological Diversity was persuaded to accept that the notion of "common heritage" as applied to biological diversity, "does not mean the establishment of collective rights to resources within national juridictions nor does it infringe upon permanent sovereignty of States over natural resources". *See* Report of the *Ad Hoc* Working Group on the Work of its Second Session in Preparation for a Legal Instrument on Biological Diversity of the Planet, UN Doc. UNEP/Bio.Div.2/3, 23 February 1990, 3, paragraph 11.

[185] The acute sensitivity of the "internationalization" process, is well illustrated by a headline referring to local resentment of the campaign to make management of Amazonian rain forests a matter of international accountability: "It's Our Forest to Burn if We Want to", *The Economist*, March 11, 1989, 42. *See also*, "8 Amazon Nations Denounce Pressure to Save Rain Forest", *N.Y. Times*, March 9, 1989, 8, col.6.

[186] *See, e.g.*, paragraph 2 of the Declaration of Brasilia Emanating from the Sixth Ministerial Meeting on the Environment in Latin America and the Caribbean Held in Brasilia on March 30 and 31, 1989, *text in 28 ILM* 1311 (1989).

[187] Of course, abandonment of outdated views of "sovereignty" is not only a prerequisite for effective protection of global environmental resources, but also a condition for worldwide enjoyment of fundamental human rights. *See* Reisman, "Sovereignty and Human Rights in Contemporary International Law", 84 *AJIL* 866 (1990).

[188] *Island of Palmas* case (Netherlands/U.S.A.), 2 UNRIAA 829, at 839.

[189] Allott, "Power Sharing and in the Law of the Sea", 77 *AJIL* 1, at 27 (1983).

[190] To this effect, the Permanent Court of International Justice in the *River Oder* case, [1929] PCIJ Ser.A, No.23, 27.

[191] Schwarzenberger, "Die Glaubwürdigkeit des Völkerrechts", in E. Diez, *et al.*, eds., *Feschrift für Rudolf Bindschedler* 91, at 95 (1980).

point, states are bound together in a global "community of necessity" and that this fact has given rise to an increasingly complex matrix of mutual rights and obligations bearing on the protection of environmental resources.

Although, as pointed out, the beginnings of some fundamental changes are discernible, decision-making related to internationally or globally sensitive natural resources is still steeped in the voluntarist and statist model characteristic of classic international law. The realities of modern international life, foremost among which must be ranked global environmental interdependence, urgently require adjustment of the international system towards greater openness to accommodate non-state actors and formal abandonment of the idea that the principle of individual state consent continues to represent a fundamental defining characteristic of the international legal system. The transition from this traditional view of the international legal system to a new, community-based or majoritarian system of international decision-making will not be easy. Nor will it be reassuring to those who believe that assurance of stability is the principal function of the law. Ultimately, however, success or failure of our mission to secure global environmental security, will depend on our determination to press for timely structural adjustment.

[2]

The Tragedy of the Commons

The population problem has no technical solution; it requires a fundamental extension in morality.

Garrett Hardin

At the end of a thoughtful article on the future of nuclear war, Wiesner and York (*1*) concluded that: "Both sides in the arms race are . . . confronted by the dilemma of steadily increasing military power and steadily decreasing national security. *It is our considered professional judgment that this dilemma has no technical solution.* If the great powers continue to look for solutions in the area of science and technology only, the result will be to worsen the situation."

I would like to focus your attention not on the subject of the article (national security in a nuclear world) but on the kind of conclusion they reached, namely that there is no technical solution to the problem. An implicit and almost universal assumption of discussions published in professional and semipopular scientific journals is that the problem under discussion has a technical solution. A technical solution may be defined as one that requires a change only in the techniques of the natural sciences, demanding little or nothing in the way of change in human values or ideas of morality.

In our day (though not in earlier times) technical solutions are always welcome. Because of previous failures in prophecy, it takes courage to assert that a desired technical solution is not possible. Wiesner and York exhibited this courage; publishing in a science journal, they insisted that the solution to the problem was not to be found in the natural sciences. They cautiously qualified their statement with the phrase, "It is our considered professional judgment. . . ." Whether they were right or not is not the concern of the present article. Rather, the concern here is with the important concept of a class of human problems which can be called "no technical solution problems," and, more specifically, with the identification and discussion of one of these.

It is easy to show that the class is not a null class. Recall the game of tick-tack-toe. Consider the problem, "How can I win the game of tick-tack-toe?" It is well known that I cannot, if I assume (in keeping with the conventions of game theory) that my opponent understands the game perfectly. Put another way, there is no "technical solution" to the problem. I can win only by giving a radical meaning to the word "win." I can hit my opponent over the head; or I can drug him; or I can falsify the records. Every way in which I "win" involves, in some sense, an abandonment of the game, as we intuitively understand it. (I can also, of course, openly abandon the game—refuse to play it. This is what most adults do.)

The class of "No technical solution problems" has members. My thesis is that the "population problem," as conventionally conceived, is a member of this class. How it is conventionally conceived needs some comment. It is fair to say that most people who anguish over the population problem are trying to find a way to avoid the evils of overpopulation without relinquishing any of the privileges they now enjoy. They think that farming the seas or developing new strains of wheat will solve the problem—technologically. I try to show here that the solution they seek cannot be found. The population problem cannot be solved in a technical way, any more than can the problem of winning the game of tick-tack-toe.

What Shall We Maximize?

Population, as Malthus said, naturally tends to grow "geometrically," or, as we would now say, exponentially. In a finite world this means that the per capita share of the world's goods must steadily decrease. Is ours a finite world?

A fair defense can be put forward for the view that the world is infinite; or that we do not know that it is not. But, in terms of the practical problems that we must face in the next few generations with the foreseeable technology, it is clear that we will greatly increase human misery if we do not, during the immediate future, assume that the world available to the terrestrial human population is finite. "Space" is no escape (*2*).

A finite world can support only a finite population; therefore, population growth must eventually equal zero. (The case of perpetual wide fluctuations above and below zero is a trivial variant that need not be discussed.) When this condition is met, what will be the situation of mankind? Specifically, can Bentham's goal of "the greatest good for the greatest number" be realized?

No—for two reasons, each sufficient by itself. The first is a theoretical one. It is not mathematically possible to maximize for two (or more) variables at the same time. This was clearly stated by von Neumann and Morgenstern (*3*), but the principle is implicit in the theory of partial differential equations, dating back at least to D'Alembert (1717–1783).

The second reason springs directly from biological facts. To live, any organism must have a source of energy (for example, food). This energy is utilized for two purposes: mere maintenance and work. For man, maintenance of life requires about 1600 kilocalories a day ("maintenance calories"). Anything that he does over and above merely staying alive will be defined as work, and is supported by "work calories" which he takes in. Work calories are used not only for what we call work in common speech; they are also required for all forms of enjoyment, from swimming and automobile racing to playing music and writing poetry. If our goal is to maximize population it is obvious what we must do: We must make the work calories per person approach as close to zero as possible. No gourmet meals, no vacations, no sports, no music, no literature, no art. . . . I think that everyone will grant, without

The author is professor of biology, University of California, Santa Barbara. This article is based on a presidential address presented before the meeting of the Pacific Division of the American Association for the Advancement of Science at Utah State University, Logan, 25 June 1968.

argument or proof, that maximizing population does not maximize goods. Bentham's goal is impossible.

In reaching this conclusion I have made the usual assumption that it is the acquisition of energy that is the problem. The appearance of atomic energy has led some to question this assumption. However, given an infinite source of energy, population growth still produces an inescapable problem. The problem of the acquisition of energy is replaced by the problem of its dissipation, as J. H. Fremlin has so wittily shown (*4*). The arithmetic signs in the analysis are, as it were, reversed; but Bentham's goal is still unobtainable.

The optimum population is, then, less than the maximum. The difficulty of defining the optimum is enormous; so far as I know, no one has seriously tackled this problem. Reaching an acceptable and stable solution will surely require more than one generation of hard analytical work—and much persuasion.

We want the maximum good per person; but what is good? To one person it is wilderness, to another it is ski lodges for thousands. To one it is estuaries to nourish ducks for hunters to shoot; to another it is factory land. Comparing one good with another is, we usually say, impossible because goods are incommensurable. Incommensurables cannot be compared.

Theoretically this may be true; but in real life incommensurables *are* commensurable. Only a criterion of judgment and a system of weighting are needed. In nature the criterion is survival. Is it better for a species to be small and hideable, or large and powerful? Natural selection commensurates the incommensurables. The compromise achieved depends on a natural weighting of the values of the variables.

Man must imitate this process. There is no doubt that in fact he already does, but unconsciously. It is when the hidden decisions are made explicit that the arguments begin. The problem for the years ahead is to work out an acceptable theory of weighting. Synergistic effects, nonlinear variation, and difficulties in discounting the future make the intellectual problem difficult, but not (in principle) insoluble.

Has any cultural group solved this practical problem at the present time, even on an intuitive level? One simple fact proves that none has: there is no prosperous population in the world today that has, and has had for some time, a growth rate of zero. Any people that has intuitively identified its optimum point will soon reach it, after which its growth rate becomes and remains zero.

Of course, a positive growth rate might be taken as evidence that a population is below its optimum. However, by any reasonable standards, the most rapidly growing populations on earth today are (in general) the most miserable. This association (which need not be invariable) casts doubt on the optimistic assumption that the positive growth rate of a population is evidence that it has yet to reach its optimum.

We can make little progress in working toward optimum poulation size until we explicitly exorcize the spirit of Adam Smith in the field of practical demography. In economic affairs, *The Wealth of Nations* (1776) popularized the "invisible hand," the idea that an individual who "intends only his own gain," is, as it were, "led by an invisible hand to promote . . . the public interest" (*5*). Adam Smith did not assert that this was invariably true, and perhaps neither did any of his followers. But he contributed to a dominant tendency of thought that has ever since interfered with positive action based on rational analysis, namely, the tendency to assume that decisions reached individually will, in fact, be the best decisions for an entire society. If this assumption is correct it justifies the continuance of our present policy of laissez-faire in reproduction. If it is correct we can assume that men will control their individual fecundity so as to produce the optimum population. If the assumption is not correct, we need to reexamine our individual freedoms to see which ones are defensible.

Tragedy of Freedom in a Commons

The rebuttal to the invisible hand in population control is to be found in a scenario first sketched in a little-known pamphlet (*6*) in 1833 by a mathematical amateur named William Forster Lloyd (1794–1852). We may well call it "the tragedy of the commons," using the word "tragedy" as the philosopher Whitehead used it (*7*): "The essence of dramatic tragedy is not unhappiness. It resides in the solemnity of the remorseless working of things." He then goes on to say, "This inevitableness of destiny can only be illustrated in terms of human life by incidents which in fact involve unhappiness. For it is only by them that the futility of escape can be made evident in the drama."

The tragedy of the commons develops in this way. Picture a pasture open to all. It is to be expected that each herdsman will try to keep as many cattle as possible on the commons. Such an arrangement may work reasonably satisfactorily for centuries because tribal wars, poaching, and disease keep the numbers of both man and beast well below the carrying capacity of the land. Finally, however, comes the day of reckoning, that is, the day when the long-desired goal of social stability becomes a reality. At this point, the inherent logic of the commons remorselessly generates tragedy.

As a rational being, each herdsman seeks to maximize his gain. Explicitly or implicitly, more or less consciously, he asks, "What is the utility *to me* of adding one more animal to my herd?" This utility has one negative and one positive component.

1) The positive component is a function of the increment of one animal. Since the herdsman receives all the proceeds from the sale of the additional animal, the positive utility is nearly +1.

2) The negative component is a function of the additional overgrazing created by one more animal. Since, however, the effects of overgrazing are shared by all the herdsmen, the negative utility for any particular decision-making herdsman is only a fraction of −1.

Adding together the component partial utilities, the rational herdsman concludes that the only sensible course for him to pursue is to add another animal to his herd. And another; and another. . . . But this is the conclusion reached by each and every rational herdsman sharing a commons. Therein is the tragedy. Each man is locked into a system that compels him to increase his herd without limit—in a world that is limited. Ruin is the destination toward which all men rush, each pursuing his own best interest in a society that believes in the freedom of the commons. Freedom in a commons brings ruin to all.

Some would say that this is a platitude. Would that it were! In a sense, it was learned thousands of years ago, but natural selection favors the forces of psychological denial (*8*). The individual benefits as an individual from his ability to deny the truth even though society as a whole, of which he is a part, suffers.

Education can counteract the natural tendency to do the wrong thing, but the inexorable succession of generations requires that the basis for this knowledge be constantly refreshed.

A simple incident that occurred a few years ago in Leominster, Massachusetts, shows how perishable the knowledge is. During the Christmas shopping season the parking meters downtown were covered with plastic bags that bore tags reading: "Do not open until after Christmas. Free parking courtesy of the mayor and city council." In other words, facing the prospect of an increased demand for already scarce space, the city fathers reinstituted the system of the commons. (Cynically, we suspect that they gained more votes than they lost by this retrogressive act.)

In an approximate way, the logic of the commons has been understood for a long time, perhaps since the discovery of agriculture or the invention of private property in real estate. But it is understood mostly only in special cases which are not sufficiently generalized. Even at this late date, cattlemen leasing national land on the western ranges demonstrate no more than an ambivalent understanding, in constantly pressuring federal authorities to increase the head count to the point where overgrazing produces erosion and weed-dominance. Likewise, the oceans of the world continue to suffer from the survival of the philosophy of the commons. Maritime nations still respond automatically to the shibboleth of the "freedom of the seas." Professing to believe in the "inexhaustible resources of the oceans," they bring species after species of fish and whales closer to extinction (9).

The National Parks present another instance of the working out of the tragedy of the commons. At present, they are open to all, without limit. The parks themselves are limited in extent—there is only one Yosemite Valley—whereas population seems to grow without limit. The values that visitors seek in the parks are steadily eroded. Plainly, we must soon cease to treat the parks as commons or they will be of no value to anyone.

What shall we do? We have several options. We might sell them off as private property. We might keep them as public property, but allocate the right to enter them. The allocation might be on the basis of wealth, by the use of an auction system. It might be on the basis of merit, as defined by some agreed-upon standards. It might be by lottery. Or it might be on a first-come, first-served basis, administered to long queues. These, I think, are all the reasonable possibilities. They are all objectionable. But we must choose—or acquiesce in the destruction of the commons that we call our National Parks.

Pollution

In a reverse way, the tragedy of the commons reappears in problems of pollution. Here it is not a question of taking something out of the commons, but of putting something in—sewage, or chemical, radioactive, and heat wastes into water; noxious and dangerous fumes into the air; and distracting and unpleasant advertising signs into the line of sight. The calculations of utility are much the same as before. The rational man finds that his share of the cost of the wastes he discharges into the commons is less than the cost of purifying his wastes before releasing them. Since this is true for everyone, we are locked into a system of "fouling our own nest," so long as we behave only as independent, rational, free-enterprisers.

The tragedy of the commons as a food basket is averted by private property, or something formally like it. But the air and waters surrounding us cannot readily be fenced, and so the tragedy of the commons as a cesspool must be prevented by different means, by coercive laws or taxing devices that make it cheaper for the polluter to treat his pollutants than to discharge them untreated. We have not progressed as far with the solution of this problem as we have with the first. Indeed, our particular concept of private property, which deters us from exhausting the positive resources of the earth, favors pollution. The owner of a factory on the bank of a stream—whose property extends to the middle of the stream—often has difficulty seeing why it is not his natural right to muddy the waters flowing past his door. The law, always behind the times, requires elaborate stitching and fitting to adapt it to this newly perceived aspect of the commons.

The pollution problem is a consequence of population. It did not much matter how a lonely American frontiersman disposed of his waste. "Flowing water purifies itself every 10 miles," my grandfather used to say, and the myth was near enough to the truth when he was a boy, for there were not too many people. But as population became denser, the natural chemical and biological recycling processes became overloaded, calling for a redefinition of property rights.

How To Legislate Temperance?

Analysis of the pollution problem as a function of population density uncovers a not generally recognized principle of morality, namely: *the morality of an act is a function of the state of the system at the time it is performed* (*10*). Using the commons as a cesspool does not harm the general public under frontier conditions, because there is no public; the same behavior in a metropolis is unbearable. A hundred and fifty years ago a plainsman could kill an American bison, cut out only the tongue for his dinner, and discard the rest of the animal. He was not in any important sense being wasteful. Today, with only a few thousand bison left, we would be appalled at such behavior.

In passing, it is worth noting that the morality of an act cannot be determined from a photograph. One does not know whether a man killing an elephant or setting fire to the grassland is harming others until one knows the total system in which his act appears. "One picture is worth a thousand words," said an ancient Chinese; but it may take 10,000 words to validate it. It is as tempting to ecologists as it is to reformers in general to try to persuade others by way of the photographic shortcut. But the essense of an argument cannot be photographed: it must be presented rationally—in words.

That morality is system-sensitive escaped the attention of most codifiers of ethics in the past. "Thou shalt not . . ." is the form of traditional ethical directives which make no allowance for particular circumstances. The laws of our society follow the pattern of ancient ethics, and therefore are poorly suited to governing a complex, crowded, changeable world. Our epicyclic solution is to augment statutory law with administrative law. Since it is practically impossible to spell out all the conditions under which it is safe to burn trash in the back yard or to run an automobile without smog-control, by law we delegate the details to bureaus. The result is administrative law, which is rightly feared for an ancient reason—*Quis custodiet ipsos custodes?*—"Who shall watch the watchers themselves?" John Adams said that we must have "a government of laws and not men." Bureau administrators, trying to evaluate the morality of acts in the total system, are singularly liable to corruption, producing a government by men, not laws.

Prohibition is easy to legislate (though not necessarily to enforce); but how do we legislate temperance? Experience indicates that it can be accomplished best through the mediation of administrative law. We limit possibilities unnecessarily if we suppose that the sentiment of *Quis custodiet* denies us the use of administrative law. We should rather retain the phrase as a perpetual reminder of fearful dangers we cannot avoid. The great challenge facing us now is to invent the corrective feedbacks that are needed to keep custodians honest. We must find ways to legitimate the needed authority of both the custodians and the corrective feedbacks.

Freedom To Breed Is Intolerable

The tragedy of the commons is involved in population problems in another way. In a world governed solely by the principle of "dog eat dog"—if indeed there ever was such a world—how many children a family had would not be a matter of public concern. Parents who bred too exuberantly would leave fewer descendants, not more, because they would be unable to care adequately for their children. David Lack and others have found that such a negative feedback demonstrably controls the fecundity of birds (*11*). But men are not birds, and have not acted like them for millenniums, at least.

If each human family were dependent only on its own resources; *if* the children of improvident parents starved to death; *if*, thus, overbreeding brought its own "punishment" to the germ line—*then* there would be no public interest in controlling the breeding of families. But our society is deeply committed to the welfare state (*12*), and hence is confronted with another aspect of the tragedy of the commons.

In a welfare state, how shall we deal with the family, the religion, the race, or the class (or indeed any distinguishable and cohesive group) that adopts overbreeding as a policy to secure its own aggrandizement (*13*)? To couple the concept of freedom to breed with the belief that everyone born has an equal right to the commons is to lock the world into a tragic course of action.

Unfortunately this is just the course of action that is being pursued by the United Nations. In late 1967, some 30 nations agreed to the following (*14*):

> The Universal Declaration of Human Rights describes the family as the natural and fundamental unit of society. It follows that any choice and decision with regard to the size of the family must irrevocably rest with the family itself, and cannot be made by anyone else.

It is painful to have to deny categorically the validity of this right; denying it, one feels as uncomfortable as a resident of Salem, Massachusetts, who denied the reality of witches in the 17th century. At the present time, in liberal quarters, something like a taboo acts to inhibit criticism of the United Nations. There is a feeling that the United Nations is "our last and best hope," that we shouldn't find fault with it; we shouldn't play into the hands of the archconservatives. However, let us not forget what Robert Louis Stevenson said: "The truth that is suppressed by friends is the readiest weapon of the enemy." If we love the truth we must openly deny the validity of the Universal Declaration of Human Rights, even though it is promoted by the United Nations. We should also join with Kingsley Davis (*15*) in attempting to get Planned Parenthood-World Population to see the error of its ways in embracing the same tragic ideal.

Conscience Is Self-Eliminating

It is a mistake to think that we can control the breeding of mankind in the long run by an appeal to conscience. Charles Galton Darwin made this point when he spoke on the centennial of the publication of his grandfather's great book. The argument is straightforward and Darwinian.

People vary. Confronted with appeals to limit breeding, some people will undoubtedly respond to the plea more than others. Those who have more children will produce a larger fraction of the next generation than those with more susceptible consciences. The difference will be accentuated, generation by generation.

In C. G. Darwin's words: "It may well be that it would take hundreds of generations for the progenitive instinct to develop in this way, but if it should do so, nature would have taken her revenge, and the variety *Homo contracipiens* would become extinct and would be replaced by the variety *Homo progenitivus*" (*16*).

The argument assumes that conscience or the desire for children (no matter which) is hereditary—but hereditary only in the most general formal sense. The result will be the same whether the attitude is transmitted through germ cells, or exosomatically, to use A. J. Lotka's term. (If one denies the latter possibility as well as the former, then what's the point of education?) The argument has here been stated in the context of the population problem, but it applies equally well to any instance in which society appeals to an individual exploiting a commons to restrain himself for the general good—by means of his conscience. To make such an appeal is to set up a selective system that works toward the elimination of conscience from the race.

Pathogenic Effects of Conscience

The long-term disadvantage of an appeal to conscience should be enough to condemn it; but has serious short-term disadvantages as well. If we ask a man who is exploiting a commons to desist "in the name of conscience," what are we saying to him? What does he hear?—not only at the moment but also in the wee small hours of the night when, half asleep, he remembers not merely the words we used but also the nonverbal communication cues we gave him unawares? Sooner or later, consciously or subconsciously, he senses that he has received two communications, and that they are contradictory: (i) (intended communication) "If you don't do as we ask, we will openly condemn you for not acting like a responsible citizen"; (ii) (the unintended communication) "If you *do* behave as we ask, we will secretly condemn you for a simpleton who can be shamed into standing aside while the rest of us exploit the commons."

Everyman then is caught in what Bateson has called a "double bind." Bateson and his co-workers have made a plausible case for viewing the double bind as an important causative factor in the genesis of schizophrenia (*17*). The double bind may not always be so damaging, but it always endangers the mental health of anyone to whom it is applied. "A bad conscience," said Nietzsche, "is a kind of illness."

To conjure up a conscience in others

is tempting to anyone who wishes to extend his control beyond the legal limits. Leaders at the highest level succumb to this temptation. Has any President during the past generation failed to call on labor unions to moderate voluntarily their demands for higher wages, or to steel companies to honor voluntary guidelines on prices? I can recall none. The rhetoric used on such occasions is designed to produce feelings of guilt in noncoopoerators.

For centuries it was assumed without proof that guilt was a valuable, perhaps even an indispensable, ingredient of the civilized life. Now, in this post-Freudian world, we doubt it.

Paul Goodman speaks from the modern point of view when he says: "No good has ever come from feeling guilty, neither intelligence, policy, nor compassion. The guilty do not pay attention to the object but only to themselves, and not even to their own interests, which might make sense, but to their anxieties" (*18*).

One does not have to be a professional psychiatrist to see the consequences of anxiety. We in the Western world are just emerging from a dreadful two-centuries-long Dark Ages of Eros that was sustained partly by prohibition laws, but perhaps more effectively by the anxiety-generating mechanisms of education. Alex Comfort has told the story well in *The Anxiety Makers* (*19*); it is not a pretty one.

Since proof is difficult, we may even concede that the results of anxiety may sometimes, from certain points of view, be desirable. The larger question we should ask is whether, as a matter of policy, we should ever encourage the use of a technique the tendency (if not the intention) of which is psychologically pathogenic. We hear much talk these days of responsible parenthood; the coupled words are incorporated into the titles of some organizations devoted to birth control. Some people have proposed massive propaganda campaigns to instill responsibility into the nation's (or the world's) breeders. But what is the meaning of the word responsibility in this context? Is it not merely a synonym for the word conscience? When we use the word responsibility in the absence of substantial sanctions are we not trying to browbeat a free man in a commons into acting against his own interest? Responsibility is a verbal counterfeit for a substantial *quid pro quo*. It is an attempt to get something for nothing.

If the word responsibility is to be used at all, I suggest that it be in the sense Charles Frankel uses it (*20*). "Responsibility," says this philosopher, "is the product of definite social arrangements." Notice that Frankel calls for social arrangements—not propaganda.

Mutual Coercion Mutually Agreed upon

The social arrangements that produce responsibility are arrangements that create coercion, of some sort. Consider bank-robbing. The man who takes money from a bank acts as if the bank were a commons. How do we prevent such action? Certainly not by trying to control his behavior solely by a verbal appeal to his sense of responsibility. Rather than rely on propaganda we follow Frankel's lead and insist that a bank is not a commons; we seek the definite social arrangements that will keep it from becoming a commons. That we thereby infringe on the freedom of would-be robbers we neither deny nor regret.

The morality of bank-robbing is particularly easy to understand because we accept complete prohibition of this activity. We are willing to say "Thou shalt not rob banks," without providing for exceptions. But temperance also can be created by coercion. Taxing is a good coercive device. To keep downtown shoppers temperate in their use of parking space we introduce parking meters for short periods, and traffic fines for longer ones. We need not actually forbid a citizen to park as long as he wants to; we need merely make it increasingly expensive for him to do so. Not prohibition, but carefully biased options are what we offer him. A Madison Avenue man might call this persuasion; I prefer the greater candor of the word coercion.

Coercion is a dirty word to most liberals now, but it need not forever be so. As with the four-letter words, its dirtiness can be cleansed away by exposure to the light, by saying it over and over without apology or embarrassment. To many, the word coercion implies arbitrary decisions of distant and irresponsible bureaucrats; but this is not a necessary part of its meaning. The only kind of coercion I recommend is mutual coercion, mutually agreed upon by the majority of the people affected.

To say that we mutually agree to coercion is not to say that we are required to enjoy it, or even to pretend we enjoy it. Who enjoys taxes? We all grumble about them. But we accept compulsory taxes because we recognize that voluntary taxes would favor the conscienceless. We institute and (grumblingly) support taxes and other coercive devices to escape the horror of the commons.

An alternative to the commons need not be perfectly just to be preferable. With real estate and other material goods, the alternative we have chosen is the institution of private property coupled with legal inheritance. Is this system perfectly just? As a genetically trained biologist I deny that it is. It seems to me that, if there are to be differences in individual inheritance, legal possession should be perfectly correlated with biological inheritance—that those who are biologically more fit to be the custodians of property and power should legally inherit more. But genetic recombination continually makes a mockery of the doctrine of "like father, like son" implicit in our laws of legal inheritance. An idiot can inherit millions, and a trust fund can keep his estate intact. We must admit that our legal system of private property plus inheritance is unjust—but we put up with it because we are not convinced, at the moment, that anyone has invented a better system. The alternative of the commons is too horrifying to contemplate. Injustice is preferable to total ruin.

It is one of the peculiarities of the warfare between reform and the status quo that it is thoughtlessly governed by a double standard. Whenever a reform measure is proposed it is often defeated when its opponents triumphantly discover a flaw in it. As Kingsley Davis has pointed out (*21*), worshippers of the status quo sometimes imply that no reform is possible without unanimous agreement, an implication contrary to historical fact. As nearly as I can make out, automatic rejection of proposed reforms is based on one of two unconscious assumptions: (i) that the status quo is perfect; or (ii) that the choice we face is between reform and no action; if the proposed reform is imperfect, we presumably should take no action at all, while we wait for a perfect proposal.

But we can never do nothing. That which we have done for thousands of years is also action. It also produces evils. Once we are aware that the status quo is action, we can then compare its discoverable advantages and disadvantages with the predicted advantages and disadvantages of the proposed reform, discounting as best we can for our lack of experience. On the basis of such a comparison, we can make a rational decision which will not involve the unworkable assumption that only perfect systems are tolerable.

Recognition of Necessity

Perhaps the simplest summary of this analysis of man's population problems is this: the commons, if justifiable at all, is justifiable only under conditions of low-population density. As the human population has increased, the commons has had to be abandoned in one aspect after another.

First we abandoned the commons in food gathering, enclosing farm land and restricting pastures and hunting and fishing areas. These restrictions are still not complete throughout the world.

Somewhat later we saw that the commons as a place for waste disposal would also have to be abandoned. Restrictions on the disposal of domestic sewage are widely accepted in the Western world; we are still struggling to close the commons to pollution by automobiles, factories, insecticide sprayers, fertilizing operations, and atomic energy installations.

In a still more embryonic state is our recognition of the evils of the commons in matters of pleasure. There is almost no restriction on the propagation of sound waves in the public medium. The shopping public is assaulted with mindless music, without its consent. Our government is paying out billions of dollars to create supersonic transport which will disturb 50,000 people for every one person who is whisked from coast to coast 3 hours faster. Advertisers muddy the airwaves of radio and television and pollute the view of travelers. We are a long way from outlawing the commons in matters of pleasure. Is this because our Puritan inheritance makes us view pleasure as something of a sin, and pain (that is, the pollution of advertising) as the sign of virtue?

Every new enclosure of the commons involves the infringement of somebody's personal liberty. Infringements made in the distant past are accepted because no contemporary complains of a loss. It is the newly proposed infringements that we vigorously oppose; cries of "rights" and "freedom" fill the air. But what does "freedom" mean? When men mutually agreed to pass laws against robbing, mankind became more free, not less so. Individuals locked into the logic of the commons are free only to bring on universal ruin; once they see the necessity of mutual coercion, they become free to pursue other goals. I believe it was Hegel who said, "Freedom is the recognition of necessity."

The most important aspect of necessity that we must now recognize, is the necessity of abandoning the commons in breeding. No technical solution can rescue us from the misery of overpopulation. Freedom to breed will bring ruin to all. At the moment, to avoid hard decisions many of us are tempted to propagandize for conscience and responsible parenthood. The temptation must be resisted, because an appeal to independently acting consciences selects for the disappearance of all conscience in the long run, and an increase in anxiety in the short.

The only way we can preserve and nurture other and more precious freedoms is by relinquishing the freedom to breed, and that very soon. "Freedom is the recognition of necessity"—and it is the role of education to reveal to all the necessity of abandoning the freedom to breed. Only so, can we put an end to this aspect of the tragedy of the commons.

References

1. J. B. Wiesner and H. F. York, *Sci. Amer.* **211** (No. 4), 27 (1964).
2. G. Hardin, *J. Hered.* **50**, 68 (1959); S. von Hoernor, *Science* **137**, 18 (1962).
3. J. von Neumann and O. Morgenstern, *Theory of Games and Economic Behavior* (Princeton Univ. Press, Princeton, N.J., 1947), p. 11.
4. J. H. Fremlin, *New Sci.*, No. 415 (1964), p. 285.
5. A. Smith, *The Wealth of Nations* (Modern Library, New York, 1937), p. 423.
6. W. F. Lloyd, *Two Lectures on the Checks to Population* (Oxford Univ. Press, Oxford, England, 1833), reprinted (in part) in *Population, Evolution, and Birth Control*, G. Hardin, Ed. (Freeman, San Francisco, 1964), p. 37.
7. A. N. Whitehead, *Science and the Modern World* (Mentor, New York, 1948), p. 17.
8. G. Hardin, Ed. *Population, Evolution, and Birth Control* (Freeman, San Francisco, 1964), p. 56.
9. S. McVay, *Sci. Amer.* **216** (No. 8), 13 (1966).
10. J. Fletcher, *Situation Ethics* (Westminster, Philadelphia, 1966).
11. D. Lack, *The Natural Regulation of Animal Numbers* (Clarendon Press, Oxford, 1954).
12. H. Girvetz, *From Wealth to Welfare* (Stanford Univ. Press, Stanford, Calif., 1950).
13. G. Hardin, *Perspec. Biol. Med.* **6**, 366 (1963).
14. U. Thant, *Int. Planned Parenthood News*, No. 168 (February 1968), p. 3.
15. K. Davis, *Science* **158**, 730 (1967).
16. S. Tax, Ed., *Evolution after Darwin* (Univ. of Chicago Press, Chicago, 1960), vol. 2, p. 469.
17. G. Bateson, D. D. Jackson, J. Haley, J. Weakland, *Behav. Sci.* **1**, 251 (1956).
18. P. Goodman, *New York Rev. Books* **10**(8), 22 (23 May 1968).
19. A. Comfort, *The Anxiety Makers* (Nelson, London, 1967).
20. C. Frankel, *The Case for Modern Man* (Harper, New York, 1955), p. 203.
21. J. D. Roslansky, *Genetics and the Future of Man* (Appleton-Century-Crofts, New York, 1966), p. 177.

[3]

TOWARDS A MEANINGFUL CONCEPT OF POLLUTION IN INTERNATIONAL LAW

By

ALLEN L. SPRINGER *

THE question has been posed by, among others, C. B. Bourne: " What are you talking about when you are talking about pollution? What is pollution? How would you define it if you are going to remove the concept of damage from it? " [1] The fact is that " pollution " is a word whose precise meaning in law, particularly international law, is not easily discerned. It has been used in a wide variety of contexts, from international conventions to pessimistic speeches about the state of the environment, to describe different levels and kinds of man-induced [2] changes in the natural world. Within a particular context, pollution assumes a meaning, either explicitly stated or implicitly developed, which may bear little resemblance to its usage elsewhere. While any definition may appear satisfactory for the purpose to which it is applied, this proliferation of usages has led some publicists to believe that the term has lost any legal value it might once have had and should be discarded. Indeed, in many cases, pollution has been replaced by other words, supposedly more precise. Yet " pollution " is an extremely important concept in the contemporary discussion of international environmental law and an integral part of many international agreements, including the Stockholm Declaration on the Human Environment of 1972.[3] The problem of what constitutes a legally significant effect on the environment cannot be solved by the simple manipulation of labels.

By setting forth the ways " pollution " has been used in an international legal context in the recent past, this paper attempts to reveal the varying approaches taken which now make it difficult to consider " pollution " a reasonably precise and generally accepted concept in international law. The classification of these approaches could

* Lecturer in Law, Department of Government and Legal Studies, Bowdoin College, Brunswick, Maine.

The author is indebted to Professor Alfred Rubin of the Fletcher School of Law and Diplomacy for his useful suggestions and careful criticism during the preparation of this paper.

1 C. B. Bourne, " Trail Smelter Arbitration: Oral Proceedings " (1971) 50 *Oregon Law Review* 291.

2 If there is any clear consensus on any aspect of what pollution is, it is the general belief that pollution in the legal sense is necessarily caused by man, either directly or indirectly. This will be assumed in the discussion that follows.

3 *Stockholm Declaration on the Human Environment*, Report of the United Nations Stockholm Conference on the Human Environment, Stockholm, June 5–16, 1972, A/Conf. 48/14.

be based on an evolution of the meaning of the term through time, or on the different attitudes taken toward environmental change in particular parts of the biosphere (atmosphere, oceans, and land), or on the degree of control and interest those using the label have had in the exploitation of the environment to be protected. Each of these factors is clearly related to the way the concept is used in a specific case and must be kept in mind in understanding its meaning in that context. Yet pollution, to be a useful concept, should have or develop a meaning which transcends and can be detached from particular usages.

An initial step must be taken to clarify the nature of the concept to be discussed. The word "pollution" has been used in two distinct senses: first, to indicate any alteration in a given environment, and, secondly, to indicate a threshold level of damage or interference which is legally significant. This paper adopts the second approach. What is important is the point at which the label is attached and the criteria deemed necessary for that attachment, not the specific label employed. Thus, some licence has been taken in incorporating into this analysis examples which appear to approach essentially the same threshold under the guise of another label. This study is limited to a description of what is meant by this threshold as an independent concept. The legal consequences which flow from the attachment of the label—questions of degrees of liability, and so forth—are important, but constitute fields of investigation which are beyond the scope of this paper. It is in the latter area that most of the discussion of international pollution to date has taken place.[4]

The paper is divided into two parts. In the first are outlined what the author considers the basic conceptual categories within which pollution has been approached in the past. The primary concern is the criteria required to pass the threshold of legal significance. The type of criteria employed is the basis on which these categories are distinguished, while the threshold level of "necessary" criteria and the area of application are used to show the range of definitions within each category. The second section of the paper discusses the two basic "reactions" to the limitations of these past approaches: wide definitions of pollution encompassing two or more types of

[4] This is not to deny the interrelation in specific cases of the threshold of label attachment and the attendant legal consequences. As Charles R. Ross shows with the 1909 Boundary Waters Treaty between the United States and Canada, a State may be willing to accept a "low" threshold of legally-significant environmental change only on the condition that the consequences of the label attachment be relatively lenient or only applied in very serious cases. Charles R. Ross, "National Sovereignty in International Environmental Decisions" (1972) 2 *Natural Resources Journal* 243. Yet it is this interrelationship which has been responsible for some of the confusion over what pollution means. To understand the meaning and significance of the label, one must attempt to set it apart from its legal consequences.

criteria, and new concepts to replace pollution. Finally, an attempt is made to place within this perspective present efforts to give the word " pollution " a generally acceptable meaning for the future, not limited by specific usages and concepts.

I. PAST APPROACHES TO POLLUTION

Five categories have been chosen to describe the range of approaches to pollution. The first two, " Pollution as any alteration of the existing environment " and " Pollution as the right of the territorial sovereign," are employed to set the extreme boundaries of the discussion and thus are presented more as ideal types than as categories of widely-shared viewpoints. The other three, " Pollution as damage," " Pollution as interference with other uses of the environment," and " Pollution as exceeding the assimilative capacity of the environment," correspond far more realistically to the major centres of opinion within the often unconscious controversy over the meaning of pollution.

A. *Pollution as any Alteration of Existing Environment*

In its purest form, this approach would allow little room for man in the natural world. By reference to it, a single drop of refined oil in the Pacific Ocean would become pollution under international law, as indeed would the most minimal change anywhere within man's reach. The distinction made earlier between pollution as any alteration and as a threshold of man-induced change breaks down here and, in this pure form, the approach is clearly meaningless as a general basis of law.

Yet in specific situations something similar to this has been adopted. A 1929 frontier agreement between Germany and Belgium contains the clause:

> Before erecting any building which might alter the present situation and have a *prejudicial* effect on the quality of the water, the Governments of both States shall come to an agreement with regard to the necessary protective measures. *In no case* is it permissible to let water *injurious to public health flow into* streams and ditches.[5]

Set forth is a very low threshold of acceptable alteration of a given body of water, mitigated only slightly by the vague reference to " prejudicial " effects. The second sentence appears, at first glance, to be setting more concrete standards for the degree of environmental effect, yet nowhere is there stated any threshold of change in the

[5] Agreement Concerning the Frontier Between Germany and Belgium, Aix-La-Chapelle, Nov. 7, 1929, League of Nations, Treaty Series (LNTS), Vol. 121, No. 795, Art. 60 (2), p. 361 (emphasis added).

river itself or any permissible degree of damage which its "polluted" waters might cause. What is said is that no amount of a particular type of water, described as "injurious to public health" may be added to streams and ditches.

A more recent example of the "purity" approach, in the highly specific area of radioactive waste, is provided by the Antarctic Treaty of 1959 which prohibits "any nuclear explosions in Antarctica and the disposal there of radioactive waste material." [6] Similarly the 1963 Treaty Banning Nuclear Weapon Tests in the Atmosphere, in Outer Space, and Under Water, "desiring to put an end to the contamination of man's environment by radioactive substances," [7] permits no nuclear explosions in the three parts of the biosphere mentioned in the title. Article I (1) (b) is particularly important in showing the environmental component of this absolute prohibition. The presence of any level of radioactive debris outside the territory of the testing State is considered unacceptable and, in itself, constitutes pollution in the sense of this paper.[8] This view of the need to keep as much of the planet free of radioactive waste as possible is further embodied in the General Assembly's Resolution on the Urgent Need for Suspension of Nuclear and Thermonuclear Tests. The Assembly's primary concern is stated to be the injury "to human and animal life" and the fear that "such fall-out may poison the Earth's atmosphere for decades to come." [9] Yet the threshold of pollution depends not upon a particular level of damage to man or the environment but upon the detonation of a nuclear weapon and the subsequent emission of radioactive fallout. Once again, a standard of absolute purity is called for.

The applicability of this approach is clearly limited in today's world to exactly the sort of specific and blatant forms of environmental degradation presented by nuclear explosions. Absolute purity can only be a useful concept when the interaction between the potential pollutant and a certain part of the biosphere would be a relatively rare, controllable, and avoidable occurrence. As long as radioactive wastes could be disposed of in the oceans and nuclear weapons tested underground, it was plausible for negotiators to accept the "absolute" standards represented in the documents discussed above. Yet, in addition to problems of political acceptability of such stan-

[6] Antarctic Treaty, Washington, Dec. 1, 1959, United Nations, Treaty Series (UNTS), Vol. 402, Art. v (1), p. 71.

[7] Treaty Banning Nuclear Weapon Tests in the Atmosphere, in Outer Space and Under Water, Moscow, Aug. 5, 1963, UNTS, Vol. 480, p. 45.

[8] *Ibid.*, Art. I (1) (b).

[9] Resolution on the Urgent Need for Suspension of Nuclear and Thermonuclear Tests, United Nations, General Assembly, Resolution No. 2828 (XXVI), Dec. 16, 1971.

dards for countries like France and China whose nuclear programmes required further atmospheric testing, the difficulty of adhering to the "purity" approach (at least as long as underground testing is permitted) was quickly revealed. An underground detonation by the USSR on January 15, 1965, in the Semipalatinsk area of Soviet Central Asia released radioactive debris detected by U.S. reconnaissance planes as having crossed Soviet borders in apparent violation of the Test-Ban Treaty's terms. However, unwilling to adopt a "strict" viewpoint which might later be applied against its own tests, the United States refrained from directly accusing the Soviet Union of a treaty violation, instead considering it an "inadvertent" and "isolated" incident. A similar stance was taken by the Soviet Union in 1966 when a U.S. explosion in Nevada vented radioactive fallout.[10] What evolved in this exchange was an understanding that something more than the detection of *any* radioactivity would be required to charge a signatory of the treaty with an illegal act. The "absolute" standards adopted earlier were, in fact, replaced by a threshold of *unacceptable* radioactivity, a threshold undefined either in terms of the amount which actually crossed an international border or the degree of the threat it posed to human or animal life.

In the case of the German-Belgian frontier treaty, another problem with the approach seems clear. To label a minimal influx of "injurious" waters "pollution" is to ignore the assimilative capacity of the stream and bestow legal significance on a situation that may not require it. Should this become a standard to maintain, many worthwhile developments along the affected waterway might well be impossible. If, instead, what the agreement seeks to prevent is an unhealthful body of water, the threshold of pollution should be defined either in terms of water quality standards for that body of water or by reference to far more precise emission standards which take into account each stream's assimilative potential.[11]

B. *Pollution as Right of Territorial Sovereign*

In contrast to the previous approach, this view in its ideal form allows no international purview over any type or degree of environmental

[10] This problem received a limited amount of publicity in several *New York Times* articles and an editorial of Jan. 22, 1965. John W. Finney, "U.S. Says Soviets May Have Broken Test-Ban Treaty," *New York Times*, Jan. 20, 1965, p. 1, col. 1; "U.S. Cautious on Fall-out from Soviet," *New York Times*, Jan. 21, 1965, p. 4, col. 4; "The Use of Nuclear Explosions," editorial, *New York Times*, Jan. 22, 1965, p. 42, col. 1; "A-Test Violation Denied by Soviet," *New York Times*, Jan. 26, 1965, p. 8, col. 3; "Soviet Test Blast is Assessed by U.S.," Mar. 10, 1966, p. 13, col. 1; "Nuclear Accident in Nevada is Assailed by Soviet Press," May 1, 1966, p. 71, col. 4.

[11] This distinction is an important one and will be explored at greater length below.

change which arises within the geographical borders of a sovereign State, regardless of the extra-territorial effects of the change. It does not speak directly to the question of pollution in areas outside of State control (the oceans, outer space, and unclaimed land), yet within the State it implies a very high or infinite threshold of alteration for which international law would be unable to hold the State responsible.

Such an extreme position finds little support in contemporary discussions of international pollution, but the "Harmon Doctrine" can be cited as within the conceptual framework of this approach. Responding to a Mexican protest over the United States' diversion of the waters of the Rio Grande, the United States Attorney-General, Judson Harmon, saw no principle of international law which would bar the United States from or make it liable for such a diversion. Comity might serve to limit such actions but "that question should be decided as one of policy only." [12] While this particular case involved the quantity of water, the implications as to quality are obvious. Those portions of rivers within United States jurisdiction could be used as the United States saw fit. International law set no limits of permissibility to the external effects such use might entail. Issued in 1895, the Harmon Doctrine reflected a far less interdependent international situation than that which would develop and be recognized in the twentieth century by the evolution of riparian rights theory.

In addition to the present unacceptability of the general viewpoint, thinking of pollution as the right of the territorial sovereign leads, as Lester points out, to the logical result that "unlimited exercise of sovereignty by an upper riparian State must limit the equally important sovereignty of the lower riparian." [13] Under Harmon's approach each State could alter the river as much as it wanted with neither being held accountable under international law for having passed the pollution threshold. Given the general directional flow of contaminating substances in moving waterways, the lower riparian is clearly placed in a disadvantageous position. At the other extreme, emphasis on the absolute territorial inviolability of the downstream State is to permit the lowest riparian to veto any use by the upper riparians, even if the stream is returned to something very close to its "natural" state before it reaches the border.[14] Further it allows the down-stream State to bring about any degree of change in the river which, since it

[12] Judson Harmon, United States Attorney-General, Dec. 12, 1895, in Moore, *International Law Digest*, Vol. 1, p. 654.

[13] A. P. Lester, "River Pollution in International Law" (1963) 57 A.J.I.L. p. 832.

[14] For good reason, such a position was found untenable in the *Lake Lanoux* Arbitration. See Brunson MacChesney, "*Lake Lanoux* Case" (1959) 53 A.J.I.L. 165–167.

then flows into the *res communis* of the sea, damages no territorial sovereign in the way necessary to serve as the basis for a claim.[15] From an ecological or economic perspective, neither extreme represents a rational approach to environmental pollution.

C. *Pollution as Damage*

Pollution as damage is a very wide category and to distinguish between the various approaches which have been taken within it one must keep in mind two interrelated questions: to what must the damage be done to be considered pollution and what level of damage is necessary? The most useful methodological distinction is made between damage to man and his property and damage to the environment.[16]

Damage to man and his property

The decision of the tribunal in the *Trail Smelter Arbitration* is a good illustration of a high threshold approach. Feeling limited by the *compromise* to a determination of the " extent to which *property* in the State of Washington has been damaged by fumes from Smelter at Trail, B.C.," [17] the tribunal, in effect, construed the term " damage " to include only " tangible injury translatable into provable monetary damages." [18] The tribunal did state that both international and United States municipal law deny any State " the right to use or permit the use of its territory in such a manner as to cause injury by fumes in or to the *territory* of another or the properties or persons thereof." [19] This implies the possibility of damage to the environment itself, at least as it exists as the property of the injured State. Yet the award of compensation under United States municipal law indicates that non-monetary damage to the evergreen population of Washington (as well as potential tourism and other aesthetic or

15 See *Trail Smelter*, n. 17 *infra*.

16 It must be pointed out that there are a number of other differences between various kinds of damage concepts which, because of the complexity of the subject and limitations of this paper, cannot be treated in any systematic way. The question of where the damage occurs, within or beyond the limits of national jurisdiction, is a very important factor, as is the part of the biosphere regulated by each concept of pollution. Further study might well be able to establish a correlation between all these factors and the actual definitions chosen.

17 Trail Smelter Arbitral Tribunal, Decision, April 16, 1938, *UNRIAA*, Vol. 3, p. 1918. (emphasis added).

18 Alfred P. Rubin, " Pollution By Analogy: The Trail Smelter Arbitration " (1971) 50 *Oregon Law Review* 272. The logic, or lack thereof, which the Tribunal employed in arriving at this decision is fully discussed in Professor Rubin's article. What is important, for our purposes, is the concept of what interests could or could not be considered as protected by that decision and thus the area within which the label " pollution " could be applied.

19 Trail Smelter Arbitral Tribunal, Decision, March 11, 1941, *UNRIAA*, Vol. 3, p. 1965. (emphasis added).

speculative interests) did not meet the criteria of our threshold concept of pollution.[20]

Further, besides requiring that such damage actually occur before the threshold could be passed,[21] the tribunal said that the claim could not be accepted unless "the case is of serious consequence and the injury established by clear and convincing evidence."[22] It should also be noted that in the dispute no question arose of the legal effect of alterations to the biosphere outside the territorial jurisdiction of any State.

The 1909 Boundary Waters Treaty between the United States and Great Britain (Canada) also approaches pollution from a damage perspective. Article IV states, "It is further agreed that the waters herein defined as boundary waters and waters flowing across the boundary shall not be polluted on either side *to the injury of health or property on the other*."[23] Of particular significance, the determination of exactly what constitutes "injury" was not made clear in the Treaty but was left to the International Joint Commission (IJC) which it established. Although the word "polluted" implies that *any* alteration might serve as the basis of an international claim, the second part of the sentence makes it clear that the legal effects would attach only when such alteration involved "injury." The word of the IJC furnishes an important view of how this threshold has been defined. As will be shown in the next section, the damage context within which the IJC's findings are framed has resulted, at times, in a real discrepancy between the standards suggested by the Treaty and those actually employed by a body desirous of lowering the threshold of pollution.[24] In any case, the threshold envisioned by this agreement seems to lie markedly below that required under the *Trail Smelter* decision, despite an apparent stipulation that the injury be done to "health or property" on the other side of the boundary. What are missing are qualifying terms like "substantial," "serious," and "established by clear and convincing evidence."

An even lower threshold is implied by an exchange of notes in 1961

20 Rubin, "Pollution By Analogy," p. 273.

21 *Ibid.*

22 Trail Smelter Arbitral Tribunal, Decision, March 11, 1941, p. 1965.

23 Treaty Between His Majesty and the United States of America Relating to Boundary Waters and Questions Arising Along the Boundary Between Canada and the United States, Washington, January 11, 1909, *United States Treaty Series*, Vol. 548, Art. IV, p. 3, (emphasis added).

24 A similar approach was taken by France, Belgium, and Luxembourg in 1950. These countries set up a Tripartite Standing Committee on Polluted Waters and entrusted a technical subcommittee with the task of drawing up pollution standards. Unlike the IJC, however, the subcommittee was not confronted with a formal and established approach to the problem. Protocol Between France, Belgium, and Luxembourg to Establish a Tripartite Standing Committee on Polluted Waters, Brussels, April 8, 1950, *UNTS*, Vol. 66, p. 285.

between the United States and Mexico over the transboundary emission of fumes from American stockyards in El Paso to Ciudad Juarez. Although Mexico did make the claim that "serious physical and economic damages" were being suffered by the city's residents and businesses,[25] the United States' reply which, in apologetic tones, declared the problem solved, accepted responsibility for something far less serious than damage as used in the *Trail Smelter* sense. Regretting "any *inconvenience* or *discomfort* that the activities of the plants might have caused," the Secretary of State, Dean Rusk, explained the meteorological reasons for the problems and included with these odours "other pollutants such as smoke . . . and traffic dust" as contributing to the air pollution of the area.[26] Yet it was the odours against which Mexico had protested and the United States felt that the test of whether or not that problem had been taken care of was to see how the people who had originally complained felt after the changes had been made. Compensatable injury, "damages," were disregarded in the final stages of the correspondence as no reference was made to any decrease in the economic or physical damage of which Mexico had complained. It was said simply that people agreed that the "*objectionable* odours have been removed."[27]

Similarly, a report by Professor Hogger to the European Conference on Air Pollution stresses the need to include "inconveniences" as legally relevant forms of pollution damage.[28] Hogger also confronts directly the problem of defining the threshold of what degree of inconvenience to consider unacceptable, a problem which Charles Ross suggests is avoidable through a switch of emphasis from water quality to emission standards.[29] Yet, while emission standards may be a preferable policy tool for combating pollution, they still require some determination of the overall level of acceptable environmental change. This is not an easy task:

> It is, indeed, in the very nature of the problem that such limits can only be determined approximately. Apart from the difficulties of logic and methodology, there is a considerable linguistic problem, in the sense that there is no generally accepted definition of such terms as "inoffensive," "presumed," etc.[30]

Absolute purity is seen as an extremely costly and unnecessary basis

[25] Chargé d'affaires *ad interim* of Mexico (Gallardo) to the Secretary of State (Rusk), note, April 6, 1961, Whiteman, *Digest of International Law*, Vol. 6, p. 257.

[26] Secretary of State to the Chargé d'affaires *ad interim* of Mexico, note, Aug. 17, 1961, Whiteman, *Digest of International Law*, Vol. 6, p. 258.

[27] *Ibid.*, p. 259 (emphasis added).

[28] Professor Hogger, *Comparison of National Laws and Regulations, Possibility of Standardising These and Drawing Up Technical and Legislative Agreements and European Conventions on Air Pollution*, presented at the European Conference on Air Pollution, Strasbourg, June 24–July 1, 1964, pp. 439–440.

[29] Ross, *National Sovereignty*, p. 252.

[30] Hogger, *Comparison of National Laws*, p. 441.

for creating standards. Hogger implies that cost-benefit considerations should really predominate in the case of " inconveniences," while one might go to greater lengths and take net economic " loss " into consideration where actual damage was done or the health of populations endangered.[31] While this seems reasonable in situations where disruptive economic changes might bring only minor improvement of a problem of limited proportions, the line between " inconvenience," " damage," and " danger " becomes an important one to draw and Hogger gives little indication of how this should be done.

Although one may question their value as useful sources of international law, several judicial decisions made within the United States municipal legal system do help illustrate the range of concepts from high to low thresholds of damage to man and his property.[32] In *Missouri* v. *Illinois* (1906), Justice Holmes emphasised the need for a case to be " of serious magnitude, clearly and fully proved," [33] before the court should intervene, a concept of great importance to the *Trail Smelter* tribunal. The inability of Missouri to draw a clear connection between its increased rate of deaths due to typhoid and the Chicago sewage resulted in the case being dismissed.[34] New York also lost its case against New Jersey in 1921 when it could not show that New Jersey's proposed sewage disposal plan " would so corrupt the waters of the Bay as to create a public nuisance by causing offensive odours or unsightly deposits on the surface or that it would seriously add to the pollution of it." [35] Despite some confusion with the separation of public nuisance from an undefined " pollution " concept, the court did imply that " offensive odours " and " unsightly deposits " could be made the basis of a valid claim if sufficiently proved.[36]

Sierra Club v. *Morton* (1972), while dismissed because the Sierra

[31] *Ibid.*, p. 442.

[32] No attempt is made to accept or refute the view of some publicists that much of the unwillingness of the Supreme Court justices, particularly Holmes, to impose a low threshold view was due less to limited definitions of pollution than to a very real concern for the role of the Supreme Court in resolving interstate disputes. See Rubin, *Pollution By Analogy*, pp. 269–271. For whatever reasons they decided as they did, the conceptions of pollution which emerge from those decisions are useful illustrations of the differences previously examined.

[33] *Missouri* v. *Illinois and the Sanitary District of Chicago*, 200 U.S. 521 (1906).

[34] *Ibid.*, pp. 525–526.

[35] *New York* v. *New Jersey and Passaic Valley Sewerage Commissioners*, 256 U.S. 313 (1921).

[36] *Ibid.* The court, in effect, set up two thresholds of unacceptable environmental change. One which it called " pollution " was measured in terms of the change in the percentage of dissolved oxygen in the water. The other involved a question of public nuisance with an unarticulated degree of " unsightliness " or " objectionability " serving as the extremely vague basis for determining what was unacceptable. New Jersey's proposed plan was viewed as bringing about effects which transcended neither threshold and implicit was the belief that, by remaining within the legal limits established by these thresholds, " injury " would not be done to the Bay.

Club was unable to demonstrate the injury which would be done to its members by a proposed Disney development in a secluded mountain site, left open the possibility of an individual being able to claim injury to himself on the basis of aesthetic and ecological changes made in the environment which might not be easily translatable into economic terms. The court stated that " aesthetic and environmental well-being, like economic well-being, are important ingredients of the quality of life in our society " and quoted the *Data Processing* case (399 U.S. 154) in arguing that " the interest alleged to have been injured ' may reflect " aesthetic, conservational, and recreational " as well as economic values.' " The court objected not to the idea that such interests could be injured in a legal sense but to the fact that the Sierra Club had not shown the connection of the injury to the individuals it represented.[37]

Damage to the environment

Reacting to the limitations placed on a concept of pollution restricted to damage to specifically " human " interests, some publicists and organisations have moved to considering damage to the environment itself as legally significant. Justice Holmes, in *Georgia* v. *Tennessee Copper Co.* (1906), saw the claim as based on injury done to Georgia as a quasi-sovereign. Yet the damage was done to the environment which was simply being defended by the State that had territorial jurisdiction over it.

> It is a fair and reasonable demand on the part of a sovereign that the air over its territory should not be polluted *on a great scale* by sulphurous acid gas, that the forests on its mountains . . . should not be further destroyed or threatened by the act of persons beyond its control.[38]

The evidence of severe damage was so substantial " as to make out a case within the requirements of *Missouri* v. *Illinois*," [39] and Georgia won the case.

The Brussels Convention Relating to Intervention on the High Seas in Cases of Oil Pollution Casualties, although clearly reflecting the active measures resulting from its potential application, also sets a relatively high threshold of damage to the environment. Parties are allowed to act only against " *grave and imminent danger* to their coastline or related interests from pollution of the sea by oil, *following* upon a maritime casualty or acts related to such a casualty, which may reasonably be expected to result in *major harmful* conse-

37 *Sierra Club* v. *Morton*, 405 U.S. 734–735 (1972).

38 *Georgia* v. *Tennessee Copper Co. and Ducktown Sulphur, Copper and Iron Co.*, 206 U.S. 238 (1906) (emphasis added).

39 *Ibid.*, p. 239.

quences." [40] On the other hand, a joint communiqué released by the United States and Canada, which significantly extends to "areas beyond the limits of national jurisdiction" as well as the territory of other States, speaks of the international responsibility of States not to do damage to the environment. The term "damage" is unqualified and suggests a lower threshold than the above convention.[41]

A number of terms have been chosen to connote varying degrees of environmental damage. The presence of "harmful" or "potentially harmful" substances in the environment has been suggested by Dr. Herbert Volchok as a useful basis for pollution but, as he admits, it is really the "relative levels" of harm to the environment that are important from a legal standpoint. Dr. Volchok does not elaborate on what these levels might be although he suggests that they should be much lower than is generally believed.[42] The term "harmful" is also employed in the 1967 Outer Space Treaty. Article 9 requires parties to carry out their exploration of celestial objects in such a way as "to avoid their *harmful contamination* and also *adverse changes* in the environment of the Earth resulting from the introduction of celestial matter." [43] Neither of the italicised terms is further defined within the Treaty but relatively precise guidelines were set up in 1964 by the Consultative Group of the Committee on Space Research (COSPAR) of the International Council of Scientific Unions to prevent the undesired contamination of outer space and were basically adhered to in the United States explorations near Mars. Efforts have also been made to limit, as much as possible, effects on the Earth's environment from returning missions, yet here as well clear-cut standards of actual acceptable damage to the environment have not been worked out.[44]

The United States National Oceanic and Atmospheric Administration (NOAA) report to the Congress on ocean dumping defines ocean pollution as "the *unfavourable alteration* of the marine environment . . . through direct or indirect effects of changes in energy patterns, radiation levels, chemical and physical constitution and dis-

[40] International Convention Relating to Intervention on the High Seas in Cases of Oil Pollution Casualties, Brussels, Nov. 29, 1969, *International Legal Materials*, Vol. 9, No. 1 (1970), Art. I (1), p. 25 (emphasis added).

[41] United States-Canadian Joint Communiqué, Train and Davis, issued on July 14, 1972, in *The International Law of Pollution*, James Barros and Douglas M. Johnston, comp. (New York: Free Press, 1974), p. 345.

[42] Herbert Volchok, statement before U.S. Senate Committee on Commerce, Sub-committee on Oceans and Atmosphere, 93rd Congress, 1st session, July 12, 13 and 28, 1973, *Ocean Pollution*, pp. 52–59.

[43] Treaty on Principles Governing the Activities of States in the Exploration and Use of Outer Space, Including the Moon and Other Celestial Bodies, Washington, London, and Moscow, Jan. 27, 1967, *UNTS*, Vol. 610, Art. IX, p. 210 (emphasis added).

[44] Frederik L. Kirgis, "Technological Challenge to the Shared Environment: United States Practice" (1972) 66 *A.J.I.L.* 309–310.

tribution, abundance, and quality of organisms." [45] Apparently including such problems as overfishing and spoliation in general, this definition also makes explicit the fact that pollution need affect man only in the most indirect way, perhaps simply by lessening his enjoyment of nature. When faced with the problem of what to consider "unfavourable" for purposes of regulation, the NOAA report says most standards are not strict enough. In particular, it argues that many of these standards ignore negative long-term effects of sub-lethal doses of substances like DDT on the entire ecology of a given ocean area, looking instead for the concentrated, acute effects on particular organisms.[46]

An even more inclusive view of pollution is advanced by Alfred Rubin who, within a damage context, would define damage to mean "any alteration in the predicted availability of natural resources." [47] Offered in a discussion of the *Trail Smelter* decision, Professor Rubin's definition was intended to allow for changes made directly on the environment for which one would not be able to assign monetary "damages." While it takes into account the sort of long-range effects that worried the NOAA, this view would also seem to label "pollution" the exploitation of any non-renewable resource. As important as this might be to frame one's thinking about the relationship between man and his environment, or, more practically, to set up a procedure requiring proof of "acceptable damage" before any activity which would have an effect on the environment could be started, it would be difficult to apply such a concept as a final legal standard.

Many of the problems in the damage approach are found where, due to lack of agreement, limited perspective, or the strict legal consequences envisioned for attaching the label, a high threshold has been chosen. Requiring "serious" or "grave" damage to make an alteration legally significant may result in the overlooking of gradual changes with perhaps even greater long-term impact. Where restricted to "damage" as tangible injury of a monetarily determinable nature, the damage viewpoint may refuse protection to much of the "unowned" area and resources of the world. At the other extreme, very low levels of acceptable damage could, depending on the legal consequences, demand a costly and relatively unrewarded "cleaning-up" operation. Emphasis on damage, unless very widely defined, offers little positive guidance about man's interaction with the environ-

[45] U.S. Department of Commerce, National Oceanic and Atmospheric Administration, "Report to the Congress on Ocean Dumping and Other Man-Induced Changes to Ocean Ecosystems (March 1974), p. 6 (emphasis added).

[46] *Ibid.*, p. 20. The report says most tests look for the dose required to kill 50 per cent. of the test organisms.

[47] Rubin, *Pollution By Analogy*, p. 292.

ment. It stresses a series of levels and degrees of prohibition, rather than providing international law with a progressive and co-operative approach to the problem of maintaining the integrity of natural systems while allowing for social and economic development.

D. *Pollution as Interference with Other Uses of Environment*

Another approach which has received substantial support focuses on pollution as that which interferes with the various uses to which a particular environment is or can be put. Largely the product of international agreements regulating busy waterways and ocean areas, this category has been characterised in most of its forms by a very short-sighted, anti-ecological bias. The environment is important only to the degree that it is useful to man's immediate interests and environmental alteration is something to be halted only if the benefits of so doing, increased efficiency or expansion of usage, outweigh the costs. The threshold concern here is the degree of interference necessary for pollution to have occurred, while a second major distinguishing feature between these views is the various uses with which it is legally significant to interfere.

The Frontier Treaty of 1960 between the Netherlands and the Federal Republic of Germany adopts a use orientation. Article 58 (2) (e) requires both parties to take steps " to prevent such *excessive pollution* of the boundary waters as may *substantially impair* the *customary use* of the waters by the neighbouring State." [48] The " customary use " orientation of this agreement is retained, although the interference threshold lowered somewhat, by the Indus Waters Treaty of the same year. Pakistan and India thereby agreed to refrain from " undue pollution . . . which might adversely affect uses similar in nature to those to which the waters were put on the effective date." [49]

The rationale behind the use approach is spelled out well by Justice Holmes in the 1931 case of *New Jersey* v. *New York*:

> A river is more than an amenity, it is a treasure. It offers a necessity of life that must be rationed among those who have power over it. . . Both states have real and substantial interests in the river that must be reconciled as best they may be. The different traditions and practices in different parts of the country may lead to varying results, but the effort is always to secure equitable apportionment without quibbling over formulas.[50]

[48] Frontier Treaty Between the Kingdom of the Netherlands and the Federal Republic of Germany, the Hague, April 8, 1960, in force Aug. 1, 1963, in *The International Law of Pollution*, p. 158 (emphasis added).

[49] The Indus Waters Treaty (1960), Karachi (Sept. 19, 1960), *The Indian Yearbook of International Affairs* (1960–1961), Vol. IX–X, p. 364.

[50] *New Jersey* v. *New York* 283 U.S. 342–343 (1931).

The court used the services of a technical expert to see what the results of New York's proposed water diversion plan would be in terms of New Jersey's uses of the Deleware watershed and found that the planned 600 million gallons per day diversion would produce somewhat serious effects on recreation and oyster fishing uses. The decision was thus to limit New York's withdrawal to 440 million gallons daily.[51] Here a *new* use of the river's waters was integrated into an overall picture of interdependent, though potentially conflicting interests.

A study prepared in 1958 for the Economic Commission for Europe recognised that every State on an international river has the right to use the river as a natural resource. Although no lower riparian could expect to receive the water in a completely natural condition, " it is accepted that each upstream country has a duty to pass on the water in a usable condition." [52] " Usable condition " was described in the following paragraph as being equal to the condition in which the water was maintained in practice in the upstream State. The minimum acceptable condition, however (described as " wholesome ") would be that the water contain " significant amounts of dissolved oxygen for at least 95 per cent. of the year." [53]

An interesting contrast to this view of the use approach is provided by a report to the same organisation made one year earlier by the Group of Experts consulted by the Executive Secretary of the ECE. Where the 1958 study spoke in relatively specific terms of what minimal standards are for a " usable " river, this report gave no such criteria and even stated that " although the discharge of, for instance, salt, to any water is theoretically pollution, if it took place to a river whose sole use was navigation then it would not qualify to be classified as pollution." [54] Neither provided an effective guarantee for future uses of the river, but the 1958 study at least showed some concern that the river be maintained above a minimal level of purity. On the other hand, where the 1957 report called pollution any change which adversely affected the existing uses of the downstream State,[55] the 1958 study required that the water be passed on in usable condition. The point may be trivial, but there seems to be a difference between the two views as to whose " use criteria " would determine whether the river was polluted.

A third definition offered to the ECE declared a river to be polluted when its water is " less suitable for any or all of the purposes to

[51] *Ibid.*, p. 50.

[52] Economic Commission for Europe, " A Study on Water Pollution Control Problems in Europe," Feb. 26, 1958, Whiteman, *Digest of International Law*, Vol. 3, p. 1049.

[53] *Ibid.*

[54] *Ibid.*, p. 1043.

[55] *Ibid.*

which it would be suitable in its natural state." [56] While this definition offers no more precise a view of the threshold at which changes would be legally significant, it clearly requires that a waterway be preserved at the highest level of purity necessary for any potential use, even if not practised by anyone at the time.

Among publicists, Charles Bourne is a firm supporter of the use approach. "Man's concern is not whether the available water is pure, but whether there is enough of usable quality to satisfy his needs." [57] For Professor Bourne, sewage disposal is just one more possible use for a waterway, a use which will have a higher or lower priority depending on the needs of those who control it. Levels of cleanliness thus have significance only in their relationship to the requirements of other uses considered valuable by the community.[58]

Professor Bourne speaks highly of the 1966 Helsinki Rules of the International Law Association (ILA) which do articulate this viewpoint in a persuasive context. After a period of soul-searching in Article IX, where the ILA stresses the need to adopt a definition of pollution which recognises injury to the environment "irrespective of its effects on subsequent users," [59] Article X makes it clear that "equitable utilisation" is the key concept when it comes to determining the actual legal threshold of pollution. Pollution which results in injury should be seen within the "overall perspective of what constitutes an equitable utilisation" [60] and thus what the ILA considers pollution for definitional purposes may not be illegal if the use which causes it is in keeping with the equitable utilisation principle.[61] The Helsinki Rules also limit the ability of a State to argue in favour of preserving a river for future use. Article VII says: "A basin State may not be denied the present reasonable use of the waters of an international drainage basin to reserve for a co-basin State a future use of such waters." [62]

A final example which must be subsumed under the use category, although it reflects a far greater concern for the natural world, is the Canadian "Arctic Waters Pollution Prevention Act." The word "pollution" is largely avoided but the Act's definition of "waste" is aimed at the threshold with which this paper is concerned. Canada's

[56] *Ibid.*

[57] Bourne, C. B., "International Law and Pollution of International Rivers and Lakes" (1971) *University of British Columbia Law Review*, p. 117.

[58] *Ibid.*, p. 118.

[59] International Law Association, Helsinki Rules on the Uses of the Waters of International Rivers, Helsinki, August, 1966, in *Report of the Fifty-Fifth Conference* (London, 1967), p. 496.

[60] *Ibid.*, p. 499.

[61] *Ibid.*, p. 500. This is somewhat qualified by a reference to "substantial" injury and it remains unclear whether this substantial injury, even if caused by a valid use of the water would be a legal delict by the injuring State.

[62] *Ibid.*, p. 492.

jurisdiction is extended over a 100-mile zone to regulate the emission of any substance or water that " would, if added to any waters, degrade or alter or form part of a process of degradation or alteration of the quality of those waters to an extent that is detrimental to their use by man or by any animal, fish, or plant that is useful to man." [63] While this definition permits Canadian authorities to react directly against pollution which may affect a given species of fish far more directly than it does Canada's use of the seas, there still remains some doubt as to the fate of living organisms that may not be considered " useful to man."

As was stated earlier, the major objection to this approach is the disregard for the biological characteristics of ecological systems that it almost always represents. It is so directed to the balancing of State and individual interests that many important components of the biosphere may never be considered. This is particularly true if the question becomes reduced to a simplistic cost-benefit analysis into which it may be extremely difficult to fit the value of an unexploited species of fish There is an economic rationality to the approach, similar to the " polluter-pays " principle put forth by the Organization for Economic Co-operation and Development,[64] which seems to ignore the very real limits of the planet's ability to absorb man-caused waste and other environmental changes.

In adopting a use orientation, the ILA and others have attempted to incorporate the " reasonable man " test into environmental planning and dispute settlement procedures. Yet " reasonable " people do now and will continue to disagree over the priority of uses for a river, for example. However successful the reasonableness standard may be in a vertically-structured municipal law context where some form of judicial authority is able to weigh these opposing views and render a binding decision, the horizontal nature of the present international legal system makes the use of this standard far less effective on an international level.

Further, while one presumes that the ILA would be hesitant to endorse the extreme " full utilisation " approach taken by Myres McDougal and Norbert Schlei in their defence of U.S. nuclear testing in the Pacific Ocean, " The Hydrogen Bomb Tests in Perspective: Lawful Measures for Security " does reveal the danger inherent in relying solely on reasonableness in formulating legal norms to protect the international environment. Viewing the " technical prescriptions " of such concepts as the " territorial sea," " freedom of the seas," and

63 " Arctic Waters Pollution Prevention Act," Canada (1970) 9 I.L.M. 544.

64 Organisation for Economic Co-operation and Development, " Guiding Principles on the Environment," May 26, 1972 (1972) 11 I.L.M. 1172.

so forth as " highly flexible policy preferences " to be manipulated by decision makers in a particular controversy, McDougal and Schlei assert that, " for all types of controversies the one test that is invariably applied by decision makers is that . . . standard of what, considering all relevant policies and all variables in context is *reasonable* as between the parties." Naturally, " security " interests have a high priority for most decision makers and the hydrogen bomb tests must be seen as " reasonable, and hence lawful, within the régime of the high seas." [65] If such a " use " of the environment can be considered " reasonable," at least by two respected publicists, what cannot? All too often " in light of all relevant factors," and similar phrases used to justify a " reasonable use " approach, in fact have resulted in a position of secondary importance for environmental " variables."

E. *Pollution as Exceeding Assimilative Capacity of Environment*

The type of concern just mentioned, the growing realisation of the frailty and interdependence of the components of the biosphere, has brought about another view of pollution as waste which, either in quantity or in kind, is such that it cannot be broken down and rendered harmless by natural processes. Barry Commoner spoke to the Senate Commerce Committee's Subcommittee on Oceans and Atmosphere about pollution as the " overloading of natural cycles." " Human beings pollute the enivronment because their activities have broken out of the closed cyclical network in which all other living things are held." [66] One of the most important of these " activities " has been the development of synthetic chemicals such as PCBs which, as C. I. Jackson points out,[67] were created and their use made widespread long before their effects on the environment were known. " Foreign " to the natural world and incapable of being broken down by normal ecological processes, their very existence may be " polluting " the planet.

Determining the existence of legally significant pollution primarily on the basis of assimilative criteria has received some support from publicists, particularly those concerned with the need to encourage developing countries to take a direct interest in the pollution problem. Rubin writes of the value of a clear understanding " that pollut-

[65] Myres S. McDougal and Norbert A. Schlei, " The Hydrogen Bomb Tests in Perspective: Lawful Measures for Security," in Myres S. McDougal and Associates, *Studies in World Public Order* (New Haven: Yale University Press, 1960), pp. 775–778.

[66] Barry Commoner, statement before U.S., Senate, Committee on Commerce, Subcommittee on Oceans and Atmosphere, 92nd Congress, 2nd session, Oct. 18 and Nov. 8, 1971, *International Conference on Ocean Pollution*, p. 77.

[67] C. I. Jackson, " Dimensions of International Pollution " (1971) 50 *Oregon Law Review* 242.

ing a neighbour's territory, befouling the seas, or despoiling the environment of one's own territory so as to endanger the ecology of the planet constituted a violation of an international obligation." [68] His view of the assimilation concept clearly transcends political boundaries giving international law purview over changes within a State's territory which may not result in provable "damage" to interests outside but do "endanger" the Earth's ecology. Ross refers to Canada's concern within the IJC that the United States' recent move from water quality to emission standards heralds an attempt to limit industrial expansion along the Great Lakes by setting extremely high international effluent standards which do not reflect the actual assimilative capacity of the lakes. Once developed, the United States appears unwilling to permit other countries to use the same development methods it did and the costs of "unnecessary" United States-sponsored pollution control seem prohibitive. "The very essence of assimilative capacity suggests certain rights or equitable entitlements," [69] and developing countries need to have some sort of "right" to alter the environment for development purposes. Nevertheless, while recognising the need to take the particular characteristics of each body of water into account in setting up water quality objectives for it, the IJC said in its report on Rainy River that such objectives "should not . . . tolerate the maximum quantity of domestic and industrial wastes that the stream can assimilate." Exactly what role assimilative criteria should play was left unclear.[70]

However useful this view may be to those concerned with either the very real problems faced by the environment on a global level or the requirements of developing countries, this approach is insufficient in itself as the basis of an international law concept of pollution. First, there is the problem of data. It is difficult to determine with any certainty what constitute the assimilative limits of a given environment. This is particularly true in the case of substances like PCBs whose environmental effects cannot be known immediately. Similarly, what may appear to be acceptable limits of a substance in terms of its detrimental effect on the ecological structure of a swiftly-flowing river may result in sizeable deposits in the ocean into which it empties and seriously disrupt the maritime ecology. To translate marginal changes in as vast a system as the world's environment back into useful standards of pollution on a local level is a difficult task.

On another level, there is a great deal of uncertainty as to when

[68] Rubin, *Pollution By Analogy*, p. 275.
[69] Ross, *National Sovereignty*, p. 254.
[70] International Joint Commission, "Report on the Pollution of Rainy River and the Lake of the Woods" (1965), in *The International Law of Pollution*, p. 104. See *infra*, p. 553 for further discussion of this report.

it can be said that actual damage has been done to the integrity of natural cycles. Is the process of eutropiphication taking place in some of the United States' most "polluted" lakes a "natural" process, simply responding to the introduction of human wastes, or is it a sign that the ecological systems of the area have been violated? If the latter, at what point should the law intervene? Before eutropiphication begins, at some level of "unacceptable" eutropiphication, or when the eutropiphication itself affects a wider circle and cannot be absorbed into the ecology?

Finally, one must object to the assimilative approach in that the threshold it seems to advocate offers little or no protection to aesthetic values and other interests which could be irreparably damaged by environmental changes that have no significant effect on particular ecological systems. The towering office building that dwarfs and disgraces the structures around it and the hamburger stands and souvenir shops which increasingly obscure man's view of and contact with nature may have little or no effect on the functioning of any natural cycle and yet constitute environmental alterations many would find unacceptable. At the same time, a sufficiently narrow assimilative approach might label the existence of a local garbage dump "pollution" since the wastes deposited there either could not be integrated "naturally" into the land or had a serious impact on the types of animal and plant life which the dump area could support.

CONCLUSION

This paper has presented five ways of approaching the question of what is legally significant pollution. Of the last three, none is completely independent of the others. Within the use concept there are assumed views of what constitutes "damage" just as the damage approach recognises, to some degree, that damage to another use of the environment may be pollution. Damage to particular aspects of the environment and exceeding the assimilative capacity of a given environment are clearly related. The ability of the learned Justice Holmes to represent both the use and damage approaches in different contexts is further evidence of their inter-connection. In some cases, it is a matter of emphasis. Yet no consistent view of pollution emerges from this past record. The differences between definitions are more than semantic; they reflect inconsistent views of what kinds and degrees of environmental change men should be allowed to make.

That is the key issue. Having decided upon a "pollution" threshold, different bodies have then chosen a variety of means to see that this threshold was made legally enforceable. Some prohibited any discharges of certain kinds or attempted to regulate discharges to keep their effects within acceptable limits. Others decided to permit discharges until they reached the chosen threshold and then to attach legal consequences designed either to encourage potential polluters to refrain from undesired environmental degradation or to force them, at least, to pay some kind of compensation for their harmful actions. Yet this becomes a matter of tactics: how, in a specific case, can man and his environment best be protected from the adverse effects of societal development? First, one must find a satisfactory way to determine the " pollution " threshold.

II. CONTEMPORARY DEFINITIONAL TRENDS

Given the confusion that the relatively short history of State practice and uncertain " general principles " of international law have created with regard to pollution, recent efforts of international bodies to implement a meaningful and useful pollution concept are instructive of the problems faced in arriving at a general definition for the future.

A. *Label Substitution*

The lack of precision which has become characteristic of the term " pollution " has led in many cases to the invention of new labels. The Canadian " Arctic Waters Pollution Prevention Act " and several of the IMCO conventions declare in their titles the intention of preventing pollution. Yet none defines pollution within the text. As an example, the International Convention for the Prevention of Pollution from Ships concerns itself with the discharge of " harmful substances " from ships, with " harmful substances " defined as " any substance which, if introduced into the sea, is liable to create hazards to human health, to harm living resources and marine life, to damage amenities or to interfere with other legitimate use of the sea." [71] This concept varies little from that put forth by other recent international agreements which employ an expanded view of pollution. Similarly, the Canadian legislation, by employing the term " waste " within a use approach, is still confronted with the problem of deciding when a given level of interference becomes illegal. The fact that Canadian authorities can set up relatively precise levels for determining a " waste " threshold is a function not of the added precision of the new term, but of the relative ease in reaching agreement on standards within a single national government.

Although this label substitution makes it no easier to describe with precision the *level* of environmental degradation considered illegal,

[71] International Conference on Marine Pollution: International Convention for the Prevention of Pollution from Ships, London, Nov. 2, 1973 (1973) 12 I.L.M. p. 1320.

it can be useful in narrowing the *scope* of environmental effects to be regulated. " Waste " can be more easily perceived as simply a form or subset of a larger concept called " pollution." This can also work the other way, as the Scandinavian Convention on the Protection of the Environment illustrates. There the primary concern is for " environmentally harmful activities " which include air and water pollution as particular types but set pollution, as such, apart from other problems like " sand drift," " vibration," and " ionising radiation." [72] This distinction is a useful one for clarifying what is meant by pollution.

B. *Combination of Approaches*

Another development, which is directed more at the threshold problem of what polluting activity is legally significant has been an increasing tendency for international groups to adopt definitions of pollution which embody two or more of the approaches described in the first section. At the 58th Conference of the International Law Association, " Draft Articles on Marine Pollution of Continental Origin " were presented which, coming from the body responsible for the relatively " use-oriented " Helsinki Rules, provides a good example of this development. After adopting a descriptive definition of pollution in Article I, the draft turns to the actual legal obligations of a State. Article II de-emphasises the equitable utilisation principle of the Helsinki Rules and, while making a distinction between the legal consequences of existing and future pollution, says that a State " shall prevent any form of existing sea-water pollution . . . which would cause substantial injury in the territory of another State or to any of its rights under international law or to the marine environment." [73] Inter-State injury receives a more prominent place and an obligation to the environment itself is put forth for the first time. " There is now more and more support for the philosophy according to which maritime waters need general protection, as they constitute . . . a sort of global resource, and the flora and fauna living in these massive quantities of waters must be protected in the interest of all." [74] Article III stresses the need for international standards for seawater pollution to be established and, with the help of a group of technical experts, sets up a list of " relevant factors " to be considered. This list takes into account a wide variety of monetary, recreational, conservation, and ecological interests, clearly not limited by a use con-

[72] Denmark-Finland-Norway-Sweden: Convention on the Protection of the Environment, Stockholm, Feb. 19, 1974 (1974) 13 I.L.M. 591.

[73] International Law Association, " Draft Articles on Marine Pollution of Continental Origin," *Report of the 58th Conference* (New York, 1972), Art. II, p. 100.

[74] *Ibid.*, Comment on Art. II, p. 101.

cept, and carefully refrains from assigning any relative importance to a particular factor over others.[75]

The IJC has gone through a similar period of transition as it has confronted a series of pollution questions along the United States-Canadian border. Oriented by the 1909 Treaty and subsequent U.S.-Canadian references to the IJC to view pollution as " injury of health or property " on either side of the border, the Commission has, at times, felt it appropriate to fit into this damage framework some aspects of what it considered pollution that seemed to stretch somewhat the pollution concept of the Treaty. The report on Rainy River contains two good examples. First, the actual existence of harmful conditions in the river is established solely by the use of various scientific standards, such as coliform concentration and dissolved oxygen content. While this evidence of " pollution " of the water is not said to be legally sufficient, the case appears to have been decided by applying these criteria. The evidence of actual injury to property is given little emphasis and no monetary value and, otherwise, much of the IJC's concern is for the river's unfit condition for bathing, recreation, and some forms of aquatic life.[76]

A second example is provided by the water quality objectives set up for the river. The importance of competing uses is clear as the " general objective " states that any waste discharged into the river should not " create conditions which will adversely affect the uses of these waters as a source of domestic or industrial water supply or for navigation, fish and wild life, bathing, recreation, agriculture, and other riparian activities." [77] The Commission seeks " to achieve the highest quality consistent with maximum benefit to all users." [78] Yet in the same section, which so clearly endorses a form of the use concept as a valuable index of pollution, the IJC still seems to find it advisable to view injury to the fish population of boundary waters within the terms of the Treaty. " Undue interference with the development of *desirable* types of aquatic life constitutes an *injury to property* even though it may be the property of the *public at large*." [79] One with an ecological bent might ask what type of aquatic life could be considered " undesirable," but the concept of freely swimming fish in an international waterway, fish that men may not like to eat or even catch, being claimed as property identifiable to one country or the other is particularly hard to rationalise and must be granted the status of " legal fiction " to mesh with the terms of the 1909 Treaty definition.

[75] *Ibid.*, Art. III (c), p. 102.
[76] IJC, *Report on Rainy River*, pp. 95–101.
[77] *Ibid.*, p. 105.
[78] *Ibid.*, p. 104.
[79] *Ibid.* (emphasis added).

Two important international dumping conventions, containing almost identical definitions of pollution, further illustrate the shift towards combining approaches. Article 1 of the 1972 Oslo Convention for the Prevention of Marine Pollution by Dumping from Ships and Aircraft requires all parties to prevent pollution by substances that "are liable to create hazards to human health, to harm living resources and marine life, to damage amenities or to interfere with other legitimate uses of the sea." [80] In addition to showing concern about damage to both humans and the environment and interference with other uses of the ocean, the Convention recognises "that the ecological equilibrium . . . of the sea [is] increasingly threatened by pollution." [81] The threshold problem is avoided somewhat by prohibiting any discharge of the substances considered most dangerous and requiring permits for the dumping of others. The only real difficulty here is in drawing up the lists. Yet, as is true of other "purity" oriented conventions, the Oslo Convention relies for its success on the relatively limited and controllable sources of the pollution to be prevented.

The 1972 Helsinki Convention on the Protection of the Marine Environment of the Baltic Sea, covering a larger range of problems, adopts a definition similar to that accepted at Oslo, expanding it somewhat to include the effects of the introduction of energy as well as substances. Eutropiphication also receives treatment as a type of "land-based pollution" and there is an explicit call for the development of uniform pollution control criteria. Once again, a list is drawn up of specific substances not to be introduced into the Baltic Sea area. Given the vague threshold and all-inclusive scope of pollution, as defined in Article 2, what is really meant by pollution is better discerned from the Annexes than the body of the Convention.[82]

Embracing similar concepts and yet lacking such explicit Annexes, the 1972 Stockholm Declaration on the Human Environment serves as a useful document to examine more carefully the implications of a widely-defined view of pollution. Principle 6 of the Declaration clearly accepts a role for assimilative criteria:

> The discharge of toxic substances or of other substances and the release of heat, in such quantities or concentrations as to exceed the capacity of

[80] Convention for the Prevention of Marine Pollution by Dumping from Ships and Aircraft, Oslo, Feb. 15, 1972 (1972) 11 I.L.M. 262. See also Convention on the Prevention of Marine Pollution by Dumping of Wastes and Other Matter, London, Nov. 13, 1972 (1972) 11 I.L.M. 1293.

[81] *Ibid.* "Annex I" listing the most dangerous substances specifically takes note of the ocean's assimilative capacity by excluding those types of a particular compound "which are rapidly converted in the sea into substances which are biologically harmless": p. 265.

[82] Convention on the Protection of the Marine Environment of the Baltic Sea Area, Helsinki, March 22, 1974 (1974) 13 I.L.M. 544–557.

> the environment to render them harmless, must be halted in order to ensure that serious or irreversible damage is not inflicted upon ecosystems.[83]

Principle 7 goes on, with respect to the oceans, to add damage and use concepts in a form easily recognisable in conventions adopted since the Stockholm Conference. "States shall take all possible steps to prevent pollution of the seas by substances that are liable to create hazards to human health, to harm living resources and marine life, to damage amenities or to interfere with other legitimate uses of the sea."[84] Principle 21 makes explicit the existence of a relationship between the right of each State to exploit its own natural resources and "the responsibility to ensure that activities within their jurisdiction or control do not cause damage to the environment of other States or of areas beyond the limits of national jurisdiction."[85]

The combination of approaches outlined in the first chapter is evident. Yet the way they are separated and employed in the Stockholm Declaration reveals a view of pollution that does not simply "throw together" past definitions but tries, perhaps unconsciously, to select the most appropriate approach for the various levels and types of adverse environmental changes faced by the world, within the very real limiting context of what would be acceptable to the national delegations. The assimilative perspective is employed in Principle 6 in terms of an overall commitment to the integrity of the biosphere, a commitment which transcends and penetrates national boundaries. Not intended as the basis for setting up specific pollution standards, it is, at least, a clear reminder of the need to set an upper limit to "discharges" which threaten fundamental changes in the ecological balance.

The emphasis on ocean pollution in Principle 7 reflects, as Louis Sohn points out, the strong concern of many nations for the deteriorating condition of that particular part of the biosphere.[86] The vague concept of damage to "amenities," seen in other conventions, is included and there is the clear intention to allow almost any kind of detrimental environmental change in the oceans to fall within "pollution," given a degree of seriousness that is only generally hinted at by terms like "damage," "harm," and "hazards." Principle 21, far from implying a move toward near absolute sovereignty of a State over the management of its environment (as Sohn suggests),[87] sets out one aspect of the dual nature of the State's relationship with the

83 *Stockholm Declaration on the Human Environment*, p. 4.
84 *Ibid.*, Principle 7, p. 4.
85 *Ibid.*, Principle 21, p. 7.
86 Louis Sohn, "The Stockholm Declaration on the Human Environment" (1973) 14 *Harvard International Law Journal*, 463–464.
87 *Ibid.*, p. 492.

environment within its territory. The right to manage its own resources requires a corresponding responsibility that those resources be managed in such a way as to prevent damage to the environment outside of its territory. This is not just a throwback to earlier conceptions of pollution as a question of the territorial integrity of a sovereign State, although it does include that part of the more "traditional" view of legally-significant pollution. Within the framework of the other principles, it simply states one more area of international purview over the actions of States with regard to the environment.

C. *For the Future*

If any consensus emerges from what has been described, it is one which is evolving towards the use of a wide variety of *types* of criteria for defining pollution. The use, damage and assimilation approaches are being employed together to expand the range of effects from man-induced environmental change which can be judged, on the basis of some threshold of damage or interference, to fall under a legally significant concept of "pollution." What kinds of changes may be considered "pollution" is a question of scope which is approached only rarely and indirectly, as in the Scandinavian Convention which, as noted above, sets pollution apart from sand drift and vibration.[88]

The viability of a general concept of pollution for international law eventually depends upon the degree to which one can arrive at international agreement on the organisation(s) and procedure(s) which will identify both human activities and their by-products which cause unacceptable environmental change, and the levels of environmental change considered unacceptable. Much recent practice and the reasoned opinions of many publicists point to the need for precise threshold values of what this unacceptable level is, to be determined case-by-case given basic working limits, by groups of highly trained experts in the field. As has been shown, organisations and commissions have either performed or required the services of these groups to decide what is and what is not legally significant pollution, what demands regulation and what does not.

A general concept of pollution must include a means for determining these thresholds and the Stockholm Conference took a step in this direction by recognising the related problems of identifying and setting

[88] This question is one which has received scant and indirect treatment within this paper as well. For reasons of space and coherence, as well as lack of source material, I have limited myself to the range of effects and the threshold of damage or interference as the key variables distinguishing past definitions. The "scope" approach just mentioned seems to offer little useful in isolating the basic trends of current thought about what pollution is. Whether pollution includes overfishing, for example, is a difficult question to answer from past practice and one not usually considered central to the views on what pollution is.

limits for pollutants " of broad international significance " and recommending procedures for these purposes. In the section entitled " Pollution Generally," the Conference, while relying heavily on the co-operation of governments with international organisations, called, in Recommendation 74, for the development of a capability within the United Nations system " to provide awareness and advance warning of deleterious effects to human health and well-being from man-made pollutants." [89] The same Recommendation speaks of a desire to " improve the international acceptability of procedures for testing pollutants and contaminants " [90] and suggests ways this could be done. Subsections (a) and (b) of Recommendation 85 are even more to the point:

> It is recommended that any mechanism for co-ordinating and stimulating the actions of the different United Nations organs in connexion with environmental problems include among its functions:
> (a) Development of an internationally accepted procedure for the identification of pollutants of international significance and for the definition of the degree and scope of international concern;
> (b) Consideration of the appointment of appropriate inter-governmental expert bodies to assess quantitatively the exposures, risks, pathways, and sources of pollutants of international significance.[91]

This, of course, is just a beginning and it will be some time before one will be able to tell at least to what degree an international harmonisation of pollution standards is possible. Given different national and individual conceptions of how best to manage the environment and the various criteria which are still used to define " pollution," there is room for scepticism. More work needs to be done in defining clearly the types of criteria on which the experts should base their studies. General principles must be formed into tight policy guidelines which look ahead to both the problems to be faced and the economic and social goals sought. Once these standards, the " pollution limits," are established, then the negotiations must begin to attach the legal consequences to their infraction. That is a separate process. A general and meaningful concept of pollution will be established when the experts, working within the conceptual framework provided by the international community, are able to draw particular thresholds of legally-significant change that are accepted for those negotiations.

[89] *Stockholm Declaration on the Human Environment*, Recommendation 74, pp. 40–41.
[90] *Ibid.*
[91] *Ibid.*, p. 84.

[4]

SHOULD TREES HAVE STANDING?—TOWARD LEGAL RIGHTS FOR NATURAL OBJECTS

CHRISTOPHER D. STONE*

INTRODUCTION: THE UNTHINKABLE

In *Descent of Man*, Darwin observes that the history of man's moral development has been a continual extension in the objects of his "social instincts and sympathies." Originally each man had regard only for himself and those of a very narrow circle about him; later, he came to regard more and more "not only the welfare, but the happiness of all his fellowmen"; then "his sympathies became more tender and widely diffused, extending to men of all races, to the imbecile, maimed, and other useless members of society, and finally to the lower animals. . . ."[1]

The history of the law suggests a parallel development. Perhaps there never was a pure Hobbesian state of nature, in which no "rights" existed except in the vacant sense of each man's "right to self-defense." But it is not unlikely that so far as the earliest "families" (including extended kinship groups and clans) were concerned, everyone outside the family was suspect, alien, rightless.[2] And even within the family, persons we presently regard as the natural holders of at least some rights had none. Take, for example, children. We know something of the early rights-status of children from the widespread practice of infanticide—

---

* Professor of Law, University of Southern California. A.B. 1959, Harvard; LL.B. 1962, Yale. Chairman, Committee on Law and the Humanities, Association of American Law Schools. The author wishes to express his appreciation for the financial support of the National Endowment for the Humanities.

1. C. DARWIN, DESCENT OF MAN 119, 120-21 (2d ed. 1874). *See also* R. WAELDER, PROGRESS AND REVOLUTION 39 *et seq.* (1967).

2. *See* DARWIN, *supra* note 1, at 113-14:

> . . . No tribe could hold together if murder, robbery, treachery, etc., were common; consequently such crimes within the limits of the same tribe "are branded with everlasting infamy"; but excite no such sentiment beyond these limits. A North-American Indian is well pleased with himself, and is honored by others, when he scalps a man of another tribe; and a Dyak cuts off the head of an unoffending person, and dries it as a trophy . . . It has been recorded that an Indian Thug conscientiously regretted that he had not robbed and strangled as many travelers as did his father before him. In a rude state of civilization the robbery of strangers is, indeed, generally considered as honorable.

See also Service, *Forms of Kinship* in MAN IN ADAPTATION 112 (Y. Cohen ed. 1968).

especially of the deformed and female.[3] (Senicide,[4] as among the North American Indians, was the corresponding rightlessness of the aged).[5] Maine tells us that as late as the Patria Potestas of the Romans, the father had *jus vitae necisque*—the power of life and death—over his children. A fortiori, Maine writes, he had power of "uncontrolled corporal chastisement; he can modify their personal condition at pleasure; he can give a wife to his son; he can give his daughter in marriage; he can divorce his children of either sex; he can transfer them to another family by adoption; and he can sell them." The child was less than a person: an object, a thing.[6]

The legal rights of children have long since been recognized in principle, and are still expanding in practice. Witness, just within recent time, *In re Gault*,[7] guaranteeing basic constitutional protections to juvenile defendants, and the Voting Rights Act of 1970.[8] We have been making persons of children although they were not, in law, always so. And we have done the same, albeit imperfectly some would say, with prisoners,[9] aliens, women (especially of the married variety), the insane,[10] Blacks, foetuses,[11] and Indians.

3. *See* DARWIN, *supra* note 1, at 113. *See also* E. WESTERMARCK, 1 THE ORIGIN AND DEVELOPMENT OF THE MORAL IDEAS 406-12 (1912).

The practice of allowing sickly children to die has not been entirely abandoned, apparently, even at our most distinguished hospitals. *See Hospital Let Retarded Baby Die, Film Shows*, L. A. Times, Oct. 17, 1971, § A, at 9, col. 1.

4. There does not appear to be a word "gericide" or "geronticide" to designate the killing of the aged. "Senicide" is as close as the Oxford English Dictionary comes, although, as it indicates, the word is rare. 9 OXFORD ENGLISH DICTIONARY 454 (1933).

5. *See* DARWIN, *supra* note 1, at 386-93. WESTERMARCK, *supra* note 3, at 387-89, observes that where the killing of the aged and infirm is practiced, it is often supported by humanitarian justification; this, however, is a far cry from saying that the killing is *requested* by the victim as his right.

6. H. MAINE, ANCIENT LAW 153 (Pollock ed. 1930). Maine claimed that these powers of the father extended to all regions of private law, although not to the Jus Publicum, under which a son, notwithstanding his subjection in private life, might vote alongside his father. *Id.* at 152. WESTERMARCK, *supra* note 3, at 393-94, was skeptical that the arbitrary power of the father over the children extended as late as into early Roman law.

7. 387 U.S. 1 (1967).

8. 42 U.S.C. §§ 1973 *et seq.* (1970).

9. *See* Landman v. Royster, 40 U.S.L.W. 2256 (E.D. Va., Oct. 30, 1971) (eighth amendment and due process clause of the fourteenth amendment require federal injunctive relief, including compelling the drafting of new prison rules, for Virginia prisoners against prison conduct prohibited by vague rules or no rules, without disciplinary proceedings embodying rudiments of procedural due process, and by various penalties that constitute cruel and unusual punishment). *See* Note, *Courts, Corrections and the Eighth Amendment: Encouraging Prison Reform by Releasing Inmates*, 44 S. CAL. L. REV. 1060 (1971).

Nor is it only matter in human form that has come to be recognized as the possessor of rights. The world of the lawyer is peopled with inanimate right-holders: trusts, corporations, joint ventures, municipalities, Subchapter R partnerships,[12] and nation-states, to mention just a few. Ships, still referred to by courts in the feminine gender, have long had an independent jural life, often with striking consequences.[13] We have become so accustomed to the idea of a corporation having "its" own rights, and being a "person" and "citizen" for so many statutory and constitutional purposes, that we forget how jarring the notion was to early jurists. "That invisible, intangible and artificial being, that mere legal entity" Chief Justice Marshall wrote of the corporation in *Bank of*

10. *But see* T. SZASZ, LAW, LIBERTY AND PSYCHIATRY (1963).

11. *See* notes 22, 52 and accompanying text *infra*. The trend toward liberalized abortion can be seen either as a legislative tendency back in the direction of rightlessness for the foetus—or toward increasing rights of women. This inconsistency is not unique in the law of course; it is simply support for Hohfeld's scheme that the "jural opposite" of someone's right is someone else's "no-right." W. HOHFELD, FUNDAMENTAL LEGAL CONCEPTIONS (1923).

Consider in this regard a New York case in which a settlor *S* established a trust on behalf of a number of named beneficiaries and "lives in being." Desiring to amend the deed of trust, the grantor took steps pursuant to statute to obtain "the written consent of all persons beneficially interested in [the] trust." At the time the grantor was pregnant and the trustee Chase Bank advised it would not recognize the proposed amendment because the child *en ventre sa mere* might be deemed a person beneficially interested in the trust. The court allowed the amendment to stand, holding that birth rather than conception is the controlling factor in ascertaining whether a person is beneficially interested in the trust which the grantor seeks to amend. *In re* Peabody, 5 N.Y.2d 541, 158 N.E.2d 841 (1959).

The California Supreme Court has recently refused to allow the deliberate killing of a foetus (in a non-abortion situation) to support a murder prosecution. The court ruled foetuses not to be denoted by the words "human being" within the statute defining murder. Keeler v. Superior Court, 2 Cal. 3d 619, 87 Cal. Rptr. 481, 470 P.2d 617 (1970). But see note 52 and accompanying text *infra*.

Some jurisdictions have statutes defining a crime of "feticide"—deliberately causing the death of an unborn child. The absence of such a specific feticide provision in the California case was one basis for the ruling in *Keeler*. *See* 2 Cal. 3d at 633 n.16, 87 Cal. Rptr. at 489 n.16, 470 P.2d at 625 n.16.

12. INT. REV. CODE of 1954, § 1361 (repealed by Pub. L. No. 89-389, effective Jan. 1, 1969).

13. For example, *see* United States v. Cargo of the Brig Malek Adhel, 43 U.S. (2 How.) 210 (1844). There, a ship had been seized and used by pirates. All this was done without the knowledge or consent of the owners of the ship. After the ship had been captured, the United States condemned and sold the "offending vessel." The owners objected. In denying release to the owners, Justice Story cited Chief Justice Marshall from an earlier case: "This is not a proceeding against the owner; it is a proceeding against the vessel for an offense committed by the vessel; which is not the less an offense . . . because it was committed without the authority and against the will of the owner." 43 U.S. at 234, quoting from United States v. Schooner Little Charles, 26 F. Cas. 979 (No. 15,612) (C.C.D. Va. 1818).

the United States v. Deveaux[14]—could a suit be brought in *its* name? Ten years later, in the *Dartmouth College* case,[15] he was still refusing to let pass unnoticed the wonder of an entity "existing only in contemplation of law."[16] Yet, long before Marshall worried over the personifying of the modern corporation, the best medieval legal scholars had spent hundreds of years struggling with the notion of the legal nature of those great public "corporate bodies," the Church and the State. How could they exist in law, as entities transcending the living Pope and King? It was clear how a king could bind *himself*—on his honor—by a treaty. But when the king died, what was it that was burdened with the obligations of, and claimed the rights under, the treaty *his* tangible hand had signed? The medieval mind saw (what we have lost our capacity to see)[17] how *unthinkable* it was, and worked out the most elaborate conceits and fallacies to serve as anthropomorphic flesh for the Universal Church and the Universal Empire.[18]

It is this note of the *unthinkable* that I want to dwell upon for a moment. Throughout legal history, each successive extension of rights to some new entity has been, theretofore, a bit unthinkable. We are inclined to suppose the rightlessness of rightless "things" to be a decree of Nature, not a legal convention acting in support of some status quo. It is thus that we defer considering the choices involved in all their moral, social, and economic dimensions. And so the United States Supreme Court could straight-facedly tell us in *Dred Scott* that Blacks had been denied the rights of citizenship "as a subordinate and inferior class of beings, who had been subjugated by the dominant race. . . ."[19]

14. 9 U.S. (5 Cranch) 61, 86 (1809).

15. Trustees of Darmouth College v. Woodward, 17 U.S. (4 Wheat.) 518 (1819).

16. *Id.* at 636.

17. Consider, for example, that the claim of the United States to the naval station at Guantanamo Bay, at $2000-a-year rental, is based upon a treaty signed in 1903 by José Montes for the President of Cuba and a minister representing Theodore Roosevelt; it was subsequently ratified by two-thirds of a Senate no member of which is living today. Lease [from Cuba] of Certain Areas for Naval or Coaling Stations, July 2, 1903, T.S. No. 426; C. Bevans, 6 Treaties and Other International Agreements of the United States 1776-1949, at 1120 (U.S. Dep't of State Pub. 8549, 1971).

18. O. Gierke, Political Theories of the Middle Age (Maitland transl. 1927), especially at 22-30. The reader may be tempted to suggest that the "corporate" examples in the text are distinguishable from environmental objects in that the former are comprised by and serve humans. On the contrary, I think that the more we learn about the sociology of the firm—and the realpolitik of our society—the more we discover the ultimate reality of these institutions, and the increasingly legal fictiveness of the individual human being. *See* note 125 and accompanying text *infra*.

19. Dred Scott v. Sandford, 60 U.S. (19 How.) 396, 404-05 (1856). In Bailey v. Poindexter's Ex'r, 56 Va. (14 Gratt.) 132, 142-43 (1858) a provision in a will that testator's

In the nineteenth century, the highest court in California explained that Chinese had not the right to testify against white men in criminal matters because they were "a race of people whom nature has marked as inferior, and who are incapable of progress or intellectual development beyond a certain point . . . between whom and ourselves nature has placed an impassable difference.[20] The popular conception of the Jew in the 13th Century contributed to a law which treated them as "men *ferae naturae*, protected by a quasi-forest law. Like the roe and the deer, they form an order apart."[21] Recall, too, that it was not so long ago that the foetus was "like the roe and the deer." In an early suit attempting to establish a wrongful death action on behalf of a negligently killed foetus (now widely accepted practice), Holmes, then on the Massachusetts Supreme Court, seems to have thought it simply inconceivable "that a man might owe a civil duty and incur a conditional prospective liability in tort to one not yet in being."[22] The first woman in Wisconsin who thought she might have a right to practice law was told that she did not, in the following terms:

> The law of nature destines and qualifies the female sex for the bearing and nurture of the children of our race and for the custody of the homes of the world . . . . [A]ll life-long callings of women, inconsistent with these radical and sacred duties of their sex, as is the profession of the law, are departures from the order of nature; and when voluntary, treason against it . . . . The

---

slaves could choose between emancipation and public sale was held void on the ground that slaves have no legal capacity to choose:

> These decisions are legal conclusions flowing naturally and necessarily from the one clear, simple, fundamental idea of chattel slavery. That fundamental idea is, that, in the eye of the law, so far certainly as civil rights and relations are concerned, the slave is not a person, but a thing. The investiture of a chattel with civil rights or legal capacity is indeed a legal solecism and absurdity. The attribution of legal personality to a chattel slave,—legal conscience, legal intellect, legal freedom, or liberty and power of free choice and action, and corresponding legal obligations growing out of such qualities, faculties and action—implies a palpable contradiction in terms.

20. People v. Hall, 4 Cal. 399, 405 (1854). The statute there under interpretation provided that "no Black or Mulatto person, or Indian shall be allowed to give evidence in favor of, or against a white man," but was silent as to Chinese. The "policy" analysis by which the court brings Chinese under "Black . . . or Indian" is a fascinating illustration of the relationship between a "policy" decision and a "just" decision, especially in light of the exchange betwen Hart, *Positivism and the Separation of Law and Morals*, 71 HARV. L. REV. 593 (1958) and Fuller, *Positivism and Fidelity to Law—A Reply to Professor Hart*, *id.* at 630.

21. Schechter, *The Rightlessness of Mediaeval English Jewry*, 45 JEWISH Q. REV. 121, 135 (1954) quoting from M. BATESON, MEDIEVAL ENGLAND 139 (1904). Schechter also quotes Henry de Bracton to the effect that "a Jew cannot have anything of his own, because whatever he acquires he acquires not for himself but for the king. . . ." *Id.* at 128.

22. Dietrich v. Inhabitants of Northampton, 138 Mass. 14, 16 (1884).

peculiar qualities of womanhood, its gentle graces, its quick sensibility, its tender susceptibility, its purity, its delicacy, its emotional impulses, its subordination of hard reason to sympathetic feeling, are surely not qualifications for forensic strife. Nature has tempered woman as little for the juridical conflicts of the court room, as for the physical conflicts of the battle field . . . .[23]

The fact is, that each time there is a movement to confer rights onto some new "entity," the proposal is bound to sound odd or frightening or laughable.[23a] This is partly because until the rightless thing receives its rights, we cannot see it as anything but a *thing* for the use of "us"—those who are holding rights at the time.[24] In this vein, what is striking about the Wisconsin case above is that the court, for all its talk about women, so clearly was never able to see women as they are

23. *In re* Goddell, 39 Wisc. 232, 245 (1875). The court continued with the following "clincher":

> And when counsel was arguing for this lady that the word, person, in sec. 32, ch. 119 [respecting those qualified to practice law], necessarily includes females, her presence made it impossible to suggest to him as *reductio ad absurdum* of his position, that the same construction of the same word . . . would subject woman to prosecution for the paternity of a bastard, and . . . prosecution for rape.

Id. at 246.

The relationship between our attitudes toward woman, on the one hand, and, on the other, the more central concern of this article—land—is captured in an unguarded aside of our colleague, Curt Berger: ". . . after all, land, like woman, was meant to be possessed. . . ." LAND OWNERSHIP AND USE 139 (1968).

23a. Recently, a group of prison inmates in Suffolk County tamed a mouse that they discovered, giving him the name Morris. Discovering Morris, a jailer flushed him down the toilet. The prisoners brought a proceeding against the Warden complaining, *inter alia*, that Morris was subjected to discriminatory discharge and was otherwise unequally treated. The action was unsuccessful, on grounds that the inmates themselves were "guilty of imprisoning Morris without a charge, without a trial, and without bail," and that other mice at the prison were not treated more favorably. "As to the true victim the Court can only offer again the sympathy first proffered to his ancestors by Robert Burns. . . ." The Judge proceeded to quote from Burns' "To a Mouse." Morabito v. Cyrta, 9 CRIM. L. REP. 2472 (N.Y. Sup. Ct. Suffolk Co. Aug. 26, 1971).

The whole matter seems humorous, of course. But what we need to know more of is the function of humor in the unfolding of a culture, and the ways in which it is involved with the social growing pains to which it is testimony. Why do people make jokes about the Women's Liberation Movement? Is it not on account of—rather than in spite of—the underlying validity of the protests, and the uneasy awareness that a recognition of them is inevitable? A. Koestler rightly begins his study of the human mind, ACT OF CREATION (1964), with an analysis of humor, entitled "The Logic of Laughter." And *cf.* Freud, *Jokes and the Unconscious*, 8 STANDARD EDITION OF THE COMPLETE PSYCHOLOGICAL WORKS OF SIGMUND FREUD (J. Strachey transl. 1905). (Query too: what is the relationship between the conferring of proper *names*, *e.g.*, Morris, and the conferring of social and legal *rights*?)

24. Thus it was that the Founding Fathers could speak of the inalienable rights of all men, and yet maintain a society that was, by modern standards, without the most basic rights for Blacks, Indians, children and women. There was no hypocrisy; emotionally, no one *felt* that these other things were men.

(and might become). All it could see was the popular "idealized" version of *an object it needed*. Such is the way the slave South looked upon the Black.[25] There is something of a seamless web involved: there will be resistance to giving the thing "rights" until it can be seen and valued for itself; yet, it is hard to see it and value it for itself until we can bring ourselves to give it "rights"—which is almost inevitably going to sound inconceivable to a large group of people.

The reason for this little discourse on the unthinkable, the reader must know by now, if only from the title of the paper. I am quite seriously proposing that we give legal rights to forests, oceans, rivers and other so-called "natural objects" in the environment—indeed, to the natural environment as a whole.[26]

---

25. The second thought streaming from . . . the older South [is] the sincere and passionate belief that somewhere between men and cattle, God created a *tertium quid*, and called it a Negro—a clownish, simple creature, at times even lovable within its limitations, but straitly foreordained to walk within the Veil.

W. E. B. DuBois, The Souls of Black Folk 89 (1924).

26. In this article I essentially limit myself to a discussion of non-animal but natural objects. I trust that the reader will be able to discern where the analysis is appropriate to advancing our understanding of what would be involved in giving "rights" to other objects not presently endowed with rights—for example, not only animals (some of which already have rights in some senses) but also humanoids, computers, and so forth. *Cf.* the National Register for Historic Places, 16 U.S.C. § 470 (1970), discussed in Ely v. Velde, 321 F. Supp. 1088 (E.D. Va. 1971).

As the reader will discover, there are large problems involved in defining the boundaries of the "natural object." For example, from time to time one will wish to speak of that portion of a river that runs through a recognized jurisdiction; at other times, one may be concerned with the entire river, or the hydrologic cycle—or the whole of nature. One's ontological choices will have a strong influence on the shape of the legal system, and the choices involved are not easy. *See* notes 49, 73 and accompanying text *infra*.

On the other hand, the problems of selecting an appropriate ontology are problems of all language—not merely of the language of legal concepts, but of ordinary language as well. Consider, for example, the concept of a "person" in legal *or* in everyday speech. Is each *person* a fixed bundle of relationships, persisting unaltered through time? Do our molecules and cells not change at every moment? Our hypostatizations always have a pragmatic quality to them. *See* D. Hume, *Of Personal Identity*, in Treatise of Human Nature bk. 1, pt. IV, § VI, in The Philosophical Works of David Hume 310-18, 324 (1854); T. Murti, The Central Philosophy of Buddhism 70-73 (1955). In Loves Body 146-47 (1966) Norman O. Brown observes:

> The existence of the "let's pretend" boundary does not prevent the continuance of the real traffic across it. Projection and introjection, the process whereby the self as distinct from the other is constituted, is not past history, an event in childhood, but a present process of continuous creation. The dualism of self and external world is built up by a constant process of reciprocal exchange between the two. The self as a stable substance enduring through time, an identity, is maintained by constantly absorbing good parts (or people) from the outside world and expelling bad parts from the inner world. "There is a continual 'unconscious' wandering of other personalities into ourselves."
>
> Every person, then, is many persons; a multitude made into one person; a corporate body; incorporated, a corporation. A "corporation sole"; every man

As strange as such a notion may sound, it is neither fanciful nor devoid of operational content. In fact, I do not think it would be a misdescription of recent developments in the law to say that we are already on the verge of assigning some such rights, although we have not faced up to what we are doing in those particular terms.[27] We should do so now, and begin to explore the implications such a notion would hold.

Toward Rights for the Environment

Now, to say that the natural environment should have rights is not to say anything as silly as that no one should be allowed to cut down a tree. We say human beings have rights, but—at least as of the time of this writing—they can be executed.[28] Corporations have rights, but they cannot plead the fifth amendment;[29] *In re Gault* gave 15-year-olds certain rights in juvenile proceedings, but it did not give them the right to vote. Thus, to say that the environment should have rights is not to say that it should have every right we can imagine, or even the same body of rights as human beings have. Nor is it to say that everything in the

a parson-person. The unity of the person is as real, or unreal, as the unity of the corporation.

See generally, W. Bishin & C. Stone, Law, Language and Ethics Ch. 5 (1972).

In different legal systems at different times, there have been many shifts in the entity deemed "responsible" for harmful acts: an entire clan was held responsible for a crime before the notion of individual responsibility emerged; in some societies the offending hand, rather than an entire body, may be "responsible." Even today, we treat father and son as separate jural entities for some purposes, but as a single jural entity for others. I do not see why, in principle, the task of working out a legal ontology of natural objects (and "qualities," *e.g.*, climatic warmth) should be any more unmanageable. Perhaps someday all mankind shall be, for some purposes, one jurally recognized "natural object."

27. The statement in text is not quite true; *cf.* Murphy, *Has Nature Any Right to Life?*, 22 Hast. L.J. 467 (1971). An Irish court, passing upon the validity of a testamentary trust to the benefit of someone's dogs, observed in dictum that "'lives' means lives of human beings, not of animals or trees in California." Kelly v. Dillon, 1932 Ir. R. 255, 261. (The intended gift over on the death of the last surviving dog was held void for remoteness, the court refusing "to enter into the question of a dog's expectation of life," although prepared to observe that "in point of fact neighbor's [sic] dogs and cats are unpleasantly long-lived. . . ." *Id.* at 260-61).

28. Four cases dealing with the Constitutionality of the death penalty under the eighth and fourteenth amendments are pending before the United States Supreme Court. Branch v. Texas, 447 S.W.2d 932 (Tex. 1969), *cert. granted*, 91 S. Ct. 2287 (1970); Aikens v. California, 70 Cal. 2d 369, 74 Cal. Rptr. 882, 450 P.2d 258 (1969), *cert. granted*, 91 S. Ct. 2280 (1970); Furman v. Georgia, 225 Ga. 253, 167 S.E.2d 628 (1969), *cert. granted*, 91 S. Ct. 2282 (1970); Jackson v. Georgia, 225 Ga. 790, 171 S.E.2d 501 (1969), *cert. granted*, 91 S. Ct. 2287 (1970).

29. *See* George Campbell Painting Corp. v. Reid, 392 U.S. 286 (1968); Oklahoma Press Pub. Co. v. Walling, 327 U.S. 186 (1946); Baltimore & O.R.R. v. ICC, 221 U.S. 612 (1911); Wilson v. United States, 221 U.S. 361 (1911); Hale v. Henkel, 201 U.S. 43 (1906).

environment should have the same rights as every other thing in the environment.

What the granting of rights does involve has two sides to it. The first involves what might be called the legal-operational aspects; the second, the psychic and socio-psychic aspects. I shall deal with these aspects in turn.

The Legal-Operational Aspects

What it Means to be a Holder of Legal Rights

There is, so far as I know, no generally accepted standard for how one ought to use the term "legal rights." Let me indicate how I shall be using it in this piece.

First and most obviously, if the term is to have any content at all, an entity cannot be said to hold a legal right unless and until *some public authoritative body* is prepared to give *some amount of review* to actions that are colorably inconsistent with that "right." For example, if a student can be expelled from a university and cannot get any public official, even a judge or administrative agent at the lowest level, either (i) to require the university to justify its actions (if only to the extent of filling out an affidavit alleging that the expulsion "was not wholly arbitrary and capricious") or (ii) to compel the university to accord the student some procedural safeguards (a hearing, right to counsel, right to have notice of charges), then the minimum requirements for saying that the student has a legal right to his education do not exist.[30]

But for a thing to be *a holder of legal rights*, something more is needed than that some authoritative body will review the actions and processes of those who threaten it. As I shall use the term, "holder of legal rights," each of three additional criteria must be satisfied. All three, one will observe, go towards making a thing *count* jurally—to have a legally recognized worth and dignity in its own right, and not merely to serve as a means to benefit "us" (whoever the contemporary group of rights-holders may be). They are, first, that the thing can institute legal actions *at its behest*; second, that in determining the granting of legal relief, the court must take *injury to it* into account; and, third, that relief must run to the *benefit of it*.

To illustrate, even as between two societies that condone slavery

30. *See* Dixon v. Alabama State Bd. of Educ., 294 F.2d 150 (5th Cir.), *cert. denied*, 368 U.S. 930 (1961).

there is a fundamental difference between S_1, in which a master can (if he chooses), go to court and collect reduced chattel value damages from someone who has beaten his slave, and S_2, in which the slave can institute the proceedings *himself*, for *his* own recovery, damages being measured by, say, *his* pain and suffering. Notice that neither society is so structured as to leave wholly unprotected the slave's interests in not being beaten. But in S_2 as opposed to S_1 there are three operationally significant advantages that the slave has, and these make the slave in S_2, albeit a slave, a holder of rights. Or, again, compare two societies, S_1, in which pre-natal injury to a live-born child gives a right of action against the tortfeasor at the mother's instance, for the mother's benefit, on the basis of the mother's mental anguish, and S_2, which gives the child a suit in its own name (through a guardian *ad litem*) for its own recovery, for damages to it.

When I say, then, that at common law "natural objects" are not holders of legal rights, I am not simply remarking what we would all accept as obvious. I mean to emphasize three specific legal-operational advantages that the environment lacks, leaving it in the position of the slave and the foetus in S_1, rather than the slave and foetus of S_2.

The Rightlessness of Natural Objects at Common Law

Consider, for example, the common law's posture toward the pollution of a stream. True, courts have always been able, in some circumstances, to issue orders that will stop the pollution—just as the legal system in S_1 is so structured as incidentally to discourage beating slaves and being reckless around pregnant women. But the stream itself is fundamentally rightless, with implications that deserve careful reconsideration.

The first sense in which the stream is not a rights-holder has to do with standing. The stream itself has none. So far as the common law is concerned, there is in general no way to challenge the polluter's actions save at the behest of a lower riparian—another human being—able to show an invasion of *his* rights. This conception of the riparian as the holder of the right to bring suit has more than theoretical interest. The lower riparians may simply not care about the pollution. They themselves may be polluting, and not wish to stir up legal waters. They may be economically dependent on their polluting neighbor.[31] And, of

31. For example, *see* People *ex rel.* Ricks Water Co. v. Elk River Mill & Lumber Co., 107 Cal. 221, 40 Pac. 531 (1895) (refusing to enjoin pollution by a upper riparian at the instance of the Attorney General on the grounds that the lower riparian owners, most of whom were dependent on the lumbering business of the polluting mill, did not complain).

course, when they discount the value of winning by the costs of bringing suit and the chances of success, the action may not seem worth undertaking. Consider, for example, that while the polluter might be injuring 100 downstream riparians $10,000 a year *in the aggregate*, each riparian separately might be suffering injury only to the extent of $100—possibly not enough for any one of them to want to press suit by himself, or even to go to the trouble and cost of securing co-plaintiffs to make it worth everyone's while. This hesitance will be especially likely when the potential plaintiffs consider the burdens the law puts in their way:[32] proving, *e.g.*, specific damages, the "unreasonableness" of defendant's use of the water, the fact that practicable means of abatement exist, and overcoming difficulties raised by issues such as joint causality, right to pollute by prescription, and so forth. Even in states which, like California, sought to overcome these difficulties by empowering the attorney-general to sue for abatement of pollution in limited instances, the power has been sparingly invoked and, when invoked, narrowly construed by the courts.[33]

The second sense in which the common law denies "rights" to natural objects has to do with the way in which the merits are decided in those cases in which someone is competent and willing to establish standing. At its more primitive levels, the system protected the "rights" of the property owning human with minimal weighing of any values: *"Cujus est solum, ejus est usque ad coelum et ad infernos."*[34] Today we have come more and more to make balances—but only such as will adjust the economic best interests of identifiable humans. For example, continuing with the case of streams, there are commentators who speak of a "general rule" that "a riparian owner is legally entitled to have the stream flow by his land with its quality unimpaired" and observe that "an upper owner has, prima facie, no right to pollute the water."[35]

32. The law in a suit for injunctive relief is commonly easier on the plaintiff than in a suit for damages. *See* J. GOULD, LAW OF WATERS § 206 (1883).

33. However, in 1970 California amended its Water Quality Act to make it easier for the Attorney General to obtain relief, *e.g.*, one must no longer allege irreparable injury in a suit for an injunction. CAL. WATER CODE § 13350(b) (West 1971).

34. To whomsoever the soil belongs, he owns also to the sky and to the depths. *See* W. BLACKSTONE, 2 COMMENTARIES *18.

At early common law, the owner of land could use all that was found under his land "at his free will and pleasure" without regard to any "inconvenience to his neighbour." Acton v. Blundell, 12 Meeson & Welsburg 324, 354, 152 Eng. Rep. 1223, 1235 (1843). "He [the landowner] may waste or despoil the land as he pleases. . . ." R. MEGARRY & H. WADE, THE LAW OF REAL PROPERTY 70 (3d ed. 1966). *See* R. POWELL, 5 THE LAW OF REAL PROPERTY ¶725 (1971).

35. *See* Note, *Statutory Treatment of Industrial Stream Pollution*, 24 GEO. WASH.

Such a doctrine, if strictly invoked, would protect the stream absolutely whenever a suit was brought; but obviously, to look around us, the law does not work that way. Almost everywhere there are doctrinal qualifications on riparian "rights" to an unpolluted stream.[36] Although these rules vary from jurisdiction to jurisdiction, and upon whether one is suing for an equitable injunction or for damages, what they all have in common is some sort of balancing. Whether under language of "reasonable use," "reasonable methods of use," "balance of convenience" or "the public interest doctrine,"[37] what the courts are balancing, with varying degrees of directness, are the economic hardships on the upper riparian (or dependent community) of abating the pollution vis-à-vis the economic hardships of continued pollution on the lower riparians. What does not weigh in the balance is the damage to the stream, its fish and turtles and "lower" life. So long as the natural environment itself is rightless, these are not matters for judicial cognizance. Thus, we find the highest court of Pennsylvania refusing to stop a coal company from discharging polluted mine water into a tributary of the Lackawana River because a plaintiff's "grievance is for a mere personal inconvenience; and . . . mere private personal inconveniences . . . must yield to the necessities of a great public industry, which although in the hands of a private corporation, subserves a great public interest."[38] The stream itself is lost sight of in "a quantitative compromise between *two* conflicting interests."[39]

The third way in which the common law makes natural objects rightless has to do with who is regarded as the beneficiary of a favorable judgment. Here, too, it makes a considerable difference that it is not

L. REV. 302, 306 (1955); H. FARNHAM, 2 LAW OF WATERS AND WATER RIGHTS § 461 (1904); GOULD, *supra* note 32, at § 204.

36. For example, courts have upheld a right to pollute by prescription, Mississippi Mills Co. v. Smith, 69 Miss. 299, 11 So. 26 (1882), and by easement, Luama v. Bunker Hill & Sullivan Mining & Concentrating Co., 41 F.2d 358 (9th Cir. 1930).

37. *See* Red River Roller Mills v. Wright, 30 Minn. 249, 15 N.W. 167 (1883) (enjoyment of stream by riparian may be modified or abrogated by reasonable use of stream by others); Townsend v. Bell, 167 N.Y. 462, 60 N.E. 757 (1901) (riparian owner not entitled to maintain action for pollution of stream by factory where he could not show use of water was unreasonable); Smith v. Staso Milling Co., 18 F.2d 736 (2d Cir. 1927) (in suit for injunction, right on which injured lower riparian stands is a quantitative compromise between two conflicting interests); Clifton Iron Co. v. Dye, 87 Ala. 468, 6 So. 192 (1889) (in determining whether to grant injunction to lower riparian, court must weigh interest of public as against injury to one or the other party). *See also* Montgomery Limestone Co. v. Bearder, 256 Ala. 269, 54 So. 2d 571 (1951).

38. Pennsylvania Coal Co. v. Sanderson, 113 Pa. 126, 149, 6 A. 453, 459 (1886).

39. Hand, J. in Smith v. Staso Milling Co., 18 F.2d 736, 738 (2d Cir. 1927) (emphasis added). *See also* Harrisonville v. Dickey Clay Co., 289 U.S. 334 (1933) (Brandeis, J.).

the natural object that counts in its own right. To illustrate this point, let me begin by observing that it makes perfectly good sense to speak of, and ascertain, the legal damage to a natural object, if only in the sense of "making it whole" with respect to the most obvious factors.[40] The costs of making a forest whole, for example, would include the costs of reseeding, repairing watersheds, restocking wildlife—the sorts of costs the Forest Service undergoes after a fire. Making a polluted stream whole would include the costs of restocking with fish, water-fowl, and other animal and vegetable life, dredging, washing out impurities, establishing natural and/or artificial aerating agents, and so forth. Now, what is important to note is that, under our present system, even if a plaintiff riparian wins a water pollution suit for damages, no money goes to the benefit of the stream itself to repair *its* damages.[41] This omission has the further effect that, at most, the law confronts a polluter with what it takes to make the plaintiff riparians whole; this may be far less than the damages to the stream,[42] but not so much as to force the polluter to desist. For example, it is easy to imagine a polluter whose activities damage a stream to the extent of $10,000 annually, although the aggregate damage to all the riparian plaintiffs who come into the suit is only $3000. If $3000 is less than the cost to the polluter of shutting down, or making the requisite technological changes, he might prefer to pay off the damages (*i.e.*, the legally cognizable damages) and continue to pollute the stream. Similarly, even if the jurisdiction issues an injunction at the plaintiffs' behest (rather than to order payment of damages), there is nothing to stop the plaintiffs from "selling out" the stream, *i.e.*, agreeing to dissolve or not enforce the injunction at some price (in the example above, somewhere between plaintiffs' damages—$3000—and defendant's next best economic alternative). Indeed, I take it this is exactly what Learned Hand had in mind in an opinion in which, after issuing an anti-pollution injunction, he suggests that the defendant

---

40. Measuring plantiff's damages by "making him whole" has several limitations; these and the matter of measuring damages in this area generally are discussed more fully at notes 83-93 and accompanying text *infra*.

41. Here, again, an analogy to corporation law might be profitable. Suppose that in the instance of negligent corporate management by the directors, there were no institution of the stockholder derivative suit to force the directors to make *the corporation* whole, and the only actions provided for were direct actions by stockholders to collect for damages *to themselves qua* stockholders. Theoretically and practically, the damages might come out differently in the two cases, and not merely because the creditors' losses are not aggregated in the stockholders' direct actions.

42. And even far less than the damages to all human economic interests derivately through the stream; *see* text accompanying notes 83-84, 120 *infra*.

"make its peace with the plaintiff as best it can."[43] What is meant is a peace between *them*, and not amongst them and the river.

I ought to make clear at this point that the common law as it affects streams and rivers, which I have been using as an example so far, is not exactly the same as the law affecting other environmental objects. Indeed, one would be hard pressed to say that there was a "typical" environmental object, so far as its treatment at the hands of the law is concerned. There are some differences in the law applicable to all the various resources that are held in common: rivers, lakes, oceans, dunes, air, streams (surface and subterranean), beaches, and so forth.[44] And there is an even greater difference as between these traditional communal resources on the one hand, and natural objects on traditionally private land, *e.g.*, the pond on the farmer's field, or the stand of trees on the suburbanite's lawn.

On the other hand, although there be these differences which would make it fatuous to generalize about a law of the natural environment, most of these differences simply underscore the points made in the instance of rivers and streams. None of the natural objects, whether held in common or situated on private land, has any of the three criteria of a rights-holder. They have no standing in their own right; their unique damages do not count in determining outcome; and they are not the beneficiaries of awards. In such fashion, these objects have traditionally been regarded by the common law, and even by all but the most recent legislation, as objects for man to conquer and master and use—in such a way as the law once looked upon "man's" relationships to African Negroes. Even where special measures have been taken to conserve them, as by seasons on game and limits on timber cutting, the dominant motive has been to conserve them *for us*—for the greatest good of the greatest number of human beings. Conservationists, so far as I am aware, are generally reluctant to maintain otherwise.[45] As the name implies, they want to conserve and guarantee *our* consumption and *our* enjoyment of these other living things. In their own right, natural objects have counted for little, in law as in popular movements.

---

43. Smith v. Staso, 18 F.2d 736, 738 (2d Cir. 1927).

44. Some of these public properties are subject to the "public trust doctrine," which, while ill-defined, might be developed in such fashion as to achieve fairly broad-ranging environmental protection. *See* Gould v. Greylock Reservation Comm'n, 350 Mass. 410, 215 N.E.2d 114 (1966), discussed in Sax, *The Public Trust Doctrine in Natural Resource Law: Effective Judicial Intervention*, 68 MICH. L. REV. 471, 492-509 (1970).

45. By contrast, for example, with humane societies.

As I mentioned at the outset, however, the rightlessness of the natural environment can and should change; it already shows some signs of doing so.

Toward Having Standing in its Own Right

It is not inevitable, nor is it wise, that natural objects should have no rights to seek redress in their own behalf. It is no answer to say that streams and forests cannot have standing because streams and forests cannot speak. Corporations cannot speak either; nor can states, estates, infants, incompetents, muncipalities or universities. Lawyers speak for them, as they customarily do for the ordinary citizen with legal problems. One ought, I think, to handle the legal problems of natural objects as one does the problems of legal incompetents—human beings who have become vegetable. If a human being shows signs of becoming senile and has affairs that he is de jure incompetent to manage, those concerned with his well being make such a showing to the court, and someone is designated by the court with the authority to manage the incompetent's affairs. The guardian[46] (or "conservator"[47] or "committee"[48]—the terminology varies) then represents the incompetent in his legal affairs. Courts make similar appointments when a corporation has become "incompetent"—they appoint a trustee in bankruptcy or reorganization to oversee its affairs and speak for it in court when that becomes necessary.

On a parity of reasoning, we should have a system in which, when a friend of a natural object perceives it to be endangered, he can apply to a court for the creation of a guardianship.[49] Perhaps we already

46. *See, e.g.*, CAL. PROB. CODE §§ 1460-62 (West Supp. 1971).

47. CAL. PROB. CODE § 1751 (West Supp. 1971) provides for the appointment of a "conservator."

48. In New York the Supreme Court and county courts outside New York City have jurisdiction to appoint a committee of the person and/or a committee of the property for a person "incompetent to manage himself or his affairs." N.Y. MENTAL HYGIENE LAW § 100 (McKinney 1971).

49. This is a situation in which the ontological problems discussed in note 26 *supra* become acute. One can conceive a situation in which a guardian would be appointed by a county court with respect to a stream, bring a suit against alleged polluters, and lose. Suppose now that a federal court were to appoint a guardian with respect to the larger river system of which the stream were a part, and that the federally appointed guardian subsequently were to bring suit against the same defendants in state court, now on behalf of the river, rather than the stream. (Is it possible to bring a still subsequent suit, if the one above fails, on behalf of the entire hydrologic cycle, by a guardian appointed by an international court?)

While such problems are difficult, they are not impossible to solve. For one thing, pre-trial hearings and rights of intervention can go far toward their amelioration. Further, courts have been dealing with the matter of potentially inconsistent judgments

have the machinery to do so. California law, for example, defines an incompetent as "any person, whether insane or not, who by reason of old age, disease, weakness of mind, or other cause, is unable, unassisted, properly to manage and take care of himself or his property, and by reason thereof is likely to be deceived or imposed upon by artful or designing persons."[50] Of course, to urge a court that an endangered river is "a person" under this provision will call for lawyers as bold and imaginative as those who convinced the Supreme Court that a railroad corporation was a "person" under the fourteenth amendment, a constitutional provision theretofore generally thought of as designed to secure the rights of freedmen.[51] (As this article was going to press, Professor Byrn of Fordham petitioned the New York Supreme Court to appoint him legal guardian for an unrelated foetus scheduled for abortion so as to enable him to bring a class action on behalf of all foetuses similarly situated in New York City's 18 municipal hospitals. Judge Holtzman granted the petition of guardianship.[52]) If such an argument based on present statutes should fail, special environmental legislation could be enacted along traditional guardianship lines. Such provisions could provide for guardianship both in the instance of public natural objects and also, perhaps with slightly different standards, in the instance of natural objects on "private" land.[53]

for years, as when one state appears on the verge of handing down a divorce decree inconsistent with the judgment of another state's courts. Kempson v. Kempson, 58 N.J. Eg. 94, 43 A. 97 (Ch. Ct. 1899). Courts could, and of course would, retain some natural objects in the res nullius classification to help stave off the problem. Then, too, where (as is always the case) several "objects" are interrelated, several guardians could all be involved, with procedures for removal to the appropriate court—probably that of the guadian of the most encompassing "ward" to be acutely threatened. And in some cases subsequent suit by the guardian of more encompassing ward, not guilty of laches, might be appropriate. The problems are at least no more complex than the corresponding problems that the law has dealt with for years in the class action area.

50. CAL. PROB. CODE § 1460 (West Supp. 1971). The N.Y. MENTAL HYGIENE LAW (McKinney 1971) provides for jurisdiction "over the custody of a person and his property if he is incompetent to manage himself or his affairs by reason of age, drunkenness, mental illness or other cause. . . ."

51. Santa Clara County v. Southern Pac. R.R., 118 U.S. 394 (1886). Justice Black would have denied corporations the rights of "persons" under the fourteenth amendment. *See* Connecticut Gen. Life Ins. Co. v. Johnson, 303 U.S. 77, 87 (1938) (Black, J. dissenting): "Corporations have neither race nor color."

52. *In re* Byrn, L. A. Times, Dec. 5, 1971, § 1, at 16, col. 1. A preliminary injunction was subsequently granted, and defendant's cross-motion to vacate the guardianship was denied. Civ. 13113/71 (Sup. Ct. Queens Co., Jan. 4, 1972) (Smith, J.). Appeals are pending. Granting a guardianship in these circumstances would seem to be a more radical advance in the law than granting a guardianship over communal natural objects like lakes. In the former case there is a traditionally recognized guardian for the object—the mother—and her decision has been in favor of aborting the foetus.

53. The laws regarding the various communal resources had to develop along their own lines, not only because so many different persons' "rights" to consumption and

The potential "friends" that such a statutory scheme would require will hardly be lacking. The Sierra Club, Environmental Defense Fund, Friends of the Earth, Natural Resources Defense Counsel, and the Izaak Walton League are just some of the many groups which have manifested unflagging dedication to the environment and which are becoming increasingly capable of marshalling the requisite technical experts and lawyers. If, for example, the Environmental Defense Fund should have reason to believe that some company's strip mining operations might be irreparably destroying the ecological balance of large tracts of land, it could, under this procedure, apply to the court in which the lands were situated to be appointed guardian.[54] As guardian, it might be given rights of inspection (or visitation) to determine and bring to the court's attention a fuller finding on the land's condition. If there were indications that under the substantive law some redress might be available on the land's behalf, then the guardian would be entitled to raise the land's rights in the land's name, *i.e.*, without having to make the roundabout and often unavailing demonstration, discussed below, that the "rights" of the club's members were being invaded. Guardians would also be looked to for a host of other protective tasks, *e.g.*, monitoring effluents (and/or monitoring the monitors), and representing their "wards" at legislative and administrative hearings on such matters as the setting of state water quality standards. Procedures exist, and can be strengthened, to move a court for the removal and substi-

---

usage were continually and contemporaneously involved, but also because no one had to bear the costs of his consumption of public resources in the way in which the owner of resources on private land has to bear the costs of what he does. For example, if the landowner strips his land of trees, and puts nothing in their stead, he confronts the costs of what he has done in the form of reduced value of his land; but the river polluter's actions are costless, so far as he is concerned—except insofar as the legal system can somehow force him to internalize them. The result has been that the private landowner's power over natural objects on his land is far less restrained by law (as opposed to economics) than his power over the public resources that he can get his hands on. If this state of affairs is to be changed, the standard for interceding in the interests of natural objects on traditionally recognized "private" land might well parallel the rules that guide courts in the matter of people's children whose upbringing (or lack thereof) poses social threat. The courts can, for example, make a child "a dependent of the court" where the child's "home is an unfit place for him by reason of neglect, cruelty, or depravity of either of his parents. . . ." CAL. WELF. & INST. CODE § 600(b) (West 1966). *See also id* at § 601: any child "who from any cause is in danger of leading an idle, dissolute, lewd, or immoral life [may be adjudged] a ward of the court."

54. *See* note 53 *supra*. The present way of handling such problems on "private" property is to try to enact legislation of general application under the police power, *see* Pennsylvania Coal Co. v. Mahon, 260 U.S. 393 (1922), rather than to institute civil litigation which, though a piecemeal process, can be tailored to individual situations.

tution of guardians, for conflicts of interest or for other reasons,[55] as well as for the termination of the guardianship.[56]

In point of fact, there is a movement in the law toward giving the environment the benefits of standing, although not in a manner as satisfactory as the guardianship approach. What I am referring to is the marked liberalization of traditional standing requirements in recent cases in which environmental action groups have challenged federal government action. *Scenic Hudson Preservation Conference v. FPC*[57] is a good example of this development. There, the Federal Power Commission had granted New York's Consolidated Edison a license to construct a hydroelectric project on the Hudson River at Storm King Mountain. The grant of license had been opposed by conservation interests on the grounds that the transmission lines would be unsightly, fish would be destroyed, and nature trails would be inundated. Two of these conservation groups, united under the name Scenic Hudson Preservation Conference, petitioned the Second Circuit to set aside the grant. Despite the claim that Scenic Hudson had no standing because it had not made the traditional claim "of any personal economic injury resulting from the Commission's actions,"[58] the petitions were heard, and the case sent back to the Commission. On the standing point, the court noted that Section 313(b) of the Federal Power Act gave a right of instituting review to any party "aggrieved by an order issued by the Commission";[59] it thereupon read "aggrieved by" as not limited to those alleging the traditional personal economic injury, but as broad enough to include "those who by their activities and conduct have exhibited a special interest" in "the aesthetic, conservational, and recreational aspects of power development. . . ."[60] A similar reasoning has

55. CAL. PROB. CODE § 1580 (West Supp. 1971) lists specific causes for which a guardian may, after notice and a hearing, be removed.

Despite these protections, the problem of overseeing the guardian is particularly acute where, as here, there are no immediately identifiable human beneficiaries whose self-interests will encourage them to keep a close watch on the guardian. To ameliorate this problem, a page might well be borrowed from the law of ordinary charitable trusts, which are commonly placed under the supervision of the Attorney General. *See* CAL. CORP. CODE §§ 9505, 10207 (West 1955).

56. *See* CAL. PROB. CODE §§ 1472, 1590 (West 1956 and Supp. 1971).

57. 354 F.2d 608 (2d Cir. 1965), *cert. denied*, Consolidated Edison Co. v. Scenic Hudson Preservation Conf., 384 U.S. 941 (1966).

58. 354 F.2d 608, 615 (2d Cir. 1965).

59. Act of Aug. 26, 1935, ch. 687, Title II, § 213, 49 Stat. 860 (*codified in* 16 U.S.C. § 8251(b) (1970).

60. 354 F.2d 608, 616 (2d Cir. 1965). The court might have felt that because the New York-New Jersey Trial Conference, one of the two conservation groups that

swayed other circuits to allow proposed actions by the Federal Power Commission, the Department of Interior, and the Department of Health, Education and Welfare to be challenged by environmental action groups on the basis of, *e.g.*, recreational and esthetic interests of members, in lieu of direct economic injury.[61] Only the Ninth Circuit has balked, and one of these cases, involving the Sierra Club's attempt to challenge a Walt Disney development in the Sequoia National Forest, is at the time of this writing awaiting decision by the United States Supreme Court.[62]

organized Scenic Hudson, had some 17 miles of trailways in the area of Storm King Mountain, it therefore had sufficient economic interest to establish standing; Judge Hays' opinion does not seem to so rely, however.

61. Road Review League v. Boyd, 270 F. Supp. 650 (S.D.N.Y. 1967). Plaintiffs who included the Town of Bedford and the Road Review League, a non-profit association concerned with community problems, brought an action to review and set aside a determination of the Federal Highway Administrator concerning the alignment of an interstate highway. Plaintiffs claimed that the proposed road would have an adverse effect upon local wildlife sanctuaries, pollute a local lake, and be inconsistent with local needs and planning. Plaintiffs relied upon the section of the Administrative Procedure Act, 5 U.S.C. § 702 (1970), which entitles persons "aggrieved by agency action within the meaning of a relevant statute" to obtain judicial review. The court held that plaintiffs had standing to obtain judicial review of proposed alignment of the road:

> I see no reason why the word "aggrieved" should have different meaning in the Administrative Procedure Act from the meaning given it under the Federal Power Act. . . . The "relevant statute," i.e., the Federal Highways Act, contains language which seems even stronger than that of the Federal Power Act, as far as local and conservation interests are concerned.

Id. at 661.

In Citizens Comm. for the Hudson Valley v. Volpe, 425 F.2d 97 (2d Cir. 1970), plaintiffs were held to have standing to challenge the construction of a dike and causeway adjacent to the Hudson Valley. The Sierra Club and the Village of Tarrytown based their challenge upon the provisions of the Rivers and Harbors Act of 1899. While the Rivers and Harbors Act does not provide for judicial review as does the Federal Power Act, the court stated that the plaintiffs were "aggrieved" under the Department of Transportation Act, the Hudson River Basin Compact Act, and a regulation under which the Corps of Engineers issued a permit, all of which contain broad provisions mentioning recreational and environmental resources and the need to preserve the same. Citing the *Road Review League* decision, the court held that as "aggrieved" parties under the Administrative Procedure Act, plaintiffs similarly had standing. Other decisions in which the court's grant of standing was based upon the Administrative Procedure Act include: West Virginia Highlands Conservancy v. Island Creek Coal Co., 441 F.2d 231 (4th Cir. 1971); Environmental Defense Fund, Inc. v. Hardin, 428 F.2d 1093 (D.C. Cir. 1970); Allen v. Hickel, 424 F.2d 944 (D.C. Cir. 1970); Brooks v. Volpe, 329 F. Supp. 118 (W.D. Wash. 1971); Delaware v. Pennsylvania N.Y. Cent. Transp. Co., 323 F. Supp. 487 (D. Del. 1971); Izaak Walton League of America v. St. Clair, 313 F. Supp. 1312 (D. Minn. 1970); Pennsylvania Environmental Council, Inc. v. Bartlett, 315 F. Supp. 238 (M.D. Pa. 1970).

62. Sierra Club v. Hickel, 433 F.2d 24 (9th Cir. 1970), *cert. granted sub nom.* Sierra Club v. Morton, 401 U.S. 907 (1971) (No. 70-34). The Sierra Club, a non-profit California corporation concerned with environmental protection, claimed that its interest in the conservation and sound management of natural parks would be adversely affected by an Interior permit allowing Walt Disney to construct the Mineral King Resort in Sequoia

Even if the Supreme Court should reverse the Ninth Circuit in the Walt Disney-Sequoia National Forest matter, thereby encouraging the circuits to continue their trend toward liberalized standing in this area, there are significant reasons to press for the guardianship approach notwithstanding. For one thing, the cases of this sort have extended standing on the basis of interpretations of specific federal statutes—the Federal Power Commission Act,[63] the Administrative Procedure Act,[64] the Federal Insecticide, Fungicide and Rodenticide Act,[65] and others. Such a basis supports environmental suits only where acts of federal agencies are involved; and even there, perhaps, only when there is some special statutory language, such as "aggrieved by" in the Federal Power Act, on which the action groups can rely. Witness, for example, *Bass Angler Sportsman Society v. United States Steel Corp.*[66] There, plaintiffs sued 175 corporate defendants located throughout Alabama, relying on 33 U.S.C. § 407 (1970), which provides:

> It shall not be lawful to throw, discharge, or deposit . . . any refuse matter . . . into any navigable water of the United States, or into any tributary of any navigable water from which the same shall float or be washed into such navigable water. . . .[67]

Another section of the Act provides that one-half the fines shall be paid to the person or persons giving information which shall lead to a conviction.[68] Relying on this latter provision, the plaintiff designated his action a *qui tam* action[69] and sought to enforce the Act by injunction

---

National Forest. The court held that because of the Sierra Club's failure to assert a direct legal interest, that organization lacked standing to sue. The court stated that the Sierra Club had claimed an interest only in the sense that the proposed course of action was displeasing to its members. The court purported to distinguish *Scenic Hudson* on the grounds that the plaintiff's claim of standing there was aided by the "aggrieved party" language of the Federal Power Act.

63. 16 U.S.C. §§ 791(a) *et seq.* (1970). *See* note 59 and accompanying text *supra.*

64. 5 U.S.C. §§ 551 *et seq.* (1970). Decisions relying upon 5 U.S.C. § 702 are listed in note 56 *supra.*

65. 7 U.S.C. §§ 135 *et seq.* (1970). Section 135b(d) affords a right of judicial review to anyone "adversely affected" by an order under the Act. *See* Environmental Defense Fund, Inc. v. Hardin, 428 F.2d 1093, 1096 (D.C. Cir. 1970).

66. 324 F. Supp. 412 (N.D., M.D. & S.D. Ala. 1970), *aff'd mem., sub nom.* Bass Anglers Sportsman Soc'y of America, Inc. v. Koppers Co., 447 F.2d 1304 (5th Cir. 1971).

67. Section 13 of Rivers and Harbors Appropriation Act of 1899.

68. 33 U.S.C. § 411 (1970) reads:

> Every person and every corporation that shall violate, or that shall knowingly aid, abet, authorize, or instigate a violation of the provisions of sections 407, 408, and 409 of the title shall . . . be punished by a fine . . . or by imprisonment . . . in the discretion of the court, one-half of said fine to be paid to the person or persons giving information which shall lead to conviction.

69. This is from the latin, "who brings the action as well for the King as for himself," referring to an action brought by a citizen for the state as well as for himself.

and fine. The District Court ruled that, in the absence of express language to the contrary, no one outside the Department of Justice had standing to sue under a criminal act and refused to reach the question of whether violations were occurring.[70]

Unlike the liberalized standing approach, the guardianship approach would secure an effective voice for the environment even where federal administrative action and public-lands and waters were not involved. It would also allay one of the fears courts—such as the Ninth Circuit—have about the extended standing concept: if any ad hoc group can spring up overnight, invoke some "right" as universally claimable as the esthetic and recreational interests of its members and thereby get into court, how can a flood of litigation be prevented?[71] If an ad hoc committee loses a suit brought *sub nom.* Committee to Preserve our Trees, what happens when its very same members reorganize two years later and sue *sub nom.* the Massapequa Sylvan Protection League? Is the new group bound by res judicata? Class action law may be capable of ameliorating some of the more obvious problems. But even so, court economy might be better served by simply designating the guardian de jure representative of the natural object, with rights of

> 70. These sections create a criminal liability. No civil action lies to enforce it; criminal statutes can only be enforced by the government. A qui tam action lies only when expressly or impliedly authorized by statute to enforce a penalty by civil action, not a criminal fine.

324 F. Supp. 412, 415-16 (N.D., M.D. & S.D. Ala. 1970). Other *qui tam* actions brought by the Bass Angler Sportsman Society have been similarly unsuccessful. *See* Bass Anglers Sportsman Soc'y of America v. Scholze Tannery, 329 F. Supp. 339 (E.D. Tenn. 1971); Bass Anglers Sportsman's Soc'y of America v. United States Plywood-Champion Papers, Inc., 324 F. Supp. 302 (S.D. Tex. 1971).

71. Concern over an anticipated flood of litigation initiated by environmental organizations is evident in Judge Trask's opinion in Alameda Conservation Ass'n v. California, 437 F.2d 1087 (9th Cir.), *cert. denied*, Leslie Salt Co. v. Alameda Conservation Ass'n, 402 U.S. 908 (1971), where a non-profit corporation having as a primary purpose protection of the public's interest in San Francisco Bay was denied standing to seek an injunction prohibiting a land exchange that would allegedly destroy wildlife, fisheries and the Bay's unique flushing characteristics:

> Standing is not established by suit initiated by this association simply because it has as one of its purposes the protection of the "public interest" in the waters of the San Francisco Bay. However well intentioned the members may be, they may not by uniting create for themselves a super-administrative agency or a *parens patriae* official status with the capability of over-seeing and of challenging the action of the appointed and elected officials of the state government. Although recent decisions have considerably broadened the concept of standing, we do not find that they go this far. [Citation.]
>
> Were it otherwise the various clubs, political, economic and social now or yet to be organized, could wreak havoc with the administration of government, both federal and state. There are other forums where their voices and their views may be effectively presented, but to have standing to submit a "case or controversy" to a federal court, something more must be shown.

437 F.2d at 1090.

discretionary intervention by others, but with the understanding that the natural object is "bound" by an adverse judgment.[72] The guardian concept, too, would provide the endangered natural object with what the trustee in bankruptcy provides the endangered corporation: a continuous supervision over a period of time, with a consequent deeper understanding of a broad range of the ward's problems, not just the problems present in one particular piece of litigation. It would thus assure the courts that the plaintiff has the expertise and genuine adversity in pressing a claim which are the prerequisites of a true "case or controversy."

The guardianship approach, however, is apt to raise two objections, neither of which seems to me to have much force. The first is that a committee or guardian could not judge the needs of the river or forest in its charge; indeed, the very concept of "needs," it might be said, could be used here only in the most metaphorical way. The second objection is that such a system would not be much different from what we now have: is not the Department of Interior already such a guardian for public lands, and do not most states have legislation empowering their attorneys general to seek relief—in a sort of *parens patriae* way—for such injuries as a guardian might concern himself with?

As for the first objection, natural objects *can* communicate their wants (needs) to us, and in ways that are not terribly ambiguous. I am sure I can judge with more certainty and meaningfulness whether and when my lawn wants (needs) water, than the Attorney General can judge whether and when the United States wants (needs) to take an appeal from an adverse judgment by a lower court. The lawn tells me that it wants water by a certain dryness of the blades and soil—immediately obvious to the touch—the appearance of bald spots, yellowing, and a lack of springiness after being walked on; how does "the United States" communicate to the Attorney General? For similar reasons, the guardian-attorney for a smog-endangered stand of pines could venture with more confidence that his client wants the smog stopped, than the directors of a corporation can assert that "the corporation" wants dividends declared. We make decisions on behalf of, and in the purported interests of, others every day; these "others" are often creatures whose wants are far less verifiable, and even far more metaphysical in conception, than the wants of rivers, trees, and land.[73]

---

72. *See* note 49 *supra*.

73. Here, too, we are dogged by the ontological problem discussed in note 26 *supra*. It is easier to say that the smog-endangered stand of pines "wants" the smog stopped

As for the second objection, one can indeed find evidence that the Department of Interior was conceived as a sort of guardian of the public lands.[74] But there are two points to keep in mind. First, insofar as the Department already is an adequate guardian it is only with respect to the federal public lands as per Article IV, section 3 of the Constitution.[75] Its guardianship includes neither local public lands nor private lands. Second, to judge from the environmentalist literature and from the cases environmental action groups have been bringing, the Department is itself one of the bogeys of the environmental movement. (One thinks of the uneasy peace between the Indians and the Bureau of Indian Affairs.) Whether the various charges be right or wrong, one cannot help but observe that the Department has been charged with several institutional goals (never an easy burden), and is currently looked to for action by quite a variety of interest groups, only one of which is the environmentalists. In this context, a guardian outside the institution becomes especially valuable. Besides, what a person wants, fully to secure his rights, is the ability to retain independent counsel even when, and perhaps especially when, the government is acting "for him" in a beneficent way. I have no reason to doubt, for example, that the Social Security System is being managed "for me"; but I would not want to abdicate my right to challenge its actions as they affect me, should the need arise.[76] I would not ask more trust of national forests, vis-à-vis the Department of Interior. The same considerations apply in the instance of local agencies, such as regional water pollution boards, whose members' expertise in pollution matters is often all too credible.[77]

The objection regarding the availability of attorneys-general as

---

(assuming that to be a jurally significant entity) then it is to venture that the mountain, or the planet earth, or the cosmos, is concerned about whether the pines stand or fall. The more encompassing the entity of concern, the less certain we can be in venturing judgments as to the "wants" of any particular substance, quality, or species within the universe. Does the cosmos care if we humans persist or not? "Heaven and earth . . . regard all things as insignificant, as though they were playthings made of straw." LAO-TZU, TAO TEH KING 13 (D. Goddard transl. 1919).

74. *See* Knight v. United States Land Ass'n, 142 U.S. 161, 181 (1891).

75. Clause 2 gives Congress the power "to dispose of and make all needful Rules and Regulations respecting the Territory or other Property belonging to the United States."

76. *See* Flemming v. Nestor, 363 U.S. 603 (1960).

77. *See* the L. A. Times editorial *Water: Public vs. Polluters* criticizing:

> . . . the ridiculous built-in conflict of interests on Regional Water Quality Control Board. By law, five of the seven seats are given to spokesmen for industrial, governmental, agricultural or utility users. Only one representative of the public at large is authorized, along with a delegate from fish and game interests.

Feb. 12, 1969, Part II, at 8, cols. 1-2.

protectors of the environment within the existing structure is somewhat the same. Their statutory powers are limited and sometimes unclear. As political creatures, they must exercise the discretion they have with an eye toward advancing and reconciling a broad variety of important social goals, from preserving morality to increasing their jurisdiction's tax base. The present state of our environment, and the history of cautious application and development of environmental protection laws long on the books,[78] testifies that the burdens of an attorney-general's broad responsibility have apparently not left much manpower for the protection of nature. (*Cf. Bass Anglers*, above.) No doubt, strengthening interest in the environment will increase the zest of public attorneys even where, as will often be the case, well-represented corporate pollutors are the quarry. Indeed, the United States Attorney General has stepped up anti-pollution activity, and ought to be further encouraged in this direction.[79] The statutory powers of the attorneys-general should be enlarged, and they should be armed with criminal penalties made at least commensurate with the likely economic benefits of violating the law.[80] On the other hand, one cannot ignore the fact that there is increased pressure on public law-enforcement offices to give more attention to a host of other problems, from crime "on the streets" (why don't we say "in the rivers"?) to consumerism and school bussing. If the environment is not to get lost in the shuffle, we would do well, I think, to adopt the guardianship approach as an additional safeguard, conceptualizing major natural objects as holders of their own rights, raisable by the court-appointed guardian.

Toward Recognition of its Own Injuries

As far as adjudicating the merits of a controversy is concerned, there is also a good case to be made for taking into account harm to the environment—in its own right. As indicated above, the traditional way of deciding whether to issue injunctions in law suits affecting the environment, at least where communal property is involved, has been to strike some sort of balance regarding the economic hardships *on human*

78. The Federal Refuse Act is over 70 years old. Refuse Act of 1899, 33 U.S.C. § 407 (1970).

79. *See* Hall, *Refuse Act of 1899 and the Permit Program*, 1 NAT'L RES. DEFENSE COUNCIL NEWSLETTER i (1971).

80. To be effective as a deterrent, the sanction ought to be high enough to bring about an internal reorganization of the corporate structure which minimizes the chances of future violations. Because the corporation is not necessarily a profit-maximizing "rationally economic man," there is no reason to believe that setting the fine as high as—but no higher than—anticipated profits from the violation of the law, will bring the illegal behavior to an end.

beings. Even recently, Mr. Justice Douglas, our jurist most closely associated with conservation sympathies in his private life, was deciding the propriety of a new dam on the basis of, among other things, anticipated lost profits from fish catches, some $12,000,000 annually.[81] Although he decided to delay the project pending further findings, the reasoning seems unnecessarily incomplete and compromising. Why should the environment be of importance only indirectly, as lost profits to someone else? Why not throw into the balance the cost *to the environment?*

The argument for "personifying" the environment, from the point of damage calculations, can best be demonstrated from the welfare economics position. Every well-working legal-economic system should be so structured as to confront each of us with the full costs that our activities are imposing on society.[82] Ideally, a paper-mill, in deciding what to produce—and where, and by what methods—ought to be forced to take into account not only the lumber, acid and labor that its production "takes" from other uses in the society, but also what costs alternative production plans will impose on society through pollution. The legal system, through the law of contracts and the criminal law, for example, makes the mill confront the costs of the first group of demands. When, for example, the company's purchasing agent orders 1000 drums of acid from the *Z* Company, the *Z* Company can bind the mill to pay for them, and thereby reimburse the society for what the mill is removing from alternative uses.

Unfortunately, so far as the pollution costs are concerned, the allocative ideal begins to break down, because the traditional legal institutions have a more difficult time "catching" and confronting us with the full social costs of our activities. In the lakeside mill example, major riparian interests might bring an action, forcing a court to weigh *their* aggregate losses against the costs to the mill of installing the

81. Udall v. FPC, 387 U.S. 428, 437 n.6 (1967). *See also* Holmes, J. in New Jersey v. New York, 283 U.S. 336, 342 (1931): "A river is more than an amenity, it is a treasure. It offers a necessity of life that must be rationed among those who have power over it."

82. To simplify the description, I am using here an ordinary language sense of causality, *i.e.*, assuming that the pollution causes harm to the river. As Professor Coase has pointed out in *The Problem of Social Cost*, 3 J. LAW & ECON. 1 (1960), harm-causing can be viewed as a reciprocal problem, *i.e.*, in the terms of the text, the mill wants to harm the river, and the river—if we assume it "wants" to maintain its present environmental quality—"wants" to harm the mill. Coase rightly points out that at least in theory (if we had the data) we ought to be comparing the alternative social product of different social arrangements, and not simply imposing full costs on the party who would popularly be identified as the harm-causer.

anti-pollution device. But many other interests—and I am speaking for the moment of recognized homocentric interests—are too fragmented and perhaps "too remote" causally to warrant securing representation and pressing for recovery: the people who own summer homes and motels, the man who sells fishing tackle and bait, the man who rents rowboats. There is no reason not to allow the lake to prove damages to them as the prima facie measure of damages to it. *By doing so, we in effect make the natural object, through its guardian, a jural entity competent to gather up these fragmented and otherwise unrepresented damage claims, and press them before the court even where, for legal or practical reasons, they are not going to be pressed by traditional class action plaintiffs.*[83] Indeed, one way—the homocentric way—to view what I am proposing so far, is to view the guardian of the natural object as the guardian of unborn generations, as well as of the otherwise unrepresented, but distantly injured, contemporary humans.[84] By making the lake itself the focus of these damages, and "incorporating" it so to speak, the legal system can effectively take proof upon, and confront the mill with, a larger and more representative measure of the damages its pollution causes.

So far, I do not suppose that my economist friends (unremittent human chauvanists, every one of them!) will have any large quarrel in principle with the concept. Many will view it as a *trompe l'oeil* that comes down, at best, to effectuate the goals of the paragon class action, or the paragon water pollution control district. Where we are apt to part company is here—I propose going beyond gathering up the loose ends of what most people would presently recognize as economically valid damages. The guardian would urge before the court injuries not presently cognizable—the death of eagles and inedible crabs, the suffering of sea lions, the loss from the face of the earth of species of commercially valueless birds, the disappearance of a wilderness area. One might, of course, speak of the damages involved as "damages" to us

83. I am assuming that one of the considerations that goes into a judgment of "remoteness" is a desire to discourage burdensome amounts of petty litigation. This is one of the reasons why a court would be inclined to say—to use the example in the text—that the man who sells fishing tackle and bait has not been "proximately" injured by the polluter. Using proximate cause in this manner, the courts can protect themselves from a flood of litigation. But once the guardian were in court anyway, this consideration would not obtain as strongly, and courts might be more inclined to allow proof on the damages to remotely injured humans (although the proof itself is an added burden of sorts).

84. *Cf.* Golding, *Ethical Issues in Biological Engineering*, 15 U.C.L.A.L. Rev. 443, 451-63 (1968).

humans, and indeed, the widespread growth of environmental groups shows that human beings do feel these losses. But they are not, at present, economically measurable losses: how can they have a monetary value for the guardian to prove in court?

The answer for me is simple. Wherever it carves out "property" rights, the legal system is engaged in the process of *creating* monetary worth. One's literary works would have minimal monetary value if anyone could copy them at will. Their economic value to the author is a product of the law of copyright; the person who copies a copyrighted book has to bear a cost to the copyright-holder because the law says he must. Similarly, it is through the law of torts that we have made a "right" of—and guaranteed an economically meaningful value to—privacy. (The value we place on gold—a yellow inanimate dirt—is not simply a function of supply and demand—wilderness areas are scarce and pretty too—, but results from the actions of the legal systems of the world, which have institutionalized that value; they have even done a remarkable job of stabilizing the price). I am proposing we do the same with eagles and wilderness areas as we do with copyrighted works, patented inventions, and privacy: *make* the violation of rights in them to be a cost by declaring the "pirating" of them to be the invasion of a property interest.[85] If we do so, the net social costs the polluter would be confronted with would include not only the extended homocentric costs of his pollution (explained above) but also costs to the environment *per se*.

How, though, would these costs be calculated? When we protect an invention, we can at least speak of a fair market value for it, by reference to which damages can be computed. But the lost environmental "values" of which we are now speaking are by definition over and above those that the market is prepared to bid for: they are priceless.

One possible measure of damages, suggested earlier, would be the cost of making the environment whole, just as, when a man is injured in an automobile accident, we impose upon the responsible party the injured man's medical expenses. Comparable expenses to a polluted river would be the costs of dredging, restocking with fish, and so forth. It is on the basis of such costs as these, I assume, that we get the figure of $1 billion as the cost of saving Lake Erie.[86] As an ideal, I think this

85. Of course, in the instance of copyright and patent protection, the creation of the "property right" can be more directly justified on homocentric grounds.

86. *See* Schrag, *Life on a Dying Lake*, in THE POLITICS OF NEGLECT 167, at 173 (R. Meek & J. Straayer eds. 1971).

is a good guide applicable in many environmental situations. It is by no means free from difficulties, however.

One problem with computing damages on the basis of making the environment whole is that, if understood most literally, it is tantamount to asking for a "freeze" on environmental quality, even at the costs (and there will be costs) of preserving "useless" objects.[87] Such a "freeze" is not inconceivable to me as a general goal, especially considering that, even by the most immediately discernible homocentric interests, in so many areas we ought to be cleaning up and not merely preserving the environmental status quo. In fact, there is presently strong sentiment in the Congress for a total elimination of all river pollutants by 1985,[88] notwithstanding that such a decision would impose quite large direct and indirect costs on us all. Here one is inclined to recall the instructions of Judge Hays, in remanding Consolidated Edison's Storm King application to the Federal Power Commission in *Scenic Hudson*:

> The Commission's renewed proceedings must include as a basic concern the preservation of natural beauty and of natural historic shrines, keeping in mind that, in our affluent society, the cost of a project is only one of several factors to be considered.[89]

Nevertheless, whatever the merits of such a goal in principle, there are many cases in which the social price tag of putting it into effect are going to seem too high to accept. Consider, for example, an oceanside nuclear generator that could produce low cost electricity for a million homes at a savings of $1 a year per home, spare us the air pollution that comes of burning fossil fuels, but which through a slight heating effect threatened to kill off a rare species of temperature-sensitive sea urchins; suppose further that technological improvements adequate to reduce the temperature to present environmental quality would expend the entire one million dollars in anticipated fuel savings. Are we prepared to tax ourselves $1,000,000 a year on behalf of the sea

87. One ought to observe, too, that in terms of real effect on marginal welfare, the poor quite possibly will bear the brunt of the compromises. They may lack the wherewithal to get out to the countryside—and probably want an increase in material goods more acutely than those who now have riches.

88. On November 2, 1971, the Senate, by a vote of 86-0, passed and sent to the House the proposed Federal Water Pollution Control Act Amendments of 1971, 117 CONG. REC. S17464 (daily ed. Nov. 2, 1971). Sections 101(a) and (a)(1) of the bill declare it to be "national policy that, consistent with the provisions of this Act—(1) the discharge of pollutants into the navigable waters be eliminated by 1985." S.2770, 92d Cong., 1st Sess., 117 CONG. REC. S17464 (daily ed. Nov. 2, 1971).

89. 354 F.2d 608, 624 (2d Cir. 1965).

urchins? In comparable problems under the present law of damages, we work out practicable compromises by abandoning restoration costs and calling upon fair market value. For example, if an automobile is so severely damaged that the cost of bringing the car to its original state by repair is greater than the fair market value, we would allow the responsible tortfeasor to pay the fair market value only. Or if a human being suffers the loss of an arm (as we might conceive of the ocean having irreparably lost the sea urchins), we can fall back on the capitalization of reduced earning power (and pain and suffering) to measure the damages. But what is the fair market value of sea urchins? How can we capitalize their loss to the ocean, independent of any commercial value they may have to someone else?

One answer is that the problem can sometimes be sidestepped quite satisfactorily. In the sea urchin example, one compromise solution would be to impose on the nuclear generator the costs of making the ocean whole somewhere else, in some other way, *e.g.*, reestablishing a sea urchin colony elsewhere, or making a somehow comparable contribution.[90] In the debate over the laying of the trans-Alaskan pipeline, the builders are apparently prepared to meet conservationists' objections half-way by re-establishing wildlife away from the pipeline, so far as is feasible.[91]

But even if damage calculations have to be made, one ought to recognize that the measurement of damages is rarely a simple report of economic facts about "the market," whether we are valuing the loss of a foot, a foetus, or a work of fine art. Decisions of this sort are always hard, but not impossible. We have increasingly taken (human) pain and suffering into account in reckoning damages, not because we think we can ascertain them as objective "facts" about the universe, but because, even in view of all the room for disagreement, we come up with a better society by making rude estimates of them than by ignoring them.[92] We can make such estimates in regard to environmental losses

90. Again, there is a problem involving what we conceive to be the injured entity. *See* notes 26, 73 *supra*.

91. N.Y. Times, Jan. 14, 1971, § 1, col. 2, and at 74, col. 7.

92. Courts have not been reluctant to award damages for the destruction of heirlooms, literary manuscripts or other property having no ascertainable market value. In Willard v. Valley Gas Fuel Co., 171 Cal. 9, 151 Pac. 286 (1915), it was held that the measure of damages for the negligent destruction of a rare old book written by one of plaintiff's ancestors was the amount which would compensate the owner for all detriment including sentimental loss proximately caused by such destruction. The court, at 171 Cal. 15, 151 Pac. 289, quoted approvingly from Southern Express Co. v. Owens, 146 Ala. 412, 426, 41 S. 752, 755 (1906):

fully aware that what we are really doing is making implicit normative judgments (as with pain and suffering)—laying down rules as to what the society is going to "value" rather than reporting market evaluations. In making such normative estimates decision-makers would not go wrong if they estimated on the "high side," putting the burden of trimming the figure down on the immediate human interests present. All burdens of proof should reflect common experience; our experience in environmental matters has been a continual discovery that our acts have caused more long-range damage than we were able to appreciate at the outset.

To what extent the decision-maker should factor in costs such as the pain and suffering of animals and other sentient natural objects, I cannot say; although I am prepared to do so in principle.[93] Given the conjectural nature of the "estimates" in all events, and the roughness of the "balance of conveniences" procedure where that is involved, the

---

> Ordinarily, where property has a market value that can be shown, such value is the criterion by which actual damages for its destruction or loss may be fixed. But it may be that property destroyed or lost has no market value. In such state of the case, while it may be that no rule which will be absolutely certain to do justice between the parties can be laid down, it does not follow from this, nor is it the law, that the plaintiff must be turned out of court with nominal damages merely. Where the article or thing is so unusual in its character that market value cannot be predicated of it, its value, or plaintiff's damages, must be ascertained in some other rational way and from such elements as are attainable.

Similarly, courts award damages in wrongful death actions despite the impossibility of precisely appraising the damages in such cases. In affirming a judgment in favor of the administrator of the estate of a child killed by defendant's automobile, the Oregon Supreme Court, in Lane v. Hatfield, 173 Or. 79, 88-89, 143 P.2d 230, 234 (1943), acknowledged the speculative nature of the measure of damages:

> No one knows or can know when, if at all, a seven year old girl will attain her majority, for her marriage may take place before she has become twenty-one years of age. . . . Moreover, there is much uncertainty with respect to the length of time anyone may live. A similar uncertainty veils the future of a minor's earning capacity or habit of saving. Illness or a non-fatal accident may reduce an otherwise valuable and lucrative life to a burden and liability.
>
> The rule, that the measure of recovery by a personal representative for the wrongful death of his decedent is the value of the life of such decedent, if he had not come to such an untimely end, has been termed vague, uncertain and speculative if not, conjectural. It is, however, the best that judicial wisdom has been able to formulate.

93. It is not easy to dismiss the idea of "lower" life having consciousness and feeling pain, especially since it is so difficult to know what these terms mean even as applied to humans. *See* Austin, *Other Minds*, in *Logic and Language* 342 (S. Flew ed. 1965); Schopenhauer, *On the Will in Nature*, in TWO ESSAYS BY ARTHUR SCHOPENHAUER 193, 281-304 (1889). Some experiments on plant sensitivity—of varying degrees of extravagance in their claims—include Lawrence, *Plants Have Feelings, Too . . .*, ORGANIC GARDENING & FARMING 64 (April 1971); Woodlief, Royster & Huang, *Effect of Random Noise on Plant Growth*, 46 J. ACOUSTICAL SOC. AM. 481 (1969); Backster, *Evidence of a Primary Perception in Plant Life*, 10 INT'L J. PARAPSYCHOLOGY 250 (1968).

practice would be of more interest from the socio-psychic point of view, discussed below, than from the legal-operational.

Toward Being a Beneficiary in its Own Right

As suggested above, one reason for making the environment itself the beneficiary of a judgment is to prevent it from being "sold out" in a negotiation among private litigants who agree not to enforce rights that have been established among themselves.[94] Protection from this will be advanced by making the natural object a party to an injunctive settlement. Even more importantly, we should make it a beneficiary of money awards. If, in making the balance requisite to issuing an injunction, a court decides *not* to enjoin a lake polluter who is causing injury to the extent of $50,000 annually, then the owners and the lake ought both to be awarded damages. The natural object's portion could be put into a trust fund to be administered by the object's guardian, as per the guardianship recommendation set forth above. So far as the damages are proved, as suggested in the previous section, by allowing the natural object to cumulate damages to others as prima facie evidence of damages to it, there will, of course, be problems of distribution. But even if the object is simply construed as representing a class of plaintiffs under the applicable civil rules,[95] there is often likely to be a sizeable amount of recovery attributable to members of the class who will not put in a claim for distribution (because their pro rata share would be so small, or because of their interest in the environment). Not only should damages go into these funds, but where criminal fines are applied (as against water polluters) it seems to me that the monies (less prosecutorial expenses, perhaps) ought sensibly to go to the fund rather than to the general treasuries. Guardians fees, including legal fees, would then come out of this fund. More importantly, the fund would be available to preserve the natural object as close as possible to its condition at the time the environment was made a rights-holder.[96]

The idea of assessing damages as best we can and placing them in a trust fund is far more realistic than a hope that a total "freeze" can be put on the environmental status quo. Nature is a continuous theatre in which things and species (eventually man) are destined to enter and

94. *See* note 39 *supra*, and Coase, note 82 *supra*.

95. *See* FED. R. CIV. P. 23 and note 49 *supra*.

96. This is an ideal, of course—like the ideal that no human being ought to interfere with any other human being. *See* Dyke, *Freedom, Consent and the Costs of Interaction*, and Stone, *Comment*, in IS LAW DEAD? 134-67 (E. Rostow ed. 1971). Some damages would inevitably be *damnum absque injuria*. *See* note 93 *supra*.

exit.[97] In the meantime, co-existence of man and his environment means that *each* is going to have to compromise for the better of both. Some pollution of streams, for example, will probably be inevitable for some time. Instead of setting an unrealizable goal of enjoining absolutely the discharge of all such pollutants, the trust fund concept would (a) help assure that pollution would occur only in those instances where the social need for the pollutant's product (via his present method of production) was so high as to enable the polluter to cover *all* homocentric costs, plus some estimated costs to the environment *per se*, and (b) would be a corpus for preserving monies, if necessary, while the technology developed to a point where repairing the damaged portion of the environment was feasible. Such a fund might even finance the requisite research and development.

(Incidentally, if "rights" are to be granted to the environment, then for many of the same reasons it might bear "liabilities" as well—as inanimate objects did anciently.[98] Rivers drown people, and flood over and destroy crops; forests burn, setting fire to contiguous communities. Where trust funds had been established, they could be available for the satisfaction of judgments *against* the environment, making it bear the costs of some of the harms it imposes on other right holders. In effect, we would be narrowing the claim of Acts of God. The ontological problem would be troublesome here, however; when the Nile overflows, is it the "responsibility" of the river? the mountains? the snow? the hydrologic cycle?[99])

Toward Rights in Substance

So far we have been looking at the characteristics of being a *holder of rights*, and exploring some of the implications that making the environment a holder of rights would entail. Natural objects would have

---

97. The inevitability of some form of evolution is not inconsistent with the establishment of a legal system that attempts to interfere with or ameliorate the process: is the same not true of the human law we now have, *e.g.*, the laws against murder?

98. Holmes, *Early Forms of Liability*, in THE COMMON LAW (1881), discusses the liability of animals and inanimate objects in early Greek, early Roman and some later law. Alfred's Laws (A.D. 871-901) provided, for example, that a tree by which a man was killed should "be given to the kindred, and let them have it off the land within 30 nights." *Id.* at 19. In Edward I's time, if a man fell from a tree the tree was deodand. *Id.* at 24. Perhaps the liability of non-human matter is, in the history of things, part of a paranoid, defensive phase in man's development; as humans become more abundant, both from the point of material wealth and internally, they may be willing to allow an advance to the stage where non-human matter has rights.

99. *See* note 26 *supra*. In the event that a person built his house near the edge of a river that flooded, would "assumption of the risk" be available on the river's behalf?

standing in their own right, through a guardian; damage to and through them would be ascertained and considered as an independent factor; and they would be the beneficiaries of legal awards. But these considerations only give us the skeleton of what a meaningful rights-holding would involve. To flesh out the "rights" of the environment demands that we provide it with a significant body of rights for it to invoke when it gets to court.

In this regard, the lawyer is constantly aware that a right is not, as the layman may think, some strange substance that one either has or has not. One's life, one's right to vote, one's property, can all be taken away. But those who would infringe on them must go through certain procedures to do so; these procedures are a measure of what we value as a society. Some of the most important questions of "right" thus turn into questions of degree: how much review, and of which sort, will which agencies of state accord us when we claim our "right" is being infringed?

We do not have an absolute right either to our lives or to our driver's licenses. But we have a greater right to our lives because, if even the state wants to deprive us of that "right," there are authoritative bodies that will demand that the state make a very strong showing before it does so, and it will have to justify its actions before a grand jury, petit jury (convincing them "beyond a reasonable doubt"), sentencing jury, and, most likely, levels of appellate courts. The carving out of students "rights" to their education is being made up of this sort of procedural fabric. No one, I think, is maintaining that in no circumstances ought a student to be expelled from school. The battle for student "rights" involves shifting the answers to questions like: before a student is expelled, does he have to be given a hearing; does he have to have prior notice of the hearing, and notice of charges; may he bring counsel, (need the state provide counsel if he cannot?); need there be a transcript; need the school carry the burden of proving the charges; may he confront witnesses; if he is expelled, can he get review by a civil court; if he can get such review, need the school show its actions were "reasonable," or merely "not unreasonable," and so forth?[100]

In this vein, to bring the environment into the society as a rights-holder would not stand it on a better footing than the rest of us mere mortals, who every day suffer injuries that are *damnum absque injuria.*

100. *See* Dixon v. Alabama State Bd. of Educ., 294 F.2d 150 (5th Cir.), *cert. denied,* 368 U.S. 930 (1961); Comment, *Private Government on the Campus—Judicial Review of University Expulsions,* 72 YALE L.J. 1362 (1963).

What the environment must look for is that its interests be taken into account in subtler, more procedural ways.

The National Environmental Policy Act is a splendid example of this sort of rights-making through the elaboration of procedural safeguards. Among its many provisions, it establishes that every federal agency must:

> (C) include in every recommendation or report on proposals for legislation and other major Federal actions significantly affecting the quality of the human environment, a detailed statement by the responsible official on—
>
> (i) the environmental impact of the proposed action,
>
> (ii) any adverse environmental effects which cannot be avoided should the proposal be implemented,
>
> (iii) alternatives to the proposed action,
>
> (iv) the relationship between local short-term uses of man's environment and the maintenance and enhancement of long-term productivity, and
>
> (v) any irreversible and irretrievable commitments of resources which would be involved in the proposed action should it be implemented.
>
> Prior to making any detailed statement, the responsible Federal official shall consult with and obtain the comments of any Federal agency which has jurisdiction by law or special expertise with respect to any environmental impact involved. Copies of such statement and the comments and views of the appropriate Federal, State, and local agencies, which are authorized to develop and enforce environmental standards, shall be made available to the President, the Council on Environmental Quality and to the public as provided by section 552 of title 5, United States Code, and shall accompany the proposal through the existing agency review processes;
>
> (D) study, develop, and describe appropriate alternatives to recommended courses of action in any proposal which involves unresolved conflicts concerning alternative uses of available resources;
>
> (E) recognize the worldwide and long-range character of environmental problems and, where consistent with the foreign policy of the United States, lend appropriate support to initiatives,

resolutions, and programs designed to maximize international co-operation in anticipating and preventing a decline in the quality of mankind's environment;

(F) make available to States, counties, municipalities, institutions, and individuals, advice and information useful in restoring, maintaining, and enhancing the quality of the environment . . . .[101]

These procedural protections have already begun paying off in the courts. For example, it was on the basis of the Federal Power Commission's failure to make adequate inquiry into "alternatives" (as per subsection (iii)) in *Scenic Hudson*, and the Atomic Energy Commission's failure to make adequate findings, apparently as per subsections (i) and (ii), in connection with the Amchitka Island underground test explosion,[102] that Federal Courts delayed the implementation of environment-threatening schemes.

Although this sort of control (remanding a cause to an agency for further findings) may seem to the layman ineffectual, or only a stalling of the inevitable, the lawyer and the systems analyst know that these demands for further findings can make a difference. It may encourage the institution whose actions threaten the environment to really *think about* what it is doing, and that is neither an ineffectual nor a small feat. Indeed, I would extend the principle beyond federal agencies. Much of the environment is threatened not by them, but by private corporations. Surely the constitutional power would not be lacking to mandate that all private corporations whose actions may have significant adverse affect on the environment make findings of the sort now mandated for federal agencies. Further, there should be requirements that these findings and reports be channeled to the Board of Directors; if the directors are not charged with the knowledge of what their corporation is doing to the environment, it will be all too easy for lower level management to prevent such reports from getting to a policy-making level. We might make it grounds for a guardian to enjoin a private corporation's actions if such procedures had not been carried out.

The rights of the environment could be enlarged by borrowing yet another page from the Environmental Protection Act and mandating comparable provisions for "private governments." The Act sets up

101. National Environmental Policy Act, 92 U.S.C. § 4332 (1970).

102. *See* Committee for Nuclear Responsibility Inc. v. Schlesinger, 40 U.S.L.W. 3214 (Nov. 5, 1971) (Douglas, J. dissent to denial of application for injunction in aid of jurisdiction).

within the Executive Office of the President a Council on Environmental Quality "to be conscious of and responsive to the scientific, economic, social, esthetic, and cultural needs of the Nation; and to formulate and recommend national policies to promote the improvement of the quality of the environment."[103] The Council is to become a focal point, within our biggest "corporation"—the State—to gather and evaluate environmental information which it is to pass on to our chief executive officer, the President. Rather than being ineffectual, this may be a highly sophisticated way of steering organizational behavior. Corporations—especially recidivist polluters and land despoilers—should have to establish comparable internal reorganization, *e.g.*, to set up a Vice-President for Ecological Affairs. The author is not offering this suggestion as a cure-all, by any means, but I do not doubt that this sort of control over internal corporate organization would be an effective supplement to the traditional mechanisms of civil suits, licensing, administrative agencies, and fines.[104]

Similarly, courts, in making rulings that may affect the environment, should be compelled to make findings with respect to environmental harm—showing how they calculated it and how heavily it was weighed—even in matters outside the present Environmental Protection Act. This would have at least two important consequences. First, it would shift somewhat the focus of court-room testimony and concern; second, the appellate courts, through their review and reversals for "insufficient findings," would give content to, and build up a body of, environmental rights, much as content and body has been given, over the years, to terms like "Due Process of Law."

Beyond these procedural safeguards, would there be any rights of the environment that might be deemed "absolute," at least to the extent of, say, Free Speech? Here, the doctrine of irreparable injury comes to mind. There has long been equitable support for an attorney-general's enjoining injury to communal property if he can prove it to be "irreparable." In other words, while repairable damage to the environment

103. 42 U.S.C. § 4342 (1970).

104. As an indication of what lower-level management is apt to do, *see* Ehrenreich & Ehrenreich, *Conscience of a Steel Worker*, 213 THE NATION 268 (1971). One steel company's "major concession [toward obedience to the 1899 Refuse Act, note 78 *supra*] was to order the workers to confine oil dumping to the night shift. 'During the day the Coast Guard patrols. But at night, the water's black, the oil's black; no one can tell.'" An effective corporation law would assure that the internal information channels within a corporation were capable of forcing such matters to the attention of high-level officials. Even then, there is no guarantee that the law will be obeyed—but we may have improved the odds.

might be balanced and weighed, irreparable damage could be enjoined absolutely. There are several reasons why this doctrine has not been used effectively (witness Lake Erie).[105] Undoubtedly, political pressures (in the broadest sense) have had an influence. So, too, has the failure of all of us to understand just how delicate the environmental balance is; this failure has made us unaware of how early "irreparable" injury might be occurring, and, if aware, unable to prove it in court. But most important I think, is that the doctrine simply is not practical as a rule of universal application. For one thing, there are too many cases like the sea urchin example above, where the marginal costs of abating the damage seem too clearly to exceed the marginal benefits, even if the damage to the environment itself is liberally estimated. For another, there is a large problem in how one defines "irreparable." Certainly the great bulk of the environment in civilized parts of the world has been injured "irreparably" in the sense of "irreversably"; we are not likely to return it to its medieval quality. Despite the scientific ring to the term, judgments concerning "irreparable injury" are going to have to subsume questions both of degree of damage and of value—to all of "us" including the environment, *i.e.*, to "spaceship earth"—of the damaged object. Thus, if we are going to revitalize the "irreparable damages" doctrine, and expect it to be taken seriously, we have to recognize that what will be said to constitute "irreparable damage" to the ionosphere, because of its importance to all life, or to the Grand Canyon, because of its uniqueness, is going to rest upon normative judgments that ought to be made explicit.

This suggests that some (relatively) absolute rights be defined for the environment by setting up a constitutional list of "preferred objects," just as some of our Justices feel there are "preferred rights" where humans are concerned.[106] Any threatened injury to these most jealously-to-be-protected objects should be reviewed with the highest level of scrutiny at all levels of government, including our "counter-majoritarian" branch, the court system. Their "Constitutional rights" should be implemented, legislatively and administratively, by, *e.g.*, the setting of environmental quality standards.

I do not doubt that other senses in which the environment might

105. In the case of Lake Erie, in addition to the considerations that follow in the text, there were possibly additional factors such as that no one polluter's acts could be characterized as inflicting irreparable injury.

106. *See* for example Justice Reed's opinion for the Court in Kovacs v. Cooper, 336 U.S. 77 (1949) (*but see* Mr. Justice Frankfurter's concurring opinion, 336 U.S. at 89-96), and United States v. Carolene Products, 304 U.S. 144, 152 n.4 (1938).

have rights will come to mind, and, as I explain more fully below, would be more apt to come to mind if only we should speak in terms of their having rights, albeit vaguely at first. "Rights" might well lie in unanticipated areas. It would seem, for example, that Chief Justice Warren was only stating the obvious when he observed in *Reynolds v. Sims* that "legislators represent people, not trees or acres." Yet, could not a case be made for a system of apportionment which *did* take into account the wildlife of an area?[107] It strikes me as a poor idea that Alaska should have no more congressmen than Rhode Island primarily *because there are in Alaska all those trees and acres, those waterfalls and forests.*[108] I am not saying anything as silly as that we ought to overrule *Baker v. Carr* and retreat from one man-one vote to a system of one man-or-tree one vote. Nor am I even taking the position that we ought to count each acre, as we once counted each slave, as three-fifths of a man. But I am suggesting that there is nothing unthinkable about, and there might on balance even be a prevailing case to be made for, an electoral apportionment that made some systematic effort to allow for the representative "rights" of non-human life. And if a case can be made for that, which I offer here mainly for purpose of illustration, I suspect that a society that grew concerned enough about the environment to make it a holder of rights would be able to find quite a number of "rights" to have waiting for it when it got to court.

Do We Really Have to Put it that Way?

At this point, one might well ask whether much of what has been written could not have been expressed without introducing the notion of trees, rivers, and so forth "having rights." One could simply and straightforwardly say, for example, that (R_1) "the class of persons competent to challenge the pollution of rivers ought to be extended beyond that of persons who can show an immediate adverse economic impact on themselves," and that (R_2), "judges, in weighing competing claims to a wilderness area, ought to think beyond the economic and even esthetic impact on man, and put into the balance a concern for the threatened environment as such." And it is true, indeed, that to say trees and rivers have "rights" is not in itself a stroke of any operational significance—no more than to say "people have rights." To solve any concrete case,

107. Note that in the discussion that follows I am referring to legislative apportionment, not voting proper.

108. In point of fact, there is no reason to suppose that an increase of Congressmen for Alaska would be a benefit to the environment; the reality of the political situation might just as likely result in the election of additional Congressmen with closer ties to oil companies and other developers.

one is always forced to more precise and particularized statements, in which the word "right" might just as well be dropped from the elocution.

But this is not the same as to suggest that introducing the notion of the "rights" of trees and rivers would accomplish nothing beyond the introduction of a set of particular rules like (R_1) and (R_2), above. I think it is quite misleading to say that "*A* has a right to . . ." can be fully explicated in terms of a certain set of specific legal rules, and the manner in which conclusions are drawn from them in a legal system. That is only part of the truth. Introducing the notion of something having a "right" (simply *speaking* that way), brings into the legal system a flexibility and open-endedness that no series of specifically stated legal rules like R_1, R_2, R_3, . . . R_n can capture. Part of the reason is that "right" (and other so-called "legal terms" like "infant," "corporation," "reasonable time") have meaning—vague but forceful—in the ordinary language, and the force of these meanings, inevitably infused with our thought, becomes part of the context against which the "legal language" of our contemporary "legal rules" is interpreted.[109] Consider, for example, the "rules" that govern the question, on whom, and at what stages of litigation, is the burden of proof going to lie? Professor Krier has demonstrated how terribly significant these decisions are in the trial of environmental cases, and yet, also, how much discretion judges have under them.[110] In the case of such vague rules, it is *context*—senses of direction, of value and purpose— that determines how the rules will be understood, every bit as much as their supposed "plain meaning." In a system which spoke of the environment "having legal rights," judges would, I suspect, be inclined to interpret rules such as those of burden of proof far more liberally from the point of the environment. There is, too, the fact that the vocabulary and expressions that are available to us influence and even steer our thought. Consider the effect that was had by introducing into the law terms like "motive," "intent," and "due process." These terms work a subtle shift into the rhetoric of explanation available to judges; with them, new ways of thinking and

109. *See* Simpson, *The Analysis of Legal Concepts*, 80 LAW Q. REV. 535 (1964).

110. Krier, *Environmental Litigation and the Burden of Proof*, in LAW AND THE ENVIRONMENT 105 (M. Baldwin & J. Page eds. 1970). *See* Texas East Trans. Corp. v. Wildlife Preserves, 48 N.J. 261, 225 A.2d 130 (1966). There, where a corporation set up to maintain a wildlife preserve resisted condemnation for the construction of plaintiff's pipe line, the court ruled that ". . . the *quantum* of proof required of this defendant to show arbitrariness against it would not be as substantial as that to be assumed by the ordinary property owner who devotes his land to conventional uses." 225 A.2d at 137.

new insights come to be explored and developed.[111] In such fashion, judges who could unabashedly refer to the "legal rights of the environment" would be encouraged to develop a viable body of law—in part simply through the availability and force of the expression. Besides, such a manner of speaking by courts would contribute to popular notions, and a society that spoke of the "legal rights of the environment" would be inclined to legislate more environment-protecting rules by formal enactment.

If my sense of these influences is correct, then a society in which it is stated, however vaguely, that "rivers have legal rights" would evolve a different legal system than one which did not employ that expression, even if the two of them had, at the start, the very same "legal rules" in other respects.

The Psychic and Socio-Psychic Aspects

There are, as we have seen, a number of developments in the law that may reflect a shift from the view that nature exists *for men.* These range from increasingly favorable procedural rulings for environmental action groups—as regards standing and burden of proof requirements, for example—to the enactment of comprehensive legislation such as the National Environmental Policy Act and the thoughtful Michigan Environmental Protection Act of 1970. Of such developments one may say, however, that it is not the environment *per se* that we are prepared to take into account, but that man's increased awareness of possible long range effects on himself militate in the direction of stopping environmental harm in its incipiency. And this is part of the truth, of course. Even the far-reaching National Environmental Policy Act, in its preambulatory "Declaration of National Environmental Policy," comes out both for "restoring and maintaining environmental quality *to the overall welfare and development of man*" as well as for creating and maintaining "conditions under which *man and nature can exist in productive harmony.*"[112] Because the health and well-being of mankind depend upon the health of the environment, these goals will often be so mutually supportive that one can avoid deciding whether our rationale is to advance "us" or a new "us" that includes the environment. For example, consider the Federal Insecticide, Fungicide, and Rodenticide

111. See Stone, *Existential Humanism and the Law,* in Existential Humanistic Psychology 151 (T. Greening ed. 1971).

112. National Environmental Policy Act, 42 U.S.C. §§ 4321-47 (1970).

Act (FIFRA) which insists that, *e.g.*, pesticides, include a warning "adequate to prevent injury to living man and other vertebrate animals, vegetation, and useful invertebrate animals."[113] Such a provision undoubtedly reflects the sensible notion that the protection of humans is best accomplished by preventing dangerous accumulations in the food chain. Its enactment does not necessarily augur far-reaching changes in, nor even call into question, fundamental matters of consciousness.

But the time is already upon us when we may have to consider subordinating some human claims to those of the environment *per se*. Consider, for example, the disputes over protecting wilderness areas from development that would make them accessible to greater numbers of people. I myself feel disingenuous rationalizing the environmental protectionist's position in terms of a utilitarian calculus, even one that takes future generations into account, and plays fast and loose with its definition of "good." Those who favor development have the stronger argument—they at least hold the protectionist to a standstill—from the point of advancing the greatest good of the greatest number of people. And the same is true regarding arguments to preserve useless species of animals, as in the sea urchin hypothetical. One *can* say that we never know what is going to prove useful at some future time. In order to protect ourselves, therefore, we ought to be conservative now in our treatment of nature. I agree. But when conservationists argue this way to the exclusion of other arguments, or find themselves speaking in terms of "recreational interests" so continuously as to play up to, and reinforce, homocentrist perspectives, there is something sad about the spectacle. One feels that the arguments lack even their proponent's convictions. I expect they want to say something less egotistic and more emphatic but the prevailing and sanctioned modes of explanation in our society are not quite ready for it. In this vein, there must have been abolitonists who put their case in terms of getting more work out of the Blacks. Holdsworth says of the early English Jew that while he was "regarded as a species of res nullius . . . [H]e was valuable for his acquisitive capacity; and for that reason the crown took him under its protection."[114] (Even today, businessmen are put in the position of insisting that their decent but probably profitless acts will "help our company's reputation and be good for profits."[115])

113. *See* note 65 *supra*.

114. W. HOLDSWORTH, HISTORY OF ENGLISH LAW 45 (5th ed. 1931).

115. Note that it is in no small way the law that imposes this manner of speech on businessmen. *See* Dodge v. Ford Motor Co., 204 Mich. 459, 499-505, 170 N.W. 668, 682-83 (1919) (holding that Henry Ford, as dominant stockholder in Ford Motor Co., could

For my part, I would prefer a frank avowal that even making adjustments for esthetic improvemens, what I am proposing is going to cost "us," *i.e.*, reduce our standard of living as measured in terms of our present values.

Yet, this frankness breeds a frank response—one which I hear from my colleagues and which must occur to many a reader. Insofar as the proposal is not just an elaborate legal fiction, but really comes down in the last analysis to a compromise of *our* interests for *theirs*, why should we adopt it? "What is in it for 'us'?"

This is a question I am prepared to answer, but only after permitting myself some observations about how *odd* the question is. It asks for me to justify my position in the very anthropocentric hedonist terms that I am proposing we modify. One is inclined to respond by a counter: "couldn't you (as a white) raise the same questions about compromising your preferred rights-status with Blacks?"; or "couldn't you (as a man) raise the same question about compromising your preferred rights-status with women?" Such counters, unfortunately, seem no more responsive than the question itself. (They have a nagging ring of "yours too" about them.) What the exchange actually points up is a fundamental problem regarding the nature of philosophical argument. Recall that Socrates, whom we remember as an opponent of hedonistic thought, confutes Thrasymachus by arguing that immorality makes one miserably unhappy! Kant, whose moral philosophy was based upon the categorical imperative ("Woe to him who creeps through the serpent windings of Utilitarianism"[116]) finds himself justifying, *e.g.*, promise keeping and truth telling, on the most prudential—one might almost say, commercial—grounds.[117] This "philosophic irony" (as Professor Engel calls it) may owe to there being something unique about ethical argument.[118] "Ethics cannot be put into words", Wittgenstein puts it; such matters "make themselves manifest."[119] On the other hand, perhaps the truth is that in any argument which aims at persuading a human being to action (on ethical or any other bases), "logic" is only an instru-

---

not withhold dividends in the interests of operating the company "as a semi-eleemosynary institution and not as a business institution").

116. I. KANT, PHILOSOPHY OF LAW 195 (Hastie Transl. 1887).

117. I. KANT, *The Metaphysics of Morality*, in THE PHILOSOPHY OF KANT § 1 at 230-31 (J. Watson transl. 1908).

118. Engel, *Reasons, Morals and Philosophic Irony*, in LANGUAGE AND ILLUMINATION 60 (1969).

119. L. WITTGENSTEIN, TRACTATUS LOGICO-PHILOSOPHICUS §§ 6.421, 6.522 (D. Pears & B. McGuinness transl. 1961).

ment for illuminating positions, at best, and in the last analysis it is psycho-logical appeals to the listener's self-interest that hold sway, however "principled" the rhetoric may be.

With this reservation as to the peculiar task of the argument that follows, let me stress that the strongest case can be made from the perspective of human advantage for conferring rights on the environment. Scientists have been warning of the crises the earth and all humans on it face if we do not change our ways—radically—and these crises make the lost "recreational use" of rivers seem absolutely trivial. The earth's very atmosphere is threatened with frightening possibilities: absorption of sunlight, upon which the entire life cycle depends, may be diminished; the oceans may warm (increasing the "greenhouse effect" of the atmosphere), melting the polar ice caps, and destroying our great coastal cities; the portion of the atmosphere that shields us from dangerous radiation may be destroyed. Testifying before Congress, sea explorer Jacques Cousteau predicted that the oceans (to which we dreamily look to feed our booming populations) are headed toward their own death: "The cycle of life is intricately tied up with the cycle of water . . . the water system has to remain alive if we are to remain alive on earth."[120] We are depleting our energy and our food sources at a rate that takes little account of the needs even of humans now living.

These problems will not be solved easily; they very likely can be solved, if at all, only through a willingness to suspend the rate of increase in the standard of living (by present values) of the earth's "advanced" nations, and by stabilizing the total human population. For some of us this will involve forfeiting material comforts; for others it will involve abandoning the hope someday to obtain comforts long envied. For all of us it will involve giving up the right to have as many offspring as we might wish. Such a program is not impossible of realization, however. Many of our so-called "material comforts" are not only in excess of, but are probably in opposition to, basic biological needs. Further, the "costs" to the advanced nations is not as large as would appear from Gross National Product figures. G.N.P. reflects social gain (of a sort) without discounting for the social *cost* of that gain, *e.g.*, the losses through depletion of resources, pollution, and so forth. As has well been shown, as societies become more and more "advanced," their real marginal gains become less and less for each additional dollar of

---

120. Cousteau, *The Oceans: No Time to Lose*, L.A. Times, Oct. 24, 1971, § (opinion), at 1, col. 4.

G.N.P.[121] Thus, to give up "human progress" would not be as costly as might appear on first blush.

Nonetheless, such far-reaching social changes are going to involve us in a serious reconsideration of our consciousness towards the environment. I say this knowing full well that there is something more than a trifle obscure in the claim: is popular consciousness a meaningful notion, to begin with? If so, what is our present consciousness regarding the environment? Has it been causally responsible for our material state of affairs? Ought we to shift our consciousness (and if so, to what exactly, and on what grounds)? How, if at all, would a shift in consciousness be translated into tangible institutional reform? Not one of these questions can be answered to everyone's satisfactions, certainly not to the author's.

It is commonly being said today, for example, that our present state of affairs—at least in the West—can be traced to the view that Nature is the dominion of Man, and that this attitude, in turn, derives from our religious traditions.

> Whatever the origins, the text is quite clear in Judaism, was absorbed all but unchanged into Christianity, and was inflated in Humanism to become the implicit attitude of Western man to Nature and the environment. Man is exclusively divine, all other creatures and things occupy lower and generally inconsequential stature; man is given dominion over all creatures and things; he is enjoined to subdue the earth. . . . This environment was created by the man who believes that the cosmos is a pyramid erected to support man on its pinnacle, that reality exists only because man can perceive it, that God is made in the image of man, and that the world consists solely of a dialogue between men. Surely this is an infantalism which is unendurable. It is a residue from a past of inconsequence when a few puny men cried of their supremacy to an unhearing and uncaring world. One longs for a psychiatrist who can assure man that his deep seated cultural inferiority is no longer necessary or appropriate. . . . It is not really necessary to destroy nature in order to gain God's favor or even his undivided attention.[122]

Surely this is forcibly put, but it is not entirely convincing as an explanation for how we got to where we are. For one thing, so far as

121. *See* J. HARTE & R. SOCOLOW, PATIENT EARTH (1971).

122. McHarg, *Values, Process and Form*, in THE FITNESS OF MAN'S ENVIRONMENT 213-14 (1968).

intellectual influences are to be held responsible for our present state of affairs, one might as fairly turn on Darwin as the Bible. It was, after all, Darwin's views—in part through the prism of Spencer—that gave moral approbation to struggle, conquest, and domination; indeed, by emphasizing man's development as a product of chance happenings, Darwin also had the effect—intended or not—of reducing our awareness of the mutual interdependency of everything in Nature. And besides, as Professor Murphy points out, the spiritual beliefs of the Chinese and Indians "in the unity between man and nature had no greater effect than the contrary beliefs in Europe in producing a balance between man and his environment"; he claims that in China, *tao* notwithstanding, "ruthless deforestation has been continuous."[123] I am under the impression, too, that notwithstanding the vaunted "harmony" between the American Plains Indians and Nature, once they had equipped themselves with rifles their pursuit of the buffalo expanded to fill the technological potential.[124] The fact is, that "consciousness" explanations pass too quickly over the less negative but simpler view of the situation: there are an increasing number of humans, with increasing wants, and there has been an increasing technology to satisfy them at "cost" to the rest of nature. Thus, we ought not to place too much hope that a changed environmental consciousness will in and of itself reverse present trends. Furthermore, societies have long since passed the point where a change in human consciousness on any matter will rescue us from our problems. More then ever before we are in the hands of institutions. These institutions are not "mere legal fictions" moreover—they have wills, minds, purposes, and inertias that are in very important ways their own, *i.e.*, that can transcend and survive changes in the consciousnesses of the individual humans who supposedly comprise them, and whom they supposedly serve. (It is more and more the individual human being, with his consciousness, that is the legal fiction.[125])

123. Murphy, *supra* note 27, at 477.

124. On the other hand, the statement in text, and the previous one of Professor Murphy, may be a bit severe. One could as easily claim that Christianity has had no influence on overt human behavior in light of the killings that have been carried out by professed Christians, often in its name. *Feng shui* has, on all accounts I am familiar with, influenced the development of land in China. *See* Freedman, *Geomancy*, 1968 PROCEEDINGS OF THE ROYAL ANTHROPOLOGICAL INSTITUTE OF GREAT BRITAIN AND IRELAND 5; March, *An Appreciation of Chinese Geomancy*, 27 J. ASIAN STUDIES 253 (1968).

125. The legal system does the best it can to maintain the illusion of the reality of the individual human being. Consider, for example, how many constitutional cases, brought in the name of some handy individual, represent a power struggle between institutions—the NAACP and a school board, the Catholic Church and a school board, the ACLU and the Army, and so forth. Are the individual human plaintiffs the real moving causes of these cases—or an afterthought?

For these reasons, it is far too pat to suppose that a western "environmental consciousness" is solely or even primarily responsible for our environmental crisis. On the other hand, it is not so extravagant to claim that it has dulled our resentment and our determination to respond. For this reason, whether we will be able to bring about the requisite institutional and population growth changes depends in part upon effecting a radical shift in our feelings about "our" place in the rest of Nature.

A radical new conception of man's relationship to the rest of nature would not only be a step towards solving the material planetary problems; there are strong reasons for such a changed consciousness from the point of making us far better humans. If we only stop for a moment and look at the underlying human qualities that our present attitudes toward property and nature draw upon and reinforce, we have to be struck by how stultifying of our own personal growth and satisfaction they can become when they take rein of us. Hegel, in "justifying" private property, unwittingly reflects the tone and quality of some of the needs that are played upon:

> A person has as his substantive end the right of putting his will into any and every thing and thereby making it his, because it has no such end in itself and derives its destiny and soul from his will. This is the absolute right of appropriation which man has over all "things."[126]

What is it within us that gives us this need not just to satisfy basic biological wants, but to extend our wills over things, to object-ify them, to make them ours, to manipulate them, to keep them at a psychic distance? Can it all be explained on "rational" bases? Should we not be suspect of such needs within us, cautious as to why we wish to gratify

When we recognize that our problems are increasingly institutional, we would see that the solution, if there is one, must involve coming to grips with how the "corporate" (in the broadest sense) entity is directed, and we must alter our views of "property" in the fashion that is needed to regulate organizations successfully. For example, instead of ineffectual, after-the-fact criminal fines we should have more preventive in-plant inspections, notwithstanding the protests of "invasion of [corporate] privacy."

In-plant inspection of production facilities and records is presently allowed only in a narrow range of areas, *e.g.*, in federal law, under the Federal Food, Drug, and Cosmetic Act, 21 U.S.C. § 374 *et seq.* (1970), and provisions for meat inspection, 21 U.S.C. § 608 (1970). Similarly, under local building codes we do not wait for a building to collapse before authoritative sources inquire into the materials and procedures that are being used in the construction; inspectors typically come on site to check the progress at every critical stage. A sensible preventive legal system calls for extending the ambit of industries covered by comparable "privacy invading" systems of inspection.

126. G. Hegel, Hegel's Philosophy of Right 41 (T. Knox transl. 1945).

them? When I first read that passage of Hegel, I immediately thought not only of the emotional contrast with Spinoza, but of the passage in Carson McCullers' *A Tree, A Rock, A Cloud,* in which an old derelict has collared a twelve year old boy in a streetcar cafe. The old man asks whether the boy knows "how love should be begun?"

> The old man leaned closer and whispered:
>
> "A tree. A rock. A cloud."
>
> . . .
>
> "The weather was like this in Portland," he said. "At the time my science was begun. I meditated and I started very cautious. I would pick up something from the street and take it home with me. I bought a goldfish and I concentrated on the goldfish and I loved it. I graduated from one thing to another. Day by day I was getting this technique. . . .
>
> . . .
>
> . . . "For six years now I have gone around by myself and built up my science. And now I am a master. Son. I can love anything. No longer do I have to think about it even. I see a street full of people and a beautiful light comes in me. I watch a bird in the sky. Or I meet a traveler on the road. Everything, Son. And anybody. All stranger and all loved! Do you realize what a science like mine can mean?"[127]

To be able to get away from the view that Nature is a collection of useful senseless objects is, as McCullers' "madman" suggests, deeply involved in the development of our abilities to love—or, if that is putting it too strongly, to be able to reach a heightened awareness of our own, and others' capacities in their mutual interplay. To do so, we have to give up some psychic investment in our sense of separateness and specialness in the universe. And this, in turn, is hard giving indeed, because it involves us in a flight backwards, into earlier stages of civilization and childhood in which we had to trust (and perhaps fear) our environment, for we had not then the power to master it. Yet, in doing so, we—as persons—gradually free ourselves of needs for supportive illusions. Is not this one of the triumphs for "us" of our giving legal rights to (or acknowledging the legal rights of) the Blacks and women?[128]

---

127. C. McCullers, The Ballad of the Sad Cafe and Other Stories 150-51 (1958).

128. Consider what Schopenhauer was writing "Of Women," about the time the Wisconsin Supreme Court was explaining why women were unfit to practice law, note 23 *supra:*

> You need only look at the way in which she is formed, to see that woman is not meant to undergo great labour, whether of the mind or of the body. She pays the debt of life not by what she does, but by what she suffers; by the pains of

Changes in this sort of consciousness are already developing, for the betterment of the planet and us. There is now federal legislation which "establishes by law"[129]

> the humane ethic that animals should be accorded the basic creature comforts of adequate housing, ample food and water, reasonable handling, decent sanitation, sufficient ventilation, shelter from extremes of weather and temperature, and adequate veterinary care including the appropriate use of pain-killing drugs. . . .[130]

The Vietnam war has contributed to this movement, as it has to others. Five years ago a Los Angeles mother turned out a poster which read "War is not Healthy for children and other living things."[131] It caught

---

> childbearing and care for the child, and by submission to her husband, to whom she should be a patient and cheering companion. The keenest sorrows and joys are not for her, nor is she called upon to display a great deal of strength. The current of her life should be more gentle, peaceful and trivial than man's, without being essentially happier or unhappier.
>
> Women are directly fitted for acting as the nurses and teachers of our early childhood by the fact that they are themselves childish, frivolous and short-sighted; in a word, they are big children all their life long—a kind of intermediate stage between the child and the full-grown man, who is man in the strict sense of the word. . . .
>
> However many disadvantages all this may involve, there is at least this to be said in its favour: that the woman lives more in the present than the man, and that, if the present is at all tolerable, she enjoys it more eagerly. This is the source of that cheerfulness which is peculiar to woman, fitting her to amuse man in his hours of recreation, and, in case of need, to console him when he is borne down by the weight of his cares.
>
> . . . .
>
> . . . [I]t will be found that the fundamental fault of the female character is that it has *no sense of justice*. This is mainly due to the fact, already mentioned, that women are defective in the powers of reasoning and deliberation; but it is also traceable to the position which Nature has assigned to them as the weaker sex. They are dependent, not upon strength, but upon craft; and hence their instinctive capacity for cunning, and their ineradicable tendency to say what is not true. ***For as lions are provided with claws and teeth, and elephants and boars with tusks, bulls with horns, and the cuttle fish with its cloud of inky fluid, so Nature has equipped woman, for her defense and protection, with the arts of dissimulation; and all the power which Nature has conferred upon man in the shape of physical strength and reason, has been bestowed upon women in this form. Hence, dissimulation is innate in woman, and almost as much a quality of the stupid as of the clever. . . .

A. SCHOPENHAUER, *On Women*, in STUDIES IN PESSIMISM 105-10 (T. B. Saunders transl. 1893).

If a man should write such insensitive drivel today, we would suspect him of being morally and emotionally blind. Will the future judge us otherwise, for venting rather than examining the needs that impel us to treat the environment as a senseless object—to blast to pieces some small atoll to find out whether an atomic weapon works?

129. Of course, the phase one looks toward is a time in which such sentiments need not be prescribed *by law*.

130. The "Purpose of the Legislation" in H.R. Rep. No. 91-1651, 91st Cong., 2d Sess., to the "[Animal] Welfare Act of 1970," 3 U.S. CODE CONG. & ADMIN. NEWS 5103, 5104 (1970). Some of the West Publishing Co. typesetters may not be quite ready for this yet; they printed out the title as "Annual Welfare Act of 1970."

131. *See* MCCALL'S, May, 1971, at 44.

on tremendously—at first, I suspect, because it sounded like another clever protest against the war, *i.e.*, another angle. But as people say such things, and think about them, the possibilities of what they have stumbled upon become manifest—in its suit against the Secretary of Agriculture to cancel the registration of D.D.T., Environmental Defense Fund alleged "biological injury to man and other living things."[132] A few years ago the pollution of streams was thought of only as a problem of smelly, unsightly, unpotable water *i.e.*, to us. Now we are beginning to discover that pollution is a process that destroys wondrously subtle balances of life within the water, and as between the water and its banks. This heightened awareness enlarges our sense of the dangers to us. But it also enlarges our empathy. We are not only developing the scientific capacity, but we are cultivating the personal capacities *within us* to recognize more and more the ways in which nature—like the woman, the Black, the Indian and the Alien—is like us (and we will also become more able realistically to define, confront, live with and admire the ways in which we are all different).[133]

The time may be on hand when these sentiments, and the early stirrings of the law, can be coalesced into a radical new theory or myth —felt as well as intellectualized—of man's relationships to the rest of nature. I do not mean "myth" in a demeaning sense of the term, but in the sense in which, at different times in history, our social "facts" and relationships have been comprehended and integrated by reference to the "myths" that we are co-signers of a social contract, that the Pope is God's agent, and that all men are created equal. Pantheism, Shinto and Tao all have myths to offer. But they are all, each in its own fashion, quaint, primitive and archaic. What is needed is a myth that can fit our growing body of knowledge of geophysics, biology and the cosmos. In

132. Environmental Defense Fund, Inc. v. Hardin, 428 F.2d 1093, 1096 (D.C. Cir. 1970). Plaintiffs would thus seem to have urged a broader than literal reading of the statute, 7 U.S.C. § 135(z) (2) (d) (1970), which refers to " . . . living man and other vertebrate animals, vegetation, and useful invertebrate animals."

E.D.F. was joined as petitioners by the National Audubon Society, the Sierra Club, and the West Michigan Environmental Action Council, 428 F.2d at 1094-95 n.5.

133. In the case of the bestowal of rights on other humans, the action also helps the recipient to discover new personal depths and possibilities—new dignity—within himself. I do not want to make much of the possibility that this effect would be relevant in the case of bestowing rights on the environment. But I would not dismiss it out of hand, either. How, after all, do we judge that a man is, say, "flourishing with a new sense of pride and dignity?" What we mean by such statements, and the nature of the evidence upon which we rely in support of them, is quite complex. *See* Austin, note 93 *supra*. A tree treated in a "rightful" manner would respond in a manner that, when described, would sound much like the response of a person accorded "new dignity." *See also* note 93 *supra*.

this vein, I do not think it too remote that we may come to regard the Earth, as some have suggested, as one organism, of which Mankind is a functional part—the mind, perhaps: different from the rest of nature, but different as a man's brain is from his lungs.

> Ever since the first Geophysical Year, international scientific studies have shown irrefutably that the Earth as a whole is an organized system of most closely interrelated and indeed interdependent activities. It is, in the broadest sense of the term, an "organism." The so-called life-kingdoms and the many vegetable and animal species are dependent upon each other for survival in a balanced condition of planet-wide existence; and they depend on their environment, conditioned by oceanic and atmospheric currents, and even more by the protective action of the ionosphere and many other factors which have definite rhythms of operation. Mankind is part of this organic planetary whole; and there can be no truly new global society, and perhaps in the present state of affairs no society at all, as long as man will not recognize, accept and enjoy the fact that mankind has a definite function to perform within this planetary organism of which it is an active part.
>
> In order to give a constructive meaning to the activities of human societies all over the globe, these activities—physical and mental—should be understood and given basic value with reference to the wholesome functioning of the entire Earth, and we may add of the entire solar system. This cannot be done (1) if man insists on considering himself an alien Soul compelled to incarnate on this sorrowful planet, and (2) if we can see in the planet, Earth, nothing but a mass of material substances moved by mechanical laws, and in "life" nothing but a chance combination of molecular aggregations.
>
> . . . As I see it, the Earth is only one organized "field" of activities—and so is the *human person*—but these activities take place at various levels, in different "spheres" of being and realms of consciousness. The lithosphere is not the biosphere, and the latter not the . . . ionosphere. The Earth is not *only* a material mass. Consciousness is not only "human"; it exists at animal and vegetable levels, and most likely must be latent, or operating in some form, in the molecule and the atom; and all these diverse and in a sense hierarchical modes of activity and consciousness should be seen integrated in and perhaps transcended by an all-encompassing and "eonic" planetary Consciousness.
>
> . . . .
>
> Mankind's function within the Earth-organism is to extract

> from the activities of all other operative systems within this organism the type of consciousness which we call "reflective" or "self"-consciousness—or, we may also say to *mentalize* and give meaning, value, and "name" to all that takes place anywhere within the Earth-field. . . .
>
> This "mentalization" process operates through what we call culture. To each region of, and living condition in the total field of the Earth-organism a definite type of culture inherently corresponds. Each region is the "womb" out of which a specific type of human mentality and culture can and sooner or later will emerge. All these cultures—past, present and future—and their complex interrelationships and interactions are the collective builders of the Mind of humanity; and this means of the *conscious Mind of the Earth*.[134]

As radical as such a consciousness may sound today, all the dominant changes we see about us point in its direction. Consider just the impact of space travel, of world-wide mass media, of increasing scientific discoveries about the interrelatedness of all life processes. Is it any wonder that the term "spaceship earth" has so captured the popular imagination? The problems we have to confront are increasingly the world-wide crises of a global organism: not pollution of a stream, but pollution of the atmosphere and of the ocean. Increasingly, the death that occupies each human's imagination is not his own, but that of the entire life cycle of the planet earth, to which each of us is as but a cell to a body.

To shift from such a lofty fancy as the planetarization of consciousness to the operation of our municipal legal system is to come down to earth hard. Before the forces that are at work, our highest court is but a frail and feeble—a distinctly human—institution. Yet, the Court may be at its best not in its work of handing down decrees, but at the very task that is called for: of summoning up from the human spirit the kindest and most generous and worthy ideas that abound there, giving them shape and reality and legitimacy.[135] Witness the School Desegregation Cases which, more importantly than to integrate the schools (assuming they did), awakened us to moral needs which, when made visible, could not be denied. And so here, too, in the case of the environment, the Supreme Court may find itself in a position to award "rights" in a way that will contribute to a change in popular consciousness. It would

134. D. Rudhyar, Directives for New Life 21-23 (1971).

135. *See* Stone, note 111 *supra*.

be a modest move, to be sure, but one in furtherance of a large goal: the future of the planet as we know it.

How far we are from such a state of affairs, where the law treats "environmental objects" as holders of legal rights, I cannot say. But there is certainly intriguing language in one of Justice Black's last dissents, regarding the Texas Highway Department's plan to run a six-lane expressway through a San Antonio Park.[136] Complaining of the Court's refusal to stay the plan, Black observed that "after today's decision, the people of San Antonio and the birds and animals that make their home in the park will share their quiet retreat with an ugly, smelly stream of traffic. . . . Trees, shrubs, and flowers will be mown down."[137] Elsewhere he speaks of the "burial of public parks," of segments of a highway which "devour parkland," and of the park's heartland.[138] Was he, at the end of his great career, on the verge of saying—just saying—that "nature has 'rights' on its own account"? Would it be so hard to do?

136. San Antonio Conservation Soc'y v. Texas Highway Dep't, *cert. denied*, 400 U.S. 968 (1970) (Black, J. dissenting to denial of certiorari).

137. *Id.* at 969.

138. *Id.* at 971.

[5]

Our Rights and Obligations to Future Generations for the Environment

Edith Brown Weiss

> This we know: the earth does not belong to man: man belongs to the earth. . . . Whatever befalls the earth, befalls the sons of the earth. Man did not weave the web of life: he is merely a strand in it. Whatever he does to the web, he does to himself.
>
> *Chief Seattle*†

We read every day about the desecration of our environment and the mismanagement of our natural resources. We have always had the capacity to wreck the environment on a small or even regional scale. Centuries of irrigation without adequate drainage in ancient times converted large areas of the fertile Tigris-Euphrates valley into barren desert. What is new is that we now have the power to change our global environment irreversibly, with profoundly damaging effects on the robustness and integrity of the planet and the heritage that we pass to future generations.

In Fairness to Future Generations argues that we, the human species, hold the natural environment of our planet in common with all members of our

† Letter from Chief Seattle, patriarch of the Duwamish and Squamish Indians of Puget Sound, to U.S. President Franklin Pierce (1855). Although the letter appears in numerous anthologies, the original has never been located.

species: past generations, the present generation, and future generations.[1] As members of the present generation, we hold the earth in trust for future generations. At the same time, we are beneficiaries entitled to use and benefit from it.

There are two relationships that must shape any theory of intergenerational equity in the context of our natural environment: our relationship to other generations of our own species and our relationship to the natural system of which we are a part.[2]

The human species is integrally linked with other parts of the natural system; we both affect and are affected by what happens in the system. The natural system, contrary to popular belief, is in many ways a hostile one. Deserts, glaciers, volcanoes, tsunamis can bring havoc to our species. Moreover, the natural environment can be toxic to our species, as through the natural toxicity of some plants and animals or the dramatic release of toxic clouds of carbon dioxide from Lake Nyos in the Cameroon, which killed 1,700 people. On the other hand, the natural system makes life possible for us. It gives us the resources with which to survive and to improve human welfare.

Our actions affect the natural system. We alone among all living creatures have the capacity to shape significantly our relationship to the environment. We can use it on a sustainable basis or we can degrade environmental quality and the natural resource base. As part of the natural system, we have no right to destroy its integrity; nor is it in our interest to do so. Rather, as the most sentient of living creatures, we have a special responsibility to care for the planet.

The second fundamental relationship is that between different generations of the human species. All generations are inherently linked to other generations, past and future, in using the common patrimony of earth.[3]

To define intergenerational equity, it is useful to view the human community as a partnership among all generations. In describing a state as a partnership, Edmund Burke observed that "as the ends of such a partnership cannot be obtained in many generations, it becomes a partnership not only between those who are living but between those who are living, those who

[1] E. Brown Weiss, In Fairness to Future Generations: International Law, Common Patrimony and Intergenerational Equity (1989).

[2] The field of human ecology studies this relationship. *See* Readings in Man, the Environment, and Human Ecology (A. S. Boughey ed. 1973) (good selection of readings in human ecology); R. & P. Watson, Man and Nature (1969) (thoughtful essay).

[3] Professor D'Amato criticizes existing theories of equity for depending on "an articulate link to the improvement of the *human* condition" (i.e., as anthropocentric), rather than on a moral relationship with nature itself. It is certainly true that *In Fairness to Future Generations* is concerned with equity among generations of the human species. But it is equity with regard to the care and use of the planet, which is explicitly rooted in the recognition that the human species is part of the natural *system*. This implies great respect for the natural system of which we are a part, but it does not imply that all other living creatures are or should be treated equally. Rather, the human species, as a part of this natural system, has a special obligation to maintain the integrity of the planet, so that all generations will be able to enjoy its fruits.

are dead, and those who are to be born."[4] The purpose of human society must be to realize and protect the welfare and well-being of every generation. This requires sustaining the life-support systems of the planet, the ecological processes and the environmental conditions necessary for a healthy and decent human environment.

In this partnership, no generation knows beforehand when it will be the living generation, how many members it will have, or even how many generations there will ultimately be. It is useful, then, to take the perspective of a generation that is placed somewhere along the spectrum of time, but does not know in advance where it will be located.[5] Such a generation would want to inherit the earth in at least as good condition as it has been in for any previous generation and to have as good access to it as previous generations. This requires each generation to pass the planet on in no worse condition than it received it in[6] and to provide equitable access to its resources and benefits. Each generation is thus both a trustee for the planet with obligations to care for it and a beneficiary with rights to use it.

Intergenerational equity calls for equality among generations in the sense that each generation is entitled to inherit a robust planet that on balance is at least as good as that of previous generations. This means all generations are entitled to at least the planetary health that the first generation had.[7] In practice, some generations may improve the environment, with the result that later generations will inherit a richer and more diverse natural resource base. In this case, they would be treated better than previous generations. But this extra benefit would be consistent with intergenerational equity, because the minimum level of planetary robustness would be sustained and later generations would not be worse off than previous generations. The converse is also possible, that later generations would receive a badly degraded environment with major loss of species diversity, in which case they would be treated worse than previous generations. This latter case would be contrary to principles of intergenerational equity. Equity among generations provides for a minimum floor for all generations and ensures that each generation has at least that level of planetary resource base as its ancestors. This concept is consistent with the implicit premises of trusteeship, stewardship and tenancy, in which the assets must be conserved, not dissipated, so that they are equally available to those who come after.

The theory of intergenerational equity finds deep roots in international law.[8] The Preamble to the Universal Declaration of Human Rights begins, "Whereas recognition of the inherent dignity and of the equal and inalienable rights of all members of the human family is the foundation of freedom, justice and peace in the world." The reference to all members of the human

[4] E. BURKE, *Reflections on the Revolution in France* 139–40 (1790), in 2 WORKS OF EDMUND BURKE 368 (London 1854).

[5] *See* J. RAWLS, A THEORY OF JUSTICE (1971).

[6] *See* Callahan, *What Obligations Do We Have to Future Generations?*, in RESPONSIBILITIES TO FUTURE GENERATIONS 73 (E. Partridge ed. 1981).

[7] *See* B. ACKERMAN, SOCIAL JUSTICE IN THE LIBERAL STATE (1980).

[8] E. BROWN WEISS, *supra* note 1, at 25–26.

family has a temporal dimension, which brings all generations within its scope. The reference to equal and inalienable rights affirms the basic equality of these generations in the human family.

The United Nations Charter, the International Covenant on Civil and Political Rights, the Convention on the Prevention and Punishment of the Crime of Genocide, the American Declaration on the Rights and Duties of Man, the Declaration on the Elimination of Discrimination against Women, the Declaration on the Rights of the Child and many other human rights documents protect the dignity of all people and the equality of their rights. The Declaration of the Principles of International Cultural Co-operation provides in Article 1 that "each culture has a dignity and value which must be respected and preserved," and that "all cultures form part of the common heritage belonging to mankind." These instruments reveal a fundamental belief in the dignity of all members of human society and in an equality of rights that extends in time as well as space. Indeed, if we were to license the present generation to exploit our natural and cultural resources at the expense of the well-being of future generations, we would contradict the purposes of the United Nations Charter and international human rights documents.

It is not enough, however, to apply a theory of intergenerational equity only among generations. It also carries an intragenerational dimension. When future generations become living generations, they have certain rights and obligations to use and care for the planet that they can enforce against one another. Were it otherwise, members of one generation could allocate the benefits of the world's resources to some communities and the burdens of caring for it to others and still potentially claim on balance to have satisfied principles of equity among generations.

Moreover, the fulfillment of intergenerational obligations requires attention to certain aspects of intragenerational equity. As is well-known, poverty is a primary cause of ecological degradation. Poverty-stricken communities, which by definition have unequal access to resources, are forced to overexploit the resources they do have so as to satisfy their own basic needs. As an ecosystem begins to deteriorate, the poor communities suffer most, because they cannot afford to take the measures necessary to control or adapt to the degradation, or to move to pristine areas.

Thus, to implement intergenerational equity, countries need to help poor communities to use the natural environment on a sustainable basis, to assist them in gaining equitable access to the economic benefits from our planet, such as potable water, and to help protect them from degraded environmental quality. As beneficiaries of the planetary legacy, all members of the present generation are entitled to equitable access to and use of the legacy. The future nationals of all countries will benefit from efforts of the present generation to protect the general planetary environment for future generations. Conversely, all will suffer if the present generation does not make such efforts.

I have proposed three basic principles of intergenerational equity. First, each generation should be required to conserve the diversity of the natural and cultural resource base, so that it does not unduly restrict the options available to future generations in solving their problems and satisfying their own values, and should also be entitled to diversity comparable to that enjoyed by previous generations. This principle is called "conservation of options." Second, each generation should be required to maintain the quality of the planet so that it is passed on in no worse condition than that in which it was received, and should also be entitled to planetary quality comparable to that enjoyed by previous generations. This is the principle of "conservation of quality." Third, each generation should provide its members with equitable rights of access to the legacy of past generations and should conserve this access for future generations. This is the principle of "conservation of access."

These proposed principles constrain the actions of the present generation in developing and using the planet, but within these constraints do not dictate how each generation should manage its resources.

These principles of intergenerational equity form the basis of a set of intergenerational obligations and rights, or planetary rights and obligations, that are held by each generation. These rights and obligations derive from each generation's position as part of the intertemporal entity of human society.

Planetary rights and obligations are integrally linked. The rights are always associated with obligations. They are rights of each generation to receive the planet in no worse condition than did the previous generation, to inherit comparable diversity in the natural and cultural resource bases, and to have equitable access to the use and benefits of the legacy. They represent in the first instance a moral protection of interests, which must be transformed into legal rights and obligations.

Planetary rights and obligations coexist in each generation. In the *inter*generational dimension, the generations to which the obligations are owed are future generations, while the generations with which the rights are linked are past generations. Thus, the rights of future generations are linked to the obligations of the present generation. In the *intra*generational context, planetary obligations and rights exist between members of the present generation. They derive from the *inter*generational relationship that each generation shares with those who have come before and those yet to come. Thus, intergenerational obligations to conserve the planet flow from the present generation both to future generations as generations and to members of the present generation, who have the right to use and enjoy the planetary legacy.

Intergenerational rights of necessity inhere in all generations, whether these be immediately successive generations or ones more distant. There is no theoretical basis for limiting such rights to immediately successive generations. If we were to do so, we would often provide little or no protection to more distant future generations. Nuclear and hazardous waste disposal, the loss of biological diversity and ozone depletion, for example, have significant effects on the natural heritage of more distant generations.

Intergenerational planetary rights may be regarded as group rights, as distinct from individual rights, in the sense that generations hold these rights as groups in relation to other generations—past, present and future.[9] They exist regardless of the number and identity of individuals making up each generation. When held by members of the present generation, they acquire attributes of individual rights in the sense that there are identifiable interests of individuals that the rights protect. However, those interests derive from the fact that those living now are members of the present generation and have rights in relation to other generations to use and benefit from the planet. The remedies for violations of these rights will benefit other members of the generation, not only the individual.[10]

Developments in international law outside the field of the environment make acceptance of intergenerational rights a natural and desirable evolution. Indeed, international human rights law—the genocide convention, and the prohibition against racial discrimination, to cite two examples—are arguably directed as much to the protection of future, as to present, generations. The extinction of, for example, an entire people is more odious in law than the murder of an equal number of people constituting a minority of each of several groups. Similarly, discrimination denies an "equal place at the starting gate" not only to the generation of the suppressed group but (by implication) also to future generations. Provisions in other human rights agreements refer to rights of children and of the elderly, and to education and training, which are implicitly temporally oriented.

One might still ask whether it is not preferable to speak only of planetary obligations toward future generations without corresponding intergenerational rights. Can intergenerational obligations exist without rights?[11] While rights are always connected to obligations, the reverse is not always true. Theoretically, an obligation need not always entail a right. For example, a moral obligation of charity does not give those who benefit a right to charity. The legal positivist Hans Kelsen hesitated to find a legal right connected to certain legal obligations.

[9] For a thoughtful analysis of group rights in relation to goods that are enjoyed together, see J. Waldron, Can Communal Goods Be Human Rights? (paper delivered at Conference on Development, Environment and Peace as New Human Rights, Oxford University, Oxford, England, May 28–31, 1987).

[10] The temporal dimension may offer a theoretical basis for unifying those human rights that we now consider to be group or social rights and for so-called new human rights. Group rights, such as cultural rights, have a temporal dimension since the community inherently extends over time. Theoretically, rights to development, to food, to health, and to the environment can be seen as intergenerational, or intertemporal, in that they are rights of access of each generation to use and benefit from our natural and cultural resources. *See* E. Brown Weiss, *supra* note 1, at 114–15.

[11] Bryan Norton, a philosopher, argues that if one accepts the conceptual model of rights as limited to individual rights (which he does), it is preferable to recognize general obligations toward the integrity of environmental systems rather than to discuss environmental protection in the framework of rights, since this framework cannot encompass such categories as future generations, whose individual members are still contingent. Norton, *Environmental Ethics and the Rights of Future Generations*, 7 Soc. Theory & Prac. 319, 337 (1981).

> If the obligated behavior of one individual does not refer to a specifically designated other individual . . . but refers only to the legal community as such, then . . . one is satisfied . . . to assume a legal obligation without a corresponding reflex right: for example in case of the legal norms that prescribe a certain human behavior toward some animals, plants, or inanimate objects by pain of punishment. It is forbidden to kill certain animals at certain times (or altogether), to pick certain flowers, to cut certain trees or to destroy certain historical monuments. These are obligations which—indirectly—exist toward the legal community interested in these objects.[12]

John Austin described some obligations as absolute duties, which exist independently of any correlative right. He defined absolute duties as those prescribing actions toward parties other than the one obliged, who are not determinate persons, such as members generally of an independent society and mankind at large.[13]

If we were to follow this analysis, we would contend that the obligations of the present generation to future generations constitute obligations or duties for which there are no correlative rights, because there are no determinate persons to whom the right attaches. Similarly, in the intragenerational context, obligations to conserve diversity, quality and access would be viewed as absolute duties for which there is no correlative right.

While this approach may be attractive, it ignores the fundamental temporal relationship that each generation has to all other generations and that gives rise to the rights of each generation to share equitably in the use of the planet and its natural resources. These rights focus discussion on the welfare of generations, what each generation is able to have and to enjoy, in a way that obligations cannot. If obligations of the present generation are not linked with rights, the present generation has a strong incentive to bias the definition of these obligations in favor of itself at the expense of future generations. Intergenerational rights have greater moral force than do obligations. They provide a basis for protecting the interests of all generations in a healthy and robust planet.

Professor D'Amato in his essay takes issue with the notion of rights of future generations to the planet by invoking Derek Parfit's famous paradox and combining it with the new theory of chaos. He argues that future generations cannot have rights because they are composed of individuals who do not exist yet and every intervention we take today to protect the environment affects the composition of these future individuals, robbing some potential members of future generations of their existence.

It is important to parse this analysis into its two component parts: that future generations cannot have rights because the individuals do not exist yet, and that actions to protect the environment for future generations will destroy the rights of some future individuals because different people will be born as a result of the intervention. The first is that future generations

[12] H. Kelsen, Pure Theory of Law 62 (M. Knight trans. 1969).

[13] 1 J. Austin, Austin's Jurisprudence, Lectures on Jurisprudence 413–15 (1873).

cannot have rights, because rights exist only when there are identifiable interests, which can only happen if we can identify the individuals who have interests to protect. Since we cannot know who the individuals in the future will be, it is not possible for future generations to have rights.

This paradox assumes the traditional conceptual framework of rights as rights of identifiable individuals. The planetary, or intergenerational, rights proposed in *In Fairness to Future Generations* are not rights possessed by individuals. They are, instead, *generational* rights, which must be conceived of in the temporal context of generations. Generations hold these rights as groups in relation to other generations—past, present and future. This is consistent with other approaches to rights, including the Islamic approach, which treats human rights not only as individual rights, but as "rights of the community of believers as a whole."[14] They can be evaluated by objective criteria and indices applied to the planet from one generation to the next. To evaluate whether the interests represented in planetary rights are being adequately protected does not depend upon knowing the number or kinds of individuals that may ultimately exist in any given future generation.

Enforcement of these intergenerational rights is appropriately done by a guardian or representative of future generations as a *group*, not of future individuals, who are of necessity indeterminate. While the holder of the right may lack the capacity to bring grievances forward and hence depends upon the representative's decision to do so, this inability does not affect the existence of the right or the obligation associated with it.

Now it may be argued that such rights do depend upon knowing at least the number of individuals in the future, because if the earth's population continues to grow rapidly, the amount of diversity and degree of quality that must be passed on will be higher than if the population in the future were at the same level or less than it is today.

But, if anything, the existence of these generational rights to the planet may constrain the population policies of present and future generations. Whether a generation chooses to meet its obligations by curtailing exploitation, consumption and waste or by constraining population growth is a decision it must make. The fact that future generations have a generational right to receive the planet in a certain condition puts constraints on the extent to which a present generation can ignore this choice.

The second part to Professor D'Amato's argument is that if we intervene to conserve the environment to protect future generations, we cannot succeed in protecting them because our intervention will cause a different group of individuals to emerge. But since the rights of future generations exist only as generational rights, it does not matter who the individuals are or how many they may be. Only at the point where the individuals are born and by definition become members of the present generation do the generational rights attach to individuals.

Professor D'Amato's response is that "[f]uture generations are not an abstraction; they consist of individuals." But they do not consist of individ-

[14] M. KHADDURI, THE ISLAMIC CONCEPTION OF JUSTICE 233 (1984).

uals until they are born, and hence it is necessary and appropriate to speak of future generations qua generations as having rights in relation to the planet.

Professor D'Amato correctly points out that the composition of future generations cannot be known in advance, in part because it is affected by actions of the present generation. Indeed, he does not make his own case as strongly as he might. For example, we do not need to limit ourselves to ascribing these effects to subtle changes in the biochemistry of conception, as Professor D'Amato does in his amusing excursion into the dynamics of egg and sperm.

Virtually every policy decision of government and business affects the composition of future generations, whether or not they are taken to ensure their rights under the guidelines enunciated above. Decisions regarding war and peace, economic policy, the relative prosperity of different regions and social groups, transportation, health, education—all influence the demographics and the composition of future generations by affecting the lives and fortunes of the present generation: who will succeed and prosper, who will marry whom, who will have children, and even who will emigrate.

In Fairness to Future Generations takes the view that our planetary obligations to future generations are owed to all the earth's future human inhabitants, whoever they may be. This opens the possibility that these decisions, too, deserve to be scrutinized from the point of view of their impact on future generations. Professor D'Amato's approach reflects an unnecessarily constrained view of human rights law that would shut off a useful and broadly acceptable theoretical underpinning to sustainable resource development. The possibility that intergenerational equity may place limits on our actions is an important new area of human rights research.

Such limitations should be applied very narrowly, lest the rights of future generations develop into an all-purpose club to beat down any and all proposals for change. But surely long-term environmental damage is a good place to begin. Future generations really do have the right to be assured that we will not pollute ground water, load lake bottoms with toxic wastes, extinguish habitats and species or change the world's climate dramatically —all long-term effects that are difficult or impossible to reverse—unless there are extremely compelling reasons to do so, reasons that go beyond mere profitability.

Professor D'Amato invokes chaos theory to justify his contention that any environmental intervention will produce different individuals in the future than would otherwise have been produced. But he overlooks the most important implication of chaos theory for the environment and for future generations: namely, that systems do not proceed on orderly, linear paths of change, but rather that they will abruptly change.[15] This can be demonstrated on a home computer, using a very simple program. It has been

[15] For catastrophe theory, see R. THOM, MATHEMATICAL MODELS OF MORPHOGENESIS (1983); for the theory of complex systems, see I. PRIGOGINE & I. STENGERS, ORDER OUT OF CHAOS: MAN'S NEW DIALOGUE WITH NATURE (1984). For a concise review of the influence of chaos theory, see *Chaos Theory: How Big an Advance?*, 245 SCIENCE 26 (1989).

suggested that there may be key breaking points in our global environmental system, beyond which systems will reorganize and substantially change their properties.[16] If we are concerned about future generations, it is important to try to predict these breaking points. More importantly, the best tool that we could give future generations to respond to abrupt changes and reorganizations is a robust planet, which requires conserving a diversity of resources so that future generations have greater flexibility in designing responses.

Professor D'Amato proposes that there is a "preverbal sense of morality" that tells us not to waste resources, degrade the environment or wantonly kill animals. But, if anything, history in the last few centuries suggests that our natural instincts are self-indulgent. We have desecrated environments, wasted resources and slaughtered animals purely for pleasure or for modest personal gain. It may be that the human species carries both a selfish gene and an altruistic one, as the sociobiologists tell us,[17] but it is hardly sufficient to rely on the generous gene to build a theory of morality to overcome the selfish genes, without more.

In Fairness to Future Generations relies on a fundamental norm of equality among generations of the human species in relation to the care and use of the natural system. But it recognizes that we are part of the natural system and that we, as all other generations, must respect this system. We have a right to use and enjoy the system but no right to destroy its robustness and integrity for those who come after us.

Whether we rely on a beneficent "preverbal sense of morality" toward the planet and its resources or on theories rooted in the welfare of the human condition and the ecological system of which people are a part, there is a shared recognition that the present generation has an obligation to care for the planet and to ensure that all peoples can enjoy its services.

EDITH BROWN WEISS*

[16] G. Gallopin, President, Fundación Bariloche, discussion with author, June 1986. This is consistent with the scientific paradigms in the theories of catastrophe and of the dynamics of complex systems far from equilibrium.

[17] *See, e.g.*, J. & J. BALDWIN, BEYOND SOCIOBIOLOGY (1981). Sociobiologists assert that there are four types of inherent behavior that explain all our social behavior: selfish, altruistic, cooperative and spiteful. Humans act so as to try to ensure that their genes will be carried forward into succeeding generations. *Id.* at 49–50.

* Of the Board of Editors.

Part II
Traditional Sources of International Environmental Law

[6]

TOWARDS NEW APPROACHES TO TREATY-MAKING IN THE FIELD OF ENVIRONMENT*

A.O. Adede, LLB, PhD **

* This article is adapted from the inaugural lectures given by the author at the School of Environmental Studies, Moi University, Eldoret, Kenya, 7–9 January 1991, as the recipient of the 1990 Elizabeth Haub Gold Medal Award in International Environmental Law. The views expressed are those of the author and do not necessarily represent those of the United Nations.

** Member of the Editorial Advisory Board of the *Yearbook*; currently Deputy Director for Research and Studies, Codification Division, Office of Legal Affairs, United Nations Secretariat, New York; formerly the Legal Adviser (Director of the Legal Division), International Atomic Energy Agency, Vienna (September 1983 to July 1987); The Legal Adviser (Head of the Legal Desk), Ministry of Foreign Affairs of the Republic of Kenya, Nairobi (September 1971 to June 1976).

1. INTRODUCTION

The objectives of this article are twofold: first, to enable the participants to have more than a glimpse of the scope and nature of the major legal and related instruments, which the international community has developed, as frameworks for international responses to the problems of environment and development, during the past 20 years. It also offers, in this connection, an assessment of the efforts which have been made towards progressive development and codification of international environmental law since the United Nations Conference on Human Environment in Stockholm 1972. Second, the article is intended to indicate the pathway which the international community has chosen towards achieving concrete results at the United Nations Conference on Environment and Development (UNCED) now called the Earth Summit, in Rio de Janeiro (2–12 June 1992). The decision by the UN to hold the Earth Summit 20 years after Stockholm, has presented the opportunity through the preparatory process towards the 1992 Rio Summit, for taking stock of what needs to be done on the basis of past lessons and in light of new challenges ahead.

Consistent with the objectives of the article outlined, it is useful to recall here briefly that the main results of the 1972 Stockholm Conference on Human Environment[1] were the establishment of the United Nations Environment Programme (UNEP) and the adoption of an Action Plan for the Human Environment. UNEP has since its establishment continued to discharge admirably its Mandate[2] of coordinating, within the UN system, international responses to the first generation environmental issues namely: pollution of water, air and soil, resulting both from industrial activities and from activities associated with poverty and under-development.[3]

1 See UN Doc. A/CONF.48/14/Rev. 1, L. Sohn, 'The Stockholm Declaration on the Human Environment', *Harvard International Law Journal*, Vol. 14, No. 3, 1973.

2 See General Assembly Resolution 2997 (XXVII), 15 December 1972.

3 For a synopsis of UNEP's legal instruments, see 'Environmental Law in UNEP', UNEP Environmental Law No. 1, 1991. See also 'International Conventions and Protocols in the field of the environment', UN Doc. A/C.2/46/31.

In the meantime, the second generation environmental issues entered the scene. They are: global warming (climate change), acid rain, and the depletion of the stratospheric ozone layer. This group of issues, to which the problem of exploitation of environment as a weapon in times of armed conflict was most recently added, began to receive closer attention from the international community. The problems which they raised brought into focus the need to initiate additional processes for public education and consciousness-raising in order to enable the international community to take effective and timely measures, both internationally and nationally, in response thereto. Such measures would require appropriate legal frameworks which may need to be either strengthened or established.

The assessment of the impacts of these new issues, indeed, leads to the realization of the fact that, although the linkage between environment and development was recognized as far back as the 1972 Stockholm Conference, 'all too little progress [has been] made toward actual integration of environmental dimensions to development policies and practices'[4] The establishment of the necessary modalities for integrating more fully environmental dimensions to development policies is the task presently assigned to the Preparatory Committee of UNCED. To this end, UNCED is working on the so-called 'Agenda 21', with specific components for adoption at Rio and for subsequent action. As will be shown later, the road to UNCED in Rio and beyond is paved with a number of new challenges which must be identified. The means for meeting the new challenges effectively must also be established. It should, in this connection, be pointed out further that the road map to Rio, which is now being improved by UNCED's preparatory process was, since Stockholm, re-charted by the World Commission on Environment and Development (WCED) which, in 1987, produced its report - *Our Common Future* - in which the concept of 'sustainable development', among others, was revitalized.[5]

The current process of devising appropriate means for addressing environment and development issues in an integrated manner has thus underscored the need for a truly interdisciplinary approach to the task. It clearly demonstrated the necessity of bringing together, for example, scientists, lawyers, economists, development strategists, ecologists, policy-makers and administrators, from both the public and the private sectors, to exchange views concerning appropriate responses to the identified problems of environment and development, and on the necessary

4 Observation by Maurice F. Strong, Secretary-General, United Nations Conference on Environment and Development, see 'From Stockholm to Rio: A Journey Down a Generation', *An Earth Summit Publication*, No. 1, 1991, p. 2.

5 Established pursuant to UN General Assembly Resolution 38/161, 19 December 1983, WCED was chaired by Gro Harlem Brundtland (then Prime Minister of Norway). The Commission submitted its report to the General Assembly, Doc. A/42/427, through the Governing Council of UNEP. The report was later published under the title: *Our Common Future*, Oxford University Press, Oxford, 1987 .

international framework for undertaking the agreed measures. The process has also underscored the need to find more effective ways for encouraging and ensuring full participation of the developing countries in the various international conferences and meetings, negotiating legal and related instruments which States would be called upon to implement, nationally and internationally, towards the achievement of the commonly shared goals.

Although geared predominantly towards the discussion of the legal aspects of the issues, efforts are made in this article to raise also the issues which are of interest to non-lawyers, thus clearly demonstrating the multi-disciplinary approach to the tasks at hand. A sample of such issues are randomly and briefly offered below:

(1) In connection with issues such as those concerning the fight against global warming, acid rain, desertification and deforestation; the preservation of biological diversity; and the protection of the stratospheric ozone layer, law meets science and economics right at the threshold, raising thereby, a number of preliminary and controversial questions. It is therefore necessary to distinguish genuine gaps in the scientific knowledge or genuine lack of knowledge about possible economic consequences of suggested preventive or corrective measures, from false claims of the existence of such gaps in knowledge. This is to guard against the use of false claims of gaps in knowledge as a convenient pretext for inaction or rejection of efforts towards the putting into place of the necessary legal frameworks for international response to these identified problems.

(2) In connection with the question of transfer of technology, the legal framework for bringing this about should recognize a number of basic views: one emphasizes the fact that technology is an indispensable ingredient of economic growth. Thus, the developing countries which lack adequate capital for acquiring environmentally sound technologies for supporting environmental protection strategies, need assistance. They need adequate financial, institutional and professional capacities for choosing and using technologies which are best suited to their needs, developed and adapted to fit local conditions, and integrated with traditional technologies and experience.[6] There is also the suggestion that the best place for the lawyers to start working on the problem of transfer of technology is to look, for example, at the treaties governing patents, intellectual property rights and trade, with full knowledge that the basic questions of transfer of the technology and the additional fund resources linked to the process are to be answered by other experts.[7]

6 Strong, *supra* note 4 at 6.

7 Observation by Mustafa K. Tolba, Executive Director, United Nations Environment Programme, made at the Symposium on Developing Countries and International Environmental Law, Beijing, 12 August 1991. See, eg, UN Doc. A/C.6/46/4.

The question is whether such technologies should be transferred to developing countries on preferential and non-commercial terms, as suggested by them, or on the basis of straight market value as argued by the industrialized countries emphasizing the proprietary nature of technology. Due regards should be given to the implications of the current efforts towards 'globalization of technology' to develop technology without borders.

(3) In addressing the questions of prevention of deforestation and desertification, it is necessary to develop new and innovative incentives or trade-offs that would guide the conduct of individuals (natural or juridical persons) whose activities have adverse effects on the forests. For example, the individuals who use the forest for survival as the source of firewood (energy) which they need for preparing their daily meals, those who clear the forest to make room for agricultural activities for subsistence, and those who cut down forest trees as the source of timber for which exist local or international lucrative markets. This use-oriented approach to the forests, for the benefit of human beings, is to be balanced and integrated with the approach of preservation of the tropical rain forests as indispensable carbon sinks and as the home of species of fauna and flora which need to be preserved.

(4) In the process of integrating environmental dimensions into development policies and practice, it is essential to avoid pursuing this goal to the extent of turning it into one of the means of introducing new forms of conditionality for the allocation of aid or development financing to developing countries.

(5) In devising appropriate measures for responding to the identified problems, it is necessary to continue to keep perspective the environmental problems of poverty for which development as such would provide the answer and the environmental problems arising from the process of development and industrialization for which other measures are necessary.

(6) While focusing on the problems of environment and development, it is necessary to assess and address the impact of the burgeoning population growth in the developing countries and its link to the causes of urban and rural poverty, through increasing and staggering demand upon various natural resources. This would be balanced with the equal concern about the patterns of production and consumption in the industrialized countries which also have impact upon certain finite natural resources.

(7) In recognizing the new grounds being broken by international law through the development of new concepts, it is necessary to evaluate the impact of the application of such concepts in both the North and the South. The new concepts are, for example,

(a) inter-generational responsibility and inter-generational equity;
(b) shared but differentiated responsibilities;
(c) common concern of mankind;

(d) precautionary principle;
(e) resource transfer;
(f) mature and environmentally sound technology;
(g) cost internalization;
(h) the global commons;
(i) polluter pays principle; and
(j) sustainable development.

The degree of application of these concepts will depend on agreement as to which among them are amenable to precise definitions which generate concrete legal obligations to be included in legally binding instruments, and those which continue to defy such definitions and are, therefore, destined to remain in the realm of general guidelines or statements of aspirations.

(8) When putting into place appropriate national legal instruments for responding to problems of environment and development, it is necessary to recognize the rights and the proper roles of individuals (natural or juridical persons) as well as those of non-governmental organizations, in bringing to the attention of governmental authorities certain cultural, social, and other values that need to be protected for the benefit of the society, which should not be easily sacrificed on the altar of development.

(9) In devising new legal instruments for international response to the identified problems of environment and development, care must be taken to strengthen or establish, as appropriate, institutional mechanisms or arrangements that would ensure the monitoring of compliance with the international obligations contained in the instrument in question to achieve their effective implementation, as well as the mechanisms for updating the instruments expeditiously to enable them to correspond to new realities.

(10) In the current exercise, it is necessary for the international community to adopt the policy of taking preventive actions without waiting for a disaster or a crisis in connection with the pollution or degradation of a specified area of the environment, recognizing adverse environmental effects which are across the boundary of States and those which concern the global commons. This would enable the international community to supplement or even replace the practice of 'react and correct' by the policy of 'forecast and prevent', relying upon exchange of information, collected through the process of monitoring of environmental activities, as may be stipulated under appropriate international legal instruments.

(11) In adopting the policy of 'forecast and prevent' it is necessary for the international community also to establish or strengthen emergency preparedness and contingency plans for taking effective remedial measures in case of environmental disasters.

(12) In an effort to reduce areas of international friction arising from activities

relating to problems of environment and development, it is necessary to encourage the process of exchange of pertinent information and the collaboration in the research for obtaining the necessary information. Together with this, efforts should be made to accept, in the appropriate international instruments, effective mechanisms for the *avoidance* of environmental disputes, and those for the *settlement* of such disputes. The mechanism should be flexible enough to allow for those ranging from resort to informal non-adjudicatory procedures, to the formal adjudicatory such as arbitration, including resort to judicial settlement by the International Court of Justice (ICJ).

The foregoing list of issues is certainly not exhaustive. It is merely illustrative of the point made here that the current process of negotiating international legal instruments for dealing with the problems of environment and development, requires a multi-disciplinary approach. It is the approach that would enable the international community to continue addressing effectively the first generation environmental issues as well as the second generation problems as briefly identified in this introduction. With this in mind, we may now pass to the analysis aimed at demonstrating that international environmental law has tended to develop, since the Stockholm Conference, in a piecemeal way and that the time has now come to put into place an appropriate multilateral legal instrument dealing comprehensively with environment and development issues in an integrated manner, in light of past lessons and directing attention to new challenges, taking into account the interest and concern of the developing countries.

2. THE PIECEMEAL APPROACH TO TREATY-MAKING IN THE ENVIRONMENTAL FIELD: PAST LESSONS

2.1 Areas, Issues and Activities Addressed by the Existing Treaties

A survey of the existing treaties in the field of environment shows that since 1972, the following broad areas or issues have been the subject of multilateral treaties (global or regional): protection of the marine environment; prevention of air pollution; protection of spheres of fauna and flora and related issues; prevention of pollution of rivers and lakes; protection of the environment from radiological emergencies from peaceful uses of nuclear emergencies and from chemical and toxic substances including hazardous wastes; and protection of the environment from military and related activities. This section will give a synopsis of the existing legal instruments.

It may be shown, for example, that the question of elaborating legal instruments for international responses to issues of environment and development was approached more boldly by some experts groups,[8] and too cautiously by others,[9] hampered by the scientific evidence controversy already mentioned. Thus, it is initially unclear whether in a particular case, what is needed or what is achievable is an umbrella/framework Convention for the protection of the environment in general, for the protection of the atmospheric environment as a whole, or for addressing only the problems of climate change. There was also the question as to what should come first – framework conventions in these areas, or specific protocols dealing with the control and elimination of particular sources of pollution and environmental degradation or specific issues.

Relying upon the existing examples of efforts since Stockholm, the following may be highlighted concerning the approach to the task of elaborating appropriate legal instruments.[10] In the protection of the marine environment, for example, specific regimes were put into place before general regimes by framework conventions were established. This was illustrated by the 1972 London Dumping Convention and the 1973 IMO Convention on Pollution from Ships (both specific), which preceded Part XII of the 1982 United Nations Convention on the Law of the Sea (a general framework convention). But the reverse had also occurred. The most recent example was the 1985 Vienna Convention on the Protection of the Ozone Layer (global framework agreement), negotiated under the auspices of UNEP, which was later followed by its 1987 Montreal Protocol (specific and reduction of CFCs). The same was true in the case of the 1979 ECE Long-Range Transboundary Air Pollution (regional framework agreement) later followed by its 1987 Helsinki Protocol (specific control and reduction of SO_2) and the 1989 Sofia Protocol (specific control and reduction of NO_2). It is generally recognized that one approach does not exclude the other, since it is possible to undertake simultaneous drafting of a

8 See eg, the 'Proposed Legal Principles for Environmental Protection and Sustainable Development', prepared by the group of Legal Experts convened by the World Commission on Environment and Development (WCED) (the Brundtland Commission) in *Our Common Future*, Annex I (1987); draft by the group of Legal Experts on Long-distance Transboundary Air Pollution convened by the International Environment Institute in Aix-les-Bains, 1988 (in the present author's file); draft of the Working Group of Legal Experts on Environmental Law convened by the Commission on Environmental Law and of the International Union for Conservation of Nature and Natural Resources (IUCN, Bonn, 29 April 1991) (in the present author's file). For the texts of these instruments see Adede, A.O. *International Environmental Law Digest* (1993).

9 See eg the results of the Toronto meeting, 27–30 June 1988, *The Changing Atmosphere Implications for Global Security*, *infra* note 24, and the *Ottawa Meeting of Legal and Policy Experts*, 20–22 February 1990, UN Doc. A/C.2/44/2.

10 For a survey of environmental treaties for the purposes of UNCED see Doc. A/CONF.151/PC/103 and Add. 1 described further pp. 112–113 *infra*.

framework agreement and a technical annex to it, addressing a particular issue, which can lend itself readily to such treatment.

2.1.1 Instruments for the protection of the marine environment

In connection with the question of protection of the marine environment, it is noteworthy that the international community had the political will to conclude, soon after Stockholm, a number of multilateral global instruments dealing with particular sources of marine pollution. The earliest ones were the 1972 London Convention on the Prevention of Marine Pollution by Dumping of Wastes and other Matter (LDC)[11] and the 1973 International Convention for the Prevention of Pollution from Ships (MARPOL).[12]

The 1972 London Dumping Convention (LDC) dealt with the problem of deliberate disposal at sea of wastes or other matter from vessels, aircrafts, platforms or other man-made structures at sea and covered all marine areas except internal waters. Under the Convention, the parties assumed obligation to prohibit the dumping of the type of wastes contained in the 'black list' (Annex I) and obligation to seek permits for the dumping of the wastes contained in the 'grey list' (Annex II) and permits for the dumping of all other wastes. The technical lists were subject to amendment as appropriate. Guidelines, in the form of non-binding legal instruments,[13] were later developed by the parties to assist them in implementing the Convention.

The 1973 the MARPOL Convention was deliberately restricted to pollution from ships in order to deal with the issues which are within the competence of the International Maritime Organization (IMO). With the establishment of UNEP after Stockholm, the question of distribution of competence between organizations and bodies within the UN system to deal with problems of the environment became necessary. Thus UNEP acquired competence over land-based source of marine pollution,[14] while the IMO dealt exclusively with marine pollution from ships – a

11 LDC was adopted on 29 December 1972 at a diplomatic conference convened and hosted by the Government of the United Kingdom of Great Britain and Northern Ireland. See 11 *International Legal Materials* (1972) (hereinafter, ILM) 1294. Prior to the Stockholm Conference there was the 1972 Convention for the Protection of Marine Pollution by Dumping from Ships and Aircrafts, II *ILM* 262 (1972).

12 MARPOL was adopted on 2 November 1973 at a diplomatic conference convened by the International Maritime Organization (ILM). See 12 *ILM* 1319 (1973).

13 See 'London Guidelines for the Exchange of Information on Chemicals in International Trade', *UNEP Publication*, Environment Law Guidelines and Principles.

14 See eg, the 1974 Convention on the Prevention of Marine Pollution from Land-Based Sources, 13 *ILM*, 352 (1974). The implementation of this convention was to be facilitated by the Montreal Guidelines for the Protection of the Marine Environment from Land-Based Sources, No. 7 of UNEP's publication on 'Environmental Law Guidelines and Principles'.

fact which was to be emphasized even in the title of the IMO Convention in question. The MARPOL Convention accordingly addresses pollution releases such as any escape, disposal, spilling, leaking, pumping, emitting, or emptying of pollutants from ships. The Convention included several annexes dealing with pollution problems associated with oil; noxious liquid substances in bulk; harmful substances carried by sea in package forms, or in freight containers, portable tanks, or on road and rail tank wagons, sewage and garbage. Furthermore, the MARPOL Convention accepted a number of innovations introduced by the shipping industry such as the load-on-top system and segregated ballast oil tankers. The Convention also provides for obligation of cooperation between the parties concerning certificates, special rules on inspection of ships, enforcement mechanisms and detection of violations.

It is important to point out here that these two specific regimes for the protection of the marine environment were indeed put in place by States before they could agree on a comprehensive general regime which they later achieved in Part XII of the 1982 United Nations Convention on the Law of the Sea (UNCLOS).[15] As the umbrella framework convention, UNCLOS addressed six sources of pollution in a series of treaty provisions some of which constituted a codification of international customary rules,[16] while others reflected progressive development of international law.[17] The six sources of pollution dealt with in the generally accepted Part XII of UNCLOS are pollution from: land-based sources; sea-bed activities within national jurisdiction; sea-bed activities beyond national jurisdiction; dumping; vessels; and atmosphere. Thus, in their efforts to develop legally-binding instruments to guide their conduct in the area of protection of the marine environment, States chose to put in place specific regimes first then followed them with a general and comprehensive regime. But as will be shown in connection with similar efforts of States to develop legally-binding instruments for the prevention of air pollution (the protection of the atmospheric environment), quite the opposite occurred.

Apart from the above-mentioned multilateral global conventions for the Protection of the marine environment and other multilateral instruments negotiated under IMO, dealing with particular issues such as liability for marine pollution damage and compensation as well as other remedial and preventive measures,[18] a number

15 Opened for signature at Montego Bay, Jamaica, 10 December 1982, not yet in force, see *The Law of the Sea*, UN Pub. Sales No. E.83.V.5 (1983).

16 See eg, Articles 192, 193 and 197 of the Convention.

17 See eg, Articles 217–220 of the Convention.

18 See eg, 1973 Protocol Relating to Intervention on the High Seas in Case of Pollution by Substances Other than Oil, 13 *ILM* 605 (1974); 1971 International Convention on the Establishment of an International Fund for Compensation for Oil Pollution Damage, 11 *ILM* 289 (1972); 1974 International Convention for the Safety of Life at Sea, 14 *ILM* 959 (1975;) and 1976 Protocol to the International Convention on Civil Liability for Oil Pollution Damage, 16 *ILM* 617 (1977).

of multilateral conventions were also concluded after Stockholm to deal with environmental issues in specific regions, or in specific areas, through regional or global instruments.[19] The bulk of the regional conventions were, however, the direct results of UNEP's Regional Seas Programme which encouraged States to conclude regional treaties for dealing with environmental concerns identified by them.[20]

Some of the common features of such regional conventions for the protection of the marine environment may serve as examples of standard treaty provisions for the protection of the marine environment.

2.1.2 *Instruments for the prevention of air pollution*

With respect to the question of protection of the atmospheric environment (prevention of air pollution) the first decade after Stockholm produced only one multilateral regional treaty. This was the Convention on Long-Range Transboundary Air Pollution (LRTAP) concluded in Geneva on 13 November 1979, under the auspices of the Economic Commission for Europe (ECE). LRTAP was aimed primarily at the problem of acid rain and was a general framework convention containing basic obligations for dealing with long-range transboundary air pollution described as,

> 'air pollution whose physical origin is situated wholly or in part within the area under national jurisdiction of one State and which has adverse effects in the area under jurisdiction of another State at such distances that it is not generally possible to distinguish the contribution of individual emission sources or groups of sources'.

19 See eg, 1973 Convention on Fishing and Conservation of the Living Resources in the Baltic Sea and Belts, 12 *ILM* 1972 (1973); 1974 Nordic Environmental Protection Conventions 11; 1980 Convention on the Conservation of Antarctic Marine Living Resources, 19 *ILM* 841 (1980); 1988 Convention on the Regulation of Antarctic Mineral Resources Activities, 27 *ILM* (1988).

20 See, eg, 1976 Barcelona Convention for the Protection of the Mediterranean Sea Against Pollution, 15 *ILM* 240 (1976); 1976 Barcelona Protocol Concerning Cooperation in Combating Pollution of the Mediterranean Sea by Oil and Other Harmful Substances in Case of Emergency 11; 1978 Kuwait Regional Convention for Cooperation on the Protection of the Marine Environment, 17 *ILM* 511 (1978); 1981 Abidjan Convention for Cooperation in the Protection and Development of the Marine and Coastal Environment of the West and Central African Region, 20 *ILM* 746 (1981); 1981 Lima Convention for the Protection of the Marine Environment and Coastal Areas of the South-East Pacific, UNEP Pub. (1984); 1982 Jeddah Regional Convention for Conservation of the Regional Environment of the Sea and the Gulf of Aden, UNEP Pub. (1984);1983 Cartagena Convention for the Protection and Development of the Marine Environment of Wider Caribbean Region, 20 *ILM* 227 (1983); 1985 Nairobi Convention for the Protection, Management and Development of the Marine and Coastal Environment of the Eastern African Region, UNEP Pub. (1986); and 1986 Noumea Convention for the Protection of Natural Resources and Environment of the South Pacific Region, 26 *ILM* 30 (1987).

The Convention does not, however, apply to pollution affecting the areas beyond national jurisdiction and explicitly excludes provisions dealing with the important question of liability which the conventions for the protection of the marine environment, by contrast, attempted to address to a varying degree as illustrated in this chapter.[21]

However, as the problem of acid rain received added attention, it became one of the three interrelated environmental issues of the second decade after Stockholm, mentioned above. The 1979 Long-Range Transboundary Air Pollution, as a *regional* framework convention, was later supplemented by protocols dealing with control and reduction of emission of specific gases and concrete international actions to combat acid rain.[22] Efforts are being made accordingly to put in place *global* framework convention for dealing with LRTAP. When the international community, through UNEP, turned its attention to the question of protection of the stratospheric ozone layer, the result was that a general framework Convention was negotiated first then followed by a specific protocol reducing emission of specific gases associated with the depletion of the ozone layer.[23] Thus, unlike the experience in the development of legal instruments for protection of the marine environment where, as indicated above, specific regimes preceded the general regime, in the case of protection of the atmosphere, the opposite occurred: the framework conventions preceded the specific protocols.

The success of the LRTAP and the ozone layer conventions and their specific protocols has encouraged the international community to strive towards establishing similar legal regimes for the protection of the atmosphere in general or for tackling the problem of climate change in particular. A definite call upon the international community to take concrete steps towards negotiating an umbrella/framework Convention for the protection of the atmosphere was made at the June 1988 Toronto Conference on the Changing Atmosphere.[24] The momentum for this

21 See pp. 89–91 *infra*.

22 See the 1985 Protocol to the 1979 Convention on Long-Range Transboundary Air Pollution on the Reduction of Sulphur Emissions of their Transboundary Fluxes by at least 30 per cent, Helsinki, 8 July 1985, and the 1988 Sofia Protocol on the Control of Emissions Nitrogen Oxides or their Transboundary Fluxes.

23 See the 1985 Vienna Convention for the Protection of Ozone Layer, 26 *ILM* 1516 (1987) and the 1987 Montreal Protocol on the Reduction of the Chlorofluorocarbons (CFCs), 26 *ILM* 1550 (1987).

24 The Conference was hosted by the Government of Canada and was co-sponsored by United Nations Environment Programme (UNEP) and World Meteorological Organization (WMO). More than 300 scientists and policy-makers from 48 countries, United Nations and related international organizations and relevant non-governmental organizations participated

exercise was carried to the February 1990 Ottawa Meeting of Experts on Environmental Law and Policy, where the idea of producing a convention on climate change rather than an umbrella convention for the protection of the atmosphere as a whole was vigorously pursued. Following further specific steps taken by both UNEP and WMO, through the work of the International Panel on Climate Change (IPCC), which the two UN bodies jointly created in 1988, earnest work on the negotiation of a convention on climate change continued. The conclusion of such an instrument became part of the preparatory work for the Second World Climate Conference in November 1990 and also remained one of the goals for the 1992 United Nations Conference on Environment and Development, as further discussed in section 3, below.

From the point of view of lessons for treaty-making techniques, it is important to observe at this juncture that the latter approach (framework conventions first, followed by specific protocols) becomes unavoidable in situations where the international community is being called upon to conclude a multilateral treaty for dealing with a problem with respect to which some States feel reluctant to address questions of detail (specific reduction of pollutants), claiming lack of conclusive scientific evidence or asking for further studies and in-depth assessment of economic and other implications of the treaty being contemplated. Accordingly, the approach may indeed be an evidence of genuine gaps in knowledge, generally recognized, and permitting only the conclusion of a framework convention embodying general principles as the first realistic step to be followed by specific protocols. But the choice of this approach may also be an evidence of lack of political will, on the part of some States, to take concrete actions through binding instruments, because of hidden reasons, while stressing on an apparent gap in knowledge (or controversy over scientific facts for example) as a convenient explanation for their reluctance to proceed with the negotiation of a multilateral instrument committing them to specific actions.

---

in the sessions of the Conference. See 'The Changing Atmosphere: Implications for Global Security – Conference Statement', 5 July 1988 version (hereinafter referred to as Conference Statement). The conference urged the international community to 'initiate the development of a comprehensive global convention as a framework for protocols on the protection of the atmosphere. The convention should emphasize such key elements as the free international exchange of information and support of research and monitoring, and should provide a framework for specific protocol for addressing particular issues, taking into account existing international law. This was vigorously pursued at the international workshop on law and policy held in Ottawa early in 1989, and at the Second World Climate Conference, Geneva, June 1990, with a view to having the principles and components of such a convention ready for consideration at the UNCED in 1992.

2.1.3 *Instruments for the protection of species of fauna and flora and related issues*

With respect to the question of environmental problems addressed through the protection of species of fauna and flora or by the preservation of global or regional natural, and cultural heritage as well as the maintenance of ecological balance and biological diversity, a handful of legal instruments were concluded after Stockholm. Such an example was the November 1972 Convention for the Protection of the World Cultural and Natural Heritage,[25] which was negotiated under the auspices of the United Nations Educational, Scientific and Cultural Organization (UNESCO). The Convention applied to natural features consisting of physical and biological formations of outstanding universal value from aesthetic and biological points of view. Then came the 1973 Washington Convention on International Trade in Endangered Species of Wild Fauna and Flora (CITES) which was mainly the work of the International Union for Conservation of Nature and Natural Resources (IUCN).

CITES is a protectionist instrument which operates under a system of permits to regulate international trade in wild fauna and flora listed in the three appendices of the Convention. Trade in the species threatened with extinction (Appendix I) is prohibited. Trade in species not yet threatened with extinction but which may soon become so threatened (Appendix II) is exceptionally permitted but strictly limited to the level that would not endanger the survival of the species therein listed. Appendix III provides a mechanism by which a party may, by domestic legislation, regulate the export of species not listed in Appendix I or Appendix II, and request the other parties to CITES to enforce the domestic legislation in question. The appendices are subject to amendments from time to time.

Three other multilateral conventions were later concluded: the 1973 Geneva International Tropical Timber Agreement;[26] the 1979 Convention on the Conservation of Migratory Species of Wild Animals;[27] the 1982 World Charter for Nature, adopted by the United Nations General Assembly.[28] As to the regional instruments in this area, the forerunner was the 1968 African Convention on the Conservation of Nature and Natural Resources.[29] Since Stockholm, the following instruments were adopted: the 1976 Convention on Conservation of Nature in the South Pacific;[30] the 1976

25 See 11 *ILM* 1358 (1972). Just prior to this before Stockholm, was the 1971 Rasmar Convention on Wetlands of International Importance Especially as Waterfront Habitat, 11 *ILM* 963 (1972).

26 See 6773 *UNTS* 63.

27 See 19 *ILM* 11 (1979).

28 See GA/RES/37/7, 28 October 1982.

29 1001 *UNRA*, p. 4.

30 See *International Protection of the Environment*, p. 10359.

Convention on the Protection of the Archaeological, Historical and Artistic Heritage of the American Nations;[31] the 1979 Convention of European Wild Life and Natural Habitats;[32] the 1980 Convention on the Conservation of Antarctic Marine Living Resources;[33] the 1982 Benelux Convention on Natural Resources and Landscape Protection;[34] and the 1985 Protocol Concerning Protected Areas and Wild Fauna and Flora in the East African Region;[35] the 1985 ASEAN Agreement on the Conservation of Natural Resources.[36]

These efforts in the area of protection of species of fauna and flora and for the preservation of natural resources were later supplemented during the second decade after Stockholm with the concern over the preservation of biological diversity. UNEP took the lead in bringing to the attention of the international community the need for a multilateral convention on this topic, having regard also to the work that was being done by the IUCN. Thus the negotiation and conclusion of such an instrument became one of UNEP's urgent activities which coincided with those of the Preparatory Work for the 1992 United Nations Conference on Environment and Development, as further noted in section 3 below.

2.1.4 *Instruments for the prevention of pollution of rivers and lakes*

A study of an impressive number of international treaties concerning international cooperation on the utilization and management of international rivers, in the period before the Stockholm Conference, disclose that such instruments dealt primarily with the question of allocation of rights and obligations of the parties in respect of their shared natural resources. Very little attention was paid to the environmental consequences of the utilization of international watercourses either for navigation or for non-navigational purposes. However, the riparian States soon became aware of the negative environmental consequences of such uses of the rivers and lakes. They thus began to conclude treaties creating, among others, river basin commissions aimed at studying environmental and other problems and suggesting appropriate preventive and remedial measures.[37]

The efforts to deal comprehensively and exclusively with the problem of pollution of international watercourses from specific sources received impetus after

31 56 *UKTS*, Cmnd 8738.
32 15 *ILM* 736 (1977).
33 19 *ILM* 837 (1980)
34 See *Environmental Law Multilateral Agreements*, W. E. Burhenne (ed.) (1982), p. 43.
35 See *New Directions in the Law of the Sea, New Series*, K. R. Simmonds (ed.) (1986)
36 *Ibid*.
37 For a collection of earlier treaties relating to the utilization of international watercourses, see *United Nations Legislative Series*, ST/LEG/SER. B/12.

Stockholm. Thus, there was the 1976 Convention for the Protection of the Rhine Against Chemical Pollution,[38] and the 1976 Convention for the Protection of the Rhine from Pollution of Chlorides.[39] The best example of a comprehensive regime is the 1987 Agreement on the Action Plan for the Environmentally Sound Management of the Common Zambezi River system,[40] negotiated under the auspices of UNEP, representing a unique effort to develop and preserve the Zambezi River system. Such a comprehensive effort is being promoted by the Economic Commission for Europe in its 'Ecosystem approach to water management', which considers the utilization of the atmosphere, water soil and living resources as affecting a single ecosystem which should be protected through balanced international measures aimed at preserving each of the elements of the single ecosystem. This is the approach taken by the International Law Commission of the UN which adopted, at first reading, a set of draft articles on the Law of the Non-Navigational Uses of International Watercourses, as presented in its report of the 46th session of the General Assembly Supp. No. 10 ((A/40/10).

2.1.5 *Instruments for the protection of the environment from radiological emergencies*

With respect to the question of notification or assistance in case of nuclear accident or radiological emergencies, there were a mosaic of bilateral agreements concluded between a number of countries during the first decade after Stockholm and before the Chernobyl nuclear accident of 1986. Although some of the bilateral instruments primarily addressed issues of nuclear safety and rules and regulations concerning installation of nuclear plants along the boarders, some of the agreements focused attention on environmental consequences of such nuclear activities.[41] It is evident, therefore, that States had already recognized the need to deal with the threats of transboundary environmental damage arising from accidental radiological emergencies from civilian nuclear activities. These bilateral agreements thus laid a firm foundation for the negotiation of two important multilateral conventions: the 1986 Convention on Early Notification of a Nuclear Accident,[42] and the Convention on Assistance in Case of a Nuclear Accident or Radiological Emergency,[43] which

38 16 *ILM* 242 (1977).

39 16 *ILM* 265 (1979).

40 540 *UNTS*, 587.

41 Eighty-five bilateral treaties on aspects of nuclear activities in the pre-Chernobyl era existed. See generally, *Bilateral, Regional and Multilateral Agreements Relating to Co-operation in the Field of Nuclear Safety*, IAEA Pub. Leg. Ser., No. 15 (1990).

42 See IAEA Doc. INFCIRC/335; 25 *ILM* 1369 (1986) opened for signature 26 September 1986.

43 See IAEA Doc. INFCIRC/336; *ibid.*, opened for signature 26 September 1986.

the International Atomic Energy Agency (IAEA) concluded immediately after the Chernobyl nuclear accident of 26 April 1986.

These two conventions which were generally recognized as landmarks in the history of treaty-making,[44] were tailored to address the specific issues among those exposed by the Chernobyl accident with respect to which the IAEA Member States believed international legal instruments were achievable as a matter of urgency. In the Notification Convention, the Member States of the IAEA singled out the need to establish a treaty obligation to notify a nuclear accident with potential transboundary effects: who to notify, how to notify and the information to be notified. The emphasis was on the early warning following a nuclear accident that might have transboundary consequences, alerting States likely to be affected and thus enabling them to take some precautionary measures addressing, in that connection, the special needs of the developing countries. In the Assistance Convention the IAEA also singled out the need to establish a multilateral legal framework of providing prompt emergency assistance: how to request the assistance, how to render it, the modalities for undertaking an assistance mission itself having regard to the applicable bilateral arrangements, the question of equipment, personnel, and also the financial aspects of assistance.

The post-Chernobyl era also witnessed an equally large number of bilateral agreements dealing with some specific details relating to questions of notification and assistance, as envisaged under the two IAEA Conventions, and, covering also matters concerning aspects of nuclear safety.[45]

With respect to multilateral instruments addressing the problem of pollution of the environment by chemical or toxic substances, attention is recalled first to the relevant provisions and annexes of the 1972 Convention for the Prevention of Marine Pollution from Ships and Aircrafts;[46] those contained in the London Convention for the Prevention of Marine Pollution by Dumping of Wastes and Other Matters;[47] those found in the 1974 Convention for the Prevention of Marine Pollution from Land-Based Sources as amended in 1986;[48] those covered under the

44 The two conventions were negotiated and concluded simultaneously in a single forum, sitting in one session lasting only four weeks. Having been concluded in September 1986, three months following the Chernobyl accident, both conventions entered into force in record time: Notification Convention, one month from the date of signature and Assistance Convention six months from the date of signature. For a legislative history of the conventions, See Adede, A.O. *The IAEA Notification and Assistance Conventions in Case of a Nuclear Accident*, (1987).

45 Sixty-two bilateral treaties addressing aspects of civilian nuclear activities in the post-Chernobyl era have been recorded. See IAEA Pub. Leg. Ser., No. 15 *supra* note 31.

46 11 *ILM* 262 (1972).

47 11 *ILM* 1294 (1972).

48 13 *ILM* 32 (1974).

1985 Ozone Layer Convention on the 1979 Long-Range Transboundary Air Pollution including their relevant protocols;[49] and the two 1976 Conventions for the Protection of the Rhine from Chemical Pollution and from Pollution by Chlorides.[50] Two global conventions were also concluded to deal specifically and comprehensively with environmental pollution from other particular hazardous substances. One of them was the 1976 Geneva Convention concerning safety in the use of asbestos,[51] negotiated under the auspices of the ILO, and the 1989 Basel Convention on the Control of Transboundary Movements of Hazardous Wastes and their Disposal,[52] negotiated under the auspices of UNEP. The Basel Convention was found unacceptable by the African countries on the ground that its premise of permitting and simply regulating the transboundary movement of such wastes exposed them to constant peril. The African countries preferred complete prohibition of transboundary movement of hazardous wastes and produced the African Convention on the Control of Transboundary Movement and Disposal of Hazardous Waste, Bamako, 1991.

2.1.6 *Instruments addressing problems of interference with the environment by military and related activities*

Apart from the multilateral treaties which, as can be seen above, addressed specific areas of the environment, there had been other efforts to deal with interference with the environment in general. Such efforts produced, for example, the 1977 Convention on the Prohibition of Military or Any Other Hostile Use of Environmental Modification Techniques (ENMOD).[53] It may be further noted that, before Stockholm, several multilateral treaties had been concluded which, although primarily dealt with the problem of nuclear testing in the effort to reduce nuclear arms race, had clear environmental implications, owing to radioactive pollution associated with the specific activities they were intended to prohibit or control.[54] Specific mention must also be made here of the 1977 Protocol I Additional to the Geneva Conventions of 12 August 1949 and relating to the Protection of Victims of International Armed Conflict (Articles 35(3) and 55), concluded under the auspices of the International Red Cross in its efforts to develop international humanitarian law. Taken together,

49 *Supra* note 12.
50 *Supra* notes 28 and 29.
51 16 *ILM* 88 (1977).
52 28 *ILM* 649 (1977).
53 See 16 *ILM* 85 (1977).
54 Such treaties include the 1963 Treaty Banning Nuclear Weapons Tests in the Atmosphere, in Outer Space and Under Water, 880 *UNTS*,385; 1967 Treaty on Principles Governing the Activities of States in the Exploration and Use of Outer Space Including the Moon and Other Celestial Bodies, 610 *UNTS*, 205; 1971 Treaty on the Prohibition of the Emplacement of Nuclear Weapons and Other Weapons of Mass Destruction in the Sea-Bed and the Ocean Floor, 13 *UKTS*.

these legal instruments illustrate the concern and success of the international community to put in place binding legal instruments to guide their conduct in their military and related activities with clear potentials of adversely affecting the environment in general. The assessment of the adequacy of the ENMOD legal regime and of the international humanitarian law regime contained in Articles 35(3) and 55 of the above-mentioned Additional Protocol I is the subject of current discussions, as mentioned in section 3 below.

The foregoing list has been intended to illustrate the areas of the environment and subject matters, with respect to which States have been able to conclude binding legal instruments after Stockholm. It also indicates that international environmental law has largely developed through specific treaties dealing with specific issues arising from human activities at a given period. Thus, there is the need to undertake the elaboration of treaties which deal comprehensively with issues of environment and development so as to generate general principles of international law to guide the conduct of the actors in this field. Such an effort was originally made by the legal experts convened under the above-mentioned World Commission on Environment and Development, the Brundtland's Commission. The most recent effort to produce another instrument, dealing comprehensively with issues of environment and development is, however, the Covenant on Environment Conservation and Sustainable Use of Natural Resources, drafted by the Group of Legal Experts convened by the Commission on Environmental Law (CEL) of the International Union for Conservation of Nature and Natural Resources (IUCN). These drafts, prepared by experts in their individual capacities and in a non-governmental setting, should provide useful bases for the work of governmental experts who may be called upon to consider the question of such a comprehensive environmental treaty. The IUCN is already submitted to the Preparatory Committee of UNCED as document A/CONF.151/AC/WG.III/4/ of 28 August 1991, for information, pending further developments after the Earth Summit.

2.2 The Anatomy of Environmental Treaties: A Survey of Standard Clause

A survey of environmental treaties concluded since Stockholm indicates that there are certain provisions which have almost become standard. Accordingly, those seeking to identify the gaps in the substantive law of the environment particularly the treaty-law,[55] may wish to consider the following profile which presents the anatomy of an environmental treaty.

55 See in this connection the background papers prepared for consideration of Working Group III of UNCED, UN Doc. A/CONF.151/PC/36; A/CONF.151/PC/77 to 80; A/CONF.151/PC/WG.III.L.1 to 7.

The duty of States to conduct activities under their jurisdiction or control in such a manner as not to cause environmental damage to other States, or to areas beyond their national jurisdiction, as was stated in the non-binding Principle 21 of the Stockholm Declaration,[56] has now become a well settled, binding obligation based on treaty law, beyond the customary international law which inspired it.[57] The clearest treaty provision on the scope of this duty is contained in Article 193 and Article 194, paragraph 2 of the 1982 United Nations Convention on the Law of the Sea, which respectively recognize that 'States have the sovereign right to exploit their natural resources pursuant to their environmental policies and in accordance with their duty to protect and preserve the marine environment', and the obligation to 'take all measures necessary to ensure that activities under their jurisdiction or control are so conducted as not to cause damage by pollution to other States and their environment, and that pollution arising from incidents or activities under their jurisdiction or control does not spread beyond the areas where they exercise sovereign rights in accordance with [the] Convention'.

In all the environmental treaties containing provisions along the lines of the above-mentioned articles of the Law of the Sea Convention, adapted to suit the subject matter or scope of the particular instrument, some other related provisions are also usually found. The checklist includes provisions on:[58]

(1) Recognition of the sovereign rights of States to exploit their natural resources pursuant to their environmental policies and the corresponding duty to protect and preserve the environment.

(2) Obligation of States to take measures to prevent, reduce and control pollution of the environment with the best practicable means at their disposal.

56 Principle 21 of the Stockholm Declaration provides that 'States have, in accordance with the Charter of the United Nations and the principles of international law, the sovereign right to exploit their own resources pursuant to their own environmental policies, and the responsibility to ensure that activities within their jurisdiction or control do not cause damage to the environment of other States or of areas beyond the limits or national jurisdiction'.

57 It may be recalled that the dictum of the International Court of Justice in the *Corfu Channel* case to the effect that it is 'every State's obligation not to allow knowingly its territory to be used for acts contrary to the rights of other States (*ICJ Reps.*,1949, 4) has been cited as a case in point, along with classical *Trail Smelter* arbitration (3 *UNRAA*, – 1905); *Island of Palmas* case (2 *ibid., 281)* and *Lac Lanoux* ,*Whitman Digest of International Law*, 262–65. These series of cases have often been cited as standing for the proposition that States have a duty under customary law not to cause transboundary environmental damage and that the violation of this duty entails international responsibility of States under international law.

58 For detailed analysis of specific examples of the treaty provisions outlined in this connection, see *A Digest of Materials and Instruments for International Responses to Problems of Environment Development 1972–1992* Adede, A.O. (Draft Publication of the International Environmental Institute, IEI, Institut de l'Environnement International, in progress by the author, 15–72).

(3) Obligation of States to ensure that, in taking the said measures to protect the environment, they do not transfer directly or indirectly, damage or hazards from one area of the environment to another, or transform one type of pollution into another.

(4) Obligation of States to ensure that, in taking the said measures to prevent, reduce, and control pollution, they refrain from unjustifiable interference with the activities carried out by other States in the area of environment and development in conformity with the rights and obligations under the instrument in question.

(5) Obligation of each State to notify promptly other States in case of activities or events in its territory likely to cause environmental damage to other States.

Another set of provisions found in environmental treaties, also adapted to suit the subject matter and scope of a particular instrument, establish the general obligation of States parties to cooperate directly or through an appropriate global or regional organization in specific activities relating to the instrument. The checklist in this set includes provisions on obligation of States parties to:

(a) Undertake research and systematic observation (monitoring) necessary for the implementation of the instrument in question;

(b) Exchange information on scientific, technical, socio-economic, commercial, and legal matters relevant to the particular instrument;

(c) Undertake the development and transfer of environmentally sound technology necessary for meeting specific obligations assumed under the treaty in question;

(d) Encourage the conclusion of additional international instruments or the harmonization of domestic policies and legislation consistent with the aims and purposes of the convention in question;

(e) Undertake environmental impact assessment of planned activities and prior notice to and consultations with parties likely to be affected by such activities;

(f) Provide assistance in case of environmental emergencies, in accordance with the legal framework established for requesting and receiving such assistance and for undertaking contingency plans;

(g) Take into account special interests and needs of developing countries;

(h) Address the question of liability and compensation in case of environmental harm;

(i) Establish procedures and mechanisms for reviewing the effectiveness of the legal regime of the treaty in question, including those relating to its revision or amendment and for speedy entry into force of such revisions or amendments;

(j) Establish procedures and mechanisms for settlement or avoidance of environmental disputes;

(k) Establish appropriate institutional and financial arrangements for the implementation of the convention in question.

The degree of generality or specificity with which any of the issues in the checklist are treated in each instrument will, no doubt, depend upon the nature of the instrument in question: whether a framework convention or a specific protocol, and/or upon the subject matter or scope of the instrument.

The anatomy of environmental treaties just outlined, is admittedly not exhaustive of all the possible treaty provisions, and was intended to offer illustrations of clauses which treaty-makers have succeeded to formulate for the protection of the environment between 1972 after the Stockholm Conference and 1990 when the international community decided to hold another conference in 1992 to address new issues of environment and development.

As discussed in section 3 below, the Preparatory Committee of UNCED adopted in its Decision 3/25, Annex II, 32 criteria for analyzing the effectiveness of the existing multilateral treaties in this field in search for the gaps in both the substantive or procedural law which need to be filled or areas of weaknesses which need to be strengthened. The forthcoming section is also illustrative of these issues.

2.3 Materials and Instruments Other than Treaties as Frameworks for International Responses to Problems of Environment and Development

The experience of UNEP, as the United Nations body with responsibility for coordinating the work of the Organization in the environment field since Stockholm, and the efforts which the international community has continued to make through the work of the other UN system organizations and bodies dealing with problems of environment and development within their competence, provide solid evidence of the usefulness of materials and instruments other than treaties ('soft law') in this field.

The materials and instruments other than treaties, are divided into three broad categories.[59] In one category are the guidelines or principles embodied in non-legally binding instruments recommended to States to take into account when negotiating agreements, enacting legislation, or formulating environmental policies on the issues concerned,[60] or adopted initially as a first step towards negotiation and conclusion of legally binding obligations, thus providing a basis for a treaty

59 For a detailed analysis of salient provisions of such non-legally binding instruments, addressing certain issues of environment and development, and presenting relevant texts, see *The Digest*, op. cit., note 58, 75–127.

60 See, eg, Principles of Conduct in the Field of the Environment for the Guidance of States in the Conservation and Harmonious Utilization of Natural Resources Shared by Two or More States, Decision of the Governing Council of UNEP of 19 May 1978, reproduced in UNEP's *Environmental Law Guidelines and Principles Series No. 2* (hereinafter cited as UNEP's *Environmental Law Series*); Conclusions of the Study of Legal Aspects Concerning the Environment Related to Offshore Mining and Drilling within the Limits of National Jurisdiction, Decision 10/14/VI of the Governing Council of UNEP of 31 May 1982, in

regime.[61] In the other category are guidelines or principles prepared by States parties to a particular treaty or convention to provide the necessary specific details for facilitating effective implementation of the treaty or convention in question.[62] In yet another category are the guidelines adopted by certain United Nations system organizations and bodies, or by other international organizations, global or regional, to implement environmental policies established by them.[63]

The specific examples of the materials and instruments other than treaties illustrate the different techniques followed by the international community in responding to problems of environment and development, indicating also issues with respect to which only such non-legally binding instruments could be adopted, and circumstances

UNEP's *Environmental Law Series No. 4*; Cairo Guidelines and Principles for Environmentally Sound Management of Hazardous Waste, Decision 14/30 of the Governing Council of UNEP, OF 17 June 1989, in UNEP's *Environmental Law Series No. 8*; Goals and Principles of Environmental Impact Assessment, Decision, 14/25 of the Governing Council of UNEP, of 17 June 1987, in UNEP's *Environmental Law Series No. 9*; and London Guidelines for Exchange of Information on Chemicals in International Trade, Dec. 14/27 of the Governing Council of UNEP, of 17 June 1987, in UNEP's *Environmental Law Series No. 10*; and FAO Code of Conduct on the Distribution and Use of Pesticides (1985).

61 See the 1983 IAEA Guidelines for Mutual Emergency Assistance Arrangements in Connection with a Nuclear Accident or Radiological Emergency, Doc. INFCIRC/310, and the 1984 IAEA Guidelines on Reportable Events, Integrated Planning and Information of Exchange in a Transboundary Release of Radioactive Materials, Doc. INFCIRC/321. These two guidelines were the basis of the two IAEA Conventions concluded after the 1986 Chernobyl nuclear accident, namely: the 1986 Convention on Early Notification of a Nuclear Accident, INFCIRC/335 and the 1986 Convention on Assistance in Case of Nuclear Accident or Radiological Emergency, INFCIRC/336.

62 See eg, Interim Guidelines for the Implementation of paras. 8 and 9 of Annex I to the 1972 London Dumping Convention, in 10 *New Direction in the Law of the Sea* 23–30 (1978); Montreal Guidelines for the Protection of the Environment Against Pollution from Land-based Sources, Decision 13/18/II of the Governing Council of UNEP of 24 May 1985, in UNEP's *Environmental Law Guidelines and Principles Series No. 7*, adopted in relation to the Paris Convention for the Prevention of Marine Pollution from Land-based Sources; the Helsinki Convention on the Protection of the Marine Environment of the Baltic Sea Area; the Athens Protocol for the Protection of the Mediterranean Sea Against Pollution from Land-based Sources, and Part XII of the United Nations Convention on the Law of the Sea; the Provisions for Cooperation Between States in Weather Modification, Dec. 8/7/A of the Governing Council of UNEP, of 29 April 1980, in UNEPs *Environmental Law Series No. 3*, adopted in relation to the Convention on the Prohibition of Military or Any Hostile Use of Environmental Modification Techniques.

63 See, eg, the 1989 World Bank Operational Directive 4.00. Annex A on Environmental Assessment; the 1990 Guidelines for Environmental Management and Sustainable Development; 1989 FAO's Code of Conduct on the Distribution and Use of Pesticides: Introduction of the 'Prior Informed Consent' (PIC) Clause; and the 1989 Council of Europe's Directive on Civil Liability for Damage and Injury to the Environment Caused by Wastes, decision of the Commission of 3 August 1989, CJ–EN (89)9.

in which such materials were later developed into legally binding instruments or conventions. As observed elsewhere 'such non-binding instruments are easier to adopt than conventions and are immediately applicable by States'.[64]

3. THE ROAD TO RIO AND BEYOND

3.1 Towards Emphasis Upon Integration of Environment and Development Policies

As briefly mentioned previously it is indeed WCED that brought into focus once again the issues concerning environmental survival under the concept of 'sustainable development' described in WCED's report as 'Development that meets today's needs without compromising the ability of future generations to meet their own needs'. Discussions on some aspects of these issues have also been conducted through the debate in the General Assembly of the United Nations (upon the initiative of the Government of Malta) leading to the adoption of Resolution 43/53 calling for 'Protection of global climate for present and future generations of mankind'.[65] Lastly, the issues were taken up in the context of the 1992 United Nations Conference on Environment and Development (UNCED) and its substantive preparatory process which began in March 1990.

On the basis of the identified environment and development issues and the stated objectives to be addressed by UNCED[66] the following have been singled out for specific attention:

(1) protection of the atmosphere by combating climate change, depletion of the ozone layer and transboundary air pollution;

(2) protection and management of land resources by, *inter alia*, combating deforestation, desertification and drought;

(3) conservation of biodiversity;

(4) environmentally sound management of biotechnology;

(5) protection of the oceans and all kinds of seas, including enclosed and semi-

64 See 'Conclusions of the Sienna Forum on International Law of the Environment', UN Doc. A/45/666, Recommendation 5, p. 4.

65 See General Assembly Resolution 43/53 of 6 December 1988, entitled 'Protection of Global Climate for Present and Future Generations of Mankind', Agenda item 143 (A.43/905). See also Doc. A/45/696 and Add.l.

66 See General Assembly Resolution 44/228 of 22 December 1989, convening the United Nations Conference on Environment and Development, Part I, Para. 12 and Para. 15. respectively.

enclosed seas and of coastal areas and the protection, rational use and development of their living resources; and

(6) environmentally sound management of wastes, particularly hazardous wastes, environmentally sound management of toxic chemicals, and prevention of illegal traffic in toxic and dangerous produces and wastes.

The Preparatory Committee of UNCED later established Working Group I to deal with the issues 1–4 above, Working Group II to handle issues 5–7 and Working Group III to deal with legal, institutional and all related matters.[67]

In the process of elaborating appropriate legal instruments for international responses to these issues, the government representatives taking part in the negotiation of such instruments have been reminded by UNCED of the following, they:

> 'should ensure an integrated approach to environment and development questions, taking into account matters such as the patterns of consumption and production, access to and transfers of environmentally sound technology, financial resources requirements, human resources development, economic instruments, attainment of food security in the context of a sustainable development of agriculture, institutional arrangements, the improvement of the living and working environment of the poor in urban slums and rural areas, through eradicating poverty, *inter alia*, by implementing integrated rural and urban development programmes, as well as taking other appropriate measures at all levels necessary to stem the degradation of the environment, protection of human health conditions and improve the quality of life'.

To make the preparatory work of UNCED more manageable, the Secretary-General of the Conference suggested and the Preparatory Committee accepted that the issues to be addressed by the United Nations Conference could indeed be organized in six principle components as follows:

(1) An 'Earth Charter', a non-legally binding declaration of basic principles for the conduct of nations and peoples in respect of environment and development;

(2) Agreements on specific legal measures, eg, an umbrella convention on climate change and a convention on biological diversity which would be negotiated prior to the Conference and signed or agreed to at the Conference;

(3) An agenda for action, 'Agenda 21', establishing the agreed work programme of the international community for the period beyond 1992 and into the twenty-first century with respect to the issues to be addressed by the Conference, with priorities,

67 See these specific issues as originally included in the mandate of the two Working Groups established by the Preparatory Committee for the United Nations Conference on Environment and Development; First session, New York, 5–16 March 1990, Doc. A/44/48, Para. 56, Para. 9, p. 14, and as later reformulated in the report of the Working Groups at the end of the sessions of the Preparatory Committee of UNCED. For the latest report see UN Doc. GAOR Supp. 48 (A/46/48), Vols. I and II.

targets, cost estimates, modalities and assignments of responsibilities; plus the means to implement this agenda;

(4) New and additional financial resources;

(5) Transfer of technology;

(6) Strengthening of institutional capacities and processes of the multilateral system.

With respect to the new problems of global warming (climate change), acid rain, depletion of the ozone layer, and the problem of deforestation and its links to the issues of climate change and to the question of conservation of biodiversity, it may be recalled here that the law meets science and economics in a complementary way towards the solving of the identified problems. Thus, threshold questions arose which needed to be settled at the outset: whether or not there is indeed a 'global warming' and what exactly are its effects; whether or not there is sufficient scientific evidence upon which the international community may take international measures through appropriate international legal instruments to combat global warming, to deal with the problems of acid rain, to prevent further depletion of the stratospheric ozone layer, to preserve biological diversity and to combat desertification through the protection of tropical rain forests, taking into account the interdisciplinary approach mentioned in the introduction.

As a result of the pioneering work of UNEP and WMO and now through the preparatory process of UNCED, these questions have been amply answered as can be seen through the actions already being taken to develop appropriate legal instruments in response to the identified problems. Thus, for example, the Inter-governmental Negotiating Committee established by the General Assembly in Resolution 45/212 of 21 December 1990, is proceeding full speed with the drafting of a convention on climate change; UNEP is also continuing its efforts to elaborate a convention on biodiversity. The Food and Agricultural Organization (FAO), for its part, has also put in motion the process of elaborating, but with little success, a global convention on the protection of tropical forests. Other instruments are also being negotiated in response to the demands of updating of provisions to address problems of environment and development. For example, there is a convention on the prevention of industrial disaster being negotiated by the International Labour Organization (ILO) to be ready by 1993; the Economic Commission for Europe (ECE) is also elaborating a convention on protection and uses of transboundary watercourses to be completed by 1992; ECE is similarly working on a revision of the 1985 Protocol on SO_2 under the 1979 Long-Range Transboundary Air Pollution Convention; and a revision of the 1958 ECE Motor Vehicle Agreement; the Council of Europe is working on a draft convention on liability of damage resulting from activities dangerous to the environment, to be ready by 1992. There is also work under way for: a revision of the 1974 Baltic Marine Environment Convention; possible merger of the 1972 Oslo and 1974 Paris Conventions on Marine Pollution in the North Sea, new protocols on offshore mining and on hazardous wastes under the 1976 Mediterranean Convention, and on land-based marine pollution, both under the 1981 West African Convention and the 1983 Caribbean Convention.

While UNCED itself is not the forum for the actual negotiation of the text of these instruments just mentioned, participants in the work of the said UN bodies receive suggestions from the preparatory process of UNCED about the kind of issues of environment and development which should be taken into account in drafting the specific legal instruments foreseen. Some of these instruments are thus expected to be completed and ready for formal adoption and signature at the UNCED – Earth Summit in Rio de Janeiro. The decision-makers are indeed being told that, on balance, it may be unwise to simply sit by and wait for that day when the scientists will be able to pronounce, with the degree of certainty they demand, their final verdict on, for example, the question of 'global warming'. That day of complete scientific certainty may not come or if it does, the opportunity to take preventive action may have been lost. Accordingly, negotiations on a climate change convention had to proceed.

It may be also observed that, in the wake of the severe environmental damage caused by Iraq during the Gulf conflict, particularly the oil spills in the Persian Gulf and the burning of Kuwaiti oil wells, Jordan proposed the inclusion of a new item entitled 'Exploitation of the environment as a weapon in times of armed conflict and the taking of practical measures to prevent such exploitation' in the Agenda of the 46th session of the General Assembly of the UN.

During the debate in the Sixth Committee, to which this item was allocated, two main trends emerged. Some States considered the existing body of international law dealing with the protection of the environment in times of armed conflict to be adequate,[68] but stressed the need for greater adherence to and compliance with the existing legal instruments. Other States believed that recent events had demonstrated the inadequacy of the relevant existing rules of international law and supported their strengthening and the elaboration of new rules.

There was a general agreement to await the results of the 26th International Conference of the Red Cross and the Red Crescent which was to be held in late November 1991 and that the Secretary-General of the UN would report to the 47th Session of the General Assembly on the results of the Conference. However, the Red Cross Conference was momently postponed indefinitely. Consequently, the Secretary-General of the UN was requested to report to the 47th Session of the

68 In particular, Protocol I Additional to the Geneva Conventions of 12 August 1949 and relating to the Protection of Victims of International Armed Conflicts of 10 June 1977 and the Convention of the Prohibition of Military or Any Other Hostile Use of Environmental Modification Techniques of 18 May 1977.

General Assembly on the activities of the International Red Cross on this issue. The item was accordingly placed on the Agenda of the 47th session of the General Assembly.[69]

Several expert groups had also taken up the question of protection of environment in times of armed conflicts, making proposals for encouraging wider acceptance and implementation of the existing treaty-law on this issue and suggesting further development of the law in this area.[70]

3.2 Contribution of the Legal Working Group of the Preparatory Committee of UNCED

Working Group III on legal institutional and related matters, established by the Preparatory Committee of UNCED, commenced its work at the third session of the Committee when it was given concrete terms of reference. According to the terms of reference, the Working Group was to:

(1) Prepare an annotated list of existing international agreements and international legal instruments in the environmental field, describing their purpose and scope, evaluating their effectiveness and examining possible areas for the further development of international environmental law, in the light of the need to integrate environment and development, especially taking into account the special needs and concerns of the developing countries;

(2) Examine the feasibility of elaborating principles on general rights and obligations of States and regional economic integration organizations, as appropriate, in the field of environment and development, and consider the feasibility of incorporating such principles in an appropriate instrument/ charter/ statement/ declaration, taking due account of the conclusions of all the regional preparatory conferences;

(3) Consider the legal and institutional issues referred to it by Working Group I, Working Group II and the plenary of the Preparatory Committee, including the legal and institutional aspects of cross-sectoral issues dealt with by the Preparatory Committee that have been identified in relevant General Assembly resolutions;

69 General Assembly Decision A/46/C.6/L/13, as recommended by the Sixth (Legal Committee) and as amended by the General Assembly Plenary on 9 December 1991, in Doc. A/46/L.39 recognizing the postponement of the Red Cross Conference.

70 See eg Conference of experts on the use of the environment as a tool of environmental warfare, Ottawa, 10–12 July 1991 (copy of executive summary on authors file); London Conference on 'A Fifth Geneva' Convention on the Protection of the Environment in Times of Armed Conflict, 3 June 1991 (copy of executive summary of author's file), and consultation on the Law Concerning the Protection of the Environment in Times of Armed Conflict, convened by the International Council of Environmental Law, Munich, 13–15 December 1991 (copy of recommendations on author's file).

(4) Review ways and means of strengthening the cooperation and coordination between the UN system and other inter-governmental and non-governmental, regional and global institutions in the field of environment and development;

(5) Review the role and functioning of the UN system in the field of environment and development and make recommendations on ways and means of further enhancing coordination and cooperation on environment and development issues in the UN system;

(6) Examine and consider strengthening institutional arrangements required for the effective implementation of the Conclusions of UNCED in the UN system.[71]

The contribution of Working Group III of the Preparatory Committee of UNCED is the main subject of analysis in this section, aimed at indicating the efforts of the international community to encourage the development of appropriate legal instruments for responding to problems of environment and development. It is important to describe here at some length, the contributions of Working Group III, in order to provide a concise legislative history of the final legal instruments which are to emerge from the Earth Summit.

The first order of business for Working Group III was, therefore, the preparation of a list of existing international agreements and international legal instruments to be evaluated and the criteria for undertaking such evaluation. A list of 100 instruments was prepared and became the basis of the work of Working Group III.[72] The 100 instruments, some of which have been the subject of analysis in section 2 above, dealing with the anatomy of environmental treaties, include treaties concluded before 1972 Stockholm Conference.

The Working Group then adopted 32 specific criteria for evaluating the effectiveness of instruments in terms of six broad considerations, namely:

(a) objectives and achievements,

(b) participation in the instruments in question,

(c) implementation of the instrument,

(d) information requested under the instruments,

(e) operation, review and adjustment of the instruments, and

(f) codification programming contained in them.

Given the importance of the useful exercise of evaluating the effectiveness of the existing legal instrument in the field of environment, in order to identify the gaps in both the substantive and procedural law, the 32 criteria are outlined below:[73]

(1) Objectives and achievement

(a) What are the basic objectives formulated in the international agreements and instruments evaluated, and how do these objectives relate to the

71 See Doc. A/46/48, Vol. I, Decision 2/3.

72 See Doc. A/CONF.151/PC/103/Add.1.

73 See Doc. A/CONF.151/PC/77, Sec.II, pp. 12–16; Doc. A/CONF.151/PC/94 (Annex II).

effective integration of environment and development?

(b) In the case of regional agreements and instruments, what is their actual and potential bearing on global environmental protection and sustainable development?

(c) Do these agreements or instruments take into account the special circumstances of developing countries?

(d) To what extent have the basic objectives (environmental/ developmental) formulated in international agreements and instruments been met, and how is goal achievement measured?

(2) Participation

(a) Is membership limited or open-ended?

(b) Are reservations possible, and to what extent have they been used.

(c) What is the current geographical distribution of membership in existing environmental agreements and instruments, especially as regards developing countries?

(d) Which incentives (eg financial, trade, technology benefits) are available to encourage participation and facilitate implementation by developing countries?

(e) Which measures have been taken to promote and support the effective participation of developing countries in the negotiation and operation of international agreements or instruments, including technical and financial assistance and other available mechanisms for this purpose?

(f) Which factors influenced the participation, especially of developing countries, in the agreement or instrument? For example:

(*i*) Financial resources required and available for participation in the agreement or instrument;

(*ii*) Technical assistance required and available for participation in the agreement or instrument;

(*iii*) Scientific assistance required and available for participation in the agreement or instrument;

(*iv*) Information on the (operation of the) agreement or instrument to governments, parliaments, press, NGOs, industries and the general public;

(*v*) Role of parliaments, press, NGOs, industries and public opinion in general;

(*vi*) Availability of reservations.

(3) Implementation

(a) To what extent has the implementation of agreements or instruments been constrained or accelerated by provisions regarding their entry into force?

(b) What are the commitments imposed on parties by these agreements and instruments, and how is compliance by parties with their commitments monitored and measured?

(c) How do parties report on their performance in implementing agreements and instruments, and to what extent have they been met by the parties?

(d) Which are the specific requirements (if any) of data supply and data disclosure, and to what extent have they been met by the parties?

(e) Which possibilities exist to promote compliance and to follow up on non-compliance, and to what extent have they been used?

(f) Which mechanisms are available to deal with disputes over implementation and to what extent have they been used?

(g) Which factors influenced the implementation? For example:

(*i*) Financial resources required and available for implementation of the agreement or instrument;

(*ii*) Technical assistance required and available for implementation of the agreement or instrument;

(*iii*) Scientific assistance required and available for implementation of the agreement or instrument;

(*iv*) Information on the (operation of the) agreement or instrument to governments, parliaments, press, NGOs, industries and the general public;

(*v*) Role of parliaments, press, NGOs, industries and public opinion in general;

(*vi*) International supervisory or implementing bodies;

(*vii*) Obligations to report on compliance and/or to supply and disclose data;

(*viii*) Non-compliance procedures and procedures for settlement of disputes (including fact-finding procedures).

(4) Information

(a) In which form and in which languages are the texts of existing agreements and instruments published and disseminated?

(b) How is current information on the operation and implementation of international agreements and instruments made available to governments, to the industries concerned and to the general public?

(c) What additional materials are available to provide guidance for the implementation of international agreements and instruments at the national level?

(d) To what extent is the above information used in international and national training and education programmes?

(5) Operation, review and adjustment

(a) Which are the institutional arrangements for international administration of existing agreements and instruments?

(b) What are the annual (1990) costs of international administration (secretariat, meetings, programmes) of agreements and instruments, and how are they financed?

(c) Which are the main benefits and the main cost elements of national participation in existing agreements and instruments, and which possibilities exist to reduce participation cost for developing countries?

(d) Which mechanisms are available to ensure that scientific knowledge and advice is taken into account in policy-making decisions under these agreements and instruments?

(e) How do these arrangements and mechanisms ensure the effective participation of
 (*i*) national authorities, especially from developing countries; and
 (*ii*) non-governmental participants, including the industries concerned and the scientific community?

(f) Which mechanisms are available to ensure periodic review and adjustment of international agreements and instruments in order to meet new requirement, and to what extent have they been used?

(6) Codification programming

(a) Which new drafts, or draft revisions of existing agreements and instruments, in the environmental field are currently under preparation or negotiation?

(b) To what extent and through which mechanisms is drafting coordinated with related work regarding other agreements and instruments?

(c) Which are the remaining gaps that need to be covered by legal provisions?

(d) To what extent are mechanisms other than formal agreements or instruments contributing to the development of international law in the field of the environment?

On the basis of the above criteria for evaluating the effectiveness of the existing agreements in the environmental field, the Secretariat of UNCED prepared a survey of the 100 instruments which were evaluated and included suggestions for follow-up action.[74] The assessment of the agreements contained in the survey, confirmed, *inter alia*, what has been underscored here about the piecemeal approach to environmental treaty-making and the need to integrate more fully development dimensions into environmental policies in response to the 1987 report of the WCED recalling the concept of 'sustainable development' and taking into account the interest and concern of the developing countries. The verdict was that, most of the existing agreements have too generalized objectives, usually buried in the preambles. Agreements should: have more precisely stated objectives; avoid excessive use of reservation clauses which affect the level of participation; contain provisions

74 For details, see Doc. A/CONF.151/PC/103/and Add. 1.

encouraging speedy entry-into-force to allow for implementation; establish more flexible procedures for settlement of disputes; require the circulation of information regarding implementation; include more expeditious procedures for amendments; contain provisions encouraging further development of the law in the subject matter covered by the instrument through additional protocols; provide for mechanisms for monitoring compliance and for periodic review of the treaty regime relying upon, which approach, streamlined, harmonized or combined administrative or supporting service and institutions; and improve upon the negotiating process of the instruments.

Apart from its assessment of the existing multilateral treaties in the field of environment, Working Group III also undertook discussions on the institutional aspects of such treaties aiming at strengthening the multilateral system for integration of environment and development policies. It received certain proposals in that regard.[75] Whether the solution was to be found in the re-establishment of a completely new international institution, in the strengthening of an existing institution such as UNEP or in the maintenance of an existing process such as UNCED, remained a troublesome issue. On the basis of a preliminary discussion in the Working Group III of the Committee, the following eight points were recommended for consideration of this issue towards an appropriate solution:[76]

(a) Some reform of UN institutions in the field of environment and development is needed, taking into account general efforts for restructuring and revitalization of the UN in the context of General Assembly Resolution 45/264.

(b) Working Group III must take into account decisions with institutional implications originating from Working Groups I and II and the Plenary.

(c) Proliferation of institutions at the global level must be avoided.

(d) There is a need to work out mechanisms to promote coordination, both at the intergovernmental level and at the level of the Secretariat and UN specialized agencies and programmes involved with environment or development.

(e) Existing international institutions at the global and regional levels in the field of environment and development, including UNEP and UNDP, should be adapted to changed circumstances in order to support sustainable development. There was consensus that UNEP must be strengthened.

(f) Among the goals of institutional reform at the global and regional levels should be enhancement of the capacity of institutions at the national level, especially in developing countries, to ensure the full integration of environment and development.

(g) Institutions and organizations outside the UN system, including the non-

75 See eg, Doc. A/CONF.151/PC/WG.III/L.19; Doc. A/CONF.151/PC/102.
76 See Doc. A/CONF.151/PC/WG.III/L10.

governmental sector, have an important role in this process.

(h) The Working Group, at the fourth session of the Preparatory Committee, will have to consider the need for institutional arrangements, both at the intergovernmental and secretariat levels for the implementation and continuous review of Agenda 21.

The analysis or the views of participants at the UNCED Preparatory Committee commenting on some of the above specific points indicate,[77] as noted above, that the whole question was destined to remain a controversial one.

In addition to its work on institutional aspects, the Legal Working Group was also charged with the duty to prepare the draft *Earth Charter* or the Rio Declaration on Environment and Development, which is one of the important components of 'Agenda 21', as mentioned earlier. Specific suggestions for inclusion in the *Earth Charter* were submitted by a number of States and have been consolidated into one document dealing with principles on general rights and obligations. On the basis of preliminary discussions in Working Group III of the Preparatory Committee, the discussion on this issue was to proceed, bearing in mind the following five points:[78]

(a) the charter or declaration containing the principles should be short and concise;

(b) the text should be closely integrated with Agenda 21;

(c) the text should be appealing and inspiring, with a view to enhancing public awareness of environment and development issues;

(d) its language and style, while ensuring legal precision of commitments, should be easily understood by the general public;

(e) the charter or declaration should, in a forward-looking manner, build on existing principles contained in documents such as the 1972 Declaration of the United Nations Conference on the Human Environment.

It was also agreed that the proposals for specific provisions concerning Principles on General Rights and Obligations would address the following issues:[79]

Principle 1, Integration of environment and development;
Principle 2, Common but differentiated responsibility;
Principle 3, Individual and group rights;
Principle 4, Responsibility to present and future generations;
Principle 5, Sovereignty and responsibility to others;
Principle 6, Precautionary principle and prior assessment;
Principle 7, Cooperation;

77 These views also took into account General Assembly Resolution 44/229, requesting the Secretary-General to submit a report on the structure and responsiveness of the UN in dealing with major environmental issues.

78 See Doc. A/CONF.151/PC/WG/III/L.13.

79 See eg, Doc. A/CONF.151/PC/WG.III/L.8/Rev.1. and Add.1.

Principle 8, Special needs of developing countries;
Principle 9, Environment and world trade;
Principle 10, Peace and security;
Principle 11, Production and consumption patterns;
Principle 12, Information and education;
Principle 13, Cost internalization;
Principle 14, Liability for damage and dispute settlement;
Principle 15, Public participation and democracy;
Principle 16, Poverty;
Principle 17, Resources transfer.

Working Group III also examined possible areas for further development of international environmental law in accordance with the now well-established standard of review, namely the need to integrate environment and development, especially taking into account the needs and concerns of developing countries. Certain objectives were identified in the survey,[80] along the lines described and expanded below.

3.3. Future Objectives and Challenges

Coming back to the objectives of the seminar, and taking into account the evidence presented here concerning the approaches to environmental law-making in light of the lessons learnt since Stockholm 1972, while looking forward to Rio de Janeiro in 1992 and beyond, the following should be borne in mind, as recognized in UNCED studies.[81]

The overall present and future objective of UNCED is to promote the integration of environment and development policies through effective international agreements and instruments,[82] especially taking into account the needs and concerns of the developing countries. To that end, effort must be made in the legal field to:

(a) Set priorities for future law-making at the appropriate level, incorporating environmental and development concerns in a balanced manner;

(b) Promote and support, in more concrete ways, the effective participation of developing countries in the negotiation and implementation of international agreements or instruments. Such support should include assured financial assistance to cover the necessary travel expenses to meetings and access to the necessary information and scientific-technical expertise on preferential terms;

80 See Doc. A/CONF.151/PC/102 para.40. Cf para. 60 *infra*.

81 See Doc. A/CONF.151/PC/103 and Add.1.

82 See generally, Integration of Environment and Development in Decision Making, Doc. A/CONF.151/PC/100 Add.8.

(c) Ensure effective implementation and compliance, regular assessment and timely review and adjustment or agreements or instruments by the parties concerned. In addition, to monitor and review domestic legal instruments giving effect to international agreements on environment and development, with a view to promoting compliance and harmonization;

(d) Improve on the substantive scope of international environmental agreements by including more effective provisions on, *inter alia*, environmental emergencies preparedness and contingency plans for assistance in case of such emergencies; environmental impact assessment by planned projects with procedures for allowing effective participation of individual citizens and non-governmental organizations; more concrete rules on liability and compensation; and equal access of governments to local judicial or administrative procedures;

(e) Improve the effectiveness of institutions, mechanisms and procedures for administration of international environmental agreements and instruments;

(f) Assist developing countries and economies in transition in their national efforts at modernizing and strengthening the legal and regulatory framework of governance for sustainable development, having regard to local social values and infrastructures;

(g) Disseminate information on effective legal and regulatory innovations in the field of environment and development, including non-coercive instruments and compliance incentives, with a view to encouraging their wider use and adaptation at the national and local level;

(h) Promote and resolve environmental disputes including potential conflicts between environment and development/trade agreements or instruments, combining options for resort to informal, non-compulsory procedures with formal compulsory procedures which provide for adjudication by ad hoc arbitral tribunals or judicial settlement by pre-constituted courts such as the International Court of Justice. Two proposals were submitted in this connection: one seeking to establish a comprehensive instrument for the settlement of all types of environmental disputes[83] while the other deals with the establishment of an independent enquiry commission.[84] They will form the basis of further discussions on this important issue. Whether the establishment of a comprehensive system reflected in the above pentagonale countries' proposals would be the preferred approach is still one of the issues to be settled. Certain governments have expressed doubts about such a system.

83 See Doc.A/CONF.151/PC/L.29, submitted by the pentagonale countries (Austria, the Czech and Slovak Federal Republic, Hungary, Italy and Yugoslavia) and Poland.

84 See Doc. A/CONF.151/PC/WG.III/L.1, submitted by the above pentagonale countries and Poland.

The Earth Summit in Rio will, as emphasized by the Secretary-General of the Conference,[85] be about environment *and* development. But there is a primary emphasis on development and economic change. For it is through the development process that we carry out activities which impact upon the environment. It is also through fundamental changes in our economic behaviour, in lifestyles and in management or development process that we can effect the positive synthesis between the environment and development that will produce life that is sustainable, both in economic and environmental things. The challenge is that we have to make the necessary efforts towards the transition to sustainable development.

The transition to sustainability, the Secretary-General further observed, requires much more effective use of resources and accountability for environmental as well as economic impacts of such use. This must depend primarily on the provision of the necessary incentives to change rather than over reliance on regulating measures. The challenge is that the system of incentives and penalties through which governments create conditions that motivate our economic life must be re-examined and re-oriented to provide the necessary incentives for transition to sustainability in both our industrial and individual behaviour.

What is called for at Rio, as stated by the Secretary-General of the Conference, is nothing less than 'eco-industrial revolution', namely, one that will not only preserve and extend the benefits created by the industrial revolution, but also create a whole new generation of economic opportunity and redress the gross imbalance between the rich and the poor. The challenge is how to redress concretely the imbalances which are incompatible with sustainable development as they are with justice and equity.

Admittedly, traditional patterns of technical assistance which often deepen dependence on foreign experts are simply not adequate. What is needed, the challenge for us to meet, is a sustainable commitment to building indigenous human and institutional capacity. Surely, the key to self-reliance is the fostering of a pool of indigenous talents that can adapt and innovate in a world where knowledge is the primary basis of competitiveness.

As we strive towards putting into place appropriate legal frameworks, for international responses to problems of environment and development, we have to keep in mind the following: the concept of national sovereignty has been an immutable and a most sacred principle of international law. There is no need for wholesale retreat from the principle. The present challenge is for us to recognize that, in many fields, particularly in the environmental field, it is simply not feasible for sovereignty to be exercised unilaterally by individual States, however powerful. Global environmental and economic security requires global cooperation which implies the

85 See Maurice F. Strong, *supra* note 4.

willingness of States to give up, in appropriate legal instruments, a little of their sovereignty, in the interest of the international community at large.

Owing to the increased publicity, environment and development issues are moving to grass roots in a growing number of countries. There is a proliferation of new citizens groups and voluntary organizations which are becoming more important agents of action as well as sources of political pressure. Some of them need, however, to be scrutinized in order to ascertain if they do not have a hidden or separate agenda from the Rio mainstream. But, on the whole, most of the citizens groups simply insist on opportunities for greater participation in the decisions which affect them and for more effective accountability of the decisions and actions by governments.

On the pervasive concept of sustainable development the following needs to be underscored: sustainable development cannot be imposed by external pressure, it must be noted in the culture, the values, the interests and the priorities of the people concerned. Developing countries cannot be denied their right to grow, nor to choose their own pathways to growth. Nor should that right be constrained by new conditions on financial flows or trade imposed in the name of environment. The challenge is how to tap the necessary support of the international community and reverse the outflow of resources that has still stifled the economic growth of developing countries.

It has been acknowledged in the UNCED documents addressing the question of integration of environment and development in decision-making,[86] that laws and regulations are among the most important instruments to transform environment and development policies into action – not only through 'command and control' methods but also as a normative framework for economic planning and market instruments. Yet although the volume of legal texts in this field is steadily increasing, much of the law-making has been ad hoc and piecemeal, or has not been endowed with the necessary institutional machinery and authority for enforcement and timely adjustment. The legal process, which ought to facilitate progress towards sustainable patterns of development, is often ill-adapted to the scale and pace of economic and social change – and to the degree of public participation and transparency of decision-making – required for this purpose.[87]

The UNCED document also notes that, while there is continuous need for law reform in all countries, developing countries have been particularly affected by the shortcomings of laws and regulations often dating back to the colonial period. In order to ensure timely adjustment, technical support is needed both for the drafting of new or revised legal instruments and for their practical implementation, including the appropriate institutions and remedies. Technical cooperation requirements in this

86 See Part B of Doc. A/CONF.151/0C/100/Add.8, Paras. 14–16
87 See these issues as further developed in Agenda 21 for Rio.

field include legal information, advisory services and specialized training and institutional capacity-building.

The document further emphasizes that the enactment and enforcement of laws and regulations (at a national/state/provincial or local/municipal level) is also essential for the implementation of most international agreements in the field of environment and development, as illustrated by the frequent treaty obligation to report on legislative measures. The survey of existing agreements undertaken in the context of UNCED preparations has indicated serious problems of compliance in this respect, and the need for improved monitoring and related technical assistance.

3.4 Conclusion: Focus upon Financial Resources as a Fundamental Issue

From the ongoing discussion within the Preparatory Committee for UNCED, in Working Groups I and II, and as demonstrated by the efforts of Working Group III, conclusion is inescapable that a lot more work is still to be done towards the fulfilment of the objectives such as outlined in this section. Thus, what seems readily achievable at the Rio Summit in June 1992, is the formal acceptance of specific commitments by the governments, on the basis of the results achieved by the three working groups, to continue pursuing, within an established period of time after Rio, the further elaboration of appropriate international legal frameworks for concrete actions for implementing 'Agenda 21'.

Lurking behind all these is the need for a general understanding of the fact that developed and developing countries will have to reach agreement on how to distribute responsibilities for global environmental damage already caused and traced to activities in the industrial countries and those traced to the activities in the developing countries.

There also needs to be an understanding on the part of the countries of the North that they will not divert the funds already earmarked for developments in the South and use such funds for dealing with newly identified environmental problems. Additional resources must thus be made available for dealing with environmental issues of 'Agenda 21' as adopted at the Earth Summit in Rio. In this connection, it is necessary to keep in mind the existing Global Environment Facility (GEF) which has been billed as an experiment offering a way to pursue development while meeting global environmental concerns. To encourage wider dissemination of the facts about GEF and the evaluation of its role beyond the Earth Summit, its concise descriptions, prepared by the World Bank, United Nations Development Programme, and United Nations Environment Programme, merits inclusion here:

> 'The Global Environment Facility is a US$1 billion-plus programme providing grants to developing countries to help them carry out programmes to relieve pressures on global

ecosystems. The GEF is jointly managed by the World Bank, the United Nations Development Programme (UNDP) and the United Nations Environment Programme (UNEP), and is funded by both industrialized and developing countries. With experience gained since its founding in November 1990, the facility is poised to play a role in helping regions and nations of the world reach agreements at the United Nations Conference on Environment and Development in June of 1992.

Working closely with each developing country, the GEF acts in four main areas: to reduce global warming; to preserve biological diversity; to protect international waters; and to prevent further depletion of the ozone layer. These activities, however, must be consistent with a country's national development priorities: it is the responsibility of all three managing agencies to ensure that the facility enhances the potential for long-term sustainable development. Specialized agencies and non-governmental organizations (NGOs) help to assess impact on local populations, advise on project design and implement projects.

To qualify for GEF financial support, both the beneficiary country and the project itself must meet strict criteria. Countries have per-capital gross domestic product (GDP) of US$4,000 or less. The project must protect the global environment in a cost-effective, technologically sound way while respecting the interests of the country's people. While most of the GEF funding goes for investment projects, other activities include technical assistance, technology transfer and training. Funds support activities which, while they benefit the environment of the world as a whole, would not otherwise be economically viable for that country. The funds are not meant to substitute for existing programme or project support, but to provide additional resources. Money has been earmarked for 53 specific projects totalling $470 million so far.

Projects currently under way include a $4.8 million project in cooperation with the World Meteorological Organization to monitor greenhouse and ozone depleting gases by setting up monitoring stations in developing countries. Projects nearing approval include a $10 million East African regional project to support the protection of biodiversity in the area and a biomass gasification programme for Brazil with an initial planning and design phase of $7 million, and calling for private sector participation.

In addition to big projects costing millions of dollars, the GEF has created a small-grants programme. This provides support for innovative small-scale activities by community groups, NGOs and NGO networks in amounts up to $50,000 each for community and national projects and $250,000 each for subregional, regional or inter-regional projects. It is funded initially at $5 million and is managed by UNDP.

Each of the GEF partners – the World Bank, UNDP and UNEP – has a distinct role to play. The World Bank administers the trust fund and is responsible for investment operations. It undertakes identification, appraisal and supervision of investment projects with the participation of UNDP and UNEP.

UNEP provides scientific and technological guidance in identifying and selecting projects, and coordinates research and data collection. It convenes a Scientific and Technical Advisory Panel of both industrialized and developing country experts to provide criteria and priorities for GEF funding.

UNDP coordinates and manages the financing and execution of technical assistance and pre-investment activities. Through its 112 field offices, UNDP plays a central role in identifying projects, communicating with recipient governments and coordinating with donors at the country level. Both UNEP and UNDP help governments to make GEF programmes fit with other environment and development activities in beneficiary countries.'

The availability of the necessary financial resources for the implementation of Agenda 21 on the basis of legal frameworks for addressing problems of environment and development, through appropriate international or national institutions, remains one of the central issues for which an effective solution must be found. The GEF experiment must, therefore, be critically evaluated, its shortcomings identified and possibly remedied.

[7]

Protection of the Stratospheric Ozone Layer and the Structure of International Environmental Lawmaking

By DAVID D. CARON*

I. INTRODUCTION

As concern for the global environment grows, there is both underway and planned a flurry of international environmental lawmaking efforts. Protection of the stratospheric ozone layer is an area in which there already has been a relatively large amount of lawmaking activity. This Article in Part I briefly reviews the stratospheric ozone depletion problem and the history of the international community's response to that threat. This review and history has been treated extensively and competently elsewhere.[1] In this sense, it is not the purpose of Part I to duplicate such work, but rather to provide the reader with an appreciation of the concerns and trends that have marked the community's response. Part II provides a restatement of the regime for the protection of the stratospheric ozone layer as it presently exists under the 1985 Vienna Convention,[2] the 1987 Montreal Protocol,[3] and the 1990 London Adjustments and Amendments to that Protocol.[4] Finally in Part III, I briefly

* Acting Professor of Law, University of California, Berkeley; Dr. Jur. 1990, Drs. 1985, Leiden University; Dip. 1984, Hague Academy of International Law; J.D. 1983, School of Law (Boalt Hall), University of California, Berkeley; M.Sc. 1980, University of Wales Center for Marine Law and Policy; B.S. 1974, U.S. Coast Guard Academy.

This Article on the current status of the international regime for the protection of the stratospheric ozone layer was solicited by the Annuaire Français de Droit International and published in French as *La protection de la couche d'ozone stratosphérique et la structure de l'activité normative internationale en matière d'environnement*, 36 ANNUAIRE FRANÇAIS DE DROIT INTERNATIONAL (1990) (forthcoming).

1. *See, e.g.*, S. ROAN, OZONE CRISIS: THE 15-YEAR EVOLUTION OF A SUDDEN GLOBAL EMERGENCY (1989).

2. Vienna Convention for the Protection of the Ozone Layer, *opened for signature* Mar. 22, 1985, U.N. Doc. UNEP/IG.53/Rev.1, at 11 (1985), S. TREATY DOC. 9, 99th Cong., 1st Sess. (1985), *reprinted in* 26 I.L.M. 1529 (1987) [hereinafter Vienna Convention].

3. Montreal Protocol on Substances that Deplete the Ozone Layer, *opened for signature* Sept. 16, 1987, S. TREATY DOC. 10, 100th Cong., 2d Sess. (1987), *reprinted in* 26 I.L.M. 1550 (1987) [hereinafter Montreal Protocol].

4. *Report of the Second Meeting of the Parties to the Montreal Protocol on Substances that*

reflect on what the community's experience with the ozone depletion problem tells us concerning the evolving structure of lawmaking in the international environmental area.[5]

II. STRATOSPHERIC OZONE DEPLETION: THE PROBLEM AND A BRIEF HISTORY OF THE INTERNATIONAL RESPONSE

A. The Stratospheric Ozone Layer and The Theory That It Could Be Depleted[6]

A diffuse layer of ozone[7] in the upper reaches of our atmosphere has shielded life on the planet from ultraviolet radiation[8] for millions of years. A seemingly unrelated event in 1928 was the development of chlorofluorocarbons (CFCs) by Dupont chemists. These extremely stable and consequently long-lived substances were hailed as technological triumphs. If one recurrent theme in the effort to protect the ozone layer is uncertainty as to the reality or extent of a threat, then it is noteworthy that for almost fifty years after the discovery of CFCs, the community was ignorant of the threat CFCs posed and, as a consequence, focused only upon the benefits they accorded. CFCs came to be used in a multitude of ways, and the amount and types of CFCs utilized grew dramatically, first after the World War II and again in the late 1960s.[9]

In 1974 however, two scientists postulated that these stable sub-

---

Deplete the Ozone Layer, U.N. Environment Programme (Agenda Item 7), U.N. Doc. UNEP/OzL.Pro.2/3, Annex II (1990) [hereinafter *London Amendments*].

5. *See also* P.H. SAND, LESSONS LEARNED IN GLOBAL ENVIRONMENTAL GOVERNANCE (1990) (addressing innovations in standard setting and implementation).

6. For a succinct description of the problem, see Rowland, *Stratospheric Ozone Depletion by Chlorofluorocarbons*, 19 AMBIO 281 (1990); Gribbin, *The Ozone Layer*, NEW SCIENTIST, May 5, 1988, Inside Science No. 9, at 1.

7. Ozone is an unstable gas composed of three atom oxygen molecules, which tends to break down into the two atom oxygen molecules which we breathe. Ozone nonetheless exists in the stratosphere because ultraviolet radiation (from which we are shielded by the ozone layer) creates ozone by breaking apart diatomic oxygen. This ozone eventually returns spontaneously to its more stable two atom configuration. But amidst this cycle there is a resultant layer of ozone. Crucially important to one's understanding is the fact that the ozone layer operates as a shield even though the concentration of ozone is only about one molecule in every 100,000. The concentration is so small that human activities have the potential to disrupt it.

8. Light from the sun covers a range of energies. Light which appears blue to the human eye, for example, is more energetic than light that appears red. Ultraviolet light, with wavelengths from below 200 nanometers up to 350 nanometers and not visible to the human eye, is highly energetic and, consequently, harmful to life.

9. CFCs have been used as propellants for aerosols, refrigerants, solvents for the cleaning of electronic components, and the manufacture of rigid and flexible foams.

stances, for the most part, ultimately reached the stratosphere; that once there, they finally became exposed to the ultraviolet radiation from which they had been shielded by the ozone layer; that this highly energetic radiation broke down the CFC molecule, releasing chlorine atoms; and that such chlorine atoms then served as catalysts in reactions which broke down ozone molecules.[10] It was estimated that each chlorine atom released could destroy 100,000 ozone molecules, ultimately depleting the ozone layer and exposing the planet to increased harmful ultraviolet radiation.[11]

Two responses to this theory quickly emerged. Some experts pointed to the dangers of failing to act quickly to protect the ozone layer. Others pointed to the costs of acting precipitously on the basis of a contested and yet unproven hypothesis. This confrontation became a key characteristic of the debate regarding CFCs and ozone depletion for most of the decade that followed. Moreover, because the issue became a clash of experts which was not accessible to laypeople, there was a lack of shared knowledge concerning the problem that in many ways foreclosed broader public participation.

B. The Focus on Aerosols: 1974 to 1981[12]

Public debate regarding regulation initially focused upon the use of CFCs as propellants in aerosols, a use that clearly resulted in releases of CFCs into the atmosphere. Not without difficulty, a number of states, including the United States,[13] Canada, and Sweden,[14] moved toward national bans on such aerosols. These efforts at unilateral action added new characteristics to the debate. First, the concern arose in U.S. governmental circles that these unilateral efforts might be counterproductive in that

10. Molina & Rowland, *Stratospheric Sink for Chlorofluoromethanes: Chlorine Atom-Catalyzed Destruction of Ozone*, 249 NATURE 810 (1974). *See also* Stolarski & Cicerone, *Stratospheric Chlorine: A Possible Sink for Ozone*, 52 CAN. J. CHEMISTRY 1610 (1974).

11. As to the potential harmful effects of increased ultraviolet radiation, see Emmett, *Health Effects of Ultraviolet Radiation*, 1 EFFECTS OF CHANGES IN STRATOSPHERIC OZONE AND GLOBAL CLIMATE 129 (J.G. Titus ed. 1986) [hereinafter 1 STRATOSPHERIC OZONE]; Waxler, *Ozone Depletion and Ocular Risks from Ultraviolet Radiation*, in 1 STRATOSPHERIC OZONE, *supra* at 147; Teramura, *Overview of Our Current State of Knowledge of UV Effects on Plants*, in 1 STRATOSPHERIC OZONE, *supra*, at 165; Worrest, *The Effect of Solar UV-B Radiation on Aquatic Systems: An Overview*, in 1 STRATOSPHERIC OZONE, *supra*, at 175.

12. For a history of this early period, see L. DOTTO & H. SCHIFF, THE OZONE WAR (1978).

13. As to U.S. actions then and generally, see Nangle, *Stratospheric Ozone: United States Regulation of Chlorofluorocarbons*, 16 B.C. ENVTL. AFF. L. REV. 531 (1989).

14. As to Swedish actions then and generally, see Ahmadzai & Hedlund, *A Profile of Measures Taken in Sweden to Protect the Stratospheric Ozone Layer*, 19 AMBIO 341 (1990).

the actions of a few states took pressure off other states to do likewise. In other words, there was a free rider problem. Second, because lawmakers and the public often could not judge the debate of experts, governments began undertaking their own studies. These studies provided more impartial and authoritative sources of knowledge regarding the subject. They would take time to complete, but their eventual release would profoundly affect the debate. In some cases, such as in the United States, a study would strongly support regulation efforts,[15] while in other states such as the United Kingdom, the study would have the opposite effect.[16]

The national debates, as might be expected, resulted in basically one of two outcomes: states generally inclined to greater regulation of CFCs, and states basically still suspicious of the theory or at least of the need for aggressive immediate action. Those states holding the former view included Canada, Finland, Sweden, and the United States; the latter view was held by much of continental Europe and the United Kingdom.[17] The states holding these two views would coalesce into two groups (respectively the Toronto group and the European Community (EC) group) during the international negotiations which followed, and, would roughly maintain their views and compositions until approximately 1987.

C. UNEP and the 1985 Vienna Framework Convention

Even as the national debates proceeded, the groundwork for an international approach was laid. The United Nations Environmental Programme (UNEP) in 1977 convened a meeting to begin the international process. The meeting resulted in the adoption of the "World Plan of Action on the Ozone Layer" and the establishment of a Global Coordinating Committee on the Ozone Layer.

As U.S. leadership and concern over the ozone problem diminished with the advent of the Reagan administration in 1981, UNEP, as a forum for action, and the UNEP efforts to formulate an international response under its Action Plan, in particular, moved to center stage.[18] In 1981

---

15. *See* NATIONAL ACADEMY OF SCIENCES, HALOCARBONS: ENVIRONMENTAL EFFECTS OF CHLOROFLUOROMETHANES (1976).

16. *See* STRATOSPHERIC RESEARCH ADVISORY COMM., U.K. DEP'T OF THE ENV'T, REPORT ON STRATOSPHERIC OZONE (1976).

17. This should not be taken to mean that the European Communities did nothing, but rather that they were not prepared to do as much. As to actions by the European Community in 1978, 1980, and 1982, see S.P. JOHNSON & G. CORCELLE, THE ENVIRONMENTAL POLICY OF THE EUROPEAN COMMUNITIES 149-51 (International Environmental Law and Policy Series, 1989).

18. For discussions of the UNEP efforts up to and including adoption of the Vienna Convention, see J. BRUNNÉE, ACID RAIN AND OZONE LAYER DEPLETION: INTERNATIONAL

UNEP established an Ad Hoc Working Group of Legal and Technical experts charged with the task of drafting a framework convention for the protection of the ozone layer. A framework convention is a document that aims not at substantive norms, but rather at establishment of the institutional framework that will result in such norms. The Working Group released the first draft of its work in October 1983, and several further drafts were produced prior to the Vienna Conference in March 1985, which ultimately adopted a framework convention.

Adoption of the Vienna Convention was bittersweet, however, because several states had sought more from the Conference. In particular, Finland, Norway, and Sweden circulated a draft protocol to the then developing framework convention (the Nordic Annex) that would have banned aerosol use of CFCs. Meanwhile, changes within the Environmental Protection Agency under the Reagan administration led the United States to join Canada in supporting the Nordic Annex. The EC states opposed the approach taken by the Annex. Ultimately a compromise was reached in the form of a Resolution of the Conference calling for the states to reassemble for the purpose of concluding a protocol regulating CFCs.

D. A Growing Sense of Urgency and the 1987 Montreal Protocol[19]

Even as work proceeded in anticipation of a second meeting to adopt a protocol, two important trends were occurring. First, a British research group in May 1985 announced that huge losses in Antarctic ozone had occurred in the springs of 1982, 1983, and 1984.[20] By late summer 1985 American satellite measurements, free of certain previous

LAW AND REGULATION 225-53 (1988). Rummel-Bulska, *The Protection of the Ozone Layer Under the Global Framework Convention*, in TRANSBOUNDARY AIR POLLUTION: INTERNATIONAL LEGAL ASPECTS OF THE CO-OPERATION OF STATES 281 (C. Flinterman, B. Kwiatkowska & J. Lammers eds. 1986); Sand, *Protecting the Ozone Layer: The Vienna Convention is Adopted*, ENVIRONMENT, June 1985, at 18; Wasermann, *UNEP: Protection of the Ozone Layer*, 17 J. WORLD TRADE L. 182 (1983).

19. For discussions of the period leading up to and immediately following the Montreal Protocol, see Bankes, *The Ozone Convention and Protocol: Further Steps Towards an International Law of the Atmosphere*, RESOURCES: NEWSL. OF THE CAN. INST. OF RESOURCES L., Spring 1988, at 1; Mintz, *Keeping Pandora's Box Shut: A Critical Assessment of the Montreal Protocol on Substances That Deplete The Ozone Layer*, 20 INTER-AM. L. R. 565 (1989).

20. Farmer, Gardiner & Shanklin, *Large Losses of Total Ozone in Antarctica Reveal Seasonal CLO_x/NO_x Interaction*, 315 NATURE 207 (1985). The data supporting this, however, was limited in that measurements were taken at only two points in Antarctica. More importantly, for several months the data was not supported by American satellite measurements.

interpretational errors, confirmed the British findings.[21] The Antarctic ozone hole created quite a stir in the scientific community since none of the atmospheric models developed up to that point would have predicted such an event. As a result, a massive international research effort was undertaken to determine whether chlorine was responsible for the hole. In this instance, there would not only be theories, but actual measurements of the chlorine in the stratosphere over Antarctica would be taken. In more general terms, the Antarctic hole was significant because, even before the scientific community could confirm that chlorine was responsible for the hole, the public had what in its view was tangible and comprehensible evidence that humanity could fundamentally alter the Earth's atmosphere. As the public increasingly voiced its concern, the states participating in the international negotiations became increasingly receptive not only to a ban on aerosol use, but, more generally, to across the board phased reductions in CFC and halon consumption and production.

The second trend also facilitated the inclination to adopt across the board phased reductions. Specifically, the major producers of CFCs had come to believe that environmentally safe substitutes for CFCs existed, and that it was for each of them in their individual interest to be the first to develop and offer such substitutes. Although it was thought that such substitutes would be several times more expensive than CFCs, it was also thought that there would be a market for them in a world that called for limits on the use of CFCs.[22] Simultaneously, numerous large users of CFCs moved to eliminate their reliance on such substances.[23]

For these reasons, the Montreal meeting was quite different from the one held only two years earlier in Vienna in that virtually all of the interested parties were now in agreement that some amount of phased reductions was appropriate. Thus, even though the final report of the international study of the Antarctic hole was not yet released,[24] a Proto-

21. Stolarski, Krueger, Schoeberl, McPeters, Newman & Alpert, *Nimbus 7 Satellite Measurements of the Springtime Antarctic Ozone Decrease*, 322 NATURE 808 (1986).

22. *See generally* Morrisette, *The Evolution of Policy Responses to Stratospheric Ozone Depletion*, 29 NAT. RESOURCES. J. 793 (1989); Monastersky, *Decline of the CFC Empire*, 133 SCI. NEWS 234 (1988); Jones, *In Search of the Safe CFCs*, NEW SCIENTIST, May 26, 1988, at 56.

23. This trend continues apace. *See, e.g.*, *Northern Telecom to Phase Out CFCs This Year*, GLOBAL ENVTL. CHANGE REP., Jan. 18, 1991, at 6; *AT&T Eliminates CFC Use in US Manufacturing Facility*, GLOBAL ENVTL. CHANGE REP., Jan. 4, 1991, at 6.

24. Preliminary reports of high chlorine concentrations by the international group in the Antarctic stratosphere did not state that the chlorine was the conclusive cause of the hole. *See* Shabecoff, *Chlorine Levels Reported High Over Antarctica*, N.Y. Times, Mar. 10, 1987, at C1, col. 1. That is not to say, however, that there was no scholarly literature pointing to chlorine as the cause. *See, e.g.*, McElroy, Salawitch, Wofsy & Logan, *Reductions of Antarctic Ozone Due to Synergistic Interactions of Chlorine and Bromine*, 321 NATURE 759 (1986).

col to the Vienna Convention calling for a fifty percent reduction in the production and consumption of specified CFCs over an approximately ten year period was adopted in Montreal in September 1987.

E. The Antarctic Ozone Hole and the Race to 1990 London Adjustments and Amendments[25]

But even as states adopted the Montreal Protocol in September 1987, two major concerns were present regarding the instrument. First, the startling findings regarding the Antarctic ozone hole, officially confirmed only after the meeting in Montreal, had not been taken fully into account in the Protocol. The negotiators were frustrated by their apparent inability to draft regimes that kept up with the revelations emerging from the scientific community. They had taken a step forward in Montreal, but they felt that they were always two steps behind in their own understanding of the problem, and at least two steps behind in their response to the problem. Thus, there was a widespread feeling that the Protocol was inadequate and would require revision.[26]

Second, the early indications by China and India, representing over one-third of humanity, that they would not become parties to the Protocol because of its failure to provide adequate assistance to developing countries, suggested that the international community might not be sufficiently cohesive to comprehensively regulate the matter. As with greenhouse gases, the international community was coming to realize that the atmospheric changes theorized were evidence of the increasing burden of a growing population on the planet, and that all such problems ultimately boiled down to a combination of the number of people in the world and the way they lived. It was apparent that any regime relating to protection of the ozone layer must include highly populated states, whether or not they presently were significant consumers or producers of ozone-depleting substances. This development was particularly important because it marked one of the few times that the industrialized world needed the cooperation and participation of the Third World. This need

25. For articles anticipating the issues that were addressed in London, see Handl, *International Efforts to Protect the Global Atmosphere: A Case of Too Little, Too Late?*, 1 EUR. J. INT'L L. 250 (1990); Nanda, *Stratospheric Ozone Depletion: A Challenge for International Environmental Law and Policy*, 10 MICH. J. INT'L L. 482 (1989); Rosencranz & Milligan, *CFC Abatement: The Needs of Developing Countries*, 19 AMBIO 312 (1990).

26. Regarding the Antarctic ozone hole, see NAT'L AERONAUTICS & SPACE ADMIN., ANTARCTIC OZONE: INITIAL FINDINGS FROM PUNTA AREAS, CHILE (1988); NAT'L AERONAUTICS & SPACE ADMIN., OZONE TRENDS PANEL REPORT (1988); Stolarski, *The Antarctic Ozone Hole*, 258 SCI. AM. 30 (1988).

allowed the third world to raise development and international equity concerns they believed had been unaddressed for too long.

As to the adequacy of the Montreal Protocol, planning for its adjustment and amendment began almost immediately. The political focus on the global environment in general, and on the protection of the ozone layer in particular, was intense from the 1987 Montreal Conference of the Parties to the 1990 London Meeting of the Parties to the Montreal Protocol. Of particular importance at this time, although less publicly dramatic than the Antarctic ozone hole, was the release of a study by the U.S. Environmental Protection Agency asserting that even assuming one hundred percent global participation in the Protocol, the presence of chlorine in the stratosphere would, by the year 2075, increase by a factor of three.[27]

Amidst these new revelations, the entry into force of the Montreal Protocol on January 1, 1989, was anticlimactic and hardly noticed. At that time, one nation after another was calling for swifter and deeper cuts in the production and consumption of ozone-depleting substances, and in some cases unilaterally adopting such measures. By the opening of the London Meeting in June 1990, the negotiating parties were in agreement not merely on accelerating the phased reductions, but on phasing out entirely the substances specified by the Montreal Protocol.[28] The primary issue was whether this phase out should be accomplished by the year 1997 or the year 2000, the latter representing the adjustment ultimately made to the Montreal schedules.[29] Simultaneously, evolving scientific knowledge regarding the threat posed by other substances led to the consensus to amend the Protocol so that it would require phase outs of other fully halogenated CFCs and carbon tetrachloride by the year 2000, and a phaseout of methyl chloroform by the year 2005.[30] Increased understanding that the substitutes thought to exist at the time of the Montreal Protocol might also be ozone-depleting[31] and significant

27. J. Hoffman & M. Gibbs, Future Concentrations of Stratospheric Chlorine and Bromine 2 (EPA Rep. 400/1-88/5, 1988). *See also* Bowman, *Global Trends in Total Ozone*, 239 Science 48 (1988).

28. *See Helsinki Declaration on the Protection of the Ozone Layer, Report of the Parties to the Montreal Protocol on the Work of Its First Meeting*, May 2, 1989, U.N. Doc. UNEP/OzL.Pro.1/5, app. 1 (1989).

29. *See infra* text accompanying notes 55-61.

30. As to methyl chloroform, see *Montreal Protocol Should Include Methyl Chloroform, Dutch Group Urges*, 13 Int'l Env't Rep. (BNA) 53 (1990); *U.S. Environmental Group Calls for Phase-Out of Methyl Chloroform*, 13 Int'l Env't Rep. (BNA) 53 (1990).

31. *See, e.g.*, *Scientists Warn of Perils Posed by Substitutes for CFCs*, New Scientist, June 30, 1990, at 33.

contributors to the greenhouse effect,[32] resulted in the designation of these substitutes as "transitional ozone-depleting substances," and in the conclusion that the transitional substances should be phased out by the year 2040, or, if possible, by the year 2020.

The apparent willingness of nonparticipating countries such as China and India to operate outside of what they perceived to be an unjust regime, was pitted against the reluctance of some developed countries such as the United States, to construct new international structures, to recognize a right of such countries to assistance and technology transfer, and to encourage linkages between participation in regimes like the Protocol and recognition of the special situation of developing countries. This reluctance was particularly strong since, at this same time, the developing world was making analogous demands for a global climate change fund.[33] In time, the United States, virtually alone, opposed the establishment of a financial mechanism. In May 1990 an apparently firm refusal to offer new monies to help developing countries phase out ozone-depleting chemicals threatened to derail the London Meeting planned for late June and early July 1990. In mid-June, however, the United States agreed to provide such monies,[34] and shifted its focus to the mechanism for the disbursement of such monies, pressing for a controlling voice in how the fund would operate.[35] Ultimately, the London meeting adopted amendments to the Protocol that provided for technology transfer, and established a fund under the supervision of a fourteen member committee drawn from the developed and developing world.[36] At the conclusion of the London Meeting, the representatives of China and India indicated their countries would sign the Protocol in 1992.[37] The reference by these delegates to the 1992 date is significant because it implies a further linkage between their willingness to join the Protocol and the develop-

32. As to the adequacy of the transition period approach, see *Scientist Says Interim CFC Substitute Should Not Increase Stratospheric Chlorine*, 14 Int'l Env't Rep. (BNA) 76 (1991). This possibility is under particular scrutiny. *See, e.g.*, *AFEAS Studies Greenhouse Contribution of CFC Alternatives*, GLOBAL ENVTL. CHANGE REP., Dec. 7, 1990, at 6.

For a tabular summary of the ozone-depleting potential, global warming potential, relative chlorine-loading potential, and reference lifetime of the various species of identified ozone-depleting substances, see Rosemarin, *Some Background on CFCs*, 19 AMBIO 280 (1990).

33. *See generally* Handl, *supra* note 25.

34. Milore, *US Agrees Extra Funds to Safeguard Ozone Layer*, NEW SCIENTIST, June 23, 1990, at 30.

35. Milne, *Nations Approach Unity on Measures to Protect Ozone*, NEW SCIENTIST, June 30, 1990, at 33.

36. *See* Rosencranz & Milligan, *supra* note 25, at 314.

37. Milne, *CFC Clampdown Eases Pressure on the Ozone Layer*, NEW SCIENTIST, July 7, 1990, at 21.

ment of a more general climate trust fund at the United Nations Conference on Environment and Development to be held in Brazil in 1992.

F. The Task Ahead

After the London Meeting, two major areas of concern remain. First, a number of groups assert that the Protocol even as adjusted and amended does not go far enough. Although the list of controlled substances has been increased and, for the most part, total phaseouts have been called for, an observer group at the London Meeting noted that the phaseout periods—generally of ten years—will allow the production of another seventeen million tons of ozone-depleting substances.[38] Such arguments arise amidst continued findings by the scientific community that the ozone layer continues to deteriorate over Antarctica,[39] the Arctic,[40] and generally,[41] and increasing evidence that the same substances that deplete ozone are major contributors to global warming.[42]

Second, there is a growing sense that agreement upon the Protocol and its adjustments and amendments, even if not completely satisfactory, may have been an easier task than will be the facilitation, monitoring, and enforcement of its implementation.[43]

---

38. *See Report of the Second Meeting of the Parties to the Montreal Protocol on the Substances that Deplete the Ozone Layer*, para. 36, at 10, UNEP/OzL.Pro.2/3, para. 36, at 10 (1990) [hereinafter *Report of the Second Meeting]*.

39. *See, e.g., 1990 Ozone Hole Continues Into December*, GLOBAL ENVTL. CHANGE REP., Dec. 21, 1990, at 5; Monastersky, *Antarctic Ozone Bottoms at Record Low*, 138 SCI. NEWS 228 (1990) (Antarctic ozone layer hole reaches record proportions); Stevens, *Ozone Losses in Arctic Are Larger Than Expected*, N.Y. Times, Sept. 6, 1990, at A25, col. 1; *Ozone Depletion Quickens at Both Poles*, NEW SCIENTIST Aug. 4, 1990, at 32.

40. *See, e.g., Scientists Detect Hole in Ozone Above Three Scandinavian Nations*, 14 Int'l Env't Rep. (BNA) 68 (1991).

41. *See, e.g.*, Stevens, *Ozone Loss Over U.S. is Found to be Twice as Bad as Predicted*, N.Y. Times, Apr. 5, 1991, at A1, col. 1; Shabecoff, *Scientists Report Faster Ozone Loss*, N.Y. Times, June 24, 1990, § 1, at 13, col. 1 (Sunday late ed.) (10% reduction in ozone since 1967 over middle latitudes).

42. *See, e.g., Total CFC Ban Needed to Halt Global Warming*, NEW SCIENTIST, Sept. 8, 1990 (CFCs will soon overtake carbon dioxide as the principal contributors to the increase in the greenhouse effect); Leggett, *Playing Roulette with the Atmosphere*, NEW SCIENTIST, July 7, 1990, at 16 (the Intergovernmental Panel on Climate Change Report indicts CFCs and many of their "substitutes" because of their contribution to global warming).

43. Additional issues on the horizon are other ozone-depleting activities such as proposals for stratospheric supersonic aircraft, *see, e.g.*, Gribbin, *Supersonic Plans 'Threaten Ozone Layer'. . .*, NEW SCIENTIST, June 9, 1990, at 24, military use of ozone-depleting substances (a category of use not clearly encompassed within the Protocol), and apparent difficulties in phasing out CFC use by vessels, *see, e.g., CFC Phaseout Schedules Present Special Problems for Ships*, GLOBAL ENVTL. CHANGE REP., Dec. 7, 1990, at 7.

For discussions of how the international regime should be implemented in the United States, see Chafee & Shimberg, *Supplementing the Montreal Protocol: The Need for Domestic*

III. A RESTATEMENT OF THE REGIME

A. The Organization of the Regime

There are two main strands to the international organizational scheme created by the Vienna Convention and the Montreal Protocol, as amended and adjusted. First, there are state parties (to the Convention, to the Protocol, and to the Protocol as amended) who meet on a regular basis and who in smaller groups meet more regularly for particular tasks. Second, there is a Secretariat which fulfills a number of duties, occasionally through ad hoc working groups, assigned to it by the state parties in the Convention and Protocol.

With respect to the parties to the ozone protection regime, there are three formal groups of parties. First, the Vienna Convention establishes a "Conference of the Parties."[44] Second, although no special name such as "Conference" is given, the term "Parties" in the Montreal Protocol means only the parties to that Protocol.[45] Third, because the Protocol was amended in London, there may be slight divergences between those states party to the Protocol and those states party to the Protocol as amended. Inasmuch as a party to the Protocol or the Protocol as amended must also be a party to the Convention, the parties to the Protocol or the Protocol as amended are subgroups of the "Conference of the Parties" to the Convention.

Both the Convention and the Protocol provide that there shall be regular meetings of the parties to the respective instruments.[46] As a practical matter, these groups of parties coordinate their meetings, and the Montreal Protocol generally calls for the meetings of Parties to the Protocol to be held in conjunction with the meetings of the Conference of the Parties to the Convention.[47] The primary distinction between the groups of parties thus reduces their standing to vote upon, or have an official voice regarding, certain issues. In particular, only Parties to the Protocol, and not those who are solely members of the Conference of the

Legislation, 19 AMBIO 310 (1990); Hahn & McGartland, *The Political Economy of Instrument Choice: An Examination of the U.S. Role in Implementing the Montreal Protocol*, 83 NW. U.L. REV. 592 (1989).

44. Vienna Convention, *supra* note 2, art. 6, para. 1, at 12, *reprinted in* 26 I.L.M. at 1531.

45. Montreal Protocol, *supra* note 3, art. 1, para. 2, *reprinted in* 26 I.L.M. at 1551. Article 1(2) is unaltered in the Protocol as amended. *London Amendments, supra* note 4, at 2.

46. Vienna Convention, *supra* note 2, art. 6, para. 1, at 15, *reprinted in* 26 I.L.M. at 1531; Montreal Protocol, *supra* note 3, art. 11, *reprinted in* 26 I.L.M. at 1557.

47. Montreal Protocol, *supra* note 3, art. 11, *reprinted in* 26 I.L. M. at 1557. Article 11 is not altered in this regard in the Protocol as amended. *London Amendments, supra* note 4, at 14.

Parties to the Convention, can vote on amendments to the Protocol.[48] Similarly, membership on the Executive Committee, which is responsible for the Multilateral Fund established by the London Amendments to the Protocol is limited to Parties to the Protocol as amended.[49]

Although there are various groups of parties, there is only one Secretariat for the Convention and the Protocol. The Secretariat functions are carried out by the UNEP and, in this sense, the Vienna Convention can be seen as merely formalizing the coordinating role held by UNEP before the Vienna Conference.[50] The duties of the Secretariat are set forth both in the Convention and the Protocol, and both of these documents allow for the Conference of Parties to the Convention or the Parties to the Protocol to assign the Secretariat other functions.[51]

Finally, the organizational structure created by the Convention and Protocol necessarily has extensive relations with two other organizational clusters. First, in order to provide a better foundation for the timely making of policy, there are relations with the public international scientific community (namely, the World Meteorological Organization and the World Health Organization), leading national scientific agencies, and private international scientific organizations. Second, in order to provide financial and technical assistance, there are relations with organizations such as the World Bank.

B. The Lawmaking Process

A number of innovative steps in lawmaking are contained in the Montreal Protocol. The general implications of these steps are discussed in Part III; the following discussion describes the formal structure of the regime as it presently exists.

The Protocol anticipates that continued revision may be necessary, and calls for the Parties periodically to assess the adequacy of the measures taken in the Protocol.[52] The Protocol provides that the parties, on

48. Vienna Convention, *supra* note 2, art. 9, paras. 2, 4, at 18-19, *reprinted in* 26 I.L.M. at 1532-33.

49. *London Amendments*, *supra* note 4, art. 10, at 12-13.

50. Vienna Convention, *supra* note 2, art. 7, para. 2, at 18, *reprinted in* 26 I.L.M. at 1532. UNEP's designation as the agency responsible for secretariat functions was only "on an interim basis." *Id.*

51. As to the duties assigned, see Vienna Convention, *supra* note 2, art. 7, at 17-18, *reprinted in* 26 I.L.M. at 1532; Montreal Protocol, *supra* note 3, art. 12, *reprinted in* 26 I.L.M. at 1558-59. Article 12 is unaltered in the Protocol as amended. *London Amendments*, *supra* note 4, at 14.

52. Montreal Protocol, *supra* note 3, art. 6, *reprinted in* 26 I.L.M. at 1556. Article 6 is basically unaltered in the Protocol as amended. *London Amendments*, *supra* note 4, at 10.

the basis of such an assessment, may decide to adjust the reductions called for in the controlled substances, and, if the parties are unable to reach agreement on such adjustments, two-thirds majority adoption of adjustments shall be binding upon all Parties to the Protocol.[53] Thus, the Parties to the Protocol have limited legislative power in this area with an objector's recourse being withdrawl generally from the Protocol. Some of the actions taken at the London Meeting were adjustments.

In contrast to this legislative-like adjustment process, there is also the more commonly encountered amendment process that becomes binding only upon those states who accept such amendments. In this regard, it is particularly important to see that although the parties may make adjustments to the controlled substances already designated, they cannot use an adjustment to designate a new controlled substance.[54] As a consequence, the actions taken at the London Meeting were in part also amendments. Many of the amendments relate to the creation of a financial mechanism, but many others relate to the addition of new controlled substances. The crucial implication, however, is that since amendments must be consented to in order to have application to any particular party, a confusing array of regimes may arise.[55]

C. The Normative Scheme

1. The Obligation to Phase Out Designated Ozone-Depleting Chemicals

The basic regulatory approach of the Montreal Protocol in 1987 was to require the Parties to the Protocol to reduce their production and consumption of five chlorofluorocarbons specified in Group I to Annex A of the Protocol, and three halons specified in Group II to Annex A of the

53. Montreal Protocol, *supra* note 3, art. 2, para. 9, *reprinted in* 26 I.L.M. at 1553-54. In the Montreal Protocol, the two-thirds majority must also represent 50% of the total consumption of the controlled substances by the Parties. In the Protocol as amended, this requirement is changed to a two-thirds majority that reflects both a majority of those states whose special situation as developing states is recognized under the Protocol as amended, *London Amendments*, *supra* note 4, art. 5, para. 1, at 9, and a majority of those states that do not fit within this category. In this way, the Protocol better reflects not only the interests of those who presently consume CFCs, but also those who forgo developing such use.

54. As to the amendment process generally, see Vienna Convention, *supra* note 2, art. 9, at 18-19, *reprinted in* 26 I.L.M. at 1532-33. As to the characterization of designating new controlled substances as amendments, see Montreal Protocol, *supra* note 3, art. 2, para. 10, *reprinted in* 26 I.L.M. at 1554, as originally drafted and as clarified by the London amendments.

55. *See Report of the Second Meeting*, *supra* note 38, dec. II/16, at 18 (recommending that the Conference of Parties to the Vienna Convention undertake to consider how to expedite the amendment procedure for protocols).

Protocol. The London Adjustments to the Protocol accelerated this timetable and deepened the cuts by requiring the parties to phase out production and consumption entirely by the year 2000. The scheduled reductions required under both the Montreal Protocol and the London Adjustments for the Group I CFCs are represented in Figure 1, while the scheduled reductions required for halons are represented in Figure 2.

The London Amendments to the Protocol added new chemicals to the regulatory scheme, specifying them in a new Annex B. A phaseout by the year 2000 is required for other fully halogenated CFCs[56] and for carbon tetrachloride,[57] while a phaseout of methyl chloroform is required by the year 2005.[58] These scheduled phaseouts are represented in Figure 3.

As illustrated by Figures 1, 2, and 3, the scheduled reductions, leading ultimately to phaseouts, are expressed in terms of percentages of calculated national levels of consumption and production in either 1986, in the case of the substances originally regulated by the Protocol, or in 1989, for the substances added to the scope of the Protocol by the London Amendments. The national calculated levels thus are particularly important bench marks for the purpose of the regulatory scheme. It is important to note how the calculated level and the reductions in that level relate to baskets of substances. Group I of Annex A, for example, designates five different CFCs. It is up to each state to decide how they will mix reductions of the five so as to meet any particular scheduled reduction in the overall calculated level. To avoid false incentives in this scheme, the formula for the calculated level places all of the various designated chemicals on the same level by multiplying the amount of each chemical produced, imported, and exported by its "ozone-depleting potential," such potentials also being specified in the annex.[59]

The use of national calculated levels is also significant because it inherently gives value to historical usage and avoids the difficult issue of equitably allocating between states a limited resource, the right to emit ozone-depleting substances. Thus, the United States could be viewed as particularly advantaged under the Montreal Protocol since a fifty percent reduction in its production and consumption would still leave it with a disproportionate per capita share of such use. This significance of course

56. *London Amendments*, *supra* note 4, art. 2C, at 4.

57. *Id.* art. 2D, at 4-5.

58. *Id.* art. 2E, at 5-6.

59. Montreal Protocol, *supra* note 3, art. 3, *reprinted in* 26 I.L.M. at 1554. Article 3 is basically unaltered in the Protocol as amended. *London Amendments*, *supra* note 4, at 6.

diminished greatly when the Protocol was adjusted and amended so as to require phaseouts rather than mere reductions.

Two constructive exceptions to the reductions schedule are expressed in terms of the calculated level. First, any party may transfer to another party any portion of its calculated level of production, so long as such transfers do not cause the parties involved to exceed collectively the production limit applicable to them as a group.[60] Second, if a party had contracted for a production facility prior to September 16, 1987, or provided for such expansion in national legislation prior to January 1, 1987, then that party may add such production to its calculated level.[61]

2. Recognition of the Special Situation of Developing Countries

The special situation of certain developing countries is recognized through the possibility of a delayed phaseout schedule for such countries. These special provisions apply to any party "that is a developing country and whose annual calculated level of consumption . . . is less than 0.3 kilograms per capita . . . ."[62] The delay works in two ways. First, these parties are allowed to exceed the target percentage reduction at any point in the schedule by a specified percentage of their initial calculated level if such action is necessary in order to satisfy "basic domestic needs."[63] Second, such developing countries, in order to meet basic domestic needs, also are entitled to delay at every point their compliance with the schedule of reductions leading to phase outs by a period of ten years.[64]

60. *London Amendments*, *supra* note 4, art. 2, para. 5, at 2. The London Amendment to this paragraph greatly simplified and perhaps broadened somewhat what originally was termed "industrial rationalization." *See CFC Trading Under the Montreal Protocol: How Does it Work?*, GLOBAL ENVTL. CHANGE REP., Dec. 21, 1990, at 1.

61. *London Amendments*, *supra* note 4, art. 2, para. 6, at 3. The facility must have been completed by December 31, 1990, and such production must not raise the party's annual calculated level of consumption above 0.5 kilograms per capita. The London Amendment to this paragraph does not reflect any significant alteration in the original provision. This provision was intended to address central planning concerns of socialist states; it is unclear what practical significance it has, particularly after the changes that have occurred in what was the socialist world.

62. Montreal Protocol, *supra* note 3, art. 5, para. 1, *reprinted in* 26 I.L.M. at 1555. Article 5(1) is basically unaltered in the Protocol as amended. *London Amendments*, *supra* note 4, at 9.

63. Montreal Protocol, *supra* note 3, art. 2, *reprinted in* 26 I.L.M. at 1552-53. Article 2 in this regard is basically unaltered in its appearances in Articles 2, 2A-2E in the Protocol as amended. *London Amendments*, *supra* note 4, at 3-6.

64. Montreal Protocol, *supra* note 3, art. 5, *reprinted in* 26 I.L.M. at 1555. Article 5 in this regard is basically unaltered in the Protocol as amended. *London Amendments*, *supra* note 4, at 9.

3. The Resolution of States to Act Beyond the Requirements of the Protocol as Adjusted and Amended

It is important to recognize that the reduction schedule set forth in the Protocol as adjusted and amended represents only the baseline. A number of states have accepted greater obligations,[65] and the Protocol urges the parties to act with greater dispatch when possible. Particularly significant in this regard is the Declaration at the London Meeting by thirteen developed countries of "[t]heir firm determination . . . to phaseout the production and consumption of all fully halogenated chlorofluorocarbons controlled by the Montreal Protocol, as adjusted and amended, as soon as possible but no later than 1997."[66] Similarly, all the parties at the London Meeting resolved to do the following: refrain from using certain other halons except for essential applications; use "transitional substances with a low ozone-depleting potential, such as hydrochlorofluorocarbons (HCFCs)," with great care and with a view to their replacement by nonozone-depleting and more environmentally suitable alternatives no later than 2040 and, if possible, no later than 2020; phase out production and consumption of methylchloroform as soon as possible; and express appreciation to those parties that have already taken measures more stringent and broader in scope than those required by the Protocol.[67]

D. Encouraging Participation and Facilitating Implementation

From the beginning, it was recognized that the shared nature of the ozone-depletion problem required widespread participation in the regime to be established by the Convention and Protocol. Encouragement of participation by developing countries, in particular India and China, required mechanisms to aid implementation of the regime by those countries. Thus, encouragement of participation and facilitation of implementation were and remain linked.

The regime encourages participation in a number of ways. First,

65. As to actions by the European Community, see *Council of Ministries Favors Regulation to Phase Out Chlorofluorocarbons by 1977*, 14 Int'l Env't Rep. (BNA) 3 (1991); *EC Environment Ministers Agree on CFC Phaseout, Vehicle Emission Cuts*, GLOBAL ENVTL. CHANGE REP., Jan. 4, 1991, at 3. As to actions by the Federal Republic of Germany, see *Strengthened German CFC Law Goes Before Parliament*, GLOBAL ENVTL. CHANGE REP., Jan. 18, 1991, at 3. As to actions by political subdivisions in the United States, see *State and Local CFC Laws on the Rise in US*, GLOBAL ENVTL. CHANGE REP., Dec. 21, 1990, at 4.

66. *Report of the Second Meeting*, *supra* note 38, paras. 48-49, at 20-21. The countries were Australia, Austria, Belgium, Canada, Denmark, the Federal Republic of Germany, Finland, Liechtenstein, the Netherlands, New Zealand, Norway, Sweden, and Switzerland.

67. *Id.* Annex VII.

because the reduction schedules are tied to either 1986 or 1989 levels of consumption and production, there is no advantage to waiting to join the regime. Second, although the parties to the regime during the phaseout periods may trade the controlled substances with one another, the Protocol, as adjusted and amended, progressively restricts trade involving controlled substances between parties and nonparties.[68] Thus, for example, by January 1, 1993, the parties, having agreed upon a list of products containing the controlled substances specified in the Montreal Protocol,[69] shall bar the import of those products from any state not party to the Protocol.[70]

Third, the Protocol not only attempts to limit the advantages of remaining outside, but for developing countries, also provides incentives to join. The Montreal Protocol originally was vague on this point, providing that the parties, recognizing the particular needs of developing countries, "shall . . . cooperate in promoting technical assistance to facilitate participation in and implementation of this Protocol."[71] In response to the positions of India and China in particular, more specific and detailed provisions for financial assistance and technology transfer were adopted at the London Meeting.[72]

E. Noncompliance, Enforcement, and Dispute Settlement

Thus far, the Parties to the Convention and the Protocol have been concerned primarily with elaboration of and formal participation in the regime. As a result, enforcement procedures at this point are not particularly developed.

The key monitoring and enforcement device at present is the requirement for parties to provide to the Secretariat statistics on production, on imports and exports to parties and nonparties, and on amounts destroyed or recycled as feedstocks.[73] Such reports will aid Secretariat

---

68. *See generally London Amendments*, *supra* note 4, art. 4, at 7-9.

69. *See* Vienna Convention, *supra* note 2, art. 10, at 19-20, *reprinted* in 26 I.L.M. at 1533 (procedures elaborating this list).

70. *London Amendments*, *supra* note 4, art. 4, para. 3, at 8. The London Amendments to article 4 primarily attempt to adapt that article to the addition of the new Annex B.

71. Montreal Protocol, *supra* note 3, art. 10, *reprinted in* 26 I.L.M. at 1557.

72. *See generally London Amendments*, *supra* note 4, arts. 10, 10A, at 12-14. Under Decision II/8A taken at the London Meeting, an "Interim Financial Mechanism" of quite similar design was established for the period January 1, 1991, to December 31, 1993, or "until such time as the Financial Mechanism is established." *Report of the Second Meeting*, *supra* note 38, dec. II/8 A, at 12. *See generally* Handl, *supra* note 25; Rosencranz & Milligan, *supra* note 25.

73. *London Amendments*, *supra* note 4, art. 7, at 10-11. The amendment to Article 7 expanded upon the original reporting requirement by recognizing the need also to follow amounts destroyed or recycled as feedstocks.

and party monitoring, and will also further nongovernmental organization involvement since such data is not regarded as confidential.[74] Unfortunately, not all parties have made such reports, or have submitted incomplete reports. The London meeting of the parties, noting these reporting difficulties, established an ad hoc group of experts to consider the reasons for the difficulties and to recommend solutions.[75]

Investigatory and dispute settlement provisions are quite limited. The Convention, with application to the Protocol,[76] provides that in the event of a dispute concerning interpretation or application of a provision, the parties (1) shall negotiate; (2) failing that, seek the good offices of, or request mediation by, a third party; and (3) failing that, submit the dispute to conciliation.[77] The parties, in accepting the Convention also may declare that they accept as a means of dispute settlement either arbitration or submission to the International Court of Justice, or both.[78] Against that backdrop, the Parties to the Protocol have been considering procedures and institutional mechanisms for determining noncompliance and for treatment of parties found to be in noncompliance.[79] Interim noncompliance provisions adopted at the London Meeting essentially provide for parties with reservations regarding implementation by other parties to report such concerns in writing to the Secretariat. The Secretariat shall transmit the submission to an Implementation Committee established by these same interim procedures, and that Committee shall consider the record with a view to securing an amicable resolution.[80] The Committee shall report on its work to the Meeting of the Parties and the parties "may . . . decide upon and call for steps to bring about full compliance . . . including measures to assist the Party's compliance . . . ."[81]

IV. THE EVOLVING STRUCTURE OF INTERNATIONAL ENVIRONMENTAL LAWMAKING

Reflection on the international effort to protect the stratospheric

74. *Report of the Second Meeting*, *supra* note 38, dec. II/9, at 12.

75. *Id.*

76. Montreal Protocol, *supra* note 3, art. 14, *reprinted in* 26 I.L.M. at 1559. Article 14 is unaltered in the Protocol as amended. *London Amendments*, *supra* note 4, at 14.

77. Vienna Convention, *supra* note 2, art. 11, at 20-21, *reprinted in* 26 I.L.M. at 1533-34.

78. *Id.* art. 11, para. 3, at 21, *reprinted in* 26 I.L.M. at 1534. At the time of the Vienna Convention, 16 countries expressed their regret at the absence of a compulsory provision for the settlement of disputes. *See id.* at 35, *reprinted in* 26 I.L.M. at 1535.

79. *See* Montreal Protocol, *supra* note 3, art. 8, *reprinted in* 26 I.L.M. at 1556.

80. *Report of the Second Meeting*, *supra* note 38, dec. II/5, at 12; *see also id.* Annex III.

81. *Id.* Annex III.

ozone layer illuminates the emerging structure of international environmental lawmaking. International environmental lawmaking is different from international lawmaking in general in at least three respects. First, environmental lawmaking must be conducted amidst great uncertainty about the reality, cause, and extent of the problem. Second, because the nature of environmental problems such as ozone depletion requires concerted action, it is necessary that at least the major contributors to the problem, present and future, be parties to the regime. Third, because it is difficult to separate environmental problems from one another and from development concerns generally, environmental lawmaking runs the risk of either being unmanageable or not system-oriented. This section discusses each of these differences in turn.

A. Lawmaking Amidst Uncertainty: The Process as the Solution

We ordinarily might expect that states seeking to address an international problem would work towards a diplomatic conference where a treaty addressing an issue could be negotiated. Without in any way implying that this "ordinary" situation is easy, the international environmental context can be far more difficult because the views of the parties as to the nature of the environmental problem not only can be quite different, but moreover, the knowledge of all environmental problems is likely incomplete even though evolving. In the "ordinary" context a central task in the lawmaking effort is to improve communication between the parties so that they may better understand each other's objectives and concerns. In negotiations concerning environmental matters, however, there is the added and quite different task of the parties seeking to discover precisely what the environment requires. In this sense, the environment is an unobtrusive, but central presence in the negotiations. It is a party that does not volunteer information, but may answer questions if asked correctly. It is also a party that refuses to negotiate.

In the case of stratospheric ozone depletion, the international community initially confronted great debate as to whether there was a problem at all, followed by debate regarding the extent of the problem. As observed by many scholars in the past several decades, the nature of many environmental problems requires action by the relevant community before it has proof of the theory. In other words, the international community, despite uncertainty about the theory, must act to confront the danger indicated by the theory. Moreover, it must act knowing that its knowledge will continue to evolve and suggest further actions. These aspects of uncertainty and evolving knowledge lead to two major differences in international environmental lawmaking efforts from lawmaking efforts generally. Both of these differences evidence an emphasis on an ongoing process of lawmaking rather than, as ordinarily the case, the one time negotiation of a treaty at a particular conference.

The first difference is the explicit incorporation of scientific inquiry into the lawmaking process. Dealing with the uncertainty necessarily present in environmental problems requires that the process not only increase the shared knowledge of the parties, but that such knowledge also accurately reflect the state of scientific understanding of the problem. This requires much greater cooperation between the lawmaking community attempting to draft a response and the scientific community seeking to understand the phenomena. Imbedding this scientific effort in an international organizational structure or in international efforts that coordinate national efforts increases the perceived legitimacy, and hence shared nature, of the resulting description of the problem. Making the scientific inquiry an integral part of an ongoing lawmaking process serves both to educate the lawmakers and to speed up the incorporation of such knowledge into the process. In the case of the ozone regime, the Protocol institutionalizes this cooperation by requiring the convening of "appropriate panels of experts" (scientific, environmental, technical, and economic) at least one year before the parties meet to reassess the sufficiency of the Protocol's controls on ozone-depleting substances.[82]

The second major difference is that the lawmaking effort that accommodates evolving knowledge through the establishment of an ongoing process of lawmaking continuously incorporates new knowledge and revises previous responses. In this sense, the Protocol calls for the parties to periodically "assess the control measures provided for in Article 2 on the basis of available scientific, environmental, technical, and economic information."[83] Thus, we see a transition from a one-conference effort to an ongoing process, and from "two steps behind" to action on the basis of evolving knowledge. In this sense, cooperation and education are recognized as important aspects of the lawmaking process in the environmental area. For all these reasons, the solution to a threat such as ozone depletion is not the particular requirements of the Montreal Protocol or the London Adjustments and Amendments to the Protocol. Rather, the solution is the process which yielded the Protocol and which already looks ahead to the next adjustments and amendments.

82. Montreal Protocol, *supra* note 3, art. 6, *reprinted in* 26 I.L.M. at 1556. Article 6 is basically unaltered in the Protocol as amended. *London Amendments*, *supra* note 4, art. 6, at 10.

83. Montreal Protocol, *supra* note 3, art. 6, *reprinted in 26* I.L.M. at 1556.

B. Consensual Lawmaking on Transcendent Problems

International environmental lawmaking is also distinct in that the nature of many environmental problems requires that at least those countries primarily contributing, or potentially contributing, to the problem participate in the regime. The environmental regime is dictated by the planet in the sense that the earth is not willing to negotiate the terms of a solution. In the previous section, it was asserted that states must negotiate a regime despite the fact that they are uncertain as to what precisely the earth requires. This section points to the need to encourage participation in global environmental regimes by at least those states which are, or potentially are, significant contributors to the problem.

In encouraging participation, the tools of the lawmaker are sticks and carrots. In other words, states either may be penalized for not joining the regime or rewarded for doing so. In the ozone protection regime, developing countries were encouraged to join through the recognition of their special needs. Moreover, although there are no sticks per se, the treaty does attempt to prevent those who remain outside from benefitting by doing so. First, there is no advantage in waiting to join the treaty since the baseline calculation from which reductions are to be made is fixed. Second, there is no trade advantage in remaining outside the convention since it restricts members from trading in areas involving the regulated substances with those outside the regime.

The more subtle implication of needing widespread participation, as discussed above, was the demand by China, India, and others for a linkage between their agreement to participate in the regime and satisfaction of other concerns, particularly, development assistance for the Third World. In the case of stratospheric ozone protection, linkage ultimately was made in the London amendments. The amendments provide for technology transfer and establish a fund to aid implementation of the Protocol by facilitating nonozone-depleting paths for growth in developing countries. The scale of linkage in the greenhouse gas negotiations will be an order of greater magnitude. The lawmaking risk presented by issue linkage is that it likely causes the scope of the agreement to increase. Moreover, the agreement, as a result, may embody compromises on linked issues and thus have the flavor of a package deal. This line of reasoning raises for some observers the possibility that greenhouse negotiations will bog down as did the Law of the Sea negotiations, and like the Law of the Sea, will result ultimately in an agreement that is too rigid because of the delicate balancing that is required. However, the sense of urgency which is associated with climate change did not exist with the

Law of the Sea issue. In this sense, the urgency of climate change likely will push negotiations along despite the recognition of the special needs of developing countries. Other possibly even broader linkages to North-South questions, however, are perhaps best avoided so as to keep manageable the already broad scope of negotiations.

C. The Tension Between Manageability of Negotiations and Systemic Thinking

One of the first lessons of environmental studies is the need to approach the environment as a system, an indivisible process. The lawmaker, however, can not approach the development of an environmentally sound relationship between humanity and the world all at once. Rather, negotiations must be limited so that the number of issues and interests involved remain at a manageable level. The danger with the slicing off of what appears to be a somewhat separable and manageable problem, however, is that systemic thinking may be lost. The question thus becomes how to best reconcile the need for manageable negotiations with the need for holistic thinking.

In the case of ozone depletion, the negotiations, at least initially, in moving to address the depletion problem did not consider whether their solutions might rest upon assumptions that would exacerbate the greenhouse gas problem. In particular, the reductions in CFC and halon use agreed to in Montreal were premised in part on the belief that ozone-safe substitutes existed. But, as already mentioned, not only did it later turn out that these substances also were ozone depleting, they also came to be seen as highly efficient greenhouse gases.

In this regard, I suggest that the regime negotiators take care to identify the major scientific, technical, environmental, and economic assumptions underlying major policy choices so that the corresponding panels of experts in these areas, already an integral part of the process, might examine such assumptions against their more general knowledge, and hence, in a more systemic fashion.

V. CONCLUSION

In the little over fifteen years since the theory of ozone depletion was put forward, the international community moved relatively quickly to order the phaseout of key ozone-depleting substances by the year 2000. In doing so, the community formed an international regime, despite uncertainty, in relation to a problem whose solution requires near universal participation. Scholarly elaboration of the lessons of that effort is needed so that the more difficult upcoming negotiations regarding greenhouse gases may be fruitful. Among others things, an international environmental lawmaking process should:

(1) address uncertainty and the evolving nature of one's knowledge by explicitly viewing such lawmaking as an ongoing process within which knowledge is advanced and becomes shared through the imbedding of scientific, technical, environmental, and economic expertise in the organizational regime;
(2) encourage participation, yet avoid unrelated linkages, by addressing related interests of special groups of states and by denying any benefit to those remaining outside the regime; and
(3) resolve the tension of manageability of negotiations and systemic thinking by the identification of factual assumptions underlying major policy directions and by placing such assumptions also within the scope of inquiry of the expert's committees imbedded in the process.

Finally, I stress that even as the international lawmaking process develops, we must remember that another whole phase, that of international and national implementation of this international normative construct, remains to be addressed.

FIGURE 1

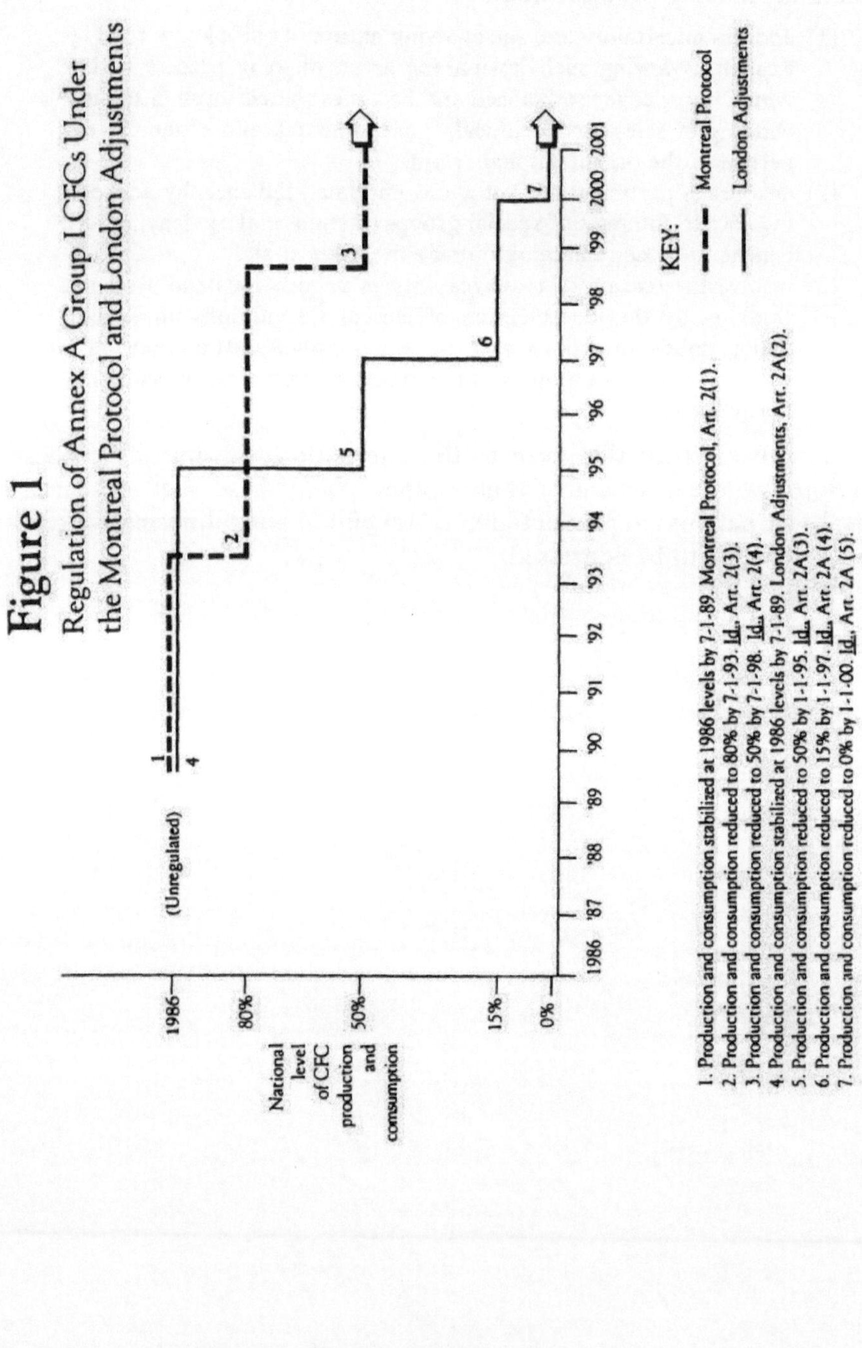
Figure 1
Regulation of Annex A Group I CFCs Under the Montreal Protocol and London Adjustments
National level of CFC production and consumption
1986
80%
50%
15%
0%
(Unregulated)
1986
'87
'88
'89
'90
'91
'92
'93
'94
'95
'96
'97
'98
'99
2000
2001
KEY:
Montreal Protocol
London Adjustments
1. Production and consumption stabilized at 1986 levels by 7-1-89. Montreal Protocol, Art. 2(1).
2. Production and consumption reduced to 80% by 7-1-93. Id., Art. 2(3).
3. Production and consumption reduced to 50% by 7-1-98. Id., Art. 2(4).
4. Production and consumption stabilized at 1986 levels by 7-1-89. London Adjustments, Art. 2A(2).
5. Production and consumption reduced to 50% by 1-1-95. Id., Art. 2A(3).
6. Production and consumption reduced to 15% by 1-1-97. Id., Art. 2A (4).
7. Production and consumption reduced to 0% by 1-1-00. Id., Art. 2A (5).

FIGURE 2

Figure 2

Regulation of Annex A Group II Halons Under the Montreal Protocol and London Adjustments

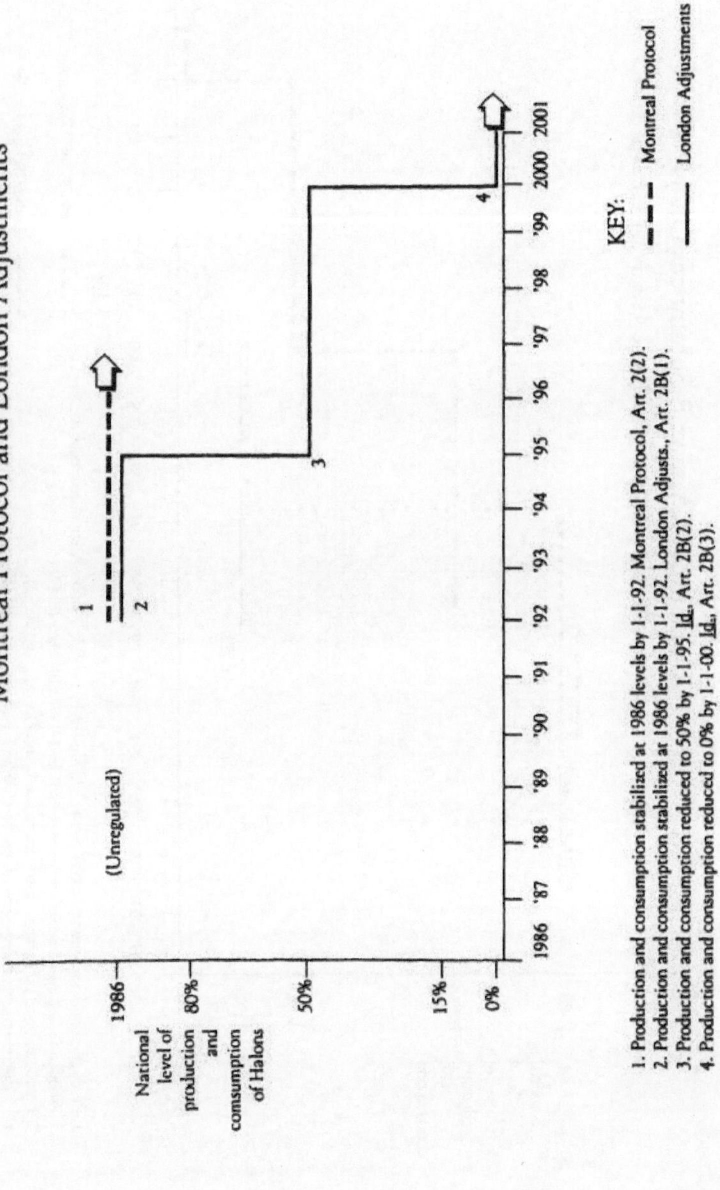

FIGURE 3

Figure 3

Regulation of Annex B Substances Under
the London Amendments to the Montreal Protocol

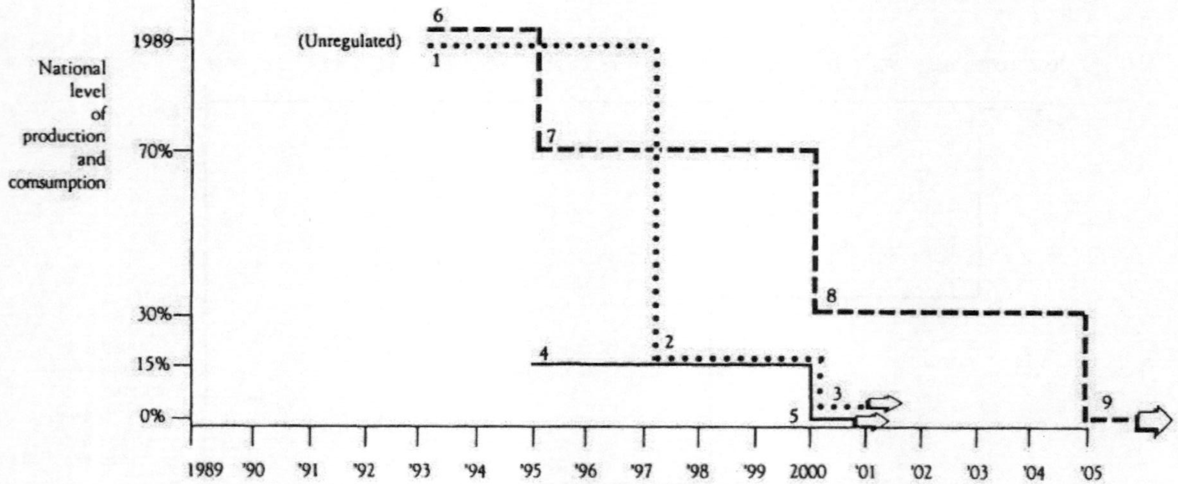

KEY:

- • • • • Other Fully Halogenated CFCs
- ——— Carbon Tetrachloride
- – – – Methyl Choloroform

1. Production and consumption stabilized at 1989 levels by 1-1-93. London Admendments, Art. 2C (1).
2. Production and consumption reduced to 15% by 1-1-97. Id., Art. 2C (2).
3. Production and consumption reduced to 0% by 1-1-00. Id., Art. 2C (3).
4. Production and consumption reduced to 15% by 1-1-95. Id., Art. 2D (1).
5. Production and consumption reduced to 0% by 1-1-00. Id., Art. 2D (2).
6. Production and consumption stabilized at 1989 levels by 1-1-93. Id., Art. 2E (1).
7. Production and consumption reduced to 70% by 1-1-95. Id., Art. 2E (2).
8. Production and consumption reduced to 30% by 1-1-00. Id., Art. 2E (3).
9. Production and consumption reduced to 0% by 1-1-05. Id., Art. 2E (4).

[8]

Customary (And Not So Customary) International Environmental Law

DANIEL BODANSKY*

In this article, Professor Bodansky reevaluates the concept of customary international environmental law. Initially, he argues that most purported customary norms – such as the duty not to cause transboundary harm and the precautionary principle – do not fit the standard account of customary international law, since they do not represent regularities in the actual behavior of states. Claims that these norms have the status of customary law reflect a different conception of "customary law," one that focuses on what states say rather than what they do. Next, Professor Bodansky examines if it makes any difference whether these principles constitute "legal" norms. He argues that the question of legal status is significant only if legal institutions exist that apply norms deemed to be "legal" in character, or if a norm has a sufficiently determinate content to guide state behavior directly. Neither of these conditions, however, generally holds true in the environmental field. Instead, the purported norms of customary environmental law represent community standards – they set the general terms of the debate about what actions are appropriate and provide the framework for the negotiation of more specific rules. Since these functions do not depend on a norm's legal status, debates about whether a norm is part of customary international law are of little consequence. The author concludes that international lawyers should spend less time debating the legal status of environmental norms and more time working to make them more precise and effective.

* Professor of Law, University of Washington School of Law. I would like to thank Joan Fitzpatrick and André Nollkaemper for their very helpful comments.

Recent years have witnessed a proliferation of international environmental agreements.[1] For each new environmental problem, a new treaty is negotiated: depletion of the stratospheric ozone layer,[2] transboundary movements of hazardous wastes,[3] climate change,[4] the loss of biological diversity,[5] desertification, and so on.[6] Although, the efficacy of these treaties remains an open question,[7] and their relative benefits versus soft law instruments are poorly understood,[8] most scholars consider treaties to be the preeminent method of international environmental lawmaking. Through the negotiation of treaties, states may develop detailed substantive rules and international supervisory machinery to address particular environmental problems.[9]

The growing importance of treaties suggests a diminished role for customary international environmental law. Nevertheless, many writers still consider custom an important source of international environmental law.[10] Claims like the following by the distinguished German scholar Rüdiger Wolfrum are not infrequent: "There is agreement in international law that, in general, transfrontier damage is prohibited. This prohibition has essentially

---

1. Since 1980, the UNEP treaty register has increased from 102 to 164. UNITED NATIONS ENVIRONMENT PROGRAM, REGISTER OF INTERNATIONAL TREATIES AND OTHER AGREEMENTS IN THE FIELD OF THE ENVIRONMENT (1993); *see also* Robert W. Hahn & Kenneth R. Richards, *The Internationalization of Environmental Regulation*, 30 HARV. INT'L L.J. 421, 424 (1989).

2. Vienna Convention for the Protection of the Ozone Layer, Mar. 22, 1985, T.I.A.S. 11097, 26 I.L.M. 1529 (1987); Montreal Protocol on Substances that Deplete the Ozone Layer, Sept. 16, 1987, 26 I.L.M. 1550 (1987).

3. Basel Convention on the Control of Transboundary Movements of Hazardous Wastes and Their Disposal, Mar. 22, 1989, U.N.E.P. Doc. IG. 80/3.

4. U.N. Conference on Environment and Development: Framework Convention on Climate Change, May 9, 1992, 31 I.L.M. 849.

5. U.N. Conference on Environment and Development: Convention on Biological Diversity, *opened for signature* June 5,1992, 31 I.L.M. 818.

6. Convention to Combat Desertification in Those Countries Experiencing Serious Drought and/or Desertification, Particularly in Africa, *opened for signature* Oct. 14, 1994, U.N. Doc. A/AC.241/15/Rev.7, 33 I.L.M. 1328 (1994).

7. Thomas Bernauer, *The Effectiveness of International Environmental Institutions: How We Might Learn More*, 49 INT'L ORG. 351 (1995).

8. *Environmental Law: When Does It Make Sense to Negotiate International Agreements?*, 87 PROC. AM. SOC'Y INT'L L. 377 (1993); Michael Bothe, *Legal and Non-Legal Norms—A Meaningful Distinction in International Relations?*, 11 NETH. Y.B. INT'L L. 65 (1980).

9. *E.g.*, PATRICIA W. BIRNIE & ALAN E. BOYLE, INTERNATIONAL LAW AND THE ENVIRONMENT 11, 84-85 (1992); Oscar Schachter, *The Emergence of International Environmental Law*, 44 J. INT'L AFF. 457, 470 (1991).

10. BIRNIE, *supra* note 9, at 87; *see also* Pierre-Marie Dupuy, *Overview of the Existing Customary Legal Regime Regarding International Pollution*, *in* INTERNATIONAL LAW AND POLLUTION 61 (Daniel B. Magraw ed., 1991); RESTATEMENT (THIRD) OF THE FOREIGN RELATIONS LAW OF THE UNITED STATES §§ 601-604 (1987).

been developed under customary international law."[11] Scholars have asserted, for example, that whales have an emerging right to life under customary international law;[12] that states must take steps to protect endangered species;[13] and, more generally, that states have a duty to provide notice and engage in consultations concerning activities that may cause transboundary harm.[14] Meanwhile, expert groups have spent considerable time and effort attempting to codify what they regard as the customary norms of international environmental law.[15]

True to their disciplinary training, international legal scholars tend to place importance on whether a norm represents customary international law and have spilled much ink debating whether particular environmental norms have achieved this status. I recently participated in one such debate concerning the customary law status of the so-called "precautionary principle."[16]

In this essay, I wish to step back and ask two broader questions: First, what do we mean when we say that a norm is part of customary international law? Second, does it matter whether a norm has achieved this status and, if so, why? My preliminary conclusion is that much less is at stake than is ordinarily supposed. Rather than continue arguing whether a particular environmental norm is part of customary international law, international legal scholars might do better to invest their time elsewhere.

---

11. Rüdiger Wolfrum, *Purposes and Principles of International Environmental Law*, 33 GER. Y.B. INT'L L. 308, 309 (1990). *See also id.* at 310 (Stockholm Principle 21 "is more than a policy programme, it has to be regarded rather as a restatement of international customary law."); BIRNIE & BOYLE, *supra* note 9, at 89 ("It is beyond serious argument that states are required by international law to take adequate steps to control and regulate sources of serious global environmental pollution or transboundary harm within their territory or subject to their jurisdiction."); Dupuy, *supra* note 10, at 63 (arguing obligation to prevent transfrontier pollution is "well-established").

12. Anthony D'Amato & Sudhir K. Chopra, *Whales: Their Emerging Right to Life*, 85 AM. J. INT'L L. 21 (1991).

13. Michael J. Glennon, *Has International Law Failed the Elephant?*, 84 AM. J. INT'L L. 1, 30 (1990).

14. *See* Wolfrum, *supra* note 11, at 313; RESTATEMENT, *supra* note 10, § 601, comment e; *cf.* Daniel G. Partan, *The "Duty to Inform" in International Environmental Law*, 6 B.U. INT'L L.J. 43, 83 (1988) (duty to inform "has finally emerged as a legal duty of all states under general international law," although its customary law status open to doubt).

15. *See, e.g.*, EXPERTS GROUP ON ENVIRONMENTAL LAW OF THE WORLD COMMISSION ON ENVIRONMENT AND DEVELOPMENT, ENVIRONMENTAL PROTECTION AND SUSTAINABLE DEVELOPMENT: LEGAL PRINCIPLES AND RECOMMENDATIONS (1987). For a general discussion of principles of international environmental law, see PHILIPPE SANDS, PRINCIPLES OF INTERNATIONAL ENVIRONMENTAL LAW (1994).

16. The precautionary principle states that when there is a threat of serious or irreversible environmental harm, lack of full scientific certainty should not be a reason to postpone action. Some scholars have argued that the precautionary principle is part of customary international law, *see, e.g.*, James Cameron & Juli Abouchar, *The Precautionary Principle: A Fundamental Principle of Law and Policy for the Protection of the Global Environment*, 14 B.C. INT'L & COMP. L. REV. 1, 20-21 (1991). I have remained somewhat skeptical. *See* Daniel M. Bodansky, *Scientific Uncertainty and the Precautionary Principle*, 33 ENVIRONMENT 4 (1991).

I. THE ORTHODOX ACCOUNT OF CUSTOMORY INTERNATIONAL LAW

In claiming that a norm, such as the duty to prevent transboundary harm or the precautionary principle, is part of customary law, what kind of claim is one making? According to the standard account of customary international law, claims about customary law are empirical claims about the ways that states (and other international actors[17]) regularly behave.[18] States, for example, generally grant immunity to foreign diplomats; refrain from exercising law enforcement functions in the territory of other states; and do not interfere with foreign vessels on the high seas. These represent significant regularities of behavior--apparently normatively based--amidst the extremely complex and often seemingly *ad hoc* interactions among states.

Anthony D'Amato, while departing in many respects from the standard account of customary international law, has forcefully captured its behavioral orientation:

> To approach the subject of custom from the simplest starting point, we look at the international scene. We could have expected to see nothing but chaos and anarchy, everybody fighting with each other all the time and nobody having any idea about what's going on – in other words, Hobbes' state of nature. But instead we see regularity. We see for the most part peace and peaceful accommodations. . . .
>
> So we say to ourselves: "Aha! Something's going on here that's not explained." There is a systemic process here. . . . We are witnessing ordered behavior. . . .
>
> Well, that's our customary-law problem: to figure out what laws account for these regularities. And so we start looking at what states do and what they claim. The laws could be anything. We don't dictate what international law is; we look for it and find it out there in the real world. International law is implicit in the interactions of these state units. Somehow they're interacting in ways that tell us that there is regularity there. If we were physicists we would say the same

17. For example, international organizations, transnational corporations and other non-governmental groups.

18. Thus, according to the standard theory, uniform and consistent state practice is the basis of custom. Asylum (Colom. v. Peru), 1950 I.C.J. 266, 277 (describing custom as a "constant and uniform usage, accepted as law"). *See generally* KAROL WOLFKE, CUSTOM IN PRESENT INTERNATIONAL LAW (2d rev. ed. 1993).

> thing. If we saw a bunch of microbes, and they were acting in a certain orderly fashion, we would say that there must be some laws regulating their behavior. . . . So today we're looking at states, and we say the same thing--that there are certain laws that seem to account for their regular behavior.[19]

In saying that customary rules represent regularities of behavior, several points should be noted. First, the approach is empirical rather than normative. It attempts to describe the existing norms that govern the relations among states, but does not advocate or prescribe new norms. Accordingly, it draws a clear distinction between *lex lata* (law as it is) and *lex ferenda* (law as it should be).[20]

Second, customary rules are not equivalent to simple behavioral regularities. Behavioral regularities are like physical laws; they can be identified by an external observer, whose "view will be like the view of one who, having observed the working of a traffic signal in a busy street for some time, limits himself to saying that when the light turns red there is a high probability that the traffic will stop."[21] In contrast, the concept of following a rule has an internal as well as an external aspect: the red light is not merely a predictor or sign of traffic stopping; it is a *signal* for traffic to stop. The doctrine of *opinio juris* serves to introduce the internal point of view into the concept of customary international law: Customary norms depend not only on state practice (that is, on observable regularities of behavior), but also on acceptance of these regularities as law by states.

Finally, customary rules represent regularities, but not necessarily uniformities, of behavior. The behavioral approach requires a general congruence between rules and behavior.[22] If a purported rule says one thing and states generally do something else, one can no longer say that the rule "governs" behavior. Nevertheless, mistakes and violations of rules are possible.

---

19. Anthony D'Amato, *Seminar on the Theory of Customary International Law in* INTERNATIONAL LAW ANTHOLOGY 73, 74 (Anthony D'Amato ed., 1994).

20. *See* South West Africa, 1966 I.C.J. 3, 34 (July 18) (drawing a sharp distinction between law and morality).

21. H.L.A. HART, THE CONCEPT OF LAW 87 (1961).

22. *Cf.* Military and Paramilitary Activities in and Against Nicaragua (Merits) (Nicar. v. U.S.), 1986 I.C.J. 4, 98 (June 27) ("The Court does not consider that, for a rule to be established as customary the corresponding practice must be in absolutely rigorous conformity with the rule. . . . [T]he Court deems it sufficient that the conduct of states should, in general, be consistent with such rules . . . .").

Although the concept of customary international law is often viewed as mystifying,[23] the emergence and application of custom are commonplace occurrences. Language provides a good example. Every time we speak, we apply an extremely complex set of customary rules of grammar and usage. These rules are not legislated or enforced by any centralized body (the attempts of the French Academy notwithstanding[24]). Instead, they emerge and continue to evolve through the regular practice of language users. Like any type of customary rule, they need to be identified and learned if one is to participate effectively in society.

In ascertaining customary law, our task is similar to that of a legal anthropologist who wishes to determine how an alien society works or of someone trying to understand a strange game or a foreign language. We must observe what actors do to see what regularities or patterns exist.[25] In watching a football game, for example, we might notice that players' actions seem to be divided into discrete "plays;" one side has the ball for several such plays in a row; during each play, the ball can be advanced by running or passing or kicking, and so on. Similarly, in learning a foreign language, we could try to observe how natives regularly use and combine words. This is presumably how infants learn vocabulary (if not grammar)--through induction from observed behavior.

Do the purported norms of customary international environmental law--such as the prohibition on transboundary harm--represent regularities in state behavior? Would the proverbial Martian coming to Earth[26] be able to induce these norms by observing what states do? The short answer seems to be "no."[27] Consider, for example, the duty to prevent transboundary pollution, generally viewed as one of the most firmly established norms of customary international environmental law. Although I am unaware of any systematic empirical study of this issue, transboundary pollution seems much more the

23. *See* ANTHONY A. D'AMATO, THE CONCEPT OF CUSTOM IN INTERNATIONAL LAW 4 (1971) ("The questions of how custom comes into being and how it can be changed or modified are wrapped in mystery and illogic."); G.J.H. VAN HOOF, RETHINKING THE SOURCES OF INTERNATIONAL LAW 85 (1983); WOLFKE, *supra* note 18, at xiii ("[I]nternational custom and customary law still raise the greatest number of doubts and controversies" of any type of international law).

24. The French Academy was founded in 1635 by Cardinal Richelieu "to maintain the purity of the language . . . and to serve as the ultimate judge of approved usage." THE NEW COLUMBIA ENCYCLOPEDIA 1012 (William H. Harris & Judith S. Levey eds., 1975).

25. *Cf.* Georg Schwarzenberger, *The Inductive Approach to International Law*, 60 HARV. L. REV. 539 (1947) (emphasizing study of judicial and arbitral decisions).

26. *See* THOMAS M. FRANCK, THE POWER OF LEGITIMACY AMONG NATIONS 41-42 (1990).

27. *Cf.* Schachter, supra note 9, at 462-63 (admitting that there is only fragmentary evidence that international environmental principles are supported by state practice and *opinio juris*).

rule than the exception in interstate relations. Pollutants continuously travel across most international borders through the air and by rivers and ocean currents. In a few cases, states have undertaken efforts to reduce these pollution flows--generally, through treaties.[28] Leaving aside the question of whether these treaties can create or are evidence of a customary norm, they apply to the relations among only a small fraction of the 180-plus countries of the world, and presumably cover only a small part of the total flow of transboundary pollution.[29] As Schachter concludes, "To say that a state has no right to injure the environment of another seems quixotic in the face of the great variety of transborder environmental harms that occur every day."[30]

If the putative rules of customary international environmental law reflected behavioral regularities, then they would have a predictive function. Based on these rules, for example, we could predict how a state would most likely behave when considering an activity with potential transboundary effects. The state would undertake an assessment, provide notice to and engage in consultations with potentially affected states, and not proceed if there were a significant risk of harm. Indeed, according to the precautionary principle, one would ordinarily expect states to refrain from actions that have the potential to cause substantial, irreversible harm even if significant uncertainties exist. Would these be sound predictions of state behavior? Quite the contrary. If one were a government lawyer providing advice to policy makers, reliance on the purported norms of customary international environmental law as the basis of one's predictions would constitute malpractice.

As a growing number of international legal scholars are recognizing, there is a divergence between the traditional theory of customary law, which emphasizes consistent and uniform state practice, and the norms generally espoused as "customary."[31] Robert Jennings has observed, "Most of what we perversely persist in calling customary international law is not only *not*

28. *E.g.*, Convention on Long-Range Transboundary Air Pollution (LRTAP), Nov. 13, 1979, T.I.A.S. 10541, 18 I.L.M. 1442; Agreement Concerning Frontier Watercourses (Fin.-U.S.S.R.), Apr. 24, 1964, 537 U.N.T.S. 231. If any behavioral regularity were in the process of emerging, it would be that states negotiate treaties in response to transboundary pollution.

29. Schachter, *supra* note 9, at 462 ("Environmental treaties, though numerous, are limited in scope and in participation. On the whole, they are not accepted as expressions of customary law and are regarded as binding for the parties alone.").

30. *Id.* at 463.

31. *See, e.g.*, Hiram E. Chodosh, *Neither Treaty Nor Custom: The Emergence of Declarative International Law*, 26 TEX. INT'L L.J. 87 (1991); N.C.H. Dunbar, *The Myth of Customary International Law*, 8 AUSTRL. Y.B. INT'L L. 1 (1983); Stephen Zamora, *Is There Customary International Economic Law?*, 32 GERMAN Y.B. INT'L L. 9 (1989).

customary law; it does not even faintly resemble a customary law."[32] Torture is said to be prohibited by customary international law[33] even though it is common throughout the world.[34] Prompt, adequate, and effective compensation is held to be required by customary international law[35] even though this formula has seldom, if ever, been applied by states in actual expropriation cases.[36] Similarly, scholars characterize the duty to prevent transboundary pollution and the precautionary principle as customary obligations when there is little support for them in the actual behavior of states. As Jennings concludes, "Perhaps it is time to face squarely the fact that the orthodox tests of custom--practice and *opinio juris*--are often not only inadequate but even irrelevant for the identification of much new law today."[37]

II. "DECLARATIVE" INTERNATIONAL ENVIRONMENTAL LAW[38]

According to the orthodox account of customary international law, few principles of international environmental law qualify as customary. Does this mean that claims about customary international environmental law are simply mistaken? Perhaps, but I would suggest that these claims may instead reflect a different conception of customary international law--one that focuses on what states say rather than what they do. While writers pay lip service to the traditional account,[39] they are really discussing a very different kind of law.

Consider the methodology used to establish the existence of customary international environmental norms. According to the traditional account, one would need to undertake a systematic survey of state behavior to determine whether a norm is part of customary law. For example, with respect to the duties to assess activities that may cause transboundary harm and to notify

32. Robert Y. Jennings, *The Identification of International Law*, *in* INTERNATIONAL LAW: TEACHING AND PRACTICE 3, 5 (Bin Cheng ed. ,1982) (emphasis in original).

33. *See, e.g.*, Filartiga v. Pena-Irala, 630 F.2d 876 (1980).

34. *See* Bruno Simma & Philip Alston, *The Sources of Human Rights Law: Custom, Jus Cogens, and General Principles*, 12 AUSTRL. Y.B. INT'L L. 82, 91-92 (1992).

35. Patrick M. Norton, *A Law of the Future or a Law of the Past? Modern Tribunals and the International Law of Expropriation*, 85 AM. J. INT'L L. 474, 488 (1991).

36. Generally expropriation cases have been resolved through lump sum settlements, in which considerably less than full compensation has been paid. RICHARD LILLICH & BURNS WESTON, INTERNATIONAL CLAIMS: THEIR SETTLEMENT BY LUMP SUM AGREEMENTS (1975).

37. Robert Y. Jennings, *What Is International Law and How Do We Know It When We See It?*, 37 ANNUAIRE SUISSE DE DROIT INTERNATIONAL 59, 67 (1981).

38. Chodosh, *supra* note 31.

39. *See, e.g.*, Dupuy, *supra* note 10, at 61 (admitting that "from a strict point of view," customary law should "consist only of those principles that receive a concrete application in the usual conduct and behavior of States.").

potentially affected states, one would need to identify the set of activities that pose a significant risk of transboundary harm and then examine how often states undertake assessments and provide notifications. Similarly, with regard to the duty to prevent significant transboundary pollution, one would need to determine whether states regularly take action to limit the pollution escaping their borders.

Needless to say, attempting to induce the rules of customary international law directly from state practice would be a Herculean task.[40] While legal writers generally claim to adhere to the traditional account, their assertions about customary international law are not based on surveys of state behavior,[41] nor does their training as lawyers equip them for this task. Even when surveys of state practice are undertaken--by committees of the International Law Association for example--the reliability of these efforts is questionable.[42] If we really wanted systematic surveys of state practice, anthropologists and historians would likely do a better job.

Lawyers tend to be good, not at empirically studying behavior, but rather interpreting and utilizing texts--for example, cases, statutes, treaties, and resolutions. And, in writing about "customary" international law, this is exactly what international lawyers do. They base their arguments on both written and oral texts, produced in some cases by states, but often by non-state actors such as courts and arbitral panels,[43] intergovernmental and non-governmental organizations,[44] and legal scholars. Their methodology is to

---

40. *Cf.* RONALD DWORKIN, TAKING RIGHTS SERIOUSLY 105 (1977) (naming his ideal judge "Hercules"). Zamora comments that only the International Law Commission "in permanent session with armies of researchers could gather and sift through all the relevant evidence to establish, in a manner acceptable to social scientists, the existence of a rule of customary international law." *See* Zamora, *supra* note 31, at 38.

41. Schwarzenberger's comment, that "the immense material from which [international custom] may be gathered has hardly yet been touched by international lawyers," still rings true today. *See* Schwarzenberger, *supra* note 25, at 563-64.

42. The following example from personal experience is illustrative. Currently, I serve on an International Law Association committee charged with examining coastal state jurisdiction over marine pollution. As the U.S. member, I was responsible for reporting on U.S. practice. Initially, I expected this would be a relatively straightforward task. The problem of coastal state jurisdiction is an old one, of which government officials are well aware and about which they might be expected to keep records. Nonetheless, it has proven surprisingly difficult to obtain systematic information about incidents of pollution of U.S. coastal waters by foreign vessels and the subsequent U.S. response. If this information is inaccessible with regard to the United States, think how much more difficult it must be to obtain for most other states. By necessity, my report focused on U.S. legislation and regulations, with only anecdotal information about actual pollution incidents.

43. *See* Norton, *supra* note 35, at 497-98 ("Virtually all of the recent opinions [of the Iran-U.S. Claims Tribunal] have placed their principal reliance on judicial and arbitral precedents.").

44. The International Law Association and the Institute of International Law are examples.

collate these texts to see whether a critical mass of authority exists in support of a given norm. A perusal of any work on customary international environmental law confirms that this methodology is the rule, not the exception. At most, scholars cite one or two celebrated incidents, such as the Chernobyl or Sandoz accidents, but provide little or no analysis of whether these incidents typify state behavior. The International Law Association, for example, concluded that the duty to notify was a norm of customary international law, citing only seven examples of state practice,[45] out of the presumably countless instances in which states have undertaken activities with a significant risk of transboundary harm. Instead, emphasis was placed on the various resolutions and treaties in which the putative customary norm appeared.[46]

Discussions of the duty to prevent transboundary pollution provide another good example of this methodology. Generally, writers begin by citing *Trail Smelter*,[47] which after more than fifty years is still the only case in which a state was held internationally responsible for causing transboundary harm.[48] Writers then cite to Principle 21 of the Stockholm Declaration,[49] now joined by the recent reiteration of this principle (very slightly modified) in the 1992 Rio Declaration.[50] For good measure, references are also usually included to the O.E.C.D. Council Recommendation Concerning Transfrontier Pollution,[51]

45. *See* Partan, *supra* note 14, at 51. Three of these examples were based on treaties. Even with respect to the four instances of notification not based on treaty, whether these were made out of a sense of international legal obligation is, according to Partan, "problematical" and "entirely speculative." *Id.* at 54.

46. *Id.* at 51-53.

47. Trail Smelter (U.S. v. Can.), 3 R.I.A.A. 1938, 1965 (Mar. 11, 1941) ("[N]o State has the right to use or permit the use of its territory in such a manner as to cause injury . . . in or to the territory of another or of the properties or persons therein, when the case is of serious consequence and the injury is established by clear and convincing evidence.").

48. The *Corfu Channel Case* (U.K. v. Alb.), 1949 I.C.J. 4 (judgment of Apr. 9), also cited by most scholars in support of the duty to prevent transboundary environmental harm, did not involve transboundary pollution. Instead, it enunciated the more general principle that a state may not knowingly allow its territory to be used to injure another state. *Id.* at 22.

49. Stockholm Declaration on the Human Environment, princ. 21, REPORT OF THE UNITED NATIONS CONFERENCE ON THE HUMAN ENVIRONMENT, Stockholm, June 5-16, 1972, U.N. Doc. A/CONF.48/14/Rev.1, U.N. Sales No. E.73.II.A.14, pt. 1, ch. 1 (1973), *reprinted in* 11 I.L.M. 1416 (1972) ("States have . . . the responsibility to ensure that activities within their jurisdiction or control do not cause damage to the environment of other States or of areas beyond the limits of national jurisdiction.").

50. Rio Declaration on Environment and Development, U.N. Doc. A/CONF.151/5/Rev.1 (1992), 31 I.L.M. 876.

51. OECD Council Recommendation C(74)224, Nov. 14, 1974, Title B(2), *in* OECD, OECD AND THE ENVIRONMENT 142 (1986) (states "should, individually and jointly, take all appropriate measures to prevent and control transfrontier pollution").

U.N. General Assembly resolutions,[52] the International Law Association's Montreal Rules of International Law Applicable to Transfrontier Pollution,[53] various treaties,[54] and the numerous international law scholars who have asserted that customary law imposes a duty to prevent transboundary environmental harm.[55]

Of course, the focus on verbal rather than physical practice could reflect not a search for a different type of legal norm, but merely a methodology for discovering the rules of state behavior. Just as one might find it easier to learn the rules of cricket by studying a rules book or by asking someone familiar with the game rather than through direct observation and induction, it may be easier to apprehend the rules of state behavior by studying what states say about customary law rather than by directly observing what they do. This would be an appropriate methodology when a state's statements and actions are congruent; when state declarations are a good guide to behavior. In the environmental realm, however, verbal claims and physical behavior often diverge. States acknowledge a duty to prevent significant transboundary harm, but continue to cause such harm; they accept resolutions recommending assessments and notification, but seldom act accordingly. Consequently, studying verbal practice appears to be a misguided methodology for discovering behavior regularities.

In my view, the focus by scholars on verbal practice is not merely methodological; it represents a fundamentally different ontology of international law--one that is discursive rather than behavioral in orientation. International environmental norms reflect not how states regularly behave, but how states speak to one another. They represent the evaluative standards used by states to justify their actions and to criticize the actions of others. Writers

---

52. *E.g.*, Co-operation in the Field of Environment Concerning Natural Resources Shared by Two or More States, G.A. Res. 3129 (XXVIII), U.N. GAOR Supp. (No. 30A), U.N. Doc. A/9030/Add.1 (1973).

53. Montreal Rules of International Law Applicable to Transfrontier Pollution, art. 3(1), Int'l Law Assn., Rep. 60th Conf., at 1-3 (1982) ("States are in their legitimate activities under an obligation to prevent, abate, and control transfrontier pollution to such an extent that no substantial injury is caused in the territory of another State.").

54. *E.g.*, U.N. Convention on the Law of the Sea, Dec. 10, 1982, art. 194(2), U.N. Doc. A/Conf.62/121, 21 I.L.M. 1261 (1982) ("States shall take all measures necessary to ensure that activities under their jurisdiction or control are conducted so as not to cause damage by pollution to other States and their environment.").

55. *See, e.g.*, BIRNIE & BOYLE, *supra* note 9, at 89-95. Dupuy, for example, cites the *Trail Smelter* and *Corfu Channel* cases, Stockholm Principle 21, several U.N. General Assembly resolutions, OECD Council recommendations, the Helsinki Final Act, and the UNEP Draft Principles of Conduct on Shared Natural Resources. Dupuy, *supra* note 10, at 64-65. As far as "concrete cases" of state practice are concerned, however, he notes that states "seem partly to ignore" the rule prohibiting transboundary pollution. *Id.* at 66.

persist in characterizing these norms as "customary," the catch-all term generally applied to any non-treaty norm,[56] but it would be more accurate to distinguish this type of norm from custom. Chodosh has suggested the term "declarative law."[57] A more pointed characterization is "myth system,"[58] since these norms represent the collective ideals of the international community, which at present have the quality of fictions or half-truths.[59]

III. THE ROLE OF "DECLARATIVE" LAW

Assuming that so-called customary international environmental norms represent regularities in discourse rather than regularities in state behavior, what difference then do these norms make? Should we care about whether this myth system counts as international law and, if so, why?

In thinking about these questions, it is useful to distinguish between three ways to implement and enforce legal norms: by courts and arbitral tribunals (third-party control); through voluntary compliance (first-party control); and through interactions among the subjects of the legal system (second-party control).[60] Third-party control--the paradigm of domestic legal systems--is the easiest situation. Where the possibility of adjudication or arbitration exists, the distinction between legal and non-legal norms matters, since courts will

---

56. *See* Chodosh, *supra* note 31, at 88. Another possibility is that these norms represent "general principles of law." *See* Partan, *supra* note 14, at 72 (duty to inform is a general principle of law). This at least brings them under the rubric of one of the accepted sources of international law (although arguably with little advance in understanding, since the category of "general principles" has no well-accepted meaning). *Cf.* Schwarzenberger, *supra* note 25, at 549 (criticizing the resort to general principles of law as a means of avoiding the need to research state practice). Most international environmental principles, however, do not fit within any of the proposed theories of "general principles of law." They are not principles of legal logic, nor do they appear to represent principles common to most national legal systems. Although traces of the precautionary principle can be found in U.S. and European environmental law, generalizing from this to the rest of the world reflects a Eurocentric view. TIMOTHY O'RIORDAN & JAMES CAMERON, INTERPRETING THE PRECAUTIONARY PRINCIPLE (1994). Finally, they do not represent principles of natural law. Although their proponents tend to defend them in natural law terms (i.e., as necessary to cope with international environmental problems), the primary authority for their legal status is positivist. Scholars justify these norms not in terms of abstract justice, but by reference to certain kinds of evidence, including U.N. General Assembly resolutions, treaties, reports of experts groups, and the writings of other international law scholars.

57. Chodosh, *supra* note 31.

58. W. MICHAEL REISMAN, FOLDED LIES 15-36 (1979) (discussing the difference between "myth system" and "operational code").

59. AMERICAN HERITAGE DICTIONARY 1196 (3d ed. 1992) (defining "myth" as a story "delineating the psychology, customs, or ideals of society" and as "a fiction or half-truth, especially one that forms part of an ideology").

60. *See* ROBERT C. ELLICKSON, ORDER WITHOUT LAW: HOW NEIGHBORS SETTLE DISPUTES 126-27 (1991) (distinguishing between systems of first-, second-, and third-party control).

enforce legal but not non-legal norms.[61] Debates about whether a norm is part of international law are not purely academic, for if one can convince a court that a norm represents the law, then that court can apply and enforce the norm.

A good illustration is the *Filartiga v. Pena-Irala* case,[62] in which the plaintiff persuaded the Second Circuit Court of Appeals that customary international law prohibits torture. The possibility of judicial enforcement gave significance to the debate about whether the prohibition on torture is customary. The same situation prevails in the Iran-U.S. Claims Tribunal, which has applied the "prompt, adequate and effective" compensation formula as part of customary international law.[63]

In my view, most writers on customary international environmental law instinctively assume a state of affairs where third-party dispute resolution is available, and subconsciously address their arguments to legal decisionmakers, such as courts and arbitrators.[64] These legal decisionmakers are the real target audience for the voluminous writings on customary international environmental law.[65] The problem is that courts and arbitral tribunals currently play only a relatively minor role in addressing international environmental issues.[66] Third-party dispute resolution has resolved few environmental problems.[67] That is why *Trail Smelter* must bear such a heavy load in current scholarship on customary international environmental law. The establishment of an environmental chamber of the International Court of Justice and the recent cases between Nauru and Australia and between Hungary and Slovakia may signal the emergence of a greater judicial role. But, at present, legal discourse that presupposes a judicial audience plays to a largely empty house.

Of course, even when judicial enforcement is unavailable, norms may still affect behavior by exerting a compliance pull on states.[68] Non-legal as well as

---

61. *See* Bothe, *supra* note 8, at 87.

62. Filartiga v. Pena-Irala, 630 F.2d 876 (1980).

63. Sedco v. National Iranian Oil Co., 10 IRAN-U.S. CL. TRIB. REP. 180 (1986 I), 25 I.L.M. 629, 631 (1986).

64. Legal arguments are also addressed to legislatures, but here the arguments are normative rather than descriptive; they concern what the law *should* be, not what it *is*.

65. *See* Hans Baade, *Codes of Conduct for Multinational Enterprises: An Introductory Survey*, *in* LEGAL PROBLEMS OF CODES OF CONDUCT FOR MULTINATIONAL ENTERPRISE 407, 413 (Norbert Horn ed., 1980) ("[W]henever the volume of learned comment outstrips the supply of 'hard' decisional law, and especially wherever scholarly discussion starts to feed on itself, it loses touch with reality.").

66. In a few international regimes, such as the European Union and the World Trade Organization, the situation is different, but these regimes remain the exception.

67. Thus far, domestic courts have infrequently applied international environmental norms, in contrast to human rights norms, which have often been the subject of litigation in U.S. courts.

68. *See* FRANCK, *supra* note 26. This factor is stressed by Mary Ellen O'Connell, *Enforcement and the Success of International Environmental Law*, 3 IND. J. GLOBAL LEGAL STUD. 47 (1995).

legal norms may exert such a pull. Moral norms, for example, can influence behavior through the operation of conscience.[69] But, arguably, the legal status of a norm enhances its influence.[70] If people feel that the "secondary" rules for the creation of law are legitimate, then they are likely to accept a rule produced through that lawmaking process, whether they like the substance of the rule or not. Much compliance with law results from this voluntary mechanism.[71]

Does declarative international environmental law exert a significant compliance pull on states? Again, I am not aware of any empirical studies of this question, but my intuition is that the answer is no. First, at least some important states do not accept the secondary rule of law formation underlying declarative law--*i.e.*, that commonly repeated statements in treaties, declarations, and the like create general norms of behavior, applicable to the entire range of state action, not just the more specific areas where the norms were originally propounded. Second, in the absence of judicial enforcement, customary norms must have a relatively high degree of specificity in order to exert a constraining influence on states.[72] Indeed, the determinacy of norms--the degree to which they establish certainty of expectations about future action--may influence compliance more than their legal or non-legal character. The declarative rules of international environmental law, however, are very general and provide little specific guidance to states.[73] States are told, for example, to avoid significant transboundary pollution, but what constitutes "significant"? They ought to undertake precautionary action, but in what circumstances and to what degree? As a result of this vagueness, states may basically do what they like and argue that their actions are consistent with customary international law.

Given the rarity of third-party dispute resolution, and the weak compliance pull exerted by "declarative" international environmental norms, the biggest

69. Similarly, political obligations undertaken in solemn form, such as the Helsinki Final Act, are often taken seriously by states and exert a compliance pull. Bothe, *supra* note 8, at 85.

70. *Id.* at 78 (states find it somewhat easier not to comply with resolutions that are not legally binding, but this is only one factor among many in determining actual compliance).

71. *See* TOM TYLER, WHY PEOPLE OBEY THE LAW (1990).

72. *See* FRANCK, *supra* note 26, at 52 (arguing that the determinacy of rules is an important factor in their legitimacy).

73. *See Developments in the Law–International Environmental Law*, 104 HARV. L. REV. 1484, 1504-05 (1991); Ian Brownlie, *A Survey of International Customary Rules of Environmental Protection*, 13 NAT. RESOURCES J. 179, 179 (1973). Dupuy argues that customary international environmental norms are no more vague than domestic norms such as good faith or due process. Dupuy, *supra* note 10, at 69. The difference, however, is that courts can give more specific meaning to domestic norms in the context of concrete cases. In contrast, the general unavailability of international adjudication implies that norms such as the duty to prevent transboundary pollution remain vague.

potential influence of these norms is on second-party control mechanisms. Most international environmental issues are resolved through mechanisms such as negotiations, rather than through third-party dispute settlement or unilateral changes of behavior. In this second-party control process, international environmental norms can play a significant role by setting the terms of the debate, providing evaluative standards, serving as a basis to criticize other states' actions, and establishing a framework of principles within which negotiations may take place to develop more specific norms, usually in treaties. Consider, for example, the role of the duty to prevent transboundary harm in the U.S.-Canada acid rain dispute. This norm did not directly constrain the United States; but it arguably had an indirect effect by providing a shared normative framework for the negotiations that led ultimately to the 1991 U.S.-Canada Air Quality Agreement.[74] To the extent the norm influenced state behavior, it was through this indirect mechanism.

My hypothesis, however, is that these functions of international environmental norms do not depend on a norm's legal status. Whether the duty to prevent transboundary pollution or the precautionary principle are part of customary international law, they will set the terms of international discussions and serve as the framework for negotiations. If so, the current debates over the legal versus non-legal status of these norms are of little consequence. They would matter if dispute resolution were more prevalent. But so long as courts and arbitrators play a minor role, these debates will remain a sideshow. Rather than continue them, our time and efforts would be better spent attempting to translate the general norms of international environmental relations into concrete treaties and actions.

---

74. U.S.-Canada Air Quality Agreement, Mar. 31, 1991, 30 I.L.M. 676 (1991).

Part III
Contemporary Sources of International Environmental Law

[9]

SOFT LAW AND THE INTERNATIONAL LAW OF THE ENVIRONMENT

*Pierre-Marie Dupuy**

INTRODUCTION

"Soft" law is a paradoxical term for defining an ambiguous phenomenon. Paradoxical because, from a general and classical point of view, the rule of law is usually considered "hard," *i.e.*, compulsory, or it simply does not exist. Ambiguous because the reality thus designated, considering its legal effects as well as its manifestations, is often difficult to identify clearly.

Nevertheless, a new process of normative creation which jurists feel uncomfortable analyzing does exist and has been developing for more or less twenty years. "Soft" law certainly constitutes part of the contemporary law-making process but, as a social phenomenon, it evidently overflows the classical and familiar legal categories by which scholars usually describe and explain both the creation and the legal authority of international norms. In other words, "soft" law is a trouble maker because it is either not yet or not only law.[1]

This heterogeneity requires that one first consider, without necessarily subscribing to any "sociological" school of thought, the social reasons for this phenomenon. There seem to be three:

The first reason is structural in nature: it is the existence and development of a ramified network of permanent institutions, both at the universal and regional levels, since the end of the Second World War.

---

* Professor of Law, University of Paris; Visiting Professor, University of Michigan Law School, 1990.

1. *See* SOCIÉTE FRANÇAISE POUR LE DROIT INTERNATIONAL, L'ÉLABORATION DU DROIT INTERNATIONAL PUBLIC (1975); E. MCWHINNEY, UNITED NATIONS LAW MAKING 78-79 (1984); CHANGE AND STABILITY IN INTERNATIONAL LAW-MAKING 66-101 (A. Cassese & J. Weiler eds. 1988); F. MUNCH, NON-BINDING AGREEMENTS 1-11 (1969); M. LACHS, SOME REFLECTIONS ON THE SUBSTANCE AND FORM OF INTERNATIONAL LAW, 99-112 (1972); O. Schachter, *The Existence of Nonbinding International Agreements*, 71 AM. J. INT'L L. 296 (1977); R. Baxter, *International Law in "Her Infinite Variety,"* 29 INT'L & COMP. L.Q. 549 (1980); Bothe, *Legal and Non-Legal Norms — A Meaningful Distinction in International Relations?*, 11 NETHERLANDS Y.B. INT'L L. 65 (1980); Weil, *Towards Relative Normativity in International Law?*, 77 AM. J. INT'L L. 413 (1983); Virally, *La Distinction entre Textes Internationaux de Portée Juridique et Textes Internationaux Dépourvus de Portée Juridique*, 60-I ANNUAIRE DE L'INSTITUT DE DROIT INTERNATIONAL [A.I.D.I.] 166 (1983); *Délibérations de l'Institut en Séances Plénières, Première Séance Plénière*, 60-II A.I.D.I. 117 (1984) (M. Virally, rapporteur); Aust, *The Theory and Practice of Informal International Instruments*, 35 INT'L & COMP. L.Q. 787 (1986).

The "UN family" of organizations plays the leading role here. These institutions offer the world community a standing structure of cooperation which makes it possible to organize permanent and on-going political, economic and normative negotiations among the member States of this community. Furthermore, the increasingly important function of non-governmental organizations provides an efficient complement to the existing intergovernmental framework by assuring, in particular, a dynamic relationship between inter-State diplomacy and international public opinion.[2]

The second reason is the diversification of the components of this world community. Since the late 1950s, the arrival of underdeveloped countries on the international stage has made it necessary to adapt and reconsider, by way of normative negotiation, a great number of international customary norms which had been elaborated at a time when these countries were not in existence as sovereign States. It is well known that these new States, having the weight of the majority without the power of the elder countries, have speculated on the utilization of "soft" instruments, such as resolutions and recommendations of international bodies, with a view toward modifying a number of the main rules and principles of the international legal order.

The last and most important element, closely linked to the previous one, is best characterized by the rapid evolution of the world economy and increasing State interdependence combined with the development of new fields of activity created by the unceasing progress of science and technology. This phenomenon requires the timely creation of new branches of international law that are adaptable and applicable to each new level of achievement reached as a result of technological advancement. Thus, international economic law[3] and international law relating to the protection of the human environment are areas in which new "soft" regulations have emerged in predominant fashion.

The inter-relationship among these three elements, even if complex, is nonetheless quite evident: the steady evolution and adaptation of these new norms necessitate a constant renegotiation which usually takes place within the many organs of international organizations. One could say that the "soft" law "wave" reflects both, on the one hand, a desire for a new type of law rendered necessary by the previ-

2. M. Bettati & P.-M. Dupuy, Les ONG et le Droit International (1986).

3. An important component of international economic law, for instance, has to do with the relationship between international law and economic development. *See generally*, La Formation des Normes en Droit International du Développement (M. Flory, A. Mahiou & J. Henry eds. 1984).

ously enunciated factors and, on the other, a certain fear that existing law is too rigid — either too difficult to be rigorously applied by the poorest countries or incapable of adapting to the rapidly evolving areas which it is supposed to cover and regulate.

It would, however, be a mistake to believe that, given these considerations, "soft" law is solely an attribute of international law. For partly the same reasons, particularly given the rapid evolution of scientific advances, one can observe its appearance in certain domains of municipal law. For example, very few countries have yet adopted precise legislation providing for normative regulation of genetic research and its applications in "assisted procreation." The preference has instead been to define, through various institutions and procedures, a variety of "soft" ethical guidelines addressed to scientists and physicians without resorting to laws, decrees or other "hard" legal instruments. That this phenomenon is common nowadays is one of the many reasons why "soft" law should not be considered a "normative sickness" but rather a symbol of contemporary times and a product of necessity.[4]

Because the existing body of international environmental law has, in part, emerged on the basis of "soft" norms, it provides a good field for observing the general sociological and juridical phenomenon termed "soft" law. The 1972 Stockholm Declaration adopted by the UN Conference on the Human Environment, for example, constitutes the normative program for the world community in this field. Although, from a formal point of view, the Declaration is only a nonbinding resolution, many of its "principles," particularly Principle 21, have been relied upon by governments to justify their legal rights and duties. The subsequent State practice has been, no doubt, influenced by such provisions. It is in this context and with the benefit of these introductory remarks that we shall briefly and successively examine the creation (I), the forms and content (II), and the legal effects (III) of "soft" law in the field of international environmental law.

I. Creation of Soft Environmental Law

A. *The Institutional Framework*

The primary function assumed by international institutions in the international "soft" law-making process has already been illustrated. In practice, the development of "soft" law norms with regard to the protection of the human environment began immediately after the Stockholm Conference, one of the consequences of which was the cre-

4. *Contra* Weil, *supra* note 1, at 413-23, 441-42.

ation of a special subsidiary organ of the UN General Assembly devoted to the promotion of both universal and regional environmental law. This body, the United Nations Environment Program ("UNEP"), has played a leading role in the promotion of regional conventions aimed at, for example, protecting seas against pollution. Although it was not supposed to develop in such a manner, UNEP has also evolved into a standing structure for negotiating draft resolutions sent, after their elaboration, to the General Assembly, where their contents have been either passed as is or expressly referred to in resolutions. A prime example of this phenomenon is provided by the 1978 UNEP Draft Principles of Conduct in the Field of the Environment for the Guidance of States in the Conservation and Harmonious Utilization of Natural Resources Shared by Two or More States.[5]

At the regional level in general and in Europe in particular, several international institutions have engaged in important activities related to environmental protection: the Organization for Economic Cooperation and Development ("OECD"), which, in particular, has adopted a series of recommendations conceived of as a follow-up to the Universal Stockholm Declaration regarding the prevention and abatement of transfrontier pollution;[6] the EEC which has adopted Programmes of Action for the Environment, on the basis of which "hard" law is later established, mainly by way of "directive";[7] and the Council of Europe, which, even before the recent, intense international cooperation in this field, was perhaps the first international intergovernmental institution to bring to the attention of States the necessity of protecting the environment.[8]

The action of non-governmental organizations ("NGOs") has also contributed to the enunciation of "soft" law principles regarding the environment. The International Law Association ("ILA"), for example, adopted an influential resolution in 1966 known as the Helsinki Rules on the Use of Waters of International Rivers[9] which was ex-

5. *Report on the Intergovernmental Working Group of Experts on Natural Resources Shared by Two or More States on the Work of its Fifth Session Held in Nairobi from January 23, to February 7, 1978* (D. Kinyanjui, rapporteur) [UNEP Governing Council decision 6/14 of May 19, 1978], *reprinted in* 17 I.L.M. 1094, 1097 (1978)[hereinafter *UNEP Draft Principles of Conduct*].

6. See ORGANIZATION FOR ECONOMIC COOPERATION AND DEVELOPMENT AND THE ENVIRONMENT (1986) [hereinafter OECD AND THE ENVIRONMENT], which contains OECD resolutions dealing with the protection of the environment.

7. *See, e.g., Council Directive of 15 July 1980 on Air Quality Limit Values and Guide Values for Sulphur Dioxide and Suspended Particulates*, 23 O.J. EUR. COMM. (No. L 229) 30 (1980).

8. *See, e.g., Resolution 71(5) on Air Pollution in Frontier Areas*, 1971 EUR. Y.B. (Council of Eur.) 263.

9. INTERNATIONAL LAW ASSOCIATION, REPORT OF THE FIFTY-SECOND CONFERENCE (HELSINKI) 477 (1966).

panded and enlarged by the same institution in 1982 with the adoption of the Montreal Rules of International Law Applicable to Transfrontier Pollution.[10] The Institute of International Law ("IIL") has played an equally important role by promulgating resolutions on the Utilization of Non-Maritime International Waters;[11] on the Pollution of Rivers and Lakes and International Law;[12] and on Transboundary Air Pollution.[13]

In this context, the regional commissions of the United Nations play a role that could become more important in the near future. This is reflected in the recent Bergen Declaration adopted on May 14, 1990, by thirty environment ministers at a meeting convened jointly by the United Nations Economic Commission for Europe and the government of Norway.[14] One can find in the terms of this declaration different considerations, guidelines and principles which echo those of other contemporary declarations such as the Declaration on Human Responsibilities for Peace and Sustainable Development proposed a year earlier by Costa Rica,[15] or the Declaration of Environmental Interdependence adopted by the Interparliamentary Conference on the Global Environment in Washington, D.C. on May 2, 1990.[16]

B. *The Soft Lawmaking Process*

As with other areas in which "soft" law plays a part, *repetition* is a very important factor in the international environmental "soft" lawmaking process. All of the international bodies referred to above should be viewed, as far as their recommendatory action in this field is concerned, as transmitting basically the same message. Cross-references from one institution to another, the recalling of guidelines adopted by other apparently concurrent international authorities, recurrent invocation of the same rules formulated in one way or another at the universal, regional and more restricted levels, all tend progressively to develop and establish a common international understanding. As a result of this process, conduct and behavior which would have

10. International Law Association, Report of the Sixtieth Conference (Montreal) 1 (1982).

11. 49-II A.I.D.I. 381 (1961).

12. 58-II A.I.D.I. 196 (1979).

13. 62-II A.I.D.I. 296 (1987).

14. *See Bergen: Weak Declaration Adopted*, 20 Envtl. Pol'y & L. 84 (1990).

15. *See Human Responsibilities for Peace and Sustainable Development*, 19 Envtl. Pol'y & L. 232 (1989).

16. *See The Interparliamentary Conference on the Global Environment*, 20 Envtl. Pol'y & L. 112 (1990).

been considered challenges to State sovereignty twenty years ago are now accepted within the mainstream.

Let us examine, by way of illustration, four substantial examples of this phenomenon in the context of international environmental "soft" law. The first example involves the principle of *information and consultation*. This principle usually manifests itself as an obligation whereby States must inform and consult one another, prior to engaging in any activity or initiative that is likely to cause transfrontier pollution, so that the country of origin of the potentially dangerous activity may take into consideration the interests of any potentially exposed country. From a more general point of view, the principle covers the additional duty to provide to these potentially exposed States all relevant and reasonably available information concerning transboundary natural resources and transfrontier environmental interference.[17]

The principle of information and consultation has been reiterated for almost twenty years by the different organizations cited above as well as by others. It can be found in many recommendations or resolutions: the aforementioned 1978 UNEP Draft Principles of Conduct on Shared Natural Resources; UN General Assembly resolutions 3129 (XXVIII) of December 1973 and 3281 (the Charter of Economic Rights and Duties of States);[18] OECD Council recommendations on Transfrontier Pollution[19] and the Implementation of a Regime of Equal Right of Access and Non-Discrimination in Relation to Transfrontier Pollution.[20] In the context of NGO activity, the same rule is

17. For a presentation of duties of States with regard to the protection of the environment, see generally Handl, *Territorial Sovereignty and the Problem of Transnational Pollution*, 69 AM. J. INT'L L. 50 (1975). *See also* Handl, *Balancing of Interests and International Liability for the Pollution of International Watercourses: Customary Principles of Law Revisited*, 13 CANADIAN Y.B. INT'L L. 156 (1975); Dupuy, *Bilan de Recherches de la Section de Langue Française du Centre D'Étude et de Recherche de L'Académie*, in LA POLLUTION TRANSFRONTIÈRE ET LE DROIT INTERNATIONAL 33 (1985) (publication of the Centre for Studies and Research in International Law and International Relations, Hague Academy of International Law); Lammers, *The Present State of Research Carried Out by the Centre for Studies and Research*, in LA POLLUTION TRANSFRONTIÈRE ET LE DROIT INTERNATIONAL, *supra*; WORLD COMMISSION ON THE ENVIRONMENT AND DEVELOPMENT, EXPERT GROUP ON ENVIRONMENTAL LAW, LEGAL PRINCIPLES FOR ENVIRONMENTAL PROTECTION AND SUSTAINABLE DEVELOPMENT (1986).

18. G.A. Res. 3129, 28 U.N. GAOR Supp. (No. 30), U.N. Doc. A/Res./3050-3199; G.A. Res. 3281, 29 U.N. GAOR Supp. (No. 31), U.N. Doc. A/9631 (1974), *reprinted in* 14 I.L.M. 251 (1975). UN bodies other than UNEP, such as the ECOSOC Commission on Transnational Corporations, also work on environmental matters and produce "soft" standards for environmental protection. *See, e.g.*, *Transnational Corporations and Issues Relating to the Environment*, U.N. Doc. E/C.10/1987/12 (1987).

19. OECD Council Recommendation C(74)224, Annex, Title E (1974), *reprinted in* OECD AND THE ENVIRONMENT, *supra* note 6, at 142, 145.

20. OECD Council Recommendation C(77)28(final), Annex, Title C (1977), *reprinted in* OECD AND THE ENVIRONMENT, *supra* note 6, at 150, 153.

contained in the already-mentioned ILA resolutions of 1966 and 1982, as well as in the IIL resolutions of 1961, 1979 and 1981.

The second example concerns, on a more specific level, *environmental impact assessment* procedures. These procedures are directly related to the principle of information and consultation since they make it possible to estimate the impact of a planned activity on the environment of a neighboring State.[21] Adherence to such procedures has been recommended several times by various sources, such as the 1978 UNEP Draft Principles of Conduct on Shared Natural Resources and the 1981 UNEP Conclusions of the Study on the Legal Aspects Concerning the Environment Related to Off-Shore Mining and Drilling within the Limits of National Jurisdiction.[22] These UNEP recommendations have both been endorsed by the UN General Assembly in its Resolution No. 37/27 of March 24, 1983, on International Co-operation in the Field of the Environment, as well as in its resolution No. 37/7 on the World Charter for Nature (articles eleven and sixteen).

Support for the same procedures can be found in the 1974 OECD Declaration on Environmental Policy and other recommendations adopted by the same organization.[23] A faithful echo of the same rule can also be found in a 1985 EEC Council Directive pertaining to the Assessment of the Effects of Certain Public and Private Projects on the Environment.[24] It would be a mistake, however, to conclude that this type of rule has only been recognized by industrialized countries; it was, for instance, recognized and recommended by the Economic Commission for Africa Council of Ministers in 1984.[25]

The third example of repetition in the international "soft" lawmaking process is provided by the principle of *non-discrimination* according to which States should not substantially differentiate between their own environment and those of other States as regards the elaboration and application of laws and regulations in the areas of prevention, reparation and repression of pollution. With regard to instances of transfrontier inland pollution, States must also allow persons concerned with such occurrences access to available administrative and

21. U.N. Doc. UNEP/ENV/GE.1/R.11/Rev.1 (1984).

22. *The Environment Program: Program Performance Report January-April 1981*, U.N. Doc. UNEP/GC.9/5/Add.5 at 36 (1981).

23. Declaration on Environmental Policy (Nov. 14, 1974), *reprinted in* OECD AND THE ENVIRONMENT, *supra* note 6, at 15.

24. *Council Directive of 27 June 1985 on the Assessment of the Effects of Certain Public and Private Projects on the Environment*, art. 7, 28 O.J. Eur. Com. (No. L 175) 40, 42 (1985).

25. *Economic Commission for Africa, Annual Report*, 69 U.N. ESCOR Supp. (No. 11) para. 2, U.N. Doc. E/ECA/CM.10/38 (1984).

judicial proceedings.[26]

The principle of non-discrimination has been introduced quite systematically in OECD Council recommendations concerned with transfrontier pollution, in particular, recommendation C(77)28. One can also find this principle in the 1978 Draft Principles Relating to Shared Natural Resources and in several of the other recommendations already mentioned.[27] It is interesting to note that, in this area and on the basis of those programmatory instruments, the same principle has been introduced in a "hard" instrument, namely the 1982 UN Convention on the Law of the Sea.[28]

The final and most recent example of convergence between non-legally-binding texts of different natures and origins is to be found in contemporary approaches to the problems surrounding the protection of the global atmosphere. The number of "soft" instruments calling on the world community to strengthen international cooperation on the basis of a new "global" approach and the perception of the world atmosphere as part of the "*common heritage of mankind*" has been increasing in the past two to three years. If this phenomenon continues, it will likely have some legal consequence, particularly with regard to the environmental responsibility that the present generation has vis-à-vis future generations.[29]

The contemporary "common heritage" approach is reflected, for example, in the UN General Assembly Resolution 43/53 of January 27, 1989, in which it is recognized "that climate change is a common concern of mankind . . . ."[30] A second reference can be found in the statement agreed to by the International Meeting of Legal and Policy Experts hosted by the Canadian government in Ottawa on February 20-22, 1989. This statement takes the form of a draft convention on the protection of the world climate and global atmosphere. It declares that "the atmosphere . . . constitutes a common resource of vital interest to mankind."[31] Another text which can be cited in this context is

26. *See* OECD, NON-DISCRIMINATION IN RELATION TO TRANSFRONTIER POLLUTION: LEADING DOCUMENTS (1978) [hereinafter OECD, NON-DISCRIMINATION].

27. OECD, NON-DISCRIMINATION, *supra* note 26, at para. 11.

28. *See, e.g., Third United Nations Conference on the Law of the Sea, United Nations Convention on the Law of the Sea*, U.N. Doc. A/CONF.62/122, arts. 194(4) and 227 (1982), *reprinted in* 21 I.L.M. 1261 (1982).

29. *See* WEISS, IN FAIRNESS TO FUTURE GENERATIONS: INTERNATIONAL LAW COMMON PATRIMONY AND INTERGENERATIONAL EQUITY (1989); D'Amato, *Do We Owe a Duty to Future Generations to Preserve the Global Environment?*, 84 AM. J. INT'L L. 190 (1990).

30. *Protection of Global Climate for Present and Future Generations of Mankind*, U.N. Doc. A/Res/43/53, para. 1 (1989), *reprinted in* 28 I.L.M. 1326, 1327 (1989).

31. STATEMENT OF THE MEETING OF LEGAL AND POLICY EXPERTS, PROTECTION OF THE ATMOSPHERE: INTERNATIONAL MEETING OF LEGAL AND POLICY EXPERTS (February 22, 1989)(Ottawa).

the Hague Declaration of March 11, 1989, signed by representatives of twenty-four States at the Hague at the initiative of France, the Netherlands and Norway. The Declaration states that it is the "duty of the community of nations vis-à-vis present and future generations to do all that can be done to preserve the quality of the atmosphere."[32] Support for the same approach can also be found in the different reports of the Intergovernmental Panel on Climatic Change established in 1989 under the co-sponsorship of the World Meterological Organization and UNEP[33] and in the Decision on Global Climate Change adopted by the UNEP Governing Council in May 1989.[34]

These various texts appear to define a new trend which may eventually lead to the negotiation of a new general multilateral convention on the protection of the world climate. The adoption of such a convention has been called for, in particular, by the Noordwijk Declaration on Climate Change adopted at a ministerial conference of representatives of sixty-seven governments from every part of the world in November 1989.[35]

But these "soft" instruments, as is the case with others usually referred to in the general context of the "soft" law phenomenon, are in many respects rather heterogeneous in nature. Their substantial convergence does not create a new binding rule of international environmental law. This remark leads both to methodological problems, which will be dealt with later in this article, and necessitates a more thorough examination of the forms and content of "soft" environmental law.

II. The Forms and Content of Soft Environmental Law

The examples provided earlier illustrate that much of "soft" law is incorporated within "soft" (*i.e.*, non-binding) instruments such as recommendations and resolutions of international organizations, declarations and "final acts" published at the conclusion of international conferences and even draft proposals elaborated by groups of experts. It is thus generally understood that "soft" law creates and delineates goals to be achieved in the future rather than actual duties, programs rather than prescriptions, guidelines rather than strict obligations. It

32. *Hague Declaration on the Environment*, 28 I.L.M. 1308, 1309 (1989).

33. *See*, IPCC (WHO/UNEP) World Climate Program Publications Series, No. IPCC-1/TD-W.267.

34. *United Nations Environment Program, Governing Council Decision on Global Climate Change*, UNEP GC Dec. 15/36 (May 25, 1989), *reprinted in* 28 I.L.M. 1330 (1989).

35. Ministerial Conference on Atmospheric Pollution and Climate Change, The Noordwijk Declaration on Climate Change (Nov. 1989).

is true that in the majority of cases the "softness" of the instrument corresponds to the "softness" of its contents. After all, the very nature of "soft" law lies in the fact that it is not in itself legally binding.

Although this assertion is generally correct, it remains necessary both from a conceptual and, in certain situations, a practical point of view, to distinguish clearly between the *substance* and the *instrument* — they are not necessarily always in perfect accordance with one another. Two kinds of situations present themselves in which this type of potential incoherence can be observed. First, there are cases where the content of a formally *non*-binding instrument has been so precisely defined and formulated that, aside from the precaution of using "*should*" instead of "*shall*" to determine the proper behavior for concerned States, some of its provisions could be perfectly integrated into a treaty.[36]

Moreover, it is extremely interesting to observe in practice, as the author has had the opportunity of doing in his capacity as legal advisor to the OECD Transfrontier Pollution Group (1974-80), that Member States' delegations approach the negotiation of those provisions with extreme care, just as if they were negotiating treaty provisions. Such behavior suggests that States do not view such "soft" recommendations as devoid of at least some political significance, if not, in the long term, any legal significance. In fact, for a few of these "soft" instruments, some States consider it necessary to formulate reservations to such texts, just as if they were creating formal legal obligations. The most famous example of this is the UN 1974 Charter on Economic Rights and Duties; this is also true for the OECD Council Recommendation C(74)224 on Some Principles Concerning Transfrontier Pollution.[37]

Second, an increasing number of treaty provisions can be found in which the wording used is so "soft" that it seems impossible to consider them as creating a precise obligation or burden on States parties. The number of conventions in which such evasive prescriptions are enunciated appears to be increasing: for instance, many provisions of Part XII of the 1982 UN Convention on the Law of the Sea (*e.g.*, articles 204(1) and 217(2)); the majority of the articles of the 1979 Economic Commission for Europe Convention on Long-Range Trans-

36. *See, e.g.*, *Principles Concerning Transfrontier Pollution*, OECD Council Recommendation C(74)224 Annex (1974), *reprinted in* OECD AND THE ENVIRONMENT, *supra* note 6, at 142; *UNEP Draft Principles of Conduct*, *supra* note 5.

37. The Spanish delegation made several reservations to the Council Recommendation. The reservations were, however, withdrawn after several years. *See* OECD Council Recommendation C(74)224 Annex (1974), *reprinted in* OECD AND THE ENVIRONMENT, *supra* note 6, at 144-47.

boundary Air Pollution;[38] as well as the provisions of the 1985 Vienna Convention on the Protection of the Ozone Layer.[39]

Such a situation can sometimes, if not often, be explained in light of the difficulties with which delegations have been confronted in trying to reach an agreement. This is certainly the case in the second of the last three cited examples. Another factor which explains the inclusion of "soft" provisions in the text of a treaty can, however, be identified: with regard to difficult and complex areas of concern, the protection of the ozone layer for example, States realize from the outset of negotiation that easy solutions do not exist and that too rigidly-defined obligations would only lead to inefficiency by deterring a significant number of concerned governments from ratifying the convention.

Thus, States prefer to define, by common agreement, programs of action which invite them to adopt, starting at the national level, adequate material and regulatory measures. One can assume that such a prudent strategy has been encouraged by the example furnished by the positive results often produced when States effectively take into account the guidelines proposed in some of the resolutions or recommendations defined within the framework of international organizations. One percieves, then, a sort of "soft" law "contagion" which affects the transformation of "soft" instruments into "hard" ones.

Even given the accuracy of this assertion, one must recognize that it does not simplify the task of defining the scope and nature of the "soft" law. It does, however, lead to the conclusion that the criteria used to identify "soft" law should no longer be *formal*, *i.e.*, based on the compulsory or non-compulsory character of the instrument, but instead *substantial*, *i.e.*, *dependent on the nature and specificity of the behavior requested of the State*, whether or not it is included in a legally binding instrument. To be more rigorous, if the norm is included in a non-binding instrument, it should be considered presumptive evidence of the "soft" nature of the norm; at the same time, the "hard" or "soft" nature of the obligation defined in a treaty provision should not necessarily be identified on the sole basis of the formally binding character of the legal instrument in which the concerned norm is integrated and articulated.

These observations lead to the conclusion that the identification of "soft" law, significant at least because it may potentially become

38. *United Nations Convention on Long-Range Transboundary Air Pollution*, U.N. Doc. ECE/HLM.1/R.1 (1979), *reprinted in* 18 I.L.M. 1442 (1979).

39. Vienna Convention for the Protection of the Ozone Layer, opened for signature Mar. 22, 1985, U.N. Doc. UNEP/1G.53/5/Rev. 1, *reprinted in* 26 I.L.M. 1529 (1987).

"hard" law in the near or distant future, should derive from a systematic case-by-case examination in which a variety of factors are carefully considered. These factors would include, among others: the source and origin of the text (governmental or not); the conditions, both formal and political, of its adoption; its intrinsic aptitude to become a norm of international law; and the practical reaction of States to its statement. These criteria should be applied, for example, to the various texts mentioned earlier calling for a mankind-oriented and global approach to world climate protection. In other words, one must avoid grouping texts of remote origins and character in order to demonstrate the development of an emerging "soft" rule.

III. The Legal Effect of Environmental Soft Law

Two different sets of problems must be considered with respect to a discussion of the legal impact of international environmental "soft" law. The first set of problems concerns the question of the influence of "soft" law on the general international law-making process. How and under what conditions do some "soft" norms become compulsory? The second set of problems is twofold: even before their evolution into "hard" laws, do existing "soft" regulations have any influence on the definition of the content of international law? If so, does this have any impact on the international responsibility of States for the commission of wrongful acts?

Again, it should be clearly noted that the international law of the environment is explored and used as an example here merely because it provides a fertile ground for analysis and not because it is a field in which "soft" law presents any particular theoretical or technical problems.

A. *Soft Law and General International Law*

The law-making process is a long-term process. This remains true even if the notion of "long-term" is a relative one — the prevailing conception of "long-term," as hinted by the International Court of Justice in the Continental Shelf case, is one which has tended to shorten over the last decades.[40]

As early as Roman times, jurists spoke of *leges in statu nascendi* (not to be confused with *lex ferenda*). It is sufficiently clear that the creative process of customary rules enables different heterogeneous elements to participate in the crystallization of the new custom. It be-

40. North Sea Continental Shelf (W. Ger. v. Den. and W. Ger. v. Neth.), 1969 I.C.J. 3, 42-43 (Judgment of Feb. 20).

comes equally obvious that the accumulation of recurrent resolutions can greatly contribute to the creation of such a new general customary rule. It should also be noted in this context that positive cross-references between *treaties* and *resolutions* (both types of instruments incorporating the same rule at the same time) are of real importance in this respect.

In the context of "soft" instruments, one could say, using the classical working of legal theory in regard to the creation of custom, that the cumulative enunciation of the same guideline by numerous nonbinding texts helps to express the *opinio juris* of the world community.

This last observation, although different in character, should be viewed in light of the one made in 1986 by the International Court of Justice with regard to several important resolutions adopted by the UN General Assembly: "The effect of consent to the text of such resolutions . . . may be understood as an acceptance of the validity of the rule or set of rules declared by the resolution by themselves."[41] One should certainly not systematically go that far in interpreting the frequent repetition of "soft" rules in different kinds of texts. However, taking into account the criteria outlined earlier at the end of Part I of this article, one should pay careful attention to indications of a new *opinio juris* likely to emerge among nations thanks to the frequent reiteration of certain identical principles.

This conclusion is somewhat problematic, however, if one takes into account the rather dogmatic concepts and legal categories presented by the classical theory identifying the "two elements" of customary law (practice and *opinio juris*) when analyzing the "soft" law phenomenon.[42] This classical theory has been systematized by the positivist school to explain a law-making process in which the measure and conception of time was substantially different, and where the rule of law appeared as the end product of a long and careful ripening process.

Today, even given the heterogeneity of the contemporary law-making process, it would not be completely accurate to conclude that the relative importance of these two elements has been reversed so that the voicing of *opinio juris* takes precedence over the material element of State practice.[43] It would be more consistent with the reality of this process to say that, through the channel of steadfast institutionalized

41. Military and Paramilitary Activities in and Against Nicaragua (Nicar. v. U.S.), 1986 I.C.J. 4, 100 (Merits of June 27).

42. *See* Haggenmacher, *La Doctrine des Deux Eléments du Droit Coutoumier dans la Pratique de la Cour Internationale*, 90 R.G.D.I.P. 5 (1986).

43. CHANGE AND STABILITY IN INTERNATIONAL LAW MAKING, *supra* note 1.

negotiation, State practice is modified by the constant pressure of diplomacy. In this respect, general international law-making is no longer, if it has ever effectively been, a process characterized by the explicit recognition of "general practice accepted as law."[44] As a result, "soft" law must also be viewed in light of the interaction of competing legal strategies pursued by different categories of States whose varied interests are not always considered by other States to be converging. In any event, it is evident that a substantial part of "soft" law today, in an impressionistic way, describes part of the "hard" law of tomorrow.

The normative emission of international institutions plays a catalytic role in this process. For example, one could argue convincingly that the information and consultation requirement has nearly reached the point beyond which it should be considered a customary norm. Evidence of this can be found in both the methodology and materials used by several groups of experts charged with the task of establishing draft codification articles describing the content of the general international law of the environment. Both the 1987 recommendations of the World Commission on Environment and Development Expert Group on Environmental Law[45] and the ILC draft articles on the law of non-navigational uses of international watercourses[46] provide major examples. Both drafts have been supported by reports and commentaries which both take into account and largely rely upon "soft" instruments emanating from international organizations, even if not necessarily consistently confirmed by actual and unanimous State practice.

This last element makes it difficult to identify among the codified principles the ones which already belong to *lex lata* and those which are still to be considered as *lex ferenda*. It does, however, sufficiently establish that the codifying bodies consider "soft" law at the very least to be a reliable indicator of actual trends in contemporary international environmental law-making. Rules and principles such as regular exchange of information, prior notification of planned activities capable of damaging the environment in a neighboring country, equal right of access to and non-discrimination between actual or potential victims of transfrontier pollution behind and across the frontiers, have

44. I.C.J. STATUTE art. 38.

45. WORLD COMMISSION ON ENVIRONMENT AND DEVELOPMENT, *supra* note 14.

46. In particular, see *International Law Commission: Sixth Report on the Law of the Non-Navigational Uses of International Watercourses*, U.N. Doc. A/CN.4/427 (1990)(S. McCaffrey, Special Rapporteur); *Draft Report of the International Law Commission on the Work of its Forty-Second Session*, U.N. Doc. A/CN.4/L.449 (1990).

been largely launched by "soft" instruments which are now explicitly cited and recalled as valuable materials in the codification process.

B. *Soft Law and International Responsibility*

A "soft" norm can help to define the standards of good behavior corresponding to what is nowadays to be expected from a "well-governed State" without having been necessarily consecrated as an in-force customary norm. Among those standards of good behavior which constitute the type of due diligence that can be expected from a State in the context of international cooperation are: prior consultation before enforcing a regulation or empowering a private person to undertake an activity which might create a significant risk of transfrontier pollution; early international notification of a polluting accident; due recourse to procedures of impact assessments; and non-discrimination between and equality of access for victims of both national and transfrontier pollution.[47] These and other standards of behavior were recognized in the context of a due diligence definition by the arbitrators in the famous Alabama Case.[48]

Another indirect effect of international "soft" law regulations should not be underestimated: the impact of these "soft" norms on national legislatures and national legislation as reference models which anticipate internationally-grounded State obligations emerging in the near future.

When evaluating due diligence in the context of determining State responsibility under international law, one must consider the standards established by "soft" norms, although not (or not yet) compulsory in themselves. No single one of these standards by itself, it seems, should suffice in identifying illicit State activity in instances where it is ignored. Such a deficiency should, however, create a presumption of illegality and, in instances where a number of such norms are violated, constitute evidence of an illicit act.[49]

Of course, the evaluation of compliance with such standards of "good behavior" falls within the jurisdiction of international judges or arbitrators. From the point of view of international environmental law, it is disturbing to note the absence of recent arbitral or jurisdic-

---

47. Dupuy, *Due Diligence in the International Law of Liability*, in LEGAL ASPECTS OF TRANSFRONTIER POLLUTION 369 (1977); Dupuy, *Le Fait Générateur de la Responsabilité Internationale des Etats*, 188 RECUEIL DES COURS 21 (1984).

48. In the United States, see, *e.g.*, Foreign Corrupt Practices Act of 1977, Pub. L. No. 95-213, 17 I.L.M. 214 (1978).

49. For an appraisal of international safety standards in the field of nuclear energy, see Handl, *Après Tchernobyl: Quelques Reflexions sur le Programme Legislatif Multilateral à L'Ordre du Jour*, 92 R.G.D.I.P. 5 (1988).

tional awards; States do not appear to be very keen on settling disputes in this area by entrusting them to independent third parties. Each State knows that rules of law and material situations are reversible and that a country victimized by transboundary pollution today could very well end up being the polluter of tomorrow.

Nevertheless, international standards based on "soft" law are not only available for use by international judges or arbitrators. They can also be of great help in every day inter-State diplomacy. They may also effectively be taken into account by municipal judges in evaluating the legality, with regard to international law, of any internal administrative action having had or able to have some damaging impact on the environment beyond national boundaries. Furthermore, municipal judges may take these international standards into account in order to give a correct interpretation to very generally formulated international obligations.

* * *

Albeit indirect, the legal effect of "soft" law is nevertheless real. "Soft" law is not merely a new term for an old (customary) process; it is both a sign and product of the permanent state of multilateral cooperation and competition among the heterogeneous members of the contemporary world community.

The existence of "soft" law compels us to re-evaluate the general international law-making process and, in doing so, illuminates the difficulty of explaining this phenomenon by referring solely to the classical theory of formal sources of public international law.

[10]

THE PRECAUTIONARY PRINCIPLE AS A NORM OF CUSTOMARY INTERNATIONAL LAW

Owen McIntyre* and Thomas Mosedale*

1. Introduction

In order to develop effective policies, decision-makers rely upon the best available scientific data. However, scientific uncertainty regarding, inter alia, epidemiological evidence of causal linkages between activities and impacts, thresholds at which damage becomes significant or irreversible, long-term cumulative or combined effects of pollutants has, by hindering agreement, historically impeded international lawmaking for the protection of the environment. Also, the ever increasing sophistication of scientific methodologies may, in some instances, lead to uncertainty over the nature of any scientific methodology used and data collected.[1] In order to avoid this 'paralysis of uncertainty', international instruments for environmental protection created since the 1980s have often permitted or compelled State parties to proceed on the basis of a 'precautionary' approach. This approach was pioneered in German national environmental law during the 1970s and 1980s as the principle of precautionary action or 'Vorsorgeprinzip'[2] and it is hardly surprising therefore that its first explicit inclusion in an international declaration was due to the insistence of the Federal Republic of Germany.[3]

The precautionary approach has its conceptual origins in the rejection of the assumptions inherent in the traditional 'assimilative capacity approach'.[4] This

* Faculty of Law, University of Manchester.

[1] For a taxonomic scheme for classifying the different kinds of scientific uncertainty, see V.R. Walker, 'The Siren Songs of Science: Toward a Taxonomy of Scientific Uncertainty for Decision-Makers' (1991) 23 *Connecticut Law Review* 567. See also, R.M. Peterman and M. M'Gonigle, 'Statistical Power Analysis and the Precautionary Principle' (1992) 24 *Marine Pollution Bulletin* 231–4.

[2] See, S. Boehmer-Christiansen, 'The Precautionary principle in Germany—Enabling Government' in T. O'Riordan and J. Cameron (eds), Interpreting the Precautionary Principle, (Cameron May: London, 1994) 31–60; K. von Moltke, 'The Vorsorgeprinzip in West German Environmental Policy', Royal Commission on Environmental Pollution, 12th Report, Best Practicable Environmental Option, Appendix 3, (HMSO: London, 1988).

[3] See, the 1987 London Ministerial Declaration, infra, n 19.

[4] Also referred to as the 'permissive principle', see P.J. Taylor, The Precautionary Principle—Implications for the Paris Commission (Greenpeace: London, 1988), who also criticises the basic ideas behind what he describes as the 'dump-monitor-act' logic of the assimilative capacity model. See also, A.R.D. Stebbing, 'Environmental Capacity and the Precautionary Principle', (1992) 24 *Marine Pollution Bulletin* 287–95.

 © *Oxford University Press 1997*

approach to environmental regulation was based on the assumption that science could accurately determine the assimilative capacity[5] of the environment and that, once determined, sufficient time for preventive action would remain. According to Ellen Hey, this approach is 'based on certain assumptions regarding the relationship between environment, science, technology and economics'.[6] Simply stated, the assimilative capacity approach assumes that: science can accurately predict threats to the environment; science can provide technical solutions to mitigate such threats once they have been accurately predicted; there will remain sufficient time to act; and, acting at this stage results in the most efficient utilization of scarce financial resources. Failures of this approach, with conclusive scientific proof of the detrimental effects of activities or substances coming too late, have led, on a sector by sector basis, to the adoption of a precautionary approach. Any precautionary approach entails a shift in emphasis or priority 'in favour of a bias towards safety and caution'.[7] Hey states that '[T]he concept requires that policy-makers adopt an approach which ensures that errors are made on the side of excess environmental protection' and that it 'may require preventive action before scientific proof of harm has been submitted'. Any formulation of the precautionary principle is, therefore, a 'tool for decision-making in a situation of scientific uncertainty' which effectively 'changes the role of scientific data'.[8] Put another way, it is 'a policy-making strategy' which 'addresses the manner in which policy-makers, for the purposes of protecting the environment, apply science, technology and economics'.[9] The precautionary approach is based upon an entirely new set of assumptions, including: the vulnerability of the environment; the limitations of science to accurately predict threats to the environment; and, the availability of alternative, less harmful processes and products.[10] Some commentators perceive the emergence of this approach as marking a paradigm shift in international environmental law from a predominantly economic and anthropocentric stance to a primarily eco-centric point of view.[11]

The adoption of such an approach had initially tended to be restricted to specific situations and activities associated with risks of very serious damage. Such an approach could thus be justified on the ground that any damage would be irreversible or could only be rectified at considerable cost.[12] However, its adoption in a wide variety of more recent international instruments and its elaboration in the Rio Declaration as a general guiding principle for taking action to protect the environment lend weight

[5] The capacity of relevant environmental media to tolerate disturbance due to anthropogenic inputs without unacceptable harm.

[6] E. Hey, 'The Precautionary Concept in Environmental Policy and Law: Institutionalizing Caution' (1992) 4 *Georgetown International Environmental Law Review* 303–18 at 308.

[7] D. Freestone, 'The Road to Rio: International Environmental Law After the Earth Summit', (1994) 6 *Journal of Environmental Law* 193 at 211. See also, H. Hohmann, Precautionary Legal Duties and Principles of Modern International Environmental Law, (Graham & Trotman: London, 1994) at 1–5.

[8] Freestone, ibid.

[9] Hey, supra, n 6 at 307.

[10] Ibid at 308.

[11] See Hohmann, supra, n 7 at 4–5; R.C. Earll, 'Common Sense and the Precautionary Principle—An Environmentalist's Perspective' (1992) 24 *Marine Pollution Bulletin* 182–6 at 183.

[12] For example, the precautionary action required for the protection of the ozone layer by the 1985 Vienna Convention for the protection of the Ozone Layer, 26 ILM (1987) 1529, and the 1987 Montreal Protocol on Substances that Deplete the Ozone Layer, 26 ILM (1987) 1550.

to the argument that it has crystallised into a principle of general customary international law.[13]

Even if it could be established beyond all doubt that a customary obligation existed, other uncertainties would remain. In particular, due to the fact that it has appeared in a variety of forms, the precise content of the obligation, if indeed such an elusive concept can be subject to substantive definition, remains a matter of uncertainty. Some commentators have usefully provided a minimal working definition or 'conceptual core' of the principle[14] though further questions remain concerning the principle's characteristics and means of application. This article is concerned with reviewing the status of the precautionary principle in customary international law and then speculating on the nature of the obligations imposed by the principle as a binding customary norm. The former requires an examination of international instruments and examples of State and international judicial practice which might provide evidence of the development of a customary rule. The latter requires an examination of the legal devices or procedures most commonly used to implement the precautionary principle in its many and varied guises.

2. Status of the Precautionary Principle in International Law

Differing formulations of the precautionary principle are to be found in a wide variety of international instruments. These include binding agreements and non-binding declarations, instruments of global and regional application, instruments relating to specific environmental media or activities, and instruments laying down general principles for environmental action. In seeking to establish whether the precautionary principle has developed into a rule of customary international law it is necessary to examine 'soft law' alongside 'hard law'. This is so because like 'no other area of international law [international environmental law] is influenced by such a multitude of guidelines, resolutions and other declarations', the grouping of which documents 'in the category of soft law (in contrast to hard law) does not do justice to the peculiarities of modern ways of making international environmental law'.[15] Hohmann, takes

[13] See, inter alia, P. Sands, Principles of International Environmental Law (Vol 1: Frameworks, Standards and Implementation) (Manchester University Press, 1995) at 212–13, D. Freestone, supra, n 7 at 209–15; H. Hohmann, supra, n 7 at 341–5; D. Freestone, 'The Precautionary Principle', in R. Churchill and D. Freestone (eds), International Law and Global Climate Change, (Graham & Trotman: London, 1991) 21 at 23–30; J. Cameron and J. Abouchar, 'The Status of the Precautionary Principle in International Law', in D. Freestone and E. Hey, (eds), The Precautionary Principle and International Law, (Kluwer: The Hague, 1996) 29–52 at 36–52; J. Cameron and W. Wade-Gery, 'Addressing Uncertainty: Law, Policy and the Development of the Precautionary Principle', in B. Dente (ed), Environmental Policy in Search of New Instruments, (Kluwer: The Hague, 1995) 95–142 at 110–16. More sceptical commentators include L. Gundling, 'The Status in International Law of the Principle of Precautionary Action', in D. Freestone and T. IJlstra (eds), The North Sea: Perspectives on Regional Environmental Cooperation (Special Issue of the IJECL)(Graham & Trotman: London, 1990) 23–30; G. Handl, 'Environmental Security and Global Change: the Challenge to International Law', 1 *Yearbook of International Environmental Law* (1990) at 23; A. Nollkaemper, 'The Precautionary Principle in International Environmental Law: What's New Under the Sun?', 22 *Marine Pollution Bulletin* (1991) 107–10 at 108; D. Bodansky, 'Remarks on New Developments in International Environmental Law', (1991) *Proceedings of the American Society of International Law* (85th Annual Meeting) 413–17 at 417.

[14] Three progressively more stringent formulations of the conceptual core of the precautionary principle are provided by Cameron and Wade-Gery, supra, n 13 at 100.

[15] Hohmann, supra, n 7 at 335.

the view that for the purpose of identifying customary law, State practice may be reduced to diplomatic practice where the following three criteria are fulfilled:

(1) the values at the basis of the resolutions concerned are shared by all States—and all States see the need to establish the legal rule quickly;
(2) there must be an absence of pre-existing customary law to be displaced . . .; and
(3) there should be limited evidence of (external) State practice.[16]

Hohmann sees the primary role of soft law instruments in the identification of custom as that of 'the solidifying of indicators for a documentation of the opinio juris' of States.[17] However, he also points out that 'the establishment of duties of customary law has also occurred through agreements . . . if indications exist for the formation of opinio juris, if an agreement adopts this rule, if the rule can be generalized and if it is contained in a global agreement or in at least two regional agreements of two different regions'. Therefore, 'rules of customary law initiated through declarations find their way into agreements and vice versa'.[18] It would seem appropriate therefore to examine contemporaneously the development and application of the precautionary principle through both hard law and soft law sources before going on to examine recent, high-profile examples of external State practice. For convenience, international instruments are listed in terms of the environmental sectors to which they relate and in a further category of general law-making instruments.

2.1. Marine pollution

The precautionary principle has received consistent support in instruments relating to maritime pollution and one of its earliest official expressions can be found in the Preamble to the 1984 Bremen Ministerial Declaration of the International Conference on the Protection of the North Sea which provided that States 'must not wait for proof of harmful effects before taking action'. Subsequently, the 1987 London Ministerial Declaration of the Second International Conference on the Protection of the North Sea specifically mentioned the precautionary approach in accepting that 'in order to protect the North Sea from possibly damaging effects of the most dangerous substances, a precautionary approach is necessary which may require action to control inputs of such substances even before a causal link has been established by absolutely clear scientific evidence'.[19] The participating States then gave an indication of how the principle was to be implemented by agreeing to 'accept the principle of safeguarding the marine ecosystem of the North Sea by reducing polluting emissions of substances that are persistent, toxic and liable to bio-accumulate at source by the use of the best available technology and other appropriate measures'.[20]

At the Third North Sea Conference, held at the Hague in 1990, Ministers again endorsed the principle and pledged to continue its application. According to Freestone, the inclusion of a commitment to continue to apply the principle in the Preamble to the Hague Declaration is significant because it renders all areas of the work of the

[16] Hohmann, ibid. On sources of international environmental law see J. Cameron and J. Abouchar, supra, n 13 at 32–6.
[17] Ibid at 336.
[18] Ibid at 337.
[19] Article VII. See D. Freestone, supra, n 13 at 23.
[20] Article XVI.1. See Freestone, ibid.

INSC subject to the principle.[21] A 1989 recommendation,[22] adopted by the Commission created under the 1974 Paris Convention for the Prevention of Marine Pollution from Land-based Sources, declared its support for the 'principle of precautionary action' and reproduced the text of paragraph XVI.1 of the 1987 London Declaration virtually verbatim.[23] Another recommendation passed at the same meeting emphasised the role of the application of the best available technology in giving effect to the general principle of precautionary action.[24] A subsequent recommendation[25] of the Paris Commission provided the first steps for a more concrete application of the principle by defining the best available technology for specific industrial sectors.

More recent instruments on maritime pollution have linked the concepts of prevention and precaution and have expressed the precautionary principle in more specific terms. For example, the 1992 OSPAR Convention[26] provides that preventive measures are to be taken where there are 'reasonable grounds for concern . . . even when there is no conclusive evidence of a causal relationship between inputs and their alleged effects'.[27] This provision is implemented by means of the Prior Justification Procedure of the Oslo Commission, the competent regional body under the convention, whereby substances may only be introduced if it has been indicated with an acceptable margin of uncertainty that they do not cause harm to the environment. Where this requirement is impracticable, it might be applied at the more general level of the application of the best available technology or practice.[28] The Oslo Commission's Prior Justification Procedure has been described as 'a most rigorous application of the precautionary principle',[29] in that it places on the party applying to dump industrial wastes the burden of proving 'both that there are no practical alternatives on land and that the materials cause no harm in the marine environment'.[30] The 1992 Baltic Sea Convention contains a similar formulation of the principle and provides that preventive measures are to be taken 'when there is reason to assume' that harm might be caused 'even when there is no conclusive evidence of a causal relationship between inputs and their alleged effects'.[31] In October 1989 the Contracting Parties to the Barcelona Convention for the Protection of the Mediterranean Sea against Pollution agreed 'to fully adopt the principle of precautionary approach regarding the prevention and elimination of contamination in the Mediterranean Sea area' and requested the Secretariat 'to review the Dumping Protocol . . . in order to identify any necessary amendments . . .'.[32] Also in October 1989, the Nordic Council's Conference on Pollution of the Seas agreed on

[21] Ibid at 25.

[22] PARCOM Recommendation 89/1 (1989).

[23] Freestone, supra, n 13 at 24.

[24] Ibid.

[25] PARCOM Recommendation 90/1 on the Definition of the Best Available Technology for Secondary Iron and Steel Plants. See A. Nollkaemper, supra, n 13 at 109.

[26] 1992 Paris Convention for the Protection of the Marine Environment of the North-East Atlantic; 32 ILM (1993) 1068.

[27] Art 2(2)(a).

[28] Nollkaemper, supra, n 13 at 110.

[29] Freestone, supra, n 13 at 25.

[30] Decision 89/1 on the reduction and cessation of dumping industrial wastes at sea, reproduced in Freestone and IJlstra, supra, n13 at 119.

[31] 1992 Helsinki Convention on the Protection of the Marine Environment of the Baltic Sea Area, Art 3(2). Reproduced as an appendix to P. Ehlers, 'The Helsinki Convention 1992: Improving the Baltic Sea Environment' (1993) 8 *The International Journal of Marine and Coastal Law* 191 at 215–43.

[32] Freestone, supra, n 13 at 27.

'the need for an effective precautionary approach' which would 'safeguard the marine ecosystem by, among other things, eliminating and preventing pollution emissions where there is reason to believe that damage or harmful effects are likely to be caused, even where there is inadequate or inconclusive scientific evidence to prove a causal link between emissions and effects'.[33] At the Second Meeting of the Parties to the 1983 Cartagena Convention for the Protection and Development of the Marine Environment of the Wider Caribbean Region, a proposal by Mexico that the precautionary principle be adopted as an operational principle for all the decisions of the parties failed to be adopted after US opposition.[34] However, the convention Secretariat was once again asked to prepare a report on the principle for the Parties.

A 1989 decision of the United Nations Environment Programme Governing Council stated that 'waiting for scientific proof regarding the impact of pollutants discharged into the marine environment could result in irreversible damage to the marine environment and in human suffering' and went on to recommend that all governments adopt the 'principle of precautionary action' as the basis of their policy on the prevention and elimination of marine pollution.[35] In his 1990 Report on the Law of the Sea, the UN Secretary General expressly recognized the 'considerable significance' of the principle for future action to protect the marine environment and conserve marine resources and reported that it had been 'endorsed by virtually all recent international forums'.[36] The Preparatory Commission for the United Nations Conference on Environment and Development was more specific when it identified as a priority the application of the precautionary approach, implemented through clean production methods, at the global, regional and national level, targeted at all synthetic and persistent substances that directly or indirectly enter the marine environment.[37]

2.2. Atmospheric pollution

The Preamble to the 1985 Vienna Convention[38] declared that the parties were '[M]indful . . . of the precautionary measures for the protection of the ozone layer which have already been taken at the national and international levels.' The 1987 Montreal Protocol[39] goes a little further, stating in the Preamble that the parties, though '[A]ware that measures taken to protect the ozone layer from depletion should be based on relevant scientific knowledge . . .', are '[D]etermined to protect the ozone layer by taking precautionary measures to control equitably total global emissions of substances that deplete it . . .' The Preamble to the Protocol also notes 'the precautionary measures . . . that have already been taken at national and regional levels'. The widely adopted 1992 Climate Change Convention[40] lists among its principles that 'Parties should take precautionary measures to anticipate, prevent or minimise the causes of climate change and mitigate its adverse effects.' However it qualifies this

[33] Ibid.

[34] Ibid.

[35] UNEP Governing Council Decision 15/27 (1989) on the Precautionary Approach to Marine Pollution. See P. Sands, supra, n 13 at 210.

[36] UN Doc A/45/721, 19 November 1990, 20, para 6. See Freestone, supra, n 7 at 210.

[37] Doc A/CONF 151/PC/WG II/L I. See Nollkaemper, supra, n 13 at 109.

[38] 1985 Convention for the Protection of the Ozone Layer; 26 ILM (1987) 1529.

[39] 1987 Protocol on Substances that Deplete the Ozone Layer; 26 ILM (1987) 154.

[40] 1992 United Nations Framework Convention on Climate Change; 31 ILM (1992) 849, Art 3(3).

commitment to precautionary action stating that '[W]here there are threats of serious or irreversible damage, lack of full scientific certainty should not be used as a reason for postponing such measures, taking into account that policies and measures to deal with climate change should be cost-effective so as to ensure global benefits at the lowest possible cost.'

2.3. Nature conservation

The 1995 Fish Stocks Agreement,[41] adopted by over one hundred States in August 1995, provides a high-profile example of such an instrument. Under Article 5(c), parties will be required, in establishing conservation and management measures for the high seas, to apply a precautionary approach and to implement agreed conservation and management measures when precautionary reference points are exceeded. Rules relating to the application of the precautionary approach are laid down in Article 6 with more detailed guidelines for the application of precautionary reference points contained in Annex 2 to the Agreement. Parties are also required to take scientific uncertainties into account when setting their fisheries policies.

Although the original text of the 1973 CITES Convention does not refer to the precautionary principle,[42] the State parties agreed in 1994 to apply the principle when considering proposals to amend the Appendices to the Convention which list endangered species for the purposes of the Convention. The 1994 Fort Lauderdale Resolution[43] recognises 'that by virtue of the precautionary principle, in cases of uncertainty, the Parties shall act in the best interest of the conservation of the species when considering proposals for amendment of Appendices I and II' and resolves 'that when considering any proposal to amend Appendix I or II the Parties shall apply the precautionary principle so that scientific uncertainty should not be used as a reason for failing to act in the best interest of the conservation of the species'. Annex 4 to the 1994 Resolution details relevant precautionary measures including, for example, a list of specific criteria, at least one of which must be satisfied before the transfer of a species from Appendix I to Appendix II can be considered. Annex 4 also details review procedures which are to apply when a species is transferred to Appendix II.

[41] Agreement for the Implementation of the Provisions of the United Nations Convention on the Law of the Sea of 10 December 1982 Relating to the Conservation and Management of Straddling Fish Stocks and Highly Migratory Fish Stocks. See G. Rose and G. Paleokrassis, 'Compliance with International Environmental Obligations: A Case Study of the International Whaling Commission' in J. Cameron, J. Werksman and P. Roderick (eds), Improving Compliance with International Environmental Law (Earthscan Publications: London, 1996) at 328. See generally, concerning the application of the precautionary principle to fisheries management, J. Cooke and M. Earle, 'Towards a Precautionary Approach to Fisheries Management' (1993) 2 *Review of European Community and International Environmental Law* No 3, 252–9; S.M. Garcia, 'The Precautionary Principle: Its Implications in Capture Fisheries Management' (1994) 22 *Ocean and Coastal Management* 99–125; G.J. Hewison, 'The Precautionary Approach to Fisheries Management: An Environmental Perspective' (1996) 11 *International Journal of Marine and Coastal Law* No 3, 301–32.

[42] 1973 Convention on International Trade in Endangered Species of Wild Fauna and Flora; 993 UNTS 243. A precautionary approach, it may be argued, has always been implicit in the Convention, particularly in relation to Appendix II which aims to regulate trade in species that may become endangered before they become so (see Article II(2)(a)), and in the 1976 'Berne Criteria' for listing species in the appendices (Resolution Conf 1.1: 'Criteria for the addition of species and other taxa to Appendices I and II and for the transfer of species and other taxa between Appendix II and Appendix I; and Resolution Conf 1.2: Criteria for the deletion of species and other taxa from Appendices I and II (both now repealed)).

[43] Resolution of the Conference of the Parties: Criteria for Amendment of Appendices I and II, agreed at the Ninth Meeting of the Conference of the Parties, Fort Lauderdale (US), 7–18 November 1994.

The 1992 Biodiversity Convention[44] does not expressly apply or refer to the principle but its Preamble states that the contracting parties are '[A]ware of the general lack of information and knowledge regarding biological diversity' and notes that 'where there is a threat of significant reduction or loss of biological diversity, lack of full scientific certainty should not be used as a reason for postponing measures to avoid or minimize such a threat.'

Birnie and Boyle cite the imposition of a moratorium on commercial whaling under the 1946 Whaling Convention,[45] by the International Whaling Commission (IWC), as an application in a wildlife context of the precautionary principle.[46] Certainly the Revised Management Procedure developed by the IWC Scientific Committee is a clear example of a precautionary mechanism for determining quota sizes.[47]

2.4. Miscellaneous

The 1991 Bamako Convention,[48] concerning hazardous wastes in Africa, requires State parties to implement the precautionary principle in two ways, by preventing the release of certain substances into the environment and by cooperating in the application of clean technology. Article 4(3)(f) provides that they should adopt and implement '. . . the preventive, precautionary approach to pollution which entails, inter alia, preventing the release into the environment of substances which may cause harm to humans or the environment without waiting for scientific proof regarding such harm. The parties shall cooperate with each other in taking the appropriate measures to implement the precautionary principle to pollution prevention through the application of clean production methods, rather than the pursuit of a permissible emissions approach based on assimilative capacity assumptions'. The Bamako Convention was adopted by the representatives of 51 African States.

A 1990 UNEP Governing Council Decision[49] on a Comprehensive approach to Hazardous Waste had earlier advocated the latter approach and urged governments to consider clean production methods as a means of implementing the precautionary principle.[50] The Governing Council noted that 'numerous international forums' had recognized the risks involved in 'waiting for conclusive scientific proof regarding the impact of contaminants entering the environment' as well as the recent adoption of an 'environment protection and enhancement approach based on precautionary, preventative action' by some nine other forums.[51]

[44] 1992 United Nations Convention on Biological Diversity; 31 ILM (1992) 822.

[45] 1946 International Convention for the Regulation of Whaling; 161 UNTS 72.

[46] P. Birnie and A. Boyle, International Law and the Environment (Clarendon: Oxford, 1992) at 455.

[47] IWC [1994] 'Annex H: The Revised Management Procedure [RMP] for Baleen Whales' *Rep Int Whal Commn* 44, 145–52, see also e.g., G.P. Donavan, 'The International Whaling Convention and the Revised Management Procedure' paper presented at Conference on Responsible Wildlife Resource Management held by European Parliament, Brussels, 29–30 March 1993, and reprinted in High North Alliance (1995) 'Additional Essays on Whales and Man' High North Alliance, Reine i Lofoten.

[48] 1991 Convention on the Ban of Import into Africa and the Control of Transboundary Movement and Management of Hazardous Wastes within Africa; 30 ILM (1991) 775.

[49] Decision SS 11/4 B (1990), 20 EPL (1990) at 157.

[50] See Birnie and Boyle, supra, n 47.

[51] UN General Assembly. Official Records: Forty-fifth Session, Supplement No 25 (A/45/25). See Freestone, supra, n 13 at 28.

The 1992 ECE Watercourses Convention[52] stipulates that, in taking all appropriate measures to prevent, control and reduce any transboundary impact, State parties shall be guided by, inter alia, '[T]he precautionary principle, by virtue of which action to avoid the potential transboundary impact of the release of hazardous substances shall not be postponed on the ground that scientific research has not fully proved a causal link between those substances, on the one hand, and the potential transboundary impact, on the other hand.'[53] Again, this formulation of the principle focuses on controlling the release (or the impact of release) of certain substances.

2.5. General international law-making

The principle has also been declared a general principle to guide the development of international environmental law. Economic Commission for Europe (ECE) ministers, representing 34 countries, stated in the 1990 Bergen Ministerial Declaration on Sustainable Development in the ECE Region,[54] that '[I]n order to achieve sustainable development, policies must be based on the precautionary principle. Environmental measures must anticipate, prevent and attack the causes of environmental degradation. Where there are threats of serious or irreversible damage, lack of full scientific certainty should not be used as a reason for postponing measures to prevent environmental degradation.'[55] In a 'Joint Agenda for Action', appended to the Declaration, the ministers gave notice of a commitment to Sustainable Industrial Activity which 'should be based on taking precautionary and preventative measures'.[56]

The 1990 Bangkok Declaration on Environmentally Sound and Sustainable Development in Asia and the Pacific, issued by a Ministerial Conference on the Environment held by the UN Economic and Social Commission for Asia and the Pacific (ESCAP) stated that ESCAP ministers '[B]elieve that, in order to achieve sustainable development, policies must be based on the precautionary principle'.[57] It was also endorsed by the OECD Environment Committee meeting at ministerial level in January 1991. In a short period of time the principle has received widespread and consistent support among the international community as a general principle of international environmental law.

The principle was incorporated into the 1992 Rio Declaration on Environment and Development as Principle 15, which states:

> In order to protect the environment, the precautionary approach shall be widely applied by States according to their capabilities. Where there are threats of serious or irreversible damage, lack of full scientific certainty shall not be used as a reason for postponing cost-effective measures to prevent environmental degradation.

[52] 1992 Convention on the Protection and Use of Transboundary Watercourses an International Lakes, 31 ILM (1992) 1312.

[53] Article 2(5)(a).

[54] Bergen Ministerial Declaration on Sustainable Development in the ECE Region, in Action for a Common Future, Report on the Regional ,Conference at Ministerial Level on the Follow-up to the Report of the World Commission on Environment and Development in the ECE Region (Norway Ministry of Environment, 1990). Reprinted in 20 *Environmental Policy & Law* 100 (1990).

[55] Para 7, Bergen Declaration.

[56] Reproduced in 20 EPL (1990) at 103.

[57] Report of the UN ESCAP Ministerial Conference on the Environment, Bangkok, 15–16 October 1990, Appendix 2 at 8–10. See D. Freestone, supra, n 13 at 29–30.

Its inclusion in the Rio Declaration is significant as it could be argued to mark the elevation of the principle to the status of a core principle of international environmental law-making. According to Freestone, '[Perhaps] the most significant way in which the Rio process may have contributed to the development of international environmental law is through the crystallization of legal principles.'[58] However, this formulation may limit the principle's application in terms of the capabilities of States and suggests that measures required under the principle would have to satisfy a cost-effectiveness test.

All European Community law-making on the environment must now be based on the precautionary principle. The 1992 Treaty on European Union (TEU) amended Article 130R(2) of the Treaty of Rome[59] to include the requirement that 'Community policy on the environment . . . shall be based on the precautionary principle . . .'. It has been added to several other guiding principles of Community law-making upon which Community policy on the environment is to be based under Article 130R(2), including the polluter pays principle, the preventative principle and the principle of integration. However, as with the other guiding principles, the precautionary principle is not defined anywhere in the Treaty with the result that its content remains unclear and its justiciability uncertain. Any obligation to act on the basis of the precautionary principle applies only to measures taken by the Community and cannot bind Member States.[60] Indeed there is even some doubt as to whether the guiding principles contained in Article 130R(2) could bind the Community institutions in the exercise of their environmental powers. In the *Peralta* case, the European Court of Justice stated that 'Article 130R confines itself to defining the general objectives of the Community in environmental matters. The responsibility for deciding upon the action to be taken is entrusted to the Council by Article 130S'.[61] Some insight into the meaning of the precautionary principle in EC law was recently provided by Commissioner Bjerregaard in an answer to a question in the European Parliament.[62] Commenting on the proposed IPPC Directive, the Commissioner stated that the proposal, and in particular Article 8, is a 'direct application' of the precautionary principle as laid down in the Treaty, since it requires control through BAT when full information on environmental impacts is not available. However, the definition of BAT agreed in the proposed Directive might be considered to be little different from BATNEEC[63] as it allows the choice of technology to be influenced considerably by economic factors and local conditions.[64] The Environment Commissioner also stated that the precautionary principle calls for risk management, based on probable rather than potential effect and pointed out that current risk assessment procedures for chemicals are contained in Technical Guidance Documents and in Directive 93/67 on testing new chemicals and Regulation 1488/94 on testing existing substances. Haigh et al, point out that, although the Commissioner's comments are not decisive in determining the meaning of the precautionary principle in EC law, they appear to place it closer to the 'weak'

58 Freestone, supra, n 7 at 209.

59 Article 130R, S & T, which first outlined an environmental policy for the Community, had been added to the original Treaty of Rome by means the 1986 Single European Act, 25 ILM (1986) 503.

60 See *R v Secretary of State for Trade and Industry ex parte Duddridge*. Reported in (1995) 7 *Journal of Environmental Law* 224–38; 1 *Environmental Judicial Review Bulletin* Issue 2, February 1995, 18–22.

61 Case C-379/92, at para 57.

62 (OJ C91 27.3.96). See Nigel Haigh et al, 'Current Survey', 4 *Env Liability* (1996), CS55.

63 'Best Available Techniques Not Entailing Excessive Cost'.

64 Haigh et al, supra, n 62.

end of the scale of possible interpretations. The Community institutions have in the past adopted measures which would appear to apply quite a strict precautionary approach. For example, Directive 86/280 provides that Member States are only allowed to grant licenses to new industrial plants which apply standards which accord with the best available technology. Also, two 1990 directives on genetically modified organisms (GMOs) set down a range of precautionary procedures to be followed in the contained use and deliberate dissemination of GMOs into the environment.[65]

Although few would argue that Community practice constitutes a source of general customary international law per se, it may nevertheless prove useful as an indicator of EC Member State practice and opinio juris. As Weeramantry J points out in his recent ICJ dissenting opinion, '[T]he provision in the Maastricht Treaty, incorporating the precautionary principle as the basis of European Community policy on the environment (Article 130r(2)) would lead one to expect that the principle thus applicable to Europe would apply also to European activity in other global theatres.'[66]

2.6. State practice and judicial opinion

In a work of this scope no attempt can be made to examine State practice in this area comprehensively. In particular, it is not possible to catalogue the number of states that have expressly incorporated the precautionary principle their domestic environmental law.[67] However a few recent examples of high-profile State reliance on the principle may easily be examined. Before the International Court of Justice, the principle has been relied upon by both Hungary, in its dispute with Slovakia over the Gabcikovo-Nagymaros project ('the *Danube Dams*' case), and by New Zealand in its case concerning French underground nuclear tests.

In the original application by Hungary to the ICJ, against what was then the Czech and Slovak Republic,[68] the precautionary principle is directly relied upon in paragraph 31, which states:

> States shall take precautionary measures to anticipate, prevent or minimise damage to their transboundary resources and mitigate adverse effects. Where there are threats of serious or irreversible damage, lack of full scientific certainty shall not be used as a reason for postponing such measures. Art. 2, paragraph 5[a] of the Convention on the Protection and Use of Transboundary Watercourses and International Lakes, signed in Helsinki on 17 March 1992, as well

[65] Directive 90/219, on the contained use of genetically modified micro-organisms, OJ L117/1 (1990); Directive 90/220, on the deliberate release into the environment of genetically modified organisms, OJ L117/15 (1990). See Cameron and Wade-Gery, supra, n 13 at 97.

[66] Infra, n 69 at 344.

[67] The principle may be argued to have evolved as part of German environmental law, quite separately from or prior to its emergence in international law; see e.g., S. Boehmer-Christiansen, supra, n 2, 31–60; and, Hohmann, supra. n 7 at 4–5. For a survey of examples of precautionary concepts in State environmental law and policy, see Cameron and Abouchar, supra, n 13 at 38–40. Regarding States with a legal system developed from the common law, perhaps the clearest example of the incorporation of the principle into domestic policy making, is in the case of Australia, where it is declared it should inform environmental policy making and programme implementation, under section 3(5)(1), of the Intergovernmental Agreement on the Environment, signed 1 May 1992, between federal, state and local government. The Agreement in particular states that the principle requires evaluation to avoid, wherever practicable, serious or irreversible environmental damage, and assessment of the risk-weighted consequences of various options.

[68] *Application of the Republic of Hungary v The Czech and Slovak Republic on the Diversion of the Danube River* reproduced in part in P. Sands, R. Tarasofsky and M. Weiss (eds), Principles of International Environment Law, Volume IIA: Documents in International Environmental Law, (MUP: Manchester, 1994) at 693–8.

as the IUCN Draft Art. 6 and Bruntland Report, Art. 10, provide support for the obligation in general international law to apply the precautionary principle to protect a transboundary resource . . .

Hungary perceives the precautionary principle as a link between what can be described as the principle of cooperation and the principle establishing the responsibility of States not to cause transboundary environmental damage. The former principle, set out in the *Lac Lanoux* decision, Article 12 of the 1991 ILC Draft Articles on the Law of the Non-Navigational Uses of International Watercourses, and, Article 3 of the Espoo convention, (which Hungary argues represents general international law in relation to dams), requires States proposing measures which may have an appreciable adverse transboundary effect to notify other potentially affected states, to share available technical data and information, and to consult and negotiate with them in good faith. It is however for the State that is being notified to evaluate the possible effects of the planned measures, and to respond to the notifying State with their findings. The latter principle of State responsibility for transboundary environmental damage, is equally clearly established as a customary international norm, appearing in Principle 21 of the Stockholm Declaration and Principle 2 of the Rio Declaration, where it is linked with the principle of State sovereignty over natural resources. Both principles are, however, in their usual formulations, underpinned by the principle of 'preventive action', i.e. a State is not only responsible for and obliged to cooperate with regard to transboundary environmental damage, but must also seek to prevent, or otherwise reduce, limit or control such damage.

In its request to the Court concerning the French nuclear tests,[69] the Court noted that New Zealand contended:

. . . that France's conduct is illegal in that it causes, or is likely to cause, the introduction into the maritime environment of radioactive material, France being under an obligation, before carrying out its new underground nuclear tests, to provide evidence that they will not result in the introduction of such material to that environment, in accordance with the 'precautionary principle' very widely accepted in contemporary international law;[70]

While the majority in the Court dismissed New Zealand's request without the need to examine the substance of its case, the three dissenting judges did go on to find that had the Court been able to hear it, New Zealand had raised a prima facie case. Of these, Koroma is the most cautious, stating only that 'there is probably a duty not to cause gross or serious damage which can reasonably be avoided . . .'.[71] He does however consider that New Zealand had done enough to establish a prima facie case, by indicating that there was growing scientific evidence 'that contamination of the marine environment is a real risk' arising from the underground tests. Palmer concludes that both the precautionary principle, and a more specific requirement for an environmental impact assessment to be carried out 'where activities may have a significant effect on the environment' may now be a principle of customary international law

[69] *Request for an Examination of the Situation in Accordance with Paragraph 63 of the Court's judgment of 20 December 1974 in* Nuclear Tests [New Zealand v France], Order 22 IX 95, ICJ Rep [1995] 288. See also M.C.R. Craven, 'New Zealand's Request for an Examination of the Situation in Accordance with Paragraph 63 of the Courts judgment of 20 December 1974 in *Nuclear Tests [New Zealand v. France]*, Order of 22 September 1995' 45 ICLQ [1996] 725–34, for a summary of the case.

[70] Para 5, ibid at 290. See also paras 34 and 35 ibid.

[71] Dissenting opinion Koroma, idem at 378.

relating to the environment.[72] As Palmer notes, it is obviously impossible for the Court to reach firm conclusions concerning this as it had not heard counter arguments to the proposition that these obligations constitute norms of customary international law, France having not addressed these points during the preliminary submissions made prior to the case being dismissed. Weeramantry however states that the precautionary principle, (which he notes is gaining increasing support as part of the international law of the environment), is a necessary response to an evidential problem clearly illustrated by this case. Proving that irreversible environmental damage is likely to arise from any given activity is very difficult for a claimant to prove as most existing information is likely to be in the possession of those seeking to carry out that activity. New Zealand had been able to place some relevant information before the Court, but it was France who was in possession of the actual information concerning the issues raised.[73] On the basis of the information before the Court, Weeramantry concluded that there was a *prima facie* requirement for an environmental impact assessment according to the current state of international environmental law.[74] The requirement for an environmental impact assessment is ancillary to the precautionary principle. Weeramantry goes on to consider whether New Zealand has established a prima facie case that the dangers raised before the Court in 1973, i.e. breach of the right of all members of the international community to be free of nuclear tests giving rise to radioactive fallout and to be preserved from unjustified radioactive contamination of the environment,[75] were now present again. He argues that there is a sufficiently well established principle of international law for the Court to act upon:

> under which, where environmental damage of any sort is threatened, the burden of proving that it will not produce the damaging consequences complained of is placed upon the author of that design. In this view of the matter, the Court would hold that the environmental damage New Zealand complains of is prima facie established in the absence of proof by France that the proposed nuclear tests are environmentally safe.[76]

Clearly Weeramantry considers that it would be for France to provide evidence to prove that the concerns raised are groundless—a task which he suggests might prove very onerous. In dealing with the question of whether the test site is a safe repository for the resulting radioactivity, able to prevent it entering the marine environment and human food chain, he notes:

> It may be that France has material with which it can satisfy the Court on that issue, but no such material has been offered. Having regard to the course of geological events, a guarantee of stability of such an island formation for hundreds of thousands of years does not seem within the bounds of likelihood or possibility.[77]

The precautionary principle has also been relied upon by the Irish government in another case involving the risk of radioactive material entering the marine environment. Ireland has made a submission to a public inquiry in the United Kingdom concerning an application to construct a facility to test the suitability of an area on

[72] Dissenting opinion Palmer, idem at 412.
[73] Dissenting opinion Weeramantry, idem at 342–4.
[74] Ibid at 345.
[75] *Nuclear Tests [New Zealand v. France] [Interim Protection]* ICJ Rep [1973] 135 at 139.
[76] Supra, n 69 at 348.
[77] Ibid at 357.

the coast of Cumbria, adjoining the Irish Sea, for suitability as a storage site for nuclear waste—the so-called 'NIREX case'.[78] Ireland argues that the principle imposes duties on the British government in relation to the application. In particular, the principle is raised in relation to three specific points. First, it is argued that the principle requires that all non-coastal sites, (where any leakage can be more easily contained and where transboundary pollution is less likely), should be investigated fully and their limitations as a storage site demonstrated before any coastal site is considered. Secondly, the lack of any evidence of consideration being given to the possible impact of the proposed development on the environment, and on the marine environment in particular, is cited as indicative of the principle not being taken into account. Finally, it is argued that the precautionary principle has shifted the burden of proof, requiring the proponents of the scheme to prove the absence of risk, rather than its opponents to demonstrate risk. It is contended, therefore, that it is only necessary for the Irish government to point out the 'mere possibility of adverse consequences to Ireland', arising from the proposed development. Thereafter it is for the applicant company, and ultimately the British government, to show there would be no contamination of the marine environment, which, Ireland contends, they have failed to do.[79] Ireland has also made submissions concerning the need for a thorough environmental impact assessment process and for the availability to the public of information concerning alternative sites, but here reliance was naturally placed primarily on European Community legislation, without the need to rely on international customary norms.

Interestingly, in the recent controversy over the industrial fishing of sand eels in the North Sea by Danish fishermen, Tony Baldry MP, the United Kingdom Minister for Fisheries, contended, in a television news report,[80] that Denmark was bound to apply the precautionary principle in regulating the exploitation of marine living resources by its nationals.

By raising the precautionary principle, Hungary, New Zealand and Ireland are each seeking to emphasise the potential dangers of the offending activities, including those dangers which are less obvious. However, at the same time they are also seeking to shift the responsibility for identifying all these potential dangers to those States wishing to carry out the activity. It is those seeking to carry out an activity who are being asked to justify themselves. Whereas *Lac Lanoux*[81] was concerned with the direct detrimental economic effects suffered by one State because of an activity carried out by another, effects which are easier for the affected State to identify and quantify, the above mentioned claims do not relate to economic loss, but to environmental damage. These States are arguing that their right to an environment unaffected by the detrimental effects of activities in another State is being infringed. However, they each contend that the potential detrimental effects are so many and so diverse that it cannot be for them to catalogue them all. Instead, they argue that it is for the State seeking

[78] *In the Matter of the Public Inquiry concerning an Appeal by the United Kingdom NIREX Ltd concerning the Construction of a Rock Characterisation Facility at Longlands Farm, Gosforth, Cumbria: Statement on Behalf of the Minister of State at the Department of Transport, Energy and Communications, Dublin, Ireland*, made by Professor Elihu Lauterpacht CBE QC; 12 January 1996,['the Irish statement'] paras 96–100.

[79] Ibid, paragraph 6 of the Conclusions.

[80] Report on Channel 4 News, 7.00 pm, 10 June 1996.

[81] *Lac Lanoux Arbitration (Spain v France)* 16 November 1957, 24 ILR [1957] 101; [1959] 53 AJIL 156. See Sands et al, Vol IIA, supra, n 68 at 615.

to expose them to the risk of environmental damage to justify its actions and have in place safeguards and mechanisms capable to protecting their interests. Not only are Slovakia, France and the United Kingdom being asked to justify their proposed actions, they are also expected to have in place mechanisms in their decision-making systems capable of anticipating and minimising risks to the environment beyond their jurisdictions.

Opinion remains divided as to whether the precautionary principle may have crystallised into a binding norm of customary international law. However, the prevalence of the principle in recent environmental treaties, declarations and resolutions as well as its inclusion in the Rio Declaration and the UNCED treaties suggests that it may indeed have attained this status. Most recent commentators concur, though often for different reasons, that it has done so. For example, Freestone cites, in support of the principle as a customary rule, earlier State practice which implicitly employed the precautionary principle such as the 1982 moratorium on commercial whaling imposed by the International Whaling Commission.[82] He also counters the argument that it could not constitute a rule of customary international law by reason of its substantive uncertainty by comparing it to the principle of self-determination which, despite a lack of clarity as to its content, is widely accepted in international law. Elsewhere he emphasises the endorsement of the principle in treaty texts and other instruments 'by the representatives of an overwhelming majority of States'.[83] Hohmann relies on the significance of 'soft-law' and diplomatic State practice in the area of international environmental law, due, in particular, to the dearth of external State practice in the area.[84] Cameron and Abouchar rely on statements of the sources of international law which are somewhat wider and more flexible than Article 38(1) of the Statute of the International Court of Justice, including Section 102 of the 1987 American Law Institute (Third) Restatement on International Law and the 1989 International Law Commission Draft Articles on State Responsibility, Part 2, Article 5(1), in endorsing the principle.[85] In addition, they allude to Brownlie's very comprehensive list of sources which can provide evidence of State practice.[86] Sands appears to cautiously support the argument that the principle's elaboration in the Rio Declaration and the Climate Change and Biodiversity Conventions provide sufficient evidence of State practice to establish the principle as custom.[87] It should also be pointed out that those authors who have staunchly resisted attributing normative status to the principle have mostly done so prior to 1992 and the UNCED process.[88] This level of academic support, coupled with recent State practice and ICJ commentary, would appear to conclusively endorse the principle's status as a norm of customary international law.

82 Achieved by amending the Schedule under Article V of the Convention so that 'catch limits for the killing for commercial purposes of whales from all stocks . . . thereafter shall be zero'. See Freestone, supra, n 7 at 213.

83 Freestone, supra, n 13 at 30.

84 Hohmann, supra, n 7 at 335–6.

85 Supra, n 13 at 33.

86 Ibid at 35–6. See I. Brownlie, Principles of Public International Law, 4th edn, (Clarendon: Oxford, 1990) at 5.

87 Supra, n 13 at 212–13.

88 See Gundling (1990), Handle (1990), Nollkaemper (1991) and Bodansky (1991), supra, n 13. However, Gundling, reviewing H. Hohmann, 'Precautionary Legal Duties . . .', in 1994 appears to have maintained his scepticism, see Handl (ed) 4 *Yearbook of International Environmental Law* (1994) 642–5 at 644.

3. Content of the Precautionary Principle

It should be obvious from an examination of the various formulations of the principle listed above that there is little common understanding of its substantive content or agreement on its theoretical origins in law.[89] However, it is contended that this lack of consistency does not detract from the principle's usefulness or from the likelihood of it enjoying the status of a norm of customary international law. It would appear that the principle can be implemented in a variety of ways and that, in order to be effective, conventional interpretations should include detailed formal implementing measures.[90] Some authors have attempted to provide convenient definitions of the principle[91] which are useful as a starting point but tell us little of its practical application or, therefore, of its implications for decision-makers. In attempting to attribute common characteristics to the principle as it appears in customary international law, it is necessary to examine the means by which States have sought to have it applied, either in the course of disputes, in 'soft law' statements on its implementation or by means of formal conventional implementing measures.

In attempting to construct a definition of the precautionary principle as a tool of decision-making, Hey identifies those general characteristics common to its many applications. She states that in order to ensure that lack of scientific certainty shall not be used as a reason for deferring measures to enhance the quality of the environment, the principle dictates that:

(1) clean production methods, best available technology and best environmental practices must be applied;
(2) comprehensive methods of environmental and economic assessment must be used in deciding upon measures to enhance the quality of the environment;
(3) research, particularly scientific and economic research that contributes to a better understanding of the long-term options available, must be stimulated; and
(4) legal, administrative and technical procedures that facilitate the implementation of this approach must be applied and, where not available, developed.[92]

The first three characteristics identified by Hey would appear to be the most appropriate and commonly utilised means of applying the principle in customary international law. Obligations, of one form or another, relating to the application of clean production methods or the setting of precautionary standards are almost always associated with the application of the precautionary principle in international instruments[93] as are precautionary environmental assessment procedures to assess planned projects, policies and measures.[94] Similarly, practically all formulations of the principle contain ancillary informational requirements. The application and development of legal,

[89] For example, Nollkaemper perceives the principle as having developed from the so-called 'no substantial harm principle', supra, n 13 at 108, while Hohmann sees it as ancillary to the goal of "intergenerational equity', supra, n 7 at 4–5, 11.
[90] For example, in relation to nature conservation treaties, see the 1995 Fish Stocks Agreement, supra, n 41, and the 1994 (CITES) Fort Lauderdale Resolution, supra, n 43.
[91] See, for example, Cameron and Wade-Gery, supra, n 13 at 100.
[92] Hey, supra, n 6 at 311.
[93] For example, the 1991 Bamako Convention, Art 4(3)(f), supra, n 48.
[94] For example, Article 17 of the EC Waste Water Treatment Directive requires that Member States establish a programme for implementing the Directive and report thereon to the Commission which subsequently reviews and assesses the information submitted and publishes its findings; Directive of the European Community on Municipal Waste Water Treatment, 21 May 1991, OJ (L 135) 40. See Hey, supra, n 6 at 315.

administrative and technical procedures is necessary to demonstrate compliance with the precautionary principle, in effect, to apply Hey's first three characteristics which comprise the substantive core of the principle, as enumerated to date. In the remainder of this article, the authors will briefly examine selected examples of the application of such precautionary standards, assessment procedures and informational requirements.

3.1. Precautionary standards

The underlying standard inherent to the precautionary principle is that unnecessary environmental change should be avoided, as it is perceived that the eventual effects of any particular change cannot be fully anticipated. However, human activity is bound to have some environmental impacts. Therefore, the standard appears to be, particularly in relation to those activities potentially having the greatest impact, that their effect should be minimised. This involves not only ensuring that their anticipated effect is minimised, but also that the risk of unanticipated effects is minimised. The most easily identifiable standards are those relating to process, and, in particular, variations on the theme of 'best available technology' (BAT). However, process standards are predominantly used in international instruments relating to the UN ECE area and to the North Atlantic and surrounding seas, including, the OSPAR Convention,[95] the Baltic Convention,[96] the Transboundary Watercourses Convention[97] and the 1979 LRTAP Convention and Protocols.[98] That process standards should predominate in this region is not surprising as States situated here are most affected by emission based pollution and are best able to afford the best technical solutions. The Bamako Convention on Hazardous Waste[99] however, refers to 'clean production methods' in relation to adopting the precautionary principle. The reference in the Climate Change Convention to the need to cooperate in 'the development, application and diffusion, including transfer, of technologies, practices and processes to control, reduce or prevent'[100] climate change, is a recognition that the best available technology is not 'available' to most developing States but needs to be made so if the problem is to be tackled.

References to 'clean production methods, best available technology and best environmental practice' are, however, of less immediate relevance to living resources. They appear to be specific to the emission of human generated material into the natural environment, rather than, as is the case with living resources, the removal of material from the environment, directly or indirectly, by human activity. However, it can be argued that what is at issue here is the need for any human activity impacting on such resources to be carried out in such a way as to minimise that impact, and,

[95] Article 2(3)(b)(ii) refers to the application of 'best available techniques and best environmental practice as so defined, including, where appropriate, clean technology'. Criteria for defining both the former terms being set out in Appendix I, supra, n 26.

[96] Article 23(3) and Annex II refer to 'best available technology', supra, n 31.

[97] Article 3(1) refers to 'low- and non-waste technology', 'best available technology' and 'best environmental practices', supra, n 52.

[98] Article 6 refers to 'best available technology which is economically feasible and low- and non-waste technology', 18 ILM 1442 (1979), while Article 2(2)(a) of the 1988 Nitrogen Oxides Protocol refers to 'best available technology which is economically feasible', UN Doc ECE/EB AIR/21, as does Article 3(3) of the 1991 Volatile Organic Compounds Protocol, UN Doc ECE/EB AIR/30.

[99] Supra, n 48.

[100] Article 4(1)(c), supra, n 40.

in particular, to minimise its potential for unplanned 'collateral' effects. Therefore, harvesting techniques should be chosen that have the minimal effect on non-target species and habitat.[101] Such measures could be argued to be as much preventive as precautionary in nature, but given that uncertainties concerning collateral effects are likely to be even greater than those concerning direct effects, they can be seen to be precautionary.

3.2. Precautionary assessment

Fundamental to the application of the precautionary principle, is the need for anticipation and assessment of the possible outcomes of any planned action. The system of Prior Informed Consent is the basis of the application of the principle under the 1992 OSPAR Convention.[102] Requirements to carry out EIA exist in international environment law separately from the precautionary principle, in particular in relation to anticipating transboundary effects of new developments[103] and those impacting upon global commons.[104] Both the Climate Change[105] and Biodiversity Conventions[106] introduce, albeit relatively weak, requirements for EIA in relation not only to specific projects, but also in relation to a broader range of state policies, programmes and actions. The link between carrying out Environmental Impact Assessments [EIAs] and the precautionary principle was emphasised by Weeramantry and Palmer in the *Nuclear Tests Application* case.[107] Palmer, in his opinion, cites Principle 17[108] of the Rio Declaration, concerning EIA, immediately after Principle 15, in which the precautionary principle is elaborated. Indeed, in each of the examples of external State practice cited above, Hungary, New Zealand and Ireland have argued that because the burden of proof rests with the State wishing to carry out a potentially harmful activity, that State should, if it wishes to claim that its actions do not present an unacceptable risk of environmental harm, provide an appropriately rigorous EIA by way of evidence.

[101] See, for example, UNGA Res 46/215 on Large-Scale Pelagic Drift-Net Fishing and its Impact on the Living Marine Resources of the World's Oceans and Seas, 20 December 1991, (UN Doc A/46/645/Add 6), Sands et al, Vol IIA, supra, n 68 at 991. Whilst not referring specifically to the precautionary principle, this resolution appears essentially to be a precautionary measure, as it might be argued is Article 5(e), 1995 Fish Stocks Agreement, supra, n 41.

[102] Supra, n 26.

[103] See, for example, Article 6, Nordic Environmental Protection Convention, 13 ILM (1974) at 511; Article 14(1), ASEAN Agreement on Nature and Natural Resources 1985, (not yet in force), Sands et al, Vol IIA, 958; UN ECE Convention on Environmental Impact Assessment in a Transboundary Context 1991 ('the Espoo Convention')(not in force), 30 ILM [1991] 802, Sands et al, Vol IIB, 1332; Art 4(4) and Annex III, UN ECE Convention on the Transboundary Effects of Industrial Accidents 1992, (not in force) 31 ILM (1992) 330, Sands et al., Vol. IIB 1351; and, Art 3(1)(h), UN ECE Convention on the Protection and Use of Transboundary Watercourses and International Lakes 1992, (not in force) Sands et al, Vol IIA 673.

[104] See Art XV(2)(d), Convention on the Conservation of Antarctic Marine Living Resources 1980, 19 ILM (1980) 841, Sands et al, Vol IIB, 1646; Art 206, UNCLOS 1982, 21 ILM (1982) 1261; Sands et al, Vol IIA, 352; Arts 2(1)(a) and 4, Convention on the Regulation of Antarctic Mineral Resource Activity 1988, not in force, 27 ILM (1988) 859, Sands et al, Vol IIB, 1662; and, Art 8 and Annex 1, Protocol on Environmental Protection to the Antarctic Treaty 1991, not in force, Sands et al, Vol IIB, 1592.

[105] Art 4(1)(f), 31 ILM [1992] 849, Sands et al, Vol IIA, 248.

[106] Art 14(1)(a), 31 ILM [1992] 822, Sands et al, Vol IIA, 845.

[107] Supra, n 69.

[108] Principle 17 states: 'Environmental impact assessment, as a national instrument, shall be undertaken for proposed activities that are likely to have a significant adverse impact on the environment and are subject to a decision of a competent national authority.'

In the case of living resources, the precautionary principle has been applied so as to oblige those wishing to utilise a resource to provide evidence of the sustainability of that use.[109] The weight of this burden will, however, vary according to the particular circumstances of each case. Where there is uncertainty as to whether a species may be threatened with extinction, its best interests must predominate, rather than the short term economic interests of those dependent upon their utilisation.[110] In addition, once a decision is reached concerning a species, the decision-making mechanisms created ensure that the results of those decisions are fed back and monitored by the decision-makers, so that corrective measures can, if necessary, be implemented.[111] The mechanisms do not only anticipate problems and deal with them, but also anticipate the inadequacy of those solutions. Furthermore, it appears inherent both in the adoption of the Revised Management Procedure by the IWC and in Annex 4 of the Fort Lauderdale criteria, that, where utilisation of a living resource has once proved to be incapable of proper and effective regulation, extreme caution is required if such utilisation is resumed. In particular, it appears that it is for those seeking to renew utilisation to show that the circumstances have changed, presumably by demonstrating that the available assessment and regulatory mechanisms have been improved.

3.3. Informational requirements

It is obvious that Hey's third feature, the commitment to actively collect and share data and stimulate research, is necessary in order to give effect to the first two. It is hardly surprising, therefore, that inclusion of the precautionary principle in an international instrument is almost always accompanied by a commitment by State parties to exchange information and cooperate in research. For example, the 1995 Fish Stocks Agreement[112] requires State parties to 'collect and share, in a timely manner, complete and accurate data concerning fishing activities, inter alia, on position, catch of target and non-target species and fishing effort . . . as well as information from national, regional and international programmes'[113] and to 'promote and conduct scientific research in support of fishery conservation and management'.[114] The Preamble to the 1992 Biodiversity Convention[115] declares the parties' awareness 'of the general lack of information and knowledge regarding biological diversity and of the urgent need to develop scientific, technical and institutional capacities to provide the basic understanding upon which to plan and implement appropriate measures'. The text of the Convention itself requires the parties to '[E]stablish and maintain pro-

[109] For example, under the IWC Revised Management Procedure, supra, n 47, and Art 6(2) & (3)(b), Fish Stock Agreement 1995, supra, n 41, quota levels should vary according to the reliability of available data, and states wishing to utilise the resource must therefore carry out ongoing scientific monitoring and research in order to maintain or increase the size of their quotas.

[110] For example, the final recital in the Preamble to the 1994 Fort Lauderdale Resolution listing criteria, supra, n 43, and implicit in the previous Berne Criteria: Resolution Conf 1.1 Criteria for the addition of species and other taxa to Appendices I and II and for the transfer of species and other taxa between Appendix II and Appendix I and 1.2 Criteria for the deletion of species and other taxa from Appendices I and II (both now repealed).

[111] For example, the use of precautionary reference points to trigger further action: Art 6(3)(d) & Annex 2 para 5, Fish Stocks Agreement, supra, n 41; Annex 4 Part B, CITES Fort Lauderdale listing criteria, supra, n 43.

[112] Supra, n 41.

[113] Article 5(h).

[114] Article 5(i).

[115] Supra, n 44.

grammes for scientific and technical education and training',[116] to '[P]romote and encourage research which contributes to the conservation and sustainable use of biological diversity',[117] and, to '. . . promote and cooperate in the use of scientific advances in biological diversity research in developing methods for conservation and sustainable use of biological resources.'[118] Indeed, it might be argued that the Climate Change Convention commits the parties to little else. The Preamble praises 'the valuable analytical work being conducted by many States on climate change' and 'the important contribution of . . . international and intergovernmental bodies to the exchange of results of scientific research and the coordination of research'. The text of the Convention requires State parties to '[P]romote and cooperate in the development, application and diffusion, . . . of technologies, practices and processes that control, reduce or prevent anthropogenic emissions of greenhouse gases . . .',[119] to '[P]romote and cooperate in scientific, technological, technical, socio-economic and other research, systematic observation and development of data archives related to the climate system and intended to further the understanding and to reduce or eliminate the remaining uncertainties regarding the causes, effects, magnitude and timing of climate change . . .',[120] and to '[P]romote and cooperate in the full, open and prompt exchange of relevant scientific, technical, socio-economic and legal information related to the climate system and climate change . . .'.[121] Chairman Satya Nandan's Negotiating Text, prepared for the 1993 UN Fish Stocks Conference in New York, had clearly linked scientific uncertainty, precautionary action and the need for scientific advancement. Article 5 stated:

> In order to protect the environment and the living marine resources, the precautionary approach shall be applied widely by States to fisheries management and exploitation in the following manner:
> (a) States shall so act as to obtain and share the best possible scientific evidence available in support of conservation and management decision-making . . .
> (b) The absence of adequate scientific information shall not be used as the reason for failing to take strict measures to protect the resources . . .[122]

4. Conclusion

It is suggested that the aim of the precautionary principle, as a general principle of international environmental law, is to minimise, and, if possible, eliminate, unnecessary human interference with a legitimate environmental interest. That is to say, wherever international law requires environmental harm to be prevented, a precautionary approach is required in order to avoid, as far as possible, that harm occurring inadvertently. The principle may represent a shift to a more eco-centric outlook but

116 Article 12(a).
117 Article 12(b).
118 Article 12(c).
119 Article 4(1)(c).
120 Article 4(1)(g).
121 Article 4(1)(h).
122 Negotiating Text prepared by the Chairman of the Conference, UN Conference on Straddling Fish Stocks and Highly Migratory Fish Stocks, New York, 12–30 July 1993. A/CONF 164/13, 29 July 1993. See Freestone, supra, n 7 at 215.

this does not mean that damage to the environment may not be sanctioned. Rather, it means that decision-makers ought, at the very least, to make themselves aware of the potential effects of what they are sanctioning, in order to be able to determine what level of environmental change or risk of change is 'necessary'. While decision-makers should ensure that they have the best available information upon which to base their decisions, they should not assume that their information is complete or infallible, and should make allowance for this. In order to be able to adopt this approach, States and other subjects of international law need to be able to demonstrate that their decision-making processes show due care and attention for the environmental consequences of their decisions. The best means of so doing is to have in place appropriate procedures and mechanisms that incorporate a precautionary approach.

This article set out to perform two functions. First, to review, particularly in the light of the Rio (UNCED) process, the status of the precautionary principle in customary international law. Secondly, to identify what can be understood, to date, of the substantive content of the obligation created by the principle. In effect, how the customary principle can be applied demonstrably in practice. It is contended that the precautionary principle has indeed crystallised into a norm of customary international law. It is further contended that effective and satisfactory implementation of the principle can be achieved, inter alia, by means of, where appropriate, precautionary assessment, the setting of precautionary standards and the discharge of ancillary informational obligations.

[11]

A Right to Environment in International Law: Current Status and Future Outlook

Paula M. Pevato

Mankind is approaching a historic turning point: the beginning of the third millennium of the common era. Today there is an especially keen desire to look into the future and try to see what it holds.

Igor Ivanovich Lukashuk, *'The Law of the International Community'*[1]

■ Introduction

International law for the protection of the environment has evolved rather rapidly during the latter part of the twentieth century. Indeed, since the Stockholm and Rio Declarations[2] were adopted in 1972 and 1992 respectively, a broad consensus of the international community has undertaken the laborious task of drafting and adopting, ratifying or implementing a plethora of hard and soft law instruments, policy documents and otherwise, at the global, regional and municipal levels. In fact, most of the standard-setting for environmental co-operation has taken place since 1972. These sources of international law express many of the aspirations contained within and inspired by both declarations. In the course of this evolution, a number of new concepts have emerged simultaneously – including the precautionary principle, the polluter-pays-principle, intergenerational equity, and of course sustainable development – concepts that have become part of the *lingua franca* circulating amongst international legal circles. Although the legal status of many of these concepts of international environment co-operation (IEC)[3] is unclear and the subject of much academic debate, their importance in providing guidance for, contributing to and encouraging IEC cannot be denied. However, forcing the issue to find a right to environment exists – implicit, express, third generation and so on – does little for the credibility the debate desperately needs at this stage. It is one thing to say that a right to environment should exist (*lex ferenda*), but quite another to insist it does exist (*lex lata*), particularly in the light of the sources of international law.

In adhering to the spirit of this special issue of *RECIEL* that aims to 'look back and look ahead', this article is both reflective and somewhat prescient, given that it will touch upon recent history, present status and future prospects of one such concept that has emerged *para*, or alongside, the progressive development of international law for the protection of the environment: the right to environment. The *leitmotif* of this article is rather straightforward: what is a right to environment in contemporary international law and policy and what is the forecast for future recognition as a human right? Given that many arguments cannot be developed fully within the scope of this article, its aim is modest: to reevaluate prevailing attitudes, both convergent and divergent tides of thought; to situate the status of this concept within current international legal theory and practice; and, to raise relevant questions for further reflection.

This article adopts a policy science perspective, viewing law as a process of authoritative decision-making wherein policy choices play an important role. The policy science approach recognizes a broader methodological basis for identifying and appraising current or emerging norms or standards, for evaluating new trends in international law encapsulated within declarations, recommendations, decisions, amongst other soft law documents. With that international legal philosophical perspective in mind, policy science would attempt to make law and jurisprudence more relevant to contemporary social, economic and political realities, and dependent upon demands and expectations of a particular society,[4] in this case in the context of balancing competing interests amongst

© Blackwell Publishers Ltd. 1999, 108 Cowley Road, Oxford OX4 1JF, UK and 350 Main Street, Malden, MA 02148, USA.

human rights, environment and various tensions to both, including trade, development, sovereignty and other tensions. Despite the uncertain legal status of a human right to environment in international law, the policy science approach would consider that decisions taken to protect and improve the environment have elevated such demands to a position of importance in the decision-making process, in conformity with the expectations of contemporary society. It may be safe to say that such policy choices have already influenced law-making and may continue to do so in the future.

■ Progress Since 1994: From Optimism to Scepticism

The UN Study on Human Rights and the Environment

In August 1994, the final report of a United Nations (UN) study on 'Human Rights and the Environment' was adopted.[5] The Ksentini final report recommended *inter alia* the recognition of a right to a healthy environment as a human right, and the adoption of a draft declaration on human rights and the environment. The special rapporteur, Fatma Zohra Ksentini, expressed her hope that 'the draft will help the United Nations to adopt, in the course of the present United Nations Decade of International Law, a set of norms consolidating the right to a satisfactory environment – defined as an integral part of the world partnership for peace, development and proress for all'. That same year, *RECIEL* published a thematic issue dedicated to 'Environmental Rights and Access to Justice', wherein the draft declaration was reproduced.[6] In that issue, as managing editor I urged the support of the draft declaration by UN Member States. However, upon reflection, it seems in retrospect both naïve and overly optimistic to believe a draft document that had not been through the rigorous negotiation processes of standard-setting within the UN could be adopted as a *fait accompli* by the Member States. As an expression of aspirations drafted by a group of people acting in their individual capacities, the draft declaration is not without merit. However, it is entirely different if the declaration is portrayed as a consensus document of UN Member States, which it is not. In that context, a declaration put forth by decision-makers who are representing the views and perspectives of members within their community would be more convincing as an expression of the demands and expectations from the policy science perspective.

When new or so-called emerging, third-generation human rights norms are at issue such as a human right to environment, it is highly doubtful that a document such as the draft declaration would be adopted *in toto* by UN Member States. That would bypass the rigorous background research, debates, consultations, drafting and adoption procedures, which is simply not the style of the UN system. Perhaps Professor Ian Brownlie has put it best when he remarked that:

> As policy goals, as standards of morality, the so-called new generation of human rights would be acceptable and one could sit round a table with non-lawyers and agree on practical programmes for attaining these good ends. What concerns me as a lawyer is *the casual introduction of serious confusions of thought*, and this in the course of seeking to give the new rights an actual legal context.[7]

In the case of more recently elaborated international human rights standards, for example the International Labour Organization's Convention on Child Labour,[8] it was clear that new international labour standards were necessary to target intolerable situations (namely child labour), and require that States Parties to the new Convention adopt and implement those standards within national law and policy. What gaps would a right to environment fill, if that is one reason for recognizing a human right to environment? Could any existing or perceived gaps in national law and policy be served by an anthropocentric solution to environmental problems that do not affect human rights alone? The point here is that there is nothing wrong with drafting documents encapsulating inspirational goals as a statement from concerned individuals, but there has to be a more compelling reason to adopt new standards and a common understanding that there is a tremendous gap in law and practice that could only be addressed via new norms. In addition, to equate the draft declaration on human rights and the environment with universally adopted 'soft' law instruments as 'soft' mechanisms of action, that in turn entail 'soft' responsibility, or to elevate the same as having some kind of legal status, would be incorrect.

Current Circumstances in the UN: a postscript

Coinciding with the Ksentini final report, by the mid-1990s the academic tide of thought seemed to have gathered momentum in favour of standard-setting for a human right to environment, at least by its proponents, as expressed within some of the legal literature. Since that time, however, the undertow has proved stronger against the adoption of any new standards in the foreseeable future. The 1997 session of the UN Commission on Human Rights (UNCHR) gives an indication of its status: no resolution was passed to consider further the issues of human rights and the environment, and the report of the 53rd session resolved via Decision 1997/102 to request that the UN Secretary-General bring the question of human rights and environment to the UN General Assembly's (UNGA) June 1997 special session on the implementation of UN Conference on Environment and Development (UNCED), in addition to the attention of the Commission on Sustainable Development (CSD), the UN Environment Programme (UNEP), the UN Development Programme (UNDP) 'and other relevant international bodies and organizations'.[9] That decision asked the Secretary-General to prepare a consolidated report 'based on the deliberations of the [UNGA] and of those international bodies and organizations for its consideration of the question of human rights and the environment at its fifty-fifty session', in other words, for the UNCHR session in 1999.[10] This stands in direct contrast to a right to development, whereby the UNGA has at least recognized it as an 'inalienable human right',[11] and continues to seek its implementation via the UNCHR (albeit with obvious difficulties and objections to date that characterize third-generation human rights).[12]

© Blackwell Publishers Ltd. 1999.

During the UNCHR's 1999 session, human rights and the environment was not listed as a separate topic; instead, it was included in discussions on 'science and environment'. The Secretary-General's report submitted in accordance with the above-mentioned decision 1997/102 made no mention of standard-setting, of the draft declaration, or of the right to environment as a human right. Instead, this particular report reiterated a number of cross-sectoral issues that were highlighted by the Ad Hoc Committee of the Whole of the Nineteenth Special Session of the UNGA, calling for a 'need for a greater integration at all policy-making levels – economic, social and environmental – and at operational levels, including the lowest administrative levels possible'.[13] The Ad Hoc Committee noted the following areas of environmental and human rights concerns in the context of integration of economic, social and environmental objectives:

- the need for a mutually supportive balance between the international and the national environment in the pursuit of sustainable development and for a dynamic and enabling international economic climate supportive of international co-operation, particularly in the fields of finance, technology transfer and debt and trade;
- the full integration of people living in poverty into economic, social and political life via a number of poverty alleviation goals including universal access to basic social services such as health care, and provision of safe water and sanitation;
- recognizing the interrelationship between economic growth, poverty, employment, environment and sustainable development, in order to encourage and promote the current decline in population growth through the expansion of education;
- finding solutions to achieve more sustainable human settlements via the transfer of technology and expertise, capacity-building, decentralization of authority and private-public partnerships to improve the provision and environmentally sound management of infrastructure and social services;
- the urgent provision of access to safe drinking water and adequate sanitation, accompanied by a number of recommendations to ensure the optimal use and protection of all fresh-water resources to meet the needs of everyone on the planet, including granting high priority to the formulation and implementation of policies and programmes for integrated watershed management; and
- to define the type of hazardous wastes controlled under the Basel Convention and to negotiate, adopt and implement a protocol on liability and compensation for damage resulting from the transboundary movement of hazardous wastes.

According to the summary record of the 55th meeting of the UNCHR in April 1999, one observer addressed the issue of human rights and the environment, recommending that the UNCHR had a responsibility to address the human rights aspects of Agenda 21. This observer urged that the mandate of the special rapporteur on illicit movement and dumping of toxic wastes (also carried out by Mrs Ksentini) be converted to a special rapporteur on human rights and the environment. However, no resolution or decision was made at the end of the 55th session in regards to human rights and the environment.[14] Nor has the provisional agenda for the 51st session of the Sub-Commission on Prevention of Discrimination and Protection of Minorities listed consideration of human rights and the environment.[15]

On the contrary, the subject of hazardous wastes was referred to in the Vienna Declaration and Programme of Action as the only express reference to human rights and the environment,[16] and consideration of the adverse effects of the illicit movement and dumping of toxic and dangerous products and wastes on the enjoyment of human rights will be reconsidered at the UNCHR's 56th session in the year 2000.[17] That resolution reaffirmed 'that illicit traffic and dumping of toxic and dangerous products constitute a serious threat to the human rights to life, health and a sound environment for every individual'.[18] Yet, it remains unclear what the right to a sound environment encapsulates in that context.

Delegates who attend UN meetings continue to express opposition to the consideration of ecological issues by the UNCHR. Most agree that environmental issues should be dealt with in an appropriate fora, chiefly UNEP or the CSD, rather than within the UNCHR, adding that 'the proclamation of a "right" to environmental quality would be a mere political gesture'.[19] The main argument against including an express right to environment within existing human rights treaties, or within a future protocol or convention, is summarized succinctly by the UK's submission to the UNCHR in response to a request for comments on the Ksentini final report. The UK Government indicated 'it does not believe that the Commission on Human Rights is the right forum for debate in this area since it does not have the necessary expertise to promote meaningful measures to ensure environmental protection'. Instead, the UK proposed that UNEP, the CSD, and conferences of the parties (COPs) contemplating international environmental treaties were the more appropriate fora. The UK viewed human rights and the environment as distracting the UNCHR 'from its core activity of protecting human rights'.[20] Related issues, such as the UNCHR debates on the illicit movement of toxic wastes, have met with similar resistance. During the debates on economic, social and cultural rights at the UNCHR's 53rd Session in 1997, several delegations expressed their tacit disapproval of continued consideration of toxic waste within that UN entity. Opponents generally agreed that the UNCHR's consideration of hazardous wastes and other issues of IEC are best handled by those bodies equipped to resolve such matters, even though these issues have ancillary effects upon human rights. For instance, the representative from Denmark indicated that whilst his country viewed the issue of toxic waste as being of a very serious nature, 'there were already a number of binding decisions enforced under the Basel Convention', and he added that the 'Commission was not the right forum for solving the problem of the dumping of toxic wastes'.[21] The US delegate commented that toxic waste was 'a complex issue ... [that] should not be addressed superficially', and in fact was already being addressed by the Basel Convention and the CSD. The UNCHR, lacking 'the ability to address it professionally', should not add toxic waste to an 'already

© Blackwell Publishers Ltd. 1999.

over-burdened agenda'. This delegate urged that the Special Rapporteur's mandate should not be renewed when it expired in 1998.[22] The Netherlands voted against the resolution on toxic wastes 'because the subject was not an appropriate one for the Commission, and was seriously addressed elsewhere'.[23] Previously, the Belgian delegation 'regretted that the Sub-Commission should have adopted a number of resolutions which had nothing to do with its mandate, such as those on ...the movement and dumping of toxic and dangerous products'.[24] The 1997 Resolution on Toxic Wastes was passed with 32 countries in favour, 12 against and 8 abstaining, whilst future consideration of this issue beyond the UNCHR's 54th and 55th sessions in 1998 and 1999 respectively was extended to encourage co-operation with other relevant UN entities, particularly in the light of the expertise within UNEP, the CSD and the Secretariat to the Basel Convention.[25]

■ Present Status of Right to Environment in International Law: A Selection of Persistent Ambiguities, Restraints and Tensions

Conceptual Issues: Defining A Right to Environment

Many questions still surround the concept of a right to environment, enmeshed within the debate on its nature and scope, in particular:

- what are the differences between legal and non-legal relations, rights and non-rights?;
- what are human rights and which rights can be classified as such?; and
- what is the environment?

Human rights are best described as rights held simply by virtue of being a human person.[26] The policy science approach refined this description by depicting human rights as 'demands of a particularly high intensity made by individuals *vis-à-vis* their governments'.[27] But which rights are human rights and why is this analysis necessary? Can one not assume that a right to environment is a human right and simply move on to seek its protection? Judge Higgins cautioned that the question of drawing a line between what are human rights and what are not is 'more than an academic matter, because the articulation of claims as human rights is part of the process of according priority to decision-making processes'.[28] To propose that modern international legal theory and philosophy support an emerging right to environment might really be suggesting that environmental priorities must be placed higher upon the decision-making agenda at the international level – with the view in mind that international law is a process of decision-making – so it is not a human right to environment that is desired; rather, its proponents may in fact mean something else. Their 'claims' are unclear on this point.[29] Nor has any consensus emerged on what is meant by the 'environment' in a human rights context. What ingredients would make the environment an acceptable **universal or inalienable** right?

At the definitional stage, one observes that a number of doctrinal problems are triggered by a right to environment, 'not the least of which is defining its limits'.[30] To date, no single definition of a right to environment has been expressed as representative of a universally accepted term. A number of conjectures have been proposed, including:

- that it should not be assumed that a right to environment is a human right, without considering definitions of human rights and environment; philosophical theories; or the reality that this concept might be something other than a human right such as a non-right or policy initiative incapable of being legally enforced, based upon a review of the sources of international law. These alternative views are usually not considered by proponents of a right to environment[31].
- that the 'definitional framework would probably be the most contentious of the issues raised in efforts to articulate this right',[32] based upon the lack of precise scientific information pertaining to the adverse effects of environmental pollution, absence of agreement of what constitutes a healthy, decent, liveable, sound or viable environment,[33] and the difficulty in defining the environment itself,[34] among other factors;
- that definitional problems associated with a right to environment should be avoided altogether by not defining this concept too precisely, because its main characteristic is that it is evolving, which is the source of its richness;[35]
- that a narrowly defined right to environment would facilitate its enforcement by machinery 'providing for an adequate judicial guarantee', thereby ensuring its effective recognition;[36]
- that the implementation of a right to environment is a precondition to the realization of all other fundamental rights and freedoms. Thus, its implementation would contribute a sense of completeness to other guaranteed human rights by establishing equality, or at least lessening the burden of inequalities among citizens, injustices often exacerbated by environmental degradation.[37] This has been suggested regardless of whether this concept were to be included within a revised human rights treaty or as a separate protocol;[38]
- that although the use of rights language can be seductive to the environmental movement, it is criticized for concentrating on rights as an end when rights are only a means to an end, that being an improved environment.[39] Critics of rights-based approaches view the use of individual rights as exclusive, restrictive metaphors precluding the invocation of 'richer and more diverse images of the nature world',[40] essentially basing the debate on an anthropocentric perspective; and
- that it is not to be interpreted as the right to an ideal environment; rather, as the right of everyone to the conservation of his or her environment,[41] or as the right to environmental protection.

The Executive Director of UNEP, Elizabeth Dowdeswell (as she then was), observed that:

© Blackwell Publishers Ltd. 1999.

> ... it is a commonly held view that international law does not yet directly protect [a right to environment]. While environmental law has revolved around a broad understanding of human needs, it is not easy to define the right to environment with sufficient precision or clarity. The concept remains imprecise without reference to a series of objectives.[42]

The absence of a precise definition of and for the environment does not diminish the importance of protecting it. Certainly, the International Court of Justice (ICJ) has stressed the 'great significance it attaches to respect for the environment, not only for States but also for the whole of mankind'.[43] In the ICJ's Advisory Opinion on nuclear weapons, it concluded

> ... the environment is not an abstraction but represents the living space, the quality of life and the very health of human beings, including generations unborn. The existence of the general obligations of States to ensure that activities within their jurisdiction and control respect the environment of other States or of areas beyond national control is now part of the corpus of international law relating to the environment.[44]

No single treaty defines the environment. Perhaps delimitation would hinder its development in both law and policy, particularly as scientific theories are refined, as new theories are formulated, as unprotected species become endangered, and so on. Alternatively, clarification may be preferred when environmental law regulates a particular aspect of the environment, or sub-environments (such as the marine environment, ozone layer, global climate change or international watercourses) or protects the inhabitants of these sub-environments (whether biodiversity, marine mammals, and so on). The difficulties in defining the environment and the reality that the environment means different things in distinct situations represent a Medusa's head to a right to environment's advocates. How can one narrowly define that which is not narrow? And regardless of definitional hurdles, would a human right to environment add anything to the multi-lateral and sectoral approach to the global, regional, sub-regional and national protection for the environment?

Sources of International Law: A Few Observations

The definitive test to determine the current status of a right to environment as *lex lata* or *lex ferenda* in international law is made by referring to the sources of international law as enumerated in Article 38(1) of the ICJ Statute (namely, custom, convention, general principles of law, judicial decisions, and teachings of highly qualified publicists). Does international law recognize a human right to environment?

Conventions

Human Rights treaties: To date, only two **regional** human rights treaties contain and expressly recognize a human right to environment, Article 24 of the African Charter and Article 11 of the Protocol of San Salvador, though neither treaty may be viewed as representative of any **global** consensus on this issue. The European Convention does not contain an express right to environment. Proposals to amend the text of the European Social Charter, by adding a right to environment, have met with firm resistance by the Committee of Ministers.[45] In 1990, the Parliamentary Assembly for the Council of Europe recommended that a European charter and convention on environmental protection and sustainable development be drafted, recognizing *inter alia* a right to environment. The Committee of Ministers rejected this recommendation.[46]

A careful analysis of the *travaux préparatoires* to the UN International Covenant on Civil and Political Rights (ICCPR) and European Convention verifies that the right to environment as a human right was not on the agenda at the drafting stages.[47] Thus, a communication brought before an international human rights treaty body will meet with obvious substantive and procedural difficulties if it alleges the violation of an 'implied' right to environment. Application of Article 32 of the Vienna Convention on the Law of Treaties[48] – whereby supplementary means of interpretation, 'including the preparatory work of the treaty and the circumstances of its conclusion', may be reviewed in the event of an ambiguous or obscure meaning – confirms that an implicit right to environment cannot be extracted either from the *travaux préparatoires* or a generous interpretation of recognized human rights. Communications linking violations of one or more human rights to environmental degradation must identify the violation of a specific human right, not an implied one.[49] It must raise a *prima facie* case under one or more rights in the treaty, not a claim *in abstracto*, or one based upon an implied right.

When the international community has gathered to discuss human rights in more recent times, it has not sought to propose and expressly recognize a right to environment as a human right. Most notably, during the UN World Conference on Human Rights, convened in Vienna 1994 and post-dating UNCED, one would have assumed that would have been the opportunity for express recognition if a sufficiently representative majority of States Parties viewed a right to environment as having legal rather than political force. Yet it is markedly absent from the Vienna Declaration and Programme of Action. By that time, the preliminary and subsequent progress reports on the UN Commission's study on human rights and the environment had been submitted (exceptionally the final report of August 1994 post-dated Vienna), but appeared to have had little influence on the programme adopted in Vienna. The international community had the opportunity to look afresh at human rights in a contemporary light in preparations for and at Vienna, post-UNCED, but did not embrace a human right to environment.

Global Environmental Treaties: The right to live in a balanced, decent, healthy, satisfactory, sound or secure environment is more often expressed within non-legally binding resolutions and declarations adopted at conferences for environmental co-operation rather than in legally binding international human rights covenants. Many other soft-law instruments, both international and regional in scope, accept that health, well-being and the dignity of people are dependent upon the protection of one's natural surroundings,[50] in recognition that 'development of the person and satisfactory conditions of life are incompatible with an environment degraded by pol-

© Blackwell Publishers Ltd. 1999.

lution'.[51] The Hague Declaration asserted 'not only the fundamental duty to preserve the ecosystem, but also the right to live in dignity in a viable global environment, and the consequent duty of the community of nations *vis-à-vis* present and future generations to do all that can be done to preserve the quality of the atmosphere'.[52] Declarations drawing links between sustainable development, the environment, health and well-being of individuals, do not necessarily imply recognition of a **human** right to environment as a new norm, or taking it one step further, a right to sustainable development.[53] These documents should not be misconstrued as representative of statements supporting the recognition of new human rights standards, particularly when they are phrased as aspirational goals within non-legally binding, soft law documents. It might be stretching things a bit too far in assuming that the proliferation of these conventional sources creates a **human** right to environment by implication based upon a contracting State's undertakings to protect and preserve the environment. From the policy science perspective, one could argue that declarations, resolutions and other soft law instruments referring to the right to live in an environment free from pollution or the right to environmental protection may be accepted as universal norms in the future, or have they been accepted to some extent already, in the context of environmental protection laws at national, subregional, regional and global levels? Thus is it really the adoption of a **human** right to environment **alone** that is the eventual and desirable result as influenced by these policy choices?

But why are these choices expressed via so much 'soft' law? The deliberate choice to adopt non-legally binding wording in the field of the environment has been interpreted by Székely to result,

> ... at least in the field of the environment, from the clear, unequivocal and decisive intention **not** to create or develop international law, and if possible **not** to allow necessarily for the eventual formation of an international legal rule.[54]

It is rather curious that a right to environment's supporters resort to conventional sources of environmental law for evidence of a human right to environment, when such sources are not concerned with standard-setting in, or implementation of, **human rights** norms and standards. Could it be, then, that one is really talking about emerging norms and standards for environmental cooperation or concepts of IEC? Professor J.G. Merrills surmised that since international law is grounded in conventional law and state practice,

> ... the seeker after environmental rights may be tempted to use the existence of agreements and principles of customary law concerned with the states' rights and duties with regard to the environment as a basis for deriving rights for individuals and groups.[55]

As enticing as this approach has proved to be for a right to environment's supporters, Professor Merrills shrewdly cautioned that such a temptation 'should be resisted'.[56] This warning may be contrasted with those views by environmental rights advocates who state that this right 'will pressure States to implement their environmental protection obligations'.[57] From the marked absence of a right to environment either in the human rights or environmental protection areas of international law, one might conclude:

- that a right to environment is a politically convenient expression of policy goals and aspirations, a political rather than a legal obligation, one that is the end result of the implementation of international obligations via municipal environmental law and policy, rather than via the recognition of a new human right;
- that a right to environment is not pursued at human rights standard-setting conferences because its consideration by organizations, chiefly UNEP and the CSD, as one of many goals of IEC is more appropriate;
- that it is more practical to pursue a right to environment's adoption from an environmental law and policy approach because the human rights approach cannot address some of the more technical questions posed by ecological problems, including scientific uncertainty that is better addressed by the precautionary principle. In practice, international human rights treaty bodies require more certainty of evidence than the mere **threat** of a violation;
- that in response to the growing awareness of the adverse effects of environmental hazards upon human existence and the natural world, international law has ascribed a general duty upon States to refrain from activities that might harm the environment, rather than a new human right, activities such as minimizing transboundary effects of air-borne pollution following the *Trail Smelter* arbitration (Principle 21, Stockholm Declaration); encouraging environmental impact assessments (EIA) as a precondition to carrying out development projects,[58] and early notification of environmental accidents after the Chernobyl disaster;[59]
- that the International Law Commission (ILC) has attempted to codify various environmental hazards in its draft articles on state responsibility and in the non-navigational uses of international watercourses, adding more standard-setting to the large body of international law in the field of the environment, again activities not focused upon a narrowly construed human right to environment;[60] and
- that international norms and standards for IEC are complemented by regional régimes, such as those in Africa, Asia, and Latin America.[61]

This growing body of law and policy suggest that IEC wears many different hats – the protection of the atmosphere, conservation of marine living resources, nuclear safety, international watercourses, and trade in hazardous waste – that a human right to environment's milliner cannot fashion to suitably address each and every issue raised by environmental degradation. As international law for the protection of the environment moves closer to sustainable development, the interrelationship between environmental and socioeconomic instruments has increasing importance, with sustainable development requiring 'a holistic rather than a sectoral approach'.[62]

Custom

State practice and *opinio juris*, Article 38(1)(b), ICJ Statute: The emergence of 'environmental constitutional

© Blackwell Publishers Ltd. 1999.

law' has given rise to questions regarding the existence of a constitutional right to environment and, consequently, the possibility of a uniform State practice as evidence of *opinio juris*. Constitutional provisions providing for environmental protection may impose the following:

- a duty upon the State only;[63]
- a duty upon citizens only;[64]
- a duty upon the State and citizens;[65]
- an individual right to a healthy environment, alone or in combination with an individual and/or collective duty of citizens and/or the State to protect the environment;[66]
- a duty to protect a favourable living environment, public health and/or well-being;[67] and,
- a duty upon State and/or citizen, in the context of preserving public property and/or natural resources.[68]

The position that a uniform constitutional practice has emerged, as proposed by right to environment proponents,[69] is not entirely convincing, given the following counter-positions:

- that, based upon the foregoing survey, whilst over 60 constitutions may refer to environmental obligations, slightly less than one-half of those 60ish surveyed expressly refer to the right of its citizens to a healthy environment. This is not necessarily indicative of any emerging, overwhelming consensus or uniform, consistent state practice of norm-creating influence;[70]
- that such provisions take various forms,[71] and when deconstructed, may not in fact recognize a **human** right to environment *per se*; rather, such rights may resemble rights to environmental protection, to the enjoyment of or access to natural parks, and so on;
- that 'environmental protection as a constitutional issue is somewhat ambiguous because it is related [*inter alia*] to structural problems of the balance of powers, the co-ordination of conflicting rights and of different dimensions of protection';[72]
- related to the previous point, that it may prove far more difficult to reconcile constitutional environmental rights with the constitutional protection of land ownership,[73] or other competing interests such as permanent sovereignty over natural resources, development and so on;
- that such provisions do not automatically create a new norm in international law without assessing whether *de facto* international consensus has evolved to support that assumption;
- that constitutional developments may be indicative of placing environmental protection higher upon States' agendas as important objectives of social policy;
- that the pursuit of a constitutional right to environment as a State objective is more conceivable than pursuing it as a human right, e.g., from a regional perspective, only a few EU Member States' constitutions contain references to the environment;[74]
- there is no correlation between States that expressly recognize a right to a healthy environment in national constitutions, and those States that elaborate on measures taken to improve the environment by drawing links between the right to life or other expressly recognized human rights, and threats presented by ecological hazards within their periodic reports to international human rights treaty bodies;[75]
- that on a regional and national basis, State practice on a right to environment illustrates that, at most, it is viewed as a cross-cutting issue, or one of several objectives of IEC, as a political rather than legal obligation that must be translated into national law;[76] and
- that a right to environment does not have the status of *jus cogens*,[77] or a peremptory norm.

Subsidiary Sources

Judicial Decisions: ICJ judgments are a constant reminder of Article 38(1)'s significance, and recent decisions post-dating the Stockholm and Rio Conferences provide no evidence that a human right to environment has been expressly recognized within the law of nations. In his separate opinion in *Gabcíkovo-Nagymaros*, Judge Weeramantry wrote:

> The protection of the environment is ... a vital part of contemporary human rights doctrine, for it is a sine qua non for numerous human rights such as the right to health and the right to life itself. It is scarcely necessary to elaborate on this, as damage to the environment can impair and undermine all the human rights spoken of in the Universal Declaration and other human rights instruments.

Judge Weeramantry did not proclaim an express right to environment, instead referring to those human rights recognized within existing human rights treaties, rights that may be adversely affected by air pollution, poor water quality, and other ecologically-related concerns. With the exception of Vice-President Weeramantry's separate opinion, the Court did not elaborate on whether the precautionary principle, sustainable development, or other norms and standards could form the basis of new peremptory norms, instead referring to them as 'concepts'.[78]

Teachings of the Most Highly Qualified Publicists in the Various Nations: In this area, it is noted that most authors have fallen into the rights trap by confusing legal claims with non-legally enforceable policy choices or moral aspirations. Robertson and Merrills sensibly surmised:

> The trouble arises ... because advocates of the 'new human rights' are confusing objectives of social policy with rights in the lawyers' sense. If one wishes to see some objective achieved – **a clean and healthy environment**, for example – it is tempting to say that this is a right which we are all entitled. **But it is not a good idea to take wishes for reality.**[79]

A right to environment 'is still very much a theme begging for a writer'.[80] Few authors have risen to the task of discussing a right to environment from a pragmatic and realistic international legal and policy perspective to 'carry on an authentic debate', and represent an exception to the rather disappointing offerings by 'scholars' researching human rights and the environment.[81]

Various questions need to be raised and/or answered in a convincing fashion. Many ambiguities persist in contemporary legal literature on a right to environment:

- whether, in the context of the time that the articles were written, a right to environment represents a moral claim without legal foundation in international law, *lex ferenda*, or otherwise;

© Blackwell Publishers Ltd. 1999.

Volume 8 Issue 3 1999

- whether the international lawyer could frame rules to meet this claim and what those legal rules would be;
- whether and why a right to environment is even necessary given the abundance of standard-setting in human rights and environmental protection.

The more pragmatic and realistic observations in the context of contemporary international law and policy recognize that a human right to environment does not exist, and going further, should not be recognized because it would add nothing to IEC.[82] From the policy science perspective, new laws might emerge as a product of a normative system reflecting social values within contemporary society. Perhaps these environmental values are already encapsulated within and expressed by the various norms and standards existing in the field of international law for the protection and preservation of the environment. In a speech to the ILO delegations in June, 1999, Amartya Sen, Nobel Laureate in Economics, noted that social acknowledgement of certain rights can be viewed as an invitation for law to catch up with social ethics as part of a decent society, adding:

> But the invitation is not merely to fresh legislation, important as it is, since the realization of rights can also be helped by other developments, such as the creation of new institutions, better working of existing institutions, and ... by a general political and social commitment to work for the appropriate functioning of social, political and economic arrangements to facilitate recognized rights.[83]

In short, rights-based formulations are not the only way of looking at environmental co-operation. A broader conceptualization, in reality, might be better for environmental protection and preservation in the long term, via policy choices and other non-rights-based solutions.

Deconstructing a Right to Environment: Who, What and From Whom

Questions that might be raised were a hypothetical right to be constructed include:

- What does a right to environment protect?
- Who are the holders of a right to environment?
- From whom is this right granted?

In the course of their arguments, most proponents have linked this right to expressly recognized human rights, most commonly the substantive rights to life and to respect for private and family life (privacy), or to procedural rights such as access to information, participation and access to justice. If one were to build a profile of a right to environment based upon the observations of its proponents, this right would mean all things to all people, but largely to the direct exclusion of other inhabitants of the natural world such as birds, whales and so on, which cannot possess human rights by virtue of not being human. When deconstructed, this right resembles more a cross-cutting issue rather than an individual human right to life. Further lack of clarity is evident within the following summary of a right to environment's elements, according to the various views of put forth by its proponents. Such a right would:

Category A: General Characteristics, Substantive and Procedural Elements

- resemble an inalienable right;[84]
- incorporate a narrow definitional framework;[85]
- be justiciable, introducing an *actio popularis* procedure;[86]
- contain characteristics of an individual and collective right;[87]
- may be referred to as 'environmental human rights';[88]
- is corollary, derivative, implied, inherent, or inseparable from substantive human rights, such as the rights to life, physical integrity, private and family life, health, food, a safe working environment, among others,[89] necessary to guarantee and/or complete other human rights,[90] and 'grounded in fundamental human rights accepted as positive law';[91]
- recognize the special relationship between indigenous peoples and their natural environment, so that the adverse effects of economic development, environmental racism or ultimately cultural extinction may be lessened or prevented;[92]
- be a right respected through a 'wiser, more equitable and more generous international refugee law';[93]
- include a temporal element, thus applicable to present and future generations, incorporating intergenerational equity,[94] described by one author as the legal articulation of sustainable development;[95]
- provide remedies for victims of environmental abuses;[96] and/or
- include procedural rights to environmental information, to participation in environmental decision-making, and access to environmental justice.[97]

Category B: Environmental 'Dimensions'

- include the right to the conservation and preservation of one's environment;[98]
- include the State's obligation to make reasonable efforts to protect the environment;[99]
- resemble the right to enjoy a certain level of environmental quality;[100]
- include 'the right not to be exposed to man-made environmental contaminants injurious to health, the right not to be subjected to life-shortening influences, [and] the right not to be subjected to extraordinary noises';[101]
- contain quantitative environmental standards regulating harmful air pollution and other types of emissions;[102]
- include the right to protection of the Earth's wild flora and fauna, 'and the right to know that natural ecosystems containing wild flora and fauna still exist in our world';[103] and/or
- include claims to enjoin environmentally dangerous activities and to mandate affirmative actions necessary for the maintenance of an adequate quality of life.[104]

Do any of these entitlements exist in other forms and are they protected? For instance, in the case of regulating harmful air pollution, certainly national law and policy, such as the US Clean Air Act, as well as regional and global conventions regulating transboundary air pollution have already addressed these issues. Thus, the

© Blackwell Publishers Ltd. 1999.

question remains: what is the gap that needs to be filled and how best could that be done?

Does the evolution of IEC concepts represent a complementary and more precise way to address new challenges and perceived gaps in law and policy for environmental protection and preservation? IEC concepts include:

- sustainable development (perhaps the nemesis of, and having overtaken completely, the debate on a right to environment?);
- the precautionary principle;
- quality of life, environmental equity, and intergenerational equity; and
- the duty to prevent harm, due diligence, and environmental security.

On the human rights side, increasingly more and more communications brought before regional and international human rights treaty bodies link the adverse effects of environmental degradation with expressly recognized human rights, particularly with the rights to life, to private and family life, and to receive and impart information, among others.[105] Ecological degradation and related issues can be **linked** with existing human rights, subsequently broadening the scope of international human rights norms and standards to incorporate contemporary issues. One might distinguish between weaker assertions that a right to life is a **corollary** or **derivative** right, and the more convincing argument that expressly recognized human rights are capable of being **linked** with ecological degradation. In other words, the assertion that a human right to environment exists is a different claim than the view that actual human rights norms and standards are capable of being associated with issues of ecological harm. In that light, a right to environment:

- resembles a cross-cutting issue with many dimensions rather than a new or emerging human right;[106] and
- is more **duplicative** than **redundant**, given that as a policy, cross-cutting objective, it may be taken into consideration when new projects, for instance, are being discussed in order to address the human rights implications of economic development.[107]

Human Rights Tensions

Finally, one must consider the human rights tensions inherent within the international legal system in order to undertake a complete analysis, such as:

- the challenges associated with the adoption, ratification, implementation and monitoring of human rights;
- international norm fatigue or standard burn-out;
- treaty congestion;
- compliance problems;
- extrajurisdictional issues.

Likewise, human rights themselves possess and create tensions:

- restrictions, limitations or 'claw-back clauses' and derogations clauses limiting or allowing opting out of international human rights obligations;
- *drittwirkung der grundrechte*, or the third party effect of State obligations, in other words human rights operating in the private sphere, and the related debates;
- anthropocentrism v. ecocentrism;
- the right to the peaceful enjoyment of one's possessions (Article 1 Protocol 1) v. the public's general interest, and issues of proportionality;
- State sovereignty, permanent sovereignty over natural resources and their exploitation;
- international trade, economic development, environmental degradation and human rights abuses;
- overlapping and complementary authority over dimensions of environmental co-operation within the CSD, UNEP and other relevant multilateral organizations; and
- rights of indigenous peoples to explore and exploit their natural resources.

Although the foregoing points cannot be developed fully within the scope of this article, a few points are worth mentioning. Limitations abound that restrict the exercise of many human rights, and there exists no absolute guarantee for their protection. Apart from those rights considered *jus cogens* or part of customary rules, such as the right to life or freedom from torture, slavery or servitude, treaty-based human rights standards are limited because they apply only to the contracting parties. A **human** right to environment would be no exception, and if recognized would be balanced against other competing rights and broader community interests, *inter alia* aboriginal rights to protect, preserve and sustainably exploit their natural resources or economic development issues. Its implementation would confront limitations as in the case of most human rights. Besides philosophical or conceptual hurdles and lengthy delays associated with the process of recognizing new human rights, classification of a right to environment as an individual human right significantly narrows its scope to persons who have been directly affected by environmental abuses, thereby excluding broader claims brought forth on behalf of nature, due to the anthropocentricity of human rights or stringent admissibility rules, for instance where damage may be indirect or where the natural environment and its wild flora and fauna have been adversely affected. Additionally, individuals may only bring a claim against a State that is a party to a treaty, further limiting its scope or *drittwirkung*. The trade-environment-human rights equation is still searching for a satisfactory compromise, one that might settle for sustainable development, undoubtedly a right to environment's nemesis. Environmental protection does not need a human right to environment, given the numerous treaties and national laws and policies that have been adopted, just as IEC does not need the construction of new trade barriers to achieve its goals. The international community's attention in relation to environmental protection is likely to focus on achieving sustainable development rather than on creating a human right to environment.

© Blackwell Publishers Ltd. 1999.

The Future of A Right to Environment: Concluding Thoughts

The debate on a right to environment is situated at the intersection of two extremely dynamic areas of public international law, namely, human rights and the environment. The legal literature at the time of writing this article near the close of the twentieth century is not, for the most part, lacking in quantity of commentary, given that much has been written on the convergence of these two areas; rather, it is quality of content, reality-based perspectives drawing upon current sources of international law, and accuracy of interpreting these sources that, taken as a whole, are questionable. Despite those articles showering accolades upon a human right to environment in international legal theory and practice, the current status of a right to environment as a universally recognized and accepted human right norm or standard in public international law remains ambiguous, and its transformation into anything other than a moral aspiration or a concept of IEC is doubtful in the foreseeable future. The right to environmental preservation, however, as a customary norm or standard of IEC may be more realistic to envisage in the next century rather than a narrowly construed anthropocentric right to environment.

This article has challenged several assumptions within the corpus of international legal literature wherein the question of a right to environment's nature and scope has been considered, raising doubts over initial euphoria regarding a human right to environment, and adding an alternative perspective to this debate. By avoiding the rights trap right altogether, one might consider a right to environment as a non-right, manifested as a broad concept operating and applied within a more contemporary normative system of international law, a system described by Professor Abi-Saab as the 'international law of cooperation'.[108] Alternatively, it might continue to evolve as a concept of IEC, representing one of many State policy objectives achieved through the ongoing implementation, interpretation and monitoring of global, regional, sub-regional and national law and policy for environmental co-operation, protection and preservation.

Taken as a whole, the sources of international law do not lend overwhelming support to the existence of a human right to environment within current international legal theory and practice as a universally recognized human rights norm or standard. Such a right, taken at face value, has enticing appeal. However, closer inspection reveals that it has more flexibility whether one describes it as a cross-cutting issue, as a dimension of many existing human rights, or as a concept of IEC. Recognition of a new human right would merely duplicate existing human rights and IEC concepts. In absence of any identifiable process whereby a right to environment has been approved through a multilateral process, such as via official diplomatic negotiations, it is rather difficult to equate mere political gestures expressing a right to environment as a common goal within non-legally binding documents to represent a widespread, tacit universal acceptance. The process of persuasion and diplomacy is encouraged on a continuous basis to ensure that the implementation and monitoring of human rights and IEC concepts take place within the 'main stream of diplomacy and international law'.[109]

The adoption of a new human right to environment would be commensurate with acknowledging the emperor's new clothes rather than an *über* right or neologism. The ultimate goal of a right to environment – the attainment of a 'decent' quality of life within a healthy, ecologically balanced environment for present and future generations, all thriving in the human and natural worlds – is already being encouraged *without an expressly recognized right to environment*. The current status of a right to environment is tantamount to that of a cross-cutting issue, one that may be linked with various expressly recognized human rights. It resembles more a policy-oriented goal of IEC rather than a universally-accepted **human rights** norm or standard in international law for the protection of human rights.

Notes

1. UN, *International Law on the Eve of the Twenty-first Century. Views from the International Law Commission* (1997), at 51 (hereafter, Lukashuk, and *International Law on the Eve of the C21st*, respectively).
2. Declaration of the United Nations Conference on the Human Environment (Stockholm, 5–16 June 1972); and Declaration of the United Nations Conference on Environment and Development (Rio de Janeiro, 3–14 June 1992), UN Doc A/CONF.151/5 (Part I, Appendix, 12 August 1992).
3. This expression is consistent with the view that certain issues not yet regulated via expressly recognized substantive obligations in international law, such as the notion of a right to a healthy environment and other concepts of IEC, are instead governed by a residual topic, the voluntary notion encompassed within 'international co-operation'. According to Professor Francesco Francioni, international co-operation guides State behaviour through 'the spirit of reasonable consideration of other parties' interests and towards the achievement of common goals', which has a relevant role in the field of environmental protection: Francioni, 'International cooperation for the Protection of the Environment: The Procedural Dimension', in Lang, Neuhold, Zemanek (eds), *Environmental Protection and International Law* (1991), 203.
4. Lynch and Maggio, 'Human Rights, Environment, and Economic Development: Existing and Emerging Standards in International Law and Global Society' (revised draft, 15 November 1997), as available on www.igc.apc.org/ciel.
5. UN Doc E/CN.4/Sub.2/1994/9 (hereafter, *Ksentini Final Report*).
6. See *RECIEL*, 3:4 (1994) 197ff.
7. Brownlie, 'The Rights of Peoples in Modern International Law', in Crawford (ed), *The Rights of Peoples* (1988), 1, 14 (emphasis added) (hereafter, Brownlie).
8. The ILO Convention concerning the Prohibition and Immediate Action for the Elimination of the Worst Forms of Child Labour, adopted in Geneva, 17 June 1999.
9. UNCHR, Decision 1997/102, 'Human Rights and the Environment', taken at the 36th meeting of the Commission on 16 April 1997.
10. *Id.*
11. See e.g. UNGA Resolution 1997/72 on the right to development.
12. UNCHR Resolution 1999/79 on the right to development.
13. UN Doc E/CN.4/1999/89 (22 December 1998), *Promotion and Protection of Human Rights: Science and Environment. Report of the Secretary-General submitted in accordance with Commission decision 1997/102*, para. 11.

© Blackwell Publishers Ltd 1999.

14. *Id.*, paras 31–3. The observer, Neil Popovic, contributed to the 1994 special issue of *RECIEL* on environmental rights and access to justice, as well as participating in the drafting of the draft declaration on human rights and the environment.
15. UN Doc E/CN.4/Sub/1999/1, *Provisional Agenda* (12 May 1999).
16. See also UN Doc A/53/372, *Follow-up to the World Conference on Human Rights* (11 September 1998).
17. Pursuant to UNCHR Resolution 1999/23, 26 April 1999, adopted by a roll-call of 36 votes to 16, with 1 abstention.
18. *Id.*, para. 4.
19. Alfredsson, n. 31 below, at 21.
20. UN Doc E/CN.4/1997/18, *Human Rights and the Environment. Report of the Secretary-General prepared in accordance with Commission resolution 1996/13* (9 December 1996), Part I.E.
21. DPI-Releases, HR/CN/97/34, *Human Rights Commission Acts on Texts Related to Unilateral Coercive Measures, Toxic Wastes, Right to Food and Extreme Poverty* (3 April 1997), comments by Tyge Lehmann (Denmark).
22. *Id.*, Nancy Rubin (United States). It was, however, renewed.
23. *Id.*, comments by Peter Van Wulften Palthe (Netherlands). The Netherlands is consistent in its position, having declared previously that the movement of toxic wastes 'seemed to be somewhat out of place in a body supposed to be dealing with human rights' and suggested that UNEP should deal with that issue: UN Doc E/CN.4/1989/SR.24 (23 February 1989), para. 103.
24. *Id.*
25. UNCHR Resolution 1997/9 on adverse effects of the illicit movement and dumping of toxic and dangerous products and wastes on the enjoyment of human rights: See also *Progress Report submitted by Mrs Fatma Zohra Ksentini, Special Rapporteur, pursuant to Commission resolution 1996/14*, UN Doc E/CN.4/1997/19 (5 February 1997); and the most recent progress report, E/CN.4/1999/46.
26. Higgins, *Problems and Process. International Law and How We Use It* (1992), 96 (hereafter, Higgins).
27. Higgins, *id.*, 105; McDougal, Lasswell and Chen, *Human Rights and World Public Order. The Basic Policies of an International Law of Human Dignity* (1980), 80ff (hereafter, McDougal). See also Sidorsky, 'Contemporary Reinterpretations of the Concept of Human Rights', in *id.* (ed.), *Essays on Human Rights. Contemporary Issues and Jewish Perspectives* (1979), 88–109, 103–7 (describing contemporary theory of human rights and recognizing that societies with moral standards have differed on many values that are present in extended lists of human rights) (hereafter, Sidorsky).
28. Higgins, n. 26 above, at 104.
29. For instance, in the course of determining an appropriate definition of a right to a healthy environment within the European Union (EU), one author admitted, 'Debates over the philosophical foundation of the definition of human rights engender a great deal of controversy. None of the many competing schools of thought command universal or even general consensus. Each perception of human rights has its flaws': Van Dyke, n. 31 below, at 325.
30. Ladeur, 'Environmental Constitutional Law', in Winter (ed.), *European Environmental Law* (1996), 15 at 18 (hereafter, Ladeur).
31. Most notably Alfredsson and Ovsiouk, 'Human Rights and the Environment', *NJIL*, 60 (1991) 18 (hereafter, Alfredsson); Cullet, 'Definition of an Environmental Right in a Human Rights Context', *NQHR*, 13 (1995) 25 (hereafter, Cullet); Downs, 'A Healthy and Ecologically Balanced Environment: An Argument for a Third Generation Right', *DJCIL*, 3 (1993) 351 (hereafter, Downs); Gormley, 'The Legal Obligation of the International Community to Guarantee a Pure and Decent Environment', *GIELR*, 3 (1990) 85 (hereafter, Gormley); Hodkova, 'Is There a Right to a Healthy Environment in the International Legal Order?', *CJIL*, 7 (1991) 65 (hereafter, Hodkova); Kiss, 'Définition et nature juridique d'un droit de l'homme à l'environnement', in Kromarek (ed), *Environnement et droits de l'homme* (1987) (hereafter, 'Définition', and *Environnement*, respectively); Leighton Schwartz, 'International Legal Protection for Victims of Environmental Abuse', *Yale JIL*, 18 (1993) 355 (hereafter, Leighton Schwartz); Maddalena, *Il diritto all'ambiente come fundamentale diritto dell'individuo et della collectività* (1983) (hereafter, Maddalena); Popovic, 'In Pursuit of Environmental Human Rights: Commentary on the Draft Declaration of Principles on Human Rights and the Environment', *CHRLR*, 27 (1996) 487 (hereafter, Popovic); Postiglione, *Il diritto all'ambiente* (1982) (hereafter, Postiglione); Shelton, 'Human Rights, Environmental Rights and the Right to Environment', *Stanford J Int'l L*, 28 (1991) 103 (hereafter, Shelton); Thorme, 'Establishing Environment as a Human Right', *DJILP* 19 (1991) 301 (hereafter, Thorme); Uibopuu, 'The Internationally Guaranteed Right of an Individual to a Clean Environment', *CLYB*, 1 (1977) 101 (hereafter, Uibopuu). For a regional perspective, see Van Dyke, 'A Proposal to Introduce the Right to a Healthy Environment into the European Convention Regime', *VELJ*, 13 (1994) 323 (hereafter, Van Dyke). Cf. Gibson, 'The Right to a Clean Environment', *Sask LR*, 54 (1990) 5 at 8 (acknowledging the formal process required to proclaim a new human right).
32. Downs, *id.*, 380.
33. *Id.*
34. Van Dyke, n. 31 above, 336; 'Définition', n. 31 above, 19.
35. *Human Rights and the Environment. Preliminary report prepared by Mrs. Fatma Zohra Ksentini, Special Rapporteur*, UN Doc E/CN.4/Sub.2/1991/8 (2 August 1991), paras 69–70 (hereafter, *Ksentini Preliminary Report*).
36. Déjeant-Pons, 'The Right to Environment in Regional Human Rights Systems', in Mahoney and Mahoney (eds), *Human Rights in the Twenty-first Century* (1993), 595, 603 (hereafter, Déjeant-Pons, and Mahoney, respectively); Shelton, n. 31 above, 106.
37. See *e.g.* Kiss in 'Définition', n. 31 above, 17, translated and repeated in *id.*, 'Concept and Possible Implications of the Right to Environment', in Mahoney, *id.*, 551 at 553 (hereafter, 'Concept'); *id.*, 'Le droit à la qualité de l'environnement: un droit de l'homme?', in Duplé (ed.), *Le droit à la qualité de l'environnement: un droit en devenir, un droit à définir* (1988), 69–70 (hereafter, 'Le droit à la qualité'); Cançado Trindade, 'The contribution of international human rights law to environmental protection, with special reference to global environmental change', in Brown Weiss, 244 at 282 (hereafter, Cançado Trindade).
38. Jacqué, 'La protection du droit à l'environnement au niveau européen ou régional', in *Environnement*, n. 31 above, 65 at 70–5.
39. Giagnocavo and Goldstein, 'Law Reform or World Re-form: The Problem of Environmental Rights', *McGill LJ*, 35 (1990) 345 at 365 (hereafter, Giagnocavo).
40. Giagnocavo, *id.*, 362. Cf. Stone, 'Should Trees Have Standing? – Toward Legal Rights for Natural Objects', *SCLR*, 45 (1972) 450; Tribe, 'Ways Not to Think About Plastic Trees', *Yale LJ*, 83 (1974) 1315.
41. 'Définition', n. 31 above, at 24–5; 'Concept', n. 37 above, at 556–7.
42. Dowdeswell, 'An Enduring Peace', in *A Healthy Environment is a Human Right* (1996), Conference Proceedings, Montréal, 26–28 October 1995, 3 at 5 (hereafter, Dowdeswell).
43. *Case Concerning the Gabcíkovo-Nagymaros Project (Hungary/Slovakia)*, Judgment of 25 September 1997, as available on www.icj-cij.org, para. 53.
44. *Legality of the Threat or Use of Nuclear Weapons, Advisory Opinion*, (1996) 35 ILM 809 (8 July 1996) (text available on www.icj-cij-org), para. 29; *ref'd* to in *Hungary/Slovakia Judgment*, *id.*, para. 53.
45. 18 October 1961, *ETS* No. 35, 529 *UNTS* 89.
46. Recommendation on the Formulation of a Draft European Charter and a European Convention on Environmental Protection and Sustainable Development, Recommendation 1130 (1990), European Parliamentary Assembly, 42nd Session, *reprinted* in *YIEL*, 1 (1990) 484. See also *Draft Proposal for a Council Directive Concerning the Access to Justice in Environmental Matters*, proposed by the Öko-Institut e.V., in co-operation with FIELD, *reprinted* in *ELNI Newsletter*, 1 (1994) 7; European Charter on Environment and Health, proposed by the WHO, *reprinted* in *ELP*, 20/1/2 (1990) 57; Charter on Environmental Rights and Obligations, proposed by the UN/ECE, *reprinted* in (1991) 21/2 *ELP* 81, adopted at the Experts Meeting of the UN/ECE in Oslo, Norway, 29–31 October 1990.
47. Bossuyt, *Guide to the 'Travaux Préparatoires' of the International Covenant on Civil and Political Rights* (1987); *Collected Edition of the Travaux Préparatoires of the European Convention on Human Rights*, vols I and II (1975), III (1976), IV (1977), V (1979), VI, VII and VIII (1985). See generally, Nowak, *Kommentar zum UNO-Pakt über bürgerliche und politische Rechte und zum Fakultativeprotok-*

© Blackwell Publishers Ltd. 1999.

oll (1989), translated in *id.*, *UN Covenant on Civil and Political Rights – CCPR Commentary* (1993).

48. (Vienna, 1969), *reprinted* in Brownlie (ed.), *Basic Documents in International Law* (1995, 4th), 389.

49. Communication No. 67/1980, *EHP v. Canada* (1990) 2 *SD* 20, where the HRC declared inadmissible, on procedural grounds, the petition of a group of inhabitants of Port Hope, Ontario, who alleged their right to life was threatened due to the inherent risks posed by the proximity of a nuclear power facility to their homes. Although the HRC noted that the case raised serious questions, the case was brought pursuant to Article 6(1), the right to life, and was dependent upon linking a guaranteed human right with environmental risk or degradation. Note that the HRC did not recognize an implied right to environment (hereafter, *EHP v. Canada*). See also Communication No 429/1990, *EW et al v. The Netherlands*, CCPR/C/47/D/429/1990, *reprinted* in (1994) 1 *IHHR* 67 (hereafter, *EW v. The Netherlands*); *Fredin v. Sweden* (No. 1) (1991) 13 *EHRR* 7784 (hereafter, *Fredin v. Sweden*); *Zander v. Sweden* (1993) 18 *EHRR* 175 (hereinafter, *Zander v. Sweden*); Appl 13728/88, *S v. France*, 17 May 1990, *reprinted* in (1991) 3 *RUDH* 236 (hereafter, *S v. France*); Appl 16798/90, *López Ostra v. Spain* (1995) 20 *EHRR* 277 (December 1994) (hereafter, *López Ostra v. Spain*).

50. See e.g. UNGA Res 45/94 (1990); European Charter on Environment and Health, n. 46 above, para. 1; Charter on Environmental Rights and Obligations, n. 46 above, Principle 1; draft Covenant on Environmental Conservation and Sustainable Use of Natural Resources (Draft 4), IUCN-Commission on Environmental Law, UN Doc A/CONF.151/PC/WG.III/4 (23 August 1991) ('Part II Fundamental Principles, Article 2 Individual Rights and Duties', para. 1; WCED Experts Group on Environmental Law of the World Commission on Environment and Development, *Environmental Protection and Sustainable Development: Legal Principles and Recommendations* (1986), 25; Déclaration de Limoges, recommendation 4; Text of a European Charter and Convention on the Environment and Sustainable Development, Council of Europe, Parliamentary Assembly, Recommendation 1130 (1990) on the Formulation of a European Charter and a European Convention on Environmental Protection and Sustainable Development, adopted 28 September 1990, Doc AREC1130.1403–28/9/90–27; *reprinted* in *YIEL*, 1 (1990) 484. See also the Langkawi Declaration on Environment, *reprinted* in Gordon and Fraser (eds), *Institutions and Sustainable Development: Meeting the Challenge* (1991); Declaration of Brasilia on the Environment, *reprinted* in (1989) 28 ILM 1311; Amazon Declaration, *reprinted* in (1989) 28 ILM 1303 (1989); Abidjan Declaration, UN Doc A/CONF.151/PC/120 (14 November 1991), 31; Manaus Declaration, UN Doc A/CONF.151/PC/123 (24 February 1992), 3.

51. Dowdeswell, n. 42 above, at 4. See also *Ksentini Preliminary Report*, n. 35 above, at 3, para. 12 (a 'healthy and well-conserved environment would be a prerequisite for a healthy life'); Symonides, 'The Human Right to a Clean, Balanced and Protected Environment', in *Diritti dell'uomo e Ambiente: La Partecipazione dei Cittadini alle Decisioini sulla Tutela dell'ambiente* (1990), 239–40.

52. Declaration of The Hague on the Protection of the Atmosphere, 11 March 1989, UN Doc A/44/340; E/1989/120, *reprinted* in (1989) 28 ILM 1309.

53. See Barbados Declaration and Programme of Action for Small Island Developing States, Bridgetown, Barbados, 26 April-6 May 1994, Principle 2; Declaration of Santa Cruz de la Sierra and Plan of Action for the Sustainable Development of the Americas, Summit Conference on Sustainable Development, Santa Cruz de la Sierra, Bolivia, 7–8 December 1996, para. 2.

54. Székely, 'Non-Binding Commitments: A Commentary on the Softening of International Law as Evidenced in the Environmental Field', in ILC, *International Law on the Eve of the C21st*, n. 1 above, 173 at 190 (emphasis in original).

55. Merrills, 'Environmental Protection and Human Rights: Conceptual Aspects', in Boyle and Anderson (eds), *Human Rights Approaches to Environmental Protection* (1966), 25 at 39 (hereafter, Merrills, and *Human Rights Approaches*, respectively).

56. *Id.* Cf. 'Définition', n. 31 above, at 22.

57. Rest, 'Improved Environmental Protection Through an Expanded Concept of Human Rights?', *EPL*, 27/3 (1997) 213 at 214.

58. See UNEP's EIA Principles; Convention on Environmental Impact Assessment in a Transboundary Context, (Espoo, 25 February 1991), UN Doc E.ECE.1250, *reprinted* in (1991) 30 ILM 800, in force 10 September 1997, in accordance with Article 18(1), 30 signatories, 18 parties; Council Directive (EIA), [1985] OJ L175/40.

59. Convention on Early Notification of a Nuclear Accident (Vienna, 26 September 1986), in force 27 October 1986, *reprinted* in (1986) 25 ILM 1377.

60. Article 19(3)(d) of the ILC's draft articles on state responsibility criminalizes serious breaches of an international obligation 'of essential importance for the safeguarding and preservation of the human environment, such as those prohibiting massive pollution of the atmosphere or of the seas'.

61. See e.g., Ascencio Herrera and Pevato, 'Legal Framework for Environmental Cooperation in Latin America: An Overivew', *RECIEL*, 5 (1996) 1; Lin, 'Implementation of Environmental Conventions: A Regional Perspective', in Kurukulasuriya (ed.), *UNEP's New Way Forward. Environmental Law and Sustainable Development* (1995), 23; Wilson, Ogolla, Brañes, Kurukulasuriya 'Emerging Trends in National Environmental Legislation in Developing Countries', in *id.*, 185.

62. Dowdeswell, n. 42 above, at 6.

63. Afghanistan, Angola, Chad, China, Germany, Greece, Honduras, Islamic Republic of Iran, Mexico, Mozambique, Namibia, Nepal, The Netherlands, Nigeria, Panama, Paraguay, Taiwan, Thailand, Ukraine.

64. Algeria, Bolivia, Guatemala, Guyana, Haiti, Laos People's Democratic Republic, Russian Federation, Vanuatu.

65. Cuba, Ethiopia, India, Seychelles, Sri Lanka.

66. Argentina, Benin, Brazil, Bulgaria, Burkina Faso, Cape Verde, Chile, Colombia, Congo, Croatia, Czeck and Slovak Republics, Ecuador, Ethiopia, Federal Republic of Yugoslavia, Mali, Mongolia, Nicaragua, Nigeria, Peru, Philippines, Poland, Portugal, Romania, Slovakia, Slovenia, South Africa, Spain, The Sudan, Togo, Turkey, Ukraine.

67. El Salvador, Equatorial Guinea, Hungary, Sweden.

68. Algeria, Bahrain, Malta, Paraguay, Poland, Taiwan, Tanzania, United Arab Emirates, Viet Nam.

69. See e.g. Thorme, n. 31 above, at 312–13; Popovic, n. 31 above, at 507, fn. 75; Martín Mateo, 'La constitucionalización positiva del Derecho ambiental', *Humana Iura*, 6 (1996) 191–200 (considering constitutions and soft law documents as evidence of a right to environment's constitutionalization in positive law). Cf. Krämer, *Focus on European Environmental Law* (1992), 5–7 (hereafter, Krämer).

70. Cf. Popovic, n. 31 above, 506–7, *esp.* fn. 75 (claiming that 'More than 60 countries...have adopted similar provisions in their constitutions', yet cites 30, or 50%, that do not expressly guarantee a right to environment).

71. For instance, the Japanese Constitution does not expressly refer to the environment, instead declaring that its citizens have 'the right to maintain the minimum standards of wholesome and cultured living': Japan Constitution, ch. III, Article 25. See further *Ksentini Final Report*, n. 5 above, at 81–9.

72. Ladeur, n. 30 above, at 33–4.

73. *Id.*, 15 at 19.

74. Krämer, n. 69 above, at 5–7. Cf. Jordano Fraga, 'El derecho a disfrutar de un medio ambiente adecuado: elementos para su articulación expansiva', *Humana Iura*, 6 (1996) 121 (commenting on the subjective nature of Article 45 of Spain's Constitution). Only four Member States contain express references to the environment within national constitutions: Greece, Article 24; Spain, Article 45; Portugal, Article 66; the Netherlands, Article 21.

75. Brazil's initial report to the HRC did not refer to environmental law or policy even though Article 225 of its Constitution recognizes the right to a healthy environment: Brazil, CCPR/C/81/Add.6; CCPR/C/79/Add.66 (24 July 1996), A/51/40, paras 306–38; CCPR/C/SR.1506 to 1508; Concluding Comments *reprinted* in (1997) 4 *IHRR* 107–11.

76. See e.g. *Canada's Green Plan* (1990); *Report of Canada to the United Nations Commission on Sustainable Development* (1994); *Stewardship and Sustainability. A Renewed Conservation Strategy for Prince Edward Island* (1994); *European Union Fifth Environmental Action Programme* [1993] OJ C/138/1; *This Common Inheritance: Britain's Environmental Strategy*, Cmnd 1200 (1990); *Germany's Responsibility for the Future – Options for Sustainable*

© Blackwell Publishers Ltd. 1999.

Management of Substance Chains and Material Flows (1994); *A Framework for Sustainable Development. Action Plan for the Caribbean Environment Programme* (1987); Latin American and Caribbean Commission on Sustainable Development, *Our Own Agenda* (1990); *Summit Conference on Sustainable Development, Santa Cruz, Bolivia 1996, Plan of Action*.

77. Cf. Thorme, n. 31 above, at 332–3. Also known as 'peremptory norms' from which no derogations are permitted under any circumstances: see Article 53, Vienna Convention on the Law of Treaties.
78. The 'need to reconcile economic development with the protection of the environment is aptly expressed in the *concept of sustainable development*': para. 140 (emphasis added).
79. Robertson and Merrills, *Human Rights in the World* (3d) (1989), 259 (emphasis added) (hereafter, Robertson and Merrills).
80. Moskowitz, *The Politics and Dynamics of Human Rights* (1968).
81. With exceptions such as Merrills, n. 55 above.
82. Birnie and Boyle, *International Law and the Environment* (1992), 190ff; and see generally, Robertson and Merrills, n. 79 above, at 255–9.
83. Address by Mr Amartya Sen, Nobel Laureate in Economics, to the International Labour Conference, 15 June 1999.
84. Pathak, 'The Human Rights System as a Conceptual Framework for Environmental Law', in Brown Weiss (ed.), *Environmental Change and International Law* (1992), 205 at 213–14 (hereafter, Pathak).
85. Van Dyke, n. 31 above, at 339; Shelton, n. 31 above, at 106.
86. Déjeant-Pons, n. 36 above, at 611–12.
87. Maddalena, n. 31 above; Loperena Rota and Herreros Ezquerro, 'Los Derechos Humanos al Medio Ambiente Adecuado y a Su Protección', *Humana Iura*, 6 (1996) 171, at 178–89.
88. Popovic, n. 31 above.
89. Downs, n. 31 above, 376–77; Gormley, n. 31 above, 112; *Ksentini Final Report*, n. 5 above, para. 261; Thorme, n. 31 above, 319–22.
90. Cançado Trindade, n. 37 above, at 282; 'Concept', n. 37 above, at 553; 'Définition', n. 31 above, at 69–70; Downs, n. 31 above, at 380; *Ksentini Final Report*, note 5 above, para. 253; Pathak, n. 84 above, at 211–13; Thorme, n. 31 above, at 310; Van Dyke, n. 31 above, at 339.
91. Downs, n. 31 above, at 380.
92. Popovic, n. 31 above, at 541.
93. Pathak, n. 84 above, at 238.
94. Van Dyke, n. 31 above, at 327 and 333–334; 'Définition', n. 31 above, at 17–18.
95. Redgwell, 'Intergenerational Equity and Global Warming', in Churchill and Freestone, *International Law and Global Climate Change* (1991), 41 at 42; Cançado Trindade, n. 31 above, at 255–71; Pathak, n. 84 above, at 226–27; Thorme, n. 31 above, at 310.
96. Leighton Schwartz, n. 31 above.
97. Jadot, 'Les procédures garantissant le droit à l'environnement', in *Environnement*, n. 31 above, 51–63; Nelkin, 'Participation du public à la mise en oevre d'un droit à l'environnement', in *id.*, 39–50; Tolentino, 'Environnement et information', in *id.*, 29–37; *Ksentini Final Report*, n. 5 above, para. 253; 'Concept', n. 37 above, 557; Déjeant-Pons, n. 36 above, 609–11; Van Dyke, n. 31 above, 336.
98. *Ksentini Final Report*, n. 5 above, para. 256.
99. Van Dyke, n. 31 above, at 341.
100. Downs, n. 31 above, at 380.
101. Thorme, n. 31 above, at 309.
102. Shelton, n. 31 above, at 135.
103. Thorme, n. 31 above, at 309–10.
104. Uibopuu, n. 31 above, at 106.
105. *EHP v. Canada*; *EW v. The Netherland*; *Fredin v. Sweden*; *Zander v. Sweden*; *S v. France*; *López Ostra v. Spain*, all n. 49 above; *Case of Balmer-Schafroth and Others v. Switzerland* (67/1996/686/876), Judgment of 26 August 1997; and *Case of Guerra and Others v. Italia* (116/1996/735/932), Judgment of 19 February 1998. For commentary see further Maljean-Dubois, 'La Convention Européenne des Droits de L'homme et le Droit a L'information en Matière d'Environnement', *RGDIP*, 4 (1998) 995.
106. Downs, n. 31 above, at 376–377; Thorme, n. 31 above, at 319.
107. 'Redundant' is defined as 'surplus to requirements; unnecessary or superfluous ... verbose or tautological' whereas 'duplicative' is defined as 'something additional of the same kind': see *The Collins Dictionary and Thesaurus* (1987). Cf. Boyle, 'The Role of International Human Rights Law in the Protection of the Environment', in *Human Rights Approaches*, n. 55 above, at 53: a 'generic right to a decent environment...would add little to what already exists in *international environmental law*. While it would have undoubted rhetorical force, such a right in international law may in reality be largely *redundant*' (emphasis added).
108. Abi-Saab, 'A "New World Order"? Some Preliminary Reflections', *HYIL*, 7 (1994) 87, 92 ('what is most needed at the present juncture ... is a qualitative shift towards the alternative perspective...for legal regulation, that of "international law of cooperation"').
109. Brownlie, n. 7 above, at 14.

Paula M Pevato, PhD, LLM, LLB, BA, of the Editorial Board and former Managing Editor, *RECIEL*, 1994–95. Dr. Pevato is currently working in the Department of Working Conditions and Environment of the International Labour Organization, Geneva. This article is written in Dr. Pevato's personal capacity and does not necessarily reflect the views of the UN or its specialized agencies.

© Blackwell Publishers Ltd. 1999.

Part IV
International Institutions and Non-Governmental Organisations

[12]

ENVIRONMENTAL PROTECTION AND DEVELOPMENT

PATRICIA BIRNIE*

[Environmental protection has been an issue for the UN which was not foreseen when it was established 50 years ago. The UN's mandate to take action in respect of the environment is not clear in its Charter. However, numerous UN organs, specialised agencies and conferences — perhaps most significantly the UN Environment Program — have approached this issue from various perspectives. One of the most significant obstacles to action by any of these has been the conflict between the goals of UN members with respect to economic development and environmental protection. Recent reforms and newly-established bodies and instruments await assessment after an appropriate period of time.]

I INTRODUCTION: LACK OF ANY REFERENCE TO 'ENVIRONMENT' IN THE UN CHARTER

It is salutary to bear in mind that the founding fathers of the United Nations (UN) could not possibly have foreseen the events that would take place during the next 50 years. Almost immediately, the decision-making basis of the Charter was undermined by the advent of the Cold War and the arms race. It was then radically changed in the 1960s and 1970s by the effects of decolonisation and the emergence of many impoverished developing countries in the Southern Hemisphere whose main aim was to promote their economic development, as the countries of the North were still successfully doing. The North/South dialogue at first took place inside the UN with little, if any, awareness of the dangers of promoting development without having regard to its deleterious side effects, namely the excessive consumption of living and non-living global resources in which rapid, uncontrolled industrialisation results, as well as the degrading effects of the pollution it generates in the form of atmospheric emissions, discharges of effluents, dumping of waste and the like. The increasing use of fertilisers and pesticides in the agricultural industry also contributed to this growth in pollution of air, water and land.

As the world population increased, especially in developing countries, and uncontrolled development proceeded, other environmental problems such as desertification, deforestation and water shortages began to manifest themselves in the South, as they had done earlier in some Northern states following their earlier industrial revolutions. Yet it was not until the convening by the UN General Assembly of the Stockholm Conference on the Human Environment (UNCHE) in 1972[1] that an environmental perspective was effectively introduced into the policies and activities of the UN and its Specialised Agencies,

* Visiting Professor at Queen Mary College, London and Visiting Fellow at the London School of Economics.

[1] GA Res 2398, 23 UN GAOR (1733rd plen mtg), UN Doc A/Res/2398 (1968).

based on the principles promulgated in the Declaration adopted by that Conference.[2] Even then, the debates and programmes aimed at promoting economic development and environmental protection proceeded almost entirely on separate tracks. Despite the urgings of many critics, the need for their coalescence to achieve development on a sustainable basis was not fully and formally recognised by the UN until the Conference on Environment and Development (UNCED), convened by the General Assembly in Rio de Janeiro in 1992,[3] adopted the Rio Declaration on Environment and Development[4] and an Action Program entitled Agenda 21.[5] These documents laid down the framework for the actions required to achieve sustainable development into the 21st century and beyond.

It is the purpose of this paper to examine why the UN took so long to tackle these problems, and why in its practice they were treated for so long as discrete issues despite their obvious symbiosis, and also to evaluate its progress in promoting both development and environmental protection during its first 50 years.

II HISTORICAL BACKGROUND.

Concluded after World War I, the main aim of the League of Nations Covenant was to establish a system of collective security to deter war and aggression. However, its loopholes had been exploited by its members, either to commit acts of aggression against other states or to avoid their responsibilities under the Covenant to take the necessary measures to deal collectively with such violations. These factors had led directly to the Second World War.

The drafters of the UN Charter were anxious, above all else, to avoid including the weaknesses of the League of Nations Covenant.[6] Thus, the UN Charter's Preamble proclaims that the primary aim of establishing the UN is 'to save succeeding generations from the scourge of war'.[7] Its first purpose is stated to be 'to maintain international peace and security, and to that end: to take effective collective measures for the prevention and removal of threats to the peace, and to bring about by peaceful means, and in conformity with the principles of justice and international law, adjustment or settlement of international disputes or situations which might lead to a breach of the peace'.[8]

Following revelation at the end of World War II of the gross breaches of basic human rights that had occurred under Hitler, the second preambular aim of the

[2] Report of the United Nations Conference on the Human Environment 15-6 June 1972, UN Doc A/Conf 48/14/Rev 1 (1972) and Corr 1 (1972); 11 ILM 1416.

[3] GA Res 228, 44 UN GAOR (85th plen mtg), UN Doc A/Res/228 (1989).

[4] UN Doc A/Conf 151/5/Rev 1, endorsed in GA Res 190, 47 UN GAOR (93rd plen mtg), UN Doc A/Res/190 (1992); 31 ILM 874.

[5] Report of the United Nations Conference on Environment and Development, Rio de Janeiro, 3-14 June 1992, UN Doc A/Conf 151/26 (Vols I, II and III) (1992).

[6] F Hinsley, *Power and the Pursuit of Peace: Theory and Practice in the History of Relations between States* (1963); F Walters, *A History of the League of Nations* (1960) *passim*.

[7] Text in Ian Brownlie (ed), *Basic Documents in International Law* (3rd ed, 1983) 1.

[8] UN Charter art 1(1).

UN was stated to be 'to reaffirm faith in fundamental human rights', reflected in the purpose that it was 'to achieve international co-operation ... in promoting and encouraging respect for human rights and for fundamental freedoms.'[9]

The League of Nations had made no reference to protection of human rights or to the need to resolve the underlying economic and social problems which contribute to war and the destabilisation of international peace and security, although it had eventually established committees to deal with some aspects of those problems. The UN, however, asserted in its Preamble its determination 'to promote social progress and better standards of life in larger freedom', and in its purposes, in Article 3, 'to achieve international co-operation in solving international problems of an economic, social, cultural and humanitarian character'. Finally, Article 1(4) stated that the UN was 'to be a centre for harmonising the actions of nations in the attainment of these common ends'.

Nowhere in the Charter is there any reference to the aim of protecting, preserving or conserving the natural environment. Thus, the UN's power to adopt any explicit policy or undertake any action directed solely toward this purpose has to be derived from a broad interpretation of the above purposes and of Article 55 which requires the UN to promote, firstly, higher standards of living, full employment and conditions of economic and social progress and development, and secondly, solutions to international economic, social, health, and related problems, and international cultural and educational co-operation. It can be assumed that environmental protection is an essential element in promotion of social progress and in the solving of economic and social problems and achieving better standards of life. However, the possibilities of inferring that environmental protection is necessary for the maintenance of international peace and security, that is, that environmental threats can be equated with other threats to international security, such as aggression, and thus can be dealt with by the Security Council under Chapter VII of the Charter, have not been explicitly exploited. Even in the Security Council Resolution[10] dealing with the oil pollution caused by the burning of oil wells in Kuwait by Iraq at the end of the Gulf War the Council did not refer specifically to any concept of 'environmental security'.[11] Likewise the UN has not attempted to add any environmental rights, such as a right to a clean and healthy environment,[12] to its declarations or covenants on human rights[13] to enable it to deal with

9 Ibid art 1(3).

10 SC Res 687, 46 UN SCOR (2981st mtg), UN Doc S/Res/687 (1991) paras 16-19; (1991) 30 ILM 852.

11 Alexandre Timoshenko, 'Ecological Security: Response to Global Challenges' in Edith Brown Weiss (ed), *Environmental Change and International Law: New Challenges and Dimensions* (1992) 413-56.

12 For this approach see Alexandre Kiss, 'An Introductory Note on a Human Right to Environment' in Brown Weiss, above n 11, 199-204.

13 Universal Declaration of Human Rights, GA Res 217A, 3 UN GAOR 135, UN Doc A/810 (1948); International Covenant on Economic, Social and Cultural Rights 1966, 993 UNTS 3; UKTS 6 (1977); (1967) 6 ILM 360; International Covenant on Civil and Political Rights 1966, 999 UNTS 171; UKTS 6 (1977); see text in Brownlie, above n 7, 230-97.

environmental issues under this heading, although some commentators now advocate this.

There was no awareness in 1945 that the UN would need to be involved in conserving resources, preventing pollution and promoting *sustainable* development. In the UN's early years, as during the League's life, few actions were taken to these ends and those which were taken were *ad hoc*, such as the establishment of some fishery commissions, agreements on migrating birds and a convention on whaling. There was no coherence among, or working programmes integrating, these activities. It was the growing concern of Non-Governmental Organisations (NGOs), especially in the United States, that prompted some governments to take the initiatives that led to the convening of the Stockholm Conference in 1972.[14] Until then, and in the period immediately thereafter, promotion of development was the first priority for developing states.

III The Paramountcy of Development in the UN in the 1960s and 1970s[15]

As decolonised states began to join the UN, they started, especially in the forum of the UN Conference on Trade and Development (UNCTAD), to demand a radical transformation in the global framework of international economic relations. Even before this, as early as 1962, the UN General Assembly had adopted, as an economic aspect of self-determination, a Resolution on Permanent Sovereignty over Natural Resources. This was proclaimed as a right of peoples and nations which 'must be exercised in the interest of their national development and of the well-being of the people concerned'.[16] It did not, however, provide for conservation of these resources or the sustainable maintenance of the yield from such living resources as fish. UNCTAD had, in May 1972, stressed the urgent need to establish generally-accepted actions to govern international economic relations systematically.[17] The advent of the UNCHE Declaration (in June 1972) did not deflect the UN General Assembly from holding a Special Session on a Declaration on Establishment of a New International Economic Order (NIEO) in 1974, or UNCTAD from adopting, in December of that year, a Charter of Economic Rights and Duties of States which emphasised the need for economic development and the right of states to choose both the goals of and the means for realising the NIEO. The Preamble of this Charter did express the General Assembly's desire to contribute to the creation

[14] Lynton Caldwell, *International Environmental Policy* (2nd ed, 1990) chs 2 and 3.

[15] See K Dadzie, 'The UN and the Problem of Economic Development' in Adam Roberts and Benedict Kingsbury (eds) *United Nations, Divided World: the UN's Role in International Relations* (2nd ed, 1993) 297-326, who traces the four main phases and essential features of the UN's involvement with economic development and comments on the issues and challenges to be faced in the future.

[16] GA Res 1803, 17 UN GAOR (1194th plen mtg), UN Doc A/Res/1803 (1962).

[17] UNCTAD Res 45 (III), 18 May 1972. See A Diaz, 'Permanent Sovereignty over Natural Resources' (1994) 24 *Environment Policy and Law* 157-72, who shows how, after the UNCHE and UNCED, the Resolution on Permanent Sovereignty over Natural Resources could be used to protect the environment.

of conditions for the protection, preservation and enhancement of the environment and Article 3 did acknowledge that in the case of natural resource exploitation states must co-operate and inform and consult with each other. However, the specific aim was optimum use of the resources, subject only to the restriction that this must not damage the legitimate interest of the other states (which could, impliedly, include their interest in protecting their environments). The virtual separation of developmental and environmental interests continued. Although, outside the UN, the International Union for Conservation of Nature (IUCN, now known as the World Conservation Union), in its World Conservation Strategy of 1980 did call for *sustainable* use of resources,[18] it was not until the World Commission on Environment and Development (WCED) published its report calling for a new approach, which it articulated as 'sustainable development', and advocated this as the goal for both developing and industrialised states, that a turning point leading to the convening of the UNCED was reached and formal adoption of this concept occurred.[19]

The UN's divergent goals of environmental protection and economic development were coalesced within this amorphous formula, the precise content of which is hard to define. The WCED had side-stepped this difficult problem by categorising it in very general and somewhat Delphic terms as a process that 'ensures that it meets the needs of the present without compromising the ability of future generations to meet their own needs.'

Even so, when this bland formula came before the Governing Council of the United Nations Environment Program (UNEP) for redefinition and a vote was called for, sustainable development was reformulated more narrowly as 'development that meets the needs of the present without compromising the ability of future generations to meet their own needs and does not imply in any way encroachment upon national sovereignty'.[20] Nonetheless, following the UNCED Rio Declaration, sustainable development became firmly established as a goal on the agenda not only of the UN itself but of its relevant specialised agencies and its numerous regional bodies, commissions and autonomous units,

18 *World Conservation Strategy: Living Resource Conservation for Sustainable Development*, prepared by the International Union for Conservation of Nature and Natural Resources (IUCN) with the advice, co-operation and financial assistance of UNEP and the World Wildlife Fund (WWF, now known as the World Wide Fund for Nature) in collaboration with FAO and UNESCO (1980); see also the updated version prepared for the UNCED, *Caring for the Earth: A Strategy for Sustainable Living* (1991).

19 World Commission on Environment and Development, *Our Common Future* (1989); see also report of the UNCED's Legal Expert Group on Environmental Law, *Environmental Protection and Sustainable Development* (1987). The General Assembly welcomed the establishment of a special commission of concerned governments and suggested the terms of reference for its work - see GA Res 165, 38 UN GAOR (102nd mtg), UN Doc A/Res38/165 (1983); 'Process of preparation on Environment and Development (1985) 14 *Environmental Policy and Law* 4. For the UNCED's progress see 'The World Commission on Environment and Development' (1985) 14 *Environmental Policy and Law*, 4; 'Legal Principles Approved by Experts Group' (1986) 16 *Environmental Policy and Law* 140. The UNCED report was debated in the UN General Assembly on 19 October, 1987; for details see 'UNEP/WCED' (1989) 19 *Environmental Policy and Law* 218.

20 P Thacher, 'The Role of The United Nations' in Andrew Hurrell and Benedict Kingsbury (eds), *The International Politics of the Environment, Actors, Interests and Institutions* (1992) 183-211, 190; Annex II to UNEP GC decision 15/2, May 1989.

some details of which are outlined in Section IV below. An understanding of this framework is a necessary pre-requisite to evaluation of the success or failure of the UN in promoting and achieving protection of the environment, which will be discussed in Section V, and in synthesising this with the developmental goals of the UN as explained above.

IV THE UN'S ORGANISATIONAL FRAMEWORK: ITS APPROPRIATENESS FOR IMPLEMENTATION OF SUSTAINABLE DEVELOPMENT

The League of Nations had been equipped only with an Assembly and Council. The Statute of the Permanent Court of International Justice (PCIJ) was established later by an independent treaty. The League had no separate functional organisations in special relationship with it other than the subsequently established International Labour Organisation. The failure of the League was attributed in part to the lack of an adequate international structure within which the underlying economic and social problems could be addressed.

The founders of the UN and other eminent persons set out to remedy this, not only by expressing the UN's aims in the wider terms referred to earlier, coupled with a commitment to co-operate to achieve them, but by ensuring — in Article 1(4) — that the UN would become 'a centre for harmonising the action of nations to achieve these common ends'. For this purpose it was equipped with a wide range of organisations including not only a General Assembly and Security Council, but also an Economic and Social Council (ECOSOC).[21]

Article 62 of the UN Charter provides that ECOSOC may: 'make and initiate studies and reports with respect to international economic, social, cultural, educational, health and related matters' to the General Assembly, UN members and concerned specialised agencies; prepare draft conventions for submission to the General Assembly with respect to matters falling within its competence; call international conferences on matters within its competence; and enter into agreements with the specialised agencies defining the terms on which they will be brought into relationship with the UN (subject to approval by the General Assembly) and co-ordinate their activities. Thus, it has the potential to play a major role in promoting not only development but also environmental protection, and in harmonising these goals to achieve sustainable development. So far, however, this potential has not been fully realised because in the past much of ECOSOC's role was largely taken over by the General Assembly. However, as ECOSOC, under Articles 70 and 71 respectively, can arrange for any UN member, as well as representatives of specialised agencies and NGOs concerned with matters within its competence, to participate in its deliberations, environmental as well as developmental concerns are likely to be pressed increasingly before it. The Secretary-General's reform initiative aimed at revitalising and restructuring the UN in economic, social and related fields is intended, *inter alia*, to re-focus ECOSOC and promote a more integrated approach to UN

21 UN Charter ch X arts 62-72.

programmes.[22] The complementary nature of the work of the General Assembly and ECOSOC, including their respective roles in decision-making, review and monitoring, is being reviewed with a view to avoiding the existing duplication.

The consequent reforms, including the slimming down of the Secretariat, should lead to these bodies being better equipped to meet the demands of executing UNCED's Agenda 21. However, it is not yet clear, given the divergent approaches adopted at UNCED by North and South which have long dominated General Assembly and ECOSOC deliberations on environmental and developmental issues, whether this will bear fruit. Nevertheless ECOSOC is well-equipped to promote continued developments because of its powers to make recommendations to the Commission on Sustainable Development (CSD), the organisation established by the General Assembly after UNCED. Since 1992 a High Level Advisory Board, approved by the General Assembly and convened by the Secretary-General, has advised the Secretary-General on aspects of sustainable development. The Secretary-General has tried to overcome one of the main criticisms of the UN 'family' of organisations, that is that it lacks co-ordination and integration of programmes, by restructuring the Secretariat to create some identity of purpose.[23] However, there is still a need, as this has proved a long-standing, intransigent problem, for a better allocation of responsibilities among UN Headquarters and the other centres located in Geneva, Vienna and Nairobi where the developmental and environmental units and agencies are located. The CSD could promote ECOSOC's efforts in these respects, but as some NGOs regard ECOSOC as a moribund body it remains to be seen whether the CSD will have the strength and energy to act sufficiently vigorously (see Section VIII below).

In addition to the above-mentioned organisations, Chapters XII and XIII of the Charter equipped the UN with an International Trusteeship System, administered by a Trusteeship Council composed of UN members administering territories placed under the system by individual agreements. The territories qualifying were those held in 1945 under League of Nations Mandate, those detached from 'enemy' states following World War II, and those voluntarily placed under trusteeship by their administering states. The objectives of the system were to further international peace and security, and to promote the political, economic, social and educational advancement of the territories' inhabitants and their progressive development towards self-government and independence, as deemed appropriate to the circumstances of each territory and

22 See in particular, 'Restructuring and Revitalisation of the United Nations in the Economic, Social and Related Fields', GA Res 264, 45 UN GAOR (75th plen mtg), UN Doc A/Res/264 (1991); Secretary-General's address to the 47th session of the UN General Assembly (1993) in (1992) 22 *Environmental Policy and Law* 302, 305. See also 'Environment and Development: Towards a Common Strategy for the South in the UNCED Negotiations and Beyond', Geneva: South Centre [1991] which stresses the South's need for *rapid* development and exploitation of the resources to achieve it, and claims that it has the environmental spaces to do this.

23 See for example 'Restructuring of the UN: extract from the Secretary-General Statement' (1992) 22 *Environmental Policy and Law* 305. In 1992-3 a Department of Policy Co-ordination and Sustainable Development was established in the UN Secretariat, headed by UN Secretary-General Desai.

its peoples and the freely expressed wishes of the people concerned, 'as may be provided by the terms of each Trusteeship agreement.'[24]

Amongst the proposals considered by some NGOs in the run up to UNCED was that the Trusteeship Council, composed of members of the UN drawn from the categories identified in Article 86, might, as its former role is now negligible, be given the task of overseeing the progress of countries towards sustainable development. This is clearly not a role for which the system was designed or equipped and UNCED never seriously considered this option. However, states retain the power to voluntarily choose to place territories for whose 'administration' they are responsible under Trusteeship, and the system's purpose is to promote the 'political, economic, social, and educational advancement of the inhabitants' in a way that is appropriate to their circumstances and their 'freely expressed wishes'. So, if the disastrous decline in the internal administration of some states through civil war and the incompetence or non-existence of government continues, or even worsens in the twenty-first century, the question remains as to whether the Trusteeship system may not, with some adaptation, permit the peoples of such a territory themselves to seek to place it under UN Trusteeship. This might be appropriate when the ravages of gross environmental and developmental failure negate any prospect of progress towards sustainable development. Meanwhile, the route taken by UNCED (see below) of establishing the Commission on Sustainable Development is a much less radical, less ambitious and less controversial method of monitoring the *status quo* with a view to commenting on or making recommendations concerning a state's progress towards sustainable development.

The remaining organs of the UN which can play a role in achieving the objectives set out in the Stockholm and Rio Declarations and Action Plans include the Secretariat, the International Court of Justice and the subsequently established International Law Commission.

The Secretariat consists of the Secretary-General and 'such staff as the organisation requires'.[25] The Secretary-General, as chief administrative officer of the organisation,[26] acts in that capacity in all meetings of the other organs and must also execute 'such other functions as are entrusted to him by these organisations', and submit annual reports to the General Assembly on the work of the UN.[27] The Secretary-General may personally 'bring to the attention of the Security Council any matter *which in his opinion may* threaten the maintenance of international peace and security'.[28] All these tasks and responsibilities may well have environmental and developmental dimensions which are likely to increase. They must be carried out in the context of the UN's new goal of achieving sustainable development following the General Assembly's endorse-

24 UN Charter art 76.
25 Ibid art 97.
26 Ibid.
27 Ibid art 98.
28 Ibid art 99 (emphasis added).

ment of the Rio Declaration and its innovative involvement in the negotiating process of, for example, the 1992 UN Convention on Climate Change which led to the establishment by the General Assembly of the International Negotiating Committee (INC) on a Framework Convention on Climate Change[29] and the servicing of the INC's work by the Secretariat in the lead up to UNCED. The General Assembly not only has the power to create subsidiary organs, which it could use for environmental purposes, but can also establish special programmes, often as autonomous units within the Secretariat. The United Nations Development Program (UNDP), UNCTAD and the UNEP are examples in point, and are playing a crucial role in the process of sustainable development.

The UN Charter requires states to settle their disputes by peaceful means which include, *inter-alia,* judicial settlement.[30] It also requires the Security Council, as it deems necessary, either to call upon disputing parties to do this or to recommend appropriate procedures, and in doing so to take into consideration that legal disputes shall, as a general rule, be referred by the parties to the International Court of Justice (ICJ).[31] The ICJ thus has an as yet under-used potential for settling legal disputes concerning environmental and developmental issues and for clarifying over time, as its decisions and opinions accumulate, the legal content, if any, of the term 'sustainable development'.[32] The UN General Assembly and Security Council and approved specialised agencies can seek advisory opinions from the Court but have not yet done so on environmental topics. WHO's recent request for an opinion on the legality of using nuclear weapons may open up this possibility for other agencies.[33] The Court's recent establishment of a panel to hear environmental disputes may also improve the situation.

The International Law Commission (ILC), composed of eminent lawyers appointed by the General Assembly, was established to promote the progressive development and codification of international law. It has the potential to clarify

29 For details of the UN and the Secretariat's involvement in the process of conducting this convention and analysis of this see, J Barrett, 'The Negotiation and Drafting of the Climate Change Convention' in R Churchill and D Freestone (eds), *International Law and Global Climate Change* (1991) 183-200. The work contains the text of many relevant documents, presented in chronological order under sub-headings, at 211-436. The growing involvement of the UN and its specialised agencies, and the complementary effect on the UN of decisions and measures of other international bodies, are thus easily discerned.

30 UN Charter art 33.

31 Ibid art 36.

32 For examples of disputes, some of which involve environmental issues or environmental significance which have been referred to the ICJ, see Roberts and Kingsbury, above n 15, 543-8. Cases with environmental/developmental significance include maritime boundary cases, which allocate, *inter alia*, exclusive access to resources; *The Anglo-Norwegian Fisheries Case* (United Kingdom v Norway) [1951] ICJ Rep 116; *The Corfu Channel Case* (Merits) (United Kingdom v Albania) [1949] ICJ Rep 4; *The Nuclear Test Cases* (Australia v France; New Zealand v France) [1974] ICJ Rep 253. The disputes between Australia and Nauru concerning exploitation of certain phosphate lands in Nauru; between Hungary and Slovakia concerning construction of a dam by the latter on the Danube (the Gabcikovo-Nagymaros Project); and between Denmark and Finland concerning construction of a bridge across the Baelts, provide more recent examples.

33 Request for an advisory opinion made by the World Health Organisation pursuant to Resolution WMA 46.40, 14 May 1993.

the concept of sustainable development. However, because the issues which the ILC is called to address are determined by the General Assembly, inherent political difficulties will no doubt prevent it from doing so.

The ILC has, however, been charged with a significant role in codifying and developing the law on state responsibility for damage to and the law concerning international water courses, and has seized the chance to introduce an environmental dimension into the texts it has elaborated on these issues.[34] However, the increasingly highly-charged political, economic, and social implications of such issues, including sustainable development, have led the General Assembly to avoid using the ILC in the recent development of relevant UN treaty law. Instead, it has convened UN conferences to gradually negotiate the texts of conventions through political processes rather than presenting already prepared drafts. Increasingly such UN conferences seek to secure consensus at all stages of this process, rather than resorting to a vote as was habitual in the early days of the UN. The contrasting approaches of the UN's brief First Conference on the Law of the Sea held in Geneva in 1958 which adopted texts prepared by the ILC,[35] and its prolonged Third Conference on the Law of the Sea (UNCLOS III), held in various venues, including New York and Geneva, between 1973-1982, which aimed at, but failed to achieve, consensus, illustrate the differences and difficulties.[36] The attempts to reach consensus (as evidenced in the Law of the Sea (LOS) Convention) and the use of the 'Framework Convention' approach where the treaty merely provides a very general framework, requiring subsequent negotiation of Protocols laying down specific measures (as for the Convention on Climate Change, discussed further below), inevitably, in the context of the increasing diversity of interests represented in the UN, leads to use of deliberately ambiguous language, often referred to as 'constructive ambiguity', as this enables acceptance of the convention because such terms are open to varying interpretations.

This approach is much criticised by environmentalists and has led to, rather than avoided, disputes and threats of unilateral actions in pursuit of a particular interpretation, as in the recent disputes between Canada, Spain and the European Union concerning alleged over-fishing on the high seas of straddling stocks and of highly migratory species which cross the boundaries of coastal zones and the high seas. However, the ILC has itself had to take account of

34 On the ILC's role in state responsibility, see Patricia Birnie and Alan Boyle, *International Law and the Environment* (1992) 139-41; ECE Convention on the Protection and Use of Transboundary Watercourses and International Lakes, opened for signature at Helsinki, 17 March 1992, Cmnd 2141, Misc No 5 (1993); (1992) 31 ILM 1312; Draft Articles on the Non-Navigational Uses of International Watercourses, UN DOC A/CN4/L492/Add. 1 (1994). The General Assembly is convening a conference in 1996 to elaborate a framework convention based on the ILC Draft.

35 For the text and brief negotiations of the four conventions on the Territorial Sea and Contiguous Zone, The High Seas, Fishing and Conservation of the Living Resources of the High Seas and The Continental Shelf see Brownlie, above n 7, 85; the four conventions appear in UN Doc A/Conf 13/L52-L55; and Misc No 15 (1958).

36 United Nations Convention on the Law of the Sea, opened for signature 10 December 1982, UN Doc A/Conf 62/122; (1982) 21 ILM 1261 (entered into force 1994). For extensive but succinct assessment see R Churchill and V Lowe, *The Law of the Sea* (1988).

divergent approaches among its members on the issues under discussion and may also resort to ambiguous language. The prolonged negotiation of the UNCLOS in 1982 reflected the deep divisions between states, which were not only divided along North and South lines — as evidenced in the endeavour to agree on the terms and conditions for Deep Seabed Mining, in the context of the General Assembly's 1970 Declaration of Principles[37] on this activity, which asserted that the Area of the Seabed Beyond National Jurisdiction was the 'common heritage of mankind', to be exploited 'only under an international regime to be established by a treaty of universal character, generally agreed upon' — but on issues ranging from navigational freedoms, archipelagic waters and exclusive economic zones, to the conduct of marine scientific research and protection of the marine environment — all key environmental and developmental issues. The divisions on these were related to the particular interests of states on the issue in question, such as distant water versus coastal state fishing interests, navigational versus coastal interests and so on.

The UN was equipped at its outset with five regional economic commissions — for Africa (ECAF), Latin America (ECLA), Western Asia (ECWA), Asia and the Pacific (ESCAP) and Europe (ECE). Their original purpose of promoting economic development was quickly supplemented after the UNCHE by promotion of programmes and measures for environmental protection. The ECAF, for example, has, since the revelation in the 1980s that some industrialised states were dumping toxic waste in some African countries, become involved in matters pertaining to pollution control and waste management, as well as environmental assessment and management of the use of natural resources. The ECE has been particularly active, concluding in 1979 the only existing Convention on Long-Range Transboundary Air Pollution (LRTAP)[38] (a framework convention which has since been supplemented by Protocols requiring their parties to reduce emissions of specific pollutants such as sulphur), and the First Convention on Environmental Impact Assessment in a Transboundary Context (Espoo Convention).[39] It has also issued a Regional Strategy for Environmental Protection and Rational Use of Natural Resources.

Making good use of the breadth of the economic, social and other powers conferred upon it, the UN has gradually established numerous committees, commissions and autonomous units within its administrative structure which have adapted at various stages to developments inside and outside the UN, at global and regional level, as the strategy for sustainable development has gradually emerged. The General Assembly, for example, adopted in 1980 a World Charter for Nature,[40] a non-binding instrument setting-out in general

37 Declaration of Principles Governing the Seabed and the Ocean, Flow, and the Subsoil Thereof, Beyond the Limits of National Jurisdiction, GA Res 2749, 25 UN GAOR (1933rd plen mtg), (1970), text in Brownlie, above n 7, 122-6; (1988) 27 ILM 701.

38 (1979) 18 ILM 1442.

39 (1991) 30 ILM 802.

40 (1983) 22 ILM 455; on the debates leading up to this concerning the terminology used ('shall' rather than 'should') and the legal status of this instrument see Caldwell, above n 14, 90.

terms the goals for sustainable use of nature, and the Global Perspective to the Year 2000 and Beyond.[41]

But an evaluation of the UN's role in environment and development cannot be confined solely to the activities of its own organs and regional bodies. The work of its specialised agencies must also be taken into account, particularly that of UNEP, an agency established by the General Assembly as an autonomous unit within the UN Secretariat, in the same way as the UNDP and UNCTAD.

V THE UN SPECIALISED AGENCIES INVOLVED IN ENVIRONMENT AND DEVELOPMENT

Space does not permit a detailed explanation of the work of the concerned agencies which, through agreements with ECOSOC, have entered into a special relationship with the UN. The 16 existing agencies have broad responsibilities, within the confines of their constituent constitutions, based on *ad hoc* conventions which define their functions, purposes and goals and establish their administrative machinery and powers. In addition to those with a clearly-defined mandate to protect the environment or promote development, others also have some tangential involvement in these tasks.[42] Apart from the financial agencies, such as the International Monetary Fund (IMF) and the World Bank, four major agencies are all directly involved in sustainable development. They are the International Labour Organisation (ILO), the Food and Agricultural Organisation (FAO), the United Nations Educational, Scientific and Cultural Organisation (UNESCO) and the World Health Organisation (WHO).

The financial institutions, after much criticism from NGOs concerning their funding, without prior environmental impact assessments, of development projects such as the building of dams and exploitation of forests, have now considerably revised their approach to such projects.[43] The ILO has developed numerous conventions and codes of practice setting standards for the health and safety of workers on land and on ships, and for protection of indigenous peoples' rights. It has unique enforcement procedures. The FAO is moving from a dominant development focus, promoting more extensive fishing and agriculture, to a sustainable approach taking account of the environmental effects of over-fishing, conservation needs, including habitat protection and the effects of pollution on fish, and also the deleterious effects of the use of chemical pesticides and fertilisers in agriculture.

UNESCO promotes both co-operation and research in the natural and social sciences, and technical assistance in training and education, and also maintains a prestigious International Oceanographic Commission (IOC) which is active

41 'The Environment Perspective to the Year 2000 and Beyond' (1988) 18 *Environmental Policy and Law* 37.

42 For details of these activities see Birnie and Boyle, above n 34, 53-63.

43 See The World Bank Environment Group, *Making Development Sustainable: The World Bank Group and the Environment* (1994); K Piddington, 'The Role of the World Bank' in Hurrell and Kingsbury, above n 20, 212-27; Dadzie, above n 15, 297-326.

in, among other things, research into marine pollution. It works closely with an inter-agency Group of Experts on the Scientific Aspects of Marine Pollution (GESAMP) which advises various bodies and which produced the first definition of 'marine pollution' (now amended), which has been widely used in UN and other conventions. The IOC's role will now be enhanced by the requirements of Ch XIII (Marine Scientific Research) of the UNCLOS 1982 following the Convention's entry into force on 16 November 1994. A World Heritage Convention concluded under UNESCO's auspices in 1972, provides for natural as well as cultural sites within the territory of its state parties to be listed for protective purposes and thus to qualify for financial support from the World Heritage Fund. Eighty-five natural sites were listed by 1991, which included Australia's Great Barrier Reef and the Daintree Rainforests.

WHO promotes the attainment of the highest possible level of health by all peoples. Clearly this requires a healthy environment or, as the UNCHE Declaration puts it, 'an environment of quality'. WHO, therefore, develops codes, sets standards and supports regulations or conventions (such as those on Conservation of Biological Diversity and Climate Change and pollution control) controlling factors adversely affecting a healthy environment, such as the use of drugs and chemicals and the discharge of pollutants which affect air and water quality. WHO also administers International Health Regulations.

The smaller International Maritime Organisation (IMO) has as its major roles the promotion of the safety of ships and prevention of pollution therefrom. It has concluded almost 40 conventions on these and related topics and has established a committee exclusively concerned with Marine Environment Protection (MEPC). It has also established the post of Special Assistant to the Director of its Marine Environment Division to advise the Director on sustainable development. The IMO's further involvement in activities promoting sustainable development is set out in a paper which was presented to the MEPC's 57th Session in March 1995.[44] The MEPC has been focusing its attention on creating means of making at least some of the recommended measures under it financially self-sustaining, for example by charging shipowners who use foreign seamen a fee to cover the training thereof in their states; by charging owners of ships using international straits a fee for the navigational aids provided therein by the coastal states; and by levying a port fee for vessels required to be inspected in ports of entry in order to conform to IMO treaty requirements.

Other intergovernmental organisations in close relation with the UN include the International Atomic Energy Agency (IAEA)[45] whose code of practice, regulations, conventions and safeguard agreements contribute to environment protection, and the General Agreement on Tariffs and Trades (GATT) which

[44] Report of the IMO to the Commission on Sustainable Development in fulfilment of GA Res 191, 47 UN GAOR (70th plen mtg), UN Doc A/Res/191 (1992), IMO DOC, MEPC 37/Inf. (1995) and Follow-Up Action to UNCED, MEPC 37/10/1, 23 March 1995.

[45] See Birnie and Boyle, above n 34, 348-57.

has recently been revised to introduce some environmentally-protective measures, though it is otherwise exclusively directed to promoting development through liberalisation of trade.[46]

These organisations have made many contributions to environment protection and, especially since 1992, to promoting this in the context of sustainable development (which commonly requires provision of financial assistance to developing states — often through establishment of technical-assistance funds provided on an *ad hoc* voluntary basis by some of the organisations' member states — as well as transfer of technology and provision of training and advice — the funds in many cases being used to facilitate these activities). However, there remains much criticism of these organisations' activities in these fields, as well as of the UN's own activities. A major source of complaint is that the UN does not use the resources it has at its disposal adequately or efficiently, nor does it co-ordinate them in relation to the actions of its own internal divisions or to the activities of the UN *vis a vis* the various bodies within the UN 'family', still less with relevant outside bodies such as the IUCN, *ad hoc* Commissions or concerned NGOs. There is thus much duplication of effort and resultant misuse and wastage of resources.[47]

It might be thought that UNEP, the specialised autonomous unit established within the UN Secretariat after the UNCHE, could fulfil this role and this was indeed the original intention of the UNCHE. For the reasons outlined below, however, this has not proved to be the case, and the co-ordinating role was left for many years to the UN's own Administrative Co-ordinating Committee (ACC), the pre- and post-UNCED reforms which will be detailed below.

[46] Benedict Kingsbury, 'Environment and Trade: The GATT/WTO Regime in the International Legal System' in Alan Boyle (ed), *Environmental Regulation and Economic Growth* (1994) 189-231; see also 'Other International Developments: GATT/WTO' (1994) 24 *Environmental Policy and Law* 313.

[47] As pointed out by Dr Holdgate, then Director General of IUCN, reflecting the view of many at the 15th Session of UNEP's Governing Council held in Nairobi in May 1989: 'Despite all the emphasis on co-ordination ..., the programmes of UN agencies, and other organisations, including my own are still conceived too independently, operated too separately and involve too many overlaps and inefficiencies ... The modest programme of my own organisation ... parallels that of UNEP in many ways.' He suggested that in the run-up to UNCED 'we should look again at our communications so that we work in greater mutual awareness, respect one another's defined mandates, make complementary use of the flexibility and commitment of the Non-Governmental Organisations and of the more formal and structured machinery of Government, and exchange results'. He proposed more use of Inter-Governmental Working Groups and establishment of priority issues, as well as 'the acceleration of programmes to bring people into an enduring harmony with their environment ... which combine economic growth, sustainable development of resources, health care and family planning' in order to avoid the undermining of environmental progress; '15th Session of the Governing Council' (1989) 19 *Environmental Policy and Law* 86, 92. See also Paul Szasz, 'Restructuring the International Organisational Framework' in Brown Weiss, above n 11, 340-84.

VI The United Nations Environment Program (UNEP)[48]

A *The United Nations Conference on the Human Environment (UNCHE)*

1 *Origins*

Environmental issues had begun to be placed on the UN's and the Specialised Agencies' agenda well before the convening of the UNCHE in Stockholm in June 1972. Atmospheric pollution was on the agenda of WHO, WMO, ICAC, IAEA, FAO, UNESCO and, outside the UN, the OECD and NATO; pollution of the marine environment was on those of IMO, FAO, UNESCO, WHO and also OECD and NATO; pollution and water resource development was on those of WHO, FAO, UNESCO and IOC; urban problems were brought before the WHO, FAO, UNESCO, and standard-setting was undertaken by IAEA, OECD, IMO, UNESCO, WHO and NATO. The preparations for the UNCHE involved a wide-ranging review and audit of environmental activities not only by the UN but also by its agencies and by national governments, mainly in developed states. Spurred by the expanding international programmes of many NGOs, the General Assembly Resolution convening the Conference recognised that there was 'an urgent need for intensified action, at national and international level to limit, and where possible, to eliminate the impairment of the human environment'.[49] The Assembly's action resulted from a report from ECOSOC, which itself was responding to a Swedish proposal to put 'the human environment on its agenda'. This the General Assembly regarded as necessary for sound economic and social development purposes though this concern was not yet articulated in the synoptic terms of 'sustainable development'. The Declaration formulated by the Conference[50] took account of the developmental concerns of developing countries however, by laying down eight principles, among its total of 26, that related to developmental issues. The UNCHE's Secretary-General, Mr Maurice Strong, had immediately established a Panel of Experts on development and environment which met in Founex, Switzerland to address, in particular, the developmental aspects of environmental problems.[51] The Panel promulgated 25 guidelines preserving developmental goals. This encouraged developing countries to participate in the Conference on the understanding that any environmentally protective measures resulting from it would not be used as the medium for inhibiting their further development by imposing extra costs upon them. Many regarded the environmental movement as a disguised attack

48 For further details see A Petsonk, 'The Role of the United Nations Environment Program (UNEP) in the Development of International Environment Law' (1990) *AUJILP* 5, 351-92; Birnie and Boyle, above n 34, 39-52; Caldwell, above n 14; for an analysis of the UNCED's achievements see L Sohn, 'The Stockholm Declaration on the Human Environment' (1973) 14 *Harvard International Law Journal* 423-515; Patricia Birnie, 'The UN and the Environment' in Roberts and Kingsbury, above n 15, 327-83 and 337-55.

49 GA Res 2398, above n 1; GA Res 2581, 24 UN GAOR (1834th plen mtg) (1969).

50 Report of the UNCHE, above n 2, 35.

51 *Development and Environment: Report and Working Papers of a Panel of Experts Convened by the Secretary-General of the United Nations Conference on the Human Environment*, Founex, Switzerland, 4-12 June 1971.

on their aspirations by the capitalist and former colonialist states, whose own rapid development by unfettered industrialisation had been a prime cause of pollution and other forms of environmental degradation. But, although many developing states were among the 113 states participating in the UNCHE, the Eastern Block did not participate because the continuing non-recognition in 1972 of East Germany had resulted in it being barred from the UN and its specialised agencies and thus it was not invited to attend. The Eastern Block states did, however, join the preparatory process.

2 *Results*

The Conference resulted in four major initiatives at the normative, institutional, programmematic, and financial levels which provided the driving force for developments in the UN during the next two decades. The need to regulate the *use* of the planet's resources in conformity with the goal of maintaining developmental opportunities was accepted as a fundamental principle, though the means of doing so were not spelled out so clearly and extensively at that stage as they were in UNCED's Agenda 21.

The first initiative was the adoption of the Stockholm Declaration of Principles. The second was the establishment of UNEP, equipped with a Governing Council and an Environment Co-ordination Board. The third was the adoption of an Action Plan for the development of environmental policy, to be administered by UNEP, and the fourth was the establishment, on a voluntary basis, of an Environment Fund. All of these were innovatory.

The General Assembly's establishment of a Preparatory Commission to make ready for the Conference resulted in activity throughout the whole UN system. Papers and proposals were prepared by the UN Secretariat, the various specialised bodies and governments, relating to all six subjects on the UNCHE agenda. These were planning and management of human settlements for environmental quality; environmental aspects of natural resource management; identification and control of pollutants and nuisances of broad international significance; educational, informational, social and cultural aspects of environmental issues of development and environment; and the international organisational implications of action proposals. The commitment to the process engendered by this, inspired by the strong personal leadership of the UNCHE's Secretariat provided by Mr Strong, led to a result which was and continues to be somewhat more positive than the critics of the UN's entry into this area had expected, but they did not overcome the entrenched difficulties inherent in the sectoral approaches outlined above. If anything, these difficulties were enhanced as the agencies struggled to appropriate the share of the required actions which they regarded as being within their scope.

UNCTAD, UNIDO, UNDP, and the World Bank and other financial bodies continued to progress further towards the NIEO asserted by the General Assembly in 1974. At the same time UNEP, established merely as an autonomous unit within the UN Secretariat, and located in Nairobi, far from the UN's main centres in New York and Geneva, in an attempt to foster the participation of developing countries, endeavoured to introduce an environmental dimension to these activities.

3 *Limitations placed on the UNEP and attempts to overcome them*

The UNEP's Governing Council generally meets annually and consists of 58 states elected triennially by the General Assembly on the basis of equitable geographic distribution. It is responsible to that body and reports to it through ECOSOC. Financial restraints recently resulted in its meeting only biennially for a period. Its tasks are broad and include promotion of environmental co-operation; recommending policies; providing policy guidance for direction and co-ordination of environmental programmes within the UN; review of the world environment situation; and promotion of scientific and other technical inputs and of exchange of knowledge and information. However, on the whole the Governing Council has tended to restrict UNEP's activities to certain priority issues and to discourage more ambitious programmes, partly because of the restricted role conferred upon UNEP by the General Assembly Resolution establishing it, and partly because of the unwillingness of participating Governments, including some Governing Council members, to fund its programme budget. The UN itself supplies only support costs such as the salaries of UNEP personnel and related costs. UNEP's terms of reference limit it to acting merely as 'a focal point' for environmental action and co-ordination within the UN system. It was not envisaged that it would act as a manager or leader. It was

> to promote international co-operation in the field of the environment and to recommend, as appropriate, policies to this end; [and] to provide general policy guidance for the direction and co-ordination of environmental programmes within a United Nations System.

It was expected to act in a secondary role as a catalyst in developing and co-ordinating an environmental focus in the programmes of other UN bodies. Mr Strong categorised its role as 'to complexify', that is, to 'remind others of, and help them to take into account all the systems interactions and ramifications implied in their work'. He observed that it was the lack of this cross-sectoral, cross-disciplinary view that had led to many environmental problems.[52]

It is not surprising, and indeed it is desirable, that UNEP in its present form should limit itself to priority issues. At first these were: human settlements; people's health and environment; territorial ecosystems, their management and control, environmental and development; oceans; energy; and industrial wastes. Revisions over the years have led to the replacement of the last two by water, air, lands and desertification, the environment, and armaments and regional technical co-operation. Political pressures deriving from other items on the UN's own agenda (for example arms control) rather than a purely environmental focus have influenced the choices of priorities. It is notable that UNEP was neither initially nor subsequently given a specific mandate to develop

52 UNEP Governing Council, *Introductory Statement by the Executive Director* (11 February 1975), UNEP/GC/31, UNEP/GC/31/Add.1, UNEP/GC/31/Add.2, UNEP/GC/31/Add.3.

international environmental law, despite its relevance to most aspects of UNEP's role. Nonetheless the necessity for promotion of both binding and non-binding instruments to achieve its purposes was immediately appreciated. These include global treaties such as the 1985 Vienna Convention for the Protection of the Ozone Layer[53] and its Protocols, which treat the whole stratospheric ozone layer as a global unity. From 1974 onwards all reference to such thorny traditional legal concepts as 'sovereignty', 'shared resources' or 'common property' is avoided, indicating that a new status is emerging for the global stratosphere — that of a common resource or of 'common interest'. This formulation avoids the question of which state has sovereignty over the airspace that the ozone layer occupies. Other such treaties include the Basel Convention on the Control of Transboundary Movement of Hazardous Wastes and Their Disposal,[54] as well as UNEP's 11 Regional Seas treaties, negotiated from 1974 onwards. The Basel treaty preceded the 1992 Convention on Global Climate Change, concluded at UNCED, which, for particular reasons referred to later, introduced the concept of 'common concern' into the UN itself. All these concepts are now applicable to environmental issues and threats that transcend boundaries and which are not susceptible to resolution by any one state, that is, they can be resolved only by international co-operation, taking account also of the economic, social and political implications for development. This allows such issues legitimately to be placed on UNEP's and the UN's agenda.

This approach has led to UNEP's pioneering of its so-called 'framework treaties', referred to above, whereby the convention itself sets out the goals to be achieved and requires states to take measures to achieve them, with specification of the precise measures (regulations, administrative actions, etc) that are required to be developed or added by the parties by adoption of subsequent protocols which, for example, list the pollutants to be eliminated or controlled.[55] This approach allowed UNEP in the 1970s and 1980s to promote a series of Regional Conventions to deter or control marine pollution as part of its 'Regional Seas' Program.[56] It is easier to get initial agreement between states, especially if membership of developing countries is required to make the agreement fully-effective, globally or regionally, if the main convention is in terms of sufficiently-low commitment, expressed with sufficient generality to allow for broad interpretation. The method is not without criticism since it leads to disputed interpretations and permits evasion or deferment of the measures required to meet the convention's goals. Constant pressure then has to be exerted to ensure that the necessary protocols are both added and complied with.

53 (1987) 26 ILM 1529.

54 (1989) 28 ILM 657.

55 Such an approach is not totally innovative. Fisheries treaties have long been based on a similar approach, with the substantial articles empowering a Commission of Member States, established by the convention, to take measures to conserve fisheries at levels allowing a sustainable catch, the precise regulations being listed in a Schedule, Annex or Protocol, which is amendable annually. Some pollution control treaties are similarly structured.

56 They are the responsibility of UNEP's Oceans and Coastal Areas Program Activity Centre (OCA/PAC). UNEP also provides some secretariat activities.

Here the UN system is at its weakest since its member states have always evinced antipathy to attempts to confer or enhance any power of active enforcement on international bodies, though monitoring and reporting to the concerned bodies is now often provided for. The problem remains, in UNEP and other UN bodies, as to what action, if any, is taken on these reports. Progress on these aspects remains disappointingly slow on all fronts.[57] Recent disputes concerning fishing for straddling stocks and highly migratory species on the high seas have highlighted these weaknesses in another sphere that is of 'common concern' and which is fully within the scope of the UN and FAO as well as UNEP. These problems will be considered in more detail in connection with discussion of UNCED's Agenda 21 and its recommendations.

In addition to binding treaties, UNEP has also adopted several sets of non-binding instruments (conveniently referred to as 'soft law') in the form of guidelines, principles, goals and conclusions. These are presented in various forms, but are in effect merely recommendations concerning desirable conduct related to such diverse subjects as shared natural resources, weather modifications, off-shore mining, land-based sources of marine pollution, banning chemicals, management of hazardous waste and environmental impact assessment.[58] All these have had some influence on legislation drafted in some states on appropriate subjects.

B *The UNCHE Declaration of Principles*[59]

This proved to be of considerable significance and influence throughout the UN system. Though formulated as a Declaration, a solemn form used in the UN to emphasise and enhance its importance (as, for example, in the Universal Declaration of Human Rights), and later endorsed by a Resolution of the General Assembly, it had only the status of the codes, namely that of a 'soft law', non-binding recommendation. In practice, however, it has proved influential. Some principles have formed the basis of guidelines developed by UNEP, and have since been incorporated into treaties, especially Principle 21. The extensive, and largely rhetorical Preamble stresses the need for both co-operation by states and action by international organisations in the common interest on problems that affect 'the common realm'. From this sprang the more recent developments already referred to: that preservation of the environment and its composite elements, especially that of areas beyond national jurisdiction, such as the climate, the ozone layer, biological diversity, the high seas including its fisheries, and highly migratory species of birds and mammals, and possibly Antarctica, is a legitimate 'common concern' of humankind, to be manifested, *inter alia*, through action taken on its behalf through the UN and its related

57 See Birnie and Boyle, above n 34, 136-87, esp 160-79 for an overview.

58 See Birnie and Boyle, above n 34, 49-52; *Environmental Law in the UNEP*, UNEP Environmental Law Unit (1991); Petsonk, above n 48.

59 Report of the United Nations Conference on the Human Environment, above n 2.

bodies.[60] The text of the UN Charter is asserted by 'the peoples of the United Nations', who are 'determined ... to promote social progress and better standards of life in larger freedom' and to this end to eschew the use of force 'save in the common interest'. The UNCHE Declaration draws on this inspirational aspect. Its first principle proclaims that

> [m]an [*sic*] has a fundamental *right* to freedom, equality and adequate conditions of life, in an environment of quality that permits a life of dignity and well-being, and he [*sic*] bears a solemn responsibility to protect and improve the environment for present and future generations.[61]

Though Principle 1 is formulated as a right, UNEP's machinery is ill-suited to realisation of it as such. Neither the UN nor the European Convention on Human Rights have included or otherwise provided for it as such. It remains, like the right to development, an inchoate 'third or fourth generational' right, the asserting of which is conceived by some to have political value.[62] The key principle, Principle 26, is also formulated as a right which is purportedly drawn from existing treaty and customary law. Thus 'States have, in accordance with the Charter of the United Nations and the principles of international law, the sovereign right to exploit their own resources pursuant to their own environmental policies'. However, while thereby recognising both sovereignty and implicitly its relation to state's developmental concerns, it introduces a balancing environmental consideration by adding 'which right is coupled with a corresponding responsibility to ensure that activities within their jurisdiction or control do not cause damage to the environment of other States or areas beyond the limits of national jurisdiction'. Principles 2 to 5 require that the earth's natural resources 'must be safeguarded for the benefit of present and future generations', 'that its capacity to produce vital renewable resources must be maintained and, if practical, restored or improved', and that humans have a responsibility to 'safeguard and wisely manage the imperilled heritage of wildlife and its habitat'. The need to take account of nature conservation in economic development planning was identified, which did not rule out exploitation of natural resources. Non-living resources such as minerals were to be used so as to avoid their exhaustion and to ensure that benefit was assured to all people.

60 See Birnie and Boyle, above n 34, 112-22, 424.

61 Report of the United Nations Conference on the Human Environment, above n 2, Principle 1 (emphasis added). For the significance of the inclusion of man's responsibility to protect the environment to preserve it for present and future generations see Edith Brown Weiss, 'Intergenerational equity: A legal framework for global environmental change' in Brown Weiss, above n 11, 385-412; Edith Brown Weiss, *In Fairness to Future Generations: International Law, Common Patrimony, and Intergenerational Equity* (1989); Edith Brown Weiss, 'Our Rights and Obligations to Future Generations for the Environment' (1990) *The American Journal of International Law* 84, 198.

62 See Alexandre Kiss, 'An introductory note on a human right to environment'; R Pathake, 'The human rights system as a conceptual framework for environmental law'; A Trindade, 'The contribution of international human rights law to environmental protection, with special reference to global environmental change' in Brown Weiss, above n 11, 199, 205 and 244 respectively.

Principles 6 and 8 relate to pollution control, calling for cessation of the discharge of toxic and other substances into the environment in quantities that exceed the environmental capacity to render them harmless, and to ensure that no irreversible damage is inflicted on ecosystems. The reference here to preservation of ecosystems, an approach long advocated by NGOs, was considered a significant step towards an ecosystem approach to environmental management. Perhaps the Principle which, despite strenuous efforts by UNEP and concerned governments and NGOs, has been promoted with the least success is Principle 22. Principle 22 requires states to further develop the international law on liability and compensation for pollution and other forms of environmental damage to areas beyond their jurisdiction caused by activities within their jurisdiction and control. Although IMO has adopted a convention relating to vessel-source pollution damage[63] and a supplementary convention establishing an independent additional compensation fund,[64] attempts by UNEP to negotiate liability protocols to its Hazardous Waste and Regional Seas Conventions have proved difficult. The UN Law of the Sea Convention postpones the issue by asserting (in Article 235) that 'States are responsible for the fulfilment of their international obligations to protect the marine environment' and requiring that they *shall* be liable but only 'in accordance with international law', without further specifics. It is equally imprecise in that although it commands states to co-operate in implementing *existing* law (of which little is laid down by treaty and much is left to the ambiguities of existing customary law), it only requires them to 'co-operate' in 'its further development'. Thus victims of pollution damage other than oil pollution damage (compensation for which under existing treaties is based on the narrow principles of the limited liability conventions and their protocols), have received little help from the UN.[65] Oil pollution damage is not a substantial threat to international areas. The only other existing convention falling partly under Principle 22 is the IAEA's Vienna Convention on Civil Liability for Nuclear Damage,[66] which is limited to impact and financial and other coverage.

Principles 8 to 15 address developmental concerns arising from the recognition that economic and social development is essential for ensuring a healthy living and working environment for humankind and for creating the necessary conditions for improving the quality of life. These are policy-oriented principles that draw attention to the need to take economic factors as well as ecological processes into account.

63 International Convention on Civil Liability for Oil Pollution Damage 1969; (1970) 9 ILM 45.

64 Convention on the Establishment of an International Fund for Compensation for Oil Pollution Damage 1971; (1972) 11 ILM 284.

65 For further discussion see Birnie and Boyle, above n 34, chs 4 and 5.

66 (1963) 2 ILM 727-45.

C *UNEP*[67]

It is important to realise that the UNEP is a programme for ensuring action on the aims set out in the Declaration of Principles and endorsed by the General Assembly and that as such it originally consisted of five elements:

- the UNCHE Declaration;
- an Action Plan setting out the policy goals in the form of 106 recommendations;
- a voluntarily subscribed Environment Fund, mainly used for supporting projects and other operational activities in pursuit of the Action Plan goals;
- a new mechanism for administering and directing the programme itself, an Environment Secretariat known as UNEP, located for political reasons in Nairobi; and
- the Environment Co-ordination Board (however this was soon abandoned in favour of use of the UN's existing machinery).[68]

1 *The Action Plan*

The Action Plan was set out in the form of three components. The first was the establishment of a Global Assessment Program known as Earthwatch, which included a Global Environmental Monitoring Service (GEMS) and what is now known as the International Referral System for Sources of Environmental Information (INFOTERRA). GEMS' aims were to gather information, provide warning of environmental crises, stimulate scientific research, evaluate and review this, and link by computer all the environmental information held nationally. This last grandiose objective was soon reduced to linking only the global sources of 'information' through a Global Resource Information Data Database (GRID), which is reported even so to be under-used. An International Register of Potentially Toxic Chemicals has been maintained amongst other activities.[69] Duties under this component of the Plan are considered to have been well discharged.

The second part of the programme — goal setting, planning, consultation, and training, education and provision of information — has been limited by the constraints imposed on UNEP's role by the General Assembly (for example, its limitation to acting only as a 'focal point'), on its priorities as determined by its Governing Council, and by states' lack of financial support for the Environment Fund.

2 *The UNEP Secretariat*

UNEP was consciously established as a small unit, with a limited role and staff (originally 100, now nearer 400, though there is a constant turn-over of

67 For a full account of its status, role and impact see Szasz, above n 47, 340-84; Birnie and Boyle, above n 34, 39-56, esp 47-52; Birnie, 'The United Nations and the Environment' in Roberts and Kingsbury, above n 15, 327-83, esp. 341-58; Thacher, above n 20, 183-211, esp 186-8.

68 See the 1982 Annual Report of the UNEP Executive Director, ch III, paras 16-18.

69 For details see Szasz, above n 47, 342-4.

personnel and not all posts can be filled at all times). It was not expected to encroach on the existing roles of the specialised agencies, either as set out in their constitutions or as developed in practice. It has no independent powers, still less supranational authority, and therefore can play only a support role in ensuring that either its proposed 'soft law' measures or the treaties developed under its auspices are implemented, applied, complied with or otherwise enforced. Its annual production of a report on the State of the World Environment is a form of monitoring, and so-called 'innovatory' practical measures of monitoring have been developed under the Ozone Convention which has established a committee to examine reports on performance from its states parties, but these have only minor effects. Nonetheless, its first Executive Directors, Maurice Strong and Mostafa Tolba, succeeded in gradually furthering the environmental awareness and perspectives, not only of the specialised agencies and other UN bodies, but of inter-governmental commissions and organisations outside the UN system, such as the European Union, OECD and the fishery conservation and pollution control commissions world-wide,[70] as well as concluding numerous codes and treaties and participating closely in the preparation of others. UNEP has worked closely with a large number of concerned organisations and bodies at all levels, including NGOs.

3 *Funding*

The aim of UNEP's Governing Council has been to ensure that UNEP adheres closely to providing only support for the programmes of others and does not establish major programmes of its own. However, it is possible for UNEP to obtain voluntary financial support tied to particular projects. Initially US$20 million was pledged to the Environment Fund, but by 1975 UNEP was approving projects costing nearly US$22million. Its budget was severely cut in the 1980s during the UN's policy of tight budgetary restraint when important regular contributors, such as the US and UK, reduced their contributions. It rose in the approach to UNCED, which highlighted the growing environmental concerns but even in 1987-90 UNEP's budget was only about US$26million, a severe cut in real terms. This rendered it impossible to address such new issues as protection of the ozone layer, hazardous waste movements, possible climatic change and threats to biological diversity, which some considered required budgets of US$100 million, without abandoning or drastically reducing existing priorities.[71] In the lead-up to UNCED the Fund was brought up to US$52.3 million, but this increased contribution only served to return it to the 1980 value.[72] The UNCED did not, as some had expected, resolve this problem or enhance UNEP's legal status and role, though clearly it will play a vital part in achieving and promoting sustainable development throughout the UN system. Funds available for promoting development, however, hugely exceed those

70 For details see Birnie and Boyle, above n 34, *passim*.

71 Szasz, above n 47, 347-51; Birnie in Roberts and Kingsbury, above n 48.

72 For details see Szasz, above n 47, 341.

available for protecting the environment.[73] This is at a time when in order to ensure, post-UNCED, that the environmental perspective is fully integrated into sustainable development policies within and outside the UN system, a major international programme of education, training and creation of public awareness of this perspective and the measures and policies to achieve it are of fast-growing importance. Nonetheless, UNEP, heeding the UNCED's Declarations and Principles relating to development and the need for development planning, has played a key role in creating awareness of the need for development funding and the need to incorporate environmental dimensions into such planning, which was generally neglected in the 1970s and early 1980s.

4 *Co-ordination*[74]

The abandoned Environment Co-ordination Board, which proved unable to achieve its mandate to co-ordinate environmental activities of the specialised agencies throughout the UN system, due to its location in Nairobi, was replaced by the Interagency Board of Designated Officials on Environmental Matters (DOEM). More than 13 UN organs and eight agencies take part in DOEM which was created as a quasi-subsidiary of the UN's own Administrative Committee on Co-ordination (ACC). ACC, under the Chairmanship of the Secretary-General, attempts to co-ordinate all the organs and organisations of the UN system at the Secretariat level under the direction of the General Assembly (assisted by the Committee for Programs Co-ordination (CPC)). Co-ordination of the UN's environmental bodies is now consistently under review in the UNCED context. The ACC, assisted by DOEM, reviews all programmes with an environmental focus that involve more than one UN body and makes recommendations concerning their co-ordination. The ACC's annual report, which is drafted by the UNEP Executive Director, assisted by DOEM, is directed to UNEP's Governing Council. The system is reported to work as well as can be expected given the limitation of its small size in relation to the vastness of the problems involved. It was improved, in the context of UNCED, when an Inter-Agency Committee on Sustainable Development was established. The members of this Committee are representatives of FAO, UNESCO, World Bank, WHO, UNDP, UNEP, IMO and IAEA, but it is open to interested ACC members and is now intended to act as the main source of advice to the ACC in discharging the duties laid upon it by UNCED to achieve sustainable development. UNEP is now also providing the Secretariat for DOEM *and* the more recent Committee of International Development Institutions on the Environment (CIDIE) on which UNEP, World Bank, UNDP and 11 other intergovernmental financial institutions are represented (the World Bank is not a member

73 Dadzie, above n 15.
74 Szasz, above n 47, 371.

of DOEM, despite its increased involvement in the environmental aspects of its activities).[75]

UNEP also promotes co-ordination in other ways, for example, through joint programmes, inter-agency meetings and consultations, and by taking part in similar processes organised by other bodies. Nonetheless, its abilities in these roles was criticised during the preparation for UNCED and numerous proposals for reform were made.[76] These proposals included one that, in order to avoid considerable overlap, the UN System-Wide Medium Term Environment Program (SWMTEP)[77] formulated under UNEP's auspices devote more attention to describing relevant UN activities (including those addressed in UNCED's Agenda 21) rather than acting as a mechanism for welding these into a coherent environmental programme. Moreover, the UNEP inspired Program for the Development of Periodic Review of Environmental law (the Montevideo Program) addressed only certain selective priority issues, such as conclusion of international agreements, development of international principles, guidelines and statements, and provision of international assistance for national legislation and administration. Although the Montevideo Program was adopted by the Governing Council in 1989 and incorporated into the SWMTEP, it continues to be subjected to the same criticisms. It has, however, been more successful in promoting the development of treaties and 'soft law' instruments, as was acknowledged by a group of legal experts which reviewed it in 1991.[78]

VII Impact of UNEP on the UN System

Though the UNCHE Declaration of Principles had addressed both environmental and developmental issues, and the need for 'co-ordination' of the concerned bodies in and outside the UN system was foreseen, neither the Declaration nor the Action Plan integrated these. Thus the UN system continued to follow a sectoral, pragmatic approach, with each sector pursuing its own programmes with the addition of an environmental dimension.[79] In its first decade the UN enhanced its environmental profile by convening a series of conferences in various venues round the world addressing: Habitat (Vancouver, 1974); Population (Bucharest, 1974); Food (Rome, 1974, in conjunction with FAO); Women (Mexico City, 1975); Desertification[80] (Nairobi, 1977); Water[81]

75 But see *Making Development Sustainable: The World Bank Group and the Environment*, above n 43.

76 See Lee Kimball, *Forging International Agreements: Strengthening Intergovernmental Institutions for Environment and Development* (1992); Szasz, above n 47; Thacher, above n 20; Peter Sand, *Lessons Learned in Global Environmental Governance* (1990).

77 See UNEP, *UN Systems-Wide Medium Term Environment Program 1990-1995* (1988).

78 UNEP/ENV. Law/2/3 (1991).

79 See Birnie in Roberts and Kingsbury, above n 48, 355-62; Szasz, above n 47, 347-51; Thacher, above n 20, 190.

80 The Convention to Combat Desertification in the Countries Experiencing Drought and/or Desertification, Particularly in Africa (1994); (1994) 33 ILM 1332.

(Mar del Plata, 1977); New and Renewable Sources of Energy (Nairobi, 1981) and the Third Conference on the Law of the Sea (New York, Geneva 1973-82). The General Assembly Special Sessions on raw materials and development calling for the NIED were also held discretely in this decade. These meetings, which were expensive in terms of time, finance and use of funds, provoked controversy, widened North/South and other political divides and resulted mostly in no more than rhetorical declarations and Plans of Action and other compromises. Though the UNCLOS III concluded by adopting a convention, it did not do so by consensus and the treaty entered into force only on 16 November 1994. This treaty, however, is one of the star achievements of this period. The oceans cover 70% of the globe, over which the UN has now established a comprehensive, integrated legal order, which, though not without its conflict-producing ambiguities, is a major contribution to world peace and security. This whole process can perhaps be said to have contributed directly or indirectly to the conclusion in the 1990s of UN conventions on rivers, desertification and, at UNCED, preservation of biological diversity. Some issues, such as population, still prove too controversial for progress on a global scale. Some minor institutions have also emerged such as the International Fund for Agriculture and Development and the Habitat Secretariat. The impact is difficult to evaluate. All that can be said is that although there was some outcome, it fell far short of the expectations of environmentalists (NGO representatives attended as observers in large numbers), mainly because of the continuing tension between environment and development.

UNEP's activities did succeed to some extent in 'greening' the appropriate specialised agencies, including the financial bodies. The World Bank, under NGO pressure and having received detailed critical reports of its policies, has set up for the first time environmental departments and posts, and allocated more funds for environmental protection and studies.[82] The regional development banks in Asia and Africa and the Inter-American Bank followed its example, at some cost, as did the wealthier European Bank for Reconstruction and Development. The World Bank took on responsibility for administration of the new, voluntarily-funded Global Environmental Facility (GEF), established in 1991 as a pilot programme pursuant to the recommendations of the WCED. GEF aims to assist developing countries to resolve a limited number of problem areas including reduction of global warming by increasing energy efficiency; protection of international waters by pollution abatement and contingency planning; provision of reception facilities, and clean-up and preservation of unique water bodies (under which a major World Bank/IMO joint initiative (WCIS) is underway to enable implementation of IMO's MARPOL Convention

[81] Convention on the Protection and Use of Transboundary Watercourses and Lakes 1992; (1992) 31 ILM 1312; ILC Draft Articles on the Non-Navigational Areas of International Watercourses, UN DOC A/CN4/L492 and Add.1 (1994), are belated outcomes.

[82] Piddington, above n 43; The World Bank Environment Group, above n 43. For a critical view of past policy see H French, *After the Earth Summit: The Future of Global Environmental Governance* (1992).

in the Wider Caribbean area); preservation of biological diversity by supporting efforts to preserve this and prevent further depletion of ecosystems; and protection of the ozone layer from further depletion by aiding developing countries to transfer from the use of CFCs to substitutes, as required under UNEP's Vienna Convention and Protocol on financial assistance. By 1993 the sums available for these purposes through the GEF added up to the total amount of SDR one billion. Responsibility for its disbursement is shared with UNDP and UNEP. The fact that it is available for only a few purposes, its voluntary basis, the lack of developing-state participation and the limited funds available have all led to criticism. Nonetheless, at a conference attended by over 70 states in 1994 when the pilot programme ended, the GEF was restructured. It will now operate on a three year basis, with funds of US$750 million contributed by donors, almost three times the original sum.[83] The major donors are the USA, Japan, the FRG, France and the UK. Some developing states will now be involved and decisions on allocation will be reached by consensus or, when this is not possible, by a complex 'double majority' voting system, which gives both developed and developing states a veto power. The new arrangements uniquely weld the UN and Bretton Woods financial practices.

The World Bank now regards itself as 'an important catalyst for integrating global environmental concerns into national development goals' through provision of grants and concessional funding through the GEF. However, financing the vast range of environmental measures now required under UNEP, UN and other conventions remains a major impediment to effective implementation of UNEP and UNCED's Action Plans and Agenda 21 respectively. New financial mechanisms are constantly sought. The range of existing and possible future mechanisms has recently been reviewed elsewhere. This reveals that some patterns of funding are now emerging, ranging from standard 'trust funds' to funds compensating states for carrying out certain environmental activities in the global interest, and highly innovative funds assisting states to protect resources that lie within the scope of their national sovereignty, as well as the GEF.[84] To these must be added the recent innovative proposals for self-financing of protection measures now being proposed. For example, within IMO proposals are under consideration for port inspection and vessel-owner levies, tourist taxes (as mooted also in the Caribbean and Mediterranean) and other forms of the 'user-pays principle' since international funding is decreasing in real terms.

Concern remains, however, at the adverse environmental impact of the further liberalisation of trade by reduction of tariffs and barriers under the updated General Agreement on Tariffs and Trade (GATT), the third element of the Bretton Woods system, and the new NAFTA agreement. This is particularly so following the ruling of the GATT dispute-settlement panel in 1991 that trade

83 For full details see The World Bank Environment Group, above n 43, 132-5.

84 Peter Sand, 'Trusts for the Earth: New Financial Mechanisms for International Environment Protection', The Josephine Onoh Memorial Lecture, University of Hull, 21 February 1994.

sanctions aimed at securing environmental benefit, in this case cessation of use of drift nets in the Mexican tuna fishery which incidentally trap dolphins, were illegal under GATT because they were discriminatory.[85] The effect of trade on the environment has thus become a new area of concern, inside and outside the UN system.

VIII THE UNITED NATIONS CONFERENCE ON ENVIRONMENT AND DEVELOPMENT

It is obvious from the above sections that although the term 'sustainable development' had not been put on the UN agenda as such during this period, the problems it encountered were gradually becoming not only increasingly apparent, but more urgent if such complex and difficult emerging problems and measures as those required for global climatic change and preserving of biodiversity were to be resolved and the necessary actions taken by developing as well as developed states, and if the measures required under the now large number of existing conventions and the new ones being called for were to be put into effect. The review of UNEP's progress on its tenth anniversary by a conference held in Nairobi led to a Declaration[86] expressing dissatisfaction with the progress made by the UNEP at that date to adapt to the new perspectives. It devoted particular attention to the problems of developing countries and their need for more equitable distribution of technical and economic resources, use of appropriate technology and environmentally-sound methods of exploitation.

The situation improved in the next decade as the new strategies pressed in the IUCN's World Conservation Strategy, the UN's Charter for Nature and its Global Perspective to the Year 2000 and Beyond, all of which embrace the idea that use of the environment and its resources should be sustainable, began to make some impact within the UN. Treaties and 'soft law' instruments inside and outside the UN introduced new concepts of 'common concern', 'the precautionary principle', 'intergenerational rights' and others. The WCED report brought these ideas together in the concept of sustainable development but the process was already underway. What was needed was a focal philosophy around which the environmental and developmental programmes of the UN and other bodies could be integrated, coupled with a blue-print of the kind of measures needed to progress this synthesis. UNCED provided these.

During an elaborate two year preparatory process, the required agenda was negotiated as well as the text of a declaration to be put before the UNCED which is to be convened by the General Assembly 20 years after the UNCHE in Rio.[87] The UNCED agenda for the so-called 'Earth Summit' was laid down in

85 GATT Panel Report on US Restrictions on Imports of Tuna (1991); 30 ILM 1598-623.

86 Nairobi Declaration on the State of the World Wide Environment, adopted 19 May 1982 by UNEP Governing Council, Tenth Session, held in Nairobi 20 May - 2 June 1982; UNEP Doc UNEP/GC 10/Inf 5 of 19 May 1982; 21 ILM 676-8.

87 For the key UNCED documents and commentary see S Johnson (ed), *The Earth Summit* (1993); see also N Robinson, *Agenda 21, Earth's Action Plan Annotated* (1993); for discussion and analysis of UNCED see Peter Sand, 'International Law on the Agenda of the UN Conference on Environment

various General Assembly Resolutions. A number of instruments were adopted after intensive negotiations during which considerable opposition was expressed by both developed and developing states to the formulation of the Rio Declaration. Many environmentalists had hoped the result would be a binding Earth Charter based on a convention, and not a 'soft law' instrument. Developing states held out successfully for inclusion of language recognising the principle of 'the common but differentiated responsibilities' of states for environmental protection in both the Rio Declaration and the Conventions on Climate Change and Biodiversity, and for some practical financial and technological manifestation of the higher responsibility on the part of developed states.

The Conference adopted several significant instruments, the most important being those discussed below.

1 *The Rio Declaration on Environment and Development*

This Declaration is comprised of 27 principles — expressed in general terms, open to various interpretations in their practical application, and carefully balanced to acknowledge the priorities of both developed and developing states — governing the behaviour of individuals concerning sustainable development. Principle 1 recognises that 'human beings are at the centre of concerns for sustainable development' and are 'entitled' to 'a healthy and productive life in harmony with nature'. Principle 2 revamps Principle 21 of the UNCHE Declaration. It provides that states have, under the UN Charter and within international law, 'the sovereign right' 'to exploit their own resources pursuant to their own environmental' and also their own 'developmental policies'. Although their responsibility to ensure that they do not damage international areas or other states' environments is retained, some commentators have expressed the fear that according equal value to developmental and environmental rights could undermine the steady improvement in the UN's protection of the environment.

The concept of meeting both the developmental and environmental needs of future generations is introduced in Principle 3, with environmental protection being required to constitute an integral but severable part of the development process in achieving sustainable development. However, a requirement that the needs of developing states must be given priority (Principle 6) may undermine this. A key new principle, the implications of which will have to be worked out in state practice and further agreements, is Principle 7 which lays down that states must co-operate 'in a spirit of global partnership'. However, Principle 7

and Development' (1992) 3 *Colorado Journal of Developmental and Environmental Law and Policy* 1; Peter Sand, 'UNCED and the Development of International Environmental Law' (1992) 3 *Yearbook of International Environment Law* 465; G Handl, 'Environmental Security and Global Change: The Challenges to International Law' (1990) 1 *Yearbook of International Environment Law*, 3; M Pallamaerts, 'International Environmental Law from Stockholm to Rio: Back to the Future?' in Peter Sands (ed), *Greening International Law*, 1-19; A Adede, 'International Environment Law from Stockholm to Rio - An Overview of Past Lessons and Future Challenges' (1992) 22 *Environmental Policy and Law* 88; M Jahnke, 'UNCED - Rio Conference on Environment and Development' (1992) 22 *Environmental Policy and Law* 204; various authors (1993) 4 *Colorado Journal of Developmental and Environmental Law and Policy* 1-215.

also adds a novel provision that in view of their different contributions to global environmental degradation, states have common but differentiated responsibilities. The developed countries acknowledge the responsibility that they bear in the international pursuit of sustainable development in view of the pressures that these societies place on the global environment and of the technological and financial resources they command. However it will be observed that there is no specific content to this commitment, though Principle 11 suggests that different environmental standards might be appropriate and Principle 8 suggests that to achieve sustainable development states 'should reduce and eliminate unsustainable patterns of production and consumption and promote appropriate demographic policies'.

Principle 15 is another key principle requiring that 'the precautionary *approach* shall be widely applied by States' (emphasis added) but adding 'according to their capabilities'. This reflects emerging state practice in the UN and other treaties and declarations. Principle 15 in effect 'defines' this approach as requiring at the global level that 'where there are threats of serious irreversible damage, lack of full scientific certainty shall not be used as a reason for postponing cost-effective measures to prevent environmental degradation'. Practical interpretation of this 'approach' is creating difficulties in pollution control and fisheries commissions since it is not clear when and where the lines are to be drawn and some go so far as to presume that the burden of proof that there is no threat of damage lies with the state undertaking the activity, not those opposing it, who would have to establish that the activity is likely to or may cause harm.[88] Principle 17 requires environmental impact assessment, but 'as a national, not international instrument' and only of proposed activities that are likely to have 'a *significant* adverse impact and are subject to a decision of a competent national authority' (emphasis added). The Declaration provides more scope for further debate and legislation than it adds to the clarity of emerging concepts. However, it does offer the possibility of striking a new balance to bridge the gaps between North and South. At this stage its impact cannot be assessed. A 'wait and see' policy has to be adopted. The same applies to the other Rio instruments. Much depends on the willingness of member states and the UN and states parties to the relevant treaties to implement and interpret their obligations in a way that makes the goals of sustainable development effective.

2 *Agenda 21*

This programme, set out in 40 chapters, covers over 100 issue areas ranging from alleviation of poverty to strengthening national and international societies'

[88] There is opposition to the precautionary principle from some scientists who consider that it does not allow effective and efficient use to be made of the earth's capacity to assimilate waste, for example, in the case of the moratorium on dumping low-level radioactive waste into the sea under the London (Dumping) Convention 1972, administered by IMO; see also K Bishop and H Hultberg, 'Ignorance, the Precautionary Principle and Subsidiarity' (1995) 24(2) *AMBIO* 92, 97, who point out that 'it is not a policy panacea ... there will never be unequivocal answers', it is 'more political than scientific'.

ability to protect the atmosphere, oceans and other waters, mountains and areas vulnerable to desertification (Chapter 12). The programme has led to conclusion of the Desertification Convention,[89] and Chapter 17 has already been influential in bringing about the first moves towards providing an integrated strategy for managing the oceans, regional seas and enclosed seas. It calls for implementation of the international law as reflected in the 1982 LOS Convention and, in particular, for a UN conference, which is now in session, to resolve the problems arising from the provisions on straddling stocks and highly migratory species, overfishing of which by foreign flag vessels is undermining some existing fisheries conservation treaties. Chapter 11 on deforestation has also facilitated conclusion of an International Tropical Timber Agreement.[90]

Unlike the situation under the Stockholm Action Plan, however, there is no one body which is specifically allocated the task of executing it. Various UN specialised agencies, which are specifically referred to as appropriate throughout the text, are expected to act upon it, fleshing out its simple framework approach. Agenda 21 does, however, include a financial chapter (Chapter 33) requiring developed states to reach a target for development aid of 0.1 percent of their gross national product by the year 2000. Though several of the Heads of Developed States attending UNCED made oral commitments to provide funds amounting to US$7 billion per annum, it has been reported that several are already defaulting on this undertaking or postponing it. Agenda 21 was expected to need US$12.5 billion to implement it. It also refers to the provision of 'Earth Increments' to bolster the International Development Association's funds, and calls for GEF reforms (which have now been partially executed, as indicated) to broaden its base *vis-à-vis* developing states. Prospects for raising the necessary financial assistance from developed states seem poor at present, but the requirements of Agenda 21 will continued to be pressed by NGOs and agencies.

What was left out of Agenda 21 was especially significant, however, and is illustrative of the continuous difficulties facing the UN system. These abandoned items included such contentious issues as population, reduction of chemical pollutants, export of hazardous wastes and the role of the military. But the Agenda does draw attention to the need to deal with 'cross-cutting' issues, recognising the inter-connections between economic, environmental, poverty and developmental issues, tries to integrate them, and greatly encourages the roles of NGOs, women and indigenous peoples and promotes respect for their rights.

89 United Nations Convention to Combat Desertification in Those Countries Experiencing Serious Drought and/or Desertification, Particularly in Africa (17 June 1994); (1994) 33 ILM 1328; see articles in (1994) 6 *Our Planet: The United Nations Environment Program Magazine for Sustainable Development (UNEP)* 1-15, esp A Henrati, 'Taking Effective Action' 5-7 and B Kjellen, 'A New Departure?' 8-9.

90 (1994) 33 ILM 1016-42; for discussion see H M Schally, 'Forests: Towards an International Legal Regime' (1993) 6 *Yearbook of International Environment Law* 4, 30-50.

3 *Forest Principles*[91]

It had been hoped that UNCED would adopt a convention on deforestation but certain developing states were opposed to this since forests are always found within areas of national sovereignty. Instead a somewhat weakly-expressed and curiously-entitled set of 'Non-legally Binding Forest Principles for a Global Convention on the Management and Conservation and Sustainable Development of All Types of Forests' was adopted.

4 *The Framework Convention on Climate Change*[92]

This originated in initiatives and drafts produced by UNEP and IUCN. Efforts to secure a General Assembly Resolution declaring the climate to be the 'common heritage of mankind', like the deep seabed, failed. The General Assembly instead recognised it as 'the common concern of mankind'[93] and took over the negotiating process from UNEP. The new concept has proved a surprisingly useful one which has been respected and repeated in the Framework Convention on Climate Change. The Convention disappointed many in that it did not set targets for reduction of carbon dioxide and other gases (although some oral commitments were made and some 'unjustifiable' limitation of free trade resulted from measures taken). The Preamble recognises that developed countries bear the major responsibility for reducing emissions and also recognises the concerns of states vulnerable to sea-level rise. However, the Convention merely recommends provision of financial assistance and technology transfer without setting specific requirements for how this is to be provided. Some states present, on signing the Convention, made declarations reserving any right of the parties to decide the amount, nature, frequency and size of the financial contributions to be made to the financial mechanism established to aid developing states parties. The vague terms in which it is drafted enabled 153 states to sign the Convention at Rio, but Protocols filling in the specifics will now need to be negotiated by its parties through the UN (as for the Ozone (UNEP) and Long Range Transboundary Air Pollution (ELE) treaties).

91 United Nations Conference on Environment and Development: Statement of Principles for a Global Consensus on the Management, Conservation and Sustainable Development of all Types of Forests; (1992) 31 ILM 881.

92 (1992) 31 ILM 849; see Sebastian Oberthur, 'Climate Change Convention: Preparation for the First Conference of the Parties' (1994) 24 *Environmental Policy and Law* 299, who suggests that differences among the Parties will continue.

93 GA Res 43, UN GAOR (70th plen mtg), UN Doc A/Res/53 (1988). For a full history of the Convention including the negotiating system established by the General Assembly, see Churchill and Freestone, above n 29.

5 *Convention on Biological Diversity*[94]

Although the Convention's provisions are subject to numerous vague qualifications such as 'as far as possible and appropriate' and no definite measures are laid down, it does require its parties to take several important actions. For example, the parties are required to develop national plans for sustainable use of biodiversity; make inventories of its components; develop *in situ* mechanisms for its conservation in and outside protected areas and establish complementary mechanisms *ex situ;* restore degraded ecosystems and endangered species; regulate releases of genetically modified organisms; preserve indigenous and local management systems and equitably share benefits with local communities. But a negative view can be taken if the confused provisions on intellectual property rights and the use of the limited GEF as the funding mechanisms are emphasised, as well as the failure to tackle such key issues as land reform, the role of local communities and the debt aspects. The First Meeting of the Conference of the Parties has now taken place in Nassau in November/December 1994, but it is unclear to what extent parties will proceed to remedy these weaknesses, spurred on by the UN. Once again assessment of its impact will have to be delayed.

6 *The Commission on Sustainable Development (CSD)*

As we have seen, the perceived weakness of the UN has been the duplication of effort in the sectorally organised, unsystematic array of UN 'in-house' bodies, specialised agencies and other entities. If 'sustainable development' is even to be aimed at, still less achieved, these weaknesses need to be remedied, but a body with more clout than the ACC and its support bodies (DOEM and CIDIE) will surely be required. However, UNCED rejected proposals for strengthening UNEP by re-instituting its Co-ordination Board (though the UN may yet do so), establishing a strong supervisory Intergovernmental Standing Committee, or adapting the roles of the Security Council or Trusteeship Council (which would be very difficult to do as it would involve amending the Charter). Instead, the UN established the CSD which now reports to ECOSOC, which then had almost 200 bodies reporting to it.[95] It is unclear how successful the UN Secretary-General's endeavours to remedy this in his 'initiative' will be. The CSD consists of representatives of 53 states elected by ECOSOC for three year terms. NGOs had hoped for some role on this but had to rest content with the setting up of a High Level Advisory Board of eminent experts on environment and

94 (1993) 31 ILM 818, for analysis see Alan Boyle, 'The Convention on Biological Diversity' in Luigi Campiglei *et al* (eds), *The Environment after Rio: International Law and Economics* (1994), 114ff; F Burhenne-Guilmin and S Casey-Lefkowicz, 'The Convention on Biological Diversity: A Hard Won Global Achievement' (1992) 4 *Yearbook of International Environment Law* 3, 42-59; M Bowman and C Redgwell (eds) *International Law and Biodiversity* (forthcoming, 1995) *passim*. For the outcome of the First Meeting of the Conference of the Parties to the Rio Convention see 'First Meeting of the Conference of the Parties to the Rio Convention' (1995) 25 *Environmental Policy and Law* 38. UNEP is reported to have prepared well. It is providing the Secretariat for this and the Climate Change Convention. Some progress was made on organisational issues. A Bahamas Declaration on the Convention on Biological Diversity was adopted.

95 GA Res 191, 47 UNGAOR (70th plen mtg) (1992), above n 44.

development to advise the Secretary-General and through him the CSD, ECOSOC and the General Assembly. The Advisory Board consists of experts drawn from all sections of society, particularly NGOs and industry.

The CSD now meets annually for two to three weeks and had its first substantive session in June 1993.[96] It is served by a discrete secretariat which also serves the new Inter-Agency Committee on Sustainable Development, which itself co-ordinates the work of the various involved UN agencies. This is funded, as far as possible, under the General Assembly's mandate, from the UN budget. The General Assembly laid upon the CSD the following tasks: to monitor the progress of the implementation of Agenda 21, and the other UNCED instruments; to review the financial and other provisions; to enhance the dialogue between the UN, NGOs and other outside bodies; and to consider information on sustainable development put forward in annual reports by governments and other documents. CSD is to adopt 'a multi-year thematic' work programme, indicating what will be discussed and when. Chapter 17 (Oceans) will be reviewed in 1996. The vastness of that task alone suggests that the review will not be particularly thorough or wide-ranging or have serious input, but we must again agree to wait and see. Issues expected to be discussed will include financial resources and transfer of technology; implementation of Agenda 21 at all levels in an integrated manner and the convening in 1997 of a high-level meeting with ministerial involvement to deliberate upon an integrated overview of Agenda 21's implementation; to consider energy policy issues; and, finally, to try to stimulate the political impetus required to promote progress on the UNCED instruments.

As the CSD has no direct route to the General Assembly or Security Council, its progress is likely to be slow, and it will not have a strong co-ordinating role within the UN. Much will depend on whether it uses the information with which it will undoubtedly be supplied by NGOs and others, to improve implementation of environmental instruments, as happened in the UN Human Rights Commission. Governments can inform the CSD of the problems they encounter in relation to Agenda 21. Although UNCED did act to strengthen the ACC under the Secretary-General's leadership it left it to states to decide on the precise way to further support the ACC and the Inter-Agency Commission.

A major unresolved problem is that UNCED left unchanged the separate and independent status of UNDP and UNEP (UNCTAD had already been reformed) and the specialised agencies. CSD can do little about the problems this creates.

IX Conclusions

Fifty is not regarded a very great age today and it is certainly a short space of time in the broader historical context. It is true that the UN has not fulfilled in

[96] For an account of this and its Second Meeting by Nitin Desai, Under-Secretary-General for Policy Co-ordination and Sustainable Development, and by Klaus Topfer, then-Chairman of the CSD; see (1995) 25 *Environmental Policy and Law* 9-10. After a slow start at the First Meeting, progress on establishing priority issues and relevant committees was made at the Second Meeting.

the field of environment and development the high hopes placed on it by environmentalists. However, given that its Charter was designed to deal with many far-different problems and purposes than those which it has to handle today, and that the Charter makes no mention of any UN role in protecting the environment, it is remarkable how far the UN has progressed towards not only doing this but also in at least endeavouring to create awareness of the need to integrate its environmental and developmental programmes to achieve the goal of sustainable development.

Although its critics draw attention to its faults and factions, it in fact has many things to offer a world as diverse as the one in which it now lives. As Hurrell and Kingsbury have pointed out, 'it would be wrong to assume that the universal rhetoric of ecological interdependency translates readily into effective international action.' There are still too many post-colonial problems acting as a wedge between North and South and above all else, the UN is a political organisation in which the wide-ranging views of its diverse members can be voiced. This is at one and the same time a vice and a virtue — a vice because too often there is more talk than action, a virtue because the UN now provides the world with a large, perhaps too large, variety of organs and fora in which the views of all regions and cultures can be represented. The UN is the only central organisation that can act on their behalf. Its record in building into its fora the consensus necessary to promote sustainable development in a polarised world, through convening of conferences and drafting of texts, is remarkable as this paper has demonstrated.

However, its future challenges will be different. There is less need for treaties, although an all-embracing framework International Covenant on Environment and Development is now being contemplated. The concepts of 'sovereignty' and 'territory' endure but are being steadily eroded by the developments outlined in this article. It remains to be seen whether in the 21st century the learning process of the UN and its member states will enable it to improve its co-ordination of its agencies *inter se* and of its own relationship to the bodies outside that are engaged in common aims. Will it be able to face the administrative and funding problems involved in achieving sustainable development? Will it be able to improve its present low role in overseeing compliance with its resolutions, action programmes and treaties? Will it be able to promote the challenging new concepts of 'common concern', 'common but differentiated responsibility', 'the precautionary principle', 'future generational rights' and 'the human right to a healthy environment'? The challenges are there. Will 'all the peoples of the world' encourage and enable it to try to resolve these problems or will most share the views of a UK Prime Minister who once said 'It is exciting to have a real crisis on your hands when you have spent half your political life dealing with humdrum issues like the environment.'[97]

97 Margaret Thatcher, Speech to Scottish Conservative Party Conference, 14 May 1982 (referring to the Falklands campaign, 1982), cited in Hugo Young *One of Us* (1990) ch 13, reproduced in A Partington (ed), *The Oxford Dictionary of Quotations* (4th ed, 1992) 691.

[13]

AUTONOMOUS INSTITUTIONAL ARRANGEMENTS IN MULTILATERAL ENVIRONMENTAL AGREEMENTS: A LITTLE-NOTICED PHENOMENON IN INTERNATIONAL LAW

By Robin R. Churchill and Geir Ulfstein[*]

Since the early 1970s a considerable number of multilateral agreements have been concluded in the environmental field that establish a common pattern of institutional arrangements. The purpose of these arrangements is to develop the normative content of the regulatory regime established by each agreement[1] and to supervise the states parties' implementation of and compliance with that regime. These institutional arrangements usually comprise a conference or meeting of the parties (COP, MOP) with decision-making powers, a secretariat, and one or more specialist subsidiary bodies. Such arrangements, because of their ad hoc nature, are not intergovernmental organizations (IGOs) in the traditional sense. On the other hand, as the creatures of treaties, such conferences and meetings of the parties, with their secretariats and subsidiary bodies, add up to more than just diplomatic conferences. Because such arrangements do not constitute traditional IGOs and yet are freestanding and distinct both from the states parties to a particular agreement and from existing IGOs, we have chosen to describe them as "autonomous." They are also autonomous in the sense that they have their own lawmaking powers and compliance mechanisms.

Multilateral environmental agreements (MEAs) that establish these autonomous institutional arrangements include the Convention on Wetlands of International Importance, of 1971 (the Ramsar Convention);[2] the Convention on the Prevention of Marine Pollution by Dumping of Wastes and Other Matter, of 1972 (the London Convention);[3] the Convention on International Trade in Endangered Species of Wild Fauna and Flora, of 1973 (CITES);[4] the Convention on the Conservation of Migratory Species of Wild Animals, of 1979 (the Bonn Convention);[5] the Convention for the Protection of the Ozone Layer, of 1985 (the Vienna Convention),[6] together with the Montreal Protocol on Substances That Deplete the

* Professor of Law, Cardiff University, United Kingdom; and Professor, Department of Public and International Law, University of Oslo, Norway; respectively. The authors have particularly benefited from discussions with Patrick Széll and Jacob Werksman, and are very grateful to Duncan French, Urfan Khaliq, Jørgen Wettestad, and Oran Young for commenting on earlier drafts of this article. They would also like to thank the secretariats of a number of environmental agreements for providing various materials. They alone are responsible for any shortcomings.

1 Most of the agreements in question establish what international relations writers describe as regimes, i.e., to cite one widely quoted definition, "governing arrangements constructed by states to coordinate their expectations and organize aspects of international behavior in various issue-areas. [Regimes] thus comprise a normative element, state practice, and organizational roles." Friedrich Kratochwil & John Gerard Ruggie, *International Organization: A State of the Art on an Art of the State*, 40 INT'L ORG. 753, 759 (1986). The normative content of the regime is therefore more than simply the provisions of the agreement concerned. This point will become clearer in part IV *infra*.

2 Convention on Wetlands of International Importance, Especially as Waterfowl Habitat, Feb. 2, 1971, TIAS No. 11,084, 996 UNTS 245 [hereinafter Ramsar Convention].

3 Dec. 29, 1972, 26 UST 2403, 1046 UNTS 120 [hereinafter London Convention].

4 Mar. 3, 1973, 27 UST 1087, 993 UNTS 243 [hereinafter CITES].

5 June 23, 1979, 1990 UKTS No. 87 [hereinafter Bonn Convention].

6 Mar. 22, 1985, 1513 UNTS 293 [hereinafter Vienna Convention].

Ozone Layer, of 1987 (the Montreal Protocol);[7] the Convention on the Control of Transboundary Movements of Hazardous Wastes and Their Disposal, of 1989 (the Basel Convention),[8] together with its Protocol on Liability and Compensation, of 1999;[9] the United Nations Framework Convention on Climate Change, of 1992 (the Climate Change Convention),[10] together with the Kyoto Protocol, of 1997;[11] the Convention on Biological Diversity, of 1992 (the Biodiversity Convention),[12] together with the Cartagena Protocol on Biosafety, of 2000;[13] the Convention to Combat Desertification in Those Countries Experiencing Serious Drought and/or Desertification, Particularly in Africa, of 1994 (the Desertification Convention);[14] and the Convention on the Prior Informed Consent Procedure for Certain Hazardous Chemicals and Pesticides in International Trade, of 1998 (the Prior Informed Consent Convention).[15]

Autonomous institutional arrangements are also found in numerous regional environmental agreements, including the conventions and protocols concluded under the Regional Seas Programme of the United Nations Environment Programme (UNEP);[16] instruments concluded under the auspices of the UN Economic Commission for Europe (ECE), such as the Convention on Long-Range Transboundary Air Pollution, of 1979 (the LRTAP Convention)[17] with its protocols, and the Convention on the Protection and Use of Transboundary Watercourses and International Lakes, of 1992;[18] treaties concluded under the Bonn Convention, such as the Agreement on the Conservation of Small Cetaceans of the Baltic and North Seas, of 1992[19] and the Agreement on the Conservation of Cetaceans of the Black Sea, Mediterranean Sea and Contiguous Atlantic Area, of 1996;[20] the Convention on the Conservation of European Wildlife and Natural Habitats, of 1979 (the Bern Convention);[21] the Bamako Convention on the Ban on the Import into Africa and the Control of Transboundary Movement and Management of Hazardous Wastes Within Africa, of 1991;[22] the

[7] Sept. 19, 1987, 1522 UNTS 293 [hereinafter Montreal Protocol]. Documentation regarding the Montreal Protocol is available online at <http://www.unep.org/ozone/>.

[8] Mar. 22, 1989, 28 ILM 657 (1989) [hereinafter Basel Convention]. Documentation regarding the Basel Convention is available online at <http://www.unep.ch/basel/>.

[9] Basel Protocol on Liability and Compensation for Damage Resulting from Transboundary Movements of Hazardous Wastes and Their Disposal, Dec. 10, 1999 <http://www.basel.int/COP5/docs/prot-e.pdf>.

[10] May 9, 1992, 31 ILM 849 (1992) [hereinafter Climate Change Convention]. Documentation regarding the Climate Change Convention is available online at <http://www.unfccc.de/>.

[11] Kyoto Protocol to the United Nations Framework Convention on Climate Change, Dec. 10, 1997, 37 ILM 22 (1998) [hereinafter Kyoto Protocol].

[12] June 5, 1992, 31 ILM 818 (1992) [hereinafter Biodiversity Convention]. Documentation on the Biodiversity Convention is available online at <http://www.biodiv.org/>.

[13] Jan. 29, 2000, 39 ILM 1027 (2000) [hereinafter Biodiversity Convention].

[14] June 17, 1994, 33 ILM 1328 (1994) [hereinafter Desertification Convention].

[15] Sept. 11, 1998, 38 ILM 1 (1999) [hereinafter Prior Informed Consent Convention].

[16] These are as follows: Convention for the Protection of the Mediterranean Sea Against Pollution, Feb. 16, 1976, 1102 UNTS 27; Kuwait Regional Convention for Co-operation on the Protection of the Marine Environment from Pollution, Apr. 24, 1978, 1140 UNTS 133; Convention for Co-operation in the Protection and Development of the Marine and Coastal Environment of the West and Central African Region, Mar. 23, 1981, 20 ILM 746 (1981); Convention for the Protection of the Marine Environment and Coastal Area of the South-East Pacific, Nov. 12, 1981, *reprinted in* PETER H. SAND, MARINE ENVIRONMENT LAW IN THE UNITED NATIONS ENVIRONMENT PROGRAMME 84 (1988); Regional Convention for the Conservation of the Red Sea and Gulf of Aden Environment, Feb. 14, 1982, *reprinted in id.* at 114; Convention for the Protection and Development of the Marine Environment of the Wider Caribbean Region, Mar. 24, 1983, 22 ILM 227 (1983); Convention for the Protection, Management and Development of the Marine and Coastal Environment of the Eastern African Region, June 21, 1985, *reprinted in* 1986 O.J. EUR. COMM. (C 253) 10; Convention for the Protection of the Natural Resources and Environment of the South Pacific Region, Nov. 25, 1986, 16 ILM 41 (1987); and Convention on the Protection of the Black Sea Against Pollution, Apr. 21, 1992, L. SEA BULL., Jan. 1993, at 31.

[17] Nov. 13, 1979, TIAS No. 10,541, 1302 UNTS 217 [hereinafter LRTAP Convention].

[18] Mar. 17, 1992, 31 ILM 1312 (1992).

[19] Mar. 17, 1992, 1995 UKTS No. 52.

[20] Nov. 24, 1996, 36 ILM 777 (1997).

[21] Sept. 19, 1979, 1982 UKTS No. 56.

[22] Jan. 29, 1991, 30 ILM 773 (1991).

Convention on the Conservation and Management of Pollock Resources in the Central Bering Sea, of 1994;[23] and the Inter-American Convention for the Protection and Conservation of Sea Turtles, of 1996.[24]

The phenomenon we have chosen to call "autonomous institutional arrangements" is one that we believe to be significant, as in comparison to traditional IGOs, it marks a distinct and different approach to institutionalized collaboration between states, being both more informal and more flexible, and often innovative in relation to norm creation and compliance. This development appears to have gone largely, if not completely, unnoticed in the general literature on international law, and even not greatly commented upon in the specialist literature on international environmental law. This article aims at drawing this development to the attention of international lawyers in general (not just environmental law specialists) and at discussing some features of autonomous institutional arrangements and legal issues raised by them. Following this introduction, parts I and II give fuller descriptions of the autonomous institutions created by the referenced MEAs and try to explain why they were established. The next four parts discuss the scope of the decision-making powers of these arrangements as regards internal matters, substantive obligations, implementation and compliance, and their external capacity. In discussing these powers, we consider whether the traditional canons of treaty interpretation apply or, rather, whether the more liberal principles of international institutional law (such as the doctrine of "implied powers") should also apply. Furthermore, since MEAs either make use of the secretariats of existing international organizations or locate their own, rather limited secretariats within such organizations, we also examine the relationship between the "host" and the institutions established by the MEA. The proper legal characterization of autonomous institutional structures receives attention as well: are they merely treaty bodies or are they international organizations with a distinct legal personality? Part VII then compares the autonomous institutional arrangements of MEAs with the not entirely dissimilar institutional arrangements found in some other areas of international law, such as disarmament treaties and the Antarctic Treaty system. The article ends with some brief conclusions. In general, our discussion of legal issues tends to focus on global, rather than regional, MEAs, and we draw examples of practice largely from those instruments; we do so partly for reasons of convenience and partly because global MEAs obviously represent more widespread practice.

An important international relations dimension clearly attaches to the institutional arrangements discussed here; for reasons partly of space and partly of lack of expertise, we are unable to explore that aspect. We concentrate, as many lawyers would tend to do, on issues related to the form and powers of these arrangements. International relations writers, on the other hand, concern themselves more with how well the arrangements function in practice and the lessons that can be learned for designing institutional arrangements for future regimes.[25]

I. THE COMMON PATTERN OF AUTONOMOUS INSTITUTIONAL ARRANGEMENTS

In this section we discuss the common structure and functions of the autonomous institutional arrangements established by the MEAs referred to above, before turning to the legal issues to which these arrangements may give rise.

[23] June 16, 1994, 34 ILM 67 (1995).

[24] Dec. 1, 1996, *reprinted in* 1 J. INT'L WILDLIFE L. & POL'Y 179 (1998).

[25] On these issues, see, for example, from a large literature, THE IMPLEMENTATION AND EFFECTIVENESS OF INTERNATIONAL ENVIRONMENTAL COMMITMENTS, pt. I, *passim* (David G. Victor, Kal Raustiala, & Eugene B. Skolnikoff eds., 1998); JØRGEN WETTESTAD, DESIGNING EFFECTIVE ENVIRONMENTAL REGIMES: THE KEY CONDITIONS (1999); Thomas Bernauer, *The Effect of International Environmental Institutions: How We Might Learn More*, 49 INT'L ORG. 351 (1995); Thomas Gehring, *International Environmental Regimes: Dynamic Sectoral Legal Systems*, 1 Y.B. INT'L ENVTL. L. 35 (1990). Many international relations writers make a distinction between organizations and institutions. No such distinction is made in this article and in general the terms are used interchangeably.

Conference of the Parties

As with a treaty creating a traditional IGO, the MEAs establish an organ on which all states parties are represented. Such a plenary organ is usually called the Conference of the Parties, but it may also have a different denomination, such as the Meeting of the Parties or the Executive Bureau. Names such as COPs and MOPs indicate a less formal function than that of a plenary organ of an IGO. Furthermore, the plenary organ of an MEA does not have a permanent seat, but meets at different venues around the world in accordance with its own decisions. The COP meets regularly, usually annually or every other year. A bureau elected by the COP may act on its behalf between its regular meetings, and serves as a facilitating organ during the COP's sessions.

The COP has a variety of functions. First, it acts in relation to internal matters, e.g., by establishing subsidiary bodies, deciding on arrangements for meetings, adopting rules of procedure for itself and subsidiary bodies, and providing guidance to those bodies and the secretariat (see part III below). Second, the COP contributes to the development of new substantive obligations by the parties by amending an MEA or by adopting new protocols (see part IV). Third, the COP supervises parties' implementation of and compliance with the MEA, and decides on the consequences of noncompliance (see part V). Finally, the COP may act at the external level by adopting arrangements with international organizations and states (see part VI).

Protocols to MEAs may have their own institutional structure. For example, the Montreal Protocol to the Vienna Ozone Convention establishes a MOP consisting of all parties to the Protocol, which shall convene its meetings in conjunction with the COP established by the Convention unless the parties decide otherwise (Art. 11(2)). In other MEAs, the plenary body of the convention may also serve as the entity that implements the protocols, as in the case of the Executive Body established by the LRTAP Convention (Art. 10). The Kyoto Protocol to the Climate Change Convention provides that the COP of the Convention shall serve as the MOP of the Protocol (Art. 13(1)), but parties to the Convention that are not parties to the Protocol may participate only as observers when the COP acts in this capacity (Art. 13(2)).

In this article the plenary body of an MEA will generally be referred to as the COP, regardless of its actual title, unless its own name (if not a COP) is considered more appropriate.

Subsidiary Bodies

Subsidiary organs may be established by the MEA itself or subsequently by the COP, and are generally of three kinds. The first is advisory, e.g., the Subsidiary Body for Scientific and Technological Advice of the Climate Change Convention and the Scientific Council of the Bonn Convention. In some cases, however, such bodies may be established by a separate arrangement outside the MEA; for example, the Intergovernmental Panel on Climate Change, which serves the Climate Change Convention, was established by UNEP and the World Meteorological Organization (before the Convention was adopted in fact).

The second type of subsidiary body is concerned with financial assistance and the transfer of technology. Thus, Article 10 of the Montreal Protocol establishes a mechanism to provide financial and technical cooperation, including a multilateral fund, which is operated by an Executive Committee. The Climate Change Convention, on the other hand, uses the Global Environment Facility (GEF), which is a separate institution but is guided by the terms of the Convention.

Third, some subsidiary bodies are responsible for implementation and compliance, such as the Implementation Committees of the Montreal Protocol (Art. 8) and the 1994 Sulphur Protocol to the LRTAP Convention (Art. 7), and the Subsidiary Body for Implementation (SBI) under the Climate Change Convention (Art. 10).

Occasionally, subsidiary bodies may be established for a purpose other than the three mentioned above, such as the Ad Hoc Group on the Berlin Mandate formed by the COP of the Climate Change Convention, whose work paved the way for the adoption of the Kyoto Protocol.

Subsidiary organs may have the same membership as the COP. But participation in them may also be more limited; the Implementation Committee of the Montreal Protocol, for example, consists of ten parties elected by the Meeting of the Parties. As to its composition, the only stipulation is that it shall be based on "equitable geographical distribution."[26] Membership in subsidiary organs may also require certain qualifications; e.g., the Scientific Council of the Bonn Convention shall consist of "qualified experts" (Art. VIII(2)).

Secretariat

A permanent secretariat may be designated in the MEA itself (as is done, for example, in CITES and the Bern and Bonn Conventions), or the MEA may establish an interim secretariat and leave the final decision to the COP (as do, e.g., the Vienna Convention and Montreal Protocol, the Climate Change Convention, and the Biodiversity Convention). Generally, however, the MEAs locate or make use of secretariats in existing IGOs, such as the United Nations (the Climate Change Convention), UNEP (CITES and the Basel and Biodiversity Conventions), the ECE (LRTAP and its Protocols), the Council of Europe (the Bern Convention), and the International Maritime Organization (IMO) (the London Convention). The Prior Informed Consent Convention establishes that the functions of a secretariat shall be undertaken jointly by UNEP and the Food and Agriculture Organization. The Ramsar Convention is unusual in that the secretariat is provided by a nongovernmental organization (NGO), the International Union for the Conservation of Nature (IUCN) (although membership in the IUCN does include states in addition to scientific, professional, and conservation bodies).[27]

The MEA concerned generally spells out the functions of the secretariat, which are to provide services to the COP and the subsidiary bodies, as well as the states parties, in the implementation and development of cooperation under the agreement. More specifically, this duty means that the secretariat engages in activities such as conducting studies, preparing draft decisions for the COP and relevant subsidiary bodies, assisting states parties, and receiving reports on the implementation of commitments. The secretariat also establishes liaison to other international organizations, financial institutions such as the GEF, other MEAs, and so forth.

Although the secretariat acts under the guidance of the COP, it is usually an integral part of an existing IGO. But the extent of that integration may vary, in both legal and factual terms. The COP of the Climate Change Convention has decided that "the Convention secretariat shall be institutionally linked to the United Nations, while not being fully integrated in the work programme and management structure of any particular department or programme."[28] The fact that several MEA secretariats are placed in a different location than their "host" organization—e.g., the secretariat of the Biodiversity Convention is based in

[26] Montreal Protocol MOP Decision II/5, Doc. UNEP/OzL.Pro.2/3 (1990) <http://www.unep.org/ozone/2mlonfin.htm>, *as amended by* Decision III/20, Doc. UNEP/OzL.Pro.3/11 (1991) <http://www.unep.org/ozone/3mnbofin.htm>. These decisions, and other decisions of the Montreal Protocol's Meeting of the Parties referred to below, as well as those of other COPs referred to in this article, are designated in accordance with the number of the meeting, in roman numerals, and the number of the decision, in arabic; hence, Decision II/5 is the fifth decision of the second MOP. Some COPs reverse the sequence and change the style of the numbers, *see, e.g.*, note 28 *infra*.

[27] *See* PATRICIA W. BIRNIE & ALAN E. BOYLE, INTERNATIONAL LAW AND THE ENVIRONMENT 77–78 (1992).

[28] Institutional Linkage of the Convention Secretariat to the United Nations, Climate Change COP Decision 14/CP.1, para. 2, UN Doc. FCCC/CP/1995/7/Add.1, at 42 <http://www.unfccc.de/resource/docs/cop1/07a01.htm>.

Montreal, whereas its "host," UNEP, is in Nairobi—may also restrict the possibilities for control by those organizations. This point is considered further in part III below.

II. WHY THE DEVELOPMENT OF AUTONOMOUS INSTITUTIONAL ARRANGEMENTS IN MEAs?

This part attempts to explain why autonomous institutional arrangements of the kind described in the previous part were developed in the MEAs listed in the introduction. It will be noted that all those MEAs were negotiated and concluded after 1970. Before that date the institutional arrangements of MEAs (of which there were more than thirty)[29] could be described in three ways. In the first, the MEA set up an IGO with legal personality. Examples include the International Whaling Commission (established by the International Convention for the Regulation of Whaling, of 1946[30]) and international fisheries commissions such as the International Commission for the Northwest Atlantic Fisheries (established by the International Convention for the Northwest Atlantic Fisheries, of 1949[31]). Such bodies were generally used to adopt detailed measures to further the aims of the treaty and exercise a degree of supervision over its implementation and observance by the parties. In the second type of institutional arrangement, an existing IGO served as the institutional underpinning for an MEA, providing an institutional framework for possible amendment of the agreement and a degree of supervision over the parties. Examples include the International Maritime Organization with respect to the International Convention for the Prevention of Pollution of the Sea by Oil, of 1954,[32] and the Food and Agriculture Organization with respect to the International Plant Protection Convention, of 1951.[33] Finally, MEAs that fell into the third category effectively had no institutional arrangements at all. Examples include the Washington Convention on Nature Protection and Wildlife Preservation in the Western Hemisphere, of 1940,[34] and the African Convention on the Conservation of Nature and Natural Resources, of 1968.[35] The lack of any institutional machinery was a real weakness of these agreements, inter alia, because it became impossible to update them, in particular the lists of species requiring protection.[36]

In general terms, the institutional arrangements of MEAs have become increasingly perceived as crucial to their effectiveness. As suggested above, the lack of proper institutions makes it very difficult to develop, update, and adapt MEAs to changing circumstances, which is necessary for two main reasons: First, knowledge of the environmental issues with which MEAs deal is constantly expanding. Second, when an MEA is initially concluded, the parties may reach only limited political agreement on how to tackle the environmental problem at issue; but over time consensus on taking stricter measures may gradually emerge. These factors explain why some MEAs take the form of framework conventions (for example, the Vienna, Climate Change, Biodiversity, and LRTAP Conventions). Thus, from time to time MEA institutions will need to adopt protocols to these framework conventions, as well as

[29] For lists of such agreements, see ENVIRONMENTAL CHANGE AND INTERNATIONAL LAW, App. B at 479–82 (Edith Brown Weiss ed., 1992) [hereinafter ENVIRONMENTAL CHANGE]; Peter M. Haas with Jan Sundgren, *Evolving International Environmental Law: Changing Practices of National Sovereignty*, *in* GLOBAL ACCORD: ENVIRONMENTAL CHALLENGES AND INTERNATIONAL RESPONSES 401, 422–25 (Nazli Choucri ed., 1993).

[30] Dec. 2, 1946, 62 Stat. 1716, 161 UNTS 72.

[31] Feb. 8, 1949, TIAS No. 2089, 157 UNTS 157. In general, international fisheries commissions, including the International Whaling Commission and the International Commission for the Northwest Atlantic Fisheries, were not explicitly endowed with legal personality by their constituent conventions; but in most cases legal personality was implicit in their functions and powers. *See* ALBERT W. KOERS, INTERNATIONAL REGULATION OF MARINE FISHERIES 161–64 (1973).

[32] May 12, 1954, Art. XXI, 12 UST 2989, 327 UNTS 3.

[33] Dec. 6, 1951, Art. VII, 150 UNTS 67.

[34] Oct. 12, 1940, TS No. 981, 161 UNTS 193.

[35] Sept. 15, 1968, 1001 UNTS 3.

[36] *See* SIMON LYSTER, INTERNATIONAL WILDLIFE LAW 110–11, 123–24 (1985).

amendments to the original text of more specific MEAs. The alternative to such institutional development of MEAs is amendment of agreements through the traditional procedure of ad hoc diplomatic conference followed by ratification—a cumbersome and slow process. Furthermore, the lack of proper institutions makes it very difficult to monitor states' implementation of and compliance with MEAs and to take action when noncompliance is established. The traditional mechanisms of state responsibility and bilateral dispute settlement (especially judicial settlement) are seen as increasingly inappropriate and ineffective, particularly because breach of an MEA often damages the interests of the international community in general, rather than those of any one state.[37]

This appreciation of the importance of strong institutional arrangements informed the series of major MEAs that were developed at and grew out of the 1972 UN Conference on the Human Environment. However, this period coincided with a time of widespread dissatisfaction with traditional intergovernmental organizations because of their cost and bureaucratic nature, which resulted in a disinclination to create new IGOs, especially perhaps in the environmental field.[38] This tendency is reflected in the fact that UNEP was set up as a subsidiary organ of the UN General Assembly[39] (and not as a UN specialized agency, which might have been expected and probably would have happened if the 1972 conference had taken place ten years earlier), and more generally in the Resolution on Institutional and Financial Arrangements adopted by the 1972 conference.[40]

Thus, it became clear that institutional arrangements for MEAs were unlikely to take the form of a traditional IGO. The alternative that evolved—what may be called the COP model—not surprisingly did not emerge full-blown, but took a little while to evolve into its now-standard form. The MEA that introduced the COP was the Ramsar Convention of 1971. However, that COP was a fairly embryonic creature at first. As originally drafted, Article 6 of the Convention stated that "[t]he Contracting Parties shall, as the necessity arises, convene Conferences on the Conservation of Wetlands and Waterfowl" and that these conferences should "have an advisory character."[41] In 1987 their experience in the working of these conferences and no doubt the operation of COPs in other MEAs led the parties to amend Article 6 so as to provide for the establishment of a "Conference of the Contracting Parties to review and promote the implementation" of the Convention, meeting at intervals of not more than three years; the reference to the advisory character of the conference was deleted.[42]

The next MEA, chronologically speaking, the London Convention of 1972, was much more developed than Ramsar. In comparison with later COPs, however, the Consultative

[37] See further, on the importance of strong institutional arrangements for MEAs, *id.* at 12–13, 277; Alan E. Boyle, *Saving the World? Implementation and Enforcement of International Law Through International Institutions*, 3 J. ENVTL. L. 229 (1991); Winfried Lang, *Diplomacy and International Environmental Law-Making: Some Observations*, 3 Y.B. INT'L ENVTL. L. 108, 115–16, 120–21 (1992); Günther Handl, *Environmental Security and Global Change: The Challenge to International Law*, 1 Y.B. INT'L ENVTL. L. 3, 5–6, 16–17 (1990); Marc A. Levy, Peter M. Haas, & Robert O. Keohane, *Institutions for the Earth: Promoting International Environmental Protection*, 34 ENV'T 12 (1992).

[38] *See* Andrew Hurrell & Benedict Kingsbury, *The International Politics of the Environment: An Introduction*, *in* THE INTERNATIONAL POLITICS OF THE ENVIRONMENT 1, 34–35 (Andrew Hurrell & Benedict Kingsbury eds., 1992); Geoffrey Palmer, *New Ways to Make International Environmental Law*, 86 AJIL 259, 282 (1992); WORLD COMMISSION ON ENVIRONMENT AND DEVELOPMENT, OUR COMMON FUTURE 9 (1987).

[39] *See* GA Res. 2997 (XXVII), UN GAOR, 27th Sess., Supp. No. 30, at 43, UN Doc. A/8730 (1972). On the origins and functioning of UNEP, see also Hurrell & Kingsbury, *supra* note 38, at 30–34, 186–88; Carol Annette Petsonk, *The Role of the United Nations Environment Programme (UNEP) in the Development of International Environmental Law*, 5 AM. U. J. INT'L L. & POL'Y 351, 354–56 (1990); Paul C. Szasz, *Restructuring the International Organizational Framework*, *in* ENVIRONMENTAL CHANGE, *supra* note 29, at 340, 340–44, 351–52.

[40] UN, REPORT OF THE UNITED NATIONS CONFERENCE ON THE HUMAN ENVIRONMENT, UN Doc. A/CONF.48/14, at 29 (1973). The contents of the resolution were subsequently substantially incorporated in Resolution 2997, *supra* note 39.

[41] Ramsar Convention, *supra* note 2, Art. 6.

[42] Amendments to Articles 6 and 7 of the Convention on Wetlands of International Importance, Especially as Waterfowl Habitat, May 28, 1987, 1996 UKTS No. 13. See further LYSTER, *supra* note 36, at 184, 203–07; M. J. Bowman, *The Ramsar Convention Comes of Age*, 42 NETH. INT'L L. REV. 1, 33–38 (1995).

Meetings of the Parties (this term was used rather than "Conference of the Parties") were given no express power to establish subsidiary bodies and their powers of supervision were more limited.

The first MEA to use the term "Conference of the Parties" was CITES in 1973. The CITES COP represents what one might call the full-fledged COP model, apart from the fact that it originally lacked the power to adopt financial provisions; the parties added this power by an amendment to the Convention in 1979. Significantly, CITES was negotiated under the auspices of UNEP, unlike the Ramsar and London Conventions. The next MEAs, chronologically speaking—the Bonn, Vienna, and Basel Conventions and the Montreal Protocol—were also all negotiated under the auspices of UNEP and all contain the COP model as their institutional arrangements. It is not surprising that having devised an institutional model for CITES that worked, UNEP utilized it in the later MEAs; as Lang notes, institutional arrangements tend to be used as precedents.[43] So widely perceived as a successful institutional model was the COP that in 1990 Working Group III of the Intergovernmental Panel on Climate Change, in its report discussing possible elements for inclusion in a Framework Convention on Climate Change, could remark that "[i]t has been the general practice under international environmental agreements to establish various institutional mechanisms. The parties to a Climate Change Convention might, therefore, wish to make provision for a Conference of the Parties, an Executive Organ and a Secretariat."[44]

Several reasons may explain the ascendancy of the COP model as the preferred institutional machinery in most global MEAs concluded since 1972, as opposed to the alternative, a traditional IGO. First, using a preexisting IGO as the institutional machinery for an MEA has the disadvantage of probably involving states not parties to the MEA concerned. Second, creating a new IGO for an MEA is probably perceived as more costly and more bureaucratic than using the COP model because it requires the acquisition of premises and possibly more staff than a COP secretariat would employ.[45] Furthermore, an IGO normally meets only at its headquarters, but a COP can (and invariably does) meet in different places. As a result, developing states frequently host meetings of COPs, whereas most global IGOs are located in developed states, a fact that has been a source of complaint among developing states. Finally, some may think that an IGO ought to meet more frequently than most COPs because of the former's more permanent appearance; the COP is a more flexible arrangement. Above all, COPs may be preferred because the model works well and is acceptable to all states. Thus, it is likely to continue to be used. Significantly, despite calls from some commentators,[46] both the 1992 UN Conference on Environment and Development and its follow-up, the 1997 Special Session of the UN General Assembly, rejected the idea of creating new intergovernmental institutions for the environment.[47]

The COP model, however, is not the exclusive form of institutional machinery for MEAs. At the global level, a few MEAs concluded since 1972 rely on an existing IGO for their institutional machinery. Examples include the 1973 International Convention for the Prevention of Pollution from Ships (MARPOL)[48] and the 1990 International Convention on Oil Pollu-

[43] Lang, *supra* note 37, at 114.

[44] INTERGOVERNMENTAL PANEL ON CLIMATE CHANGE, WORKING GROUP III, FORMULATION OF RESPONSE STRATEGIES: LEGAL AND INSTITUTIONAL MECHANISMS 255 (1990), *reprinted in* INTERNATIONAL LAW AND GLOBAL CLIMATE CHANGE 295, 299 (Robin Churchill & David Freestone eds., 1991) [hereinafter GLOBAL CLIMATE CHANGE].

[45] COPs that meet frequently may not differ so much in cost because premises have to be hired for the meetings and members of the secretariat, which is usually located elsewhere, must be transported to them, often at considerable expense.

[46] *E.g.*, Lee A. Kimball & William C. Boyd, *International Institutional Arrangements for Environment and Development: A Post-Rio Assessment*, 1 REV. EUR. COMM. & INT'L ENVTL. L. 295 (1992); Palmer, *supra* note 38, at 278–82.

[47] AGENDA 21, ch. 38.1(I), 1 REPORT OF THE UNITED NATIONS CONFERENCE ON ENVIRONMENT AND DEVELOPMENT, UN Sales No. E.93.I.8 (1993); GA Res. S–19/2, pt. IVA, 36 ILM 1639 (1997).

[48] Nov. 2, 1973, 12 ILM 1319 (1973) (in particular Arts. 2(7), 4(3), 6(4), 8(2), 11, 12(2), 16, 17).

tion Preparedness, Response and Co-operation,[49] for both of which the International Maritime Organization serves as the institutional machinery, and the 1986 Conventions on Early Notification of a Nuclear Accident and on Assistance in the Case of a Nuclear Accident,[50] for which the International Atomic Energy Agency serves as the institutional machinery. Unlike the MEAs with autonomous institutional arrangements listed in the introduction, none of these four treaties (except MARPOL) is a regulatory agreement and they therefore have a much slighter need for strong institutional machinery. MARPOL is probably located in the IMO because it replaces the 1954 oil pollution Convention, for which the IMO served as the institutional machinery.

As far as we are aware, no global MEA has been concluded since 1972 that establishes a new IGO for its institutional machinery, no doubt for the reasons alluded to above. New IGOs have, however, been established on various occasions at the regional level, especially in relation to fisheries and marine pollution. Examples include the Northwest Atlantic Fisheries Organization, established by the 1978 Convention on Future Multilateral Cooperation in the Northwest Atlantic Fisheries;[51] the Commission on the Conservation of Antarctic Marine Living Resources, established by the 1980 Convention of the same name;[52] and the Paris Commission, originally established by the 1974 Convention for the Prevention of Marine Pollution from Land-based Sources[53] and continued by the 1992 Convention for the Protection of the Marine Environment of the North-East Atlantic (which replaces the 1974 Convention).[54] Such regional IGOs are often much less formal and bureaucratic than their global counterparts, and in fact the distinction between these IGOs and autonomous institutional arrangements is much less clear-cut.

III. The Powers of MEA Institutions on the Internal Plane

For the regime established by an MEA to function effectively, decisions at the internal level, i.e., of an organizational and procedural character, must be taken. Such decisions may relate to the work of the MEA institutions (e.g., adoption of the rules of procedure, the financial rules, and the budget); to the determination of the rights and obligations of member states (e.g., exclusion or suspension of voting and other rights); to representatives of member states (e.g., approval of credentials and election of officers to the bureau); to the admittance of observers from NGOs, IGOs, and non-member states; and to officials in the secretariat (e.g., hiring and firing).

The autonomous institutional arrangements (AIAs) of MEAs are hierarchical, with the COP as the supreme body. Some of the MEAs specify this structure, such as the Climate Change Convention (Art. 7(2)) and the Desertification Convention (Art. 22(2)). In other MEAs it may be inferred from provisions establishing that the subsidiary bodies and the secretariat act under the guidance of the COP, e.g., the Bonn Convention (Arts. VII(5)(c), IX(4)(k)).

The powers of the COP at the internal level are explicitly set out in treaty articles relating to, for example, the adoption of the rules of procedure, financial regulations and the budget, the establishment of new subsidiary bodies, and the provision of guidance to these bodies and the secretariat. Some MEAs also contain a catchall provision authorizing the COP to "consider any additional action that may be required,"[55] "fulfil such other functions

[49] Nov. 30, 1990, 30 ILM 733 (1991) (in particular Arts. 2(6), 12, 14).

[50] Sept. 26, 1986, 25 ILM 1370, Art. 4, and 1377, Art. 5 (1986).

[51] Oct. 24, 1978, Art. II, S. Exec. Doc. T, 90th Cong. (1979), Cmnd. 7569.

[52] May 20, 1980, Arts. VII, VIII, 33 UST 3476, 1329 UNTS 47.

[53] June 4, 1974, Arts. 15–18, 1978 UKTS No. 64.

[54] Sept. 22, 1992, Arts. 10–12, 1999 UKTS No. 14.

[55] London Convention, *supra* note 3, Art. XIV(4)(f).

as may be appropriate under the provisions of the present Convention,"[56] or "[e]xercise such other functions as are required for the achievement of the objective of the Convention."[57] Through such specific and general powers, the COP is generally provided with authority at the internal level corresponding to that found in the constitutions of IGOs.

In the case of traditional IGOs, international institutional law has developed a doctrine of "implied powers" under which an effective interpretation of the treaty establishing the IGO is adopted that emphasizes its object and purpose.[58] As stated by the International Court of Justice (ICJ) in its Advisory Opinion *Legality of the Use by a State of Nuclear Weapons in Armed Conflict*:

> The powers conferred on international organizations are normally the subject of an express statement in their constituent instruments. Nevertheless, the necessities of international life may point to the need for organizations, in order to achieve their objectives, to possess subsidiary powers which are not expressly provided for in the basic instruments which govern their activities. It is generally accepted that international organizations can exercise such powers, known as "implied" powers.[59]

The Court applied this doctrine at the internal level in the *Effect of Awards* case, where it concluded that the United Nations had an implied power to establish administrative tribunals to settle disputes with its staff.[60] The law of international institutions also derives dynamism from the weight it gives to the practice of organs of these institutions.[61] In the *Namibia* case, the Court relied on such practice in accepting that abstention by a permanent member did not prevent the Security Council from adopting decisions under Article 27(3) of the UN Charter.[62]

Can such a doctrine of implied powers be applied to the AIAs established by MEAs, in particular the COP? One possible approach would be to ask whether such institutional arrangements should properly be called IGOs, and thus be governed by international institutional law. It has been argued that "[t]hese institutional arrangements are, in effect, international organisations."[63] The UN Office of Legal Affairs, in an opinion of November 4, 1993, stated that the Climate Change Convention established an "entity/organization" with international legal personality; and, in an opinion of December 18, 1995, it added that the bodies established by this Convention "have certain distinctive elements attributable to international organizations."[64]

Are these views correct? There is no legal or generally accepted definition of an international organization. We have chosen to rely on the definition given by Schermers and Blokker in their authoritative treatise on the subject. They define international organizations as "forms of cooperation founded on an international agreement creating at least one

[56] LRTAP Convention, *supra* note 17, Art. 10(2)(c).

[57] Climate Change Convention, *supra* note 10, Art. 7(2)(m).

[58] Concerning this feature of international institutional law, see C. F. AMERASINGHE, PRINCIPLES OF THE INSTITUTIONAL LAW OF INTERNATIONAL ORGANIZATIONS 44–48 (1996); HENRY G. SCHERMERS & NIELS M. BLOKKER, INTERNATIONAL INSTITUTIONAL LAW 158–63 (3d rev. ed. 1995); N. D. WHITE, THE LAW OF INTERNATIONAL ORGANISATIONS, ch. 5 (1996).

[59] 1996 ICJ REP. 66, 79, para. 25 (July 8).

[60] Effect of Awards of Compensation Made by the U.N. Administrative Tribunal, Advisory Opinion, 1954 ICJ REP. 47, 53 (July 13).

[61] *See* AMERASINGHE, *supra* note 58, at 48–55; SCHERMERS & BLOKKER, *supra* note 58, at 718–19.

[62] Legal Consequences for States of the Continued Presence of South Africa in Namibia (South West Africa) Notwithstanding Security Council Resolution 276 (1970), Advisory Opinion, 1971 ICJ REP. 16 (June 21).

[63] PHILIPPE SANDS, PRINCIPLES OF INTERNATIONAL ENVIRONMENTAL LAW: FRAMEWORK, STANDARDS AND IMPLEMENTATION 92 (1995). A similar view is expressed by Szasz, *supra* note 39, at 347. *See also* Jacob Werksman, *The Conference of Parties to Environmental Treaties*, *in* GREENING INTERNATIONAL INSTITUTIONS 55, 55 (Jacob Werksman ed., 1996) (stating that "these MEAs establish independent intergovernmental bodies . . . with the potential to develop powers over states that may far exceed those of more formally established international institutions" (citation omitted)).

[64] *See* notes 156, 178 *infra* and corresponding text.

organ with a will of its own, established under international law."[65] The COP and its subsidiary bodies are self-governing since states parties may influence the work of these organs only by acting through them, and they do not take instructions from the international organization hosting their secretariat.[66] One could argue that an international treaty conference is also a self-governing body,[67] without being considered an IGO. The AIAs of MEAs, however, are established by an international agreement, which is also a requirement under the above definition. Consequently, these bodies fulfill the necessary criteria for an IGO and would thus aspire to the application of international institutional law.

But does the fact that the states parties to MEAs have chosen not to establish formal IGOs prevent such application? Arguably, the legal regimes of MEAs could be seen as "self-contained," in the sense that MEAs are subject only to the law of treaties and not to international institutional law.[68]

First, however, we submit that the law of AIAs resembles that of IGOs more than it does the general law of treaties. MEAs are obviously treaties, but decisions of COPs and subsidiary bodies at the internal level are not. As a result, the law of treaties does not directly apply to such decisions. Furthermore, the law of AIAs takes a hierarchical form: the MEA serves as *lex superior* and decisions by the COP, subsidiary bodies, and the secretariat constitute stepwise levels of authority. Such a hierarchy between the constitution of an IGO and decisions of its organs is unknown in the law of treaties, but forms a distinct feature of international institutional law.

Second, the functions of AIAs at the internal level are similar to those of IGOs, and to a large extent dissimilar to the ones known in the law of treaties. Although the law of treaties deals with some of the functions of AIAs, such as treaty amendment, it does not address such issues as the establishment of subsidiary bodies; the adoption of rules of procedure, financial rules, and the budget; and the binding character of such decisions. International institutional law is far better equipped to handle such questions.

Finally, we find no indication that states parties to MEAs, by not establishing formal IGOs, intended to create less effective bodies at the internal level. On the contrary, it should be assumed that the parties wanted to establish an effective and dynamic institutional framework, and thus that both the doctrine of implied powers and reliance on the practice of the treaty bodies should apply. Accordingly, the law of international institutions should be applied to AIAs at the internal level.

Among the consequences of applying international institutional law with its "implied powers" is first of all that it would supplement the law of treaties. For example, while several MEAs explicitly provide for the power to establish subsidiary bodies, such as the Climate Change Convention in Article 7(2)(i), this power should also be assumed in the absence of a specific provision.[69] The right to establish subsidiary bodies may, however, be based on such a catchall provision as was mentioned above. Indeed, in MEAs containing such a provision, the doctrine of implied powers will have limited relevance.

The application of international institutional law may also furnish certain presumptions in matters that are not clear in an MEA (or the rules of procedure of the COP), for ex-

[65] SCHERMERS & BLOKKER, *supra* note 58, at 23; *see also* AMERASINGHE, *supra* note 58, at 9.

[66] See "Powers of the Host Organization," the next section below.

[67] *See* ROBBIE SABEL, PROCEDURE AT INTERNATIONAL CONFERENCES 19 (1997).

[68] On "self-contained" regimes, see United States Diplomatic and Consular Staff in Tehran (U.S. v. Iran), 1980 ICJ REP. 3, 39–41 (May 24). *See also* Martti Koskenniemi, *Breach of Treaty or Non-Compliance? Reflections on the Enforcement of the Montreal Protocol*, 3 Y.B. INT'L ENVTL. L. 123, 134–37 (1992) (discussing the relationship between the noncompliance procedure of the Montreal Protocol and, on the other hand, the law of treaties and the law of state responsibility).

[69] *See* AMERASINGHE, *supra* note 58, at 140; SCHERMERS & BLOKKER, *supra* note 58, at 743. In fact, the CITES COP has established subsidiary bodies even though it has no explicit power to do so (and its catchall power allows it to do no more than "make recommendations for improving the effectiveness" of the Convention, *see* CITES, *supra* note 4, Art. XI(3)(e)). It must be assumed that such establishment was based on implied powers.

ample, the legal nature of decisions by the COP and its subsidiary bodies. Article 6(2)(f) of the Ramsar Convention gives the COP the power both to make "recommendations" and to adopt "resolutions," which might suggest that "resolutions" are binding and "recommendations" are not. Yet this and similar differences in wording in other MEAs should not generally be assumed to have been intended to indicate different powers to adopt binding decisions on the internal plane. As with IGOs, internal decisions, such as guidance by the COP to subsidiary bodies and the secretariat, should be considered to be binding unless the MEA or the relevant decision itself specifically indicates that it was intended to be nonbinding.[70]

Applying international institutional law to AIAs may lead to outcomes that would not be accepted under the law of treaties. Thus, it has been argued that under the doctrine of implied powers a state can be expelled from an international organization even in the absence of an express provision in its constitution if the party through its behavior prevents the organization from executing its functions.[71] Under the law of treaties, on the other hand, the only basis for expulsion would be a material breach of the treaty (Vienna Convention on the Law of Treaties, Art. 60(2)).[72]

Finally, to turn from the substance of the powers of AIAs to the procedures by which they are exercised, the rules of procedure adopted by the COP generally provide for procedural decisions to be taken by a simple majority.[73] Consequently, quite extensive powers may be exercised by majority voting, such as adopting a binding work program for developing new substantive commitments, establishing subsidiary organs and determining their composition, and, presumably, expelling states parties.[74] Decisions on substantive matters require a qualified majority, but generally consensus is applied in both procedural and substantive matters.[75]

Powers of the Host Organization

The supremacy of the COP means that the international organization hosting the secretariat may exercise only the powers flowing from this particular function, and has no powers to instruct the COP or its subsidiary bodies. Thus, the UN General Assembly and Secretariat have no right to instruct these bodies even though the United Nations hosts several MEA secretariats (through UNEP, the ECE, or directly in the case of the Climate Change Convention). As the UN Secretary-General has noted in relation to the latter Convention, "the Conference of the Parties to the Convention (COP) has an independent legal character and is not a subsidiary of the General Assembly or of any other body."[76]

As regards the secretariat, however, matters are different. Both the COP and the host organization possess powers in relation to the secretariat. The COP and its subsidiary bodies must be considered to have the authority to instruct the secretariat in substantive matters, as well as in procedural questions, e.g., preparations for meetings of the COP, assistance to states parties, and contact with other international organizations and MEAs. On the other hand, as the host organization employs the officials of the secretariats, it has the right to appoint, promote, and terminate staff. In the case of the Climate Change Convention, the

[70] *See* AMERASINGHE, *supra* note 58, at 192; SCHERMERS & BLOKKER, *supra* note 58, at 744.

[71] *See* SCHERMERS & BLOKKER, *supra* note 58, at 104–05.

[72] See part V *infra* for further discussion of this matter.

[73] See, for example, Rule 40(1) of the Rules of Procedure of both the Basel Convention and the Biodiversity Convention. For the former, see <http://www.basel.int/text/rules.html>. For the latter, see UN Doc. UNEP/CBD/COP/1/17, Annex III (Jan. 1995), <http://www.unep.ch/bio/cdbrepi.htm>. In the absence of formally adopted rules of procedure, the Climate Change Convention applies draft rules contained in UN Doc. FCCC/CP/1996/2. Draft Rule 42 on majority voting, however, is not applied. *See* Report of the Conference of the Parties on Its Fifth Session, UN Doc. FCCC/CP/1999/6, para. 14.

[74] Koskenniemi, *supra* note 68, at 139, holds that suspension of rights is a matter of substance under the Montreal Protocol and would require a qualified majority.

[75] See part IV *infra* for further discussion.

[76] Note by the Secretary-General, UN Doc. A/AC.237/79/Add.1, at 7 (1994).

COP has requested that the UN Secretary-General "appoint, after consultation with the Conference of the Parties through its Bureau, the head of the Convention secretariat, with the title of Executive Secretary."[77] The latter is vested with the authority to appoint certain categories of the secretariat's staff, but appointments are made on behalf of the UN Secretary-General.[78] The UN Staff Regulations apply to all secretariats hosted by the United Nations, including the ECE and UNEP. Similarly, the IUCN Staff Rules apply to the secretariat of the Ramsar Convention.[79] As a consequence of the staff being its employees, the host organization must also have the right to direct officials in personnel and administrative matters.[80] Hence, it may in general instruct officials in how to carry out their work. The interface between the instructions to the secretariat from the COP and its subsidiary bodies, and instructions to officials from the host organization, may obviously harbor a potential for conflict.

Where the secretariat of an existing international organization is designated as the secretariat of an MEA (e.g., the IMO secretariat in the case of the London Convention), that secretariat does not cease to be part of the host organization. Consequently, if the host and the COP or its subsidiary bodies impose contradictory instructions, the relevant officials would be obliged, under the internal law of the organization, to carry out its instructions. These instructions, however, could violate the commitments undertaken by the organization in agreeing to serve as a host organization for the COP. The possibilities for contradictory instructions may be reduced by appropriate rule making in the host organization, such as the internal job descriptions in the ECE specifying the tasks of officials in servicing the LRTAP Convention.[81]

As mentioned above in part I, the COP of the Climate Change Convention has decided that "the Convention secretariat shall be institutionally linked to the United Nations, while not being fully integrated in the work programme and management structure of any particular department or programme."[82] This semi-independent status arguably means that the United Nations has no right to instruct the officials of the secretariat. Support for limiting the powers of the United Nations to administrative matters may be found in a suggestion by the Secretary-General on the institutional linkage between the two bodies:

> 5. The head of the Convention secretariat shall be accountable:
>
> (a) to the Conference of the Parties for the implementation of the policies and programme of work approved by the Conference;
>
> (b) to the Secretary-General as the chief administrative officer of the Organization, including for the observance of the Financial and Staff Regulations and Rules of the United Nations.[83]

Another possible source of conflict may be the magnitude of the resources, in terms of both personnel and money, that should be allocated to tasks defined by the COP. The COP generally has the powers to adopt the budget and financial regulations. While the COP will control the financial contributions from states parties, the host organization wields general control over resources that it allocates to secretarial work under the MEA. Depending upon the resources and priorities of the organization, this control may be to the benefit or the disadvantage of MEAs. To the extent that it is supposed to provide secretarial resources, denying them may be considered a breach of its obligations as a host organization.

[77] Decision 14/CP.1, *supra* note 28, para. 7.

[78] *See* Letter from Richard Kinley, Climate Change Convention secretariat (Dec. 4, 1998) (on file with authors).

[79] *See* E-mail from Julia Tucker, Ramsar secretariat (May 28, 1999) (on file with authors).

[80] *See* Kinley, *supra* note 78; fax from Gilbert M. Bankobeza, UNEP (Feb. 9, 1999) (on file with authors).

[81] *See* Letter from Lars Nordberg, UN/ECE (Jan. 28, 1999) (on file with authors).

[82] *See* note 28 *supra* and corresponding text.

[83] Letter to the President of the Climate Change COP from the Special Adviser to the Secretary-General (Apr. 5, 1995), UN Doc. FCCC/CP/1995/5/Add.4, annex.

As far as we are aware, potential conflicts of the kinds described above have not (yet) emerged as a serious problem in practice.

IV. Decision-Making Powers of MEA Institutions Relating to the Parties' Substantive Obligations

In addition to decisions concerning internal matters described in the previous section, COPs are authorized by many MEAs to take decisions relating to states parties' substantive obligations under those agreements. Indeed, as explained above, one of the reasons autonomous institutional arrangements are included in MEAs is to develop the norms they contain.

The Amendment of MEAs and the Adoption of Protocols

One type of substantive decision-making power is that given to COPs to decide on amendments to MEAs. This power is found in most of the global MEAs referred to in the introduction.[84] The procedures by which such amendments are to be adopted and come into force vary from agreement to agreement, but in broad outline they are similar. Under the Ramsar, London, and Bonn Conventions, and CITES, the COP is to adopt amendments by a two-thirds majority. Under the later agreements, amendments are to be adopted by consensus if at all possible: failing consensus, they are to be adopted by either a two-thirds majority (the Montreal Protocol and the Biodiversity and Desertification Conventions) or a three-quarters majority (the Vienna, Basel, and Climate Change Conventions). In the case of all the agreements, amendments adopted by these procedures do not enter into force until ratified by the same proportion of parties as is required for their adoption, and then are in force only for those parties that have ratified them.

In practice, this power has been used to amend several of the agreements.[85] Such treaty-amendment procedures are neither novel nor unique to MEAs. Indeed, these procedures essentially reflect the general procedures for treaty amendment laid down in the Vienna Convention on the Law of Treaties,[86] though in institutionalized and more streamlined form, and are broadly comparable to those laid down in the constituent treaties of international organizations, which frequently provide for their amendment through the adoption of the provisions concerned by the principal organ(s) of the organization, followed by ratification by a certain proportion of the member states.[87] Nevertheless, in practice the treaty-amending procedures of MEAs have involved some unusual, and possibly novel, features. The main example concerns the Montreal Protocol. In 1990 some important amendments to the Protocol were adopted by the second Meeting of the Parties.[88] According to Article 9(5) of the Vienna Ozone Convention, amendments to the Montreal Protocol require ratification by two-thirds of its parties to enter into force. At the time the amendments were adopted, there were fifty-eight parties to the Protocol: thus, their entry into force would have required forty ratifications. However, many of the parties were eager for the

[84] *See, e.g.*, Ramsar Convention, *supra* note 2, Art. 10 *bis* (added by the Protocol of Dec. 3, 1982, TIAS No. 11,084); London Convention, *supra* note 3, Art. 15; CITES, *supra* note 4, Art. XVII; Bonn Convention, *supra* note 5, Art. X; Vienna Convention, *supra* note 6, Art. 6(4); Montreal Protocol, *supra* note 7, Art. 11(4)(h); Basel Convention, *supra* note 8, Art. 15(5); Climate Change Convention, *supra* note 10, Art. 15; Biodiversity Convention, *supra* note 12, Art. 23(4)(d); Desertification Convention, *supra* note 14, Art. 22(2)(f).

[85] *E.g.*, Ramsar Convention, *supra* note 2 (in 1987); London Convention, *supra* note 3 (in 1978); CITES, *supra* note 4 (in 1979); Basel Convention, *supra* note 8 (in 1995); Montreal Protocol, *supra* note 7 (in 1990, 1992, 1997, 1999).

[86] *Opened for signature* May 23, 1969, Arts. 39–40, 1155 UNTS 331.

[87] *See, e.g.*, UN Charter Arts. 108–09; Convention on the International Maritime Organization, Mar. 6, 1948, Art. 52, 9 UST 621, 289 UNTS 48; Council of Europe Statute Art. 41.

[88] Montreal Protocol MOP Decision II/2, Doc. UNEP/OzL.Pro.2/3, *supra* note 26, *reprinted in* 1993 UKTS No. 4.

amendments to enter into force quickly, and notwithstanding Article 9(5) of the Vienna Ozone Convention, succeeded in persuading the meeting to provide in Article 2 of the amendments that they would enter into force once ratified by twenty parties. The meeting overcame objections to this course of action by regarding Article 2 as an agreement *inter partes* modifying Article 9(5) of the Vienna Ozone Convention, as provided for in Article 41(1)(*b*) of the Vienna Convention on the Law of Treaties.[89] Article 2(3) provides that following entry into force after ratification by twenty parties, the amendments enter into force for each remaining party upon ratification by that party. Such ratifications have been fairly slow in coming. One of the changes made by the 1990 amendments was to add a number of ozone-depleting substances to the list of controlled substances regulated by the Protocol. It might have been expected, in the light of the traditional consensual approach to treaty participation, that only those states that had ratified the 1990 amendments could participate in decisions at subsequent Meetings of the Parties to make changes in the regulations governing the controlled substances added by those amendments. In fact, however, so as to reflect the interest of all the parties to the Montreal Protocol in its future development, all parties, regardless of whether or not they have ratified the 1990 amendments, have been allowed to participate in the consensus procedures used to adjust these regulations.[90]

Besides having the power to alter parties' substantive obligations by adopting amendments to agreements, COPs may add to parties' obligations by adopting protocols to agreements. The latter power is found predominantly, although not exclusively, in those MEAs that were drawn up in the form of framework treaties because of the lack or uncertainty of scientific knowledge concerning the environmental problem at issue and/or the lack of agreement on the action to be taken to tackle that problem when the MEA was concluded. Global MEAs that enable the COP to adopt protocols include the Vienna Convention (Art. 8), the Basel Convention (Art. 15(5)(d)), the Climate Change Convention (Art. 17), and the Biodiversity Convention (Art. 23(4)(c)). Curiously, none of these agreements contains any provisions that spell out the procedure for the adoption of protocols, although all except the Climate Change Convention specify in detail how the protocols may be amended, once adopted. The matter thus falls to be regulated by the rules of procedure of the COP.[91] In general, these provide for the adoption of protocols by consensus if at all possible, failing which they may be adopted by a two-thirds or three-quarters majority. Protocols, like treaty amendments, clearly require ratification to enter into force. The number of ratifications required for entry into force, in the absence of provisions on the matter in the parent convention, is specified in the protocol itself. So far four protocols have been adopted by COPs under global MEAs: the Montreal Protocol adopted by the COP of the Vienna Convention, the Kyoto Protocol adopted by the COP of the Climate Change Convention, the Protocol on Liability and Compensation adopted by the COP of the Basel Convention, and the Cartagena Protocol on Biosafety adopted by the COP of the Biodiversity Convention.[92] Many protocols have been adopted in respect of regional MEAs, but diplomatic conferences have done so rather than COPs.[93]

[89] *See* Jill Barrett, *The Negotiation and Drafting of the Climate Change Convention*, *in* GLOBAL CLIMATE CHANGE, *supra* note 44, at 183, 190. But this justification for the action of the Meeting of the Parties has been questioned, *see* Gehring, *supra* note 25, at 48. Subsequent amendments to the Montreal Protocol have the same provisions relating to entry into force as the 1990 amendments.

[90] See further Werksman, *supra* note 63, at 65–67. An analogous situation has occurred in the Ramsar COP. *See* M. J. Bowman, *The Multilateral Treaty Amendment Process: A Case Study*, 44 INT'L & COMP. L.Q. 540, 549–50 (1995).

[91] See further on this point Patrick Széll, *Decision Making Under Multilateral Environmental Agreements*, 26 ENVTL. POL'Y & L. 210, 213 (1996).

[92] For these Protocols, see *supra* notes 7, 9, 11, 13, respectively.

[93] For example, the Protocols to UNEP's Regional Seas Conventions, *supra* note 16, and the Protocols to the LRTAP Convention, *supra* note 17.

Lawmaking Powers

The powers of COPs to adopt amendments and protocols to MEAs are only indirect lawmaking powers, as these measures require ratification by states parties to become legally effective. Some COPs, however, have genuine lawmaking powers: one, fairly common, form is the power to amend the annexes attached to MEAs such as the London, Bonn, and Basel Conventions, CITES, and the Montreal Protocol. These annexes usually contain more technical measures, which may require amendment or updating as a result of increased knowledge, greater political agreement, or some other change in circumstances. In some cases, such as the numerous amendments to the lists of species receiving protection in the annexes to CITES and the Bonn and Bern Conventions, the COP's power to amend may be relatively minor in terms of affecting the parties' substantive obligations and interests. But this is not always so; for example, the decisions of the CITES COP concerning changes in the listing of whale and elephant products provoked considerable debate and controversy. In other cases, the COP's power of amendment may clearly have a major impact on and radically change the obligations of parties to the MEA concerned. For example, the Consultative Meeting of the Parties to the London Convention, by amending its annexes, both introduced a scheme for regulating the incineration of waste at sea and later banned such incineration;[94] in addition, the consultative meeting has phased out the dumping of industrial and radioactive wastes.[95] These constitute major changes in the Convention. Another example of the COP's power to amend the parties' obligations extensively is demonstrated by the Montreal Protocol. The Protocol, as originally drafted, stipulated that the production and consumption of the five main chlorofluorocarbons (CFCs, which are ozone-depleting gases) was to be reduced by 50 percent of 1986 levels by 1999. However, "adjustments" made to the Protocol by the Meeting of the Parties in 1990 and 1992 determined that production and consumption of these CFCs should be phased out completely by 1996.[96] Similar far-reaching changes have subsequently been required for the use of other ozone-depleting substances listed in the various annexes to the Protocol.[97]

The procedure by which the COP adopts amendments to annexes (or adjustments in the case of the Montreal Protocol) is the same as that for the adoption of amendments to the agreement, except that they do not need to be ratified by the states parties. Such amendments are binding on all parties unless objected to within a certain period of time. However, parties to the Montreal Protocol that are unhappy with an adjustment may not object to it and so not be bound. Their only option would be to denounce the Protocol.[98] This situation is rather remarkable. Since adjustments can be adopted in theory by a two-thirds majority at a Meeting of the Parties, the majority can bind the minority against its will. In practice, this has not yet happened, as all adjustments so far have been adopted by consensus. According to Széll, the reason why the Montreal Protocol does not allow its parties to object to adjustments is that "at the time of adopting the Protocol all prospective Parties knew that

[94] London Consultative Meeting of the Parties Res. LDC.5(3) (1978), 1979 UKTS No. 71; Res. LDC.50(16) (1993), 1995 UKTS No. 90.

[95] London Consultative Meeting of the Parties Res. LDC.49(16), 51(16) (1993), 1995 UKTS Nos. 89, 91, respectively.

[96] Montreal Protocol MOP Decision II/1, Doc. UNEP/OzL.Pro2/3, *supra* note 26, *reprinted in* 1 Y.B. INT'L ENVTL. L. 612 (1990); Montreal Protocol MOP Decisions IV/2, IV/3, Doc. UNEP/OzL.Pro.4/15 (1992) <http://www.unep.org/ozone/4mop_cph.htm>, *reprinted in* 3 Y.B. INT'L ENVTL. L. 805, 806 (1992). "Adjustments" relate to changes in the timetable and targets set out in Article 2 of the Protocol for reducing the production and consumption of ozone-depleting substances; "amendments" refer to other changes in the Protocol.

[97] For a table showing the results of the changes made in the phasing out of ozone-depleting substances by adjustments to the Protocol up to and including 1997, see Sebastian Oberthür, *Montreal Protocol: 10 Years After*, 27 ENVTL. POL'Y & L. 432, 433 (1997).

[98] It should be noted, however, that under Article 19, a state must have been a party for at least four years before it may withdraw from the Protocol.

the trend of the instrument was in the direction of eventual total elimination of production and consumption of all the controlled substances."[99]

Apart from having a general power to make law by amending the annexes of MEAs (or in the case of the Montreal Protocol by "adjusting" that part of the main body of the Protocol relating to the timetable for phasing out the production and consumption of ozone-depleting substances), COPs may occasionally be authorized to make new rules by specific provisions of MEAs. For example, Article 17 of the Kyoto Protocol enables the COP to adopt "rules" relating to the operation of the system for trading in emissions of greenhouse gases. The use of the word "rules" suggests that such a measure is intended to be legally binding. This interpretation is also supported by substantive considerations: seemingly, a party that observes the "rules" on emissions trading can hardly be accused of noncompliance with the Protocol. Besides rule making in a fairly strict sense, COPs may be authorized to adopt measures that relate to the implementation of the parties' substantive obligations and that, while not strictly legislative, have a certain normative content. Thus, under Article 4(2)(d) of the Climate Change Convention, the COP is to "take decisions regarding criteria for joint implementation" of commitments by parties listed in Annex I. Such criteria were adopted in Decision 5/CP.1 of 1995.[100]

In addition to these specific powers, all the more recent MEAs empower the COP to undertake any additional action that may be required to achieve the purpose of the agreement. Whether this general power includes lawmaking is controversial, as is shown by the Basel Convention. Apparently acting under this power, the Basel COP at its second meeting in 1994 adopted Decision II/12 prohibiting the transboundary movement of hazardous waste from OECD to non-OECD member states.[101] However, this action was controversial, some states arguing that the decision was not legally binding because the COP could not alter parties' substantive obligations by utilizing the general power to take action to achieve the objectives of the Convention. The third COP in 1995 sought to resolve the controversy by adopting an amendment to the Convention that incorporated the substance of Decision II/12.[102] However, this amendment has not yet entered into force, and as of March 2000 had received only twenty of the sixty-two ratifications necessary to do so.[103] In a less controversial action, which may also have been based on this general power of the COP, the MOP of the Montreal Protocol decided in 1990 to establish an Interim Multilateral Fund.[104]

As was seen in the previous part, COPs have implied powers in relation to internal decision making. Like formal IGOs, they may enjoy similar powers in relation to matters concerning substantive obligations. COPs have taken various lawmaking decisions that apparently were intended to be, and seem to be regarded as, legally binding. Since no express provision in the relevant MEA authorized their adoption, these decisions could be regarded as being based on implied powers. Perhaps the best example of such a decision is the quota systems adopted by CITES for trade in various animal products such as ivory.[105] Although the

[99] Széll, *supra* note 91, at 213; *see also* RICHARD ELLIOT BENEDICK, OZONE DIPLOMACY: NEW DIRECTIONS IN SAFEGUARDING THE PLANET 90 (1991). Compare Werksman, *supra* note 63, at 62, who speaks of the adjustment process as being tailored to the "scientific imperative of ozone depletion."

[100] Climate Change COP Decision 5/CP.1, UN Doc. FCCC/CP/1995/7/Add.1, *supra* note 28, at 18.

[101] Basel COP Decision II/12 (1994), *reprinted in* 5 Y.B. INT'L ENVTL. L. 868 (1994).

[102] For the 1995 amendment, see 6 Y.B. INT'L ENVTL. L. 779 (1995).

[103] See further Werksman, *supra* note 63, at 63–64. *See also* KATHARINA KUMMER, INTERNATIONAL MANAGEMENT OF HAZARDOUS WASTES 63–65 (1995); Louise de La Fayette, *Legal and Practical Implications of the Ban Amendment to the Basel Convention*, 6 Y.B. INT'L ENVTL. L. 703, 705–10 (1995).

[104] Montreal Protocol MOP Decision II/8, Doc. UNEP/OzL.Pro.2/3, *supra* note 26, *reprinted in* 1 Y.B. INT'L ENVTL. L. 602 (1990); *see also* Gehring, *supra* note 25, at 49. The fund was an interim one and remained in being only until the amendments to the Protocol establishing a permanent fund, which were adopted at the same time as Decision II/8, came into force. Decision II/8, like Decision II/12 of the Basel COP, does not state on which provision of the agreement it is based.

[105] *See* SANDS, *supra* note 63, at 380; *see also* LYSTER, *supra* note 36, at 248–49.

implied-powers doctrine could serve as the legal basis of this and other examples, it is a somewhat uncertain foundation for them. A state party unhappy with such a decision could argue that, as it was not expressly authorized by the MEA concerned, the COP was acting *ultra vires* and/or was disregarding the amendment procedure of the MEA (insofar as the decision could be seen as amending the agreement). For this reason, it may be better to regard any such decisions that have not been challenged as agreements in simplified form between parties to the MEA, rather than as decisions based on implied powers. The question whether implied powers constitute a possible basis for decision making does not loom as large for those MEAs (of which CITES is not one) that contain a general provision of the kind described above permitting any action to achieve the purposes of the agreement.

The various lawmaking powers of COPs described here[106] are comparable to those enjoyed by many traditional IGOs in the environmental field. For example, the International Maritime Organization can alter marine-pollution conventions by the so-called tacit amendment procedure, by which the amendments enter into force for all parties unless objected to within a certain period of time. Similarly, the International Whaling Commission and various international fisheries commissions may adopt resource management measures that bind all their members unless objected to. Even the remarkable provisions of the Montreal Protocol under which all parties are bound by adjustments without the possibility of objection do not lack precedent among IGOs; for example, both the International Civil Aviation Organization and the International Atomic Energy Agency have the power to take certain rule-making decisions by majority vote that bind all parties without the possibility of objection.[107]

Procedurally, as has been seen, COPs usually take the various kinds of lawmaking decisions outlined above by consensus if at all possible, failing which a two-thirds or three-quarters majority must be obtained. Unlike amendments to an agreement, these decisions do not require ratification. Since many of the rule-making decisions adopted by the simplified procedure are far-reaching in nature, Széll has suggested that the same procedure could be used for amendments to agreements, dispensing with the requirement of ratification.[108] This suggestion has much to commend it and seems to fall within the realm of the politically possible. The requirement of ratification often means that amendments are slow to enter into force; for example, the 1987 amendments to the Ramsar Convention took seven years to enter into force and the 1978 amendments to the London Convention have not yet done so. It may also mean that amendments are not ratified by (and so are not binding on) all parties to the agreement. For example, as of May 31, 2000, the 1990, 1992, and 1997 amendments to the Montreal Protocol had been ratified by 139, 106, and 37 parties, respectively, out of a total of 175 parties; nonratifiers are therefore not bound to phase out production and consumption of the many ozone-depleting substances added by those amendments. Széll has also wondered whether the procedure for adopting adjustments to the Montreal Protocol (i.e., precluding any opting out by states parties) could be used in other agreements.[109] While such a possibility exerts a certain attraction, it is unlikely to prove acceptable to states, except perhaps in highly unusual situations such as that of the Montreal Protocol,

[106] While all the various powers discussed here are described as "lawmaking," some writers make a distinction between legislative powers (which enable a majority of states to bind a minority, leaving the minority no possibility of opting out of the measure by objecting to it) and quasi-legislative powers (under which decisions taken by the majority can be objected to). See Julia Sommer, *Environmental Law-Making by International Organizations*, 56 ZEITSCHRIFT FÜR AUSLÄNDISCHES ÖFFENTLICHES RECHT UND VÖLKERRECHT [ZAÖRV] 628, 634–35 (1996) and literature cited there.

[107] On ICAO, see D. W. BOWETT, THE LAW OF INTERNATIONAL INSTITUTIONS 145–47 (4th ed. 1982). On the IAEA, see Paul C. Szasz, *International Norm-Making*, *in* ENVIRONMENTAL CHANGE, *supra* note 29, at 41, 65. See further Paolo Contini & Peter H. Sand, *Methods to Expedite Environment Protection: International Ecostandards*, 66 AJIL 37, 41–53 (1972); Palmer, *supra* note 38, at 273–74 and literature cited there.

[108] Széll, *supra* note 91, at 212; *see also* PETER H. SAND, LESSONS LEARNED IN GLOBAL ENVIRONMENTAL GOVERNANCE 14–18 (1990).

[109] Széll, *supra* note 91, at 213.

because it makes too great an inroad into the traditional international law principle of consent, which states still strongly embrace despite urgings to the contrary.[110] In any case, current experience suggests that such a development would offer little practical advantage, as states rarely avail themselves of the opportunity to object to measures adopted by COPs, probably because most of these measures are adopted by consensus.

The Interpretation of Agreements

COPs engage from time to time in interpretation of the provisions of MEAs in ways that relate to and affect the substantive obligations of their parties. In some cases, this power of interpretation is expressly conferred by the MEA. Thus, Article 10(1) of the Montreal Protocol (as amended in 1990) authorizes the MOP to interpret the term "agreed incremental costs" (incurred by developing state parties in complying with the Protocol) by establishing "[a]n indicative list of . . . incremental costs."[111] Such a list was adopted in 1992.[112] Interpretations so authorized by the MEA clearly appear to be intended to be legally binding.

More commonly, a COP will interpret an MEA not because the agreement authorizes it, but because experience in the operation of the MEA or scientific, technical, or other developments are perceived as requiring it. For example, the CITES COP has adopted interpretations of the provisions of the Convention relating to the conditions for entry into force of amendments[113] and the criteria for amending the appendices,[114] and the Consultative Meeting of the Parties to the London Convention has effectively expanded the definition of "dumping" under the Convention by deciding that this term covers the disposal of waste into or under the seabed from the sea but not from land by tunneling.[115] Are such interpretations legally binding? Unlike interpretations specifically authorized by an MEA, they cannot derive binding force from the agreement as such. However, an interpretation adopted by a COP could be considered subsequent practice by the parties to a treaty, which, according to Article 31(3)(*b*) of the Vienna Convention on the Law of Treaties, is an element that may be taken into account in interpreting the treaty. On the other hand, if international institutional law applies, the COP, like an IGO organ, would be regarded as the author of the practice, not the states parties, and the law of treaties would therefore not be applicable. In either case, provided the interpretation adopted by the COP is uncontested and not modified by further practice, it is likely to be regarded as authoritative.

In all legal systems, interpretation may be so far-reaching that it comes close to being an exercise in legislation. In this respect international law in general, and decision making by COPs in particular, are no exception. The interpretation of the London Convention referred to above approaches legislation. In such cases, the action of the COP might be better regarded as an agreement *inter partes* modifying or supplementing the MEA within the meaning of Article 39 or Article 41(1)(*b*) of the Vienna Convention on the Law of Treaties, rather than subsequent practice within the meaning of Article 31(3)(*b*) or the practice of an organ under international institutional law.

As regards the procedure for adopting decisions containing interpretations of the MEA, it will normally be set out in the rules of procedure of the COP. In the more recent MEAs,

[110] *See* Handl, *supra* note 37, at 33; Palmer, *supra* note 38, at 270–78.

[111] Montreal Protocol Parties: Adjustments and Amendments to the Montreal Protocol on Substances That Deplete the Ozone Layer, 30 ILM 537, 550 (1991).

[112] Doc. UNEP/OzL.Pro.4/15, *supra* note 96, Annex VIII, *reprinted in* 3 Y.B. INT'L ENVTL. L. 822 (1992).

[113] CITES COP Res. CITES.CONF.4.27 (Apr. 1983) <http://www.wcmc.org.uk/CITES/eng/resols/resol4.shtml>.

[114] CITES COP Res. CITES.CONF.9.24 (Nov. 1994) <http://www.wcmc.org.uk/CITES/eng/resols/resol921.shtml#9.24>; *see also* Sommer, *supra* note 106, at 637, 647.

[115] London Consultative Meeting of the Parties Res. LDC.41(13) (1990), *reprinted in* 6 INTERNATIONAL ORGANIZATIONS AND THE LAW OF THE SEA: DOCUMENTARY YEARBOOK 332 (1990).

such decisions, as matters of substance, should normally be submitted for adoption by consensus, before resorting to majority voting.

Soft-Law Measures

From time to time, COPs adopt measures that do not lack some legal significance for the substantive obligations of states parties but, as is clearly demonstrated by their content or nomenclature, are not intended to be legally binding—in other words, soft-law measures. COPs turn to such measures for the same reasons that soft law is used generally in international environmental law—and international law in general (e.g., because states are unwilling to commit themselves to a "hard" obligation)—and they have the same legal significance (e.g., a soft-law measure may serve as a catalyst for developing a treaty or lead to the generation of a new rule of customary international law).[116] Examples of soft-law measures adopted by COPs include the CITES Guidelines for Transport and Preparation for Shipment of Live Animals and Plants (1980),[117] the Ramsar Framework for Implementation of the Convention (1984),[118] and the resolutions of the Consultative Meeting of the Parties to the London Convention that call for a moratorium on the dumping of radioactive waste (1983 and 1985).[119] The last of these progressed from soft to hard law by becoming incorporated in amendments to the Convention's annexes in 1993.[120]

Some Questions of Procedure

As has been pointed out, in practice COPs normally try to take decisions by consensus if possible (and under the more recent MEAs the COP is legally required to make every effort to reach consensus before resort is had to voting). This feature of COPs deserves some comment.

Consensus has been used informally in various UN bodies, such as the United Nations Conference on Trade and Development and the United Nations Development Programme, since the mid-1960s: it made its first formal appearance in the Rules of Procedure for the Third United Nations Conference on the Law of the Sea, adopted in 1973.[121] Since then consensus has been increasingly used; it first appeared in an MEA of the kind discussed in this article in the LRTAP Convention of 1979. Consensus decision taking has replaced straightforward majority voting as a result, in Buzan's pithy phrase, of "the divorce of power from voting majorities";[122] in such a situation, taking decisions by majority voting becomes undesirable because of the risk of alienating powerful minorities that may simply ignore those decisions. In view of the consequent need for "a technique that [would] ensure very broadly based support for decisions in a highly divided system,"[123] consensus decision making developed. While this procedure promotes the taking of decisions that are likely to be universally acceptable, it does have some drawbacks. It is likely to slow down the reaching of decisions and to lead to decisions that represent the lowest common denominator and

[116] On the use of soft law in international environmental law, see, from a considerable literature, BIRNIE & BOYLE, *supra* note 27, at 26–30; Handl, *supra* note 37, at 7–8; Palmer, *supra* note 38, at 269–70; SAND, *supra* note 108, at 16–17; and Szasz, *supra* note 107, at 69–72.

[117] CITES COP Doc. Plen.2.6 (Rev.), item XIX (1980); *see* Michael Bowman, *Conflict or Compatibility? The Trade, Conservation and Animal Welfare Dimensions of CITES*, 1 J. INT'L WILDLIFE L. & POL'Y 9 (1998).

[118] Ramsar COP Recommendation 2.3, Doc. C.4.12 (1984), *reprinted in* 12 ENVTL. POL'Y & L. 118 (1984).

[119] London Consultative Meeting of the Parties Res. LDC.14 (7) (1983) & LDC.21 (9) (1985), *reprinted in* IMO, THE LONDON DUMPING CONVENTION: THE FIRST DECADE AND BEYOND 207, 208 (1991).

[120] *See* note 95 *supra* and corresponding text.

[121] *See* Barry Buzan, *Negotiating by Consensus: Developments in Technique at the United Nations Conference on the Law of the Sea*, 75 AJIL 324, 325–26 (1981).

[122] *Id.* at 326.

[123] *Id.* at 327.

are vague or, to use Birnie and Boyle's phrase, " 'constructively' ambiguous."[124] Consensus decision making also raises the questions of, first, what is meant by consensus, and, second, how long the search for consensus must continue before resort may be had to voting. As regards the first question, consensus is usually taken to mean the absence of formal objection to a proposed decision (which is not necessarily the same as unanimity).[125] As regards the second question, no precise answer can obviously be given.

When consensus cannot be reached, there is a case, if voting is resorted to, for requiring special majorities or weighting the votes to try to ensure that decisions receive broad support from the more powerful and interested states or groups of states. Such techniques have been developed for some IGOs such as the International Sea-Bed Authority and the World Bank's Global Environment Facility, but so far their use by the COPs of MEAs has been very limited. The only example appears to be the MOP of the Montreal Protocol, which has employed both a form of weighted voting and double majorities. Thus, under Article 2(9) of the Protocol (in its original form) decisions on the "adjustment" of the timetable for phasing out the production and consumption of ozone-depleting substances that could not be reached by consensus were to be taken by voting, provided that two-thirds of the parties voted in favor and that such parties represented at least 50 percent of the consumption of the substances in question. In 1990 this form of weighted decision making was replaced by a requirement of a double majority. Decisions on this matter (and on some others, such as the financial mechanism) now require a two-thirds majority that itself must include a majority of developing state parties and a majority of developed state parties. There seems to be a good case for considering extending such forms of decision making to other COPs, particularly those that find it difficult to reach consensus. However, it may not be so easy to decide the form that weighted voting or special majorities should take for MEAs that cover a broad spectrum of issues and interests, such as the Biodiversity and Desertification Conventions.[126] Moreover, where decisions are taken by majority vote, the possibility in most MEAs for states parties to object to, and so not be bound by, those they do not like serves as a safety valve to prevent the minority from feeling tyrannized by the majority. The absence of such objection procedures in the Montreal Protocol probably helps to explain why so far it appears to be the only MEA whose COP utilizes special voting procedures.

V. Supervision by MEA Institutions of Implementation of and Compliance with Substantive Obligations

There is a need for procedures and mechanisms to monitor and facilitate states parties' implementation of and compliance with their substantive obligations under multilateral environmental agreements.[127] Most MEAs assign a general supervisory role to the COP in this regard.[128] To enable the COP to fulfill this role, many MEAs require the parties to

[124] BIRNIE & BOYLE, *supra* note 27, at 37.

[125] *See* Széll, *supra* note 91, at 212; SCHERMERS & BLOKKER, *supra* note 58, at 506, 512–15. It is also of interest that at the fourth meeting of the Climate Change Convention COP, held in 1998, Switzerland protested against a decision that had been adopted by consensus but did not formally object to it.

[126] *See* Széll, *supra* note 91, at 213.

[127] This section deals only with institutional aspects of the topic. For a broader perspective, see, from a growing literature, ENGAGING COUNTRIES: STRENGTHENING COMPLIANCE WITH INTERNATIONAL ENVIRONMENTAL ACCORDS (Edith Brown Weiss & Harold K. Jacobson eds., 1998); IMPROVING COMPLIANCE WITH INTERNATIONAL ENVIRONMENTAL LAW (James Cameron, Jacob Werksman, & Peter Roderick eds., 1996); Martti Koskenniemi, *New Institutions for Implementation Control and Reaction*, *in* GREENING INTERNATIONAL INSTITUTIONS, *supra* note 63, at 236; Kamen Sachariew, *Promoting Compliance with International Environmental Standards: Reflections on Monitoring and Reporting Mechanisms*, 2 Y.B. INT'L ENVTL. L. 31 (1991); Patrick Széll, *Compliance Regimes for Mulilateral Environmental Agreements—A Progress Report*, 27 ENVTL. POL'Y & L. 304 (1997).

[128] *See, e.g.*, CITES, *supra* note 4, Art. XI(3); Bonn Convention, *supra* note 5, Art. VII(5); Basel Convention, *supra* note 8, Art. 15(5); Climate Change Convention, *supra* note 10, Art. 7(2)(e–g); Biodiversity Convention, *supra* note 12, Art. 23(4).

report on their implementation of the agreement. For example, Article 7 of the Montreal Protocol stipulates that the parties shall provide data on their annual production, imports, and exports of controlled substances, and Article 13 of the Basel Convention requires annual reports on transboundary movements of hazardous waste. In many MEAs these reports are to be considered by the COP, often after examination by a specialist subsidiary body, such as the Subsidiary Body for Implementation under the Climate Change Convention. Such consideration may reveal that a party is not complying with its obligations.

Where noncompliance is alleged, either as a result of a national report or in some other way (e.g., information provided by an NGO), the matter could in theory be resolved through traditional forms of dispute settlement. MEAs, however, offer fairly limited possibilities for binding dispute settlement. Normally, negotiation is the preferred procedure for settling disputes, although some MEAs call for binding resolution by mutual consent of the disputing parties; e.g., CITES (Art. XVIII(2)) and the Bonn Convention (Art. XIII) provide for submission of the dispute to arbitration, and the Basel Convention (Art. 20(2)) provides for submission to the ICJ or arbitration. Some agreements stipulate that the disputing parties may accept compulsory binding resolution by prior unilateral declaration, with provision for compulsory (but nonbinding) conciliation if they have chosen a different means of settlement or have not made a declaration; see, for example, the 1994 Sulphur Protocol to the LRTAP Convention (Art. 9(2) and (5)), the Vienna Ozone Convention (Art. 11(3) and (4)), the Biodiversity Convention (Art. 27(3) and (4)), and the Climate Change Convention (Art. 14). Only one MEA requires unconditional binding settlement of disputes on the basis of a unilateral request, namely, the Bern Convention, which in Article 18(2) provides for compulsory arbitration unless the parties agree otherwise. Unlike the noncompliance procedures discussed below, the dispute settlement procedures just described confer no real role on MEA institutions.

Rather than place much emphasis on traditional dispute settlement procedures, some MEAs establish specific bodies to determine and deal with cases of noncompliance with substantive commitments. Article 8 of the Montreal Protocol, for example, provides that "[t]he Parties, at their first meeting, shall consider and approve procedures and institutional mechanisms for determining non-compliance with the provisions of this Protocol and for treatment of Parties found to be in non-compliance."[129] In accordance with this provision, the Meeting of the Parties has established a noncompliance mechanism/procedure whose institutional component, the Implementation Committee, considers allegations of noncompliance (which may be referred to it by any state party or the secretariat) and recommends any action to be taken to the MOP.[130] Noncompliance mechanisms either have also been established or are provided for in the 1994 Sulphur Protocol to the LRTAP Convention (Art. 7(1)), the 1996 Protocol to the London Convention (Art. 11(1)), and the Desertification Convention (Art. 27). The Climate Change Convention and the Kyoto Protocol provide for a "multilateral consultative process" with a similar purpose.[131] In our view, subsidiary bodies for operating noncompliance mechanisms could also be established without an explicit provision in the MEA, on the basis of "implied powers."[132]

The advantages of using noncompliance mechanisms rather than traditional dispute settlement procedures are twofold. First, because questions of compliance with MEA commitments are multilateral in character and usually affect all parties equally rather than any particular party or parties specifically, they should preferably be addressed in a multilateral context, rather than in a bilateral dispute settlement procedure. Second, noncompliance procedures

[129] Montreal Protocol, *supra* note 7, Art. 8.

[130] Montreal Protocol MOP Decision II/5, *supra* note 26; Montreal Protocol MOP Decision IV/5, Doc. UNEP/OzL.Pro4/15, *supra* note 96.

[131] Climate Change Convention, *supra* note 10, Art. 13; Kyoto Protocol, *supra* note 11, Art. 16.

[132] *See* text at notes 58–72 *supra*.

may promote the resolution of compliance problems in a cooperative, rather than an adversarial, manner.[133]

The nonconfrontational approach is reflected in the mandate of the Implementation Committee of the Montreal Protocol, which is to seek an "amicable solution";[134] that of the Implementation Committee established under the LRTAP Convention, which is to address noncompliance with a view to securing a "constructive solution";[135] and that of the Multilateral Consultative Process under the Climate Change Convention, whose deliberations are to be conducted in a "facilitative, cooperative, non-confrontational, transparent and timely manner, and be non-judicial."[136]

Furthermore, the outcome of the procedure is directed more toward assistance than sanctions. The 1996 Protocol to the London Convention, for example, provides that the COP may offer "advice, assistance or co-operation" to parties and nonparties.[137] The Multilateral Consultative Process under the Climate Change Convention refers to "appropriate assistance."[138] The "indicative list of measures" under the Montreal Protocol, however, refers not only to supportive measures (A), but also to cautions (B) and suspension (C):

> A. Appropriate assistance, including assistance for the collection and reporting of data, technical assistance, technology transfer and financial assistance, information transfer and training.
>
> B. Issuing cautions.
>
> C. Suspension, in accordance with the applicable rules of international law concerning the suspension of the operation of a treaty, of specific rights and privileges under the Protocol, whether or not subject to time limits, including those concerned with industrial rationalization, production, consumption, trade, transfer of technology, financial mechanism and institutional arrangements.[139]

The noncompliance procedure of the LRTAP Convention seems rather open-ended in establishing that the Executive Body may "decide upon measures of a non-discriminatory nature to bring about full compliance with the protocol in question, including measures to assist a Party's compliance."[140] The report of the Executive Body, however, states that "[i]t was understood by the delegations . . . that the Executive Body's decisions concerning compliance were not legally binding unless a provision in the protocol in question rendered them so."[141] Similarly, the Kyoto Protocol provides that "procedures and mechanisms" on noncompliance established under its Article 18 entailing "binding consequences" shall be adopted by an amendment to the Protocol.[142]

One might ask whether the noncompliance procedures establish "self-contained" regimes, which would preclude recourse to sanctions under general international law such as the suspension or termination of a treaty following a material breach in accordance with Article

[133] Noncompliance mechanisms have been criticized, however, for blurring the adjudicative and conciliatory functions and for not taking account of the interests of the international community in general, *see* Christine Chinkin, *Alternative Dispute Resolution Under International Law*, *in* REMEDIES IN INTERNATIONAL LAW: THE INSTITUTIONAL DILEMMA 123, 128–34 (Malcolm Evans ed., 1998).

[134] Montreal Protocol MOP Decision IV/5, *supra* note 130, para. 8.

[135] LRTAP Executive Body Decision 1997/2, annex, para. 3(b) <http://www.unece.org/env/lrtap/conv/report/eb53_a3.htm>.

[136] Climate Change COP Decision 10/CP.4, UN Doc. FCCC/CP/1998/16/Add.1, annex, para. 3, *obtainable from* <http://www.cop4.org>.

[137] Nov. 7, 1996, Art. 11(2), 36 ILM 710 (1997).

[138] Climate Change COP Decision 10/CP.4, *supra* note 136, annex, paras. 6, 12.

[139] Montreal Protocol MOP Decision IV/5, *supra* note 130.

[140] LRTAP Executive Body Decision 1997/2, annex, *supra* note 135, para. 11.

[141] LRTAP Executive Body, Report of the Fifteenth Session, UN Doc. ECE/EB.AIR/53, para. 48 (Jan. 7, 1998) <http://www.unece.org/env/lrtap/conv/report/ebair53.htm>.

[142] Kyoto Protocol, *supra* note 11, Art. 18.

60 of the Vienna Convention on the Law of Treaties, or the use of countermeasures under the law of state responsibility. That question, however, falls outside the ambit of this article.[143] We focus instead on the extent to which the use of sanctions provided for by the law of international institutions is allowed.

We concluded earlier that international institutional law should apply in establishing the powers of AIAs at the internal level.[144] We would argue that this approach should also hold true when considering the power to adopt sanctions if substantive obligations are violated. First, the law of treaties is not directly applicable to the breach of a binding decision by a COP or other MEA body, as opposed to the breach of a treaty obligation. While certain binding substantive decisions are formally amendments to an MEA, such as decisions on the protection of species under the Bern Convention (Art. 17), other substantive decisions are not, such as the rules for emissions trading under the Kyoto Protocol (Art. 17).[145] Second, cooperation on noncompliance more closely resembles solutions to corresponding problems in traditional IGOs than dispute settlement for breach of a treaty, since account must be taken of the need for continuing cooperation under the MEA in controlling the observance of existing obligations and developing new commitments.[146] Furthermore, various incentives and sanctions are available under MEA cooperation that are unknown in the law of treaties. Third, the parties to MEAs, by establishing AIAs rather than formal IGOs, should not be considered to have intended them to be less effective institutions. Finally, while so far the measures adopted in response to a breach have been rather cautious, this should not be taken as an indication that the parties intended that the COPs could not adopt stronger measures. However, if a list of indicative measures to be taken has been adopted (as in the case of the Montreal Protocol), the use of other kinds of measures may be restricted until it has been amended.

We may thus conclude that international institutional law applies to breaches of substantive obligations in MEAs. This conclusion then raises the question of the kinds of sanctions that should be considered available under such law.

A mild kind of sanction is the "shaming" represented by merely naming a state in noncompliance. As regards formal IGOs, some commentators have argued that the competence to determine noncompliance is implied in the right to discuss the report of a supervisory organ.[147] This sanction may also be used when a situation of noncompliance has been brought to an end, as was done in the case of the Czech Republic under the Montreal Protocol.[148]

Discretionary powers to provide financial and technological assistance, or other services or privileges, may afford positive incentives to parties to comply with their commitments. But denial of assistance and privileges, or making them conditional, may serve as negative leverage: this sanction should probably be accepted as available even in the absence of explicit competence.[149] Conditions were attached to assistance to Russia under the Montreal Protocol, requiring further actions by that state to implement its obligations.[150]

More radical sanctions have also been imposed by international organizations, with or without an explicit basis, such as suspension of voting rights or representation, or of other rights and privileges of membership.[151] Under the Montreal Protocol, the MOP has cautioned several countries with economies in transition, in accordance with the indicative list

[143] On this question, see Koskenniemi, *supra* note 68.

[144] *See* text at notes 63–72 *supra*.

[145] *See* part IV *supra*.

[146] *See* SCHERMERS & BLOKKER, *supra* note 58, at 866.

[147] *See id.* at 898.

[148] *See* Montreal Protocol MOP Decision VIII/24, Doc. UNEP/OzL.Pro8/12 (1996), <http://www.unep.org/ozone/8mop_snj.htm>.

[149] *See* SCHERMERS & BLOKKER, *supra* note 58, at 906, 913–14.

[150] *See* Montreal Protocol MOP Decision VIII/25, Doc. UNEP/OzL.Pro8/12, *supra* note 148.

[151] *See* SCHERMERS & BLOKKER, *supra* note 58, at 906–12, 916–18.

of measures in subparagraph B, that measures consistent with subparagraph C, including suspension of the right to trade in ozone-depleting substances under Article 4 of the Protocol, might be considered.[152] The reference in subparagraph C to "the applicable rules of international law concerning the suspension of the operation of a treaty," rather than to the appropriate law of international institutions, seems unnecessarily restrictive.[153]

In certain circumstances, international institutional law allows the suspension or expulsion of states parties from cooperation under the MEA concerned.[154] This sanction may be the most dramatic, but not necessarily the most effective, since it would prevent the supervision of such states' activities in matters covered by the MEA. Thus, MEA COPs, like international organizations, should generally avoid this sanction.[155]

International institutional law should also be applied in interpreting explicit restrictions on the application of sanctions. Article 18 of the Kyoto Protocol, as stated above, establishes that measures with "binding consequences" shall be adopted by amending the Protocol. International institutional law could be used to interpret what is meant by "binding" in this context. It could thus be argued that sanctions such as suspension of assistance and possibly also of the use of the "Kyoto mechanisms," e.g., emissions trading, are not binding, at least to the extent that such assistance and mechanisms are considered to be "privileges" rather than "rights."

At present, much of the above discussion is rather theoretical, as the only MEA whose noncompliance mechanisms have been invoked so far in practice is the Montreal Protocol.

VI. The External Capacity of MEA Institutions

The opinion of the UN Office of Legal Affairs of November 4, 1993, mentioned above (UNOLA I), stated that the Climate Change Convention established "an international entity/organization with its own separate legal personality, statement of principles, organs and a supportive structure in the form of a Secretariat (Articles 3, 7–10)."[156] In this part we consider whether, as this statement suggests, MEA institutions, like IGOs, may possess international legal personality and therefore act on the external plane, especially in the form of entering into formally binding agreements (i.e., treaties) with states (e.g., on privileges and immunities), or with international organizations (such as the organization hosting the secretariat), or with financial institutions (for example, the GEF). We begin by examining the wording of MEAs and then go on to consider the doctrine of implied powers and the practice of MEA institutions.

Wording of MEAs

In UNOLA I, the UN Office of Legal Affairs refers to the 1986 Vienna Convention on the Law of Treaties Between States and International Organizations or Between International Organizations, which states that the capacity of an international organization to conclude treaties is governed by the "rules of the organization" (Art. 6).[157] The latter are defined, in

[152] Montreal Protocol MOP Decisions X/20, 21, 23–28 (1998) <http://www.unep.org/ozone/10mop-rpt.htm>, concerning Azerbaijan, Belarus, Estonia, Latvia, Lithuania, the Russian Federation, Ukraine, and Uzbekistan. As pointed out by Werksman, the application of trade measures may conflict with commitments under GATT/World Trade Organization. Jacob Werksman, *Compliance and Transition, Russia's Non-Compliance Tests the Ozone Regime*, 56 ZAÖRV 750, 773 (1996).

[153] *See* text at note 139 *supra*.

[154] *See* text at note 71 *supra*.

[155] *See* SCHERMERS & BLOKKER, *supra* note 58, at 97; AMERASINGHE, *supra* note 58, at 124.

[156] United Nations Office of Legal Affairs, Arrangements for the Implementation of the Provisions of Article 11 of the UN Framework Convention on Climate Change Concerning the Financial Mechanism, para. 4 (Nov. 4, 1993) (on file with authors) [hereinafter UNOLA I]; *see also* UN Doc. A/AC.237/50 (1993).

[157] Vienna Convention on the Law of Treaties Between States and International Organizations or Between International Organizations, Mar. 21, 1986, 25 ILM 543 (1986).

particular, as the constituent instruments, decisions and resolutions adopted in accordance with them, and established practice of the organization (Art. 2(1)(j)).

The opinion continues:

> 6. The United Nations Framework Convention on Climate Change of 9 May 1992 provides in Article 7 that the Conference of the Parties (COP) is established as the *supreme body* of the Convention with the responsibility to keep under regular review the implementation of the Convention with the authority to make, within its mandate, the decisions necessary to promote the effective implementation of the Convention. In addition to the wide range of functions referred to in Article 7, paragraph 2 (a–l) of the Convention, including *inter alia* the establishment of cooperative relations with competent international organizations and bodies, the COP can also exercise such other functions as are required for the achievement of the objective of the Convention (Article 7, paragraph 2-m).[158]

On the basis of the provisions mentioned, the opinion concluded that the COP had the legal capacity, within the limits of its mandate, to enter into agreements with other entities possessing the authority to do so.

It should be noted, first, that UNOLA I refers to the 1986 Vienna Convention on the Law of Treaties Between States and International Organizations or Between International Organizations (which is not in force), even though AIAs, including COPs, have not been established as formal international organizations. This accords with our characterization of AIAs as self-governing bodies, and thus as informal organizations.

Second, MEAs do not contain any explicit provisions setting out their international legal personality or their treaty-making capacity. Treaties establishing formal international organizations, however, also commonly lack such provisions.[159]

Third, several provisions in the Climate Change Convention—and other MEAs—may be taken to provide a treaty-making capacity for the COP, thus implying that AIAs have international legal personality. UNOLA I refers to the catchall phrase in the Climate Change Convention (Art. 7(2)), which states that the COP "shall make, within its mandate, the decisions necessary to promote the effective implementation of the Convention." To this end, it shall "(m) Exercise such other functions as are required for the achievement of the objective of the Convention."[160]

In addition to being very broad, this wording does not distinguish between decisions on the internal plane, those concerning substantive obligations, and those related to actions on the external plane. Whereas the terms "effective implementation of the Convention" and "achievement of the objective of the Convention" indicate extensive powers, the references to "necessary" and "required" arguably impose restrictions on these powers. Nothing suggests, however, that these restrictions preclude legal capacity to act on the external plane. Similar wording can be found in several other MEAs, such as the Bonn and Desertification Conventions, which provide respectively that their COPs may decide on "any additional measure that should be taken to implement the objects of this Convention" and "such other functions as may be necessary for the achievement of the objective of the Convention."[161]

UNOLA I also refers to more specific functions of the COP listed in Article 7(2), subparagraphs (a) to (l) of the Climate Change Convention, including the competence to "(l) [s]eek and utilize, where appropriate, the services and cooperation of . . . competent inter-

[158] UNOLA I, *supra* note 156, para. 6.

[159] *See* AMERASINGHE, *supra* note 58, at 85; SCHERMERS & BLOKKER, *supra* note 58, at 978.

[160] UNOLA I, *supra* note 156, para. 6 (quoting Climate Change Convention, *supra* note 10, Art. 7(2)).

[161] Bonn Convention, *supra* note 5, Art. VII(5)(h); Desertification Convention, *supra* note 14, Art. 22(2)(j); *see also* LRTAP Convention, *supra* note 17, Art. 10(2)(c); Vienna Convention, *supra* note 6, Art. 6(2)(k); Montreal Protocol, *supra* note 7, Art. 11(3)(j); Basel Convention, *supra* note 8, Art. 15(5)(c); Kyoto Protocol, *supra* note 11, Art. 13(4); Prior Informed Consent Convention, *supra* note 15, Art. 18(5)(c).

national organizations and intergovernmental and non-governmental bodies."[162] It is not stated in what form such cooperation should be conducted, but binding agreements, i.e., treaties, are not excluded. International organizations and intergovernmental bodies would include formal international organizations, as well as bodies established by other MEAs.

Reference should also be made to Article 8(2)(f) of the Convention, which authorizes the secretariat to "enter, under the overall guidance of the Conference of the Parties, into such administrative and contractual arrangements as may be required for the effective discharge of its functions." Nothing is said about limiting such arrangements to domestic law instruments; thus, the wording also seems to allow the secretariat to enter into binding international agreements to the extent "required" for the "effective" discharge of its functions. Similar provisions are contained in the Desertification Convention (Art. 23(2)(e)), the Vienna Ozone Convention (Art. 7(1)(e)), and the Basel Convention (Art. 15(5)(d)).

As can be seen, the wording of MEAs covers both general and specific powers relevant to the legal capacity of COPs at the external level. Since the general powers contained in catch-all phrases relate to what is necessary for the effective implementation of the MEA, powers on the external plane, including entering into treaties, seem to be included. The specific powers refer to arrangements, but they include contractual arrangements with international bodies, which should also indicate a treaty-making capacity.

Even if the view is taken that MEA institutions, or at least certain ones, do not enjoy international legal personality and treaty-making capacity by virtue of express provisions in the relevant agreement, they may still possess such personality and capacity as a result of implied powers.

Implied Powers

The doctrine of implied powers found its authoritative expression in the *Reparations* case,[163] which concerned the United Nations' capacity to bring international claims, i.e., its powers on the external plane. This reliance on the object and purpose ("effective interpretation") of the constitutive treaty has since been generally accepted as a basis for determining the external capacity of IGOs. We argued earlier that this doctrine should be applied when determining the internal powers of MEA institutions, as well as their powers to adopt substantive decisions. But what about their capacity on the external plane?

As already mentioned, the absence of an explicit provision on international legal personality, while common in formal IGOs, has not prevented them from having such personality. It is difficult to see a greater need for an explicit basis in the case of MEA institutions. States parties should therefore not be surprised to learn that they have allocated more powers to AIAs than they have expressly conferred on them.

Second, the fact that AIAs have been established rather than new formal IGOs should not be a reason for denying implied powers to AIAs; they were established instead of formal IGOs because of the need for "institutional economy" rather than a desire to establish less effective institutions. Just like formal IGOs, AIAs need to act on the external plane; for example, in relation to the organization hosting the secretariat, international financial institutions, the state where the secretariat is located, and the bodies of other MEAs. AIAs should be able to enter into binding agreements, i.e., treaties, with such entities.

We may thus conclude that, in addition or as an alternative to express powers, MEA institutions have implied powers to act on the external plane, including the capacity to enter into treaties when necessary to carry out their functions. We now turn to actual practice in the exercise of these powers.

[162] UNOLA I, *supra* note 156, para. 6 (citing Climate Change Convention, *supra* note 10, Art. 7(2)(l)).

[163] Reparation for Injuries Suffered in the Service of the United Nations, Advisory Opinion, 1949 ICJ Rep. 174 (Apr. 11).

The Practice of MEA Institutions

Arrangements with the host organization. The secretariats designated in MEAs, or established by their COPs, formally constitute a part of another international organization, i.e., the host organization. It is necessary both for the host organization to accept this responsibility and for it to make arrangements with the COP relating to the functioning of the secretariat. The making of such arrangements is provided for, inter alia, in Article 11(3) of the Climate Change Convention, Article 23(3) of the Desertification Convention, and Article 19(3) of the Prior Informed Consent Convention.

The MEAs do not define the legal character of an organization's consent to host or provide a secretariat and the consequent arrangements. In practice, these matters have not yet been the subject of a binding, or even a nonbinding, agreement entered into and signed by representatives of the AIAs and the host organization. Instead, consultations between the two parties have led to parallel decisions setting out their mutual relationship. Thus, as we have seen, in Decision 14/CP.1, the COP of the Climate Change Convention decided that "the Convention secretariat shall be institutionally linked to the United Nations, while not being fully integrated in the work programme and management structure of any particular department or programme."[164] The General Assembly responded by adopting Resolution 50/115 of December 20, 1995, which "[e]ndorse[d] the institutional linkage between the Convention secretariat and the United Nations, as advised by the Secretary-General and adopted by the Conference of the Parties."[165] Arrangements between the parties are reflected in subsequent COP decisions, such as Decision 14/CP.2, Establishment of the Permanent Secretariat and Arrangements for Its Functioning.

Nothing is said in these decisions about the international legal personality of the COP. Two self-governing bodies, however, rather than the states parties to the MEA and the host organization, entered into these arrangements. Furthermore, the character of the arrangements is international and not domestic. There may be some doubt as to whether they are binding or nonbinding. At present, such arrangements take the form of parallel decisions (though obviously underpinned by a mutual understanding) rather than formal agreements, but there seems to be no reason why in principle the competence to conclude a binding agreement should not be considered to fall within the powers of the COP.

Arrangements with financial institutions. The Climate Change Convention establishes that a mechanism for the provision of financial resources, including the transfer of technology, is "defined," and that arrangements shall be agreed upon between the COP and the "entity or entities" entrusted with the operation of this mechanism (Art. 11(1) and (3)). The Biodiversity Convention establishes that there shall be a financial mechanism and that the COP shall decide on appropriate arrangements after consultation with the institution entrusted with the operation of this mechanism (Art. 21(1) and (3)).

The opinion of the UN Office of Legal Affairs referred to above as UNOLA I concerned the arrangements between the COP of the Climate Change Convention and the GEF as the financial mechanism. In this opinion it is stated:

> In light of the above, as far as the question of the legal capacity of the COP is concerned, it may be concluded that in accordance with the relevant provisions of the Convention, the COP has the legal capacity, within the limits of its mandate, to enter into agreements and other arrangements with entities, such as states, intergovernmental and non-governmental organizations and bodies, which also have the authority to do so.[166]

[164] *See* note 28 *supra* and corresponding text.

[165] GA Res. 50/115, UN GAOR, 50th Sess., Supp. No. 49, Vol. 1, at 174, UN Doc. A/50/49 (1995) (emphasis omitted).

[166] UNOLA I, *supra* note 156, para. 7; *see also* Jacob Werksman, *Consolidating Governance of Global Commons: Insights from the Global Environment Facility*, 6 Y.B. INT'L ENVTL. L. 27, 54–60 (1995).

In a subsequent opinion of August 23, 1994 (UNOLA II), the UN Office of Legal Affairs recommended that the COP enter into "a legally-binding treaty instrument" on its relationship with the GEF:

> It may be stated with sufficient certainty that complex issues, such as accountability, observance of compliance with the eligibility criteria for funding, procedures for the reconsideration of particular funding decisions and, last but not least, procedures for joint determination and periodical review of the aggregate GEF funding necessary and available for the implementation of the Convention, will have to be regulated in an agreement concluded for these purposes. . . . [T]o ensure the effective operation of the GEF as a source of funding of the activities under the Convention, the above-captioned issues should be spelled out in a legally-binding treaty instrument.[167]

In 1996 a memorandum of understanding (MOU) was entered into by the COP and the Council of the GEF.[168] MOUs are generally meant to signify nonbinding, rather than binding, arrangements. But their legal character depends on the intention of the parties, which must also be determined on the basis of factors other than their name, especially their wording.[169] The MOU between the COP of the Climate Change Convention and the Council of the GEF contains provisions on its modification, entry into effect, and termination, which are usual in binding agreements. The relevant decision of the COP adopts the MOU, "thereby bringing it into force."[170] However, the tenor of the wording indicates its nonbinding character by using "will" and "should" rather than "shall," although it also states that the two secretariats "shall" cooperate. Furthermore, the fact that the Council of the GEF is a party strongly suggests that the MOU is meant to be nonbinding; for, according to UNOLA II, "the founders of the restructured GEF did not provide it with the legal capacity to enter into legally binding arrangements or agreements. . . . Thus, if a cooperative arrangement or agreement is negotiated by the GEF with the COP, subsequently it will have to be formalized by the World Bank."[171] Since the MOU was to come into force by acceptance of the COP and the Council of the GEF, and needed no confirmation by the World Bank, it should be considered to be nonbinding. On the other hand, nowhere is it suggested that the nonbinding status of the arrangement was chosen because the COP lacked competence to enter into binding agreements.[172]

Arrangements with the host state. When an MEA secretariat (or other subsidiary body) is located in a state other than the seat of the headquarters of the organization hosting that secretariat, arrangements must be reached, inter alia on privileges and immunities, with that other state. The incorporation of these arrangements in binding agreements under international law, with the COP as a party, would be evidence of its international legal personality. Two such arrangements will be examined to see if this is the case: the 1998 Agreement between the Multilateral Fund for the Implementation of the Montreal Protocol and Canada,[173] and the 1996 Agreement between the United Nations, the Federal Republic of Germany, and the secretariat of the Climate Change Convention.[174]

[167] UN Doc. A/AC.237/74, annex, para. 16 (1994) [hereinafter UNOLA II].

[168] Memorandum of Understanding Between the Conference of the Parties to the United Nations Framework Convention on Climate Change and the Council of the Global Environment Facility, Decision 12/CP.2, annex, UN Doc. FCCC/CP/1996/15/Add.1 (1996).

[169] *See* Anthony Aust, *The Theory and Practice of Informal International Instruments*, 35 INT'L & COMP. L.Q. 787, 800–04 (1986).

[170] Climate Change COP Decision 12/CP.2, *supra* note 168, para. 2; *see also* Biodiversity COP Decision III/8, Doc. UNEP/CBD/COP/3/38, at 61 (1996), <http://www.biodiv.org/Decisions/COP3/pdf/COP-3-AllDecisions-e.pdf>.

[171] UNOLA II, *supra* note 167, paras. 18, 19.

[172] See the documents presented by the secretariat to the Subsidiary Body for Implementation and the COP, respectively, UN Docs. FCCC/SBI/1995/3, FCCC/CP/1996/9.

[173] Agreement Regulating Matters Resulting from the Establishment in Canada of the Multilateral Fund and Its Organs, Nov. 23, 1998, Can.–Multilateral Fund for the Implementation of the 1987 Montreal Protocol on Substances That Deplete the Ozone Layer (on file with authors).

[174] Agreement Concerning the Headquarters of the Convention Secretariat, UN–FRG–Secretariat of UN Framework Convention on Climate Change, June 20, 1996 (on file with authors) [hereinafter 1996 Agreement].

The Montreal Protocol does not make use of the GEF as a financial mechanism but specifies, instead, that the parties shall establish a mechanism for providing financial and technical cooperation, which shall include a multilateral fund (Art. 10(1) and (2)). Such a fund was established by the MOP and situated in Canada,[175] whereas the secretariat of the Protocol is located in Kenya at the headquarters of its host organization, UNEP. The MOP subsequently decided that the fund shall enjoy "such legal capacity as is necessary for the exercise of its functions and the protection of its interests, in particular the capacity to enter into contracts, to acquire and dispose of movable and immovable property and to institute legal proceedings in defence of its interests."[176] Furthermore, the fund as well as its officials shall enjoy such privileges and immunities as are necessary for the fulfillment, respectively, of its purposes and their functions.

The 1998 Agreement between the multilateral fund and Canada regulates the privileges and immunities of the fund, its officials, representatives of member states, and experts. It establishes rights and obligations regarding the fund that are typical of a headquarters agreement of an international organization, such as inviolability of the office premises (Art. 3), exemption from taxes and duties (Art. 5), operation of communication facilities (Art. 6), and privileges and immunities necessary for officials to exercise their functions independently (Arts. 9 and 10).

Although the Agreement does not state that it is governed by international, rather than domestic, law, this conclusion is inescapable. It follows, first, from the object and purpose of the Agreement, since the independence purportedly conferred on the fund would not be achieved if Canada were entitled to eliminate the privileges and immunities by unilateral domestic acts. Second, the Agreement establishes in several provisions that the fund and its representatives shall have protection similar to that enjoyed by diplomatic missions and agents or international organizations and their representatives (e.g., Arts. 3(2), 6(1) and (2), 9(1) and (2), and 10). Third, the duty of persons enjoying privileges and immunities under the Agreement to respect the laws and regulations of Canada applies without prejudice to those privileges and immunities (Art. 12), which gives priority to the latter. Finally, under the procedure laid down in the Agreement for settling disputes by means of arbitration, when the parties cannot agree on the third member of the arbitral tribunal, that member shall be appointed by the president of the International Court of Justice. All these factors indicate that the Agreement is an instrument under international law.

We may thus conclude that the Agreement is a treaty entered into by the multilateral fund, on the basis of a decision of the MOP of the Montreal Protocol. It is difficult to accept that the MOP could have the capacity to establish an entity with international legal personality without itself having such personality. The MOP's decision and the subsequent Agreement should thus be regarded as evidence of the international legal personality of the MOP of the Montreal Protocol.

Although the United Nations hosts the secretariat of the Climate Change Convention, it is located in Bonn, which necessitated the conclusion of proper arrangements with the Federal Republic of Germany. The COP invited the executive secretary of the interim secretariat to consult the German authorities regarding these arrangements.[177] The executive secretary requested advice from the UN Office of Legal Affairs to clarify the legal personality and capacity of the Convention secretariat. The opinion of December 18, 1995 (UNOLA III), stated that the bodies established by the Convention "have certain distinctive elements attributable to international organizations. However, it is clear that none of these bodies is

[175] Montreal Protocol MOP Decision IV/18, Doc. UNEP/OzL.Pro.4/15, *supra* note 96.

[176] Montreal Protocol MOP Decision VI/16, Doc. UNEP/OzL.Pro.6/7 (1994), <http://www.unep.org/ozone/6mop_nbo.htm>.

[177] Climate Change COP Decision 16/CP.1, UN Doc. FCCC/CP/1995/7/Add.1, para. 2.

de jure a UN subsidiary organ."[178] Specifically in relation to the secretariat, the opinion reasoned that, "[i]n view of the distinct nature of the Convention bodies and notwithstanding the fact that the Convention Secretariat is 'institutionally linked to the United Nations', the legal regime enjoyed by the United Nations under applicable agreements cannot be automatically attached to the Convention Secretariat."[179]

The nature and status of the secretariat therefore required clarification. One possible way suggested in UNOLA III would have been for the COP or the Subsidiary Body for Implementation to adopt a decision "conferring the required juridical personality and legal capacity upon the Convention Secretariat and according it such privileges and immunities as are necessary for the fulfilment of its purposes."[180] In this context, attention was drawn to the above-mentioned decision by the MOP of the Montreal Protocol conferring juridical personality and legal capacity on the multilateral fund and vesting it with the necessary privileges and immunities. However, the SBI referred to the "exceptional circumstances" and the "urgency of concluding the legal arrangements arising from the location of the secretariat in Germany" and requested that the executive secretary enter into an appropriate agreement with Germany on the necessary legal capacity and privileges and immunities.[181]

The agreement subsequently concluded, the 1996 Agreement between the United Nations, Germany, and the secretariat of the Climate Change Convention, states that the United Nations Volunteers Programme Headquarters Agreement[182] (UNV Agreement) shall be applicable, *mutatis mutandis*, to the Convention secretariat, subject to the specific provisions of the 1996 Agreement (Art. 3(1)). It provides that the secretariat shall have legal capacity in Germany (Art. 4), and privileges and immunities are accorded to the secretariat, its officials, representatives of member and observer states, and persons invited to participate in the work of the Convention (Arts. 3 and 5).

This Agreement was approved by the COP in its Decision 15/CP.2, paragraph 1. Paragraph 2 states that the COP should consider "whether the functions that have to be carried out by the secretariat necessitate that it be given juridical personality on the international plane."[183] In the SBI, the executive secretary has stated that different legal opinions have been expressed on the international legal personality of the secretariat and welcomed consideration of the question by the parties.[184]

Arguably, the COP queried the international legal personality of the secretariat in paragraph 2 of Decision 15/CP.2. At least so far, it has not followed the advice in UNOLA III to give the secretariat international legal personality, as in the case of the multilateral fund under the Montreal Protocol. On the other hand, the COP did approve the Agreement entered into by the secretariat.

Is the Agreement then an international agreement or one entered into under domestic law? While the latter is a perfectly possible answer, it would make the Agreement subject to German domestic legislation, and as such incapable of providing the protection sought. Furthermore, as an instrument subject to domestic law, it would deviate from most other agreements on privileges and immunities. The Agreement also refers in several provisions

[178] Institutional and Budgetary Matters: Arrangements for Relocation of the Convention Secretariat to Bonn, UN Doc. FCCC/SBI/1996/7, para. 11(2) (1996).

[179] *Id.*, para. 11(5).

[180] *Id.*

[181] Report of the Subsidiary Body for Implementation on the Work of Its Second Session, UN Doc. FCCC/SBI/1996/9, para. 66(c).

[182] Agreement Concerning the Headquarters of the United Nations Volunteers Programme, Nov. 10, 1995, UN-FRG [hereinafter UNV Agreement] (on file with authors).

[183] Climate Change COP Decision 15/CP.2, UN Doc. FCCC/CP/1996/15/Add.1, para. 2.

[184] Report of the Subsidiary Body for Implementation on the Work of Its Third Session, UN Doc. FCCC/SBI/1996/12, para. 46.

to protection under international law.[185] Finally, its status would seem to be explicitly settled by the 1996 Agreement itself, since Article 6(4) establishes that any disputes shall be resolved in accordance with Article 26(2) of the UNV Agreement. Article 26(2) provides that disputes shall be resolved by arbitration "on the basis of the applicable rules of international law."[186]

It could also be argued that the signature by the representative of the Climate Change Convention's secretariat was redundant, and that legally the 1996 Agreement was concluded by only two parties, the United Nations and Germany. In fact, the Agreement was entered into under Article 4(3) of the UNV Agreement between the United Nations and Germany, which provides that the Agreement "may also be made applicable *mutatis mutandis* to other intergovernmental entities, institutionally linked to the United Nations, by agreement among such entities, the Government and the United Nations."[187] However, the title of the 1996 Agreement, its three signatures, the COP's acceptance of the Agreement, and its entry into force upon notification by all three signatories under Article 6(6), all indicate that the institutions of the Convention are a party on a par with the other two parties. Nevertheless, one may find it hard to believe that the secretariat, as a non-self-governing international body, could have the international legal capacity to become a party to the Agreement. To the extent that the secretariat is not *de jure* a UN subsidiary body, as stated in UNOLA III, it should be considered a subsidiary of the COP. Consequently, the COP with its subsidiary bodies should be considered as a whole to be a party to the Agreement.

The 1996 Agreement can therefore be understood to constitute evidence that the COP has the international legal capacity to enter into agreements on privileges and immunities.

Arrangements with other MEAs. A United Nations task force has recommended that the international community strive toward strengthening linkages between MEAs to facilitate synergies and promote coherence of policies.[188] MEA secretariats have been given the function of ensuring the necessary coordination with other relevant international "bodies," in particular by entering into the necessary administrative and contractual arrangements; see, for example, the Vienna Ozone Convention (Art. 7(1)(e)), the Basel Convention (Art. 16(1)(d)), and the Biodiversity Convention (Art. 14(1)(d)). These provisions do not state that the referenced "bodies" are COPs of other MEAs. So far few, if any, such links appear to have been established, so that no conclusions can be drawn from the cited provisions about the possible treaty-making powers of MEA institutions.

The Biodiversity Convention provides that the COP shall contact the executive bodies of other relevant conventions so as to enter into "appropriate forms of cooperation" with them.[189] This provision has formed the basis for memoranda of cooperation with the secretariats of relevant MEAs, such as the Ramsar and Bonn Conventions and CITES.[190] The memorandum of cooperation with the Ramsar secretariat is called an "agreement" and requires a year's written notice for termination (Art. 6), which could indicate its binding character.[191] On the other hand, the term "memorandum of cooperation" and its wording, which uses phrases such as "will" and "will seek to promote" instead of "shall," together with its purpose, lead to the conclusion that it is a nonbinding arrangement. This conclusion also seems to hold

[185] *E.g.*, UNV Agreement, *supra* note 182, Arts. 4, 13, 14. *Cf.* 1996 Agreement, *supra* note 174, Art. 3.

[186] UNV Agreement, *supra* note 182, Art. 26(2).

[187] *Id.*, Art. 4(3).

[188] Report of the United Nations Task Force on Environment and Human Settlements, UN Doc. A/53/463, annex, para. 30 (1998).

[189] Biodiversity Convention, *supra* note 12, Art. 23(4)(h).

[190] *See* Biodiversity COP Decision II/13, Doc. UNEP/CBD/COP/2/19, at 24 (1995), <http://www.biodiv.org/cop2/COP2_decisions_e.pdf>, *reprinted in* 6 Y.B. INT'L ENVTL. L. 830 (1995); Biodiversity COP Decision III/21, para. 2, Doc. UNEP/CBD/COP/3/38, *supra* note 170, at 112; Biodiversity COP Decision IV/15, para. 3 (1998) <http://www.biodiv.org/Decisions/COP4/html/COP-4-Dec-15.html>.

[191] *See* UNEP, A PROGRAMME FOR CHANGE: DECISIONS FROM THE FOURTH MEETING OF THE CONFERENCE OF THE PARTIES TO THE CONVENTION ON BIOLOGICAL DIVERSITY 119–22 (UNEP/IUC/98/8, 1998).

true for the other memoranda of cooperation entered into by the secretariat of the Biodiversity Convention. It should not necessarily be taken to indicate a lack of international legal personality but, rather, that internationally binding agreements are not necessary or desirable for such coordination between secretariats.

In sum, MEAs do not contain any provisions explicitly establishing the international legal personality or treaty-making capacity of their institutions. But both general and specific powers conferred on COPs (and some other bodies) may be interpreted to include such personality and capacity. The doctrine of implied powers as developed for formal IGOs should also be applied to MEA institutions as a source of international legal personality in addition to or in lieu of express powers. That such institutions have international legal personality and the right to enter into treaties is further confirmed by practice.

If MEA institutions did not have international legal personality, it would be necessary instead to consider the collective of states parties to the MEA as parties to agreements that have been concluded. This interpretation, however, would be a very artificial construct. Alternatively, the international organization hosting the secretariat could be seen as having entered into the agreements, rather than the MEA institution. But this approach would not be tenable as regards arrangements between the COP and the host organization. Furthermore, it could infringe the self-governing character of the COP. This quality is especially important when it comes to agreements with international financial institutions or bodies of other MEAs. It could be argued that agreements on privileges and immunities with host states take a standard form and should not be considered as encroaching on the self-governing status of the COP. However, there are policy aspects even to the drafting and enforcement of such agreements, and they may apply to persons other than officials of the secretariat, such as representatives of member states. Hence, it should be concluded that agreements should be (and have been) entered into by the COP, rather than by the organization hosting the secretariat.

In spite of not being established as formal IGOs, the institutions of MEAs should be considered to possess international legal personality and the capacity to act on the external plane, particularly in relation to the conclusion of agreements in the form of treaties with other subjects of international law.

VII. Are Autonomous Institutional Arrangements of MEAs Unique?

We now consider whether the autonomous institutional arrangements found in MEAs that were described above are unique to environmental agreements or whether they can be found in agreements in other areas of international law.

Some human rights treaties[192] and some arms control treaties[193] provide for their parties to meet from time to time for the purpose, typically, of considering proposed amendments to the treaty and/or of electing members of some supervisory body.[194] While at first glance these arrangements might appear to be embryonic forms of the autonomous institutional arrangements of MEAs, they are in fact very different. First, meetings of the parties to human rights and arms control treaties generally take place on an ad hoc basis and are usually called by a UN body. By contrast, the COPs of MEAs are autonomous bodies, deciding themselves whether and when to convene and meeting normally on a regular basis. Second, unlike the COPs of MEAs, meetings of parties to human rights and arms control treaties

[192] *E.g.*, Convention Against Torture, *opened for signature* Dec. 10, 1984, Arts. 17, 29, 1465 UNTS 85; Convention on the Rights of the Child, Nov. 20, 1989, Arts. 43, 50, 1577 UNTS 3.

[193] *E.g.*, Treaty on the Non-Proliferation of Nuclear Weapons, July 1, 1968, Art. VIII, 21 UST 483, 729 UNTS 161; Convention on Prohibitions or Restrictions on the Use of Certain Conventional Weapons Which May Be Deemed to Be Excessively Injurious or to Have Indiscriminate Effects, Oct. 10, 1980, Art. 8, 19 ILM 1523 (1980).

[194] A somewhat similar situation also applies to the 1982 UN Convention on the Law of the Sea.

have no permanent secretariat to assist their functioning. Third, the role of human rights and arms control meetings of parties in developing the normative content of the relevant regime is limited to considering possible amendments to the constitutive treaty. COPs, as we have seen, play a much broader role in developing the normative content of environmental regimes. Last, unlike COPs in MEAs, meetings of the parties to human rights and arms control treaties take no real part in supervising parties' implementation of the treaty concerned. To be sure, human rights treaties do provide for a supervisory organ, but it is quite separate from and independent of the meeting of the parties and normally consists of a limited number of individuals serving in their personal capacity. Indeed, such organs are autonomous vis-à-vis both the parties to the relevant treaty and the organization under whose auspices the treaty was concluded. Under MEAs, however, the COP is seen as the most appropriate forum to determine allegations of noncompliance, which may amount to challenges to the normative content of the regime.[195] Employing Sommer's typology of institutional arrangements,[196] we may say that meetings of parties to human rights and arms control treaties can be classified as "ad hoc conferences," whereas the COPs of MEAs are "treaty-management organizations."

As far as we are aware, there are only a handful of treaty arrangements outside the environmental field that bear any real similarity to the autonomous institutional arrangements of MEAs described above and that may therefore be classified as "treaty-management organizations" rather than "ad hoc conferences" or traditional IGOs (the third category of Sommer's threefold classification).

The first of these treaty arrangements, chronologically speaking, is the General Agreement on Tariffs and Trade (GATT).[197] Between its adoption in 1947 and the birth of the World Trade Organization in 1994, the GATT displayed many of the organizational features of the MEAs considered above. Above all, it was not a formal intergovernmental institution. Instead, periodic meetings of the parties were held under Article XXV and were serviced by a permanent secretariat and supported by various subsidiary bodies. The meetings of the parties developed the normative content of the Agreement, and through the subsidiary bodies exercised a supervisory role over its implementation and observance by the parties. In general, decision making was by consensus. These similarities with the COP of an MEA, however, amount to something of an accident. It was originally assumed that the International Trade Organization would be created (as an IGO) and would provide the appropriate institutional machinery for the GATT; but mainly because of opposition by the United States, the International Trade Organization never came into being.[198] The institutional role it would have assumed is now fulfilled by the World Trade Organization (an IGO).

A second example of a treaty with institutional arrangements somewhat similar to those of an MEA is the Antarctic Treaty of 1959.[199] Under Article IX of the Treaty, the consultative parties meet regularly.[200] Like the COP of an MEA, these meetings have developed the normative content of the Antarctic regime, first, by the adoption of more than 150 "recommendations" under Article IX(1) and, second, by serving as the forum for the negotiation of further treaties, such as the 1980 Convention for the Conservation of Antarctic Marine Living Resources and the 1991 Protocol on Environmental Protection. The 1980 Convention establishes its own institutional arrangement, a commission with legal personality (i.e., an

[195] *See* Gehring, *supra* note 25, at 54.

[196] Sommer, *supra* note 106, at 629–33.

[197] General Agreement on Tariffs and Trade, Oct. 30, 1947, TIAS No. 1700, 55 UNTS 188.

[198] *See* BOWETT, *supra* note 107, at 118; *see also* M. A. G. VAN MEERHAEGHE, INTERNATIONAL ECONOMIC INSTITUTIONS 90–95 (2d ed. 1971).

[199] Antarctic Treaty, Dec. 1, 1959, 12 UST 794, 402 UNTS 71.

[200] It should be noted that consultative parties do not comprise all parties to the Treaty, but the original 12 parties, together with such other parties as conduct "substantial scientific research activity" in Antarctica. *Id.*, Art. IX(1), (2).

IGO),[201] but the Protocol is served by the consultative parties to the 1959 Treaty as the principal institutional arrangement, although it also set up a Committee for Environmental Protection.[202] Like a COP, the meetings of the consultative parties have a supervisory role, which is fairly limited in the case of the 1959 Treaty and rather more extensive in the case of the Protocol.[203] Unlike a COP, the meetings of the consultative parties are not serviced by a permanent secretariat. The establishment of such a body has been mooted, but the consultative parties have resisted it so far.[204] Thus, the institutional arrangements of the Antarctic Treaty, and especially its Protocol (which in any case may arguably be classified as an MEA), in many respects resemble the autonomous institutional arrangements of MEAs. The rationale for the Antarctic institutional arrangements—to provide flexibility for future development[205]—also finds parallels in the rationale for the COP model in MEA institutional arrangements.

As mentioned at the beginning of this part, several arms control treaties provide for occasional meetings of the parties to review their provisions. Some more recent arms control treaties, however, go considerably farther in their institutional provisions. The Ottawa Convention on land mines of 1997[206] provides for its parties to meet regularly to consider any matter relating to the application or implementation of the Convention. While these meetings have a role in reviewing implementation of and compliance with the Convention, the parties report on their implementation to the UN Secretary-General, not the meeting of the parties, and the noncompliance procedure, in its initial stages and some aspects of its later stages, operates through the Secretary-General, not the meeting. Compared with an MEA COP, the meeting of the parties enjoys a limited degree of autonomy, which is further shown by the fact that meetings are convened by the Secretary-General. Moreover, the meeting of the parties has no subsidiary bodies, nor does it have a secretariat (in effect, the UN Secretary-General fulfills this role). Unlike an MEA COP, the meeting of the parties to the Ottawa Convention appears to have no role in developing the normative content of the Convention. The only provision for such development is by amending the Convention, but amendments are to be adopted by a Special Amendment Conference and not the meeting of the parties as such. A second arms control treaty, the Protocol on mines, booby traps and other devices to the 1980 Convention on conventional weapons, as amended in 1996,[207] establishes institutional arrangements that are broadly comparable to those of the Ottawa Convention but less detailed and lacking a noncompliance mechanism.

Mention should also be made of two further arms control treaties whose institutional arrangements resemble something of a hybrid between a traditional IGO and a COP. The 1993 Convention on chemical weapons[208] and the 1996 Comprehensive Test Ban Treaty[209] each establish an "Organization," with a permanent headquarters and "such legal capacity and such privileges and immunities as are necessary for the exercise of its functions,"[210] to

[201] Convention on the Conservation of Antarctic Marine Living Resources, *supra* note 52, Arts. VII–XXI.

[202] Protocol on Environmental Protection to the Antarctic Treaty, Oct. 4, 1991, Arts. 10–12, 30 ILM 1455 (1991) [hereinafter 1991 Protocol].

[203] *See* Antarctic Treaty, *supra* note 199, Art. IX(3); 1991 Protocol, *supra* note 202, Arts. 12, 15.

[204] On the carrying out of secretariat functions in the Antarctic Treaty system, see R. T. Scully, *Alternatives for Co-operation and Institutionalization in Antarctica: Outlook for the 1990s*, *in* ANTARCTIC RESOURCES POLICY 281, 284–85 (Francisco Orrego Vicuña ed., 1983). *See also* JEFFREY D. MYHRE, THE ANTARCTIC TREATY SYSTEM: POLITICS, LAW AND DIPLOMACY, chs. IV, IX (1986).

[205] *See* Scully, *supra* note 204, at 283.

[206] Convention on the Prohibition of the Use, Stockpiling, Production and Transfer of Anti-Personnel Mines and on Their Destruction, Sept. 18, 1997, 36 ILM 1507 (1997).

[207] Protocol on Prohibitions or Restrictions on the Use of Mines, Booby-Traps and Other Devices, May 3, 1996, 35 ILM 1206 (1996).

[208] Convention on the Prohibition of the Development, Production, Stockpiling and Use of Chemical Weapons and on Their Destruction, Jan. 13, 1993, 32 ILM 800 (1993) [hereinafter Chemical Weapons Convention].

[209] *Opened for signature* Sept. 24, 1996, 35 ILM 1439 (1996) [hereinafter Test Ban Treaty].

[210] Chemical Weapons Convention, *supra* note 208, Art. VIII(48); Test Ban Treaty, *supra* note 209, Art. II(54).

achieve the object and purpose of the treaties, to ensure the implementation of their provisions, and to provide a forum for consultation and cooperation between states parties. Each organization has three organs—the Conference of the States Parties, the Executive Council, and the Technical Secretariat. The functions of the Conference of the States Parties, which pertain to supervising the implementation of and compliance with the treaty and to developing its normative content, are not dissimilar to those of an MEA COP. The Executive Council to some extent resembles the bureau of an MEA COP, but it also plays an important role in the noncompliance procedure and may conclude "agreements" on certain matters with states and international organizations.[211]

Finally, we briefly call attention to the autonomous institutions (not IGOs) that have been set up by decisions of the states concerned rather than by a treaty, and that do not operate by reference to a treaty. Examples include the Conference on Security and Co-operation in Europe[212] and the Arctic Council (set up in 1996).[213] While these institutions display some of the characteristics of MEA institutions, the obvious difference is that they have no role in developing the normative content of a treaty or of ensuring compliance with it (although they do have roughly comparable roles in relation to a variety of soft-law instruments).

Of the various agreements outside the environmental field surveyed here, the institutional arrangements of GATT before 1994 come closest to those of an MEA, although the form of the GATT arrangements was largely a historical accident. The institutional arrangements of the Antarctic Treaty and certain recent arms control treaties resemble the autonomous institutional arrangements of MEAs to some extent, but they also differ from AIAs in significant ways.

VIII. Conclusion

A special feature of many MEAs is that they establish an institutional framework of what we have called autonomous institutional arrangements, in the form of COPs, subsidiary bodies, and secretariats, to develop and control their parties' environmental commitments, rather than setting up formal IGOs of the traditional kind. Some treaties other than MEAs also establish institutional arrangements that are not formal IGOs. Meetings of the parties and control bodies are provided for in several treaties, but except for the institutional arrangements of the former GATT institutions, the Antarctic Treaty, and some recent arms control treaties, we have not found any institutional framework essentially similar to AIAs.

In spite of their formal denomination, we nevertheless conclude that these self-governing, treaty-based AIAs of MEAs may be considered to be IGOs, albeit of a less formal, more ad hoc nature than traditional IGOs. This conclusion is based on Schermers and Blokker's definition of an international organization as a form of cooperation founded on an international agreement (the MEA), creating at least one organ with a will of its own (the COP) established under international law. This conclusion is further supported by the character, functions, and practice of these AIAs. Thus, while due account should be taken of the special characteristics of these arrangements, international institutional law should apply to them and supplement the law of treaties when it comes to assessing their powers. On this basis, AIAs have a wide range of both explicit and implied powers. These include powers at the internal level for purposes such as the establishment of subsidiary bodies and the adoption of rules of procedure and a budget; powers to develop substantive obligations through

[211] Chemical Weapons Convention, *supra* note 208, Art. VIII(34); Test Ban Treaty, *supra* note 209, Art. II(38).

[212] The CSCE came into being following the adoption of the Helsinki Final Act, Aug. 1, 1975, 14 ILM 1292 (1975). It became more fully institutionalized after the adoption of the Charter of Paris, Nov. 21, 1990, 30 ILM 190 (1991). In 1994 the CSCE was converted into the Organization for Security and Co-operation in Europe. See further Dominic McGoldrick, *The Development of the Conference on Security and Co-operation in Europe—From Process to Institution, in* LEGAL VISIONS OF THE NEW EUROPE 135 (Bernard S. Jackson & Dominic McGoldrick eds., 1993).

[213] Declaration on the Establishment of the Arctic Council, Sept. 19, 1996, 35 ILM 1382 (1996).

various forms of lawmaking and treaty interpretation; powers to supervise the implementation of and compliance with those obligations (especially by the use of noncompliance mechanisms rather than traditional dispute settlement procedures); and powers on the external plane to enter into arrangements with states, international organizations, and the institutions of other MEAs (some of which may be regarded as genuine treaty-making powers).

We must emphasize, however, that one should not lose sight of the special characteristics of these arrangements and that, accordingly, the powers of AIAs are not necessarily identical to those of formal IGOs in all respects. Furthermore, whereas the law of treaties may also be considered insufficient in determining the legal status and powers of treaty-based bodies that differ from AIAs, caution is advised in applying *in toto* bodies of law developed for other purposes, such as international institutional law. Diversity in treaty cooperation seems to require diversity in legal response.

Such a treaty-based institutional framework may be regarded as an aspect of a more general development in international law. It has been argued that traditional international law concentrated mostly on preservation of the peaceful coexistence of states, whereas their increasing interdependence requires an international law of cooperation.[214] The creation of institutions for the development and control of obligations in treaties may be seen as part of this more cooperative international law. It remains to be seen whether an institutional framework comparable to that developed in international environmental law will be applied more extensively in other fields of international law. In any case, these institutional arrangements demonstrate that international cooperation may take innovative forms designed for specific needs, presenting challenges to the international lawyer.

[214] *See* WOLFGANG FRIEDMANN, THE CHANGING STRUCTURE OF INTERNATIONAL LAW 60–62 (1964).

[14]

COMPLIANCE CONTROL MECHANISMS AND INTERNATIONAL ENVIRONMENTAL OBLIGATIONS

GÜNTHER HANDL*

I. INTRODUCTION

With the appreciable acceleration of international environmental law-making in the late 1980s, and in particular, the flurry of international legal initiatives occasioned by the 1992 United Nations Conference on Environment and Development (UNCED) as well as the post-UNCED legislative follow-up, "treaty congestion"[1] and even more

* Eberhard Deutsch Professor of Public International Law, Tulane Law School, New Orleans, Louisiana.

1. *See, e.g.*, Brown Weiss, *Environmental Equity: The Imperative for the Twenty-First Century*, *in* SUSTAINABLE DEVELOPMENT AND INTERNATIONAL LAW 17, 23 (W. Lang, ed., 1995).

so, "compliance control"[2] have become buzz words in international environmental legal discourse. Both terms—two sides of the same coin, really—connote justified concern in the international community over the effectiveness of international environmental obligations, in particular those embodied in legislative treaties.[3]

As a significant international issue, compliance control—the international monitoring and supervision of states parties' implementation of and compliance with international treaty-based obligations[4]—has, of course, arisen with regard to multilateral treaty relations before, most notably in the fields of arms control,[5] human rights[6] and international labor relations.[7] However, an idiosyncratic combination of factors make compliance control a matter of special concern in the context of international environmental law. First, as international environmental regulations become more technical and detailed, therefore more complex,

2. *See, e.g.*, A. CHAYES & A. HANDLER CHAYES, THE NEW SOVEREIGNTY: COMPLIANCE WITH INTERNATIONAL REGULATORY AGREEMENTS (1995); Günther Handl, *Controlling Implementation of and Compliance with International Environmental Commitments: The Rocky Road from Rio*, 5 COLORADO J. INT'L ENV. L. & POLICY 305 (1994); DAVID G. VICTOR, INTERNATIONAL INSTITUTE FOR APPLIED SYSTEMS ANALYSIS, THE EARLY OPERATION AND EFFECTIVENESS OF THE MONTREAL PROTOCOL'S NON-COMPLIANCE PROCEDURE ER-96-2 (May 1996).

3. Martti Koskenniemi, a generally perspicacious observer of international legal developments, has noted that "what is needed now is less the adoption of new instruments than more effective implementation of existing ones." Martti Koskenniemi, *Breach of Treaty or Non-Compliance? Reflections on the Enforcement of the Montreal Protocol*, 3 Y.B. INT'L ENVTL. L. 123 (1993).

4. In general, it might be appropriate to differentiate between "implementation," as the first step towards rendering an international obligation effective domestically, and (subsequent) "compliance" with, or abidance by, the international obligation concerned. Thus, at UNCED the wording of subparagraph (a) of what was then chapter 39, paragraph 7 of Agenda 21 ("Implementation Mechanisms") initially included a reference to "compliance with international legal instruments." However, that reference was deleted and replaced by "effective, full and prompt implementation" as the larger, overarching concept. Similarly, within the context of discussions on the multilateral consultative process under Article 13 of the U.N. Climate Change Convention, "implementation" and "compliance" have been used interchangeably. *See, e.g.*, Questionnaire on the Establishment of a Multilateral Consultative Process Under Article 13, Note by the Secretariat, U.N. Doc. FCCC/AG13/1996/1, para. 6 (ii) (1996) [hereinafter Note by the Secretariat].

"Compliance control" as used in the present Article follows this trend and thus will denote international efforts and procedures aimed at securing both implementation of and compliance with treaty-based obligations.

5. *See, e.g.*, Winfried Lang, *Compliance with Disarmament Obligations*, 55 ZEITSCHRIFT F. AUSLÄNDISCHES ÖFFENLICHTLICHES RECHT U. VÖLKERRECHT 69 (1995).

6. *See, e.g.*, Philip Alston & Bruno Simma, *The First Session of the United Nations Committee on Economic, Social and Cultural Rights*, 81 AM. J. INT'L L. 747 (1987).

7. *See, e.g.*, CESARE P.R. ROMANO, INTERNATIONAL INSTITUTE FOR APPLIED SYSTEMS ANALYSIS, THE ILO SYSTEM OF SUPERVISION AND CONTROL: A REVIEW AND LESSONS FOR MULTILATERAL ENVIRONMENTAL AGREEMENTS, ER-96-1 (May 1996).

they entail a commensurately greater need for international control of individual states' compliance.[8] Second, as the economic cost of compliance with such environmental regulations rises, states have an increased interest in making sure that other states, subject to the same international regulations, live up to their obligations, thereby ensuring competition on a level playing field.[9] Third, and perhaps most significantly, normative changes within environmental treaty regimes[10] tend to be frequent and often the result of informal steps taken by the conference of the parties (COP),[11] thus are apt to give rise to questions about the scope, if not the very existence, of the obligations at stake.[12] In

---

8. *See, e.g.*, Kamen Sachariew, *Promoting Compliance with International Environmental Legal Standards: Reflections on Monitoring and Reporting Mechanisms*, 2 Y.B. INT'L ENVTL. L. 31 (1991). Indeed, the assessment and evaluation of information reported by states parties as evidence of compliance with their obligations will increasingly demand a high degree of technical know-how and sophistication on the part of those members of the institutional mechanism entrusted with the control function.

9. *See* Report of the Seventh Meeting of the Parties to the Montreal Protocol on Substances that Deplete the Ozone Layer, U.N. Doc. UNEP/OzL.Prof.7/INF.1, at 7, para. 27 (1995) (statement of Patrick Széll).

10. To international lawyers, the term "regime" usually signals an international treaty, a shared general interest underlying regulation that aspires to *erga omnes* validity, as well as an institutional mechanism for the promotion of the treaty's objectives. *See* Winfried Lang, *Diplomacy and International Environmental Law-Making: Some Observations*, 3 Y.B. INT'L ENVTL. L. 108, 117 (1992); *see also* Thomas Gehring, *International Environmental Regimes: Dynamic Sectoral Legal Systems*, 1 Y.B. INT'L ENVTL. L. 35, 47 (1990). By contrast, political scientists might define a regime as "principles, norms, rules and decision-making procedures around which actors' expectations converge in a given area of international relations." Stephen Krasner, *Structural Causes and Regime Consequences: Regimes as Intervening Variables*, *in* INTERNATIONAL REGIMES 1, 2 (S. Krasner ed., 1983).

11. One of the latest and best known examples of such decision-making is Decision II/12 adopted at the Second Meeting of the Conference of the Parties to the Basel Convention on the Control of Transboundary Movements of Hazardous Wastes and Their Disposal in March 1994. Decision II/12, *reprinted in* 5 Y.B. INT'L ENVTL. L. 868 (1994). It aims at banning—with immediate effect—the export from OECD to non-OECD countries of hazardous wastes for final disposal, and to phase out all such exports destined for "recycling" or "recovery operations" by December 31, 1997. A number of countries, however, expressed their reservations about the legal status of such a far-reaching decision, arguing that such a fundamental change to the Basel Convention would require activation of the formal amendment process. Largely in response to these criticisms, in November 1995, the Third Meeting of the Conference of the Parties by Decision III/1, *reprinted in* 6 Y.B. INT'L ENVTL. L. 779 (1995), adopted an almost identical amendment to the Basel Convention which now has to undergo formal ratification, approval, etc. by the parties in accordance with Article 17 of the Convention. *See* Basel Convention on the Control of Transboundary Movements of Hazardous Wastes and Their Disposal, *opened for signature* Mar. 22, 1989, art. 17, S. Treaty Doc. No. 5, 102d Cong., 1st Sess., 28 I.L.M. 657, 673 (1989), U.N. Doc. UNEP/IG.80/3 [hereinafter Basel Convention].

12. Indeed, the complexity of the present legal situation under the Basel Convention's regulation of hazardous waste exports might be characterized as having given rise to different circles of membership in the regime, or different layers of normativity. For a discussion of some of those

such a situation compliance control serves not just verification of a state's abidance by its obligations, but also—preliminarily—ascertainment of the existence of the norm(s) potentially in dispute, as well as of the exact nature and scope of the individual state's obligations flowing therefrom.

An effective system of compliance control is, of course, itself premised on various procedural elements, especially the reporting of basic information by the parties, and its "operational links" with other components of the regulatory regime involved, such as financial mechanism(s), science and technology assessment panels, etc.[13] The present Article, however, does not concern itself with all interrelated aspects of this larger review process. Rather, its focus will be on the typical institutional mechanism, the so-called non-compliance procedure, which has evolved as a keystone in some multilateral environmental agreements (MEAs) and will likely serve as a model for others.

II. NON-COMPLIANCE PROCEDURES IN MULTILATERAL ENVIRONMENTAL AGREEMENTS: GENERAL CONSIDERATIONS

Today, establishment of some form of "internal" compliance control procedure[14] appears generally recognized as an indispensable element of MEAs.[15] Thus, most recent MEAs feature or are likely to

---

issues, see, for example, Louise de La Fayette, *Legal and Practical Implications of the Ban to the Basel Convention*, 6 Y.B. INT'L ENVTL. L. 701 (1995).

13. *See* Hugo Schally, *The Role and Importance of Implementation Monitoring and Non-Compliance Procedures in International Environmental Regimes*, *in* THE OZONE TREATIES AND THEIR INFLUENCE ON THE BUILDING OF INTERNATIONAL ENVIRONMENTAL REGIMES, Österreichische aussenpolitische Dokumentation (Special Issue) 82, 87 (W. Lang ed., 1996).

14. "Internal" procedure refers to a mechanism that is controlled by the parties to the MEA themselves, as against a third party or "external" procedure, such as traditional (third party) dispute settlement. For some of the salient distinguishing features, see, for example, Gehring, *supra* note 10, at 50-54.

15. Thus, Agenda 21 exhorts states to "[e]stablish efficient and practical reporting systems on the effective, full and prompt implementation of international legal instruments." Agenda 21, ch. 39, para. 8(a). In a similar vein, the 1993 Lucerne ECE Ministerial Declaration urges contracting parties to environmental conventions to adopt non-compliance procedures which (1) aim to avoid complexity; (2) are non-confrontational and transparent; (3) leave the competence for taking decisions to the determination of the contracting parties; (4) leave it to contracting parties to consider what technical and financial assistance may be required within the context of the specific agreement; and (5) include a transparent and revealing reporting system and procedures as agreed to by the parties. *See* Declaration by the Ministers of the Environment of the Region of the United Nations Commission for Europe (UN/ECE) and the Member of the Commission of the European Communities Responsible for the Environment, 7, para. 23.1 (April 30, 1993); *see generally* United Nations Economic Commission for Europe, Committee on Environmental Policy, Implementation of and Compliance with Environmental Conventions in the ECE Region, U.N. Doc. CEP/WG.1/R.4/Add. 1 (1995).

feature a free-standing non-compliance procedure (NCP), administered by a special, dedicated institutional mechanism.[16] The first such non-compliance procedure was established as part of the Montreal Protocol on Substances that Deplete the Ozone Layer.[17] It has since served as a model for others, such as the 1994 Protocol to the 1979 UN ECE Convention on Long-Range Transboundary Air Pollution on Further Reduction of Sulphur Emissions (1994 Sulphur Protocol).[18] It has also inspired agreement on, or calls for, the establishment of similar non-compliance mechanisms or procedures as part of the 1991 ECE Protocol on Volatile Organic Compounds,[19] the UN Framework Convention on Climate Change,[20] the UN Convention to Combat Desertification,[21] the Basel Convention on Transboundary Movement

---

16. One exception to this trend is the 1992 Convention for the Protection of the Marine Environment of the North-East Atlantic (OSPAR), which provides only for a compliance procedure centered on the Convention's Commission made up of representatives of each of the contracting parties. *See* Convention for the Protection of the Marine Environment of the North-East Atlantic, Sept. 22, 1992, art. 23, *reprinted in* 3 Y.B. INT'L ENVTL. L. 759, 779 (1992). Within the context of the UN Economic Commission for Europe Protocol on Volatile Organic Compounds, the Executive Body (EB) of the Convention on Long-Range Transboundary Air Pollution takes on a similar function, albeit, and in contrast to the OSPAR Convention, only "[a]s a first step," until the parties set up a separate mechanism for monitoring compliance. *See* Protocol to the 1979 Convention on Long-Range Transboundary Air Pollution concerning the Control of Emissions of Volatile Organic Compounds or Their Transboundary Fluxes, art. 3, para. 3, 31 I.L.M. 573, 577-78 (1992) [hereinafter VOC Protocol].

17. *See* Report of the Fourth Meeting of the Parties to the Montreal Protocol on Substances that Deplete the Ozone Layer, U.N. Doc. UNEP/OzL.4/15 (1992) [hereinafter Montreal Protocol Report], Annex IV, *reprinted in* 3 Y.B. INT'L ENVTL. L. 819 (1992).

18. *See* Protocol to the 1979 UN ECE Convention on Long-Range Transboundary Air Pollution on Further Reduction of Sulphur Emissions, 33 I.L.M. 1540 (1994) [hereinafter 1994 Sulphur Protocol]; *see also* Decision Taken by the Executive Body at the Adoption of the Protocol, June 14, 1994, on the Structure and Functions of the Implementation Committee, as well as Procedures for its Review of Compliance, *in* Protocol on Further Reduction of Sulphur Emissions, U.N. Doc. ECE/EB.AIR/40 [hereinafter Decision Taken by the Executive Body].

19. *See* VOC Protocol, *supra* note 16, art. 3, para. 3, 31 I.L.M. at 577-78.

20. *See* U.N. Framework Convention on Climate Change, May 9, 1992, arts. 10, 13, S. Treaty Doc. No. 38, 102d Cong., 2d Sess., 31 I.L.M. 849, 863, 866 (1992), U.N. Doc. A/AC 237/18, *reprinted in* 3 Y.B. INT'L ENVTL. L. 684, 694, 696 (1992) [hereinafter Climate Change Convention]. As regards the multilateral consultative process envisaged in Article 13, the First Meeting of the Conference of the Parties established an ad hoc open-ended working group of technical and legal experts "to study all issues relating to the establishment of a multilateral consultative process and its design." *See* Decision 20/CP.1, para. 1, U.N. Doc. FCCC/CP/19995/7/Add.1, 59.

21. *See* Convention to Combat Desertification in Those Countries Experiencing Serious Drought and/or Desertification, Particularly in Africa, *opened for signature* Oct. 14, 1994, 33 I.L.M. 1328 (1994), U.N. Doc. A/AC 241/15/Rev. 7. This Convention calls upon the Conference of the Parties to "consider and adopt procedures and institutional mechanisms for the resolution of questions that may arise with regard to the implementation of the Convention." *See id.* art. 27, 33 I.L.M. at 1354.

of Hazardous Wastes and Their Disposal,[22] and the international convention on the mandatory application of the prior informed consent principle whose text is expected to be finalized in 1997.[23]

The NCP offers a number of very significant advantages as regards the "management" of legal relations among the parties to the MEA. Typically, the NCP aims less at branding a state party as "defaulting on its obligations," and at imposing sanctions or providing remedies for past infractions, than at helping the incriminated party come into compliance and protecting the future integrity of the regime against would-be defectors. The NCP is hence forward- rather than backward-looking. It embodies a quintessentially collective approach, rather than being steeped in the traditional paradigm of bilateralism—the relationship between the non-complying state and the directly injured other state or states.

These characteristics are of major importance, because normative provisions of an environmental regulatory regime undergo frequent adaptation and expansion in response to new scientific insights or technological developments.[24] Compliance issues, therefore, can be expected to be relatively common and differ vastly in their individual significance for the regime as a whole. The routine invocation of traditional dispute settlement procedures to deal with such a range of issues of non-implementation and non-compliance thus will not be a realistic option either legally or politically. After all, the process of invoking principles of international state responsibility and liability is cumbersome and essentially confrontational, and, therefore, can be employed only occasionally and as an avenue of last resort. Indeed, invocation of state responsibility may be an inappropriate response

22. *See* Basel Convention, *supra* note 11, art. 19; *see also* Decision III/11 of the Third Conference of the Parties calling upon the Consultative Sub-group of Legal and Technical Experts, "to study all issues related to the establishment of a mechanism for monitoring implementation of and compliance with the Basel Convention . . . and to report its findings to the fourth meeting of the Conference of the Parties. . . ." Decision III/11, Monitoring the Implementation of and Compliance with the Obligations Set Out by the Basel Convention, *reprinted in* 6 Y.B. INT'L ENVTL. L. 786 (1995).

23. *See* Tentative Draft Key Articles for a PIC Instrument (bracketed) art. 17 (on "Compliance Measures"), U.N. Doc. UNEP/FAO/PIC/INC.26.

24. At the same time, MEAs become increasingly technical in nature (in the sense of establishing ever more specific conduct-related obligations) as latent conceptual ambiguities are redressed through further refinement of technical provisions. Note, for example, on-going efforts at defining reliably "waste" as against "non-waste," a key parameter for the operationalization of the Basel Convention. *See, e.g.*, Hazardous Waste Characterization Under the Basel Convention, U.N. Doc. UNEP/CHW/WG.4/7/3 (1995).

because non-compliance might be as much due to a state's lack of capacity, as it might be the result of its intentional or negligent disregard of its obligations.[25] Similarly, in the context of most international environmental treaties, the absence of appropriate reciprocity between injuring and injured state(s) will make reliance on traditional compliance strategies unworkable. For example, suspension of the operation of a multilateral agreement for the protection of the environment, as one of the permitted sanctions for a material breach of the treaty by a party,[26] would make little sense, and indeed might be counterproductive.

There is, finally, also the important issue of standing that arises in connection with claims of state responsibility. From a traditional perspective on the international law of state responsibility, non-compliance with obligations arising under a multilateral treaty presents itself as entailing essentially a bilateral legal relationship between the wrongdoer and the (directly) injured state(s), a fact that is emphasized, inter alia, by the restrictive view of "injured state" in the practice of international courts.[27] As a result, the vindication of international community interest in protecting environmental resources may be beyond the individual state's ability to invoke the defaulting state's international responsibility to obtain redress for non-compliance, unless the incriminated conduct rises also to the level of infringing the rights of the complaining state concerned.[28] Admittedly, recent state practice

---

25. *See, e.g.*, A. Handler Chayes et al., *Active Compliance Management in Environmental Treaties*, *in* SUSTAINABLE DEVELOPMENT AND INTERNATIONAL LAW 75, 80 (W. Lang ed., 1995).

26. *See* Vienna Convention on the Law of Treaties, May 23, 1969, art. 60, para. 2, U.N. Doc. A/CONF. 39/27, 1155 U.N.T.S. 331 (1969) (entered into force on Jan. 27, 1980).

27. *See, e.g.*, South West Africa cases (Second Phase), [1966] I.C.J. 4, 34, paras. 50-52; Case Concerning Military and Paramilitary Activities in and Against Nicaragua, [1986] I.C.J. 14, 127, para. 249.

Indeed, during debates in the International Law Commission (ILC) on a closely related issue—the concept of the "injured state" for the purpose of determining the legal consequences of acts characterized as crimes in draft Article 19 of Part One of the draft Articles on State Responsibility—several members of the Commission objected to the Special Rapporteur's view that all states were injured by an international crime. They insisted that "a clear differentiation between States directly injured and those acting as *defensores leges* was called for." Report of the International Law Commission on the Work of Its Forty-Seventh Session, U.N. GAOR, 50th Sess., Supp No. 10, at 112, para. 279, U.N. Doc. A/50/10 (1995). *A fortiori*, as regards the consequences flowing from a mere delict of a state, this distinction should carry weight.

28. Kamen Sachariew rightly points to the fact that multilateral treaties often do have bilateral (as opposed to "integral") structures, or in other words, represent treaties which set up rules essentially for bilateral application. *See* Kamen Sachariew, *State Responsibility for Multilateral Treaty Violations: Identifying the 'Injured State' and Its Legal Status*, 35 NETHERLANDS INT'L L. REV. 273, 277 (1988). A much-cited example of such a treaty is the 1982 Law of the Sea Convention, *opened for signature* Dec. 10, 1982, U.N. Doc. A/CONF. 62/122 (1982), 21 I.L.M. 1261.

indicates, as Gaetano Arangio-Ruiz, the International Law Commission's Special Rapporteur on State Responsibility, has emphasized, that

> there are rules [of international law] apparently escaping the . . . pattern of bilateralism[,] . . . rules which, in the pursuit of 'general' or 'collective' interests, create obligations compliance with which is in the legally protected interest—and in that sense the legal right—of all States to which the rule is addressed.[29]

However, such universalization of "injured state" as the reflection of a legally recognizable collective interest of states, is—according to the International Law Commission—dependent on there being an express stipulation to this effect in the MEA concerned.[30] Not every MEA, however, gives expression to such an entitlement. A case in point is the Basel Convention which is not self-evidently a MEA specifically designed to protect the global environment,[31] thus expressing the collective interest of states parties thereto. In short, non-compliance with the provisions of an MEA cannot automatically be equated with an infringement of a legally recognizable interest of any and all parties to the convention concerned.

Moreover, even if one were to assume that a breach of an obligation arising under any MEA inevitably entailed also a breach of the rights of all states parties (other than the authoring state),[32] the problem would simply resurface in terms of what remedies these differently affected or injured states might be entitled to. In the end, the judgment of the International Court of Justice in the *Nicaragua* case[33] leaves little room for doubt that, as a general rule, there continues to exist a legal

---

29. Gaetano Arangio-Ruiz, Fourth Report on State Responsibility, U.N. Doc. A/CN.4/444/Add.2, at 22, para. 132 (1992).

30. *See, e.g.*, Draft Articles on State Responsibility, Part 2, art. 5, para. 2(f) (as provisionally adopted by the ILC in 1985); [1985] 2 Y.B. INT'L L. COMM'N (part 2) 25; *see also id.* at 27, para. 24 (the ILC commentary).

31. On the other hand, while the Basel Convention ostensibly aims principally at protecting public health and the environment in would-be importing countries, there is no denying, of course, that it fosters and protects also a collective interest of states in minimizing any potential long-term transnational repercussions of untoward local impacts associated with transboundary movements of hazardous wastes and their disposal.

32. This is, however, the view taken by Gaetano Arangio-Ruiz, who considers multilateral "treaties on the environment" to be covered by Article 5, paragraph 2(f) of the Draft Articles on State Responsibility. *See, e.g.*, Gaetano Arangio-Ruiz, Third Report on State Responsibility, [1991] 2 Y.B. INT'L L. COMM'N (part 1) 27, para. 91.

33. *See* Case Concerning Military and Paramilitary Activities in and Against Nicaragua, [1986] I.C.J. 14, 127, para. 249.

difference in the status of the state that suffers material damage[34] as a result of non-compliance by another state with its obligations,[35] and that of states which would be "affected" by the simple fact of being parties to the agreement concerned.[36] On that difference, however, turns the position of the (not directly) "affected state," with regard to both substantive secondary rights (flowing from the fact of non-compliance) and the right to take counter-measures against the non-complying state.[37]

In the final analysis, the non-compliance procedure's major attraction lies in the fact that it enables the meeting of the parties to fine-tune "enforcement" of the various normative standards of the MEA. Such flexibility however, comes also at a price:[38] A possible perception among parties that the details, if not the principle, of compliance with obligations arising under the MEA might be negotiable, a perception which could work at cross-purposes with compliance control efforts. However, in assessing costs and benefits, it should be remembered that while the NCP might well contribute to the "softening" of the international normativity of individual rules and regulations of the MEA, it keeps intact the regime as a whole. Indeed, the NCP might well be characterized as "an effort at continued consensus building . . .;" or, in other words, "a process that straddles traditional law-making and law-enforcement functions."[39] Moreover, it should be posited right away that a NCP would not supplant, but rather would compliment traditional dispute settlement procedures.[40] In this supplementary capacity, then, it is an indispensable mechanism of peer review for the vindication of the collective interest of state parties, provided the procedure is invocable informally, and is reasonably open and transparent.

34. A state injured in this sense might involve the state of import or, conceivably, of transit, or a third state neighboring the state of import.

35. Reference here is, of course, to wrongful non-compliance, since non-intentional and non-negligent non-compliance would not trigger the state's international responsibility.

36. Report of the International Law Commission on the Work of Its Forty-Fourth Session, U.N. GAOR, 47th Sess., Supp No. 10 at 97, para. 271, U.N. Doc. A/47/10 (1992) (summary of the ILC's discussion of draft Article 5*bis* proposed by the ILC's special rapporteur on state responsibility).

37. *See* Arangio-Ruiz, Third Report on State Responsibility, *supra* note 32, at 28, paras. 94-95.

38. For a critical review, see Koskenniemi, *supra* note 3, at 123.

39. *See* Handl, *supra* note 2, at 329.

40. For further details, see *infra* Part IV.

III. TYPICAL FEATURES OF THE NON-COMPLIANCE PROCEDURE

A. *Initiation of the Review Process*

The central role in an MEA's compliance control system will be played by a standing body,[41] such as the Montreal Protocol's "Implementation Committee." Typically, review by such a committee will be initiated either by a complaint by one party against another, or by the secretariat of the MEA in any situation where it suspects a party of non-compliance. A third way to initiate the review process envisaged in the Montreal Protocol's procedure is self-reporting by a party defaulting on its obligations despite its best bona fide efforts to the contrary. In a first such case instance, in 1995 Belarus, Bulgaria, Poland, and Russia jointly made a submission pursuant to paragraph 4 of the Protocol's non-compliance procedure.[42]

Additionally, it might be advisable to authorize the implementation committee to initiate a review sua sponte if, upon its own periodic review of the secretariat's analytical summaries of information provided by the parties in fulfillment of the latters' reporting obligations under the MEA concerned,[43] the committee concludes there is evidence of possible non-implementation or non-compliance and provided neither a party, nor the convention secretariat on its own, has taken the necessary steps to bring the case formally before the implementation committee. Such authorization would appear particularly desirable in light of experience with the Montreal Protocol's NCP which suggests that the respective convention secretariat, or any other intermediate body authorized to receive such information, might not always be able or

41. Although ad hoc panels of review have at times been under consideration as an alternative to the standing committee structure, to date existing or proposed implementation/compliance procedures of MEAs incorporate the latter rather than the former institutional approach. *See* Jacob Werksman, *Designing a Compliance System for the Climate Change Convention*, FIELD Working Paper, 10-11 (undated).

42. *See* Report of the Seventh Meeting of the Parties to the Montreal Protocol on Substances that Deplete the Ozone Layer, U.N. Doc. UNEP/OzL.Pro.7/12, paras. 39-44 (1995).

43. As to the various MEAs' reporting procedures and the essential role the convention secretariats play thereunder, see, for example, Article 13 of the Basel Convention and Decision I/16 of the Conference of the Parties. Decision I/16, Transboundary Movements of Hazardous Wastes Destined for Recovery Operations, *available in* 3 Y.B. INT'L ENVTL. L. Documentation Diskette (Doc. 21); Intergovernmental Negotiating Committee on the Elaboration of an International Convention to Combat Desertification in Those Countries Experiencing Serious Drought and/or Desertification, Particularly in Africa, Procedures for Communication of Information and Review of Implementation, U.N. Doc. A/AC.241/49/Rev.1 (1996); Climate Change Convention, *supra* note 20, arts. 8, 12.

willing to follow through on evidence suggestive of non-compliance and formally submit the "case" for review by the implementation committee.

B. *The Implementation Committee/Mechanism*

1. Size and Composition

Factors of significant import to the effectiveness of the NCP are the size and composition of the implementation committee. The Montreal Protocol's Implementation Committee is limited to ten parties, elected for two years by the meeting of the parties.[44] The Climate Change Convention's Subsidiary Body of Implementation (SBI) is open to participation by all parties (Article 10, paragraph 1). However, the institutional structure for the multilateral consultative process that is most likely to emerge from on-going discussions within the Ad Hoc Group on Article 13—a subsidiary body of the Conference of the Parties[45]—is likely to feature a limited membership.[46] Though the size of the 1994 Sulphur Protocol's Implementation Committee still remains to be determined, the parties are expected to follow the lead taken by the Convention's Executive Body at the adoption of the Protocol in 1994,[47] and establish a limited membership committee.

In any event, it is self-evident that the effectiveness of the committee is inversely proportional to its size, as a smaller committee is more likely to be able to take appropriate action in response to a non-compliance situation than a committee of unlimited membership. A larger committee membership might, of course, ensure better reflection of the various interests at stake. Moreover, if the committee addresses matters affecting the rights or interests of state parties globally or the international community at large, an expanded, even open-ended committee might make sense. Thus, regarding the Climate Change Convention's Article 13, it has been suggested that questions of implementation that concern all parties directly "should be discussed at an open-ended forum. . . ."[48] Conversely, if the issues before the committee tend to be of a primarily bilateral nature, a small committee structure would likely be the most appropriate model.

---

44. *See* Montreal Protocol Report, *supra* note 17, Annex IV, art. 5.
45. *See* Note by the Secretariat, *supra* note 4, para. 9.
46. *See id.* para. 18.
47. *See* Decision Taken by the Executive Body, *supra* note 18.
48. Note of the Secretariat, *supra* note 4, para. 8.

Of similar importance is the committee's composition which may affect the credibility of its action in individual cases, indeed its very institutional authority. On top of "equitable geographical representation" which is specifically mentioned as a requirement for the make-up of the Montreal Protocol's Implementation Committee,[49] special attention might also have to be accorded to providing for adequate representation of those countries whose interests are likely to be most significantly affected by the MEA. For example, as regards the prospective non-compliance procedure for the Basel Convention, major hazardous waste producing/exporting as well as importing parties ought to be represented on the committee. Finally, given the fact that attendance at the meeting of the Montreal Protocol's Implementation Committee has proved problematical, it might be desirable to have members of the MEA's implementation committee serve in their individual capacities rather than as representatives of their states.[50] The only other conceptually advanced NCP, that of the 1994 Sulphur Protocol, provides for members of its implementation committee to serve as country representatives.[51] No consensus has yet emerged on this issue from the Climate Change Convention debates.[52]

Apart from the specifics of state representation on the committee, the question arises also as to whether non-governmental organizations (NGOs) and others should be given observer status. The Montreal Protocol itself does not envisage participation by non-state actors in the work of its Implementation Committee. One reason for exclusive state representation on the Montreal Protocol's Implementation Committee lies in the confidentiality problems posed by the sensitive technical and commercially valuable information that the Committee has to handle. Indeed, it appears unlikely that in the context of other MEAs correspondingly sensitive issues are likely to arise as a matter of necessity. Nevertheless, the granting of such status to NGOs could lead to an undue politicization of the committee's proceedings—the very risk that the

---

49. *See* Montreal Protocol Report, *supra* note 17, Annex IV, art. 5. Presently, the Committee includes representatives of Austria, Bulgaria, Canada, Peru, Philippines, Sri Lanka, Tanzania, Ukraine, Uruguay, and Zambia.

50. *See* Patrick Széll, *Implementation Control: Non-Compliance Procedure and Dispute Settlement in the Ozone Regime*, *in* THE OZONE TREATIES AND THEIR INFLUENCE ON THE BUILDING OF INTERNATIONAL ENVIRONMENTAL REGIMES, *supra* note 13, at 49 (pointing out the likelihood that a committee composed of individuals would display more independence, whilst "demonstrable subservience to the Meeting of the Parties" is a major factor for the Montreal Committee's acceptability); *see also* Schally, *supra* note 13, at 86-87.

51. *See* Decision taken by the Executive Body, *supra* note 18, para. 1.

52. *Cf.* Note of the Secretariat, *supra* note 4, para. 19.

choice of a small, limited-membership committee seeks to minimize. Thus, while making room for non-state observers on the implementation committee might detrimentally affect the nature of the proceedings as well as its outcome, any such "undue" impact would have to be weighed against the gain in legitimacy of the decision-making process itself.

2. Powers and Jurisdiction

The committee which would receive, consider, and report on submissions bearing on non-implementation or non-compliance, as well as, possibly, situations it has identified on its own as giving rise to concern, should be entitled to request additional information, as necessary, either through the secretariat or directly from the party or parties concerned. The Montreal Protocol's NCP limits its Committee to information-gathering through the offices of the Secretariat.[53] It provides, however, also for information-gathering by the Committee in the territory of the party suspected of non-compliance, albeit only upon the invitation of the latter.[54] This fact-finding option might be especially important to verifying parties' compliance with obligations arising under other environmental regulatory regimes.

Upon completing its review of a situation of possible non-implementation or non-compliance, the implementation committee will report its findings, including any recommendations, to the meeting of the parties. For example, paragraph 9 of the Montreal Protocol's NCP and Article 7, paragraph 1 of the 1994 Sulphur Protocol specifically authorize the respective implementation committees to formulate recommendations for the attention of the meeting of the parties.[55] Similarly, the Climate Change Convention's SBI is called upon to make recommendations to the Conference of the Parties on possible responses to the findings of its own review of the adequacy of key provisions of the Convention and their implementation.[56] More pertinently, there appears to be substantial agreement on the idea that "the committee, institution or body that is to be established to implement the Article 13 process would provide

53. *See* Montreal Protocol Report, *supra* note 17, Annex IV, art. 7(c).

54. *See id.* art. 7(d).

55. Indeed, Hugo Schally, the President of the Montreal Protocol's Implementation Committee, calls these recommendation the "*raison d'être* of the NCP." *See* Schally, *supra* note 13, at 88.

56. *See* Conclusion of Outstanding Issues and Adoption of Decisions, Draft Decision on Agenda Item 5(a)(v) submitted by the Chairman of the Committee of the Whole, Conference of the Parties, 1st Sess., Annex I, para. B(3)(b), at 7, U.N. Doc. FCCC/CP/1995/L.5/Rev.1 (1995) [hereinafter Conclusion of Outstanding Issues and Adoption of Decisions].

recommendations that would ultimately be presented to the COP for adoption."[57] Moreover, under the Montreal Protocol, the review by the Implementation Committee is to aim at "securing an amicable settlement . . . on the basis of respect for the provisions of the Protocol,"[58] thereby authorizing the Committee to broker its very own settlement of the issue prior to consideration by the meeting of the parties.[59]

As regards the Committee's powers of review, it would be preferable not to limit it to matters of compliance in the narrow sense only.[60] The 1994 Sulphur Protocol entrusts a broad review function to its Implementation Committee.[61] By the same token, although the Montreal Protocol's special review process is identified as a "non-compliance procedure," its Implementation Committee's jurisdiction would appear to extend well beyond "mere" compliance issues to matters of non-implementation of the Protocol.[62] There is no denying, at any rate, that the general trend is towards giving the implementation committee wide powers of review. For example, the First Meeting of the COP of the Climate Change Convention significantly strengthened the SBI's role of review.[63] More significantly still, in their responses to the Secretariat questionnaire about the Article 13 process, responding states parties and NGOs seem to indicate a clear preference for a broad mandate for the implementing body/committee to be established.[64]

C. *Access to and Transparency of the Proceedings before the Committee*

Maximizing transparency of the Committee proceedings without endangering the non-confrontational nature of the procedure should be an inalienable feature of the system of review, as greater transparency enhances the credibility not just of the NCP, but of the

57. Note by the Secretariat, *supra* note 4, para. 24.

58. Annex IV, *supra* note 17, para. 8.

59. *See* Winfried Lang, *Compliance Control in Respect of the Montreal Protocol* (Apr. 1995) (paper delivered at Massachusetts Institute of Technology on file with author).

60. *See supra* note 4.

61. *See* 1994 Sulphur Protocol, *supra* note 18, art. 7, para. 1.

62. Thus, the initiation of the review procedure, Annex IV, para. 1, refers to "reservations regarding another Party's implementation of its obligations under the Protocol;" in paragraph 2 to "implementation of a particular provision of the Protocol . . . at issue;" and in paragraph 3 to "possible non-compliance by any Party with its obligations under the Protocol." Montreal Protocol Report, *supra* note 17, Annex IV.

63. *See* Conclusion of Outstanding Issues and Adoption of Decisions, *supra* note 56, Annex I, para. B(3)(b) & Annex II, para. B.

64. *See* Note of the Secretariat, *supra* note 4, paras. 6-8.

MEA as a whole. It poses, however, also a major challenge. If the implementation committee is one of limited membership (as it should be), it goes without saying that, as a matter of procedural fairness, a party that is not a member of the Committee but whose conduct is under review should be entitled to participate in the consideration of the relevant submission before the Committee. Conversely, that party should not have any say in the subsequent elaboration and adoption of recommendations on the matter. A provision expressly to this effect is part of the Montreal Protocol's NCP,[65] as well as of the proposed procedure for the 1994 Sulphur Protocol.[66]

Access to and openness of the proceedings are a matter of considerable sensitivity. So is, specifically, the question of access to information upon which the implementation committee bases its recommendations. The Montreal Protocol expressly provides for Committee reports to "be made available to any person upon request."[67] This requirement, however, limits the availability of "information exchanged by or with the Committee that is related to any recommendation" to requesting parties only. On the other hand, as alluded to before, the sensitivity of access to information subject to routine review and analysis, clearly varies from MEA to MEA. For example, in the context of the Basel Convention or the Desertification Convention, the degree of sensitivity of the information involved is likely to be substantially lower, and thus might not justify anything less than full disclosure of all pertinent information, subject only to restrictions necessary to protect bona fide expectations of confidentiality of information that was received in confidence.

Moreover, given the extremely important role that NGOs have traditionally played in monitoring compliance with MEAs (for example, CITES or the Basel Convention), it would be highly conducive to maximizing the effectiveness of the proceedings to permit NGOs to submit pertinent information directly to the implementation committee concerned. If prior screening of NGO-supplied information were necessary, submissions could be routed through the convention secretariat or a similar intermediate body which in turn could summarize such information (and information on its own action thereto) and transmit these summaries to the implementation committee.

---

65. *See* Montreal Protocol Report, *supra* note 17, Annex IV, paras. 10-11.

66. *See* 1994 Sulphur Protocol, *supra* note 18, paras. 9-10; *see also* Decision Taken by the Executive Body, *supra* note 18.

67. *See* Montreal Protocol Report, *supra* note 17, Annex IV, para. 16.

D. Setting Outer Parameters for the Non-implementation/Non-compliance Procedure

If the NCP is apt to raise concerns about the degree to which the procedure might politicize the application of the legal norms and standards of the regime, an authoritative stipulation to what situations might indicate possible non-implementation and non-compliance, as well as any in advance clarification of what measures the parties in toto might wish to take in response, might go a long way towards assuaging some of these concerns.

1. Situations Indicative of Non-implementation/Non-compliance

One question that cannot be readily answered by extrapolation from any one environmental regime is whether a review procedure should be guided by a list of "possible situations of non-implementation/non-compliance." As is well known, in 1992 the Fourth Meeting of the Conference of the Parties to the Montreal Protocol failed to agree on an "indicative list" of situations of non-compliance, although the Ad Hoc Working Group of Legal Experts on Non-Compliance had drawn up a provisional list that identified seven such situations.[68] The specifics of the respective NCP of the 1994 Sulphur and VOC Protocols await clarification by the parties upon entry into force of the Protocols[69] (Article 7, paragraph 3 and Article 3, paragraph 3, respectively), while the modus operandi of the Climate Change Convention's SBI, and, more significantly, that of the multilateral consultative process of Article 13, are still evolving. As a result, in none of these regimes has the issue of such a guiding document been authoritatively addressed.

Because a non-compliance procedure is generally perceived as a highly flexible mechanism, an indicative list of possible situations of non-compliance might be viewed as introducing an undue constraining factor. However, such concern would be misplaced. While flexibility may be a defining characteristic of the "response" phase, flexibility is not and should not be the hallmark of the assessment and evaluation phase in the

---

68. The COP's failure may have been due to concern over the desirability and feasibility of qualifying *ex ante* situations of non-compliance; or, more likely, it may have been due to disagreement over whether non-payment of contribution under Article 10 of the Montreal Protocol should be included in the list.

69. However, the VOC Protocol lays down some procedural parameters of the mechanism for monitoring compliance that the parties are to adopt. *See* VOC Protocol, *supra* note 16, art. 3, para. 3.

non-compliance process. Rather, the nature of the tasks involved during the latter is quasi-judicial. The increasingly technical standards that help define states' obligations under most MEAs, moreover, contribute to making this phase an intrinsically less flexible, less "political" part of the procedure.

When seen in this light, it should be evident that the compilation of such a list of non-compliance indicators could actually benefit the effectiveness of the NCP. Regulatory demands on parties to an MEA can be expected to continue to grow and, in particular, to vary increasingly in terms of their significance to the fundamental objectives of the regime. In view of this, it may be essential for the credibility of this phase of the NCP as a non-politicized, unbiased review of state conduct—as well as convenient for the parties themselves—to highlight which conduct would prima facie be deemed irreconcilable with obligations arising under the MEA, and which conduct—infractions in a technical sense only—might not rise to the level of sufficient concern to subject it to the NCP.

2. Measures in Response to Non-implementation/Non-compliance

Annex V of the Report of the Fourth Meeting of the Parties to the Montreal Protocol sets forth the measures that the meeting of the parties might take in respect of non-compliance: Provision of appropriate assistance to the non-complying party, issuance of cautions, or imposition of sanctions (suspension of rights and privileges under the Protocol).[70] So far, none of the other MEA's NCPs has evolved to a corresponding level of detailed regulation.

As previously noted, the Montreal Protocol's flexible response is ultimately an expression of the intrinsic multilateral nature of the interests affected by a party's non-compliance: Rather than focusing on restoring the rights of the individual party or parties injured, the "remedies" listed aim at protecting the future integrity of the regime by encouraging the non-complying party to return to good standing. The Montreal Protocol's indicative list of measures also represents the symbolic reaffirmation of the overriding community interest in controlling the sanction process: Unilateral counter-measures, if not altogether preempted, must at least cede precedence to multilateral responses to non-compliance.

70. *See* Montreal Protocol Report, *supra* note 17, Annex V ("Indicative List of Measures that Might be Taken by a Meeting of the Parties in Respect of Non-compliance with the Protocol").

IV. DISPUTE SETTLEMENT AND NON-COMPLIANCE PROCEDURE

A key assumption underlying the adoption of a NCP is that rather than replacing the traditional dispute settlement provisions of the MEA concerned, the NCP will merely provide an additional procedure for resolving differences about the interpretation and application of the agreement. Thus the Montreal Protocol, as well as the 1994 Sulphur Protocol, consider the NCP as a distinct and separate process without prejudice to the operation of the respective dispute settlement procedure (DSP).[71] Similarly, Article 13 of the Climate Change Convention (the multilateral consultative process) and Article 14 (dispute settlement) are not mutually exclusive.[72]

Nevertheless, the interrelationship of the NCP and dispute settlement provisions raises a number of conceptual issues. First, whereas each state party could successfully initiate the NCP by communicating its reservation about another party's implementation/compliance to the Secretariat,[73] the complaint by a state not suffering a material prejudice may be inadmissible in dispute settlement proceedings pursuant to the MEA. The reason for this, as noted before, is that the MEA concerned may not vest a legal right or interest in state parties generically in respect of non-compliance by another party.

Second, the question arises whether the specific remedies provided by the NCP would prevent a party from resorting to the dispute settlement provisions of the MEA to vindicate rights or legal interests under general international law. Most MEAs' NCPs feature an express reservation clause regarding traditional dispute settlement procedures.[74] Presumably, a state party would thus not be prevented from having recourse to the dispute settlement provisions irrespective of the stage of the proceedings pending before the implementation committee, the only exception being the case where the party invoking the DSP had itself

71. *See id.* Annex IV, pmbl.; 1994 Sulphur Protocol, *supra* note 18, art. 7, para. 4.

72. For the common perception that the two procedures overlap but are clearly different in nature and scope, see, for example, Note of the Secretariat, *supra* note 4, at paras. 33-40 and Intergovernmental Negotiating Committee for a Framework Convention on Climate Change, Note by the Interim Secretariat, Consideration of the Establishment of a Multilateral Consultative Process for the Resolution of Questions Regarding Implementation (Article 13), U.N. Doc. A/AC.237/59, at 9, para. 26 (1994).

73. *See* Montreal Protocol Report, *supra* note 17, Annex IV, para. 1.

74. As regards the Montreal Protocol's NCP, see *supra* note 70.

initiated the NCP.[75] This follows not only from the reservation clause, but also from the fact that a matter before the implementation committee as a political organ, "is not sub judice if discussed, nor res judicata if decided."[76]

A third question is whether the NCP could be invoked, and more specifically, collective counter-measures imposed by the COP (upon recommendation of the implementation committee), only upon the exhaustion of the dispute settlement remedies. The text of the Montreal Protocol's NCP, for example, does not provide specific guidance on this issue, but its paragraph 12 clearly envisages parallel proceedings.[77] Indeed, it should be self-evident that by adopting a NCP, the parties to an MEA waive their right to have differences over non-compliance settled exclusively pursuant to dispute settlement procedures.[78] Martti Koskenniemi has persuasively argued that parallel proceedings before the Montreal Protocol's Implementation Committee and under the dispute settlement provisions would not be problematic, except for the situation in which a de facto determination of a party's compliance with its obligations is being made by the Committee while the matter has also been submitted to binding arbitration or decision by a court. In that latter situation, the jurisdictional conflict would have to be resolved in favor of the dispute settlement procedure.[79]

The question of prior exhaustion of DSP remedies is brought into even sharper focus when the COP (as the most likely institution to which the implementation committee will report) considers the adoption of "measures in response" to non-compliance. In a situation in which an injured individual state contemplates counter-measures for breach of a treaty which itself provides for a third-party dispute settlement mechanism, prior exhaustion of the DSP is quite possibly a prerequisite

---

75. In this situation the party would be estopped from invoking the DSP while the Implementation Committee remains seized of the complaint. *See* Koskenniemi, *supra* note 3, at 158.

76. *Id.* at 157 (citing D. CIOBANU, PRELIMINARY OBJECTIONS TO THE JURISDICTION OF THE UNITED NATIONS POLITICAL ORGANS 131 (1975)).

77. "The Parties involved in a matter referred to in paragraphs 1, 3, or 4 [i.e., the initiation of the non-compliance procedure] shall inform . . . the Meeting of the Parties of the results of proceedings taken under Article 11 of the [Vienna] Convention [the dispute settlement provision] regarding possible non-compliance. . . ." Montreal Protocol Report, *supra* note 17, Annex IV, para. 12.

78. *See* Koskenniemi, *supra* note 3, at 158.

79. Koskenniemi suggests that in such a case the NCP ought to be merely suspended, not terminated, to allow the committee to make a recommendation to the Conference of the Parties on the basis of the findings by the arbitral or judicial organ. *See id.* at 159.

for a permissible recourse to unilateral retaliatory measures.[80] The same cannot be said of a multilateral treaty which, while expressly envisaging the possibility of collective counter-measures by the parties, also provides for a binding third-party dispute settlement procedure. Rather, only if proposed measures amount to collective counter-measures,[81] and provided a judicial or arbitral tribunal is seized of the matter as well, will *lis pendens* bar the taking of counter-measures. The parties' collective response pursuant to the NCP would have to be stopped, or at least suspended, until after DSP remedies have been exhausted should the DSP prove ineffective.

Quite obviously, the relationship between dispute settlement procedure and the non-compliance procedure raises some intractable issues that need to be taken into account in devising any compliance control mechanism. Although it might not be necessary or even desirable to spell out in detail how NCP and DSP would interrelate, the parties would do well to set out in writing their understanding of the basic principles involved.

V. CONCLUSION

As MEAs evolve progressively into regulatory regimes that circumscribe in detailed fashion state conduct bearing on the realization of the respective MEA's key objectives, the need for effective implementation/compliance control becomes a matter of urgency. To

---

80. Bruno Simma, for example, claims that "[i]t is obvious that in these cases, the requirement of *ex ante* recourse to third-party settlement must be upheld under any circumstances (made more palatable, if need be, by the possibility of resorting to interim measures of protection)." Simma, *Counter-Measures and Dispute Settlement: A Plea for a Different Balance*, 5 EUR. J. INT'L L. 102, 104 (1994). *See also* Derek W. Bowett, *Economic Coercion and Reprisals by States*, 13 VA. J. INT'L L. 1, 11 (1972).

In should be noted, however, that this deference to the DSP is not a total one. For example, in the *Case Concerning the Air Services Agreement of 27 March 1946*, the Tribunal, addressing the issue of the permissibility of reprisals while the case was *sub judice*, noted:

> To the extent that the tribunal has the necessary means to achieve the objectives justifying the countermeasures, it must be admitted that the right of the parties to initiate such measures disappears. . . . As the object and the scope of the power of the tribunal to decide . . . may be defined quite narrowly, however the power of the parties to initiate or maintain countermeasures, too, may not disappear completely.

Case Concerning the Air Services Agreement of 27 March 1946 Between the United States and France, 54 I.L.R. 304, para. 96 (1978).

81. In other words, such a the situation presents itself where the only proposed measures represent sticks (e.g. suspension of the rights of the non-complying party), rather than carrots (e.g. financial incentives or assistance to encourage or enable compliance).

be effective, compliance control—review of information reported by states parties as to adequacy and veracity, assessment of the exact legal requirements of the MEA, and evaluation of information reported against the MEA's standards—must match the increasingly technical complexity of the regime and must be seen as being carried out impartially and objectively. Such control efforts are conceivable only within a special, dedicated institutional framework.

[15]

THE ROLE OF NON-GOVERNMENTAL ORGANIZATIONS IN THE DEVELOPMENT OF INTERNATIONAL ENVIRONMENTAL LAW

A. DAN TARLOCK*

I. INTRODUCTION: GLOBAL ENVIRONMENTALISM OPENS THE DOOR FOR NON-GOVERNMENTAL ORGANIZATIONS

This Essay explores the role of Non-Governmental Organizations [NGOs] in the establishment and enforcement of global environmental priorities. It examines the deficiencies in classic international law that NGOs are helping to overcome as well as the different roles that NGOs now play in priority setting and the enforcement of international norms. It concludes with the suggestion that as NGOs acquire more political power, we need to develop minimal standards to assess NGO performance.

Protection of the global environment from continuing degradation is the most difficult problem facing the international community.[1] The most distinctive aspect of global environmental protection is that it is primarily scientifically driven. International environmental standards have been greatly influenced by priorities established by cosmopolitan scientific elites and to a lesser extent by advocates of global social equity.[2] For this reason, calls for increased levels of global environmental protection challenge both the ways in which individual countries use natural resources and the distribution of resource use between north and south. These pleas thus challenge the basic assumptions of domestic legal systems as well as those of classic international law and the post-World War II structure of international organizations.

* Distinguished Professor of Law, Chicago-Kent College of Law, Illinois Institute of Technology; A.B. 1962, L.L.B. 1965, Stanford University.

I would like to thank Ms. Susan Hahn-Reizner, J.D. Chicago-Kent College of Law, 1992, for her research skills in locating a great deal of valuable information about the activities of non-governmental organizations (NGOs).

1. See WORLD RESOURCES INSTITUTE, WORLD RESOURCES 1990-91 (1990), for an excellent narrative and quantitative survey of global environmental degradation. Vice President Albert Gore develops this theme in THE EARTH IN THE BALANCE: ECOLOGY AND THE HUMAN SPIRIT (1992).

2. Equity has become a much more pervasive theme in the global environmental debate. WORLD RESOURCES, *supra* note 1, at 1, observes that "[t]he world's environmental dilemma is that the scale on which natural resources are being consumed and wastes are being produced is already immense, yet many poor countries still lack and desperately need the benefits of industrialization and economic development."

The developing set of environmental principles adopted in a host of international fora, most recently in Rio de Janeiro, set resource use priorities that have the potential to intrude deeply on the traditional autonomy of the nation-state. This makes it difficult for international law to accommodate environmental protection because the preservation of nation-state autonomy has been the principal objective of modern international law. Environmentalists, in contrast, view this objective as subordinate to the prevention of global degradation. Environmental norms are initially established to address problems that are defined without regard to national boundaries. These norms initially address physical not political problems. For problems such as global warming, a ton of soft coal burned in China is the same as a ton burned in England.

Science alone, of course, cannot control the definition and responses to environmental problems. Because they are fundamentally resource allocation and distribution conflicts, they are political problems. Nations will therefore address them in the context of their own self-interest. Thus, these problems must be addressed within the context of national and international legal systems and politics. However, science-driven legal and political problems are different from other problems for two reasons. First, the experience with global environmental standards shows that individual nations have less of an ability to control the global agenda by blocking efforts to establish high environmental standards. Second, nations also have less control over the range of acceptable internal responses. The ability of political systems to respond by non-action is constrained. If the science is right, then the political response must be adequate to address the problem as scientifically defined; half a loaf is the same as no loaf.

The international community's response to ozone depletion illustrates these differences at work. The 1987 Montreal Protocol is a science-driven international agreement that subordinates self-interest to science. Disturbing scientific research led the United Nations Environmental Program to make ozone depletion a priority and broke down national resistance, in both the developed and developing world, to banning a wide range of chloroflurocarbons (CFCs). This is the first international agreement to take preventative action to minimize a risk, rather than to respond to an existing condition of global resource degradation. Since 1987, the international community has moved to ban the offending chemicals at an accelerating rate.[3] The politics of ozone protection were in-

3. RICHARD E. BENEDICK, OZONE DIPLOMACY: NEW DIRECTIONS IN SAFEGUARDING THE PLANET 105 (1991).

tense and complex and all countries took "unscientific" self-interest positions at various times, but in the end both industrialized and developing countries, aided by a unique technology-transfer process, participated in strengthening the Montreal Protocol. The former United States Ambassador, who represented the United States at the Montreal Protocol Negotiations, observed that the "new wave of ecological consciousness" meant that "failing to accept a share of responsibility and opting actively to threaten the ozone layer would not be an easy course for a government to follow."[4]

The expanding role of science in defining environmental problems is changing the politics of environmental priority setting and enforcement by increasing the influence of NGOs.[5] NGOs helped to spur action to accelerate the phase-out of CFCs and play an increasingly powerful role in setting the global environmental agenda. For example, the ratio of NGO participants to United Nations and government officials at the June 1992 United Nations Conference on Environment and Development in Rio de Janeiro was approximately one to one. NGOs are now permanent players in the international arena as they are in the United States. Ironically, their domestic role was originally conceived of as a temporary antidote to correct the failure of scientific management to encompass environmental values. Domestic NGO activism was a way to "jump start" government agencies which were unresponsive to environmental values because they had degenerated from progressive regulatory agencies to ossified mission agencies. Once these agencies broadened their values, it was hoped that they would once again merit the trust of the public to manage resources scientifically. The opposite happened. NGOs became permanent players in the regulatory game with the capacity to influence all phases of policy, and NGO participation in law making has now become a political theory. The existence of strong NGOs has been identified as a hallmark of democratic government and thus a necessary condition for effective environmentalism.[6]

4. *Id.* at 152.

5. After this article was written, David Tolbert, Lecturer in Law at the University of Hull, England, published part of his L.L.M. dissertation on NGOs as *Global Climate Change and the Role of International Non-Governmental Organizations, in* INTERNATIONAL LAW AND GLOBAL CLIMATE CHANGE 95 (Robin Churchill & David Freestone eds., 1991). Much of his extensive research and analysis tracks my argument, although we differ modestly in the need to subject NGOs to minimal standards of conduct.

6. Ibrahim J. Wani, *Poverty, Governance, the Role of Law, and International Environmentalism: A Critique of the Basil Convention on Hazardous Wastes*, 1 KAN. J.L. & PUB. POL'Y 37, 45 (1991).

II. The Paradox of NGOs: Power Without Legal Status

NGOs lack legal personality in classic international law and in the theory of international organizations, but their lack of formal status has not hindered their growing influence in foreign countries and international organizations. NGOs thrived in the United States and in Europe[7] because they had a legal status which served as the basis of a broader political role. In contrast, international NGOs lack an international legal personality, but they have been able to build on the legitimacy of domestic NGOs to project themselves into the international arena.

NGO participation in the establishment and enforcement of global environmental priorities is modeled after the experience with citizen standing and intervention in the United States. Domestic and international NGOs seek to exercise the same kind of legal and political influence, but the legal position of NGOs in the international community is different. In the United States, NGOs have a tenuous constitutional status and thus are subject to the discipline of the legal as well as the political process. International and many foreign NGOs generally lack any legal status and sometimes operate on the margins of established political processes. This extra-legal character of NGOs has both positive and negative consequences: NGOs are at the mercy of international organization and foreign domestic rules on access and participation; however, their lack of legal status allows them to define their role unconstrained by the law. This allows them to develop more creative and effective approaches to environmental protection than those offered through litigation, especially before international tribunals.

NGO success and involvement in both international organizations and individual nations has generally been hailed as a positive development because they fill such a large void in both domestic and international environmental competencies. This is a powerful justification for their role. Adequate responses to environmental problems require large allocations of scarce resources. NGOs help allocate scarce resources to environmental issues in advance of the nation-centered international community. They police international organizations and provide valuable information and other assistance to developing nations. To date, NGOs have been a positive force in bringing environmental issues onto domestic and international political agendas since so much in current

7. The role of private individuals in the enforcement of European Community environmental law is discussed in Frederick M. Abbott, *Regional Integration and the Environment: The Evolution of Legal Regimes*, 68 CHI. KENT L. REV. 173 (1992).

economic and political organizations is hostile to effective environmentalism. There is, however, a need for a more critical assessment of their role.

My thesis is that NGOs have progressed from influencing the articulation of environmental aspirational standards of conduct, to the formulation and implementation of policies both in international organizations and individual nation-states, through moral and scientific persuasion, to the exercise of power. NGOs now have the capacity to influence multinational organization policy and to intervene directly in choices traditionally reserved to individual sovereign states under international law. They cannot alone overcome the difficulty of international law to adapt to the imperatives of protection, but they exercise real power in the international community. In the main, the growth of NGOs has been a positive factor in the development of international environmental protection regimes, but there is reason for caution. Because they exercise real political power, the role of NGOs must be assessed critically, and ultimately they must be held to some standards of performance.

III. NGOs Find a Niche

International environmental priorities are an interesting example of the influence of intense preference groups in the establishment of environmental priorities transcending the inability of formal governmental institutions to respond to scientific information. These groups have great success in shaping the environmental agenda of individual states, convention and treaty processes, and the work of the United Nations. Environmental NGOs can be traced back to the formation of the International Union for the Conservation of Nature in 1948, but the first United Nations conference on the environment gave their current status. Since the 1972 Stockholm conference, NGOs have played an increasingly important role in the development of global environmental standards and institutions as well as in the implementation of policies in individual countries. NGO success can be attributed to advantages that they possess over action by nation states. First, in the formulation of standards of performance, they can articulate powerful universal, single-purpose standards. They need not trade-off environmental to other objectives because they are not bound by the need of political leaders, elected and non-elected, to avoid offending powerful constituencies. Second, for the same reason, there is little incentive to subordinate science to other considerations. Third, NGOs can often work with local environmental groups, who lack both resources and political legitimacy, to support environmental initiatives. Greenpeace's work with local NGOs in Central America to monitor attempts to import toxic wastes into the region is an example of this role.[8]

NGOs fill a niche in international law created by the state-centered notion of international law. The replacement of the relatively decentralized power centers that were called states in the Middle Ages by powerful sovereign states during the Renaissance was one of the defining moments in western history. Classic international law, which crystallized in the nineteenth century, reflects this moment and has remained frozen in it. The two World Wars have produced the United Nations and a number of international organizations which play an increasingly powerful role,[9] but respect for state sovereignty remains at the center of international law.[10] The international legal system remains bound by the principles of absolute nation-state sovereignty except for vague and virtually unenforceable limitations when a state causes transnational harm.[11]

NGOs do not accept international law and the international community as they find it. Environmental advocates reject the primacy of exclusive national sovereignty. Sovereignty is often seen as a barrier to the formulation and implementation of effective environmental policies. The current expectation is that national self-interest will be reflected in standards that represent and processes that reflect the lowest common denominator standard. Reliance on traditional international cooperation processes creates a highly centralized international environmental protection process which ensures that nations will almost inevitably reach consensus on only the lowest common denominator standards and thus will "underinvest" in environmental protection. Since Grotius' *De Jure Belli ac Pacis*, international law has been concerned with the establishment of the ground rules of "civilized" conflict among nations.[12] Only general or lowest common denominator standards are accepted as law. The eighteenth and nineteenth century triumph of John Locke's idea of constitutional governments with limited power changed the theory of international law by making consensus the only criterion of legitimacy.

8. *Greenpeace Claims Foreign Companies Dumping Waste in Seven Latin Nations*, 15 Int'l Envtl. Rep. (BNA) 16 (Jan. 15, 1992).

9. *See generally* PAUL F. DIEHL, THE POLITICS OF INTERNATIONAL ORGANIZATIONS: PATTERNS AND INSIGHTS (1989).

10. PHILLIP TAYLOR, NONSTATE ACTORS IN INTERNATIONAL POLITICS: FROM TRANSREGIONAL TO SUBSTATE ORGANIZATIONS 3 (1984).

11. *See, e.g.*, IAN BROWNLIE, PRINCIPLES OF PUBLIC INTERNATIONAL LAW 58-70 (4th ed. 1990).

12. J. C. RANDALL, THE MAKING OF THE MODERN MIND: A SURVEY OF THE INTELLECTUAL BACKGROUND OF THE PRESENT AGE 197-201 (1926) remains a masterful examination of the intellectual origins of modern international law.

Constitutional governments thus robbed the most powerful nations of their power to transcend international relations.

From the sweep of world history, the aspiration for "civilized" conflict among nations is a grand one. However, from an environmental perspective, the ideal of achieving a slightly less worse human condition must be rejected as inadequate. If the warnings of scientists on issues such as global warming, ozone depletion, and rain forest destruction are correct, we can only aspire to higher not minimal standards of national performance. Thus, global environmental protection poses an even more difficult challenge to the international legal system than the effort to limit war. International environmental law seeks ways to bring all nations up to high standards of environmental protection consistent with notions of inter-generational and inter-regional equity. This aspiration is reflected in the current efforts to promote sustainable development in both the developed and developing world.

The direct doctrinal underpinning for the recognition of NGOs in international law, is the theory of the "private attorney general" as articulated by Judge Jerome Frank,[13] although ironically the Supreme Court is moving away from the private attorney general theory in the direction of the "statist" theory of classic international law.[14] No such concept can exist in international law because only states have standing to sue before the International Court of Justice (ICJ).[15] However, the wide spread de jure and de facto democratization of the judicial process and the increasingly prominent role of multi-national organizations has made it possible to analogize from domestic to international law. The Grotian idea that individuals as states are part of international society, rejected in the nineteenth century, also supports the recognition of international legal status for NGOs.[16]

NGOs' arguments for a formal legal status ultimately build on two post-World War II attacks on the premise of classic international law that co-existence is the objective of the international legal system as well

13. The leading case is Associated Industries v. Ickes, 134 F.2d 694, 704 (2d Cir. 1943). *See generally* Roger C. Cramton & Barry B. Boyer, *Citizen Suits in the Environmental Field: Peril or Promise*, 2 ECOLOGY L.Q. 407 (1972); Cass R. Sunstein, *Standing and the Privatization of Public Law*, 88 COLUM. L. REV. 1432 (1988). For an application of this model to international NGOs, see David A. Wirth, *Legitimacy, Accountability, and Partnership: A Model for Advocacy on Third World Environmental Issues*, 100 YALE L.J. 2645 (1991).

14. *See, e.g.*, Lujan v. National Wildlife Fed., 497 U.S. 871 (1990); Lujan v. Defenders of Wildlife, 112 S. Ct. 2130 (1992).

15. *See* Phillipe J. Sand, *The Environment, Community and International Law*, 30 HARV. INT'L L.J. 393, 397 (1989).

16. Hedley Bull, *The Importance of Grotius in the Study of International Relations*, *in* HUGO GROTIUS AND INTERNATIONAL RELATIONS 65, 83-87 (Hedley Bull et al. eds.,1990).

as on the Grotian idea of an international society. The first post-World War II development is the McDougall "deconstruction" of international law. McDougall and his school accepted co-existence among the major power blocks as the objective of international law, but applied American realist jurisprudence to include both de jure and de facto actors. The second is the argument of the late Wolfgang Friedman that as international law progressed from co-existence to cooperation, the category of entities with an international legal personality expanded.[17] From this perspective, NGOs can be seen as an extension of the growing status of international organizations.[18] As a leading treatise observes, "There is no general rule that the individual cannot be a 'subject of international law'. . . ."[19]

While American theories of citizen standing provide the primary legal rationale for NGO legitimacy, the ability to capitalize on this position derives from the science-driven nature of environmental politics. Most environmental problems have secured a place on political and policy agendas only because members of an educated elite believe what scientists warn. Environmental agendas are formulated at the top and then supported by the most educated segments of an electorate. They seldom come from the bottom up, although in the former Soviet Union and Eastern European block countries environmentalism was one of the only means of general protest against communist control.[20] For example, ozone depletion is a problem because scientists predict that continued ozone depletion will cause serious health risks and contribute to global warming. Scientists, however, only influence, they do not control the policy agenda. The environmental protection agenda is set by political institutions which respond to specific constituencies with perceptions of the problem that are science-based but not limited by the canons of scientific evidence.

There is a growing literature on the factors which influence the rise and fall of issues on political agendas, and this literature explains the influence of NGOs. The basic conclusion of this research is familiar to the parents of teenage children: both legislators and teenagers have short attention spans and respond primarily to noise. Increasingly, noise is a function of information not just numbers. Environmental issues are char-

17. WOLFGANG FRIEDMAN, THE CHANGING STRUCTURE OF INTERNATIONAL LAW (1964).

18. At the present time, however, international law only recognizes organizations that are a permanent association of nation states and exercise similar powers. BROWNLIE, *supra* note 11, at 680-83.

19. *Id.* at 67.

20. *See* MURRAY FESHBACH & ALFRED FRIENDLY, JR., ECOCIDE IN THE USSR (1992).

acterized as political problems when there is a perceived crisis. Historically, the crisis has been a specific disaster, such as an oil spill, but, contrary to public choice and interest group political theory,[21] knowledgeable interest groups can serve as "information brokers" and "exercise important influence in the legislative process."[22]

IV. NGOs: New Voices, New Actors

NGOs perform at least four related functions. They bring neglected as well as transcendent perspectives to bear in different fora, they monitor the environmental impacts of various activities, and they participate directly in resource allocation.[23] In short, they increasingly perform roles traditionally assigned to state agencies.

A. *Infusion of Alternative Perspectives into Narrow Mission Programs*

The case for NGOs rests on the premise that non-governmental entities have a positive role to play in contributing new information and perspectives to policy formulation. This role is a major extension of their traditional role as information synthesizers. NGOs have deep roots in the international community; they reflect a long tradition of international scientific meetings and semi-official international organizations, but their role has evolved to one of claimed parity with established governmental institutions. The modern NGO as a direct political actor with non-state interests in the international affairs emerged at the 1972 United Nations Conference on the Environment in Sweden. NGOs did not have a substantial direct influence on the conference[24] but they gained a legitimacy that they lacked before Stockholm.

The Stockholm Conference is generally counted as one of the most successful environmental conferences. It projected environmental concern into international politics where it remains an expanding priority. It also articulated a set of principles that remain the starting point for discussions of international law and treaty standards and it institutionalized

21. *See* Richard J. Tobin, The Expendable Future: U.S. Politics and the Protection of Biological Diversity 15-26 (1990), which used agenda theory to explain why endangered species protection is a very small dot on the congressional radar screen.

22. *See* Daniel A. Farber, *Politics and Procedure in Environmental Law*, 8 J. Law, Econ. & Org. 59, 72 (1992).

23. Tolbert, *supra* note 5, at 98-106, identifies four NGO functions beyond traditional scientific advisory functions: (1) the identification of environmental issues and general principles of international environmental law, (2) ombudsmen or guardian activities, (3) creation of international standards and norms, and (4) enforcement of international standards.

24. Lynton K. Caldwell, International Environmental Policy: Emergence and Dimensions 58 (2d ed. 1990).

this concern within the United Nations through the U.N. Environmental Program. Much of the success of the conference was the result of careful preparation and masterful diplomacy by conference secretary general Maurice Strong. However, the presence and participation by NGOs created a precedent that remains.

NGOs now seek political parity to counter the narrow self-interest politics of nation states. If politics is all interest groups, then all interest groups should have access to decision making processes. In the United States the opening of both administrative and judicial processes to interest group plaintiffs was justified because it furthered interest group liberalism. Environmental advocates in both Europe and the developing world have admired and emulated this model. As a Ugandan emigree teaching in the United States recently put it, "[e]ffective environmentalism is virtually impossible without basic democratic conditions."[25]

The international law argument for NGOs' status is also a major extension of the argument for citizen or public interest standing in the United States. United States law draws a sharp distinction between adjudication and political action which will not hold in the international context. In the United States, the case against the citizen suit is that it politicizes the judiciary. This is a false concern since courts are limited to cases and controversies under Article III. To cabin citizen standing, United States courts grant "injured" public interest plaintiffs standing only to enforce existing statutory mandates ignored by the agency. Citizen standing is justified by notions of pluralism that define legitimate decisions as those based on all legitimate view points. The idea of judicial participation in the establishment and enforcement of environmental priorities appeals to environmentalists in strong central administrative states as well, and this argument has become the basis for the integration of NGOs into the international community.

The analogy between domestic citizen standing and NGO participation in international law-making is apt, but concerns about the NGO role are more justified because there are no institutional constraints on NGO roles. This is a matter of considerable concern because in many international agencies the split between politics and technical expertise is a matter of great concern, and it is harder to maintain the line between the two. International organizations often provide an effective forum for developing countries to vent their frustrations, and NGOs can veer from articulating scientific positions that try to bring disparate interests together to articulating polarizing positions. NGO actions reflect the full

25. Wani, *supra* note 6, at 41.

range of contributions and have generally been hailed as positive. However, NGOs are not bound by the limitations of domestic law because their international legal status is different. At the present time NGOs participate at the discretion of the international organizations of the states. Some organizations have procedures to accredit NGOs.

NGO access is often more difficult, but once access is obtained, NGOs are free to use their influence to define agendas as they choose. Under the United States model, citizen suits are open to all who have standing and the law of standing does not screen directly for citizen competence. The idea of a case limits what the NGOs can do in a law suit. No similar limitation exists at the international level. The limitations, such as they are, are solely on access to a process. International organizations have adopted Professor Jaffe's suggestion that courts screen citizen plaintiffs. This allows agencies to limit participation to those most likely to advance the work of the agency but this procedure is biased in favor of well-financed groups.

Putting fresh alternative approaches on the table has been the bread and butter activity of NGOs. Most governments still pursue short-term economic development with little serious consideration of alternatives such as sustainable development. For example, a group of Spanish NGOs issued a report which not only criticized the Madrid-Seville high-speed train, but offered a detailed blueprint for sustainable rural development. The report recommends that rural areas participate in the coastal and urban boom in Spain by being allowed to market their natural value and products to urban dwellers under carefully controlled conditions.[26]

One of the major success stories of NGOs has been the role that they have played in the transformation of the World Bank's mission, which is under continuing criticism for its support of projects with large adverse environmental and social consequences. NGOs lobbied the Bank directly as well as the United States Congress, and in the past few years Congress has enacted legislation requiring that U.S. agencies urge the Bank to adopt environmentally responsive lending policies.[27] Since 1986, the Bank has taken impressive steps to make sustainable development the operating standard for future loans. My colleague Bartram Brown has evaluated efforts to politicize the technical mission international organizations. He distinguishes between political activity which is unrelated to the mandate of the agency and impairs its ability to carry out its mission

26. *Development Plans Being Pursued at Expense of Environment, Groups Claim*, 15 Int'l Envtl. Rep. (BNA) 18 (Jan. 15, 1992).
27. 22 U.S.C.S. § 2621-m (Law. Co-op. 1992).

and that which enhances mandates. NGO pressure, aided by United States legislation, is an example of beneficial political pressure because "the Bank's ability to function and to fulfill its mandate has been enhanced by these reforms. It is true, of course, that the Bank's Charter never specifically mentions protecting the environment . . . nonetheless, this objective is very much consistent"[28] with its mandate to improve the world standard of living through useful projects.

B. The Articulation of Universal Perspectives

NGOs play a role which is both similar and more powerful than public interest plaintiffs in domestic law. In domestic law, public interest adds a perspective to that of the agency by presenting the court with an ignored statutory or constitutional value. This is a familiar role for NGOs and commentators have urged that international agencies allow wide-spread NGO participation. In the international arena, NGOs often play a more transcendent role. They offer a fundamentally different perspective from ones urged by nation states. One of the major criticisms of international environmental law making[29] is that it is overly constrained by the state sovereignty which allows states to put state interest first in international negotiations. When agreement is reached, it reflects the lowest common denominator. NGOs, in contrast, are not bound by state interest but can articulate and advocate a global perspective. This can be a modest role such as the presentation of neutral scientific information to break a deadlock over the science of an issue or the articulation of the heretical idea that there should be no compromise on environmental issues.

The flip side of transcendence is, of course, ideological intransigence which can conflict with the underlying science as well as with legitimate non-environmental concerns. The positions taken by international wildlife organizations at the 1992 Kyoto Convention on International Trade in Endangered Species (CITES) illustrate the problem of NGO inflexibility. Several southeast African nations wanted to relax the CITES ban on trade in elephant hides and tusks. Relaxation was successfully opposed by many wildlife conservation NGOs, supported by thirty United States Senators, who saw the problem as a standard anti-species conservation move. However, the issue is more complicated. The nations, the United States Fish and Wildlife Service, and other NGOs saw the issue

28. *See* BARTRAM BROWN, THE UNITED STATES AND THE POLITICIZATION OF THE WORLD BANK: ISSUES OF INTERNATIONAL LAW AND POLICY 238 (1992).

29. *Developments in the Law: International Environmental Law*, 104 HARV. L. REV. 1484, 1490 (1991).

as a sustainable development problem and were willing to entertain the counter-environmentally intuitive proposal that limited trade in Elephant products was not inconsistent with species conservation.[30] There is no requirement that politics produce rational or right decisions, but the ability of NGOs to block creative science-based solutions is troublesome.

C. Direct Participation in Enforcement

NGOs are playing an increasing role in the enforcement of international environmental standards. There is no basis for this role in international law but nonetheless NGOs have carved out a role. Under United States law and the laws of a few European countries, citizen organizations have a statutory enforcement role through the ability to bring citizen suits. There is no corresponding role in international law both because of the principle that only states have standing and the law of effective judicial and administrative enforcement mechanisms. Paradoxically, the non-role of the International Court of Justice and the limited enforcement powers of the United Nations Environmental Program have given NGOs the flexibility to play more diverse and creative roles.

NGO participation in the area of environmental norms is the easiest to justify, especially in developing countries which lack an effective regulatory infra-structure. NGOs are free to do what international law proscribes—to intervene in a nation's affairs which would fall under that nation's exclusive sovereignty under classic international law. NGOs are not bound by the non-intervention principles of international law. They are free to lobby international organizations as well as to use their influence to shape domestic political agendas. For example, recently a coalition of local and international environmental groups played a significant role in persuading the government of Honduras to reject a United States corporation's proposal to construct a large pulp and paper mill because the project threatened to destroy a tropical forest.[31]

D. Direct Participation in Resource Allocation

NGOs have played their most creative role in pioneering incentives for developing nations to adopt environmental practices. Inter-generational equity requires that environmental protection be integrated with economic development. The north-south split is the most difficult un-

30. Stephen R. Weisman, *Bluefin Tuna and African Elephants Win Some Help at a Global Meeting*, N.Y. TIMES, Mar. 11, 1992, at A8.

31. *Ecological Concerns Prompt Government to Reject Proposals from West*, 15 Int'l Envtl. Rep. (BNA) 192-93 (Apr. 8, 1992).

resolved environmental issue and the resolution of this issue increasingly drives global environmental issues. The issue has been framed as a classic redistribution issue: the north took resources from the south through colonialism and transformed them through technology and must now make restitution. The actors have been states and state-controlled multinational organizations such as the World Bank. Since World War II, there has been limited technology transfer in the form of foreign assistance. After the OPEC oil embargo and consequent rise in the price of oil, money flowed into private and public banks and was recycled to developing countries in the form of loans. These loans are now a crushing debt burden for many countries and puts intense pressures on countries to continue to exploit rapidly their natural resources bases. This burden has also provided a small but growing window of opportunity for NGOs to change internal resource use priorities.

In 1984, Thomas Lovejoy proposed a new form of private debt relief: debt-for-nature swaps. In brief, NGOs purchase from a bank a portion of the debt of developing countries faced with a write-off or write-down prospect. Developing country "paper" is plentiful and relatively cheap. The NGO must fund a debt instrument with hard currency that the developing country would like to retire as quickly as possible, often high interest, short term bonds. After the NGO purchases the instrument, it is converted into the local currency of the debtor country and the debt service is applied to purchase land threatened by development or to finance a conservation program. Debtor countries gain the benefit of servicing its debt with local rather than hard currency, subject to NGO control over the country's natural resources. Banks may deduct the original amount of the debt donated rather than the current fair market value of the debt.[32] This strategy has been adopted by the United States government because it makes the best of a bad situation, helping developing nations with crushing debt burdens, and offers a modest way to support sustainable development projects.

In 1987, Conservation International purchased $650,000 of Bolivian debt for Citicorp at an 85% discount and cancelled the debt in return for Bolivia's promise to protect 3.7 million acres of rain forest surrounding the Beni Biosphere reserve. The World Wildlife Fund used the proceeds of its swap to fund an Ecuadorian NGO. A Mexican environmental group, Pronatura, negotiated a $3,000,000 swap with its government in 1991.

Debt-for-nature swaps are unlikely to be a major vehicle for devel-

32. Rev. Rul. 87-124, 1987-2 C.B. 205.

oping country debt relief but they have considerable potential to save high priority natural areas such as rain forests. From a legal point of view the most interesting aspect of debt-for-nature swaps is the creative NGO circumvention of the basic principle of international law, proclaimed by the United Nations at the height of the Cold War,[33] that each nation has the right to exploit its natural resources. Debt-for-Nature-Swaps have been criticized as a new form of economic imperialism,[34] but the device is preferable to traditional economic development which was dictated by the donor country and the World Bank. There are, however, many difficult issues to be faced in the future. For example, the traditional model of resource preservation, the protected enclave such as a national park, has limited application to the rain forests and other productive but environmentally sensitive areas of the developing world.

V. CONCLUSION

The late twentieth century is another defining moment in world history. The international community is both fragmenting into the worst excesses of nineteenth century nationalism and coming together around a series of basic norms. Science and technology limit state monopolies on power, and it will be increasingly difficult for states to maintain resource use policies which deviate from international environmental norms. NGOs have a major and positive role to play in this process. At the present time, their activity needs only to be encouraged and monitored. However, as they acquire more real power, they must be brought into established legal systems so that they can be subjected to standards of accountability. NGOs should not be held to the standards of national states or international organizations, but minimum norms of responsible environmental participation should be developed to monitor their performance.[35]

Because information is the source of NGO power, their use of information should be the measure of their activities. NGOs have a responsibility to use the best available information to advance the norms of environmentalism such as biodiversity protection, sustainable development and a decent level of freedom from exposure to harmful substances. They are not limited to "good science" since environmentalism is at base

33. *Permanent Sovereignty Over Natural Resources*, G.A. Res. 1803, UN GAOR 17th Sess., Supp. No. 17, at 15, U.N. Doc. A/5217 (1962).

34. *See* Michael Chamberlain et al., *Sovereign Debt Exchanges*, 1988 U. ILL. L. REV. 415-41.

35. *But cf.* Tolbert, *supra* note 5. Mr. Tolbert argues that because NGOs possess limited formal powers "any attempt to regulate NGOs, without a substantial increase in their rights and powers, appears to be unjustified." *Id.* at 95, n.2.

an ethical theory of science, but NGO activities must adhere to some higher standard than simply "interest" if they are to maintain their legitimacy.

Name Index